Syngress knows what passing the exam means to you and to your career. And we know that you are often financing your own training and certification; therefore, you need a system that is comprehensive, affordable, and effective.

Boasting one-of-a-kind integration of text, DVD-quality instructor-led training, and Web-based exam simulation, the Syngress Study Guide & DVD Training System guarantees 100% coverage of exam objectives.

The Syngress Study Guide & DVD Training System includes:

- **Study Guide with 100% coverage of exam objectives** By reading this study guide and following the corresponding objective list, you can be sure that you have studied 100% of the exam objectives.

- **Instructor-led DVD** This DVD provides almost two hours of virtual classroom instruction.

- **Web-based practice exams** Just visit us at **www.syngress.com/ certification** to access a complete exam simulation.

Thank you for giving us the opportunity to serve your certification needs. And be sure to let us know if there's anything else we can do to help you get the maximum value from your investment. We're listening.

www.syngress.com/certification

SYNGRESS®

SYNGRESS®

COVERS ALL
100%
CERTIFIED
EXAM OBJECTIVES

MCSA/MCSE

Managing and Maintaining a Windows Server
2003 Environment for an MCSA
Certified on Windows 2000

STUDY GUIDE & DVD TRAINING SYSTEM

Will Schmied
Robert J. Shimonski   Technical Editor

KEY	SERIAL NUMBER
001	TH33SLUGGY
002	Q2T4J9T7VA
003	82LPD8R7FF
004	Z6TDAA3HVY
005	P33JEET8MS
006	3SHX6SN$RK
007	CH3W7E42AK
008	9EU6V4DER7
009	SUPACM4NFH
010	5BVF3MEV2Z

PUBLISHED BY
Syngress Publishing, Inc.
800 Hingham Street
Rockland, MA 02370

Managing and Maintaining a Windows Server 2003 Environment for an MCSA Certified on Windows 2000 Study Guide & DVD Training System

Printed in the United States of America

1 2 3 4 5 6 7 8 9 0

ISBN: 1-932266-56-9

Technical Editor: Robert J. Shimonski
Technical Reviewer: Laura E. Hunter
Acquisitions Editor: Catherine B. Nolan
DVD Production: Michael Donovan

Cover Designer: Michael Kavish
Page Layout and Art by: Patricia Lupien
Copy Editor: Judy Eby
Indexer: Rich Carlson
DVD Presenters: Will Schmied,
    Robert J. Shimonski

Acknowledgments

We would like to acknowledge the following people for their kindness and support in making this book possible.

Karen Cross, Meaghan Cunningham, Kim Wylie, Harry Kirchner, Kevin Votel, Kent Anderson, Frida Yara, Jon Mayes, John Mesjak, Peg O'Donnell, Sandra Patterson, Betty Redmond, Roy Remer, Ron Shapiro, Patricia Kelly, Andrea Tetrick, Jennifer Pascal, Doug Reil, David Dahl, Janis Carpenter, and Susan Fryer of Publishers Group West for sharing their incredible marketing experience and expertise.

Duncan Enright, AnnHelen Lindeholm, David Burton, Febea Marinetti, and Rosie Moss of Elsevier Science for making certain that our vision remains worldwide in scope.

David Buckland, Wendi Wong, Daniel Loh, Marie Chieng, Lucy Chong, Leslie Lim, Audrey Gan, and Joseph Chan of Transquest Publishers for the enthusiasm with which they receive our books.

Kwon Sung June at Acorn Publishing for his support.

Jackie Gross, Gayle Voycey, Alexia Penny, Anik Robitaille, Craig Siddall, Darlene Morrow, Iolanda Miller, Jane Mackay, and Marie Skelly at Jackie Gross & Associates for all their help and enthusiasm representing our product in Canada.

Lois Fraser, Connie McMenemy, Shannon Russell, and the rest of the great folks at Jaguar Book Group for their help with distribution of Syngress books in Canada.

David Scott, Annette Scott, Geoff Ebbs, Hedley Partis, Bec Lowe, and Mark Langley of Woodslane for distributing our books throughout Australia, New Zealand, Papua New Guinea, Fiji Tonga, Solomon Islands, and the Cook Islands.

Winston Lim of Global Publishing for his help and support with distribution of Syngress books in the Philippines.

Special thanks to Daniel Bendell from Assurance Technology Management for his 24x7 care and feeding of the Syngress network. Dan expertly applies the principles of our books in a highly professional manner and under severe time constraints while keeping a good sense of humor.

Author and DVD Presenter

Will Schmied (BSET, MCSE, CWNA, TICSA, MCSA, Security+, Network+, A+), is the President of Area 51 Partners, Inc. (www.area51partners.com), a provider of wired and wireless networking implementation, security and training services to businesses in the Hampton Roads, Virginia, area. Will holds a Bachelor's degree in Mechanical Engineering Technology from Old Dominion University in addition to various IT industry certifications.

Will has previously authored and contributed to several other publications from Syngress Publishing, including, *Building DMZs for Enterprise Networks* (ISBN: 1-931836-884), *Implementing and Administering Security in a Microsoft Windows 2000 Network: Exam 70-214 Study Guide and DVD Training System* (ISBN: 1-931836-84-1), *Security+ Study Guide and DVD Training System* (ISBN: 1-931836-72-8), and *Configuring and Troubleshooting Windows XP Professional* (ISBN: 1-928994-80-6). Will has also worked with Microsoft in the MCSE exam development process.

Will currently resides in Newport News, Virginia, with his wife, Chris, their children, Christopher, Austin, Andrea, and Hannah. When he's not busy working, you can find Will enjoying time with his family.

Will would like to add special thanks to the following individuals:

For my wife Chris—thank you for your endless support and encouragement. You are my guiding light even during the hardest of times.

Thank you to the entire staff at Syngress publishing—you made this project an easy one.

Thanks to my fantastic Technical Editor, Robert Shimonski, for keeping me honest and making this work even better than I had hoped for.

Technical Editor and DVD Presenter

Robert J. Shimonski (TruSecure TICSA, Cisco CCDP, CCNP, Symantec SPS, NAI Sniffer SCP, Nortel NNCSS, Microsoft MCSE, MCP+I, Novell Master CNE, CIP, CIBS, CNS, IWA CWP, DCSE, Prosoft MCIW, SANS.org GSEC, GCIH, CompTIA Server+, Network+, Inet+, A+, e-Biz+, Security+, HTI+) is a Lead Network and Security Engineer for a leading manufacturing company, Danaher Corporation. At Danaher, Robert is responsible for leading the IT department within his division into implementing new technologies, standardization, upgrades, migrations, high-end project planning and designing infrastructure architecture. Robert is also part of the corporate security team responsible for setting guidelines and policy for the entire corporation worldwide. In his role as a Lead Network Engineer, Robert has designed, migrated, and implemented very large-scale Cisco and Nortel based networks. Robert has held positions as a Network Architect for Cendant Information Technology and worked on accounts ranging from the IRS to AVIS Rent a Car, and was part of the team that rebuilt the entire Avis worldwide network infrastructure to include the Core and all remote locations. Robert maintains a role as a part time technical trainer at a local computer school, teaching classes on networking and systems administration whenever possible.

Robert is also a part-time author who has worked on over 25 book projects as both an author and technical editor. He has written and edited books on a plethora of topics with a strong emphasis on network security. Robert has designed and worked on several projects dealing with cutting edge technologies for Syngress Publishing, including the only book dedicated to the Sniffer Pro protocol analyzer. Robert has worked on the following Syngress Publishing titles: *Building DMZs for Enterprise Networks* (ISBN: 1-931836-88-4), *Security+ Study Guide & DVD Training System* (ISBN: 1-931836-72-8), *Sniffer Pro Network Optimization & Troubleshooting Handbook* (ISBN: 1-931836-57-4), *Configuring and Troubleshooting Windows XP Professional* (ISBN: 1-928994-80-6), *SSCP Study Guide & DVD Training System* (ISBN: 1-931836-80-9), *Nokia Network Security Solutions Handbook* (ISBN: 1-931836-70-1) and the *MCSE Implementing and Administering Security in a Windows 2000 Network Study Guide & DVD Training System* (ISBN: 1-931836-84-1).

Robert's specialties include network infrastructure design with the Cisco product line, systems engineering with Windows 2000/Server 2003, NetWare 6, Red Hat Linux and Apple OSX. Robert's true love is network security design and management utilizing products from the Nokia, Cisco, and Check Point arsenal. Robert is also an advocate of Network Management and loves to 'sniff' networks with Sniffer-based technologies. When not doing something with computer related technology, Robert enjoys spending time with his fiancée Erika, or snowboarding wherever the snow may fall and stick.

Technical Reviewer

Laura E. Hunter (CISSP, MCSE, MCT, MCDBA, MCP, MCP+I, CCNA, A+, Network+, iNet+, Security+, CNE-4, CNE-5) is a Senior IT Specialist with the University of Pennsylvania, where she provides network planning, implementation, and troubleshooting services for various business units and schools within the University. Her specialties include Microsoft Windows NT and 2000 design and implementation, troubleshooting and security topics. As an "MCSE Early Achiever" on Windows 2000, Laura was one of the first in the country to renew her Microsoft credentials under the Windows 2000 certification structure. Laura's previous experience includes a position as the Director of Computer Services for the Salvation Army and as the LAN administrator for a medical supply firm. She also operates as an independent consultant for small businesses in the Philadelphia metropolitan area and is a regular contributor to the TechTarget family of websites.

Laura has previously contributed to the Syngress Publishing's *Configuring Symantec Antivirus, Corporate Edition* (ISBN 1-931836-81-7). She has also contributed to several other exam guides in the Syngress Windows Server 2003 MCSE/MCSA DVD Guide and Training System series as a DVD presenter, contributing author, and technical reviewer.

Laura holds a bachelor's degree from the University of Pennsylvania and is a member of the Network of Women in Computer Technology, the Information Systems Security Association, and InfraGard, a cooperative undertaking between the U.S. Government other participants dedicated to increasing the security of United States critical infrastructures.

Special Contributors

Michael Cross (MCSE, MCP+I, CNA, Network+) is an Internet Specialist/Computer Forensic Analyst with the Niagara Regional Police Service. He performs computer forensic examinations on computers involved in criminal investigations, and has consulted and assisted in cases dealing with computer-related/Internet crimes. In addition to designing and maintaining their Web site at www.nrps.com and Intranet, he has also provided support in the areas of programming, hardware, network administration, and other services. As part of an Information Technology team that provides support to a user base of over 800 civilian and uniform users, his theory is that when the users carry guns, you tend to be more motivated in solving their problems.

Michael also owns KnightWare (www.knightware.ca), which provides computer-related services like Web page design; and Bookworms (www.bookworms.ca), where you can purchase collectibles and other interesting items online. He has been a freelance writer for several years, and published over three dozen times in numerous books and anthologies. He currently resides in St. Catharines, Ontario Canada with his lovely wife Jennifer and his darling daughter Sara.

Jeffery A. Martin (MCSE, MCDBA, MCT, MCP+I, MCP, MCNE, CNE, CNA, CNI, CCNA, CCNP, CCI, CCA, CTT, A+, Network+, I-Net+, Project+, Linux+, CIW, ADPM) has been working with computers and computer networks for over 15 years. Jeffery spends most of his time managing several companies that he owns and consulting for large multinational media companies. He also enjoys working as a technical instructor and training others in the use of technology.

Chris Peiris (MVP) currently lectures on Distributed Component Architectures (.NET, J2EE, and CORBA) at Monash University, Caulfield, Victoria, Australia. He also works as an independent consultant for .NET and EAI implementations. He is been awarded the title "Microsoft Most Valuable Professional" (MVP) for his contributions to .NET Technologies. He has been designing and developing Microsoft solutions since 1995. His expertise lies in developing scalable, high-performance solutions for financial institutions and media groups. He has written many articles, reviews and columns for various online publications including 15Seconds, Developer Exchange (www.Devx.com) and Wrox Press (www.wrox.com). He co-authored the book *C# Web Service with .NET Remoting and ASP.NET* (Wrox Press). It was followed by *C# for Java Programmers* (Syngress Publishing, 1-931836-54-X) as a primary author. Chris frequently presents at professional developer conferences on Microsoft technologies.

MCSA/MCSE 70-292 Exam Objectives Map and Table of Contents

All of Microsoft's published objectives for the MCSA/MCSE 70-292 Exam are covered in this book. To help you easily find the sections that directly support particular objectives, we've listed all of the exam objectives below, and mapped them to the Chapter number in which they are covered. We've also assigned numbers to each objective, which we use in the subsequent Table of Contents and again throughout the book to identify objective coverage. In some chapters, we've made the judgment that it is probably easier for the student to cover objectives in a slightly different sequence than the order of the published Microsoft objectives. By reading this study guide and following the corresponding objective list, you can be sure that you have studied 100% of Microsoft's MCSA/MCSE 70-292 Exam objectives.

Exam Objective Map

Objective Number	Objective	Chapter Number
1	**Managing Users, Computers, and Groups**	1
1.1	Create and manage groups	1
1.1.1	Identify and modify the scope of a group	1
1.1.2	Find domain groups in which a user is a member	1
1.1.3	Manage group membership	1
1.1.4	Create and modify groups by using the Active Directory Users and Computers Microsoft Management Console (MMC) snap-in	1
1.1.5	Create and modify groups by using automation	1
1.2	Create and manage user accounts	1
1.2.1	Create and modify user accounts by using the Active Directory Users and Computers MMC snap-in	1
1.2.2	Create and modify user accounts by using automation	1

Objective Number	Objective	Chapter Number
1.2.3	Import user accounts	1
1.3	Troubleshoot user authentication issues	1
2	**Managing and Maintaining Access to Resources**	2
2.1	Troubleshoot Terminal Services	2
2.1.1	Diagnose and resolve issues related to Terminal Services security	2
2.1.2	Diagnose and resolve issues related to client access to Terminal Services	2
3	**Managing and Maintaining a Server Environment**	3
3.1	Manage software update infrastructure	8
3.2	Manage servers remotely	3
3.2.1	Manage a server by using Remote Assistance	3
3.2.2	Manage a server by using Terminal Services remote administration mode	3
3.2.3	Manage a server by using available support tools	3
3.3	Manage a Web server	4
3.3.1	Manage Internet Information Services (IIS)	4
3.3.2	Manage security for IIS	4
4	**Managing and Implementing Disaster Recovery**	5
4.1	Perform system recovery for a server	5
4.1.1	Implement Automated System Recovery (ASR)	5
4.1.2	Restore data from shadow copy volumes	5
4.1.3	Back up files and System State data to media	5
4.1.4	Configure security for backup operations	5
5	**Implementing, Managing, and Maintaining Name Resolution**	6
5.1	Install and configure the DNS Server service	6
5.1.1	Configure DNS server options	6
5.1.2	Configure DNS zone options	6

Objective Number	Objective	Chapter Number
5.1.3	Configure DNS forwarding	6
5.2	Manage DNS	6
5.2.1	Manage DNS zone settings	6
5.2.2	Manage DNS record settings	6
5.2.3	Manage DNS server options	6
6	**Implementing, Managing, and Maintaining Network Security**	**7**
6.1	Implement secure network administration procedures	7
6.1.1	Implement security baseline settings and audit security settings by using security templates	7
6.1.2	Implement the principle of least privilege	7
6.2	Install and configure software update infrastructure	8
6.2.1	Install and configure software update services	8
6.2.2	Install and configure automatic client update settings	8
6.2.3	Configure software updates on earlier operating systems	8

Contents

Foreword   **xxix**

About the Study Guide and DVD Training System   **xxxvii**

Chapter 1 Managing Users, Computers, and Groups   **1**

	Introduction	2
1.1	Creating and Managing Groups	2
	Group Types	3
1.1.1	Group Scopes	6
	Using Domain Local Groups	6
	Using Global Groups	8
	Using Universal Groups	8
	Default Groups	10
1.1.2/ **1.1.3/** **1.1.4/** **1.1.5**	Managing and Modifying Groups	14
	Changing the Domain Functional Level	15
1.1.4	Creating New Groups	17
1.1.3	Adding Members to Group	19
	Removing Members from Groups	23
	Converting Group Type	23
1.1.1	Changing Group Scope	26
	Deleting Groups	27
1.1.4	Modifying Group Properties	28
1.1.2	Finding Groups in Which a Particular User is a Member	30
	Assigning User Rights and Permissions to a Group	31
1.2/1.2.1/ **1.2.2**	Creating and Managing User Accounts	36

XV

Default User Accounts 36
Managing and Modifying User Accounts 37

1.2.1/   Creating New User Accounts 37
1.2.2

Resetting the User Account Password 39
Copying a User Account 41
Disabling or Enabling A User Account 42
Configuring User Account Properties 44
    The General Tab 44
    The Address Tab 45
    The Account Tab 45
    The Profile Tab 48
    The Telephones Tab 49
    The Organization Tab 49
    The Member Of Tab 50
Deleting User Accounts 50
Assigning User Rights and Permissions to a User Account 52

1.3   Troubleshooting User Authentication Issues 52
Creating and Managing Computer Accounts 53
    Creating and Modifying Computer Accounts Manually 54
    Creating Computer Accounts by Joining to the Domain 55

1.1.5/1.2.2 Importing and Exporting Active Directory Data 58
/1.2.3

Summary of Exam Objectives 61
Exam Objectives Fast Track 61
Exam Objectives Frequently Asked Questions 64
Self Test 66
Self Test Quick Answer Key 71

Chapter 2 Managing and Maintaining   **73**
Terminal Services Access
Introduction 74
The Need for Terminal Services:
  A Survey of Computing Environments 75
    Centralized Computing versus Distributed Computing 75
    Mixed Environments 80
    Terminal Services Design Issues 81
  Introduction to Windows Server 2003 Terminal Services 83
    Terminal Server 83
    Terminal Server Session Directory 86

Installing and Configuring a Terminal Server 87
Installing the Terminal Server 87
2.1/2.1.1/ Configuring the Terminal Server 92
2.1.2

Using the Terminal Services Configuration Console 93
Configuring Server Settings with the
Terminal Services Configuration Console 99
Using the Terminal Services Manager Console 101
2.1/2.1.1/ Advanced Terminal Server Configuration via Group Policy 102
2.1.2

Terminal Services Computer Options 102
2.1.2 Terminal Server Licensing 105
Using the Terminal Server Licensing Tool 106
2.1/2.1.1 Troubleshooting Terminal Services 110
2.1.2

Not Automatically Logged On 110
"This Initial Program Cannot be Started" 111
Clipboard Problems 111
License Problems 111
Security Issues 112
Summary of Exam Objectives 114
Exam Objectives Fast Track 115
Exam Objectives Frequently Asked Questions 118
Self Test 120
Self Test Quick Answer Key 125

Chapter 3 Managing and Maintaining Remote Servers   127
Introduction 128
3.2.3 Types of Management Tools 128
Administrative Tools Folder 129
Custom MMC Consoles 131
Command-Line Utilities 134
Wizards 134
Windows Resource Kits 135
The Run as Command 135
Administration Tools Pack (adminpak.msi) 136
Windows Management Instrumentation 136
Computer Management Console 137
3.2 Using Terminal Services Components for Remote Administration ...137

Terminal Services Components 137
   Remote Desktop for Administration 138
   Remote Assistance 138
3.2.2 Using Remote Desktop for Administration 140
   Configuring Remote Desktop for Administration 140
   Allowing Users to Make Remote
     Desktop for Administration Connections 140
   Advantages of Remote Desktop Administration
     over Other Remote Administration Methods 142
   Remote Desktop Security Issues 143
3.2.1 Using Remote Assistance 144
   How Remote Assistance Works 144
   Configuring Remote Assistance for Use 145
   Asking for Assistance 146
   Using Windows Messenger to Request Help 147
   Using E-mail to Request Help 149
   Using a Saved File to Request Help 152
   Completing the Remote Assistance Connection 154
   Managing Open Invitations 157
   Remote Assistance Security Issues 158
3.2/3.2.2 Using Terminal Services Client Tools 160
   Using the Remote Desktop Connection Utility 160
   Installing the Remote Desktop Connection Utility 161
   Launching and Using the
     Remote Desktop Connection Utility 162
   Configuring the Remote Desktop Connection Utility 164
   Using the Remote Desktops Console 170
   Adding a New Connection 172
   Configuring a Saved Remote Connection's Properties 173
   Connecting and Disconnecting 175
   Using the Remote Desktop Web Connection Utility 176
   Installing the Remote Desktop Web Connection Utility ...176
   Using the Remote Desktop
     Web Connection Utility from a Client 177
   Using Web Interface for Remote Administration 181
3.2.3 Using Emergency Management Services 183
   Summary of Exam Objectives 187
   Exam Objectives Fast Track 188

Exam Objectives Frequently Asked Questions 190
Self Test 192
Self Test Quick Answer Key 197

Chapter 4 Managing and Maintaining Web Servers   199
Introduction 200
What is New in IIS 6.0? 200
   New Security Features 200
      Advanced Digest Authentication 201
      Server-Gated Cryptography 202
      Selectable Cryptographic Service Provider 203
      Configurable Worker Process Identity 203
      Default Lockdown Status 203
      New Authorization Framework 204
   New Reliability Features 205
      Health Detection 206
      New Request Processing Architecture:
         HTTP.SYS Kernel Mode Driver 206
   Other New Features 207
      ASP.NET and IIS Integration 208
      Unicode Transformation Format-8 (UTF-8) 208
      XML Metabase 208
Installing and Configuring IIS 6.0 209
   Installation Methods 210
      Using the Configure Your Server Wizard 210
      Using the Windows Component Wizard to Install IIS 6.0 ...215
      Using Unattended Setup to Install IIS 6.0 217
3.3 /3.3.1 Managing IIS 6.0 219
   Creating New Sites and Virtual Servers with IIS Manager 220
      Creating New Web Sites
         Using the Web Site Creation Wizard 220
      Creating New FTP Sites
         Using the FTP Site Creation Wizard 224
      Creating New SMTP Virtual Servers
         Using the New SMTP Virtual Server Wizard 227
      Creating New NNTP Virtual Servers
         Using the New NNTP Virtual Server Wizard 229
   Common Administrative Tasks 232
      Enabling Web Service Extensions 232

Creating Virtual Directories 233
Hosting Multiple Web Sites 235
Configuring Web Site Performance 238
Working with ASP.NET 238
Backing Up and Restoring the IIS Metabase 239
Enabling Health Detection 241

3.3.2 Managing IIS Security 243
User Authentication Methods 244
Anonymous Authentication 244
Basic Authentication 245
Integrated Windows Authentication 246
Digest Authentication 246
.NET Passport Authentication 248
Using Client Certificate Mapping 248
Configuring User Authentication 249
Configuring IP Address/Domain Restrictions 252
Configuring SSL-Secured Communications 253

3.3.1 Troubleshooting IIS 6.0 258
Troubleshooting Content Errors 258
Static Files Return 404 Errors 258
Dynamic Content Returns a 404 Error 259
Sessions Lost Due to Worker Process Recycling 259
ASP.NET Pages are Returned as Static Files 260
Troubleshooting Connection Errors 260
503 Errors 260
401 Error – Sub-authentication Error 262
Client Requests Timing Out 262
Troubleshooting Other Errors 263
File Not Found Errors for UNIX and Linux Files 263
ISAPI Filters Are Not Automatically
Visible as Properties of the Web Site 263
The Scripts and Msadc Virtual
Directories Are Not Found in IIS 6.0 263

Summary of Exam Objectives 264
Exam Objectives Fast Track 266
Exam Objectives Frequently Asked Questions 266
Self Test 268
Self Test Quick Answer Key 273

Chapter 5 Managing and Implementing Disaster Recovery 275

Introduction 276
Creating a Backup Plan 276
    Backup Basics 277
    Backup Types 278
    Backup Media 279
        Media Types 280
        Offsite Storage 282
        Media Rotation 282
4.1 Using the Windows Backup Utility 287
4.1.3   Understanding System State Data 288
4.1.3   Backup Configuration Options 289
        Configuring the General Options 290
        Configuring the Restore Options 292
        Configuring the Backup Type Options 293
        Configuring the Backup Log Options 293
        Configuring the Exclude File Options 294
4.1.3   Using the Backup Utility in Advanced Mode 295
4.1.3   Using the Backup Utility in Wizard Mode 303
4.1.4   Configuring Security for Backup Operations 308
    Restoring Backup Data 309
4.1.1 Using Automated System Recovery 312
4.1.2   Working with Volume Shadow Copy 314
    Making Shadow Copies of Shared Folders 315
        Enabling Shadow Copies on the Shared Resource 315
        Changing Settings for Shadow Copies 318
    Deploying the Client Software for Shadow Copies 322
    Restoring Previous Versions of a File 322
    Shadow Copies Best Practices 324
Summary of Exam Objectives 325
Exam Objectives Fast Track 326
Exam Objectives Frequently Asked Questions 328
Self Test 329
Self Test Quick Answer Key 336

Chapter 6 Implementing, Managing, and Maintaining Name Resolution   337

	Introduction	338
5.1	Introducing and Planning the DNS Service	339
	The DNS Hierarchical Namespace	340
	Determining Namespace Requirements	342
	Determining Zone Type Requirements	345
5.1.3	Determining Forwarding Requirements	348
	Installing the DNS Service	352
5.1.1	Configuring DNS Server Options	360
	The Interfaces Tab	360
5.1.3	The Forwarders Tab	360
	The Advanced Tab	363
	The Root Hints Tab	365
	The Debug Logging Tab	365
	The Event Logging Tab	367
	The Monitoring Tab	367
5.1.2	Configuring Zone Options	368
	Configuring Forward Lookup Zone Options	368
	The General Tab	369
	The Start of Authority (SOA) Tab	372
	The Name Servers Tab	374
	The WINS Tab	376
	The Zone Transfers Tab	377
	Configuring Reverse Lookup Zone Options	378
	The General Tab	378
	The SOA Tab	379
	The Name Servers Tab	379
	The WINS-R Tab	380
	The Zone Transfers Tab	381
5.2	Managing the DNS Service	381
5.2.3	Managing DNS Server Options	381
	Connecting to Remote DNS Servers	382
	Removing Servers from the DNS Management Console	383
	Configuring Aging and Scavenging for All Zones	383
	Manually Initiating Record Scavenging	384
	Updating the DNS Server Zone File	384
	Clearing the DNS Server Local Cache	385

Launching the *nslookup* Command 385
Starting, Stopping, or Pausing DNS Servers 385
5.2.1 Managing DNS Zone Settings 386
5.2.2 Managing DNS Record Settings 386
Summary of Exam Objectives 390
Exam Objectives Fast Track 391
Exam Objectives Frequently Asked Questions 395
Self Test 396
Self Test Quick Answer Key 402

**Chapter 7 Implementing, Managing,
and Maintaining Network Security   403**

Introduction 404
6.1.2 Using the Principle of Least Privilege 404
6.1/6.1.1 Implementing Security with Security Templates 405
Introduction to Security Templates 406
The Security Configuration Manager Tools 409
The Security Configuration and Analysis Snap-in 411
The Security Templates Snap-in 419
Group Policy Security Extensions 420
The secedit.exe Command 424
Configuring Security Templates 428
Account Policies 428
Local Policies 431
Event Log 442
Restricted Groups 443
System Services 448
Registry 450
File System 452
Deploying Security Templates via Group Policy 454
6.1/ 6.1.1 Auditing Security Events 458
Auditing Areas 458
Audit Account Logon Events 459
Audit Account Management 460
Audit Directory Service Access 462
Audit Logon Events 462
Audit Object Access 463
Audit Policy Change 465
Audit Privilege Use 466

Audit Process Tracking 466

Audit System Events 467

Planning for Auditing 468

Configuring and Implementing Auditing 469

Summary of Exam Objectives 473

Exam Objectives Fast Track 474

Exam Objectives Frequently Asked Questions 476

Self Test 478

Self Test Quick Answer Key 485

Chapter 8 Managing and Implementing Software Updates
487

Introduction 488

6.2   Installing, Configuring, and Managing
the Software Update Infrastructure 488

6.2.1   Installing Software Update Services 489

6.2.2   Installing and Configuring the Automatic Update Client 497

3.1   Managing Software Update Services 507

Viewing the Synchronization Logs 507

Viewing the Approval Logs 508

Monitoring the SUS Server 509

Examining the Event Logs 510

Viewing the SUS IIS Logs 512

Troubleshooting SUS and Automatic Updates 512

6.2.3   Managing Updates for Legacy Clients 513

Windows Update 514

Windows Update Catalog 518

Systems Management Server
and Third-party Applications 521

Summary of Exam Objectives 522

Exam Objectives Fast Track 523

Exam Objectives Frequently Asked Questions 524

Self Test 525

Self Test Quick Answer Key 534

Appendix A MCSA Command-Line Reference
535

Introduction 536

Active Directory Management 536

dsadd 537

dsadd computer 537

dsadd contact 538

dsadd group 539

dsadd ou 540

dsadd user 540

dsadd quota 542

dsmod 543

dsmod computer 543

dsmod contact 543

dsmod group 544

dsmod ou 545

dsmod server 546

dsmod user 546

dsmod quota 548

dsmod partition 548

dsrm 549

dsmove 549

dsquery 550

dsquery computer 550

dsquery contact 551

dsquery group 552

dsquery ou 553

dsquery site 553

dsquery server 554

dsquery user 555

dsquery quota 556

dsquery partition 556

dsquery ★ 557

dsget 558

dsget computer 558

dsget contact 559

dsget group 560

dsget ou 561

dsget server 562

dsget user 563

dsget subnet 564

dsget site 565

dsget quota 565

dsget partition 566

gpresult 567

whoami 567

csvde and ldifde 568

DNS Management 570

dnscmd 570

dnscmd /ageallrecords 571

dnscmd /clearcache 572

dnscmd /config 572

dnscmd /createbuiltindirectorypartitions 578

dnscmd /createdirectorypartition 578

dnscmd /deletedirectorypartition 578

dnscmd /directorypartitioninfo 579

dnscmd /enlistdirectorypartition 579

dnscmd /enumdirectorypartitions 579

dnscmd /enumrecords 579

dnscmd /enumzones 580

dnscmd /info 581

dnscmd /nodedelete 581

dnscmd /recordadd 581

dnscmd /recorddelete 582

dnscmd /resetforwarders 582

dnscmd /resetlistenaddresses 583

dnscmd /startscavenging 583

dnscmd /statistics 583

dnscmd /unenlistdirectorypartition 584

dnscmd /writebackfiles 584

dnscmd /zoneadd 584

dnscmd /zonechangedirectorypartition 585

dnscmd /zonedelete 585

dnscmd /zoneexport 586

dnscmd /zoneinfo 586

dnscmd /zonepause 586

dnscmd /zoneprint 586

dnscmd /zoneresettype 586

dnscmd /zonerefresh 587

dnscmd /zonereload 587

dnscmd /zoneresetmasters 587

dnscmd /zoneresetscavengeservers 588

dnscmd /zoneresetsecondaries 588

dnscmd /zoneresume 589

dnscmd /zoneupdatefromds 589

dnscmd /zonewriteback 589

dnslint 589

nslookup 590

IIS 6.0 Management 593

iisweb.vbs 593

iisweb /create 593

iisweb /delete, /start, /stop, /pause 594

iisweb /query 594

iisvdir.vbs 595

iisvdir /create 595

iisvdir /delete 595

iisvdir /query 596

iisftp.vbs 596

iisftp /create 596

iisftp /delete, /start, /stop, /pause 597

iisftp /query 597

iisftp /setadprop 598

iisftp /getadprop 598

iisftpdr.vbs 598

iisftpdr /create 598

iisftpdr /delete 599

iisftpdr /query 599

iisback.vbs 600

iisback /backup 600

iisback /restore 601

iisback /delete 601

iisback /list 601

iiscnfg.vbs 601

iiscnfg /export 602

iiscnfg /import 602

iiscnfg /copy 603

iiscnfg /save 603

Security Template Management 603

secedit 604

secedit /analyze 604

secedit /configure 605
secedit /export 605
secedit /import 606
secedit /validate 607
secedit /GenerateRollback 607
Windows Backup Management 607
ntbackup 607

Self Test Appendix   **609**
Index   **681**

Foreword

Congratulations! By picking up this book you have taken a big step in keeping your Windows skills up to date. Whether you are an IT guru with years of experience, a neophyte fresh to the exciting world of IT, or somewhere in the middle, this book will help you get to your destination by providing you with the information and tools you need to pass the 70-292 exam, *Managing and Maintaining a Microsoft Windows Server 2003 Environment for an MCSA Certified on Windows 2000*.

Exam 70-292 is a new exam introduced by Microsoft in February 2003 as the only requirement for Microsoft Certified Systems Administrators (MCSAs) currently certified on Windows 2000 Server to upgrade their certification to MCSA on Windows Server 2003. Currently, certified Microsoft Certified Systems Engineers (MCSEs) on Windows 2000 Server must take this exam and the 70-296 exam, *Planning, Implementing, and Maintaining a Microsoft Windows Server 2003 Environment for an MCSE Certified on Windows 2000* to complete their upgrade to an MCSE on Windows Server 2003.

This book was written by a team of authors who are extremely familiar with Windows Server 2003 and Windows 2000 Server. Rest assured that this book contains the best information available and is based on real-world scenarios and applications that you may likely face one day.

What is the MCSA/MCSE?

The Microsoft Certified Professional (MCP) program turned 10 years old in the spring of 2002. From its humble beginnings, the MCP program has grown into one of the largest and most prestigious IT certification programs. Microsoft leads the way in the number and subject matter of exams delivered, with one or more exams to fit just about every person. Today, Microsoft has a dozen different IT certification tracks, ranging from networking to office suites. The MCSA and MCSE tracks specifically deal with the networking side of Microsoft's product line.

MCSA Background

At the time of this writing, Microsoft's newest networking certification track (the MCSA) is two years old. In those two years, it has quickly gained popularity as a solid foundation for those who are tasked with the day-to-day administration and maintenance of Windows Server 2003 and Windows 2000 Server networks.

Typical duties of the MCSA certified individual include managing, supporting, and troubleshooting daily needs associated with the operation of a Windows Server 2003 or Windows 2000 Server network. Microsoft specifies that an MCSA typically have at least 6 to 12 months of hands-on experience managing and supporting workstations and servers in an existing Windows Server 2003 or Windows 2000 Server infrastructure. This is a key distinction from the MCSE certification, which may involve designing and implementing new Windows Server 2003 or Windows 2000 Server infrastructures.

Some typical job titles that MCSAs may have include:

- Systems administrator
- Network administrator
- Information Systems administrator
- Network operations analyst
- Network technician
- Technical support specialist

MCSE Background

The MCSE certification dates back to the Windows NT 3.51 days, and possibly earlier. The MCSE certification came under fire during the Windows NT 4.0 track due to the ease of obtaining it. Many people simply memorized the material and took the exams, achieving the MCSE certification without having enough (or in some cases, any) hands-on experience with the product. Microsoft took great pains when it rolled out the Windows 2000 MCSE track to ensure that it corrected these issues by changing the testing experience. New question types and larger, more complex question banks were implemented in an effort to make the MCSE certification meaningful. With the introduction of the Windows Server 2003 certification track, it appears that Microsoft intends to continue this progression by introducing new exam question types such as hot area, active screen, and drag-and-drop types. More information about the testing innovations that Microsoft is working on can be found at www.microsoft.com/traincert/mcpexams/faq/innovations.asp.

The typical duties of the Windows Server 2003 MCSE include planning, designing, and implementing Windows 2000 server solutions and architectures. In other words, an MCSE certified individual should expect to spend more time designing and implementing new solutions than would the MCSA certified individual. This explains why the exam requirements for the MCSE certification include a design exam in which the candidate must not only understand the networking problems at hand, but also the business problems to be dealt with. To this end, Microsoft recommends that the MCSE-certified individual have one or more years of real-world hands-on experience analyzing business and technical requirements to support the planning, designing, and implementing of solutions capitalizing on Microsoft products and technologies—not just to include Windows Server 2003.

Some typical job titles that MCSEs may have include:

- Systems engineer
- Network engineer
- Systems analyst
- Network analyst
- Technical consultant

The Path to MCSA/MCSE

The MCSA and MCSE each have their own certification requirements, as outlined in the following sections.

The MCSA Track

To become certified as an MCSA on Windows Server 2003, you must pass three core exams and one elective exam. The required core exams consist of one client operating system exam and two networking system exams. A combination of specific CompTIA exams may be used as the elective, or the elective may be chosen from the given list of elective exams. If previously taken, exam 70-240 can be used as credit in the form of the 70-210 exam towards the MCSA requirements. As well, the 70-292 exam is an upgrade exam for currently certified MCSAs on Windows 2000 Server and is the only required exam for the upgrade to MCSA on Windows Server 2003 status.

The core exams consist of one client operating system exam and two network system exams. You will need to pass one of the following client operating system exams:

- Exam 70-210 Installing, Configuring, and Administering Microsoft Windows 2000 Professional
- Exam 70-270 Installing, Configuring, and Administering Microsoft Windows XP Professional

You also need to pass the following two core network systems exams.

- Exam 70-290 Managing and Maintaining a Microsoft Windows Server 2003 Environment

- Exam 70-291 Implementing, Managing, and Maintaining a Microsoft Windows Server 2003 Network Infrastructure

You also need to pass one elective exam from the following list:

- Exam 70-086 Implementing and Supporting Microsoft Systems Management Server 2.0

- Exam 70-227 Installing, Configuring, and Administering Microsoft Internet Security and Acceleration (ISA) Server 2000, Enterprise Edition

- Exam 70-228 Installing, Configuring, and Administering Microsoft SQL Server 2000 Enterprise Edition

- Exam 70-284 Implementing and Managing Microsoft Exchange Server 2003

- Exam 70-299 Implementing and Administering Security in a Microsoft Windows Server 2003 Network

Alternatively, you can substitute one of the following combinations of CompTIA exams for the required elective exam:

- A+ and Network+

- A+ and Server+

- Security+

For help in getting your CompTIA certifications put towards your MCSA certification, see the CompTIA Web site at www.comptia.org/certification/mcsa. You can get the latest news on the MCSA certification track from the Microsoft MCSA Web site, located at www.microsoft.com/traincert/mcp/mcsa/default.asp.

Once you have met all of the requirements for achieving MCSA certification, you will receive an e-mail confirmation of your new MCSA status from Microsoft approximately 72 hours after successfully completing the last requirements. You can also expect to receive your MCSA welcome kit from Microsoft confirming your MCSA status, in about 6 to 8 weeks in North America, sometimes longer than this worldwide.

The MCSE Track

The MCSE certification is considered a premier certification, and thus requires a total of seven MCP exams to complete as outlined here. You must pass one core client operating system exam, four core network system exams, one core design exam and one elective exam.

You need to pass one required client operating system exam from the following choices:

- Exam 70-210 Installing, Configuring, and Administering Microsoft Windows 2000 Professional

- Exam 70-270 Installing, Configuring, and Administering Microsoft Windows XP Professional

You need to pass these four core network system exams:

- Exam 70-290 Managing and Maintaining a Microsoft Windows Server 2003 Environment

- Exam 70-291 Implementing, Managing, and Maintaining a Microsoft Windows Server 2003 Network Infrastructure

- Exam 70-293 Planning and Maintaining a Microsoft Windows Server 2003 Network Infrastructure

- Exam 70-294 Planning, Implementing, and Maintaining a Microsoft Windows Server 2003 Active Directory Infrastructure

You will also need to pass one of the following core design exams:

- Exam 70-297 Designing a Microsoft Windows Server 2003 Active Directory and Network Infrastructure

- Exam 70-298 Designing Security for a Microsoft Windows Server 2003 Network

Lastly, you will need to pass one elective exam from the following list:

- Exam 70-086 Implementing and Supporting Microsoft Systems Management Server 2.0

- Exam 70-227 Installing, Configuring, and Administering Microsoft Internet Security and Acceleration (ISA) Server 2000, Enterprise Edition

- Exam 70-228 Installing, Configuring, and Administering Microsoft SQL Server 2000 Enterprise Edition

- Exam 70-229 Designing and Implementing Databases with Microsoft SQL Server 2000 Enterprise Edition

- Exam 70-232 Implementing and Maintaining Highly Available Web Solutions with Microsoft Windows 2000 Server Technologies and Microsoft Application Center 2000

- Exam 70-284 Implementing and Managing Microsoft Exchange Server 2003

- Exam 70-297 Designing a Microsoft Windows Server 2003 Active Directory and Network Infrastructure

- Exam 70-298 Designing Security for a Microsoft Windows Server 2003 Network

- Exam 70-299 Implementing and Administering Security in a Microsoft Windows Server 2003 Network

Alternatively, you can substitute the following CompTIA exam for a required elective exam:

- Security+

You can get the latest news on the MCSE certification track from the Microsoft MCSE Web site, located at www.microsoft.com/traincert/mcp/mcse/default.asp. Note that although some exams are listed under more than one requirement, you can use an exam to fulfill only one requirement. Also, many exams are either/or, meaning that you can use either Exam 70-210 or Exam 70-270 to fulfill a requirement.

Once you have met all of the requirements to achieve MCSE certification, you will receive e-mail confirmation of your new MCSE status from Microsoft approximately 72 hours after successfully completing your last requirements. You can also expect to receive a MCSE welcome kit from Microsoft confirming your MCSE status in about 6 to 8 weeks in North America, sometimes longer than this worldwide.

Registering For Exams

MCP exams are administered by two third-party organizations, VUE and Thompson-Prometric. You can register for an exam online or by telephone. At the time of this writing, MCP exams cost $125.00 each to register, although the prices are periodically adjusted.

- VUE, www.vue.com, 800-837-8734 (United States and Canada). See www.vue.com/contact/ms for a list of worldwide MCP exam registration phone numbers.

- Thompson-Prometric, www.2test.com, 800-755-EXAM (United States and Canada). See www.prometric.com/candidates/contactus2.asp?aoc=gen&pnum =2&PgpName=contactus for a list of worldwide MCP exam registration phone numbers.

MCP Status

If this is your first Microsoft MCP exam, you will become an MCP upon the successful completion of this exam. You will receive an e-mail confirmation of your new MCP status from Microsoft approximately 72 hours after successfully completing the exam. You will also receive your MCP welcome kit from Microsoft in approximately 6 to 8 weeks in North America, sometimes longer than this worldwide, confirming your MCP status.

Exam Day Experience

If you are unfamiliar with the examination process and format, taking your first MCP exam can be quite an experience. You should plan on arriving at your testing center at least 15 minutes before your scheduled exam time. Remember to bring two forms of identification with you, as testing centers are required by the vendor (Microsoft in this case) to verify your identity.

Types of Questions

You should expect to see a variety of question types on this exam, as Microsoft tends to use multiple question types to further discourage cheating on exams. Some types of questions that you may encounter include:

- **Multiple Choice** This is the standard exam question followed by several answer choices. You will see questions that require only one correct answer and also questions that require two or more correct answers. When multiple answers are required, you will be told this in the question, such as "Choose all correct answers" or "Choose three correct answers."

- **Hot Area** This type of exam question presents a question with an accompanying image and requires you to click on the image in a specific location to correctly answer the question. CompTIA regularly uses this type of question on the A+ exams.

- **Active Screen** This type of question requires you to configure a Windows dialog box by performing tasks to change one or more elements in the dialog box.

- **Drag-and-Drop** This type of exam question requires you to select objects and place them into the answer area as specified in the question.

Exam Experience

The exam itself is delivered via a computer. You will be allowed to use the Windows calculator at all times during the exam, but all other functions of the testing computer are locked out during the testing process. The testing center will have some means in place to monitor the testing room, either via video camera or one-way mirror glass, to discourage cheating. Before starting the exam, you may be asked to complete one or more short surveys. The time spent completing these surveys is separate from the time you will be allotted to complete the exam itself. If you are not taking the exam in English you may be entitled to extra testing time, make sure you talk to the testing center personnel about this issue. You may also be asked to complete one or more surveys following the exam. Again, any surveys you are asked to complete after the exam will not take away from your exam time. You will know immediately after completion of the exam whether or not you have passed and will receive an official score report from the testing center. However, it will take several business days for your online transcript to be updated on Microsoft's Web site. You can access your online transcript at www.microsoft.com/traincert/mcp/mcpsecure.asp.

Final Thoughts

While studying for your 70-292 exam, be sure to get as much hands on experience as you can with not only Windows Server 2003, but also with Windows XP Professional, Windows 2000 Professional, and Windows 2000 Server. You might be surprised by some questions that expect you to have a detailed knowledge of Windows Server 2003 and Windows 2000 Server. Setting up a small two- or three-computer test lab will benefit you greatly by allowing you to perform some tasks you would not otherwise be able to.

I would like to wish you the best of luck in pursuing your certification goals and thank you for choosing this text to help you take the next step toward those goals. Everyone involved in this project has put their best efforts into creating and delivering a thorough and useful work that not only covers the exam objectives, but also provides additional information that we believe will be useful to you to in keeping your network running smoothly.

Will Schmied
July 2003

About the Study Guide and DVD Training System

In this book, you'll find lots of interesting sidebars designed to highlight the most important concepts being presented in the main text. These include the following:

- **Exam Warnings** focus on specific elements on which the reader needs to focus in order to pass the exam.

- **Test Day Tips** are short tips that will help you in organizing and remembering information for the exam.

- **Configuring & Implementing** contain background information that goes beyond what you need to know from the exam, providing a deep foundation for understanding advanced design, installation, and configuration concepts discussed in the text.

- **New & Noteworthy** discussions and explanations of features and enhancements to Windows Server 2003.

- **Head of the Class** discussions are based on the author's interactions with students in live classrooms and the topics covered here are the ones students have the most problems with.

Each chapter also includes hands-on exercises. It is important that you work through these exercises in order to be confident you know how to apply the concepts you have just read about.

You will find a number of helpful elements at the end of each chapter. For example, each chapter contains a *Summary of Exam Objectives* that ties the topics discussed in that chapter to the published objectives. Each chapter also contains an *Exam Objectives Fast Track,* which boils all exam objectives down to manageable summaries that are perfect for last minute review. *The Exam Objectives Frequently Asked Questions* answers those questions that most often arise from readers and students regarding the topics covered in the chapter. Finally, in the *Self Test* section, you will find a set of practice questions written in a multiple-choice form that will assist you in your exam preparation These questions are designed to assess your mastery of the exam objectives and provide thorough remediation, as opposed to simulating the variety of question formats you may encounter in the actual exam. You can use the *Self Test Quick Answer Key* that follows the *Self Test* questions to quickly determine what information you need to review again. The *Self Test Appendix* at the end of the book provides detailed explanations of both the correct and incorrect answers.

Additional Resources

There are two other important exam preparation tools included with this Study Guide. One is the DVD included in the back of this book. The other is the concept review test available from our Web site.

- **Instructor-led training DVD provides you with almost two hours of virtual classroom instruction.** Sit back and watch as an author and trainer reviews all the key exam concepts from the perspective of someone taking the exam for the first time. Here, you'll cut through all of the noise to prepare you for exactly what to expect when you take the exam for the first time. You will want to watch this DVD just before you head out to the testing center!

- **Web based practice exams.** Just visit us at **www.syngress.com/certification** to access a complete Windows Server 2003 concept multiple choice review. These remediation tools are written to test you on all of the published certification objectives. The exam runs in both "live" and "practice" mode. Use "live" mode first to get an accurate gauge of your knowledge and skills, and then use practice mode to launch an extensive review of the questions that gave you trouble.

Chapter 1

MCSA/MCSE 70-292

Managing Users, Computers, and Groups

Exam Objectives in this Chapter:

1.1   Create and manage groups

1.1.1   Identify and modify the scope of a group

1.1.2   Find domain groups in which a user is a member

1.1.3   Manage group membership

1.1.4   Create and modify groups by using the Active Directory Users and Computers Microsoft Management Console (MMC) snap-in

1.1.5   Create and modify groups by using automation

1.2   Create and manage user accounts

1.2.1   Create and modify user accounts by using the Active Directory Users and Computers MMC snap-in

1.2.2   Create and modify user accounts by using automation

1.2.3   Import user accounts

1.3   Troubleshoot user authentication issues

Introduction

It seems natural to start a book for network administrators with the nuts and bolts of administration—groups and accounts. Windows Server 2003 follows in the footsteps of Windows 2000 Server by providing network administrators with intuitive and easy-to-use tools that can be used to accomplish these tasks within a graphical user interface (GUI). Windows Server 2003 also has the ability to perform these tasks from the command line using interactive commands, or pre-written scripts and batch files.

This chapter works extensively with users and groups, and presents the information required for the "Managing Users, Computers, and Groups" objective of the 70-292 exam. Additionally, this chapter examines some common user authentication issues.

Extended Command Line Functionality

Some of the biggest improvements in Windows Server 2003 are the significant enhancements made to the command line utilities. The following new command line tools have been added to make the administrator's job easier:

- **dsadd** Can be used to add new objects into Active Directory such as contacts, computers, groups, organizational units, and users.

- **dsmod** Can be used to modify an existing object in Active Directory.

- **dsrm** Can be used to remove an existing object from Active Directory.

- **dsmove** Can be used to move a single object in Active Directory within the same domain from one location to another. Can also be used to rename an object without moving it.

- **dsquery** Can be used to query Active Directory per the specified criteria to locate a specific object or object type.

- **dsget** Can be used to display the properties of a specific object in Active Directory.

EXAM 70-292 OBJECTIVE 1.1

Creating and Managing Groups

Before network administrators can begin working with groups in Windows Server 2003, they need to understand what groups are and why they are used. A group is a collection of user and/or computer accounts, contacts, and other groups that are managed as a single object. The users and computers that belong to the group are known as *group members*. In Windows, as with most operating systems, groups are used to simplify the administrative process of assigning permissions and rights to a large number of user and computer accounts at the same time, resulting in these groups' members having inherited (or implicit) permissions from the group. Groups make rights management easier and less prone to error.

A set of default groups, known as *local groups*, is created during the installation of Windows Server 2003. Computers that are part of an Active Directory domain environment also have a set of default groups; however, these default groups are objects that reside within the Active Directory database structure. Additional groups can be created as required for both workstation- and domain-based computers. For the purposes of this discussion, it is assumed that you are working with an Active Directory environment when discussing the creation and management of groups.

When using groups in Active Directory, the following three major benefits are provided:

1. Security groups allow network administrators to simplify and reduce administrative requirements by assigning permissions and rights for a shared resource (think printer or file share) to the group rather than to each individual user that requires access. In this way, all users (and groups) that are members of the group receive the configured permissions and rights through inheritance. This is much more efficient and accurate than explicitly assigning permissions and rights to users on an individual basis. This also provides the network administrator with the ability to move users in and out of groups as their job and task requirements dictate.

2. Security groups allow network administrators efficiently delegate administrative responsibilities for performing specific tasks in Active Directory. As an example, an administrator might have a group of six help desk workers that they wish to assign the ability to reset user passwords. By placing these six users in a group and then delegating this ability to the group, they can easily allow these users to perform this specific task that might otherwise be outside their standard permissions. Again, using groups this way allows the network administrator to move users in and out of the group as required.

3. Security and distribution groups allow network administrators to quickly create e-mail distribution groups by assigning an e-mail address to the group itself. All members of that group that are mailbox-enabled will receive e-mail that is sent to the group's e-mail address. This is an added ability of security groups and the only usage for distribution groups (discussed later in the "Group Type" section).

When talking about groups, there are two basic characteristics to keep in mind: *type* and *scope*, which are discussed in the next sections.

Group Types

There are two types of groups available for use in both workgroup and domain environments:

■ **Distribution Groups** Distribution groups are used for distributing messages to group members. Distribution groups are used with e-mail applications, such as Microsoft Exchange, to send e-mail to all members of a group in a quick and efficient manner by sending an e-mail to the group e-mail address. All members of the distribution group that are mailbox-enabled receive the e-mail message. Distribution groups are not security-enabled, and therefore cannot be listed on the Discretionary Access Control Lists (DACLs) that are used by Windows to control access to resources.

- **Security Groups** Security groups can be used for the distribution of e-mail as described for distribution groups, but can also be listed on DACLs, thus allowing them to control access to resources. Security groups can be used to assign user rights to group members. User rights include actions such as *Backup files and directories* or *Restore files and directories*, both of which are assigned to the Backup Operators group by default. As mentioned previously, the network administrator can delegate rights to groups to allow the members of the group to perform a specific administrative function that is not normally allowed by their standard user rights. Network administrators can also assign permissions to security groups to allow them to access network resources such as printers and file shares. Permissions, which should not be confused with user rights, determine which users can access specified resources and what they can do (read, write, execute, and so on) to that resource. By assigning these permissions to a group instead of individual users, the network administrator can ensure that all members of the group have the required permissions.

TEST DAY TIP

Workgroup environments are those that do not use a directory service such as Active Directory. Computers that are part of a workgroup cannot share account or group information between them, thus the settings would need to be configured on each computer individually. Workgroups are also commonly referred to as *peer-to-peer networks*. This type of network is usually best suited for very small groups of computers, including those that are geographically remote from the core network or otherwise isolated from it.

In contrast to workgroups, a domain environment typically relies heavily on a directory service such as Active Directory for user and computer management and security enforcement. In a Windows Server 2003 Active Directory domain environment, accounts and groups need only be created once in Active Directory and are then available for use throughout the entire network. Computers in a domain environment still have local accounts and groups, with the exception of domain controllers, thus allowing users to log into the local computer should they need to. This also allows domain administrators to install applications and perform other management tasks on computers in the domain.

When creating a new group, network administrators have the option to create it either as a distribution group or a security group. When the domain functional level (discussed in the "Changing the Domain Functional Level" section) is Windows 2000 native or higher, the administrator will be able to convert distribution groups to security groups and vice versa. If the domain functional level is set to Windows 2000 mixed, no conversions can be performed.

New & Noteworthy...

Domain and Forest Functionality

Domain and forest functionality is a new feature being introduced in Windows Server 2003. Having different levels of domain and forest functionality available within an Active Directory implementation allows for different features being available to the network.

As an example, if all of a network's domain controllers are Windows Server 2003 and the domain functional level is set to Windows Server 2003, then all domain features become available. For example, you can only make use of the new ability to rename a domain controller if the domain functional mode is set to Windows Server 2003. If the entire Active Directory forest is set at the Windows Server 2003 functional level, you also gain the new ability to rename entire domains. The specifics of how domain functionality levels affect groups is discussed in the "Group Scopes" section of this chapter.

There are three domain functional levels available:

- **Windows 2000 Mixed** The default domain functional level; allows for Windows NT 4.0 backup domain controllers (BDCs), Windows 2000 Server domain controllers, and Windows Server 2003 domain controllers.

- **Windows 2000 Native** The minimum domain functional level at which universal groups become available, along with several other Active Directory features; allows for Windows 2000 Server and Windows Server 2003 domain controllers.

- **Windows Server 2003** The highest domain functional level, providing the most features and functionality; allows only Windows Server 2003 domain controllers.

Once the domain functional level has been raised, domain controllers running earlier operating systems cannot be used in that domain. For example, should a network administrator decide to raise the domain functional level to Windows Server 2003, Windows 2000 Server domain controllers cannot be added to that domain.

Group Scopes

Unlike group types, which are fairly simple to understand, group scopes can be frustrating to those new to working with Windows Server 2003 and Active Directory. The scope of the group identifies the extent to which the group is applied throughout the domain tree or forest. There are three group scopes:

- **Universal Groups** Universal groups can include other groups and user/computer accounts from any domain in the domain tree or forest. Permissions for any domain in the domain tree or forest can be assigned to universal groups.

- **Global Groups** Global groups can include other groups and user/computer accounts from only the domain in which the group is defined. Permissions for any domain in the forest can be assigned to global groups.

- **Domain Local Groups** Domain local groups can include other groups and user/computer accounts from Windows Server 2003, Windows 2000 Server, and Windows NT domains. Permissions for only the domain in which the group is defined can be assigned to domain local groups.

Table 1.1 outlines the behavior and usage of the scopes of groups as the domain functional level changes. The following guidelines will help the network administrator to make better decisions when trying to figure out how to use each group scope:

- Using Domain Local groups

- Using Global groups

- Using Universal groups

Each of these guidelines are discussed in detail in the following sections.

Using Domain Local Groups

A Domain Local group should be used to manage access to resources located within a single domain. Consider the following example on how Domain Local groups can be used: a network administrator has a network file share for which they want to configure access for 20 user accounts. They manually configure the share permissions to allow each of the 20 user accounts to have the required access. Later, they need to configure the permissions on a second network file share for the same 20 user accounts. They now need to perform the manual permissions assignment again for the 20 users. The easier, more accurate and secure way to assign the permissions needed would be to create a Domain Local group and assign it the required permissions on the file shares. After doing this, the administrator could create a Global group and place the 20 user accounts into that Global group. Adding the Global group to the Domain Local group results in all 20 users inheriting the Domain Local group's assigned permissions, which therefore allows them to gain access to the two file shares. This

Table 1.1 Group Scope Behaviors versus Domain Functional Level

Domain Status	Behavior	Universal Group	Global Group	Domain Local Group
Windows Server 2003 or Windows 2000 native	Group membership	Members can include user accounts, computer accounts, and other Universal groups from any domain.	Members can include used accounts, computer accounts, and other Global groups from the domain.	Members can include user accounts, global accounts, computer groups, and Universal groups from the same domain.
Windows 2000 mixed Global	Group membership	Universal groups cannot be created.	Members can include user and computer accounts from the same domain.	Members can include user accounts, computer accounts, and groups from any domain.
Windows Server 2003 or Windows 2000 native	Group nesting	Can be added to other groups.	Can be added to other groups.	Can be added to other Domain Local groups.
Windows Server 2003 or Windows 2000 native	Group permissions	Can be assigned permissions in any domain.	Can be assigned permissions in any domain.	Can be assigned permissions only in the same domain.
Windows Server 2003 or Windows 2000 native	Group scope changes	Can be changed to Global groups as long as no group members are other Universal groups. Can be converted to Domain Local Groups with no restrictions.	Can be changed to Universal groups as long as the group is not a member of any other Global Group.	Can be changed to Universal groups as long as no group members are other Domain Local groups.
Windows 2000 mixed	Group scope changes	Not allowed.	Not allowed.	Not allowed.

is much faster and more accurate than attempting to manually configure permissions for 20 users on two different file shares. Now imagine how this example could be scaled up to include dozens, perhaps hundreds, of shared objects in a network.

Using Global Groups

Global groups should be used to manage objects that will likely require frequent maintenance and management operations, such as user accounts and computer accounts. Global groups are not replicated beyond the boundaries of their own domains. Thus, changes can be made to Global group members without creating large amounts of replication traffic to the domain Global Catalog servers. (This is in direct contrast to Universal groups, which are discussed later in this chapter) Permissions and user rights that are assigned to Global groups are only valid in the domain in which they are assigned. Global groups (or Universal groups) should be used when applying permissions on domain objects that are replicated to the Global Catalog.

Using Universal Groups

Universal groups are best used to consolidate Global groups into one location. Since user accounts are added to Global groups, membership changes in the Global groups do not have an effect on the Universal group. Consider an example where there are two domains, east and west, with Global groups GFinanceEast and GFinanceWest, respectively. User accounts are added to their respective Global group. The two Global groups are then added to one Universal group named UFinance. The UFinance Universal group can be used anywhere within this enterprise and changes that are made to the GFinanceEast and GFinanceWest Global groups do not cause replication to occur for the UFinance group—this provides a bandwidth (and cost) savings.

Membership in Universal groups should not change often as changes to Universal groups are replicated to every Global catalog server in the forest, a potentially very bandwidth-intensive operation.

Configuring & Implementing...

Nesting Groups

You've seen how groups can have other groups as members. This concept is known as *group nesting*. Groups can be nested to help consolidate large numbers of user and computer accounts to reduce replication traffic. The type of nesting that can be performed is determined by the domain functional level of the domain.

If the domain functional level is set to Windows 2000 native or Windows Server 2003, groups can have the following members:

- **Domain Local Groups** Other Domain Local groups in the same domain, Global groups from any domain, Universal groups from any domain, user accounts from any domain, and computer accounts from any domain.

- **Global Groups** Other Global groups in the same domain, user accounts in the same domain, and computer accounts in the same domain.

- **Universal Groups** Other Universal groups from any domain, Global groups from any domain, user accounts from any domain, and computer accounts from any domain.

If the domain functional level is set to Windows 2000 mixed, distribution groups can also have the same membership as detailed for Windows 2000 native or Windows Server 2003 functional level security groups.

If the domain functional level is set to Windows 2000 mixed, security groups can have the following members:

- **Domain Local Groups** Other Global groups from any domain, user accounts from any domain, and computer accounts from any domain.

- **Global Groups** User accounts in the same domain and computer accounts in the same domain.

TEST DAY TIP

The discussion about group types and group scopes applies only to Active Directory domain controllers and member servers. Group features such as group nesting and the distinction between security groups and distributions groups are not available elsewhere. Stand-alone servers and workstations participating in a workgroup environment can only use local groups. Local groups can only be assigned permissions on that local computer. The bottom line is that in a non-Active Directory environment, network administrators are limited to configuring rights and permissions on a computer-by-computer basis.

Default Groups

Several default groups are created during the creation of an Active Directory domain. These groups should be used as much as possible to control access to shared resources and to grant rights to perform specific administrative tasks. Many of these default groups are assigned a specific set of user rights that allow group members to perform the tasks for which the group was created. For example, any user that is a member of the Backup Operators group will have the right to perform backup and restore operations for domain controllers, even though they might not otherwise be able to perform this task.

The default groups are created in two places in Active Directory: the *Builtin* container and the *Users* container. Figure 1.1 shows the Active Directory Users and Computers console; from this location the network administrator can perform all group, user account, and computer account management tasks (discussed later in the "Managing and Modifying Groups" section of this chapter).

Figure 1.1 The Active Directory Users and Computers Console

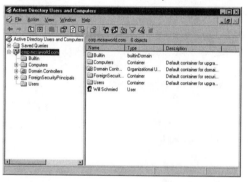

Table 1.2 details the default groups that are created in the Builtin container.

Table 1.2 The Default Groups Located in the Builtin Container

Group Name	Group Function
Account Operators	The members of this group can create, modify, and delete user accounts, computer accounts, and groups located in the User or Computers containers and all Organizational Units in the domain except for the Domain Controllers Organizational Unit. Account Operators cannot make any changes to the Administrators or Domain Admins groups, and they cannot make modifications to members of these groups.
Administrators	The members of this group have full and complete control over all domain controllers in the domain. The Domain Admins and Enterprise Admins groups are members of the Administrators group by default.

Continued

Table 1.2 The Default Groups Located in the Builtin Container

Group Name	Group Function
Backup Operators	The members of this group have user rights to back up and restore files on all domain controllers in the domain, regardless of what their individual user rights allow them. Additionally, members of the Backup Operators group can logon to domain controllers and shut them down.
Guests	The Guest group includes the Domain Guests group and the Guest account by default.
Incoming Forest Trust Builders	The members of this group can create one-way (incoming) forest trusts to the root domain of the forest tree.
Network Configuration Operators	The members of this group can configure changes to the Transmission Control Protocol/Internet Protocol (TCP/IP) settings as well as renewing and releasing Dynamic Host Control Protocol (DHCP) leases on all domain controllers in the domain.
Performance Monitor Users	The members of this group have the ability to mon itor the performance on all domain controllers in the domain, both locally and remotely.
Performance Log Users	The members of this group can manage the performance counters, logs, and alerts on all domain controllers in the domain, both locally and remotely.
Pre-Windows 2000 Compatible Access	The members of this group are provided with read-only access to all user and computer accounts in the domain. This group provides compatibility with computers run ning Windows NT 4.0 and earlier.
Print Operators	The members of this group can manage printers in the domain. Print Operators also have the ability to log on locally to domain controllers in the domain and shut them down.
Remote Desktop Users	The members of this group can remotely logon to domain controllers in the domain using Remote Desktop (RDP).
Replicator	The Replicators group is a service group that is used to support directory replication functions and is used by the File Replication Service (FRS) domain controllers in the domain.
Server Operators	The members of this group can log on locally to domain controllers. They are allowed to create and delete shared resources, start and stop specific services, backup and restore files, format disks, and shut down computers.

Continued

Table 1.2 The Default Groups Located in the Builtin Container

Group Name	Group Function
Users	The members of this group are provided the ability to perform most common tasks such as executing applications, using network and local printers, and accessing network shares. The Domain Users group and the Authenticated Users group are members of the Users group. User accounts automatically become members of the Users group upon creation.

Table 1.3 details the default groups that are created in the Users container.

Table 1.3 The Default Groups Located in the Users Container

Group Name	Group Function
Cert Publishers	The members of this group can publish certificates for users and computers.
DnsAdmins	The members of this group can perform administrative tasks on DNS servers.
DnsUpdateProxy	The members of this group are DNS clients that are permitted to perform dynamic updates on behalf of other clients, such as DHCP servers.
Domain Admins	The members of this group have full and complete control over the entire domain. The Domain Admins group is a member of the Administrators group on all computers once they are joined to the domain. The Administrator account is a member of the Domain Admins group.
Domain Computers	The Domain Computers group contains all workstations and member servers that are joined to the domain. All computer accounts created in the domain are automatically placed in this group by default.
Domain Controllers	The Domain Controllers group contains all domain controllers in the domain.
Domain Guests	The Domain Guests group contains all domain guests.
Domain Users	The Domain Users group contains all domain users. All user accounts created in the domain are automatically placed in this group by default.
Enterprise Admins	The members of this group have full control of all domains in the forest tree. The Enterprise Admins group is a member of the Administrators group on all domain controllers in the forest by default. Additionally, the Administrator account is a member of the Enterprise Admins group.

Continued

Table 1.3 The Default Groups Located in the Users Container

Group Name	Group Function
Group Policy Creator Owners	The members of this group can modify Group Policy in the domain. The Administrator account is a member of this group by default.
IIS_WPG	This group is installed when IIS 6.0 is installed and functions as the worker process group.
RAS and IAS Servers	The members of this group (Remote Access Server [RAS] and IAS servers) are allowed to access the remote access properties of users.
Schema Admins	The members of this group have the ability to modify the Active Directory schema. The Administrator account is a member of the Schema Admins group by default.

Default groups are also created on stand-alone servers. Although the primary focus of this exam is on Windows Server 2003 in an Active Directory environment, there are still many times when knowledge of the local default groups will be useful. Table 1.4 details the default local groups. These groups are listed in the Groups node of the Local Users and Groups console.

Table 1.4 The Default Local Groups

Group Name	Group Function
Administrators	The members of this group have full control of the com puter and perform any task on the server. The Administrator account is a member of this group by default.
Backup Operators	The members of this group can back up and restore files on the computer, regardless of any permissions that protect those files.
DHCP Administrators	The members of this group have administrative access to the DHCP service.
DHCP Users	The members of this group have read-only access to the DHCP service, allowing them to view information and properties without being able to make configuration changes.
Guests	The members of this group do not have a real profile, using only a temporary profile. The Guest account is a member of this group.
HelpServicesGroup	The HelpServicesGroup allows the setting of user rights that are common to support applications. Members should not be added to this group.

Continued

Table 1.4 The Default Local Groups

Group Name	Group Function
Network Configuration Operators	The members of this group can make changes to TCP/IP settings and renew and release DHCP leases on the computer.
Performance Monitor Users	The members of this group can monitor performance counters on the computer, both locally and remotely.
Performance Log Users	The members of this group can manage performance counters, logs, and alerts on a computer, both locally and remotely.
Power Users	The members of this group can create new user accounts and modify and delete the accounts they have created. Additionally, they can create local groups and then add or remove users from the local groups they have created. Members of the Power Users group can create and administer shared resources; however, they cannot take ownership of files, back up or restore files, or load or unload device drivers.
Print Operators	The members of this group can manage printers and print queues on the local computer.
Remote Desktop Users	The members of this group can remotely logon to the computer using RDP.
Replicator	The Replicator group supports replication functions. User accounts of actual users should not be added to this group.
Terminal Server Users	The members of this group are those users who are currently logged onto the system using Terminal Services.
Users	The members of this group are provided the ability to perform most common tasks such as executing applications, using network and local printers, and accessing network shares. The Domain Users group and Authenticated Users group are members of the Users group. User accounts automatically become members of the Users group upon creation.
WINS Users	The members of this group have read-only access to the to WINS service, allowing them to view information and properties without being able to make configuration changes.

EXAM
70-292
OBJECTIVE
1.1.2
1.1.3
1.1.4
1.1.5

Managing and Modifying Groups

The Active Directory Users and Computer console, as seen in Figure 1.2, identifies the tools available for working with groups in Active Directory.

Figure 1.2 The Active Directory Users and Computers Console

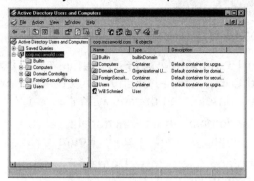

The most common tasks performed in relation to groups include the following:

- Creating new groups
- Adding members to groups
- Removing members from groups
- Converting the group type
- Changing the group scope
- Deleting groups
- Modifying group properties
- Finding groups in which a particular user is a member
- Assigning user rights and permissions to a group

Before performing any of these administrative tasks, the network administrator should know how to change the domain functional level of their domain in order to support Universal groups and scope type changes.

Changing the Domain Functional Level

If a domain contains only Windows 2000 Server and Windows Server 2003 domain controllers, the domain functional level should be raised. Raising the domain functional level from Windows 2000 mixed to Windows 2000 native or Windows Server 2003 allows the network administrator to increase the functionality of their domain and their domain controllers. They will be able to create Universal groups and also gain the ability to convert groups from distribution groups to security groups and vice versa, as well as the ability to change the group scope. Exercise 1.01 details the process involved in changing the domain functional level of an Active Directory domain.

EXERCISE 1.01

RAISING THE DOMAIN FUNCTIONAL LEVEL

1. Click **Start | Programs | Administrative Tools | Active Directory Users and Computers** to open the Active Directory Users and Computers console seen previously in Figure 1.2.

2. Click on the domain whose functional level you wish to change (refer back to the highlighted domain in Figure 1.2).

3. Click **Action** and select **Raise Domain Functional Level** from the menu, as seen in Figure 1.3.

Figure 1.3 Raising the Domain Functional Level

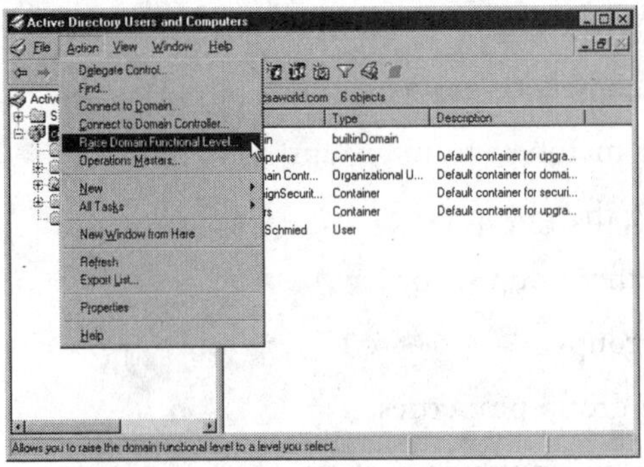

4. The Raise Domain Functional Level window opens, as seen in Figure 1.4. From the drop-down box, select the functional level you wish to configure. Note that you can only go up in functional level—you can never go back down. By selecting **Windows 2000 native**, you will no longer be allowed to have Windows NT 4.0 domain controllers on the network. By selecting **Windows Server 2003**, you can have only Windows Server 2003 domain controllers on the network. Click **Raise** after making your selection.

Figure 1.4 Selecting the New Domain Functional Level

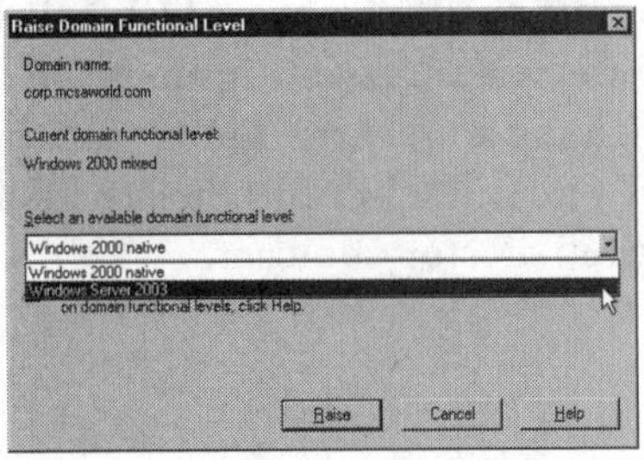

NOTE

You must be a member of the Account Operators group, the Domain Admins group, or the Enterprise Admins group in order to perform most of the administrative actions discussed in the following sections. You can also perform this task if you have been delegated the authority to do so.

Creating New Groups

The exam objectives for exam 70-292 expect you to be able to create and modify users both from within the Active Directory Users and Computers console and from the command line. To create a new group from within the GUI, perform the procedure outlined in Exercise 1.02.

EXERCISE 1.02

CREATING GROUPS WITH ACTIVE DIRECTORY USERS AND COMPUTERS

1. Open the **Active Directory Users and Computers** console.

2. Expand the console tree until you locate the node in which you want to create the new group.

3. Right-click on the node and select **New | Group** from the context menu, as seen in Figure 1.5.

4. The New Object – Group window opens, as seen in Figure 1.6.

Figure 1.5 Starting the New Group Creation Process

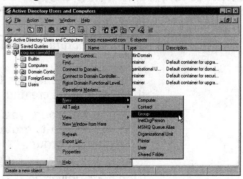

Figure 1.6 Entering the New Group Information

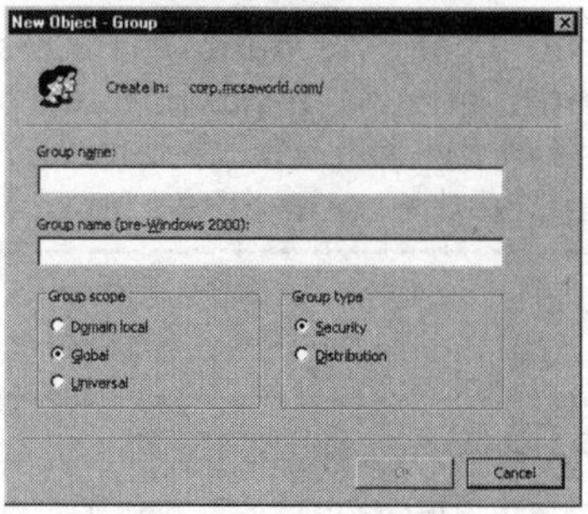

5. Enter the **Group name**. By default, the pre-Windows 2000 Group name is the same; however, you can change it as required to make it compatible with Network Basic Input/Output System (NetBIOS) naming requirements.

6. Select the **Group scope** and **Group type** as required. Click **OK** to create the new group.

New groups can also be created from the command line using the *dsadd* command. The syntax required to create a new group is as follows:

```
dsadd group GroupDN [-secgrp {yes | no}] [-scope {l | g | u}] [-samid SAMName] [-desc Description]
```

The function of each switch is explained briefly in Table 1.5. Appendix A contains a complete listing of the *dsadd* command and its switches.

Table 1.5 *dsadd* Switches for Adding a New Group

Switch	Function
Group	Required modifier; instructs *dsadd* that it is to work with groups.
GroupDN	Required item; specifies the distinguished name of the group to be created.
-secgrp {yes	no}	Specifies the group type. A **yes** answer (the default) indicates a security group and a **no** answer indicates a distribution group.
-scope {l	g	u}	Specifies the scope of the group: Domain Local, Global, or Universal.

Continued

Table 1.5 *dsadd* Switches for Adding a New Group

Switch	Function
-samid *SAMName*	Specifies the Security Accounts Manager (SAM) name to be used for the group—this will become the pre-Windows 2000 group name. If not specified, this name is derived from the distinguished name.
-desc *Description*	Specifies the description of the group being created.

Figure 1.7 demonstrates the usage of the *dsadd* command to add a new domain local security group named West Region Sales using the following command:

```
dsadd group "CN=West Region Sales,DC=corp,DC=mcsaworld,DC=com" -samid WestSales -
secgrp yes -scope 1 -desc "This group contains all members of the Western Resgion
Sales department"
```

Figure 1.7 Creating a New Group from the Command-Line

 TEST DAY TIP

Anytime there are blank spaces in an entry as seen in Figure 1.7 (West Region Sales), the entire entry must be placed in quotation marks. Thus, the entire distinguished name must be placed in quotation marks in order for Windows to properly parse the command and produce the desired results.

For more information on using the *dsadd* command, refer to Appendix A.

EXAM 70-292
OBJECTIVE 1.1.3

Adding Members to Group

Once a group is created, members are added to it. It is important to remember that group members can be user accounts, computer accounts, or other groups as allowed. Exercise 1.03 walks through the process of adding user accounts and groups to the previously created West Region Sales group using the Active Directory Users and Computers console.

ADDING GROUP MEMBERS WITH ACTIVE DIRECTORY USERS AND COMPUTERS

1. Open the **Active Directory Users and Computers** console.
2. Expand the console tree until you locate the group to have members added.
3. Double-click on the group to open its Properties dialog box.
4. Switch to the **Members** tab, as seen in Figure 1.8.

Figure 1.8 Adding Members to a Group

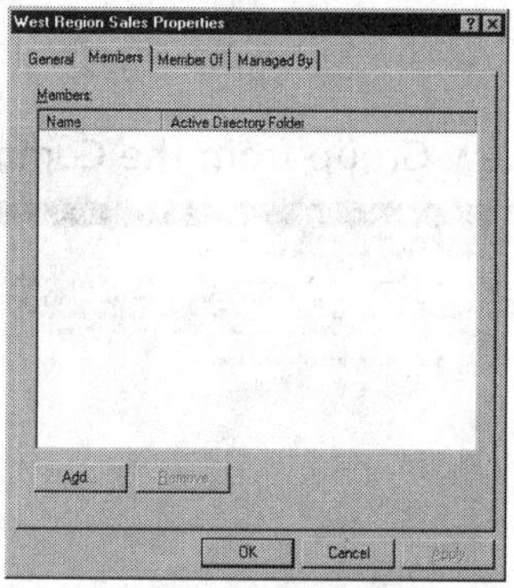

5. Click the **Add** button to open the Select Users, Contacts, Computers or Groups dialog box. To search for users, click the **Advanced** button. Click **Find Now** to search for appropriate members, as seen in Figure 1.9.

Figure 1.9 Locating Members to Add to the Group

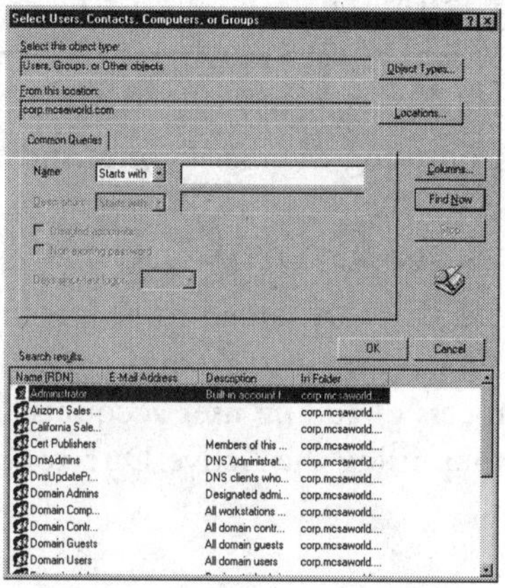

6. To add an account or group, double-click it. To add multiple accounts or groups, click on them one at a time while pressing the **Ctrl** key. Remember that you must abide by the rules for nested groups outlined in the "Group Scopes" section earlier in this chapter. After making your selections, click the **OK** button.

7. After the Select Users, Contacts, Computers or Groups dialog box collapses, click **OK** to confirm and add the selected accounts and groups. The results will be shown as seen in Figure 1.10.

Figure 1.10 Viewing Group Members

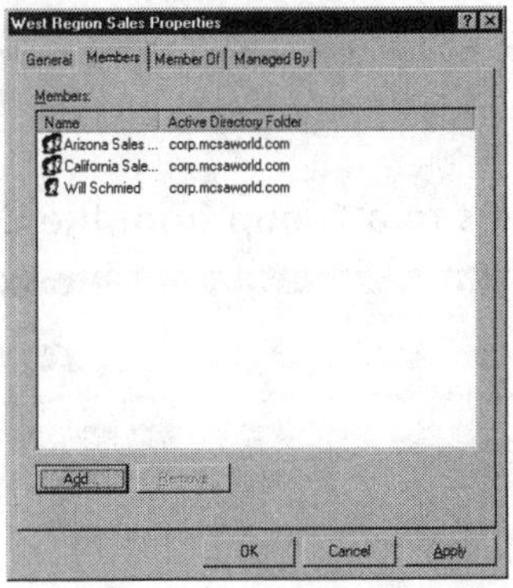

8. Click **OK** or **Apply** to accept the membership change.

9. You can also make this group a member of another group by switching to the **Member Of** tab, as seen in Figure 1.11. The process is the same as the rules for adding nesting groups as outlined in the "Group Scopes" section earlier in this chapter.

Figure 1.11 Adding the Group to Another Group

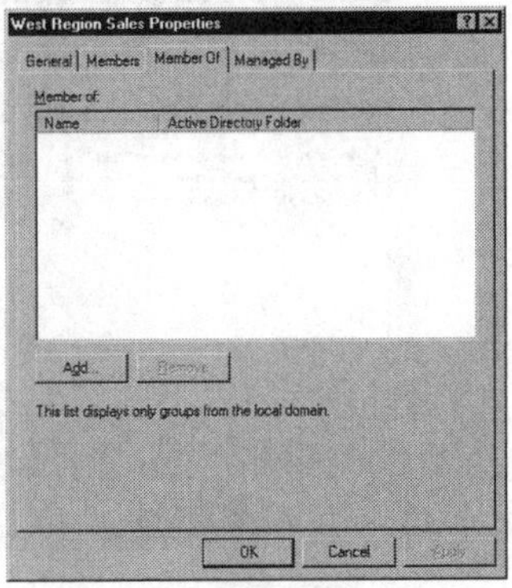

Members can also be added to an existing group from the command-line using the *dsmod* command. The syntax required to add a member to a group is as follows:

```
dsmod group GroupDN -addmbr MemberDN
```

The function of the switches is self-explanatory, as they represent the distinguished name of the group to add the member to and the distinguished name of the member to be added. Appendix A contains a complete listing of the *dsmod* command and its switches. Figure 1.12 demonstrates using the *dsmod* command twice to add two user accounts to the West Region Sales group using the following commands:

```
dsmod group "CN=West Region Sales,DC=corp,DC=mcsaworld,DC=com" -addmbr "CN=Rick
Smith,CN=Users,DC=corp,DC=mcsaworld,DC=com"
```

```
dsmod group "CN=West Region Sales,DC=corp,DC=mcsaworld,DC=com" -addmbr "CN=Jeff
Smith,CN=Users,DC=corp,DC=mcsaworld,DC=com"
```

Figure 1.12 Adding Users to a Group from the Command-Line

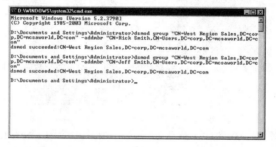

A quick check of the West Sales Region Group Members tab, seen in Figure 1.13, indicates that the user accounts were successfully added to the group.

Figure 1.13 Verifying the Results of the *dsmod* Command

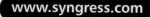

Removing Members from Groups

The process for removing a member from a group using the Active Directory Users and Computer console is simple: highlight the member or members to be removed on the **Group Members** tab, seen previously in Figure 1.12, and click the **Remove** button. You will be prompted to confirm your actions before they are carried out.

To remove group members from the command line, use the *dsmod* command. This time, however, the command being issued would look like:

```
dsmod group "CN=West Region Sales,DC=corp,DC=mcsaworld,DC=com" -rmmbr "CN=Jeff
Smith,CN=Users,DC=lab1,DC=corp,DC=mcsaworld,DC=com"
```

Figure 1.14 shows this command in action.

Figure 1.14 Removing Group Members from the Command-Line

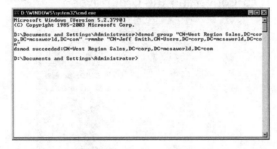

Again, a check of the Group Members tab will confirm that the user has in fact been removed from the group. You will not be prompted to verify your intent to remove a group member when issuing the command from the command line.

Converting Group Type

If the domain functional level is Windows 2000 native or higher, security groups can be converted to distribution groups at will, and vice versa. Recall that distribution groups do not have DACL entries and can only be used for e-mail distribution. Security groups can be used for e-mail distribution as well, and can also be used to effectively manage user rights, assignments, and permissions. Converting a group from one type to another can be easily accomplished from the Active Directory Users and Computers console, as discussed in Exercise 1.04.

EXERCISE 1.04

CONVERTING GROUP TYPE FROM ACTIVE DIRECTORY USERS AND COMPUTERS

1. Open the **Active Directory Users and Computers** console.

2. Expand the console tree until you locate the group whose type you wish to convert.

3. Double-click on the group to open its **Properties** dialog box.

4. On the **General** tab, seen in Figure 1.15, you will be able to change the group type.

Figure 1.15 Converting the Group Type

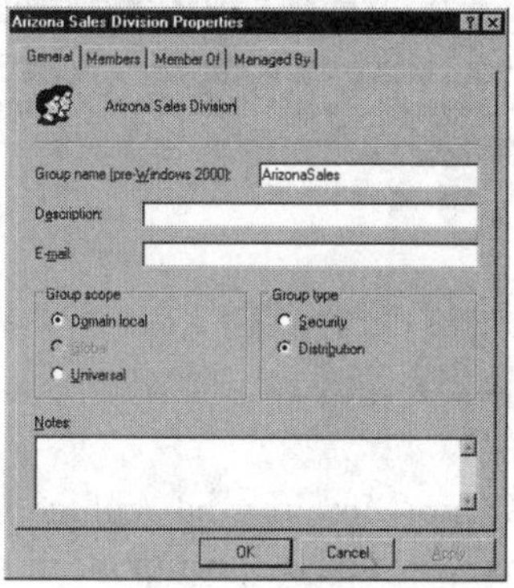

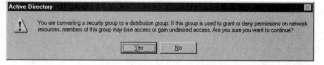

5. For conversions from Distribution to Security, you simply make the change and click **OK** or **Apply**.

6. For conversion from Security to Distribution, make the change and click **OK** or **confirm**. You will be warned, as seen in the warning dialog of Figure 1.16, that users may gain or lose access to resources in an unwanted way. This is due to the fact that you are removing the DACLs from the group by converting it to a distribution group.

Figure 1.16 The Conversion Warning Dialog Box

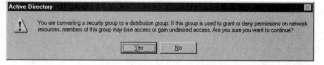

7. If you want to make the conversion to a distribution group, click **Yes**.

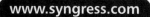

Head of the Class...

About DACLs

A DACL is an internal listing that is attached to files, folders, and other directory services objects on volumes that are formatted with the NTFS file system. DACLs are configured by administrators and used to specify which users and/or groups are allowed to perform different actions on the file, folder, or object in question. The implementation of a DACL varies from files and folders to other objects due to the specific requirements of other objects. For example, files and folders have the Read access permission, but printers do not.

Each DACL is made up of Access Control Entries (ACEs). Each ACE specifies the security identifier (SID) of the security principal (user or group) that it applies to as well as the level of access to the file, folder, or object that is permitted for that specific security principal.

Group type conversions can also be performed from the command-line using the *dsmod* command. The syntax required to perform the conversion is as follows:

```
dsmod group GroupDN [-secgrp {yes | no}]
```

Again, the function of the switches are self-explanatory as they represent the distinguished name of the group to be converted and the type of group conversion being made. Appendix A contains a complete listing of the *dsmod* command and its switches.

Figure 1.17 demonstrates using the *dsmod* command twice, first to convert a distribution group into a security group and then back into a distribution group using the following commands:

```
dsmod group "CN=Arizona Sales Division,DC=corp,DC=mcsaworld,DC=com" -secgrp yes
dsmod group "CN=Arizona Sales Division,DC=corp,DC=mcsaworld,DC=com" -secgrp no
```

Figure 1.17 Converting the Group Type from the Command-Line

A check of the group type from the **General** tab will confirm that the change has been made. You will not receive any warning dialogs when converting the group type from the command-line.

EXAM 70-292 OBJECTIVE 1.1.1

Changing Group Scope

Just as a network administrator might want to convert the group type, they may also need to change the group scope over time. If the domain functional level is Windows 2000 native or higher, they will be able to use Universal groups. A network administrator can change the scope of a group (within the guidelines established in Table 1.1) from the Active Directory Users and Computers console by performing the steps outlined in Exercise 1.05.

EXERCISE 1.05

CHANGING THE GROUP SCOPE FROM ACTIVE DIRECTORY USERS AND COMPUTERS

1. Open the **Active Directory Users and Computers** console.
2. Expand the console tree until you locate the group whose scope you wish to change.
3. Double-click on the group to open its Properties dialog box.
4. On the **General** tab, as seen in Figure 1.18, you can change the group scope.

Figure 1.18 Changing the Group Scope

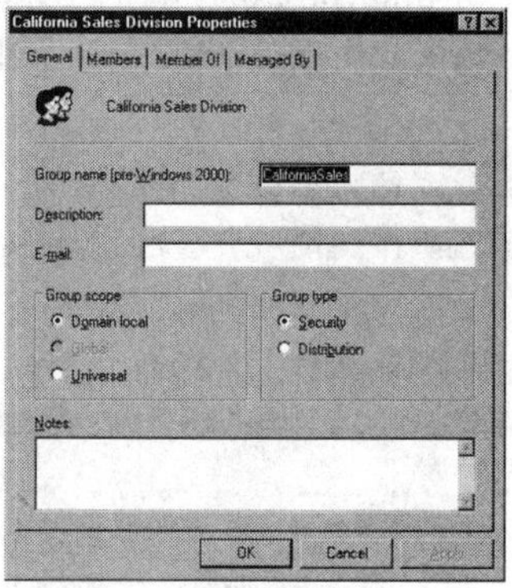

5. Change the group scope as desired and click **OK** or **Apply** to accept the changes. Remember, you can only change the group scope as previously outlined in Table 1.1.

Group scope changes can also be performed from the command line using the *dsmod* command. The syntax required make scope changes is as follows:

```
dsmod group GroupDN [-scope {l | g | u}]
```

The function of the switches are self-explanatory, as they represent the distinguished name of the group to be converted and the type of scope to change the group to. Appendix A contains a complete listing of the *dsmod* command and its switches.

Figure 1.19 demonstrates using the *dsmod* command three times: first to (unsuccessfully) change a Domain Local group into Global group, second to (successfully) change this same Domain Local group into a Universal group, and lastly to (successfully) change the Universal group into a Global group using the following commands:

```
dsmod group "CN=California Sales Division,DC=corp,DC=mcsaworld,DC=com" -scope g
dsmod group "CN=California Sales Division,DC=corp,DC=mcsaworld,DC=com" -scope u
dsmod group "CN=California Sales Division,DC=corp,DC=mcsaworld,DC=com" -scope g
```

Figure 1.19 Changing the Group Scope from the Command-Line

A check of the group scope from the General tab will confirm that the change has been made. Changing from a domain local group to a global group is not supported by the *dsmod* command.

Deleting Groups

A group can easily be deleted from within the Active Directory Users and Computers console as outlined in Exercise 1.06. Note that deleting a group does not cause any members of the group to be deleted from Active Directory—only to be removed from that group and lose any rights and permissions that may have been applied to them if the group is a security group. If the group is a distribution group, e-mails will no longer be able to be sent to the group e-mail address.

EXERCISE 1.06

DELETING GROUPS FROM ACTIVE DIRECTORY USERS AND COMPUTERS

1. Open the **Active Directory Users and Computers** console.

2. Expand the console tree until you locate the group to be deleted.

3. Right-click on the group and select **Delete** from the context menu.

4. When prompted if you want to delete the group, click **Yes**.

A group can also be deleted from the command-line using the *dsrm* command. The syntax required to delete a group is as follows:

```
dsrm GroupDN
```

Appendix A contains a complete listing of the *dsrm* command and its switches. Figure 1.20 demonstrates using the *dsrm* command to remove the Washington Sales Division group using the following command:

```
dsrm "CN=Washington Sales Division,DC=corp,DC=mcsaworld,DC=com"
```

Figure 1.20 Removing a Group Using the Command-Line

A check of Active Directory Users and Computers will show that the group has been deleted. As can be seen, you will be required to confirm the deletion when using the *dsrm* command.

Modifying Group Properties

After a group is created, the properties may need to be changed. Most commonly, these changes include supplying an e-mail address for the group and denoting someone as being the person responsible for the group. These changes can be easily made from Active Directory Users and Computers as outlined in Exercise 1.07.

EXERCISE 1.07

MODIFYING GROUP PROPERTIES

1. Open the **Active Directory Users and Computers** console.

2. Expand the console tree until you locate the group to have its scope changed.

3. Double-click on the group to open its **Properties** dialog box.

4. On the **General** tab (seen in Figure 1.21), you can enter an e-mail address to be used to distribute e-mail to all mailbox-enabled members of the group.

Figure 1.21 Entering a Group E-mail Address

5. If you want to list a user as being responsible for the group, switch to the **Managed By** tab. Go through the process to locate and add a user as demonstrated earlier in Exercise 1.03. You will see the pertinent details, as seen in Figure 1.22, after confirming the responsible user.

Figure 1.22 Viewing the Group Manager Details

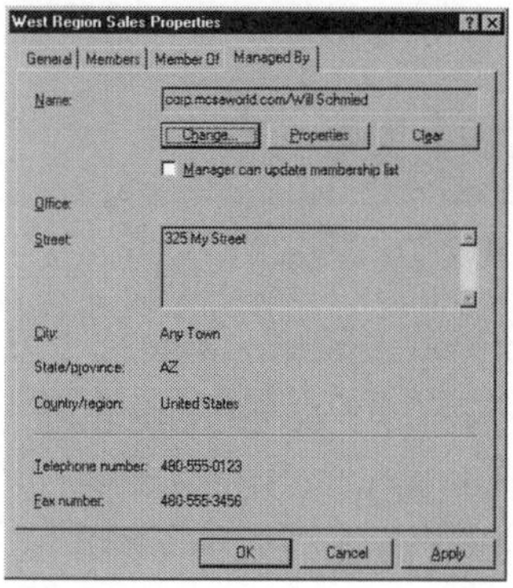

EXAM
70-292
OBJECTIVE
1.1.2

Finding Groups in Which a Particular User is a Member

The ability to determine which groups a user is a member of can be helpful in many situations, including troubleshooting permissions and user rights assignments. To determine which groups a user is member of (this also applies for computers) from the Active Directory Users and Computers console, perform the steps in Exercise 1.08.

EXERCISE 1.08

DETERMING THE GROUPS A USER IS A MEMBER OF

1. Open the **Active Directory Users and Computers** console.
2. Expand the console tree until you locate the user in question.
3. Double-click the user to open the **Properties** dialog box.
4. Switch to the **Member Of** tab, seen in Figure 1.23, to quickly determine what groups the user is a member of.

Figure 1.23 Viewing User Group Membership Details

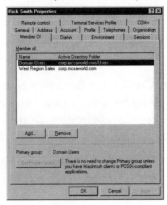

To determine what groups a user is a member of from the command-line, use the *dsget* command. The syntax required is as follows:

```
dsget user UserDN -memberof
```

Appendix A contains a complete listing of the *dsget* command and its switches. Figure 1.24 demonstrates using the *dsget* command to determine the group membership of user Rick Smith using the following command:

```
dsget user "CN=Rick Smith,CN=Users,DC=corp,DC=mcsaworld,DC=com" -memberof
```

Figure 1.24 Determining Group Membership from the Command-Line

Assigning User Rights and Permissions to a Group

Although somewhat beyond the scope of the 70-292 exam, the assignment of user rights and permissions to a group is important. After learning about groups in an effort to make administration of a network easier and more exact, it is only natural that we conclude the discussion of groups with a brief examination of how user rights and permissions can be assigned to them.

Assigning user rights to a group can be done in several places, each at a different level within the overall Active Directory domain hierarchy. The following list contains some locations and ways that user rights can be assigned to a group:

- **Default Domain Controller Security Settings Console** Located in the Administrative Tools folder, this console can be used to configure user rights assignments for all domain controllers. Domain controllers are located in the Domain Controllers container in Active Directory Users and Computers.

- **Default Domain Security Settings Console** Located in the Administrative Tools folder, this console can be used to configure user rights that will be applied to the domain as a whole.

- **Local Security Policy Console** Located in the Administrative Tools folder, this console can be used to configure user rights that will be applied only to the local computer.

- **Group Policy Objects (GPOs)** GPOs can be applied at various levels in Active Directory, such as the domain level or to a specific Organizational Unit. Within each GPO, user rights can be assigned that will affect all objects the GPO has been applied to.

- **Security Templates** Security Templates can be used to quickly and uniformly apply security settings to all objects they have been applied to. Security Templates can be applied directly to a local computer or imported into a GPO for application to all objects the GPO is applied to. Security Templates are discussed in more detail in Chapter 7.

Exercise 1.09 presents the basic process to configure user rights at the domain level using the Default Domain Security Policy console. Recall that there are many other options available as far as where and how to apply user rights to a group.

EXERCISE 1.09

APPLYING USER RIGHTS TO A GROUP

1. Click **Start | Programs | Administrative Tools | Domain Security Policy** to open the Default Domain Security console seen in Figure 1.25.

Figure 1.25 Locating the User Rights Node

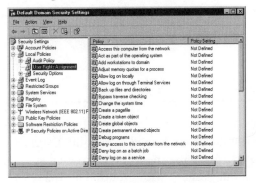

2. Expand the nodes to locate the **User Rights Assignment** node shown in Figure 1.25.

3. Locate the User Right you wish to define, and double-click it to open it for editing. As seen in Figure 1.26, place a check in the **Define these policy settings** option.

Figure 1.26 Adding User Rights to a Group

4. Click the **Add User or Group** button to open the Add User or Group dialog box. If you know the name you want to configure the rights for, enter it and click **OK**. If not, click then click the **Browse** button to open the standard **Select Users, Computers or Groups** dialog box, which will allow you to search for the user or group to add.

Figure 1.27 Locating the User or Group

More often than not a group is used to simplify the management of access to shared resources on a network. Assigning these permissions takes a different approach than has been seen thus far in our dealings with groups. This is a setting that needs to be configured directly on the object in question, such as a file share or shared printer for example. Exercise 1.10 walks through assigning NT File System (NTFS) permissions to a group for a shared network resource named SalesDocs

EXAM WARNING

Do not confuse user rights and NTFS permissions. User rights define actions that users or groups are allowed to perform, such as logon locally, shutdown the computer, and so on. Permissions (both NTFS and share) define a level of access that is allowed for the user or group to an object, such as a file, folder, or printer. Moreover, do not confuse NTFS and share permissions. NTFS permissions can be applied only on NTFS volumes such as those in Windows 2000, Windows XP, and Windows Server 2003, and apply to a user whether the resource is being accessed interactively (at the local computer) or remotely (over the network). Share level permissions can be applied on Windows 9x computers, as well and only apply to resource access over the network.

EXERCISE 1.10

ASSIGNING NTFS PERMISSIONS TO A GROUP

1. Open Windows Explorer and locate the shared resource that you want to configure NTFS permissions on—in this example a shared folder.

2. Right-click on the folder and select **Properties** from the context menu.

3. Switch to the **Security** tab as seen in Figure 1.28.

Figure 1.28 Configuring NTFS Permissions

4. To add a group to the DACL, click the **Add** button. This opens the Select Users, Contacts, Computers or Groups dialog box as discussed previously in Exercise 1.03.

5. Locate and add the group that you wish to assign permissions to.

6. After adding the group, you will see the results on the **Security** tab, as seen in Figure 1.29.

Figure 1.29 Configuring the Required Permissions for the New Group

7. Configure the required permissions for the group and click **OK** to accept the changes.

Creating and Managing User Accounts

Up to this point, we have discussed groups only. Groups can be used to collect large numbers of accounts for ease of administration. Networks exist to make the sharing of information easier. As in the previous discussion of groups, the following sections examine user accounts from the perspective of an Active Directory domain environment.

Before discussing creating and managing user accounts, let's examine the default user accounts that are found in the Windows Server 2003 environment.

Default User Accounts

Several default user accounts are created during the installation of Windows Server 2003 and the creation of an Active Directory domain. Table 1.6 lists the most common default user accounts that are created, although several more may be created depending on the specific applications and services installed on the computer.

Table 1.6 The Default User Accounts

User Name	User Description
Administrator	A built-in account that is provided for administering the computer and domain. This account is a member of the following groups: Administrators, Domain Admins, Domain Users, Enterprise Admins, Group Policy Creator Owners, and Schema Admins.
Guest	A built-in account that is used for guest access to the computer and domain. This account is a member of the following groups: Domain Guests and Guests. The guest account is disabled by default.
IUSR_*computername*	A built-in account that is used to allow anonymous access to Internet Information Services (IIS) resources. This account is a member of the following groups: Domain Users and Guests.
IWAM_*computername*	A built-in account that is used by IIS to start out-of-process applications. This account is a member of the following groups: Domain Users and IIS_WPG.
krbtgt	A built-in account that serves as the Kerberos Key Distribution Center (KDC) service account. This account is a member of the Domain Users group.
SUPPORT_*xxxxxxxx*	A built-in account that is used for the Help and Support Service. This account is a member of the following groups: Domain Users and HelpServicesGroup. The SUPPORT account is disabled by default.

Managing and Modifying User Accounts

It is fairly safe to say that, in most cases, a network administrator will work with user accounts on a daily basis in most networks. Users are the lifeblood of a network—the very reason the network exists is to provide information and other resources to users in a secure and efficient way. As such, there are several common tasks to perform when administering user accounts:

- Creating new user accounts
- Resetting a user account password
- Copying a user account
- Disabling or enabling a user account
- Configuring user account properties
- Deleting user accounts
- Assigning user rights and permissions to a user account

Each of these tasks is discussed in the following sections. We will also examine using two additional command line-based utilities to perform bulk import and export of Active Directory information, including user accounts.

Creating New User Accounts

Creating a new user accounts one at a time is one that can be accomplished from either the Active Directory Users and Computer console or from the command line. The process to create a new user account from the Active Directory Users and Computers console is detailed in Exercise 1.11.

EXERCISE 1.11

CREATING A NEW USER ACCOUNT WITH ACTIVE DIRECTORY USERS AND COMPUTERS

1. Open the **Active Directory Users and Computers** console.
2. Expand the console tree until you locate the location in which you wish to create the new user.
3. In our example, we are going to create a new user in the Sales Organizational Unit. Right-click on the node where you want to create the new user and select **New | User**. The New Object – User dialog box opens. Supply the user's name and logon name and click **Next** to continue.

Figure 1.30 Creating a New User Account

4. In the next window, as seen in Figure 1.31, supply the password for the user. Good practice dictates that the password assigned here be a temporary one by selecting the **User must change password at next logon** option, which is selected by default. If you are creating an account that is not to be used yet, network security can be increased by disabling it at this time. After entering your selections, click **Next** to continue.

Figure 1.31 Specifying Password Related Items

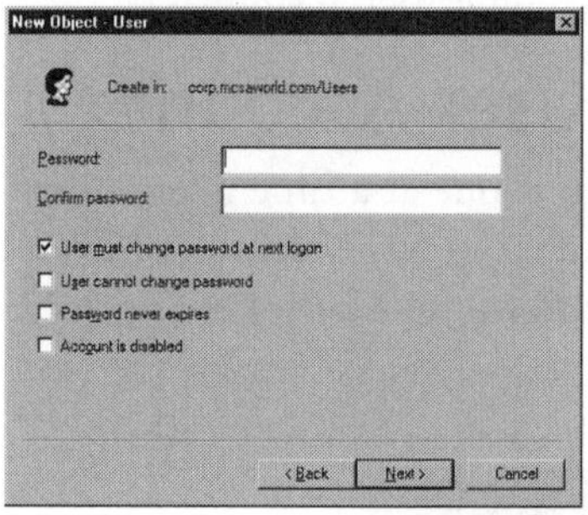

5. You will be given the chance to review your configuration from a summary page. If all is well, click **Finish** to create the user. You can click **Back** to go back and make changes as required.

Alternatively, user accounts can be created one at a time from the command-line using the *dsadd* command. The specific context to be used to create a new account is:

```
dsadd user UserDN [-UPN UPN] [-samid SAMName] -pwd {Password|*}
```

The *UserDN* and *SAMName* modifiers have been previously explained. The *UPN* modifier specifies the users User Principal Name (UPN), such as user@mydomain.com; the *pwd* modifier specifies the account password, or if set as * specifies that you want to be prompted to enter the password. Figure 1.32 demonstrates using the *dsadd* command to create a new user, Roger Smith, in the Sales OU using the following command:

```
dsadd user "CN=Roger Smith,CN=Users,DC=corp,DC=mcsaworld,DC=com" -UPN
rogersmith@corp.mcsaworld.com -samid rogersmith -pwd *
```

Figure 1.32 Creating a New User from the Command Line

As seen in the example, we exercised the ability to specify a password at the time of account creation. A quick check of the Sales OU would determine that the new user, Roger Smith, was in fact created as indicated here. It should be noted that many other attributes of the user object that could have been supplied with the *dsadd* command were left out in this example. Appendix A has a complete listing and explanation of the available *dsadd* options.

Resetting the User Account Password

It happens more than any administrator wants to talk about: resetting user passwords. In some organizations with particularly challenging password complexity requirements, this can become a burden on network administrators. Even in those organizations where the password policies are not nearly as stringent, users will still forget their passwords. Additionally, the network administrator will oftentimes need to reset the password on an expired or locked out user account. Fortunately, you can you quickly and easily reset a user's password from within the Active Directory Users and Computers console as discussed in Exercise 1.12.

EXERCISE 1.12

RESETTING USER PASSWORDS WITH ACTIVE DIRECTORY USERS AND COMPUTERS

1. Open the **Active Directory Users and Computers** console.

2. Expand the console tree until you locate the user in question.

3. Right-click on the user and select **Reset Password** from the context menu to open the **Reset Password** dialog box seen in Figure 1.33.

Figure 1.33 Resetting User Passwords Does
Not Require You to Know the Current Password

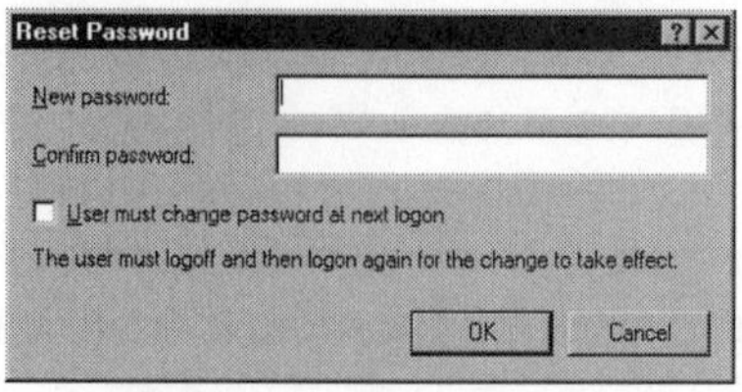

4. Enter the new password. For enhanced security, select the **User must change password at next logon** option. Click **OK** to reset the user's password.

A user's password can also be easily reset from the command-line using the *dsmod* command with the following syntax:

```
dsmod user UserDN -pwd NewPassword -mustchpwd {yes|no}.
```

The *–mustchpwd* modifier denotes whether or not the user will be forced to change their password during the next logon attempt. Figure 1.34 demonstrates using the *dsmod* command to reset the password of user Roger Smith using the following command:

```
dsmod user "CN=Roger Smith,CN=Users,DC=corp,DC=mcsaworld,DC=com" -pwd *
-mustchpwd yes
```

Figure 1.34 Resetting the User Account Password from the Command-Line

```
D:\WINDOWS\system32\cmd.exe                                          _ □ ×
Microsoft Windows [Version 5.2.3790]
(C) Copyright 1985-2003 Microsoft Corp.

D:\Documents and Settings\Administrator>dsmod user "CN=Roger Smith,CN=Users,DC=c
orp,DC=mcsaworld,DC=com" -pwd * -mustchpwd yes
Enter User Password:

Confirm user password:

dsmod succeeded:CN=Roger Smith,CN=Users,DC=corp,DC=mcsaworld,DC=com

D:\Documents and Settings\Administrator>_
```

Again, the password was supplied interactively during the reset procedure. Also, the user will be forced to change their password the next time they logon to the domain. Appendix A has a complete listing and explanation of the available *dsmod* options.

Delegating Administrative Authority

Although referenced several times in this chapter, you may be wondering exactly what delegation is when it comes to Active Directory. It works the same way in Active Directory as it does in real life. Say, for example, that you are the department head in a large manufacturing conglomerate. You have thousands of people who work for you and an administrative assistant that helps to keep you on track, making sure that you get the things done that you need to. You might, in many cases, delegate some of your authority to your administrative assistant to allow them to handle some things for you and take some of the burden off your shoulders. This also allows a continuity of operations to a certain degree should you be unavailable for a period of time.

Active Directory works the same way. Users have specific user rights that are assigned to them through their membership in certain groups. Users can have specific explicit user rights configured on their accounts individually. The Delegation of Control Wizard allows you to easily and accurately delegate administrative responsibility to groups and users. For example, it is fairly common for members of the help desk staff to be delegated the ability to reset users passwords. This saves the higher-level network administrators from being burdened with low-level administrative tasks. This delegation can be easily accomplished in three easy steps:

1. Create a new group called **Password Reset**.

2. Place all applicable help desk member user accounts in the newly created group.

3. Run the **Delegation of Control Wizard** to delegate the right to reset user passwords to the Password Reset group.

Copying a User Account

Many organizations have standardized the way that they create and configure user accounts by creating an *account template*. An account template is nothing more than a user account that has been created and configured in a specific fashion and then used to create new accounts without the administrative burden of needing to configure each new account in a similar fashion. Although the need for this is somewhat offset by the diligent usage of groups and configuring rights and permissions on the group level, there may be the need to copy a user account, creating a new user account with the same features except that the new user account will posses a different SID. User accounts can be copied from the Active Directory Users and Computers by performing the steps outlined in Exercise 1.13.

COPYING USER ACCOUNTS FROM ACTIVE DIRECTORY USERS AND COMPUTERS

1. Open the **Active Directory Users and Computers** console.

2. Expand the console tree until you locate the user in question.

3. Right-click on the user and select **Copy** from the context menu to open the Copy Object – User dialog box as seen in Figure 1.35.

Figure 1.35 Copying a User Account to Create a New User Account

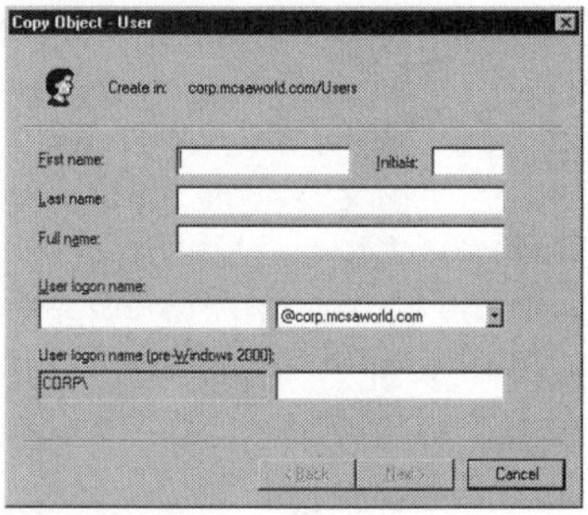

4. You will need to supply the same information for the copy process as you did when creating a new user account.

By default, only the most common attributes are copied during the user account copy process. These include log on hours, workstation restrictions, and account expiration date. You can modify which attributes are copied to the newly created user from the Active Directory Schema snap-in. This is, however, beyond the scope of the 70-292 exam. There is no corresponding command line alternative for copying user accounts.

Disabling or Enabling A User Account

A network administrator may need to disable a user account for any number of reasons. Commonly, they will disable user accounts when the user is gone for an extended period of time, or as a security measure to keep unused accounts from becoming a weakness in their network security plan. The administrator can quickly disable a user account from the Active Directory Users and Computers console by right-clicking on the account and selecting **Disable Account** from the context menu. Similarly, they can enable a disabled user account by right-clicking on the account and selecting **Enable Account**. They can also disable or enable a user account from the Account tab on the Properties dialog page as seen in Figure 1.36.

Figure 1.36 Disabling a User Account from the Properties Dialog Box

An account can also be disabled or enabled from the command-line using the *dsmod* command with the following syntax:

```
dsmod user UserDN -disabled {yes|no}.
```

Figure 1.37 demonstrates using the *dsmod* command to disable the user account of Roger Smith using the following command:

```
dsmod user "CN=Roger Smith,CN=Users,DC=corp,DC=mcsaworld,DC=com" -disabled yes
```

Figure 1.37 Disabling the User Account from the Command-Line

EXAM WARNING

Be aware that disabling a user account only prevents it from being used—it does not alter or otherwise change the user account in any other way. Network administrators should always disable newly created user accounts if they are being pre-staged and will not be used immediately. Additionally, they should always disable user accounts for users that are currently on vacation or otherwise not logging into the network. Disabled user accounts serve to increase the overall security of the network by preventing these unused (and typically unmonitored) accounts from being subjected to password guessing and other attacks.

Configuring User Account Properties

When user accounts are created using the Active Directory Users and Computers console or using the minimum required command syntax of the *dsadd* command, many user attributes and information items still need to be configured. Most of these items can be configured using the *dsadd* command at the time of account creation, or the *dsmod* command after the fact. The following sections examine the configuration process entirely from the Active Directory Users and Computers console.

Within Active Directory Users and Computers, locate the user account that you wish to configure account properties for and double-click it to open the Properties dialog box as seen in Figure 1.38.

NOTE

The Remote Control, Terminal Services Profile, COM+, Dial-in, Environment, and Sessions tabs contain configuration options that are beyond the scope of the 70-292 exam and will not be examined here.

The General Tab

The General tab of the account Properties dialog box, seen in Figure 1.38, allows the network administrator to configure basic user information such as first and last name, display name, a description of the account, office location, telephone number, e-mail address, and Web page information.

Figure 1.38 Configuring the General User Account Properties

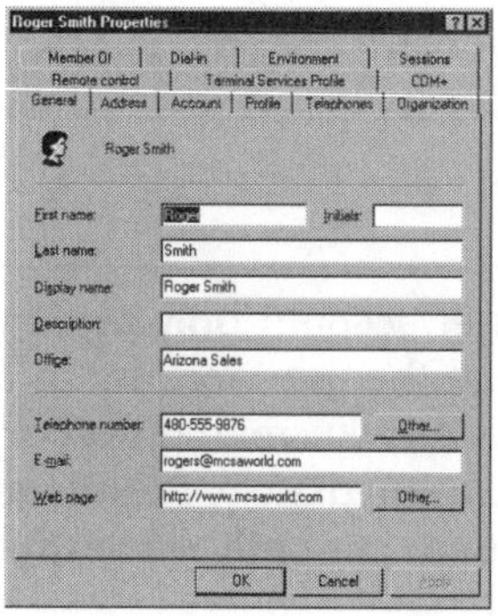

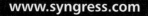

The Address Tab

The Address tab of the account Properties dialog box, seen in Figure 1.39, allows the network administrator to configure a complete mailing address for the user.

Figure 1.39 Configuring the Address User Account Properties

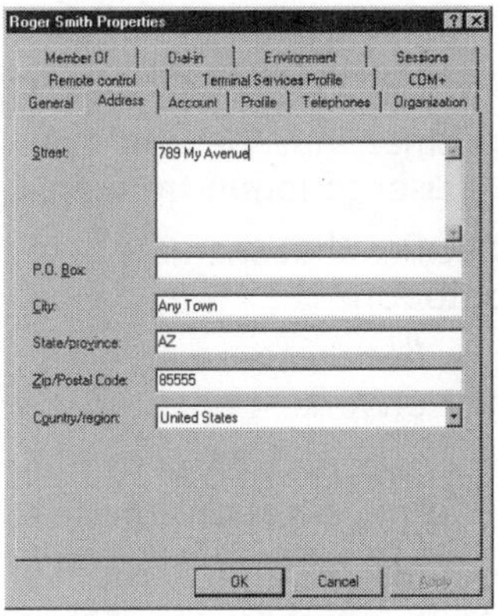

The Account Tab

The Account tab of the account Properties dialog box, seen in Figure 1.40, allows the network administrator to modify account attributes such as the logon name, the pre-Windows 2000 log-on name, logon hours, logon location restrictions, account expiration date, and several other account options.

Figure 1.40 Configuring the Account User Account Properties

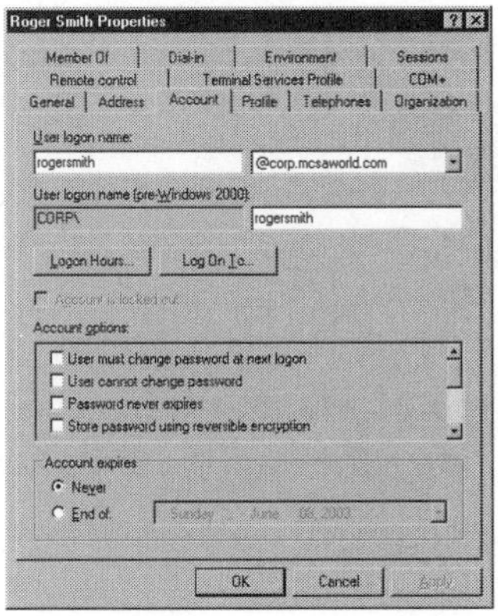

The account options that can be configured are explained in detail in Table 1.7.

Table 1.7 User Account Options

Account Option	Option Description
User must change password at next logon	Specifies that the user must change their password the next time they logon to the network.
User cannot change password	Specifies that the user is not allowed to change their password.
Password never expires	Specifies that the configured password never expires.
Store passwords using reversible encryption	Specifies that the user's password is to be used to allow the user to logon from an Apple computer.
Account is disabled	Specifies that the user account is not to be made available for logon.
Smart card is required for interactive logon	Specifies that a smart card must be used to logon to the network.
Account is trusted for delegation	Specifies that services running under this account can perform operations on behalf of other user accounts.
Account is sensitive and cannot be delegated	Specifies that the account shall not be assigned for delegation by another account.
Use DES encryption types for this account	Specifies that support for the Data Encryption Standard (DES) encryption algorithms is to be provided.
Do not require Kerberos preauthentication	Specifies that support is to be provided for alternate implementations of the Kerberos protocol.

Account logon restrictions can also be configured on the user account that can limit both the hours the user can logon to the network and also the computers in the network from which the user can logon. Exercise 1.16 presents the required steps to configure these options.

EXERCISE 1.16

CONFIGURING USER LOGON TIME AND COMPUTER RESTRICTIONS

1. On the **Account** tab of the user Properties dialog box, click the **Logon Hours** button to open the Logon Hours for User dialog box, seen in Figure 1.41.

Figure 1.41 Examining the Default Logon Hours Configuration

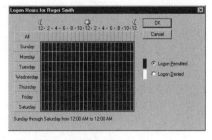

2. Blue squares represent those times when a user is allowed to logon to the network, while white squares represent those times when the user is not allowed to logon. By default, logon is allowed 7 days per week, 24 hours per day.

3. To configure a log-on hours restriction, click the **Logon Denied** button.

4. Select a starting day and time (Monday, 6 A.M. for example) and drag the cursor to highlight the time you wish to allow logon. Click the **Logon Permitted** button to make the changes, as seen in Figure 1.42. In this example, Roger Smith will now be allowed to logon only during the time period of Monday – Friday, from 6 A.M. – 6 P.M.

Figure 1.42 Configuring the Logon Hours for a User Account

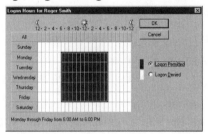

5. Click **OK** to accept the changes.

6. To configure a log-on computer restriction, which will limit the computers the user can logon to the network from, click the **Log On To** button on the **Account** tab of the user **Properties** dialog box.

7. The Logon Workstations dialog box, seen in Figure 1.43, will open allowing you enter the NetBIOS names of the computers this user will be allowed to logon in from.

Figure 1.43 Configuring Account Logon Workstation Restrictions

8. To enter computer names, select the **The following computers** button.

9. Enter the NetBIOS computer name, such as MCSAWKS042, for each computer that is to be allowed user logon. Note that the NetBIOS computer name MCSAWKS042 would belong to the computer with the following Fully Qualified Domain Name (FQDN) in this example domain: MCSAWKS042.corp.mcsaworld.com.

10. Click OK to accept the logon computer restrictions

The Profile Tab

The Profile tab of the account Properties dialog box, seen in Figure 1.44, allows the network administrator to specify a profile path, logon script, and home folder for the account.

Figure 1.44 Configuring the Profile User Account Properties

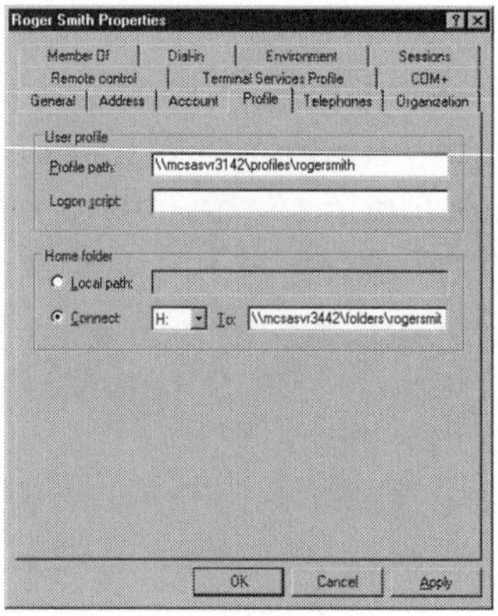

The Telephones Tab

The Telephones tab of the account Properties dialog box, seen in Figure 1.45, allows the network administrator to enter several different telephone numbers for a user including home, fax, pager, and mobile and IP phone numbers.

Figure 1.45 Configuring the Telephones User Account Properties

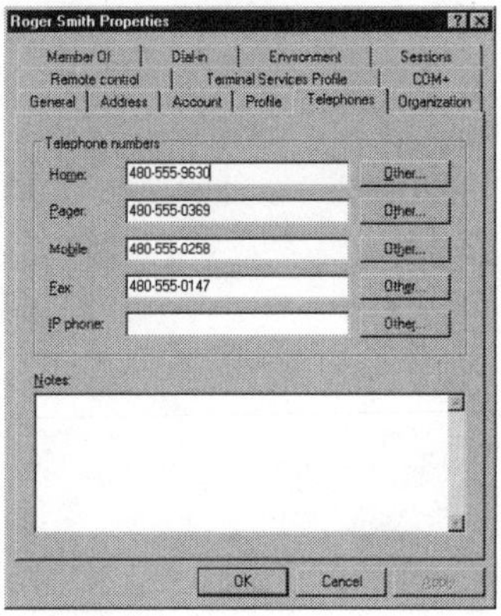

The Organization Tab

The Organization tab of the account Properties dialog box, seen in Figure 1.46, allows the network administrator to configure title and departmental information about the user. Additionally, they can enter the user's supervisor. On the Organization tab of the selected supervisor, the user's name will appear in the Direct reports area.

Figure 1.46 Configuring the Organization User Account Properties

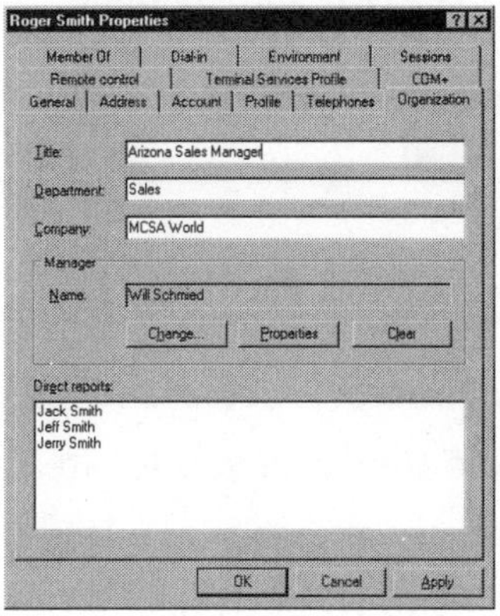

The Member Of Tab

The Member Of tab of the account Properties dialog box, seen in Figure 1.47, allows the network administrator to add or remove this user from groups. Additionally, they can also change the user's Primary group if the user is one that logs onto the network using Services for Macintosh or runs POSIX-compliant applications.

Figure 1.47 Configuring the Member Of User Account Properties

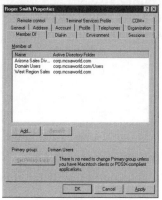

Deleting User Accounts

Occasionally, user accounts must be deleted, most commonly when a user no longer works for an organization. It is important to delete an inactive user account as soon as possible. For example, company policy might dictate that user accounts are to be disabled starting the day a user leaves the company. After 45 days if the user has not returned to the company, the user account is deleted to prevent its misuse. Exercise 1.17 outlines the process to delete a user using Active Directory Users and Computers.

EXERCISE 1.17

DELETING USERS FROM ACTIVE DIRECTORY USERS AND COMPUTERS

1. Open the **Active Directory Users and Computers** console.
2. Expand the console tree until you locate the user to be deleted.
3. Right-click on the user and select **Delete** from the context menu.
4. When prompted if you want to delete the user, click **Yes**.

Configuring & Implementing...

Reassigning User Accounts

As an alternative to deleting user accounts, an administrator may consider reassigning them. Consider the situation in which a user leaves the company and is immediately replaced by another user in the same job function. If this user's account has been extensively configured and has explicitly configured permissions, the administrator may find it difficult to create and configure the new account for the replacement worker in an exactly similar fashion. They can just rename the account and change the account password and reassign it to the new user.

To rename a user account and allow it to be reassigned, right-click on the user account and select **Rename** from the context menu. After renaming the account the Rename User dialog box will appear, allowing the network administrator to change the following key account items:

- Full name
- First name
- Last name
- Display name
- User logon name
- User logon name (pre-Windows 2000)

After this information is entered, the administrator can then go back and change any other items, such as telephone numbers, addresses, and so on. By reassigning a user account, they can quickly and accurately ensure that new users receive the exact same rights and permissions as their predecessors.

A user account can be deleted from the command-line using the *dsrm* command with the following syntax:

```
dsrm ObjectDN.
```

Figure 1.37 demonstrates using the *dsrm* command to delete the user account of Roger Smith using the following command:

```
dsrm "CN=Roger Smith,CN=Users,DC=corp,DC=mcsaworld,DC=com"
```

Figure 1.48 Deleting a User Account from the Command Line

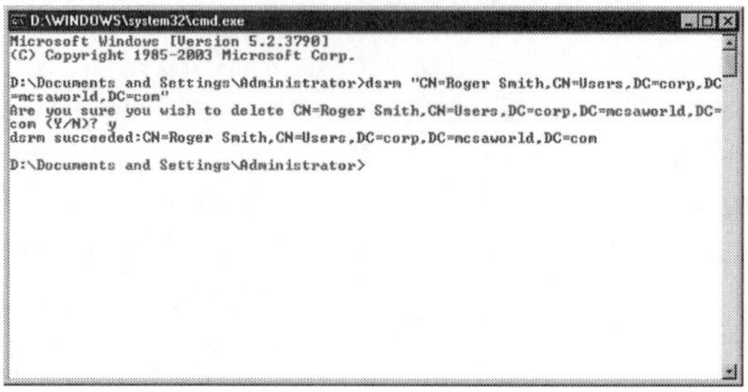

```
D:\WINDOWS\system32\cmd.exe

Microsoft Windows [Version 5.2.3790]
(C) Copyright 1985-2003 Microsoft Corp.

D:\Documents and Settings\Administrator>dsrm "CN=Roger Smith,CN=Users,DC=corp,DC
=mcsaworld,DC=com"
Are you sure you wish to delete CN=Roger Smith,CN=Users,DC=corp,DC=mcsaworld,DC=
com (Y/N)? y
dsrm succeeded:CN=Roger Smith,CN=Users,DC=corp,DC=mcsaworld,DC=com

D:\Documents and Settings\Administrator>
```

The network administrator will be prompted when using the *dsrm* command to ensure they are sure about deleting the account—once it is gone, it cannot be brought back except through a restoration action.

Assigning User Rights and Permissions to a User Account

User rights and permission assignment is done in the same fashion as that for groups, as seen previously in this chapter in Exercise 1.09 and Exercise 1.10 with the exception that you would select the applicable user instead of the applicable group.

Troubleshooting User Authentication Issues

It is safe to assume that at one time or another a network administrator will have problems with a user that cannot successfully logon to the network. While any number of things may cause this problem behavior, there are several key items that can be quickly checked to rule out the easy—and the obvious—problems that may occur.

- The user may not be allowed to logon to the specific computer interactively. If the user does not have the user right to perform interactive logons, they will receive an error dialog informing them of this situation. The network adminis-trator should check to ensure that the user has the correct user rights. If the user rights assignment is correct, they should ensure that the user is not trying to logon to a server or domain controller that they should not normally be using interactive logon for.

- The user may be using the wrong account type for the logon attempt. This problem typically occurs when a user is attempting to use a local user name and password combination to perform a network logon. If the user is using the correct credentials (network credentials), the network administrator should check to ensure that the Global Catalog (GC) server(s) are available. When the GC is unavailable, only users with administrative credentials will be able to logon to the network.

- The user's account may be disabled or locked out. The network administrator should check the Account tab of the user Properties dialog box to ensure that the account is not locked out or disabled. If the user account is locked out, the network administrator should check the Security Log to determine if the account is disabled, determine the reason why, and enable the account if permissible.

- The user may not be allowed to logon to the network during the current time period. User log-on hour restrictions may be preventing the user from performing the network logon. From the Account tab of the user Properties dialog box, the network administrator should click the **Logon Hours** button to verify the current logon hours configured for the user.

- The user may not be allowed to logon to the network from the computer being used. User logon workstation restrictions may be configured that do not allow the user to use the current computer to perform a network logon. From the Account tab of the user Properties dialog box, the network administrator should click the **Log On To** button to view the current list of allowed logon computers.

If none of these items correct the problems that the user is experiencing, the network administrator may also need to perform network troubleshooting to determine whether or not network connectivity or congestion problems may the root of the problem. For more information on TCP/IP addressing and network connectivity troubleshooting, see *MCSA/MCSE Exam 70-291 Study Guide & DVD Training System: Implementing, Managing, and Maintaining a Windows Server 2003 Network Infrastructure,* Syngress Publishing 2003, ISBN: 1-931836-92-2.

Creating and Managing Computer Accounts

Computer accounts serve the same basic function as user accounts: they are used to determine the rights and permissions that a computer will have in the domain. Although computer accounts can be created for any Windows computer on a network, only Windows 2000 or better computers will be able to fully participate in Active Directory and receive security and management configuration from Active Directory. Windows 9x and Windows NT computers will require the use of System Policies to configure security and management options. You can learn more about System Policies at www.microsoft.com/technet/prodtechnol/windowsserver2003/proddocs/server/tattooing.asp.

Computer accounts can be created in one of two ways: manually though usage of the Active Directory Users and Computers console or from the command-line, or automatically by joining a Windows 2000, Windows XP, or Windows Server 2003 computer to a domain. Each of these events is examined in more detail in the following sections.

Creating and Modifying Computer Accounts Manually

Computer accounts can be manually created in much the same fashion as user accounts. A network administrator can create a computer account from the Active Directory Users and Computers console, or from the command-line as desired. Exercise 1.18 presents the required steps to create a new computer account from the Active Directory Users and Computers console.

EXERCISE 1.18

CREATING COMPUTER ACCOUNTS FROM ACTIVE DIRECTORY USERS AND COMPUTERS

1. Open the **Active Directory Users and Computers** console.

2. Expand the console tree until you locate the location in which you wish to create the new computer.

3. Right-click on the node and select **New | Computer** from the context menu to open the New Object – Computer dialog box, seen in Figure 1.49.

Figure 1.49 Creating a New Computer Account

4. Enter the computer name and pre-Windows 2000 information. If this is a pre-Windows 2000 computer, select the appropriate option. If this computer is a Windows NT 4.0 BDC, select the appropriate option. After making your selections, click **Next** to continue.

5. On the Managed page, seen in Figure 1.50, click **Next** to continue without making any configuration changes. You would only need to enter information in this location if the computer were being pre-staged for Remote Installation Service (RIS) installation of an operating system.

Figure 1.50 You Can Pre-stage RIS Installation Computers If Desired

6. From the summary page, click **Finish** to complete the computer account creation process.

Computer accounts can also be created from the command-line by using the *dsadd* command with the following syntax:

```
dsadd computer ComputerDN
```

Figure 1.51 demonstrates using the *dsadd* command to create the computer account for a computer with a NetBIOS name of A51WXP3142 in the Sales OU using the following command:

```
dsadd computer CN=MCSAWXP3142,CN=Computers,DC=corp,DC=mcsaworld,DC=com
```

Figure 1.51 Creating a Computer Account from the Command-Line

Creating Computer Accounts by Joining to the Domain

As an alternative to creating a computer account manually, a network administrator may also create a computer account automatically by joining the computer to a domain.

Exercise 1.19 presents the required steps to join a Windows 2000 Professional client computer to a Windows Server 2003 domain. The process is similar for Windows XP Professional and Windows Server 2003 computers.

EXERCISE 1.19

JOINING A COMPUTER TO THE DOMAIN

1. On the computer to be joined to the domain, log on using an account that has local Administrative credentials.

2. Open the **System** applet in the Control Panel and click on the **Network Identification** tab.

3. Click the **Properties** button to open the Identification Changes dialog box seen in Figure 1.52. As seen in this example, this computer is currently part of a workgroup.

Figure 1.52 Joining the Computer to a Domain

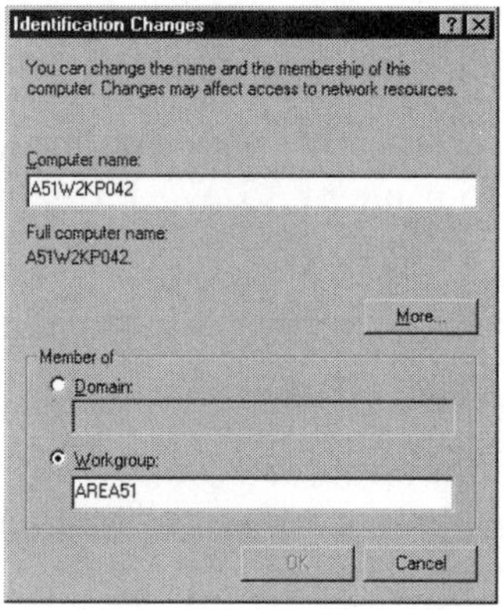

Figure 1.53 You will need to supply the proper credentials

4. Select the **Domain** button, enter the domain name that the computer is to be joined to, and click **OK**.

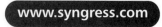

5. You will be prompted for the credentials of a user authorized to add computers to the domain. Supply them as seen in Figure 1.53.

6. Click **OK**. After some delay, depending on network conditions, you will receive the Welcome dialog box seen in Figure 1.54.

Figure 1.54 The Computer has Successfully been Joined to the Domain

7. Click **OK** to acknowledge the successful joining. You will be informed that you will need to restart the computer to complete the process.

8. Close the System applet and restart the computer.

9. When you log on next time from that computer, you will be logging onto your domain.

TEST DAY TIP

You can supply your user credentials in either of two ways in most instances: as shown in Figure 1.53 using what is referred to as the User Principal Name (UPN), or in the older, traditional Windows authentication way using DOMAIN\USER. You may find as you work your way around Windows that one way may not work in some instances where the other will. Both provide the same information to be used to authenticate the user.

EXAM WARNING

By default, members of the Account Operators group can add computers only to the Computers container (the default location for computers) or to Organizational Units. Authenticated Users in a domain are assigned the "Add workstations to a domain user" right and can add up to 10 new computer accounts to the domain with no action from an administrator. In this instance, new computer accounts are placed in the same container as the user account.

Importing and Exporting Active Directory Data

Realizing that administrators may need to import and export data into and out of Active Directory and other Lightweight Directory Access Protocol (LDAP) directory services, Microsoft has provided two utilities to accomplish just that task.

- **csvde (CSV Directory Exchange)** *csvde* uses files formatted in the Microsoft comma-separated value (CSV) format. The advantage of the CSV format is that it is supported by many other applications such as Microsoft Excel and Microsoft Access, thus allowing network administrator's to manipulate data in these applications before importing it. The downside to using *csvde* is that it only allows the addition of new objects; whereas *ldifde* allows the modification of existing objects.

- **ldifde (LDAP Data Interchange Format Directory Exchange)** *ldifde* can be used to extend the Active Directory schema, export data from Active Directory into other LDAP applications and services, and to populate the Active Directory database with LDAP data from other directory services. LDIF is an Internet standard file format used to perform batch import and export operations that conform to LDAP standards.

The full syntax of the *csvde* command is as follows:

```
csvde [-i] [-f FileName] [-s ServerName] [-c String1 String2] [-v]
[-j Path] [-t PortNumber] [-d BaseDN] [-r LDAPFilter] [-p Scope]
[-l LDAPAttributeList] [-o LDAPAttributeList] [-g] [-m] [-n] [-k]
[-a UserDistinguishedName Password] [-b UserName Domain Password] [-?]
```

The *ldifde* command also posesses the exact same syntax:

```
ldifde [-i] [-f FileName] [-s ServerName] [-c String1 String2] [-v]
[-j Path] [-t PortNumber] [-d BaseDN] [-r LDAPFilter] [-p Scope]
[-l LDAPAttributeList] [-o LDAPAttributeList] [-g] [-m] [-n] [-k]
[-a UserDistinguishedName Password] [-b UserName Domain Password] [-?]
```

The switches and modifiers for both commands are also the same as detailed in Table 1.8.

Table 1.8 *csvde/ldifde* Switches and Modifiers

Switch/Modifier	Description
Basic Global Parameters	
-i	Specifies import mode is to be used; if not specified export mode is assumed.
-f FileName	Specifies the file name for the import or export operation.

Continued

Table 1.8 *csvde/ldifde* Switches and Modifiers

Switch/Modifier	Description
-s *ServerName*	Specifies the domain controller that is to be used to per- form the import or export operation.
-c *String1 String2*	Specifies that all instances of *String1* to be replaced with *String2*.
-t *PortNumber*	Specifies a port number to connect on. The default is port 389 for LDAP and 3268 for Global Catalog serves.
-v	Sets verbose mode.
Export Related Parameters	
-d *BaseDN*	Specifies the distinguished name of the search base for data export.
-r *LDAPFilter*	Specifies an LDAP search filter for data export.
-p *Scope*	Specifies the search scope; the scope options are Base, OneLevel, or SubTree.
-l *LDAPAttributeList*	Specifies the list of attributes to return in the results of an export query.
-o *LDAPAttributeList*	Specifies the list of attributes to omit from the results of an export query.
-m	Specifies to omit attributes that only apply to Active Directory objects such as the ObjectGUID, ObjectSID, pwdLastSet, and samAccountType attributes.
-n	Specifies that the export of binary values to be omitted.
-j *Path*	Specifies the log file path and name.
-g	Specifies that paged searches are to be omitted.
Import Related Parameters	
-k	Specifies that errors during the import operation should be ignored and processing should continue.
Credentials Parameters	
-a *UserDistinguishedName Password*	Specifies that the command is to be run using *UserDistinguishedName* and *Password*. By default, the cre- dentials of the user currently logged on are used.
-b *UserName Domain Password*	Specifies that the command is to be run as Username Domain Password. By default, the credentials of the user currently logged on are used.

The following code example demonstrates what the CSV file might look like for the addition of three users into Active Directory.

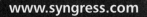

```
dn,cn,givenName,sn,description,objectClass,SAMAccountname,userPrincipalName
```

```
"CN=Richard Smith,CN=Users,DC=corp,DC=mcsaworld,DC=com","Richard
Smith",Richard,Smith,"West Regional Sales
Manager",user,richardsmith,richardsmith@corp.mcsaworld.com
```

```
"CN=Howard Smith,CN=Users,DC=corp,DC=mcsaworld,DC=com","Howard
Smith",Howard,Smith,"East Regional Sales
Manager",user,howardsmith,howardsmith@corp.mcsaworld.com
```

```
"CN=Toby Smith,CN=Users,DC=corp,DC=mcsaworld,DC=com","Toby Smith",Toby,Smith,"South
Regional Sales Manager",user,tobysmith,tobysmith@corp.mcsaworld.com
```

As can be seen, the first line defines the data fields of the rest of the file, just the same as any other flat database file in CSV format. Figure 1.55 demonstrates the command syntax used to perform the import, and the results of the process.

Figure 1.55 Using *csvde* to Import Data into Active Directory

In this example, three user accounts that were imported were all created and disabled. They need to be either manually or programatically enabled before being used. Also, no passwords were provided in this example. It is important to be aware that all accounts created this way will also be marked as requiring a password change upon the first logon.

TEST DAY TIP

Do not try to memorize every last detail of the *csvde* and *ldifde* commands. Instead, be aware of what they are used for and what differentiates them from each other. As well, be familiar with some of the more important (and commonly used) switches such as *-i*, *-f*, *-j* and *-k*.

Summary of Exam Objectives

This chapter covers a large amount of information that a network administrator will use on a daily basis. The largest purpose for networks is managing the creation of and access to shared resources. An examination of groups, user accounts, and computer accounts provides the necessary foundation to begin to work with Windows Server 2003 and networks as a whole.

In the Windows Active Directory domain model, groups are used as the first means to collect together users for the assignment of user rights and permissions. A group is a collection of user and/or computer accounts, contacts and even other groups that are managed as a single object. The users and computers that belong to the group are known as group members. In Windows, as with most operating systems, groups are used to simplify the administrative process of assigning permissions and rights to a large number of user and computer accounts at the same time, resulting in these groups' members having inherited (or implicit) permissions from the group. This is contrary to the older, and much more labor intensive practice of applying permissions and rights directly to users, which are then known as explicit permissions. A set of default groups known as local groups is created during the installation of Windows Server 2003. Computers that are part of an Active Directory domain environment also have a set of default groups; however these default groups are objects that reside within the Active Directory database structure.

Every user and computer in an Active Directory domain requires its own account. These user and computer accounts can be most easily managed by adding them to previously configured groups. User accounts are used for more than just network authentication and access control; they also contain pertinent contact and other information such as a telephone number and e-mail address that can be used to locate and contact users through searches of Active Directory. Many times, user authentication problems can be traced back to very simple and easily correctable problems.

The *csvde* and *ldifde* commands can be used to import and export data from LDAP compatible directory services, including Active Directory. While *ldifde* can be used to extend the Active Directory schema and modify existing objects, *csvde* can only be used to create new objects. The strength of *csvde* lies in the CSV file format that it uses which can be opened and modified by other applications, such as Microsoft Excel or Microsoft Access.

Exam Objectives Fast Track

Creating and Managing Groups

☑ Distribution groups are used for distributing messages to group members. Distribution groups are used with e-mail applications, such as Microsoft Exchange, to send an e-mail to all members of a group in a rapid and efficient fashion by sending an e-mail to the group e-mail address. All members of the distribution group that are mailbox-enabled will receive the e-mail message. Distribution groups are not security enabled, and therefore cannot be listed on the DACLs that are used by Windows to control access to resources.

☑ Security groups can also be used to for the distribution of e-mail as described for distribution groups, but can be listed on DACLs, thus allowing them to be used to control access to resources. Security groups can be used to assign user rights to group members. User rights include actions such as "Backup files and directories" or "Restore files and directories," both of which are assigned to the Backup Operators group by default. The network administrator can delegate rights to groups to allow the members of that group to perform a specific administrative function that is not normally allowed by their standard user rights. The network administrator can also assign permissions to security groups to allow them to access network resources such as printers and file shares.

☑ Universal groups can include other groups and user/computer accounts from any domain in the domain tree or forest. Permissions for any domain in the domain tree or forest can be assigned to universal groups.

☑ Global groups can include other groups and user/computer accounts from only the domain in which the group is defined. Permissions for any domain in the forest can be assigned to global groups.

☑ Domain Local groups can include other groups a user/computer accounts from Windows Server 2003, Windows Server 2000, and Windows NT domains. Permissions for only the domain in which the group is defined can be assigned to Domain Local groups.

☑ Several default groups are created in an Active Directory infrastructure and are located in both the Builtin and Users containers. In a workgroup environment, several default groups are created in the Local Users and Groups node of the Computer Management console.

☑ New in Windows Server 2003, group management can be carried out from the command-line, as well as from within Active Directory Users and Computers.

Creating and Managing User Accounts

☑ User accounts are much simpler to understand and work with than groups.

☑ Several default users are created during the installation of Windows Server 2003. They are located in the Users container in Active Directory and include the following: Administrator, Guest, IUSR_*computername,* IWAM_*computername,* krbtgt, and SUPPORT_*xxxxxxxx.*

☑ The IUSR_*computername* account is used to allow anonymous access to IIS resources. This account is a member of the Domain Users and Guests groups:.

☑ The IWAM_*computername* account is used by IIS to start out-of-process applications. This account is a member of the Domain Users and IIS_WPG groups.

☑ The SUPPORT_*xxxxxxxx* account is used for the Help and Support Service. This account is a member of the Domain Users and HelpServicesGroup groups. The SUPPORT account is disabled by default.

☑ New in Windows Server 2003, user account management can be carried out from the command line as well as from within Active Directory Users and Computers.

☑ Account logon restrictions can be configured for user accounts that can limit both the hours during which the user can logon to the network, and also the computers in the network from which the user can logon.

Creating and Managing Computer Accounts

☑ Computer accounts are created and managed in much the same fashion as for user accounts.

☑ Computer accounts can be created automatically for Windows 2000, Windows XP, and Windows Server 2003 computers when they are joined to an Active Directory domain.

☑ Computer accounts can be created manually for all Windows computers if desired. If the computer is a pre-Windows 2000 computer or an NT 4.0 BDC, the correct options should be selected to denote it as such.

☑ New in Windows Server 2003, computer account management can be carried out from the command line as well as from within Active Directory Users and Computers.

Importing and Exporting Active Directory Data

☑ *csvde* is a command line tool that can be used to import and export data from Active Directory in Microsoft CSV format. The advantage of the CSV format is that it is supported by many other applications such as Microsoft Excel and Microsoft Access, thus allowing the network administrator to manipulate data in these applications before importing it. The downside to using *csvde* is that it only allows the addition of new objects—*ldifde* allows the modification of existing objects.

☑ *ldifde* is a command line tool that can be used to extend the Active Directory schema, export data from Active Directory into other LDAP applications and services, and to populate the Active Directory database with LDAP data from other directory services. LDIF is an Internet standard file format for performing batch import and export operations that conform to LDAP standards.

Exam Objectives Frequently Asked Questions

The following Frequently Asked Questions, answered by the authors of this book, are designed to both measure your understanding of the Exam Objectives presented in this chapter, and to assist you with real-life implementation of these concepts. You will also gain access to thousands of other FAQs at ITFAQnet.com.

Q: It seems like creating groups, assigning them user rights and permissions, and then placing users in the groups is an awful lot of work. Why can't I just manage the user rights and permissions directly on the users themselves?

A: You can, however it will quickly become a very time- and labor-intensive process as the number of users in your network grows. Also, by managing user rights and permissions through group membership, you can absolutely ensure that all members of the group have the correct configuration. Lastly, you can quickly add or remove users from a group as required to change the user rights and permissions that are assigned to individual users, such as in the case where an employee moves from one job to another within the company.

Q: I have an employee that just quit the company last week. Should I delete her user account from Active Directory?

A: Yes and no. The most prudent thing to do in the short term would be to disable the user account, which effectively prevents it from being used to logon to the network. In this way, you will have the account available for a predetermined amount of time to see if the user is returning, or if you can perhaps reassign the account to the replacement employee.

Q: Why would I ever want to rename a user account and reassign it to another user?

A: In most cases you will not need to do this. In this case, however, where the user has had specific configuration performed directly on their user account (user rights, permissions, and so on) you may actually benefit from reusing the account after changing the key elements: user name, logon, and other personal details.

Q: How can I use the command line utilities to quickly create large numbers of user accounts?

A: You can create a batch file or script using the *dsadd* command to create and completely populate a user account with all pertinent information items. If the batch file or script can be stored in a secure location, you can even enter default password information directly into the script itself, forcing the user to change the password at the first logon. By default, all user accounts created programmatically are disabled, further adding security to them if they will not be used immediately. You can, however, have them created in the enabled state should you desire.

Q: How can the *csvde* and *ldifde* tools help me?

A: They can be used to quickly export and import large amounts of data from one LDAP-compliant directory service to another. Active Directory and Exchange Server can both create and work with CSV files that can be used by the *csvde* command. *csvde* and *ldifde* can also be used, with a little bit of experience, to create new Active Directory objects in bulk.

Q: Do all Active Directory manipulations have to be performed locally on a domain controller?

A: No, and in fact they should not be performed locally on a domain controller if it all possible. Domain controllers, just like other critical servers, should be physically isolated and secured from normal access by the use of locked server racks and specially located and secured server rooms. You can perform all network management and configuration tasks from a workstation connected to the network as long as you possess the required user rights and permissions.

Self Test

A Quick Answer Key follows the Self Test questions. For complete questions, answers, and explanations to the Self Test questions in this chapter as well as the other chapters in this book, see the Self Test Appendix.

Creating and Managing Groups

1. You are an assistant network administrator for Billy's Jeans, Inc. You have been tasked with creating three new groups, one for each of the following divisions: Sales, Marketing, and Production. The Sales group is to be configured with permissions required to access a shared network folder named Sales. The Marketing group is to be configured only for e-mail distribution to its members. The Production group is to be configured for both e-mail distribution and with the required permissions to access the Sales folder. Which of the following set of actions presents the correct steps to accomplish the requirement you have been tasked with?

   A. Create a security group named Sales and configure the Sales folder with the required permissions for this group. Create a security group named Marketing and configure the Sales folder with the required permissions for this group. Create a distribution group named Production and configure the Sales folder with the required permissions for this group. Additionally, configure an e-mail address for the Production group.

   B. Create a distribution group named Sales and configure the Sales folder with the required permissions for this group. Create a distribution group named Marketing and configure an e-mail address for this group. Create a security group named Production and configure the Sales folder with the required permissions for this group. Additionally, configure an e-mail address for the Production group.

   C. Create a security group named Sales and configure the Sales folder with the required permissions for this group. Create a distribution group named Production and configure an e-mail address for this group. Create a security group named Marketing and configure an e-mail address for this group.

   D. Create a security group named Sales and configure the Sales folder with the required permissions for this group. Create a distribution group named Marketing and configure an e-mail address for this group. Create a security group named Production and configure an e-mail address for this group. Additionally, configure the Sales folder with the required permissions for the Production group.

2. Hannah is preparing to configure user rights and permissions for 1,600 users that are spread out over five different departments: Sales, Marketing, Production, Engineering, and Administration. Each department is composed of two divisions: East and West. The network is also composed of two child domains under the root domain: East and West. The network has a total of ten divisions. How can Hannah create groups to use in assigning user rights and permissions without causing excessive directory replication between the two child domains? (Choose two correct answers)

   A. Hannah should create universal groups for all ten divisions.

   B. Hannah should create two universal groups, UEast and Uwest, and place the five respective departmental groups in them.

   C. Hannah should create global groups for all ten divisions.

   D. Hannah should create two global groups, GEast and Gwest, and place the five respective departmental groups in them.

3. You are preparing to assign user rights and permissions to 150 users on your network. Which of the following reasons explain why assigning the rights and permissions to a group and then placing the users into the group is the best course of action? (Choose three correct answers)

   A. Configuring user rights and permissions on groups is more accurate than configuring user rights and permissions on individual user accounts.

   B. Configuring user rights and permissions on groups requires less administrative time and labor to perform.

   C. Configuring user rights and permissions on groups allows you to quickly manage which users get these rights and permissions by adding or removing them from the group.

   D. Configuring user rights and permissions on groups prevents attackers from using the user accounts in an unauthorized fashion.

4. Austin is attempting to create a new group for his network that he wants to place several global groups into. When he tries to create the new group as a universal group, the option to do so is not available. What is the most likely reason for this problem?

   A. Austin's domain is operating in the Windows NT 4.0 native functional mode.

   B. Austin's domain is operating in the Windows 2000 mixed functional mode.

   C. Austin's domain is operating in the Windows Server 2003 functional mode.

   D. Austin's domain is operating in the Windows 2000 native functional mode.

5. Andrea has created a new security group for several help desk staff in her company. She has configured the required user rights and permissions on this security group and placed the help desk staff user accounts into the group. When Andrea tries to send an e-mail message to the security group, she gets a bounce back informing her that no such user was found. What is the most likely reason for this problem?

   A. One of the users in the group is not mailbox enabled.

   B. The group does not have an e-mail address configured for it.

   C. The group is not a distribution group.

   D. None of the users in the group are mailbox enabled.

6. Jon is creating several dozen new domain local security groups for his network. What command line utility could Jon use to create these groups for him?

   A. dsadd group *GroupDN* -secgrp yes -scope l -samid *SAMName* -desc *Description*

   B. dsadd group *GroupDN* -secgrp yes -scope g -samid *SAMName* -desc *Description*

   C. dsadd group *GroupDN* -secgrp no -scope l -samid *SAMName* -desc *Description*

   D. dsadd group *GroupDN* -secgrp yes -scope u -samid *SAMName* -desc *Description*

7. You have been tasked with determining the group membership status of several hundred employees within your organization. You have determined that it would be more efficient to perform this task from the command line. Which command line utility can be used to determine which groups a specified user is a member of?

   A. dsquery

   B. dsget

   C. dsmod

   D. dsrm

8. Andrew is a member of the help desk staff for Tim's Tents, Inc. Where can Andrew look to determine what groups that a user is a member of from within the Windows GUI?

   A. The Member Of tab in the group Properties dialog box.

   B. The Member Of tab in the user Properties dialog box.

   C. The Account tab in the user Properties dialog box.

   D. The Managed By tab in the group Properties tab.

Creating and Managing User Accounts

9. Which of the following user accounts is used to provide anonymous access to IIS resources and is a member of the Domain Users and Guests groups?

   A. IWAM_*computername*

   B. SUPPORT_*xxxxxxxx*

   C. IUSR_*computername*

   D. krbtgt

10. You have just completed a clean installation of Windows Server 2003 on a new server in your organization. Several default user accounts are created by the installation process. Which of the following default users are disabled by default? (Choose two correct answers.)

    A. Administrator

    B. Guest

    C. IUSR_*computername*

    D. SUPPORT_*xxxxxxxx*

11. You are in the process of creating new user accounts from the command line using the *dsadd* command. If the −*pwd* ★ modifier is specified, what is the net result?

    A. The password is to be randomly assigned.

    B. The password is to be left blank.

    C. The password is to be taken from another list.

    D. The password is to be supplied during the creation process.

12. You are a help desk staff member for your organization. A member of the Advertising department has requested that her password be changed. Which of the following items of information will you need to know in order to reset the password for her?

    A. The user's current password.

    B. The user's e-mail address.

    C. The user account name.

    D. The user's supervisor's name.

Creating and Managing Computer Accounts

13. Which of the following computers can have computer accounts in Active Directory? (Choose all correct answers.)

    A. Windows 2000 Professional

    B. Windows XP Professional

    C. Windows 98

    D. Windows 95

14. In what two ways can computer accounts be created in Active Directory? (Choose two correct answers.)

    A. By joining a Windows 95 computer to the domain.

    B. By joining a Windows 2000 Professional computer to the domain.

    C. Through manual creation from Active Directory Sites and Services.

    D. Through manual creation from Active Directory Users and Computers.

Importing and Exporting Active Directory Data

15. Chris is preparing to import a CSV file containing data from another LDAP-compliant directory service into the Active Directory of her domain. What is the minimum command that she will need to issue to perform the importation of the data in the file named userlist.csv?

    A. csvde –f *filename*

    B. ldifde –i –f *filename*

    C. csvde –i –f *filename*

    D. csvde –i

Self Test Quick Answer Key

For complete questions, answers, and explanations to the Self Test questions in this chapter as well as the other chapters in this book, see the Self Test Appendix.

1. **D**
2. **B, C**
3. **A, B, C**
4. **B**
5. **B**
6. **A**
7. **B**
8. **B**

9. **C**
10. **B, D**
11. **D**
12. **C**
13. **A, B, C, D**
14. **B, D**
15. **C**

Chapter 2

MCSA/MCSE 70-292

Managing and Maintaining Terminal Services Access

Exam Objectives in this chapter:

2.1 Troubleshoot Terminal Services

2.1.1 Diagnose and resolve issues related to Terminal Services security

2.1.2 Diagnose and resolve issues related to client access to Terminal Services

☑ Summary of Exam Objectives

☑ Exam Objectives Fast Track

☑ Exam Objectives Frequently Asked Questions

☑ Self Test

☑ Self Test Quick Answer Key

Introduction

Windows Server 2003 is a robust operating system that builds off of the successes (and failures) of previous Windows operating systems. One of the most useful improvements in Windows Server 2003 is in the area of Terminal Services. Although Terminal Services is not a completely new feature, having been around since Windows NT (as an add-on) and integrated in Windows 2000 Server, Windows Server 2003 Terminal Services is more powerful and easier to use than ever before.

Regarding Terminal Services, it is important to understand two things prior to studying—how the service works, and its basic configuration principles. These two background information items are examined before looking at the troubleshooting end of the Terminal Service, which directly relates to the exam objectives for exam 70-292. Windows Terminal Services is, in some respects, similar to Citrix MetaFrame (www.citrix.com), where applications are loaded on a main server (sometimes consisting of a cluster of load balanced servers) for thin clients to access and use. This concept dates back to the IBM mainframe concept, with green screen *dumb terminals*, where all applications resided on a centralized system. For those unfamiliar with the term "dumb terminal," it refers to a terminal with no real intelligence located on the system, for instance a central processing unit (CPU) or hard drive storage. All processing is done on the central system (mainframe) and only screen changes (referred to as *screenshots*) are sent to the dumb terminal.

Terminal Services is available in two major modes—one that provides applications to clients, and one that provides for remote administration. This chapter is primarily concerned with the former role known as *Terminal Server* (formerly known as Application Server Mode in Windows 2000 Server). The use of Terminal Services for remote administration of servers and workstations are examined later in Chapter 3. As it pertains to the Terminal Server mode of Terminal Services, this chapter examines installation, configuration, and troubleshooting of Terminal Services.

TEST DAY TIP

A lot of time is spent in the beginning of this chapter to bring you up to speed on Terminal Services, what has changed in Windows Server 2003, design issues, and the background behind the service. Although 90 percent of this information will not directly relate to an exact test question, it is all valuable information.

The test objectives for Terminal Services that are listed at the beginning of this chapter and online at www.microsoft.com/traincert/exams/70-292.asp relate to more advanced areas than previously seen for the Windows 2000 MCP exams. You must be able to perform troubleshooting operations after installation and configuration has been completed. If you are not comfortable with the Terminal Services features of Windows 2000 Server, you should read up on it at www.microsoft.com/windows2000/technologies/terminal/default.asp.

The Need for Terminal Services: A Survey of Computing Environments

When working with any major service, the network administrator must first understand how it works and how it should be deployed before entering into a production installation. Terminal Services is no exception to this rule. This chapter discusses how the service came about, and why it is so important to understand it. It is critical that the administrator understand how Terminal Services works to be able to plan deployments and troubleshoot problems.

> **NOTE**
>
> An additional detailed discussion on remotely managing servers is found in Chapter 3, "Managing and Maintaining Remote Servers."

Centralized Computing versus Distributed Computing

This section looks at centralized versus distributed computing environments to help you understand the importance of Terminal Services, and why it is such an integral component of Windows Server 2003. Before beginning, a proper definition of centralized and distributed computing is required to illustrate their differences. This section examines some background information on this set of environments that will help you eliminate obvious wrong answers during your exam experience. Additionally, you will gain an understanding of the important role that Terminal Services plays in a production network, thus providing you with some ammunition to help you justify the cost of the solution to your management team.

This section examines the following areas of concern:

- **Centralized Computing** In the centralized computing model, all network resources are located on one or more central servers or mainframes. Clients access these resources remotely and have little intelligence and little to no processing power. All processing and storage of data are done on the centralized server or servers and only screenshots of the resulting outcome are transmitted back to the client. The clients are generally referred to as *thin clients* or dumb terminals. This is the truest form of Terminal Services.

- **Distributed Computing** In the distributed computing model, network resources are still located on the central server, however, some processing is done by both the servers and the network clients. The clients are generally referred to as *fat clients* and typically consist of a standard PC or workstation. Data is stored on the central servers that are providing the services, but the manipulation of the data is done on the local workstation. This is a fairly common model in use today:

consider the situation of network clients connecting to a centralized Microsoft Exchange server for mail and messaging.

- **Mixed Environment**   In the mixed environment model, both a centralized and a distributed computing environment coexist together on the same network. This is a combination of thin clients and fat clients, and can utilize resources as required. By some accounts, network administrators have the best of both worlds. Consider the example of a mixed environment that places thin clients on a manufacturing floor that only run a process control application from a centralized server, with fat clients located in offices that access files on network file servers, manipulating the data locally on the workstation.

⚠ EXAM WARNING

Although this information will not be explicitly tested on the exam, these definitions are necessary for the proper planning of a Terminal Services infrastructure.

Before the days of fully loaded computer rooms stocked with the latest blade servers, 1U rack-mounted systems, and so on, there was the mainframe, which was responsible for creating a centralized computing environment where all resources existed, including the main CPU where all the data was processed. This is not to be mistaken for mainframe centralized computing systems that have since been declared obsolete with the advent of distributed computing solutions. Today there is a potpourri of different types of systems the network administrator can use, and there has even been a push to go back to the original centralized model, as evidenced by the strong market presence of Citrix and the enhancement made in Terminal Services in Windows Server 2003. The market for Terminal Services is growing larger every year, as the need to keep applications current is becoming more important to many managers looking at their Total Cost of Ownership (TCO).

Figure 2.1 illustrates the concept of a centralized computing environment where all processing is done on the mainframe and only the resultant screenshots are returned to the dumb terminals. There are a few other important points to note about the environment illustrated in Figure 2.1:

- There are two small local area networks (LANs) separated geographically and connected via a wide area network (WAN) link.

- In the core location, a mainframe exists where all the resources are located.

- In the core location, dumb terminals are present, which access the resources located on the mainframe.

- In the remote location, a front-end controller is present that allows communication with the remote mainframe across the WAN link.

- The bulk of the computing power is located on the mainframe, and hence the bulk of the cost as well. The mainframe will likely be costly to install, maintain, and fix if required.

Figure 2.1 The Centralized Computing Environment

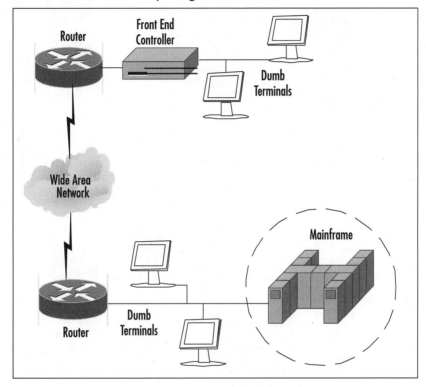

The distributed computing environment is completely different from the centralized computing solution. However, it does have some similarities that will affect the network administrator's decision to implement and maintain it. Figure 2.2 illustrates the distributed computing environment. The biggest difference here is in the placement of resources and where the processing is done.

Figure 2.2 The Distributed Computing Environment

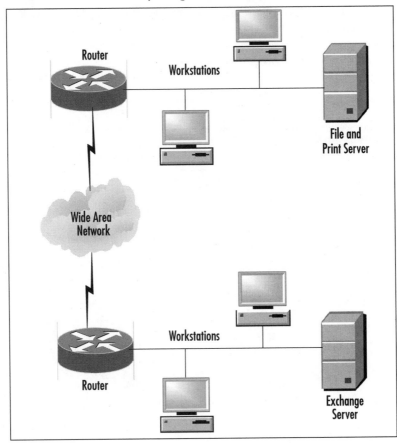

Taking a closer look at Figure 2.2, let's finalize what we need to know about a distributed computing environment.

- In the example there are two small LANs separated geographically and connected via a WAN link.

- In both locations, servers respond to user requests for resources they are allowed to access and use.

- There are PCs on both LANs (not dumb terminals) that incorporate more than just a monitor, keyboard, and network connection. In some cases these PCs are just as powerful, if not more so, than some of the servers being used. PCs contain their own storage, CPU, and so forth.

- The processing of information by the end user can be distributed between the servers they access for resources, or on their own machine with installed applications and so on.

- A distributed computing solution also means that the costs are distributed among the PCs and servers. The PCs and servers both have a considerable amount of intelligence and computing strength, with PCs running desktop applications such as Outlook or Word and servers running server applications such as Exchange or Dynamic Host Configuration Protocol (DHCP). This results in servers that are less costly to operate, maintain, and fix. However, the network administrator must make a more significant investment in desktop PCs and be prepared to support them over time.

Returning to the centralized computing environment previously shown in Figure 2.1, let's implement Windows Server 2003 Terminal Services. The results are illustrated in Figure 2.3 as a centralized computing environment with Windows Server 2003 in use, utilizing Terminal Services in the Terminal Server mode of operation. As you will notice, dumb terminals and mainframes are no longer thin clients and Terminal Services servers now come into play.

NOTE

For an example of a thin client sold by HP/Compaq, visit http://h18004.www1. hp.com/products/thinclients/. You can also run a search online for other vendors like Sun Microsystems, IBM, and so on.

Figure 2.3 The Centralized Computing Environment with Windows Server 2003

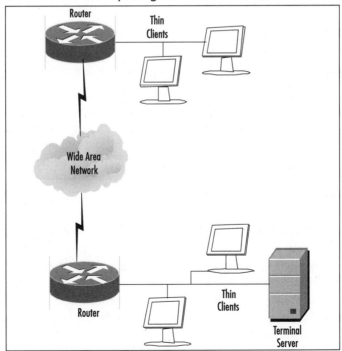

In the mode shown in Figure 2.3, applications are loaded on the Terminal Server and thin clients access the server (via login). From here the thin clients are able to access, utilize, and manage applications and data from the Terminal Server. Though this sounds similar to a mainframe environment (which it resembles), there a few major differences to be aware of:

- Thin clients (not dumb terminals) are used to access the Terminal Server. You have to go back in history (or work in a site that still utilizes dumb terminals) to appreciate what was affectionately called the "green screen." Basic text was shown on the terminal, and was all you had to work with.

- A solution like this means that most of the costs associated with running this solution are placed on the Terminal Server, where all the intelligence and computing strength is. The hardware used to run the Terminal Server client is fairly inexpensive.

NOTE

You could imply from this section that thin clients are the only things you can use with Windows Server 2003 Terminal Services. This is not true, but you may want to design the network to save cash and lower your budget on a project of this scope by utilizing thin clients. You can use your PC also, but again, this ruins the return on investment (ROI) you get from implementing this solution in the first place. The way to justify this solution is to have a mixed environment

Mixed Environments

Mixed environment is not a term you that need to memorize, or something that will appear on the exam, but rather more of a *real world reality*. It is important to understand that all the previously described environments (Figures 2.1 through 2.3) can be mixed, as shown in Figure 2.4. In this particular example, note that there are thin clients getting the resources they need from the Terminal Server, while the PCs are getting what resources they need from the File Server. Provided that the routers have paths to both locations and everything is configured properly, there is no reason why an infrastructure like this cannot be used. If your network infrastructure looks anything like most others, you are probably operating in a mixed environment where you are using what you need, where you need it.

This type of implementation implies that you possess some solid design skills for the purpose of understanding network architectures, and that you will not always implement a solution unless it deals with and provides a solution to a specific need. Many systems administrators and engineers who would like to implement thin client technologies are aware that the true driver for implementing the technology is to save money. Placing a Terminal Services-based thin client solution in your current infrastructure can significantly lower your TCO, but you may still have a high amount of value placed on your other resources such as existing file servers and so on.

Figure 2.4 A Mixed Environment

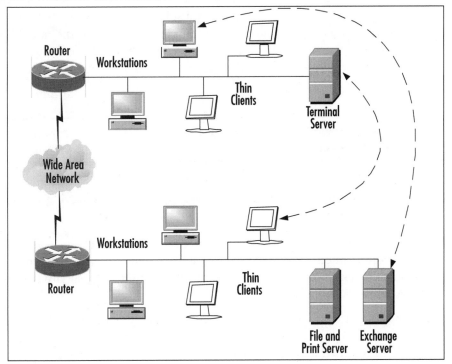

The network depicted in Figure 2.4 already had a fully functional distributing computing environment; however, the thin client solution has been introduced to provide an application to a specific group of users across the network. Implementing a thin client solution saved money, time, and resources in this case, and there was no added cost in removing the current network that was addressing a business need already in place.

NOTE

You are not expected to know all the details discussed regarding distributed versus centralized computing environments for the MCSA 70-292 Exam.

Terminal Services Design Issues

Now that you understand the basic design issues around Terminal Services, let's take a look at a very complex layout where your knowledge of Terminal Services design will be put to the test. The purpose of this it to make you are aware of the issues you most likely will see when you roll out Terminal Services. If you are planning on deploying an application to a remote site, you will need to take many factors into account.

The points made in this section offer insight into ways that you can prevent massive problems on your network by rolling out thin client solutions to all your sites. You will have to consider bandwidth to be one of the most critical analysis points for the future. You must verify that the Terminal Services-based solution, which uses centralized computing, can travel over the WAN without errors, in order to give you the best experience possible.

NOTE

Lack of proper bandwidth is almost always the culprit when you experience latency on your terminal sessions.

Remember the following key analysis and design points when deploying Terminal Services:

- If you roll out Terminal Services, you will need to continually analyze your bandwidth consumption and traffic flow. Some WAN links are not currently ready to support the traffic that Terminal Services will add to it; you may have to upgrade some existing WAN links.

- Inexpensive PCs can be bought at a comparable cost as a thin client to give remote sites some time (or life support) if your true intention is to just replace PCs. This is not always the best solution if you have to upgrade all of your WAN links to T1s.

- Deploying Terminal Services, if utilized completely, will most likely affect other applications and services on WAN links that may not have been previously affected.

EXAM WARNING

Learning how to troubleshoot Terminal Services begins with the ability to analyze the design, placement, and practical use of the service in order to spot potential problems. In simple terms, not planning out the service before implementing it can lead to troubleshooting-based problem with Terminal Services.

Since screenshots have to traverse the network to get from the server to the client utilizing the service, you have to think about the bandwidth available on the network so you know how latency will affect it. For example, if your WAN link is saturated, you may see Terminal Services suffer in the form of disconnects, hesitation with keystrokes, and so on. Always test and consider this for future implementations, especially if you are going to be providing applications over the network to your clients.

Introduction to Windows Server 2003 Terminal Services

With Terminal Services, it is important to note that Windows Server 2003 will allow you to enhance your company's software deployment ability. Not only will it allow for more flexibility, but this flexibility can be gained in both the management and application modes available.

When discussing Terminal Services in Windows Server 2003, you should be aware of the following major components and features:

- Remote Assistance
- Remote Desktop for Administration
- Terminal Server
- Terminal Services Licensing
- Terminal Server Session Directory

Remote Assistance and Remote Desktop for Administration are examined later in Chapter 3. The remaining three items: Terminal Server mode, Terminal Services Licensing, and the Terminal Service Session Directory, are examined throughout the remainder of this chapter.

Terminal Server

The Terminal Server mode is one that few people understand and even fewer people use. However, that may soon change as the cost of maintaining full-featured desktop workstations and licensing the most current version of application software gets more expensive, making Terminal Server a more attractive solution. In brief, Terminal Server allows the network administrator to deliver Windows-based applications or the Windows desktop itself to clients that do not have the processing power to run Windows locally.

Terminal Server mode is supported in the following versions of Windows Server 2003:

- Windows Server 2003 Standard Edition
- Windows Server 2003 Enterprise Edition
- Windows Server 2003 Datacenter Edition

Terminal Server is not supported on Windows Server 2003 Web Edition; Web Edition is a stripped down, and therefore less expensive, version of Windows Server 2003 that has been optimized for providing Internet Information Server (IIS)-based services to clients.

But, what exactly is new and noteworthy with regards to the Terminal Server mode in Windows Server 2003? Consider the following points:

- **Naming Conventions have Changed** It seems that with every successive version of Windows, many components get new names. In the case of Terminal Services, the Terminal Server mode was previously referred to as Terminal Services Application mode in Windows 2000. In addition, Remote Desktop for Administration has replaced what was previously referred to as Remote Administration mode in Windows 2000.

- **Rapid, Centralized Deployment of Applications** When the Terminal Server mode is used, you have the power to add greater flexibility to your network and the systems and applications. Say you have a single application that remote users need to use over a Virtual Private Network (VPN) or at remote sites. Would you rather place a server locally at each site and incur those costs, or could you let the users create a session with the Terminal Server to utilize the application and then disconnect when done? Another benefit of providing applications via Terminal Server is that the application can be updated on the server with hotfixes, Service Packs, and other updates without the need to visit remote desktop clients or roll out complex (and sometimes bandwidth consuming) updates via Group Policy, System Update Service (SUS), or some other means such as System Management Server (SMS).

- **Low-bandwidth Access to Data** When the Terminal Server mode is used, the bandwidth consumption over a switched LAN is almost transparent. When operating over a WAN link, you may need to analyze and consider upgrading the link, although in most cases this will not be a problem as the screenshots are sent as very compressed data. Terminal Server does not require an excessive amount of bandwidth to make available the functionality it offers.

- **Windows Anywhere** When the Terminal Server mode is used, you have a wider reach to include those users who may not be using Windows 2000 or Windows XP. Terminal Services support is provided for a number of devices, such as a the old Pentium 133MHz workstation running Windows 95 to a brand new iPAQ that provides support for 802.11b connectivity. The ability to deliver the Windows experience to a broad base of users can be helpful in those environments where the cost of upgrading 600 desktops to Windows 2000 just to utilize a new application is not worth the cost or effort. TCO and ROI are a large part of IT budgets these days and providing solutions that keep costs down while providing an acceptable level of functionality will go a long way towards staying in budget.

- **Increased Scalability** What good is any solution if users cannot access it? That is the question to keep in mind when deploying any mission critical solution, Terminal Services included. Scalability is often examined from one of the following two points of view:

1. *Scaling up* is to build up a server by adding more random access memory (RAM), additional CPUs, more and faster network adapters, and more storage devices. As you scale up a server, the cost goes up, thus making the term easy to remember.

2. *Scaling out* a solution refers to expanding the number of systems that are part of the solution. Additional servers are added to the Terminal Services solution and a technology such as Network Load Balancing (NLB) is used to distribute requests and load amongst all participating servers, as illustrated in Figure 2.5.

Figure 2.5 A NLB Terminal Server Cluster

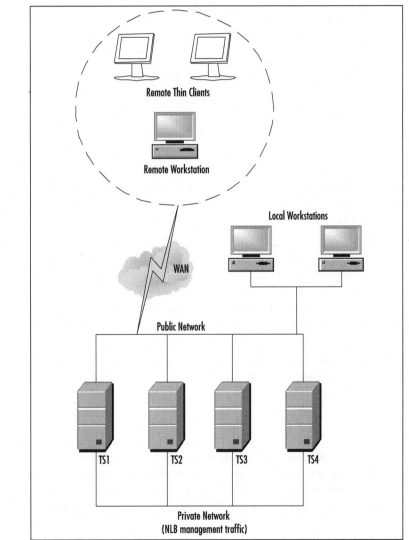

- **Improved Manageability** The bulk of the Terminal Server-related options can be configured and managed directly through Group Policy settings, allowing the administrator to configure the desired settings and have them applied to their network users during the subsequent Group Policy refresh event. Advanced users may want to consider taking advantage of the powerful management features provided by the Windows Management Instrumentation (WMI) that allows for complete remote management capability through scripting.

TEST DAY TIP

Make sure that you are familiar with the new Windows Server 2003 Terminal Services features for this exam.

Terminal Server Session Directory

The Terminal Server Session Directory is a new feature that was created to allow users to easily reconnect to a disconnected session if they are using a NLB Terminal Server farm (refer back to Figure 2.5). When a request is made for an application hosted by the Terminal Server cluster, the request is actually sent to the Virtual Internet Protocol (IP) address that represents the entire cluster. NLB uses a mathematical algorithm to determine which of the available nodes should receive the new client request, and hands off the request to the appropriate server's dedicated IP address, which is specific to each server in the cluster. If the client disconnects the session and later wants to reconnect, the default behavior of NLB is to run the request through the algorithm again, possibly putting the new session on a different Terminal Server. The Terminal Server Session Directory function prevents this problem by allowing the clients to reconnect to the Terminal Server that their existing session is located on.

The session directory for Windows Server 2003 maintains a list of sessions, indexed by user name. Once this indexing takes place, a user who has terminated a session with the Terminal Server is able to reconnect and resume the previous session so that work in that session can be completed. The session directory is best placed on a server that is not part of the NLB cluster group, although it can be placed on one of the members if required (although not recommended).

TEST DAY TIP

Although not likely to be on the test, you should be aware of the capabilities that the session directory gives you. For more information see the following Microsoft Knowledge Base articles: http://support.microsoft.com/default.aspx?scid=kb;en-us;301926 and http://support.microsoft.com/default.aspx?scid=kb;en-us;301923.

Installing and Configuring a Terminal Server

This section examines the installation and configuration of the Terminal Server service. It starts off by installing the Terminal Server and then examines the configuration options that are available for the Terminal Server.

Installing the Terminal Server

There are two different ways to install Terminal Server: using the Manage Your Server utility or using the Windows Component Wizard. Each of these methods are examined in Exercises 2.01 and 2.02, respectively.

EXERCISE 2.01

INSTALLING A TERMINAL SERVER USING MANAGE YOUR SERVER

1. Click **Start | Programs | Administrative Tools | Manage Your Server** to start the Manage Your Server utility, as seen in Figure 2.6.

   Figure 2.6 The Manage Your Server Utility

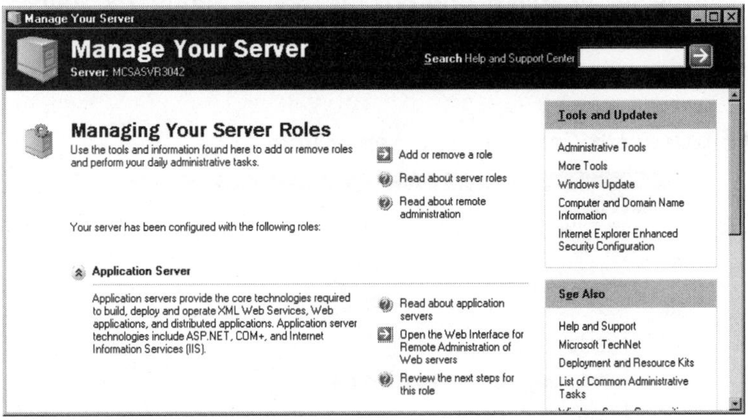

2. To start adding the Terminal Server role to your server, click the **Add or remote a role** link.

3. The Preliminary Steps dialog box appears, as seen in Figure 2.7, prompting you to ensure that you are ready to proceed. Click **Next** to continue.

Figure 2.7 Verifying Preliminary Steps

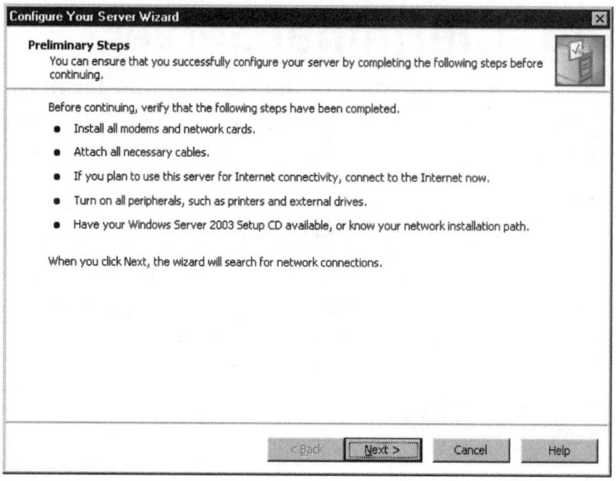

Configure Your Server Wizard

Preliminary Steps
You can ensure that you successfully configure your server by completing the following steps before
continuing.

Before continuing, verify that the following steps have been completed.

- Install all modems and network cards.
- Attach all necessary cables.
- If you plan to use this server for Internet connectivity, connect to the Internet now.
- Turn on all peripherals, such as printers and external drives.
- Have your Windows Server 2003 Setup CD available, or know your network installation path.

When you click Next, the wizard will search for network connections.

< Back   Next >   Cancel   Help

4. The Configure Your Server Wizard dialog box will appear briefly while your server is analyzed. If any problems are found, you will be informed of them before proceeding. You need to click **Continue** if any problems are found.

5. On the Server Role dialog box, as seen in Figure 2.8, you can start the installation process of the Terminal Server. Select the **Terminal server** option and click **Next** to continue.

Figure 2.8 Configuring a Server Role

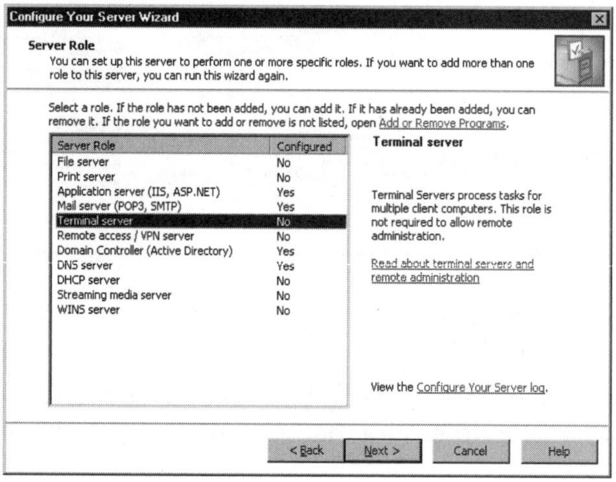

Configure Your Server Wizard

Server Role
You can set up this server to perform one or more specific roles. If you want to add more than one
role to this server, you can run this wizard again.

Select a role. If the role has not been added, you can add it. If it has already been added, you can
remove it. If the role you want to add or remove is not listed, open Add or Remove Programs.

Server Role	Configured
File server	No
Print server	No
Application server (IIS, ASP.NET)	Yes
Mail server (POP3, SMTP)	Yes
Terminal server	No
Remote access / VPN server	No
Domain Controller (Active Directory)	Yes
DNS server	Yes
DHCP server	No
Streaming media server	No
WINS server	No

Terminal server

Terminal Servers process tasks for
multiple client computers. This role is
not required to allow remote
administration.

Read about terminal servers and
remote administration

View the Configure Your Server log.

< Back   Next >   Cancel   Help

6. The Summary of Selections dialog box appears informing you of your selections. Click **Next** to continue.

7. You may be prompted with a warning, as seen in Figure 2.9, informing you that the server will require a restart to complete the installation process. Click **OK** to continue.

Figure 2.9 Acknowledging the Restart Warning

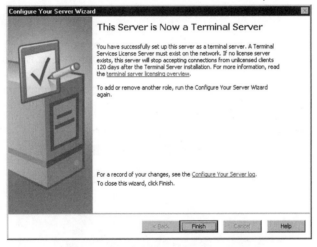

8. The Windows Components Wizard appears to finalize the installation. Click **Next** if required.

9. After the restart, you will see the dialog box, as seen in Figure 2.10. Click **Finish** to close the dialog box.

Figure 2.10 Terminal Server Installation Complete

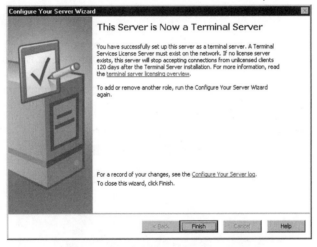

NOTE

You have now configured a server role, but where is the proof of this configuration? See the log located at %systemroot%\ debug.configureyourserver.log for information on what the Manage Your Server utility has done.

To install the Terminal Server from the Windows Component Wizard complete the steps outlined in Exercise 2.02. Installing the Terminal Server via the Windows Component Wizard is the preferred method as it offers greater control over the installation.

EXERCISE 2.02

INSTALLING A TERMINAL SERVER USING WINDOWS COMPONENTS WIZARD

1. Click **Start | Settings | Control Panel | Add or Remove Programs** to open the Add or Remove Programs applet.

2. Click the **Add/Remove Windows Components** button to start the Windows Components Wizard.

3. When the Windows Components Wizard opens, scroll down and select **Terminal Server**, as seen in Figure 2.11. Click **Next** to continue.

NOTE

The installation of the Terminal Server Licensing component is examined later in this chapter.

Figure 2.11 Selecting the Terminal Server Option

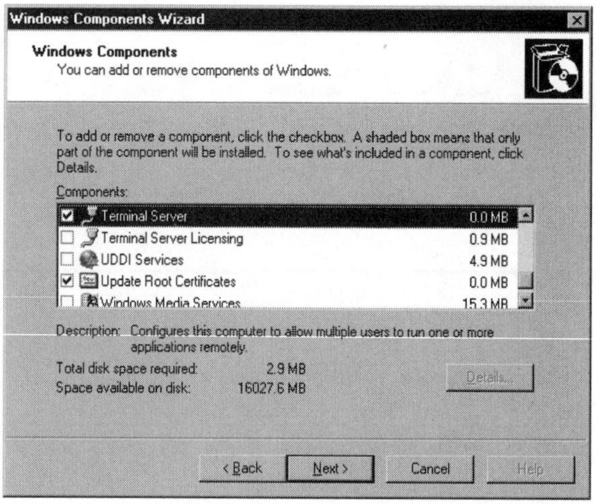

![Windows Components Wizard dialog box showing component selection with Terminal Server checked. Windows Components - You can add or remove components of Windows. To add or remove a component, click the checkbox. A shaded box means that only part of the component will be installed. To see what's included in a component, click Details. Components: Terminal Server 0.0 MB (checked), Terminal Server Licensing 0.9 MB, UDDI Services 4.9 MB, Update Root Certificates 0.0 MB (checked), Windows Media Services 15.3 MB. Description: Configures this computer to allow multiple users to run one or more applications remotely. Total disk space required: 2.9 MB, Space available on disk: 16027.6 MB. Buttons: Back, Next, Cancel, Help, Details]

4. The Terminal Server setup dialog box appears, as seen in Figure 2.12, warning you of the consequences of your selection as follows:

This option installs Terminal Server, which configures the computer to run programs for multiple simultaneous users. Note: By default only members of the local Administrators group will be able to connect to this Terminal Server. You will need to add user accounts to the local Remote Desktop Users group to allow users to connect to this Terminal Server. Do not install Terminal Server if you only need Remote Desktop for administration, which is installed by default, and may be enabled by opening the Remote tab of the System control panel applet and enabling remote connections.

Program Installation: If you continue with this installation, programs that are already installed on your server will no longer work and will have to be reinstalled. You must use Add or Remove Programs in Control Panel whenever you install programs to use on a Terminal Server.

Licensing: To continue using Terminal Server after an initial grace period of 120 days from today, you must set up a server running Terminal Server Licensing. For details see Terminal Server Help.

It is very important that you read and understand the information that this dialog box is presenting as it will affect the way your Terminal Server performs and behaves. Click **Next** to continue.

Figure 2.12 Viewing the Terminal Server Setup Warning

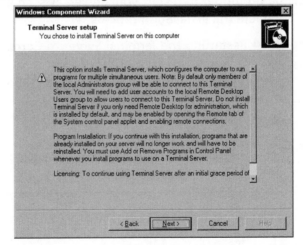

5. On the next dialog box, you must select what level of permission you are willing to allow for the applications that are to be run on the Terminal Server. The default option of **Full Security** provides the most security for your Terminal Server, but may not allow some legacy applications to run properly. The **Relaxed Security** option allows users and applications to have more access to the Registry and therefore may allow legacy applications to run properly—at the cost of decreased environment security. Make your selection and click **Next** to continue.

Figure 2.13 Selecting the Default Permissions for the Terminal Server

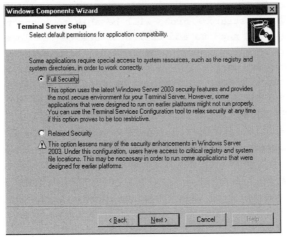

6. The Windows Component Wizard now installs the Terminal Server on your server.

7. Click **Finish** when prompted by the Windows Component Wizard.

8. You will be prompted to restart your server, as seen in Figure 2.14. Click **Yes** to complete the installation process.

Figure 2.14 Restarting the Terminal Server to Complete the Installation

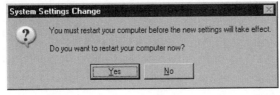

EXAM
70-292
OBJECTIVE
2.1
2.1.1
2.1.2

Configuring the Terminal Server

With the Terminal Server now installed, it is time to begin the configuration process. The easiest place to start is the Manage Your Server utility. As seen in Figure 2.15, there are four basic options to choose from.

Figure 2.15 Using the Manage Your Server utility to Configure the Terminal Server

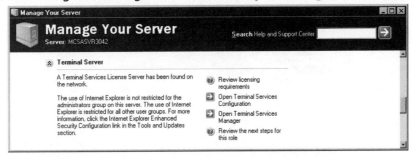

These options include:

- **Review Licensing Requirements** A Help-based function discussing the specifics of Terminal Services licensing (discussed in more detail later in the "Terminal Service Licensing" section of this chapter).

- **Open Terminal Services Configuration** Opens the Terminal Services Configuration console, where the majority of configuration tasks can be performed for the Terminal Server. This is discussed in more detail in the "Using the Terminal Services Configuration Console" section of this chapter.

- **Open Terminal Services Manager** Opens the Terminal Services Manager console that allows the network administrator to manage the users, sessions, and resources for Terminal Servers in their enterprise. This is discussed more in the "Using the Terminal Services Manager Console" section of this chapter.

- **Review the Next Steps for this Role** A Help-based function to review the future steps that should be performed.

Using the Terminal Services Configuration Console

The Terminal Services Configuration console, as seen in Figure 2.16, allows the administrator to perform the basic configuration of their Terminal Server. The following sections discuss all of the available options in this area in detail.

NOTE

You will need to use Group Policy to be able to set more advanced Terminal Services options, as discussed in the "Advanced Terminal Server Configuration via Group Policy" section of this chapter.

Figure 2.16 Using the Terminal Service Configuration Console

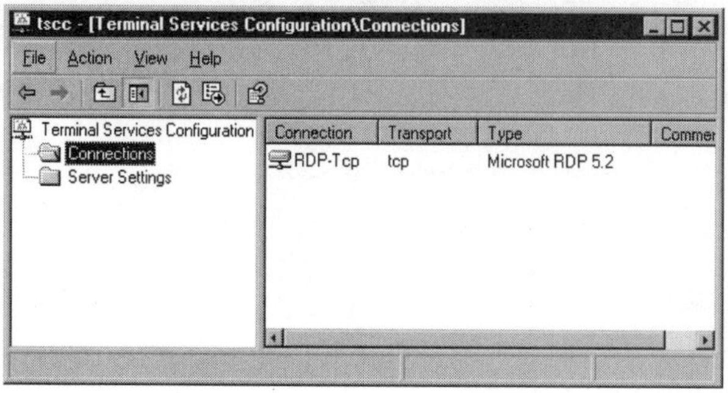

Selecting the **Connections** node and double-clicking the **RDP-Tcp** object opens the RDP-Tcp Properties dialog box, as seen in Figure 2.17. This dialog box has eight tabs that are used to configure the Terminal Services connection properties, each of which are discussed in the following sections.

The General Tab

The General tab, as seen in Figure 2.17, offers some basic configuration options for the Terminal Server.

Figure 2.17 The General Tab of the RDP-Tcp Properties Dialog Box

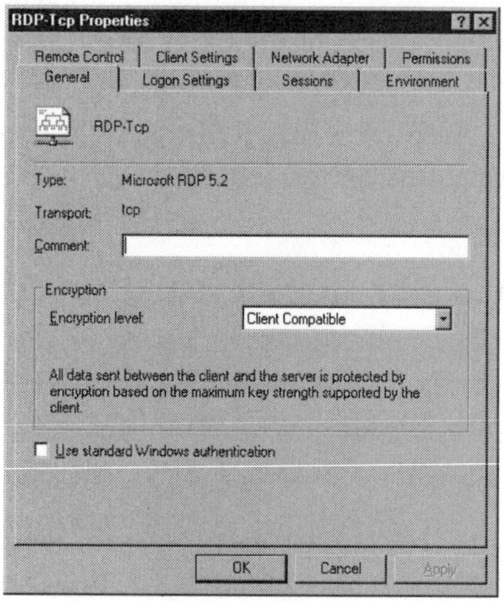

From this tab, the network administrator is able to enter a comment about the connection type, select the encryption level to be used for the connection type, and enable standard Windows authentication. The available encryption options are:

- **Low** Data sent between the client and server is encrypted using 56-bit encryption.

- **Client Compatible** Data sent between the client and server is encrypted at the maximum key strength that the client supports.

- **High** Data sent between the client and server is encrypted using strong 128-bit encryption.

- **Federal Information Processing Standard (FIPS) Compliant** Data sent between the client and the server is encrypted using the FIPS encryption algorithms.

The Logon Settings Tab

The Logon Settings tab, as seen in Figure 2.18, allows the network administrator to configure how log-on credentials are supplied to the session.

Figure 2.18 The Logon Settings Tab of the RDP-Tcp Properties Dialog Box

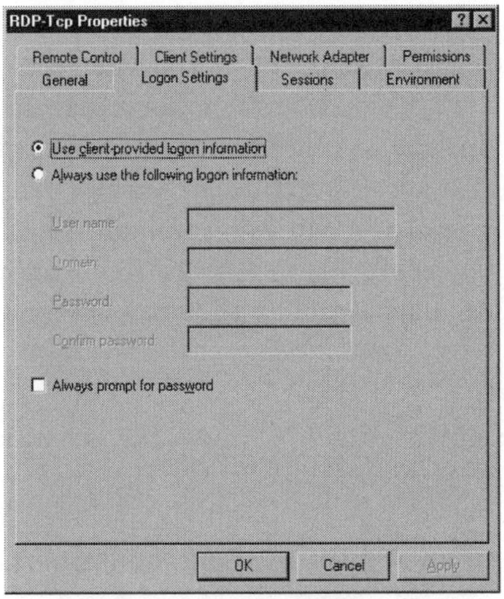

Selecting the **Use client-provided logon information** option specifies that logon credentials are to be retrieved from the client, such as through Remote Desktop Connection or the Client Connection Manager. Selecting the **Always use the following logon information** option specifies a fixed set of logon credentials that are to be used for making connections. Selecting the **Always prompt for password** option specifies that the user is to always be prompted for a password even if a password is configured.

The Sessions Tab

The Sessions tab, as seen in Figure 2.19, allows the network administrator to override client-configured settings associated with time limits and session maintenance.

Figure 2.19 The Sessions Tab of the RDP-Tcp Properties Dialog Box

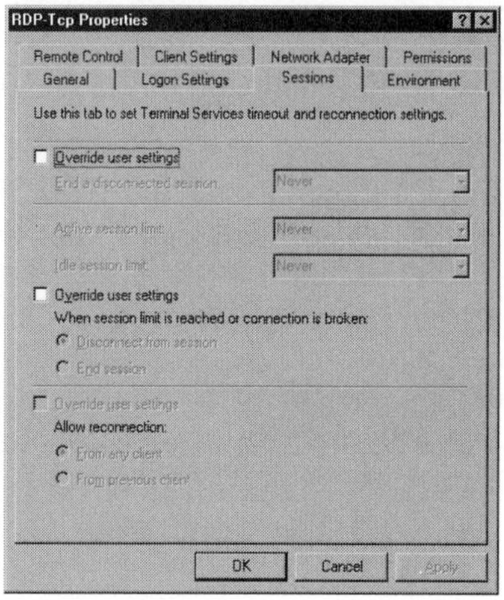

Selecting the **Override user settings** option specifies that the settings configured in the other sections of the tab are to override the settings that are configured via Group Policy for time limits. Selecting the second **Override user settings** option specifies that the settings configured below it are to override the settings that are configured via Group Policy for the action that is to occur when a session limit is reached or a connection is broken. Selecting the third **Override user settings** option allows the network administrator to configure from where clients will be allowed to reconnect to an existing session.

The Environment Tab

The Environment tab, as seen in Figure 2.20, allows the network administrator to override the settings that are configured via Group Policy for the initial program path and file name.

Figure 2.20 The Environment Tab of the RDP-Tcp Properties Dialog Box

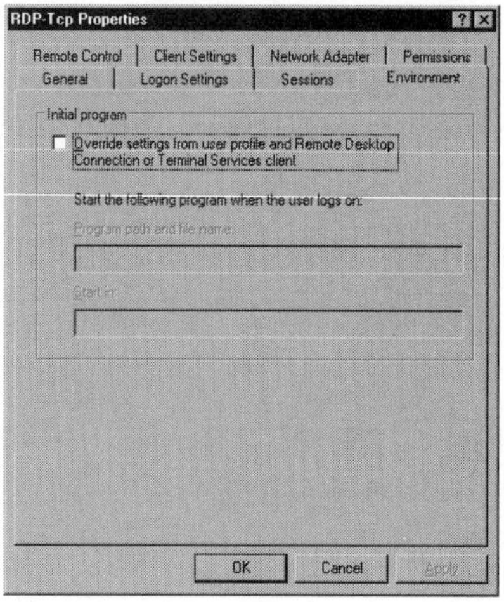

The Remote Control Tab

The Remote Control tab, as seen in Figure 2.21, allows the network administrator to configure the remote control settings for this connection.

Figure 2.21 The Remote Control Tab of the RDP-Tcp Properties Dialog Box

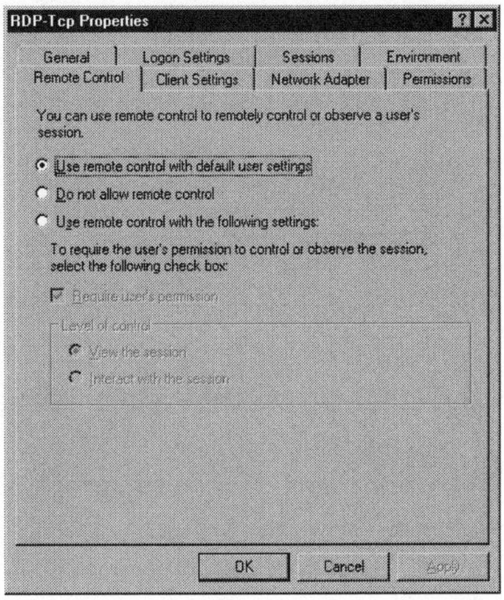

Selecting the **Use remote control with default user setting** option specifies that remote control settings are to be retrieved from Group Policy. Selecting the **Do not allow remote control** option specifies that remote control is not to be allowed on this connection. Selecting the **Use remote control with the following settings** option specifies that remote control is to be allowed with the settings the network administrator configures below it. **The Require user's permission** option specifies that the user must give permission allowing the session to be remotely controlled. The **View the session** option specifies that the remote user can view the session, but not control it. The **Interact with the session** option specifies that the remote user can control the remote users session.

The Client Settings Tab

The Client Settings tab, as seen in Figure 2.22, allows the network administrator to configure settings relating to the user's experience during the Terminal Server connection.

Figure 2.22 The Client Settings Tab of the RDP-Tcp Properties Dialog Box

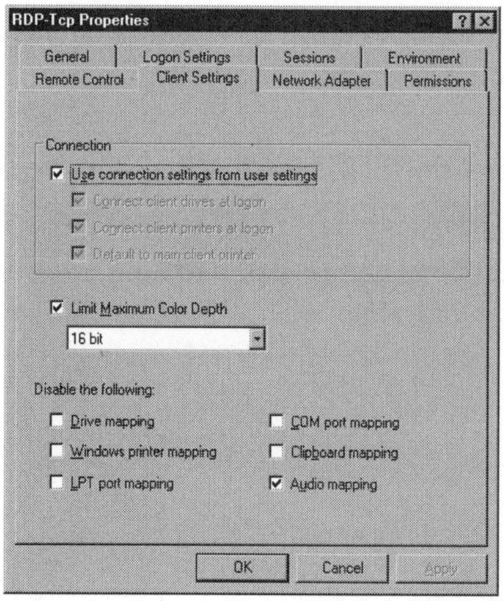

The **User connection settings from user setting** option specifies that the connection settings are to be retrieved from the Group Policy configuration. The **Limit Maximum Color Depth** option limits the maximum color depth for the remote clients; this setting can be used to reduce required bandwidth for screenshots. The network administrator can also select to disable additional options, further controlling the bandwidth usage.

The Network Adapter Tab

The Network Adapter tab, as seen in Figure 2.23, allows the network administrator to configure which network adapters are to be used for the connection and how they are to behave.

Figure 2.23 The Network Adapter Tab of the RDP-Tcp Properties Dialog Box

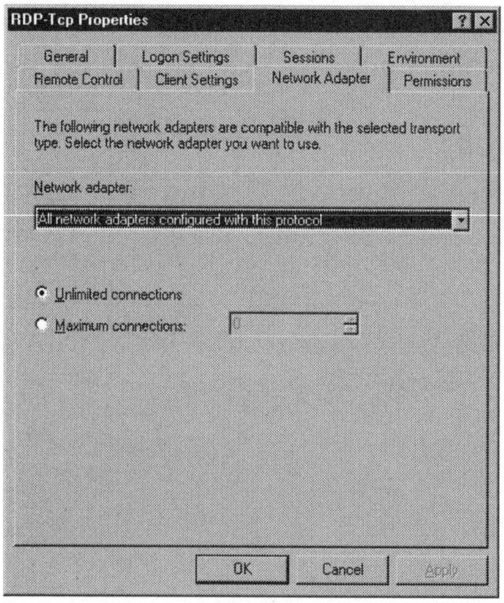

The network administrator can select all network adapters that are configured for RDP-Tcp or a specific adapter from the **Network adapter** drop-down list. They can also configure the maximum number of connections that are to be allowed using the **Unlimited connections** and **Maximum connections** options.

The Permissions Tab

The Permissions tab, as seen in Figure 2.24, provides the standard NT File System (NTFS) permissions setting dialog that allows the network administrator to control which users can connect to the Terminal Server and what level of permissions they are to have.

Figure 2.24 The Permissions Tab of the RDP-Tcp Properties Dialog Box

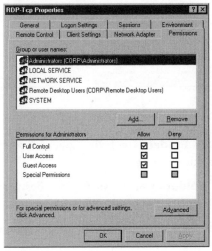

Configuring Server Settings with the Terminal Services Configuration Console

The RDP-Tcp properties are not the only thing that can be configured from the Terminal Service Configuration console. The network administrator can also configure several server settings from the Server Settings node, as seen in Figure 2.25.

Figure 2.25 Configuring the Terminal Service Server Settings

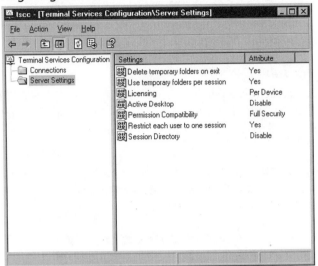

The following settings are available for configuration:

- **Delete Temporary Folders on Exit** Specifies whether temporary folders are to be deleted upon disconnecting from a session.

- **Use Temporary Folders per Session** Specifies whether a new set of temporary folders should be created for each session.

- **Licensing** Specifies whether Terminal Server licensing is to be per device or per user.

- **Active Desktop** Specifies whether or not the Active Desktop is to be allowed for remote connections.

- **Permission Compatibility** Specifies the permission compatibility mode that the Terminal Server is to operate in as configured previously and has the following options: **Full Security** and **Relaxed Security** (discussed previously).

- **Restrict Each User to One Session** Specifies whether or not users should be limited to one concurrent session at a time.

- **Session Directory** Allows the network administrator to enable and configure the Terminal Server Session Directory, as seen in Figure 2.26. Refer back to the "Terminal Server Session Directory" section of this chapter for more information.

Figure 2.26 Configuring the Terminal Server Session Directory Settings

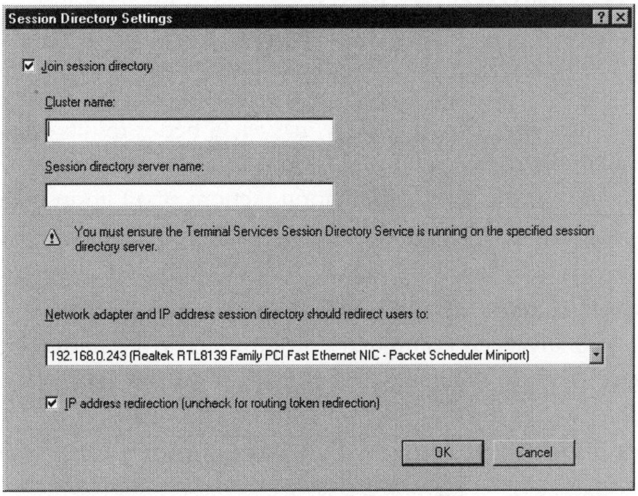

Using the Terminal Services Manager Console

The Terminal Services Manager console, as seen in Figure 2.27, allows the network admin-istrator to view information about and manage Terminal Servers that are in trusted domains. They can monitor users, sessions, and applications on each server and perform various management actions from this console.

Figure 2.27 Configuring the Terminal Server Session Directory Settings

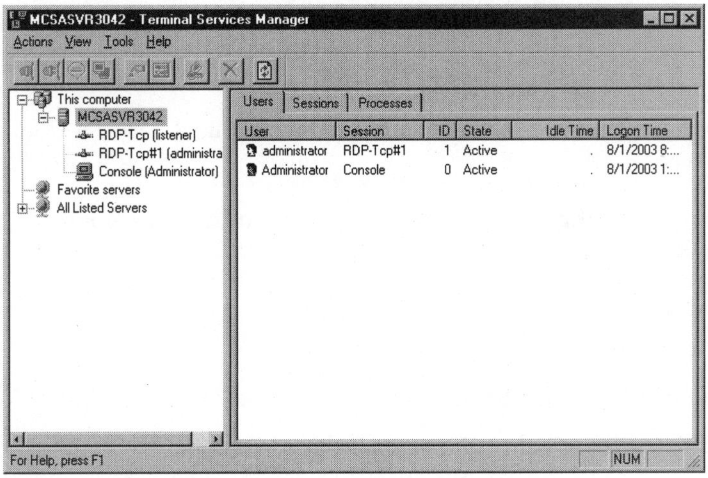

Advanced Terminal Server Configuration via Group Policy

Although the Terminal Services Configuration console can be used to implement basic Terminal Services settings, using Group Policy may yield better results while providing a wealth of additional configuration options. Terminal Services options are located in both the Computer Configuration and User Configuration sections of a Group Policy Object (GPO).

Terminal Services Computer Options

The Terminal Services node of the Computer Configuration section of a GPO, as seen in Figure 2.28, has several advanced configuration options that the network administrator may find useful (and necessary) for maintaining and managing a Terminal Server.

Figure 2.28 Configuring the Terminal Services Computer Options in Group Policy

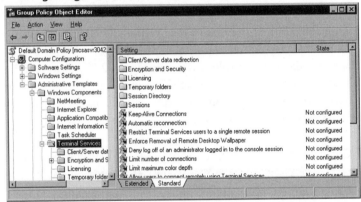

The following options are available to configure Terminal Services from the Computer Configuration section:

- Computer Configuration\Administrative Templates\Windows Components\Terminal Services node:

  1. Keep-Alive Messages

  2. Automatic reconnection

  3. Restrict Terminal Services users to a single remote session

  4. Enforce Removal of Remote Desktop Wallpaper

  5. Deny log off of an administrator logged in to the console session

  6. Limit number of connections

  7. Limit maximum color depth

8. Allow users to connect remotely using Terminal Services

9. Do not allow local administrators to customize permissions

10. Remove Windows Security item from Start menu

11. Remove Disconnect item from Shut Down dialog

12. Set path for Terminal Services Roaming Profiles

13. Terminal Services User Home Directory

14. Sets rules for remote control of Terminal Services user sessions

15. Start a program on connection

■ Computer Configuration\Administrative Templates\Windows Components\ Terminal Services\Client/Server data redirection node:

1. Allow Time Zone Redirection

2. Do not allow clipboard redirection

3. Do not allow smart card device redirection

4. Allow audio redirection

5. Do not allow COM port redirection

6. Do not allow client printer redirection

7. Do not allow LPT port redirection

8. Do not allow drive redirection

9. Do not set default client printer to be default printer in a session

■ Computer Configuration\Administrative Templates\Windows Components\ Terminal Services\Encryption and Security node:

1. Always prompt client for password upon connection

2. Set client connection encryption level

■ Computer Configuration\Administrative Templates\Windows Components\ Terminal Services\RPC Security Policy node:

1. Secure Server (Require Security)

■ Computer Configuration\Administrative Templates\Windows Components\ Terminal Services\Licensing node:

1. License Server Security Group

2. Prevent license upgrade

■ Computer Configuration\Administrative Templates\Windows Components\ Terminal Services\Temporary folders node:

1. Do not use temp folders per session

2. Do not delete temp folder upon exit

■ Computer Configuration\Administrative Templates\Windows Components\ Terminal Services\Session Directory node:

1. Terminal Server IP Address Redirection

2. Join Session Directory

3. Session Directory Server

4. Session Directory Cluster Name

■ Computer Configuration\Administrative Templates\Windows Components\ Terminal Services\Sessions node:

1. Set time limit for disconnected sessions

2. Set time limit for active sessions

3. Set time limit for idle sessions

4. Allow reconnection from original client only

5. Terminate session when time limits are reached

TEST DAY TIP

You should not stress over being able to remember all of the available Terminal Services options presented here. Instead, be aware of their existence and purpose.

The Terminal Services node of the User Configuration section of a GPO, as seen in Figure 2.28, has many more advanced configuration options that the network administrator may use to maintain and manage a Terminal Server.

Figure 2.29 Configuring the Terminal Services User Options in Group Policy

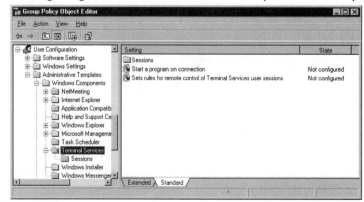

The following options are available to configure Terminal Services from the User Configuration section:

- User Configuration\Administrative Templates\Windows Components\Terminal Services node:

  1. Start a program on connection

  2. Remote control settings

- User Configuration\Administrative Templates\Windows Components\Terminal Services\Sessions node:

  1. Set time limit for disconnected sessions

  2. Set time limit for active sessions

  3. Set time limit for idle sessions

  4. Allow reconnection from original client only

  5. Terminate session when time limits are reached

Terminal Server Licensing

EXAM
70-292
OBJECTIVE
2.1.2

To fully understand Terminal Services, the network administrator must know how to license it and utilize the licensing services on the server. This can be very confusing if they have never worked with Terminal Services before. With the release of Microsoft Windows Server 2003, they need to understand the nuances associated with Terminal Services licensing so as not to wind up without the proper licensing they need.

- Every Windows Server 2003 Terminal Server must possess a valid Windows Server License.

- A Terminal Server Client Access License (TS CAL) is required to connect to a Terminal Server with a remote graphical user interface (GUI) session, except for a console session. This is a major change from Terminal Services in Windows 2000, when every Windows 2000 and Windows XP client was automatically granted a TS CAL by default.

- TS CALs are now available in Per User and Per Device options to coincide with the Windows CAL options available with the release of Windows Server 2003.

  1. A TS Device CAL permits one device used by any user to conduct Windows Sessions on any of the servers.

  2. A TS User CAL permits one user using any device to conduct Windows Sessions on any of the servers.

  3. Any combination of TS Devices and TS User CALs can be used at the same time on a single server.

- The Terminal Server External Connector (TS-EC) License can be purchased to enable external users to access a company's Terminal Servers, without the need to purchase individual TS CALs for them or their devices. One TS-EC license must be purchased for every Terminal Server that is accessible to the external user. An example of an external user is a person who is not an employee or similar personnel of the company or its affiliates. The TS-EC License replaces the TS Internet Connector license in Windows 2000.

NOTE

As of this writing, this is the current licensing plan in effect for Terminal Services. We have kept this short because the licensing plans may change, and often do. To make sure you are 100 percent compliant, you should visit the Microsoft main licensing page to check the most current information when you plan on licensing a production server. You can use the following URLs for more information: www.microsoft.com/windowsserver2003/howtobuy/licensing/ts2003.mspx, www.microsoft.com/windowsserver2003/howtobuy/licensing/overview.mspx, and https://activate.microsoft.com.

Using the Terminal Server Licensing Tool

Now that you are aware of the specifics of Windows Server 2003 Terminal Services licensing, you are ready to move on and examine the Terminal Server Licensing console. You must install Terminal Server Licensing if you have not done so already, by performing the steps outlined in Exercise 2.03.

New & Noteworthy...

Selecting Enterprise or Domain Licensing

Before you install your Terminal Server License Server, you should ensure that you understand the different server types that you can choose from: Enterprise License Server or Domain License Server.

The Enterprise License Server is appropriate if your network is comprised of several domains. The Enterprise License Server can provide licenses for the Terminal Servers located in any domain in the enterprise, provided the domain is a Windows Server 2003 or Windows 2000 domain. Terminal Servers poll Active Directory every 60 minutes looking for an Enterprise License Server, even when one has been previously located.

The Domain License Server is appropriate if you must maintain a separate license server for each domain in your enterprise. The drawback to this method is that Terminal Servers can access Domain License Servers only if they are in the same domain as the license server. If your network still has Windows NT 4.0 domains or

Continued

---

workgroups, then the domain license server is the only type you will be able to use. Terminal Servers search for a Domain License Server every 15 minutes until they find one. After the Domain License Server is located, the Terminal Servers will search for it every 2 hours.

EXERCISE 2.03

INSTALLING TERMINAL SERVER LICENSING

1. Click **Start | Settings | Control Panel | Add or Remove Programs** to open the Add or Remove Programs applet.

2. Click **the Add/Remove Windows Components** button to start the Windows Components Wizard.

3. When the Windows Components Wizard opens, scroll down and select **Terminal Server Licensing**. Click **Next** to continue.

4. You will be prompted to specify the scope of the licensing server, as seen in Figure 2.30. You can create the licensing server for either the entire enterprise or only for your domain or workgroup. Click **Next** to continue.

Figure 2.29 Configuring the Licensing Server Scope

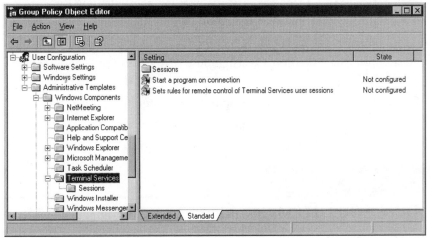

5. Click **Finish** when prompted to close the Windows Components Wizard.

TEST DAY TIP

If you are only using Remote Desktop for Administration, then you will not need a Terminal Server License Server for these connections.

After installation, the Terminal Server Licensing console can be found in the Administrative Tools folder by clicking **Start | Programs | Administrative Tools | Terminal Server Licensing**. The Terminal Server Licensing console is seen in Figure 2.31.

Figure 2.31 The Terminal Services Licensing Console

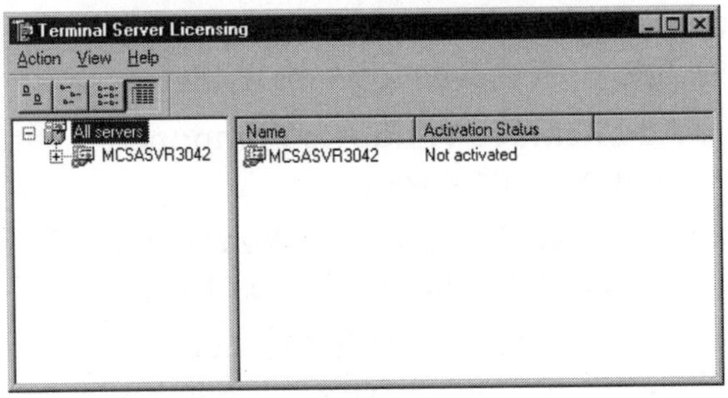

The installation of the Terminal Server Licensing console does not actually grant you any licenses. Exercise 2.04 outlines the process by which you will activate your Terminal Server Licensing server, by acquiring and installing TS CALs from the Microsoft Clearinghouse. Once the TS Licensing server is installed, the following three steps must occur to activate the Terminal Services Licensing server.

1. Activate your Terminal Server Licensing server by requesting a special digital certificate from the Microsoft Clearinghouse that allows the license server to securely install TS CALs.

2. Connect to the Microsoft Clearinghouse and acquire TS CAL tokens.

3. Distribute TS CAL tokens to requesting clients.

EXERCISE 2.04

ACTIVATING YOUR TERMINAL SERVER LICENSING SERVER

1. Open the Terminal Server Licensing console by clicking **Start | Programs | Administrative Tools | Terminal Server Licensing**.

2. Right-click on the licensing server you want to activate and select **Activate Server** from the context menu. The Terminal Server License

Server Activation Wizard starts. After reading the important text contained on the Welcome page of the Wizard, click **Next** to continue.

3. On the Connection method dialog box, as seen in Figure 2.32, you must select the connection method you want to use. Selecting the **Automatic connection** option allows the server to automatically connect to the Microsoft Clearinghouse and complete the procedure. You can also select to use your Web browser or a Telephone to active the licensing server. After making your selection, click **Next** to continue.

Figure 2.32 Selecting the Connection Method

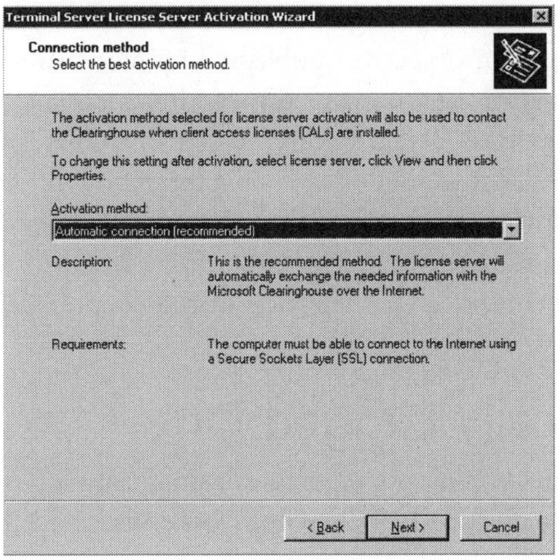

> **NOTE**
>
> If you are still using a pre-release version of Windows Server 2003 such as RC2, you will not be able to connect to the Microsoft Clearinghouse servers to acquire Terminal Services licensing until you have installed the Release to Manufacturing (RTM) version of Windows Server 2003.

4. Continue with the licensing process as prompted by the Wizard.

One Terminal Server Licensing Server can provide TS CALs for multiple Terminal Servers; however, you may want to install the licensing server component on a server that is not actively providing Terminal Services in order to increase performance.

NOTE

When you activate a license server, Microsoft provides the server with a digital certificate that validates server ownership and identity. The license server can then make subsequent transactions with the Microsoft Clearinghouse to acquire additional TS CALs in the future.

EXAM
70-292

OBJECTIVE
2.1
2.1.1
2.1.2

Troubleshooting Terminal Services

Troubleshooting Terminal Services components is never an easy task. The complexity of Terminal Services often makes for strange occurrences, that are difficult to track down. Nonetheless, some of the exam objectives published by Microsoft relate to troubleshooting Terminal Services, so this is an important section with which you should become familiar.

The most important keys to understanding how to troubleshoot Terminal Services come from the background knowledge in this chapter. Knowing how it all works is essential to answering the troubleshooting questions correctly. This section provides an overview of common problems and solutions that are drawn from Microsoft's support materials, that have not been previously covered in earlier parts of the chapter, and that relate to the exam objectives.

Not Automatically Logged On

A common problem occurs when you want to automatically log on to the server, but you are still prompted for your user credentials when you connect to the Terminal Server. There are a number of possible causes and solutions.

If you are using a Windows NT 4.0 Terminal Services client, be aware that these clients are not always able to detect and pass on the underlying system logon credentials to the Windows Server 2003 Terminal Server, even if your system log-on credentials are the same as those for the Terminal Server. In the Windows NT 4.0 Client Connection Manager, select **Automatic logon** on the General tab in the Properties box for the connection. Enter the appropriate logon credentials in the User name, Password, and Domain text boxes.

If you are using a Windows 2000 Terminal Service client or the Remote Desktop Client, it is possible that you entered the incorrect credentials on the General tab. If you mistyped the user name or password, the Terminal Server will not be able to verify your credentials and will prompt you for the correct ones. The solution is to edit the User name, Password, and/or Domain text box(es) on the General tab of the client utility.

Another possibility is that your client settings are configured correctly, but Group Policy is configured to require users to enter at least part of the credentials (the password). Group Policy settings override client settings. The only way to correct this is to remove the Group Policy setting that is enforcing this restriction.

"This Initial Program Cannot be Started"

Occasionally a client may receive a message stating "This initial program cannot be started." At the client level, a user can specify that program be launched when they connect to a server instead of receiving a desktop. Likewise, an administrator can specify this at the connection level for all users that connect to a specific listener connection. Finally, this can also be set in Group Policy.

The error may be caused by something as simple as an input error. You should first check to ensure that the path and executable names specified are correct. If you have entered them incorrectly, they will be pointing to a file that does not exist. This will make it impossible for Windows Server 2003 to launch the application.

Another possibility is that the correct permissions are not set on the executable file. If Windows cannot access the file, it will not be able to launch the program for you. You should verify that the appropriate Read and Execute permissions are applied to both the file and the working directory (if specified). If neither of these two possible solutions resolve the issue, the application may have become corrupt. Try to launch the application from the server console. If it will not open, you may need to uninstall and reinstall the application.

Clipboard Problems

Ordinarily, when text is copied to the clipboard in a session, it is synchronized with the local clipboard on the client. Because the text is available on each clipboard, it should be available to paste into local applications as well as applications running remotely in a session. You should note that it works the same way when you copy text to the clipboard locally. It is synchronized with the clipboard running in the Terminal Services session and can be used in either local or remote applications.

Microsoft states that there are instances in which text that is copied to the clipboard in a remote session is unable to be pasted into an application on the local client. Currently there is no fix available for this problem. First, try to reinstall the client application you are using. If it is still malfunctioning, try to uninstall the client application and reinstall it.

License Problems

Once a Terminal Server License Server is installed and activated with the appropriate number of licenses, things typically work well without any problems. You may, however, still encounter some licensing-related issues that bear discussion. Recall that the Terminal Server requires a TS CAL for each who client logs on a Terminal Server—each client must possess a valid TS CAL, issued by a Terminal Server Licensing Server, before they will be permitted to log on to the Terminal Server. If you receive messages similar to those below, you have license component problems.

- The remote session was disconnected because there are no TS CALs available for this computer. Please contact the server administrator.

■ The remote session was disconnected because there are no Terminal Server License Servers available to provide a license. Please contact the server administrator.

Error messages such as these can indicate several different types of issues. First, verify that the license server is online and able to communicate on the network. It is also important to verify name resolution during this step. Next, ensure that the license server component has been activated properly. Check event logs on the license server and look for more subtle problems that simple connectivity checks will not spot.

Verify that the license server has a sufficient number of valid client licenses for your network, and that the licenses are valid. The Terminal Server draws licenses from the license server, so you should also ensure that these two servers can communicate with each other. Finally, do not forget to check the clients. It is possible that the clients never received a valid license. After you have installed a Terminal Server, unlicensed clients are granted a 120-day grace period (from the date of first logon) during which they are allowed to make connections to the Terminal Server without a valid TS CAL. After this 120-day grace period has ended, the Terminal Server will no longer allow these clients to connect to it unless it can locate a Terminal Server Licensing Server to issue valid TS CALs to the clients. Should your clients start to have problems connecting to Terminal Servers around this 120-day time, the lack of valid TS CALs should be your first thing you check.

TEST DAY TIP

When faced with a troubleshooting question on the exam, focus on whether or not it is a connectivity issue. Underlying connection problems are often the root cause when you have problems in a Terminal Services environment.

Security Issues

As already discussed, Terminal Server in Windows Server 2003 supports four levels of client-server encryption. A mismatch between the server settings and the client's capabilities will prevent the client from being able to make a connection to the Terminal Server, especially in cases where older legacy clients are still in use. Recall that the four available encryption settings are:

■ Low

■ Client Compatible

■ High

■ FIPS Compliant

Additional details on these encryption levels can be found in the "The General Tab" section earlier in the chapter.

TEST DAY TIP

You cannot change the encryption level using other Group Policy or Terminal Services configurations if FIPS compliance has already been enabled by the "System cryptography: Use FIPS-compliant algorithms for encryption, hashing, and signing" GPO.

If you have any doubts about the encryption level capabilities of your clients, try setting this value to **Client Compatible** and attempting to make a connection then. If this fixed the problem, you may want to consider upgrading the encryption capabilities of your clients.

Summary of Exam Objectives

Terminal Services is a Windows component that allows users and administrators to connect to network resources using the Remote Desktop Protocol (or ICA, with Citrix client software) and obtain a desktop from a remote server. The connection transmits cursor and keyboard input from the client to the server, and transfers the image of the desktop with any running applications back to the client. This is called a screenshot. All applications that are run from within a session are executed on the server.

The Terminal Server role must be installed and configured after installation of the operating system. If the Terminal Services License component is not installed and configured correctly, Terminal Server connections will no longer be allowed 120 days after the first client connects. The Terminal Server role can be installed from either the Manage Your Server utility or via Add or Remove Programs in Control Panel. The Terminal Server License component can only be installed from Add or Remove Programs. There are three basic client tools that can be used to establish a Terminal Services connection (discussed in greater detail in Chapter 3).

The Terminal Services Manager console is the primary graphical tool for managing users who are connected to a server. It can be used to manage multiple servers simultaneously through a single interface. As an administrator, you can use this utility to monitor, connect to, disconnect from, log off, remotely control, and reset sessions. The Terminal Services Configuration utility can be used to configure new listener connections (RDP-Tcp connections) or modify the properties of existing ones, and control settings on a per-connection basis (applying to all users who connect to the Terminal Server via the connection). User account extensions are installed by default and add several tabs related to Terminal Services to the user account properties interface. These tabs enable you to control a wide range of Terminal Services settings on an individual per-user basis.

You can also use Group Policy to manage Terminal Services settings. Most settings that can be configured at the client, user account, or connection property levels have a corresponding Group Policy setting. When settings conflict between these various levels, the Group Policy settings always take precedence. There are some settings that can only be configured using Group Policy. In addition to these graphical utilities, Microsoft makes a wide range of command-line utilities for Terminal Services available. These are primarily designed for use in creating administrative scripts to automate tasks.

Finally, it is especially important to have a good understanding of the Terminal Services architecture. This makes it easier to troubleshoot problems that occur. Simple connection issues between a Terminal Server and the license server can cause severe problems. Because Terminal Services environments are much more complex than standard client-server environments, they often exhibit strange problems that require hours of research. The reasons for this are easy to understand when you consider that you have multiple users essentially using the same computer at the same time.

Exam Objectives Fast Track

The Need for Terminal Services: A Survey of Computing Environments

☑ When using a centralized computing model all of your resources are located on a central server or mainframe. Clients access resources remotely. The clients have very little intelligence or little if any processing power. All processing of data and its storage are done on the centralized CPU, Server, Terminal Server, or mainframe and only screenshots of output are sent to the client. Clients are generally thin clients or dumb terminals.

☑ Using a centralized computing environment will mean that most of the costs associated with running this solution are placed on the Terminal Server, where all the intelligence and computing strength is.

☑ When using a distributed computing model, you still have resources located on servers, but processing is done on both the server and the client. Clients are generally called "fat clients" and are characterized by a PC or workstation with its own CPU and disk storage. Files can be opened on the server, but the processing is done on the local PC.

☑ A mixed environment is one in which you can have a mainframe with dumb terminals, thin clients with a Terminal Server, or PCs with servers in a client/server formation.

Introduction to Windows Server 2003 Terminal Services

☑ Learning how to troubleshoot Terminal Services begins with the ability to analyzing the design, placement, and practical use of the service in order to spot potential problems.

☑ Since screenshots have to traverse the network to get from the server to the client utilizing the service, you have to think about the bandwidth available on the network so you know how latency will affect it. For example, if your WAN bandwidth is too saturated, you may see Terminal Services suffer in the form of disconnects, hesitation with keystrokes, and so on.

☑ Windows Server 2003 offers Remote Desktop for Administration. This was formerly known as Terminal Services in Remote Administration mode, and allows you to remotely administer any server you have it configured on. This service was designed to allow you to manage your servers without actually being at the console.

☑ Another portion of the Terminal Service is the Terminal Server Session Directory. The Terminal Server Session Directory is a new feature that was created to allow users to easily reconnect to a disconnected session within a NLB Terminal Server farm.

☑ When implementing the Session Directory Service, the Session Directory Server you configure should be a highly available network server that is not a Terminal Server for best results.

Installing and Configuring a Terminal Server

☑ In order for a Windows Server 2003 computer to function properly as an application server, both the Terminal Server role and Terminal Server Licensing component must be installed.

☑ The Terminal Server role can be installed from either the Manage Your Server utility or the Add or Remove Programs applet (or utility) in Control Panel.

☑ The Terminal Server Licensing component can only be installed via Add/Remove Programs in Control Panel.

☑ If the Terminal Server Licensing component is not installed or proper licenses are not configured on it, Terminal Server connections will be rejected when the evaluation period expires (120 days after the first client connection occurs).

☑ Terminal Services Manager is the primary session management tool. It allows an administrator to monitor, connect to, disconnect from, log off, remotely control, and reset sessions.

☑ The Terminal Services Configuration utility is used to create listener (RDP-Tcp) connections on the server, and configure server settings that apply to all users who use a particular connection. There can only be one listener connection bound to each network card.

☑ Connections can be used to control a wide range of user settings, from encryption levels to how long the user can remain connected.

☑ Settings at the connection level, when enabled, override settings at the user and client property levels.

☑ Terminal Services user account extensions are installed and enabled by default. They add additional tabs to the user account properties and enable administrators to control a wide range of settings on an individual basis. Most user level settings can be overridden at the connection level.

☑ Group Policy can be used to control many of the same settings that can be configured at the connection, user, and client levels. When settings conflict between Group Policy and one of these other levels, the Group Policy settings take precedence.

Terminal Server Licensing

- ☑ To install Licensing, go to **Start | Control Panel | Add or Remove Programs** and select the **Add Windows Components** icon. Once you do, simply add the Terminal Services Licensing option. You have to know how to configure Licensing for the exam.

- ☑ The Licensing tool can be found by going to **Start | Administrative Tools | Terminal Server Licensing**. This tool helps you keep track of License usage.

- ☑ With the Terminal Services Licensing tool, you can install and configure licensing fairly quickly and with little effort. Once configured, you are essentially creating a "license server" for your organization.

- ☑ When you activate a license server, Microsoft provides the server with a digital certificate that validates server ownership and identity. If you use this certificate, a license server can make subsequent transactions with Microsoft to receive client licenses for the servers that have Terminal Services enabled.

- ☑ You cannot deactivate or reactivate a license server by using either the fax or World Wide Web (WWW) connection methods. If you reactivate a license server, a record of your license is retained. Licenses that were already issued remain valid. If you have any unissued licenses, these licenses are also valid, but Microsoft must reissue them.

Troubleshooting Terminal Services

- ☑ Licensing error messages can occur because the Terminal Server cannot contact the license server, or because the client's license has become corrupt.

- ☑ If clipboard mapping fails between the client and server, the client may have become corrupted and should be removed and reinstalled. However, you do not have full clipboard functionality between the local computer and the Terminal Server session. You can cut and paste data, but not files and folders.

Exam Objectives
Frequently Asked Questions

The following Frequently Asked Questions, answered by the authors of this book, are designed to both measure your understanding of the Exam Objectives presented in this chapter, and to assist you with real-life implementation of these concepts. You will also gain access to thousands of other FAQs at ITFAQnet.com.

Q: There seem to be a number of different utilities that can be used to connect to Terminal Services and establish a session. Which one is the primary client tool for end users?

A: The Remote Desktop Connection utility is the primary end user connection tool. It comes pre-installed with Windows XP and Windows Server 2003 and can be installed on Windows 9*x*, NT, and 2000 computers. It can be used to save connection settings to a file so that reconfiguration is not necessary when connecting to different servers. It also has a wide range of options that allow for optimization over almost any bandwidth. It includes several improvements over the Windows 2000 Terminal Services client, including the ability to redirect audio from the server to the client.

Q: Yesterday I was able to connect to our Terminal Server with no problems, but this morning no one can log on. We keep getting a license message. What's going on?

A: It sounds as if you may have hit the 120-day limit. In a nutshell, you have 120 days from your first Terminal Server client connection to install and configure the Terminal Server License component. Microsoft provides this evaluation period so you can try the Terminal Server role and decide whether you want to use it before having to purchase TS CALs. After this time, you will not be able to establish a session unless you install the License Server component and install at least one client license.

Q: What is the best utility to use for managing existing client connections?

A: Terminal Services Manager is designed for just this purpose. It allows you to monitor, connect to, disconnect from, log off, remotely control, and reset sessions. Using it, you can manage all of your servers from one interface.

Q: Can Group Policy be used to manage Terminal Services?

A: In Windows Server 2003, there are approximately 50 dedicated Terminal Services settings in Group Policy. Using them, you can manage just about everything you can possibly imagine. These Group Policy settings override conflicting settings in other utilities, allowing for centralized management consistency.

Q: I am considering clustering two Terminal Services servers in a NLB cluster. I would like to make sure that this solution is reliable, as the Terminal Server will be hosting some mission critical applications. It should be highly available, hence the NLB cluster, and it should be reliable. What advancements in Windows Server 2003 are available to add reliability to my NLB clustered Terminal Server solution?

A: The Session Directory Service runs on all editions of Windows Server 2003. However, in order to participate in a Session Directory Service the server must be running Windows Server 2003, Enterprise Edition or Windows Server 2003, Datacenter Edition, including the 64-bit editions of the Windows Server 2003 family. To participate in a Session Directory-enabled farm, you must be using Windows Server 2003, Enterprise Edition, or Windows Server 2003, Datacenter Edition. Also, make note that when you are working with the Session Directory Service, the Session Directory Server you configure should be a highly available network server that is not a Terminal Server.

Q: As a newly minted MCSA on Windows Server 2003, I need to design and configure a Terminal Server solution in a new company. There are 20 existing workstations, and there is a need for a total of 50 users. All 50 users need to have access to file and print services, Active Directory, and a new financial application called "Money-Maker." This application is updated with new software updates once a week. There is also a need for 5 CAD workstations for the production engineering team. What would you recommend that I design for this solution?

A: You need to design a mixed environment. Simply put, a mixed environment is one in which you can have a mainframe with dumb terminals, thin clients with a Terminal Server, or PCs with servers in a client/server formation. You basically have the best of all worlds and you utilize needed resources where you need them, taking advantage of all solutions and the best they have to offer. You are basically fitting your business needs as you see fit with any technology that is best of breed.

Q: I am trying to configure the Windows Server 2003 Remote Desktop Connection client but cannot connect at the color resolution I am choosing. For some reason, no matter what I choose, I cannot connect using that resolution. What could the problem be?

A: When you connect to a Windows Server 2003-based computer by using the Windows Server 2003 Remote Desktop Connection client, you can select the resolution you want, but you may not receive this resolution when you connect. This is because you are not guaranteed any color resolution other than what the server can negotiate and configure at that time. There are many other variables that go into this selection, so you may not always get the resolution you want.

Self Test

A Quick Answer Key follows the Self Test questions. For complete questions, answers, and explanations to the Self Test questions in this chapter as well as the other chapters in this book, see the Self Test Appendix.

The Need for Terminal Services: A Survey of Computing Environments

1. Jim is the systems administrator for NVC Corporation, the makers of world famous widgets. NVC Corporation has 20 Windows Server 2003 servers, and 200 Windows XP Professional and Windows 2000 Professional client workstations. Management would like to deploy services to three new remotes sites. The need is to deploy a single application to five remote users at each site. Jim has been tasked with designing a brand new Terminal Services infrastructure. Jim needs to choose a computing model. Which model does Jim require?

   A. Centralized Computing Model

   B. Distributed Computing Model

   C. Mixed Environment

   D. Terminal Services should not be used here

2. Jake is the systems engineer for Runners Inc. Runners Inc. has 30 Windows Server 2003 servers, and 500 Windows XP Professional and Windows 2000 Professional client workstations. Jake's boss has asked him to help in the development of a new solution for two small branch offices that will be used to deploy two applications to approximately 10 users at each office. Jim has been asked to explain what the most cost would be associated with. What is the best answer Jim could offer?

   A. The clients

   B. The Terminal Server

   C. A PC workstation at each site

   D. You should not use a Terminal Server solution

Introduction to Windows Server 2003 Terminal Services

3. Several components use the Terminal Services service in Windows Server 2003. Which of the following are used primarily for remote administration? (Select all that apply.)

    A. Remote Desktop for Administration

    B. Remote Assistance

    C. The Terminal Server Role

    D. The RDP protocol

4. One of your co-workers asks how to install Terminal Services on his newly installed Windows Server 2003 server so he can perform administrative tasks on the server. Which of the following is the correct advice to give him?

    A. Add the Terminal Server role from the Manage Your Server utility.

    B. Add the Terminal Server role from the Add or Remove Programs utility.

    C. The Terminal Server role is installed by default.

    D. Do nothing.

5. A co-worker asks you what type of system can be used as a thin client to a Windows Server 2003 Terminal Server. Which of the following answers would you give her? (Select all that apply.)

    A. A PDA running Windows CE

    B. A PDA running Windows Pocket PC

    C. A desktop computer running Macintosh OS X

    D. A desktop computer running Windows 95

Installing and Configuring a Terminal Server

6. Will is the systems administrator for Wiley's, the makers of world famous pretzels. Wiley's has 20 Windows Server 2003 servers, and 200 Windows XP Professional and Windows 2000 Professional client workstations. Will needs to ensure that clients can connect to his Terminal Servers using only 128-bit encryption. What encryption option should he select?

    A. High

    B. FIPS Compliant

    C. Low

    D. Client Compatible

7. Andrew is the systems administrator for NVC Corporation, the makers of widgets. NVC Corporation has 20 Windows Server 2003 servers, and 200 Windows XP Professional and Windows 2000 Professional client workstations. Andrew needs to configure a Server Role. Where in the Windows Server 2003 interface can Andrew configure a Server Role?

   A. He can use the Control Panel.

   B. He can use the Administrative Tools MMC.

   C. He can use the Local Security MMC.

   D. He can use the Manage Your Server utility.

8. Barbara is the systems engineer for Runners, Inc. Runners, Inc. has 30 Windows Server 2003 servers, and 500 Windows XP Professional and Windows 2000 Professional client workstations. Barbara needs to deploy two new Windows Server 2003 systems to two remote offices, one in each. She is sending the servers to the remote sites and has hired Jimmy, a MCSE certified consultant to set up and configure the two servers. Jimmy needs to set up one as a File and Print Server and the other as a Terminal Server. From which utility can Jimmy quickly set up and deploy the two servers using Server Roles?

   A. He can use the Active Directory Sites and Services console.

   B. He can use the Active Directory Users and Computers console.

   C. He can use the Manage Your Server utility.

   D. Barbara needs to do it remotely; she can use the Maintain Your Server console.

9. You have been asked to create and configure a new Terminal Services connection that will allow users to connect only with 128-bit encryption. Which of the following utilities will you use to accomplish this task?

   A. Terminal Services Manager

   B. Terminal Services Configuration

   C. Terminal Server Licensing

   D. Remote Desktops MMC

10. You recently implemented a Terminal Server at your company. Right from the start, you notice that performance is slow. You carefully benchmarked and stress tested your beta system, and you thought you had planned for any amount of capacity that would be required. Upon further investigation, you notice that most of the resources are being taken up by disconnected sessions, some of which are days old. You decide to set a timeout for the termination of disconnected sessions. Which of the following could you use to set the timeout? (Select all that apply.)

A. The properties of user accounts

B. The properties of connections in the Terminal Services Configuration utility

C. Group Policy

D. The server properties in the Terminals Services Manager utility

11. One of your co-workers has been reading up on Terminal Services and asks if she can run a few questions by you to see if she understands the concepts. Which of the following statements will you tell her are accurate? (Select all that apply.)

A. Many Terminal Services settings have a corresponding setting in Group Policy.

B. In Group Policy, Terminal Services settings can be found under both the User and Computer Configuration nodes.

C. When different Terminal Services settings are specified at the user properties, connection properties and Group Policy levels, the connection properties are the effective settings.

D. Group Policy can be used to prevent an administrator from being forcibly logged off from a console session when another administrator is attempting to connect.

12. Jess is the systems engineer for Runners, Inc. the makers of really fast sneakers. Runners, Inc. has 30 Windows Server 2003 servers, and 30 Windows 98 PCs, and 500 Windows XP Professional and Windows 2000 Professional client workstations. Jess needs to configure 56-bit encryption for his clients. What encryption option should Jess select?

A. FIPS Compliant

B. Client Compatible

C. High

D. Low

Terminal Server Licensing

13. Another administrator in a different region of the country is installing the Terminal Server role. Knowing that you recently did this, the administrator asks for your advice. You mention to him that he must also be sure to install the Terminal Server License component. What will you tell him about installing this component?

A. That the License Server role must be installed from the Manage Your Server utility.

B. That Terminal Server License must be selected and installed from Add or Remove Programs.

    C. That the License Server is automatically installed with Terminal Services.

    D. That the License Server does not come with Windows Server 2003 and must be purchased separately.

Troubleshooting Terminal Services

14. Several months ago, you installed the Terminal Server role on one of the servers at your company. This morning, clients are having difficulty connecting to Terminal Services but are still able to use file and print services on the server. The error message says it is a licensing issue but you are sure that you properly licensed your Windows Server 2003 server, as well as all of your client systems. What might be causing this? (Select all that apply.)

    A. The temporary evaluation period has expired.

    B. You failed to properly configure Terminal Services client licenses on the license server.

    C. The server was installed with a temporary license code, which has expired.

    D. You did not properly install a license server.

15. Your network uses Windows NT clients running the Terminal Services Client Connection Manager utility. The user working next to you notices that when you connect to a Terminal Server, you are automatically logged in, while she is always prompted for a password. She asks if you can help to configure her system to automatically log on as well. Which of the following will you recommend?

    A. Configure **Automatic logon** on the **General** tab in the **Properties** of the connection, and enter the appropriate logon credentials in the **User name**, **Password** and **Domain** text boxes.

    B. Log on to her Windows 2000 client using your user name and password.

    C. Configure **Always use the following logon information:** on the Logon Settings tab in the connection properties of the Terminal Services Configuration utility.

    D. Configure the **User name**, **Domain**, **Password**, and **Confirm password** text boxes on the Logon Settings tab for the connection in the Terminal Services Configuration utility.

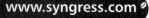

Self Test Quick Answer Key

For complete questions, answers, and explanations to the Self Test questions in this chapter as well as the other chapters in this book, see the Self Test Appendix.

1.	**A**	9.	**B**
2.	**B**	10.	**A, B, C**
3.	**A, B**	11.	**A, B, D**
4.	**D**	12.	**D**
5.	**A, B, C, D**	13.	**B**
6.	**A**	14.	**A, B, D**
7.	**D**	15.	**A**
8.	**C**		

Chapter 3

MCSA/MCSE 70-292

Managing and Maintaining Remote Servers

Exam Objectives in this Chapter:

3.2 Manage servers remotely

3.2.1 Manage a server by using Remote Assistance

3.2.2 Manage a server by using Terminal Services remote administration mode

3.2.3 Manage a server by using available support tools

- ☑ Summary of Exam Objectives
- ☑ Exam Objectives Fast Track
- ☑ Exam Objectives Frequently Asked Questions
- ☑ Self Test
- ☑ Self Test Quick Answer Key

Introduction

The network administrator's daily tasks can be made easy or difficut depending on the number and quality of administrative tools they have available for performing those tasks. In Windows Server 2003, Microsoft provides administrators with a wealth of graphical and command-line utilities for carrying out their job duties. (Appendix A provides a detailed listing of some of those utilities.) The Administrative Tools menu contains predefined management consoles for configuring and managing most of Windows Server 2003's services and components, including Active Directory tools, Domain Name System (DNS) tools, Security policies, Licensing, Routing and Remote Access, Terminal Services, Media Services, and more. Administrators can also create customized Microsoft Management Consoles (MMCs), that makes it easier to perform tasks and delegate administrative tasks to others. Network administrators can create consoles for specific purposes and enable only limited user access to them. For those who prefer the power and flexibility of the command-line utilities, many of these same administrative tasks can be performed, as well as other tasks that have no graphical user interface (GUI) interface. Windows Server 2003 includes a large number of command-line utilities, including dozens of new ones that were not included in Windows 2000 Server.

But what does the network administrator do when they cannot physically access a server to perform their required administrative tasks? Microsoft provides a wealth of remote administrative tools (and tools that have the ability to connect to remote servers). This chapter examines the general types of management tools that are available for keeping servers and networks running smoothly. It then covers the remote management tools that are available for Windows Server 2003.

NOTE

The use of the command line for management is not just limited to those administrators with the budget to support third-party add-ons such as KiXtart (www.kixtart.org). Windows Server 2003 makes it easier than ever to create powerful script- and batch file-based management solutions from the command line with its wide selection of tools and intuitive online help system.

EXAM
70-292

OBJECTIVE
3.2.3

Types of Management Tools

A number of administrative tools are available, which are located in many different places. It can be daunting for a new Windows Server 2003 system administrator to know where to start to look. Experience brings familiarity, but even experienced administrators occasionally discover a tool that they have not seen before. This section reviews where most of the common administrative tools are located, including:

- Administrative Tools folder

- Custom MMC consoles

- Command-line utilities

- Wizards

- Windows Resource Kits

- The "Run as" command

- Administration Tools Pack (adminpak.msi)

- Windows Management Instrumentation (WMI)

- Computer Management Console

Administrative Tools Folder

The Administrative Tools folder contains many of the most common administrative tools. This folder can be located by clicking **Start** | **Programs** | **Administrative Tools**. Figure 3.1 shows the tools that may be found on a domain controller in the Administrative Tools folder. Another way to access the Administrative Tools folder is by clicking **Start** | **Settings** | **Control Panel** and then double-clicking the **Administrative Tools** icon.

Figure 3.1 Tools in the Administrative Tools Folder

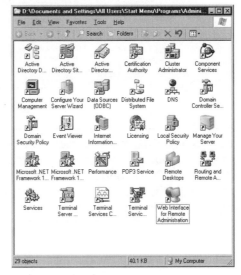

NOTE

The items in the Administrative Tools menu folder are shortcuts, rather than the programs or console files themselves. Many of the actual management console files (.MSC files) are located in the %systemroot%\system32 folder, as seen in Figure 3.2.

The location of the .MSC files can be found by right-clicking the shortcut in the right pane (shown in Figure 3.2), selecting **Properties**, and then checking the **Target** field on the **Shortcut** menu.

Figure 3.2 Locating the Administrative Tools

![Screenshot of D:\WINDOWS\system32 folder window showing a list of .msc files including azman.msc, certmgr.msc, certsrv.msc, certtmpl.msc, ciadv.msc, compmgmt.msc, dcpol.msc, devmgmt.msc, dfrg.msc, dfsgui.msc, diskmgmt.msc, dnsmgmt.msc, domain.msc, dompol.msc, dsa.msc, dssite.msc, eventvwr.msc, filesvr.msc, fsmgmt.msc, gpedit.msc with their sizes and Microsoft Common Console types.]

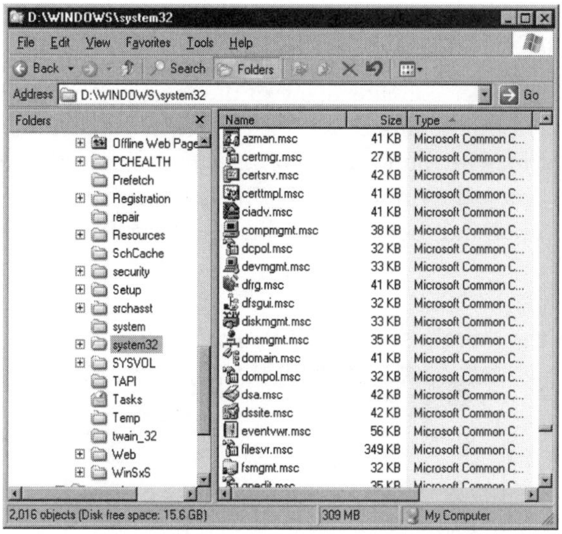

NOTE

If you want specific tools to be available in the menu only when the Administrator account (or another specific account) is logged on, you can copy the shortcuts for those tools from the **All Users | Start Menu | Programs | Administrative Tools** folder to the same folder under that user's profile (for example, **Administrator | Start Menu | Programs | Administrative Tools**).

Several of the management tools located in the Administrative Tools folder are discussed later in this chapter.

Custom MMC Consoles

The MMC is the framework for nearly all Windows graphical administrative tools. It provides an empty console where the network administrator can add their favorite or necessary administration tools. The idea is that all administrative tools have a common look and feel and that the management tool for an administrative task, such as adding users and groups, is written as a snap-in for an MMC. The administrator can then choose which snap-ins to have in a console, or use one of the many pre-configured ones found in the Administrative Tools folder. Some of the MMC snap-ins can be used to manage remote computers as well as the local computer (assuming they have the appropriate rights). Many vendors of third-party management tools are also starting to provide snap-ins for their products, that can be added to MMC consoles.

NOTE

Some of the tools in the Administrative Tools folder, such as the Licensing tool, are standalone programs that do not work with an MMC. When you look at the properties of those shortcuts, you will find that the target files are executables (.EXEs) instead of MMCs (.MSCs).

After an MMC has been created, it can be saved as a standalone file and even e-mailed to another administrator to use. Possession of an MMC file does not in itself give a user any additional rights. For example, if a network administrator e-mails an MMC file with the Disk Management snap-in to a non-administrative user, that user will not be able to complete any disk management tasks even though they can see the snap-in.

MMC consoles can also be configured to prevent anyone from changing them. A console can be saved in one of four modes, each of which has varying restrictions. Table 3.1 shows the four modes and the functionality of each. You can create your own customized MMC consoles by performing the steps outlined in Exercise 3.01.

Table 3.1 MMC Console Modes

Console Mode	Functionality
Author mode	Full access to the MMC and the ability to change all aspects.
User mode - full access	Full access to the windowing commands but cannot add or remove snap-ins.
User mode - limited access, multiple windows	Access only to the areas of the console as it was when saved. Can create new windows but not close existing windows.
User mode - limited access, single window	Access to the console as it was when saved. Cannot open new windows.

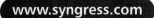

Exercise 3.01

Creating a Custom MMC

1. Click **Start | Run** and type **mmc** in the dialog box. An empty MMC console appears, as seen in Figure 3.3.

Figure 3.3 Creating a Customized MMC

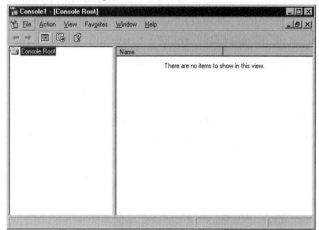

2. Select **File | Add/Remove Snap-in**.

3. In the Add/Remove Snap-in dialog-box, click the **Add** button.

4. In the Add Standalone Snap-in dialog box, scroll through the list and select a snap-in you want contained in your custom console and then click the **Add** button.

5. Continue to add snap-ins as desired.

6. Click **Close** in the Add Standalone Snap-in dialog box, and then click **OK** in the Add/Remove Snap-in dialog box.

7. Your customized MMC console is now ready and may look similar to Figure 3.4.

Figure 3.4 Examining the Customized MMC Console

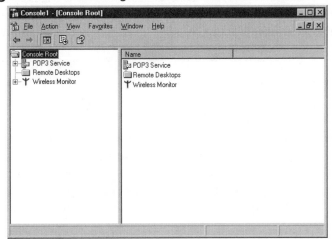

8. To save this console for future use, select **File | Save**. In the File name field, type **CustomConsole** and then click **Save**. The console is saved, by default, in the Administrative Tools folder of the currently logged in user.

9. To change the mode the console operates in, select **File | Options**. The Options dialog box appears, as seen in Figure 3.5, allowing you to change the mode.

Figure 3.5 Configuring the Console Mode

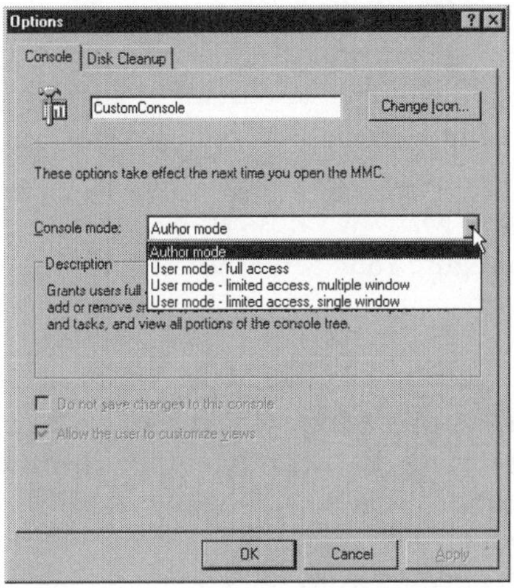

10. Close the console, saving it if prompted.

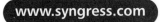

TEST DAY TIP

Make sure that you are familiar with creating custom MMC consoles to manage local and remote servers. Practice creating your own consoles and adding snap-ins to manage the local computer and remote servers.

Command-Line Utilities

As the name suggests, command-line utilities are designed to be run in a command window or as part of batch files or scripts. Administrators are forever looking for ways to simplify administration, and using command lines in batch files is a very good way of handling routine, repetitive tasks. Some administrative tasks can be performed by using only a graphical interface, some by using only a command-line utility, and others can be done using either.

Some command-line utilities are written using a language that must be run using a scripting host such as Windows cscript, and others run as compiled programs or executables. Command-line utilities are harder to find because they are not in any of the Start menus (although they can be added). A good place to look for information is in Windows Help and Support. A search on Command-line Reference provides an alphabetical listing of Windows command-line tools. In addition, Appendix A of this book has a command line utility reference.

Wizards

Wizards guide the network administrator through potentially complex tasks by taking them through a series of dialog boxes where they answer questions or make choices. Wizards are essentially wrappers around the underlying graphical- or command-line-based tool. Each version of Windows increases the number of wizards in an attempt to make administration easier for the inexperienced administrator. However, in some cases it can be quicker for the experienced administrator to perform a task directly using the appropriate administrative tools rather than using a wizard. Many wizards can be accessed by opening the Manage Your Server tool and the Configure Your Server Wizard in the Administrative Tools folder.

NOTE

As the Microsoft Windows operating system evolves, more wizards are added because the operating system itself continues to grow more complex. Understanding the wizards available will help you perform complex tasks quickly at first. As you increase your skills, you may find yourself moving onto other means to accomplish these tasks, such as from the command-line.

Windows Resource Kits

The Windows Server 2003 Resource Kit and the Windows Server 2003 Deployment Kit each provide a wealth of tools for administrators to use to manage Windows servers in a large network. If you are responsible for many servers, you should definitely consider acquiring the Resource Kit for your products. You can visit the Microsoft Resource Kit Web page at www.microsoft.com/windows/reskits/default.asp.

The Run as Command

It is good practice for administrators not to log on using an account that has administrative rights. This prevents accidental changes to the file server, viruses having more access than they otherwise would have, and so on. Administrators should log on using an ordinary user account, and when they need to perform an administrative task they can also use the **Run as** option to choose an administrator account. **Run as** is available by right-clicking an item in the **Start** menu, as seen in Figure 3.6.

Figure 3.6 The Run as Command

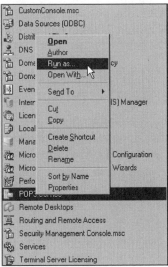

The **Run as** option will not appear in the right-click context menu for every Start menu item, only for executables, management consoles, and other programs that can be run. The *runas* command can also be used in a command prompt for command-line utilities. Start a command prompt and then type **runas /user:administrator cmd**. This starts a new command prompt with administrator privileges.

Administration Tools Pack (adminpak.msi)

The Windows Server 2003 Administration Tools Pack (sometimes referred to as the Admin Pack) is used on client computers running Windows XP Professional to provide management tools for Windows Server 2003 computers. The client computer the administrator is installing the Administrative Tools Pack on must have Windows XP Service Pack 1 applied. The Administration Tools Pack can be installed from the adminpak.msi file, which is found on the Windows Server 2003 CD or in the system32 folder of a computer running Windows Server 2003. Double-click the **adminpak.msi** file to install the tools.

After the tools are installed, all of the Administrative Tools mentioned earlier in this section are available on the Windows XP computer and the network administrator can perform server and network administrative tasks from the Windows XP client. In particular, this includes tools for server-based services such as DNS, dynamic host control protocol (DHCP), and Active Directory.

TEST DAY TIP

The Windows Server 2003 Administration Tools Pack can only be installed on computers running Windows XP Professional or later. However, they can be used to manage servers running Windows 2000 Server as well as Windows Server 2003.

Windows Management Instrumentation

WMI provides an object-based method for accessing management information in a network. It is based on the Web-Based Enterprise Management (WBEM) standard specified by the Distributed Management Task Force (DMTF) organization, and is designed to enable the management of a wide range of network devices. WMI is Microsoft's implementation of WBEM for Windows operating systems.

WMI is used with programs or scripts to retrieve management information or change configurations of Windows computers. But using WMI is not trivial and requires programming skills. WMI can be used at the command-line by typing **WMIC** at a command prompt, but this requires knowledge of the WMI database of objects. For more information on this topic, refer to Microsoft's WMI Software Development Kit. Some enterprise Microsoft tools such as Systems Management Server (SMS) and the Health Monitor for the Back Office suite of products use WMI to manage computers. For more information on WMI, go to www.microsoft.com/windows2000/techinfo/howitworks/management/wmiscripts.asp.

Computer Management Console

The Computer Management console is available on client and server computers to perform management tasks and is itself a pre-configured MMC console. Click **Start | Program |**

Administrative Tools | Computer Management to open the Computer Management console. Alternatively, you can right-click the **My Computer** icon and select **Manage**.

You can also use the Computer Management console to connect to another computer (providing you have the appropriate rights). Select **Action | Connect to another computer** and then enter the name of the remote computer in the Another computer dialog box, or browse for it by clicking the **Browse** button.

Using Terminal Services Components for Remote Administration

How often have you had to walk to the other end of a building to perform a server task or, even worse, had to drive or fly to another office? One of the main goals for any administrator is to be able to manage all of the servers without leaving their desk—this provides for faster administration and the ability to lock servers away in a secure server room. Windows Server 2003 provides a variety of methods to remotely manage servers depending on the scenario.

Most of what is new in Windows Server 2003 Terminal Services relates to remote administration. Microsoft really listened to customer feedback and created major improvements to Terminal Services. The test objectives focus on two major Terminal Services components: Remote Desktop for Administration and Remote Assistance. Although a predecessor to Remote Desktop for Administration (Terminal Services in remote administration mode) existed in Windows 2000, many changes were made for Windows Server 2003. Remote Assistance is a new component for Microsoft's server operating systems that was initially released with Windows XP.

Terminal Services Components

The Terminal Services service in Windows Server 2003 supports a number of components. These include:

- Remote Desktop for Administration (formerly called Remote Administration mode in Windows 2000)

- Remote Assistance (a feature introduced in Windows XP)

- The Terminal Server role (formerly called Application Server mode in Windows 2000)

The exam objectives focus on your ability to use Terminal Services components to remotely administer a Windows Server 2003 system. Consequently, you can expect an emphasis on client and server applications relating to the Remote Desktop for Administration and Remote Assistance features. However, it is important to understand that Terminal Services do not end there. Many organizations use Terminal Services to deploy multi-user Application servers, as discussed previously in Chapter 2.

Remote Desktop for Administration

Remote Desktop for Administration is the key component of Terminal Services that enables remote server administration. It is installed by default, but is disabled. Remote Desktop for Administration must be manually enabled and configured by an administrator before you can connect to it. This component allows a maximum of two concurrent connections for the purposes of remotely administering the server. By default, when a Terminal Services client connects to this component, a new session is created and a copy of the Windows Server 2003 desktop is displayed in a window on the client machine.

It is important to note that this copy of the desktop is not the actual server desktop that the user would see if they were sitting down at the server's keyboard—that session is called the console. This is an important distinction, because often the operating system or an installed application will send a popup message to the server console. An administrator connecting to the server using Terminal Services will not see the console by default, and thus will not see the pop-up messages. They also will not see any applications that might be running on the console session unless they use a Remote Desktop Protocol (RDP) 5.1 or later client to run a remote console session.

In Windows 2000, there was no way to remotely view the console session. However, one of the new Terminal Services client utilities (discussed in more detail later in the chapter) includes this capability. This is a dramatic improvement that enables administrators to more fully take advantage of Terminal Services for remote administration. Because this feature was missing from earlier versions, many companies had no choice but to use third-party software to connect to the console sessions on their Windows servers.

NOTE

An example of a third-party software used to connect to and control remote servers was "PC Anywhere," a product used to perform the same tasks that now come with the operating system by default.

Remote Assistance

Remote Assistance depends on and uses the Terminal Services service. However, the way the administrator connects to it is substantially different from the methods used to establish a session with Remote Desktop for Administration or a client session connecting to the multi-user Terminal Server. Remote Assistance allows a user at one computer (the Novice) to ask for help from a user at another computer (the Expert or the Assistant), on the local area network (LAN) or across the Internet. This request can be made through Windows Messenger, e-mail, or through a transferred file. The Expert can also offer Remote Assistance without receiving an explicit request from the Novice if Group Policy settings are configured to allow offering of Remote Assistance, and the Expert user is listed as an assistant in the Offer Remote Assistance policy or is a local administrator. However, the

Novice must grant permission; the Expert can never take over the Novice's computer without the Novice's agreement. This differs from Remote Desktop in that administrators and users on the Remote Desktop Users list can start a remote session without getting permission from the person who is using the computer locally.

When an Expert receives a request from a Novice, they can initiate a connection to the Novice's computer. Once connected, the Expert is able to view the actual desktop and applications that are being used by the Novice on their computer. In addition, a special application is launched on the Novice's computer that allows them to chat with the Expert and control the session, either via text messages or audio (as long as both computers are equipped with full-duplex sound cards, speakers, and microphones). If the Novice desires, the Expert can be allowed to control the Novice's desktop and applications, including taking control of the Novice's cursor. In addition, files can be transferred easily between the two through the Remote Assistance interface.

Remote Assistance requires that both computers be running Windows XP or Server 2003. Because security is always a concern in the business environment, Remote Assistance invitations can require that the assistant provide a password to prevent an imposter from connecting to the computer while pretending to be the assistant. The amount of time for which a Remote Assistance invitation will remain valid can also be specified. Users also have the option of turning off the Remote Assistance feature entirely.

NOTE

Both Remote Desktop and Remote Assistance are also included in the Windows XP Professional operating system (only Remote Assistance is included in Windows XP Home Edition). However, whereas a Windows Server 2003 computer can have two Remote Desktop for Administration sessions running simultaneously, only one Remote Desktop session at a time can connect to an XP Professional system. In addition, when connecting via Remote Desktop to an XP Professional computer you will see all the applications that are running on the desktop of that XP computer just as if you were sitting at that local machine. If Word is open on the local desktop, it will be open in the Remote Desktop Connection session. Conversely, when you connect to a Windows Server 2003 via the Remote Desktop, you will not see applications that are open on the local (console) session. When a remote session is connected to an XP computer, the local session is locked and cannot be accessed until the remote session is terminated. With Windows Server 2003, an administrator sitting at the console can continue to do tasks while the remote administrator runs a session.

Using Remote Desktop for Administration

As mentioned, no installation is necessary for the Remote Desktop for Administration component of Terminal Services. It is installed with the operating system by default. However, for security purposes it is not enabled. Once it is enabled, members of the Administrators group can connect and use it. Non-administrators must be specifically granted access.

Configuring Remote Desktop for Administration

To configure Remote Desktop for Administration, click **Start | Control Panel | System** and click the **Remote** tab. To enable the feature, simply check the box next to **Allow users to connect remotely to this computer** located in the Remote Desktop section of the tab, as shown in Figure 3.7.

Figure 3.7 Enabling Remote Desktop for Administration

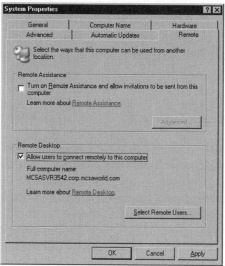

Allowing Users to Make Remote Desktop for Administration Connections

When Remote Desktop for Administration is enabled, any user accounts that are members of the Administrators built-in group on the server will be allowed to establish a remote session. However, other accounts must be explicitly approved for access by adding them to the Remote Desktop Users group on the server. To grant a user access using this method, perform the steps outlined in Exercise 3.02.

EXERCISE 3.02

ADDING USERS TO THE REMOTE DESKTOP USERS GROUP

1. Click **Start** | **Programs** | **Administrative Tools** | **Computer Management** to open the Computer Management console.

2. Expand the following nodes: **Systems Tools** | **Local Users and Groups** | **Groups**, as seen in Figure 3.8.

Figure 3.8 Locating the Remote Desktop Users Group

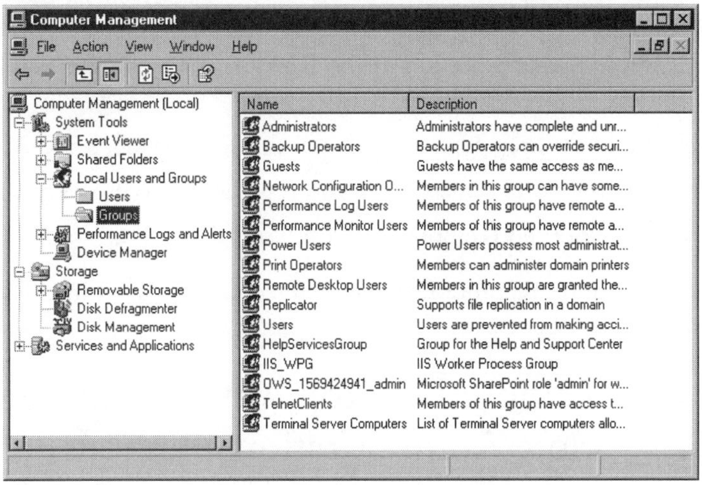

3. Right click the **Remote Desktop Users** group. From the context menu, select **Add to Group** to open the Remote Desktop Users Properties dialog box, as seen in Figure 3.9.

Figure 3.9 Adding Users to the Remote Desktop Users Group

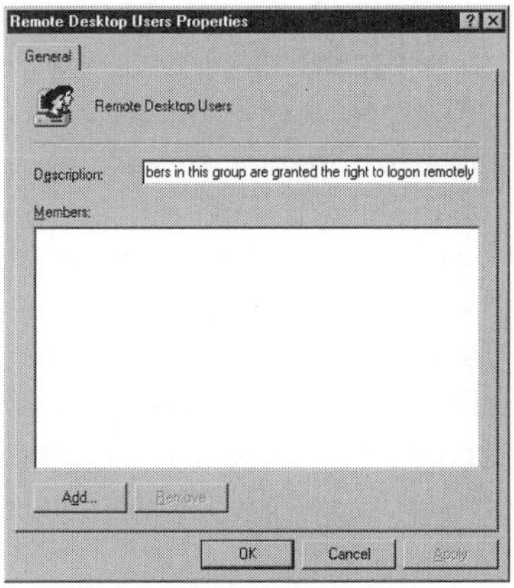

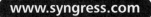

4. Click the **Add** button to open the standard Select Users, Computers or Groups dialog box.

5. Type (or search for and select) the account name of the user to whom you wish to grant access.

6. Click **OK** to close the Remote Desktop User Properties dialog box.

An easier way to access the Remote Desktop Users group and grant access is to use an option provided in the Remote tab of the System applet, seen previously in Figure 3.7. To use this method, perform the following steps:

1. In the Remote Desktop section of the **Remote** tab, click the **Select Remote Users** button.

2. In the Remote Desktop Users dialog box that appears, click the **Add** button.

3. Type (or search for and select) the account name of the user requiring access.

4. Click **OK** to close the Remote Desktop Users dialog box.

The methods of creating Remote Desktop connections are examined later in the "Using Terminal Services Client Tools" section of this chapter.

Advantages of Remote Desktop Administration over Other Remote Administration Methods

Windows Server 2003 includes many ways to remotely administer servers. Server administration tools (including Active Directory Users and Computers, Active Directory Sites and Services, Active Directory Domains and Trusts and many others) can be installed on a client computer. A network administrator can use the Computer Management console on one computer on the network to connect to and manage another. They can also use command-line tools to connect to and manage computers across the network.

Many administrators prefer Remote Desktop for Administration because they are able to see and use the entire server desktop exactly as if they were sitting at the console. They can do things such as promote or demote a domain controller, defragment the server's disk, install applications, run a backup job, or upgrade the operating system. They can change configurations that are difficult or impossible to configure by other remote methods, such as Control Panel settings. They can control the server from a computer on which they would not want to install the administrative tools. With the Remote Desktop Web Connection, the administrator does not even have to have Remote Desktop Connection or the Terminal Services client installed on the computer from which they initiate a Terminal Service session; only Internet Explorer 5.0 or later is required. Because of the efficiency of the latest version of RDP, performance over the LAN is almost as fast as if they were physically sitting at the server.

Remote Desktop Security Issues

When enabled, Remote Desktop for Administration opens Transmission Control Protocol (TCP) port 3389 and listens for connection requests. This port is a significant target and is often sought during port scans. Most open ports link to applications that must be attacked in complex ways to permit administrator level access to a computer—but this service is designed to actually provide it, which makes it a prime target for attackers. There are several best practices that should be followed to maximize the security of this component.

Remember, with the exception of administrators, users must be authorized to connect using Remote Desktop for Administration. This is accomplished by adding a user's account to the Remote Desktop Users group using one of the methods previously mentioned. If a user does not require this access, their account should never be a member of this group. The administrator should control membership in this group through Group Policy or review it manually on a regular basis.

It is important to enforce strong security precautions on all accounts that are allowed to connect using Remote Desktop for Administration. Strong passwords and the use of account lockout are essential to make it difficult for an attacker to successfully use a brute force attack to gain system access. Administrators should be required to logon using a standard user account and perform administrative duties in the session using the Run as feature. This ensures maximum security of the administrator credentials, minimal damage to the Windows Server 2003 computer if the session is hijacked, and that Trojans and other malicious code are more difficult to install accidentally when using the session.

All users should be required to use the most recent client available for their platform. This will ensure that the latest security features are available to them. It should be standard policy to check frequently for software updates to both client and server components, as these may contain critical security fixes. In addition, users should be discouraged from storing their logon credentials in the properties of the client. This allows anyone with physical access to the user's machine to establish a session. It also stores sensitive information such as their username and domain in a clear text file with an RDP extension in the user's My Documents folder.

Finally, denial of service (DoS) is a significant possibility when using Remote Desktop for Administration because it allows for only two sessions to exist on the server. Both active and disconnected sessions count. So if a company has three administrators and two of them leave disconnected sessions, the third will not be able to connect using Terminal Services until one of the existing sessions has been terminated. The solution to this may appear to be setting the time out value so that sessions are reset shortly after they enter the disconnected state. However, this can cause serious problems.

An administrator may establish a session, begin an installation process, and then disconnect to allow the installation to finish unmonitored. The previous settings would terminate the session, including the installation routine it was running, with potentially disastrous effects for the server. Special circumstances like these must be taken into account when configuring policies. Because session timeout values can be set at the user property level, Microsoft recommends the use of a special shared administrative account for such circumstances as this. The strategy applies a timeout for disconnected sessions that are started by every user account except the shared account, which has no timeout settings applied. In this way, there should always be one connection available to a server, even though the second allowed connection is being consumed by a session involving the shared administrative account.

Using Remote Assistance

As with Remote Desktop for Administration, the Remote Assistance components of Windows Server 2003 are installed with the operating system. And similar to Remote Desktop for Administration, Remote Assistance needs to be enabled and configured before the feature can be used.

Two major components comprise the default installation: the Terminal Services service and the Remote Desktop Help Session Manager service. In addition to installing these two components, Microsoft also creates a special user account for connections involving Remote Assistance, called *SUPPORT_xxxxxxxx*. On your system, the x's will be replaced with a unique alphanumeric code, and the account name will appear as something similar to this: SUPPORT_388945a0. This account will be disabled until Remote Assistance is enabled. Although Remote Assistance is based on and uses Terminal Services, it works very differently from the Remote Desktop for Administration or the Terminal Server role.

TEST DAY TIP

Be sure that you are familiar with Remote Assistance. As a new component in the Windows server family that directly relates to test objectives, it is likely to be featured in one or more exam questions.

How Remote Assistance Works

Remote Assistance allows a user at one computer (the Novice) to request help from a user at another computer (the Expert). The underlying technologies are Windows Terminal Services and the RDP. Although these are the same technologies that were originally developed for thin client computing and that are used for Remote Desktop for Administration and Terminal Server, Remote Assistance is *not* a thin client solution. In fact, both computers must be running Windows XP or Windows Server 2003. Another difference between Remote Assistance and traditional Terminal Services is that typically, the session is initiated when the Novice sends an Invitation to the Expert soliciting their assistance. The Novice must typically be present at the machine that needs assistance to allow the Expert to access their system after the Expert receives and accepts the Invitation. With Remote Desktop for Administration or the Terminal Server role, a user can connect from a wide range of client systems without permission, provided the user has a valid username and password.

Using Remote Assistance, the Expert actually views and (if allowed) interacts with the same desktop and applications that the Novice is using, at the same time. This is very different from the other forms of Terminal Services, in which a connection is established to a unique session on the Terminal Services computer. During a Remote Assistance session, both the Novice sitting at the keyboard and the remote assistant (Expert) can control the computer at the same time.

As with any form of Terminal Services, RDP is still used so that only screen updates are sent to the client (which in this case is the Expert) while keystrokes and mouse movements are sent back to the server (which in this case is the Novice).

Configuring Remote Assistance for Use

Remote Assistance is relatively easy to configure; the same tab can be used that is used to configure Remote Desktop for Administration. To enable Remote Assistance, click **Start | Settings | Control Panel**, and select the **Remote** tab in the **System** properties applet. Select the check box next to **Turn on Remote Assistance and allow invitations to be sent from this computer**, as seen in Figure 3.10.

Figure 3.10 Enabling Remote Assistance

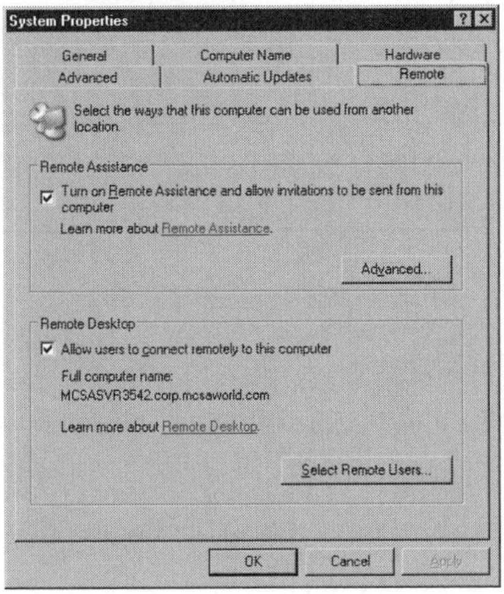

Invitations do not stay valid indefinitely. They have an expiration time of one hour by default, but the Novice can alter the expiration time of the Invitations, from 0 minutes to 99 days. The acceptance and opening of a session in response to an Invitation does not cause it to expire; it is good until it reaches the specified expiration time. In other words, if you save an Invitation to a file with an expiration time of 30 days, that Invitation can be used to establish Remote Assistance connections as many times as desired within that 30-day timeframe. To modify the default expiration time, click the **Advanced** button, as seen in Figure 3.10, to open the Remote Assistance Settings dialog box, as seen in Figure 3.11. Choose the desired number (0 to 99) and interval (minutes, hours, or days) and click **OK**.

Figure 3.11 Configuring Remote Assistance Settings

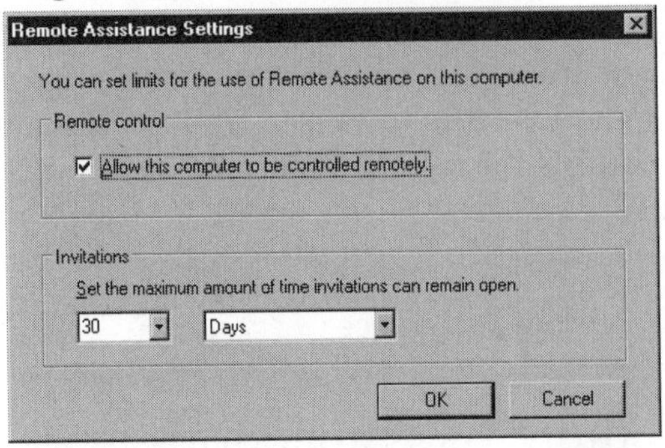

In addition to modifying the expiration time, the Remote Assistance Settings dialog box can be used to allow (or not allow) the Expert to control the Novice's desktop and applications during a Remote Assistance session. When the **Allow this computer to be controlled remotely** box is checked, the Expert will be allowed to send mouse and keyboard input to the Novice's system and interact directly with their desktop and applications. When it is unchecked, the Expert will be able to see the Novice's desktop and any actions the Novice performs, but cannot control the cursor or send keyboard commands.

NOTE

It is important to be aware that, when you enable Remote Assistance, the **Allow this computer to be controlled remotely** checkbox is enabled by default.

Asking for Assistance

A Novice can use a variety of methods to request help by sending an Invitation using Remote Assistance:

- The request can be sent using Windows Messenger
- The request can be sent via e-mail
- The request can be saved to a file

To create an Invitation, click **Start | Help and Support**. On the right side of the **Help and Support Center** utility, click **Remote Assistance** under the Support heading. In the next screen, click the **Invite someone to help you** link. You will then be able to select the method that you want to use in asking for assistance, as shown in Figure 3.12.

NOTE

Windows Messenger is not installed by default in Windows Server 2003. If you want to send a request for Remote Assistance using Windows Messenger, you need to first install it. Be careful not to install MSN Messenger—you must install Windows Messenger.

Figure 3.12 Starting Remote Assistance

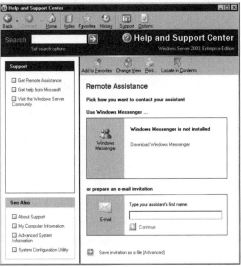

EXAM WARNING

Although a Remote Assistance session can be solicited using an Invitation sent in a file or via e-mail, Microsoft emphasizes sending an invitation using Windows Messaging. Make sure you are very familiar with all of the details of this method of solicitation.

Using Windows Messenger to Request Help

Windows Messenger is a chat program available at no cost from Microsoft that is similar to ICQ and AOL Instant Messenger. (MSN Messenger is a separate but related application; both use the .NET Messenger Service.) When you use Windows Messenger for Remote Assistance, the Invitation travels through a messaging server infrastructure that can include the Internet, or can work with a Microsoft Exchange Server within the LAN. Expert and Novice data packets that contain connection information are exchanged through this infrastructure. However, once these have been exchanged, the actual RDP connection attempt and subsequent session take place directly between the Novice and Expert computers.

Windows Server 2003 does not install Windows Messenger by default. If the administrator has not installed it prior to arriving at the Remote Connection screen, they will only see a link notifying them that it is not installed and prompting them to download and install it. If Windows Messenger is installed, the user from whom they wish to solicit help must be on the network and logged on to their Windows Messenger client. If this is the case, the administrator can click the name of the contact from which they want to solicit assistance, followed by the **Invite this person** link. The invitee can then accept the Invitation. A Remote Assistance dialog box displays on the screen until the Expert invitee accepts or until the administrator clicks the **Cancel** button on the dialog box.

The network administrator can also request assistance from within the Windows Messenger application by double-clicking on a contact to establish a conversation with the Expert and then selecting the **Ask for Remote Assistance** link on the right side of the conversation window. This adds a notification to their conversation window, with a link on which they can click to cancel the request. They will also be notified in the conversation window when the Expert receives and accepts their request.

Remember that Remote Assistance only works on computers running Windows XP and Server 2003. If an invitation is sent to a person at a computer running the Windows 2000 operating system or earlier or a non-Microsoft operating system, it will not be received.

If an administrator does not have Windows Messenger installed, they can begin the process from the Help and Support Center by clicking on the **Download Windows Messenger** link, after beginning the process of asking for Remote Assistance, as seen previously in Figure 3.12. This opens an Internet Explorer window with a Web page that displays the Windows XP version of Windows Messenger for download. At the time of this writing, a Windows Server 2003 version of Windows Messenger is not available; however, the Windows XP version works just fine.

Responding to a Request for Help Using Windows Messenger

If the invited Expert has the Windows Messaging application running, a request from a Novice for assistance will be displayed in a Conversation window on the Expert's system. The Expert can click the **Accept** link in the window to initiate the connection, or click the **Decline** link to reject it, as seen in Figure 3.13. If the Invitation is neither accepted nor declined before the invitation expires, the Expert will be unable to establish a connection in response to that Invitation.

Figure 3.13 Accepting the Remote Assistance Invitation

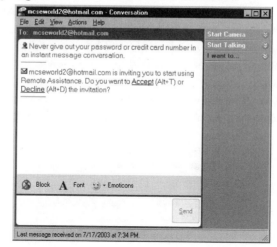

Using E-mail to Request Help

To use e-mail to send a Remote Assistance invitation, the administrator must first have a default mail client configured on the Windows Server 2003 computer. This mail client can be Microsoft Outlook Express, which is installed with Windows, Outlook (installed as separate application or with Microsoft Office), or a third party e-mail application. To create a Remote Assistance Invitation using e-mail, complete Exercise 3.03:

EXERCISE 3.03

SENDING AN E-MAIL REQUEST

1. Click on **Start | Help and Support Center**.

2. On the right side of the Help and Support Center screen, click **Remote Assistance** under the Support heading.

3. In the next screen that is displayed, click the **Invite someone to help you** link.

4. In the next screen, in the Prepare an e-mail invitation section, type the first name of the person you want to use as an Expert in the Type your assistant's first name in the text box and click on the **Continue** link.

5. The following screen, as seen in Figure 3.14, contains two sections. The first is titled "Set the invitation to expire" and contains a drop-down box for specifying a number between 0 and 99, and an interval drop-down box with selections for minutes, hours, or days. This means that the possible time period during which the invitation is valid ranges anywhere

from 0 minutes to 99 days. Verify that the second section of this screen is enabled by default by selecting **Require the recipient to use a password**. The intent is that, should the invitation accidentally fall into the wrong hands, a password would still be required to use it. Obviously, you should not include the password in the e-mailed invitation. Instead, you should communicate it to the person in some other manner (for example, by telephone). The password is entered twice, once in the Type password text box and again in the Confirm password text box.

Figure 3.14 Creating an E-mail Remote Assistance Invitation

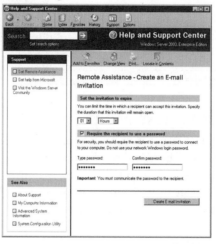

6. After the password had been entered into each box, the **Create E-mail Invitation** button at the bottom of the can be clicked. An e-mail message opens on your computer, as seen in Figure 3.15. You need to enter the recipient's e-mail address and any additional information you want to the message before sending it.

Figure 3.15 Sending an E-mail Remote Assistance Invitation

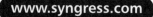

7. After you have sent the e-mail, the process of asking for Remote Assistance using the e-mail method is complete.

Responding to a Request for Help from an E-mail Request

When e-mail has been used to send you an invitation for Remote Assistance, a short e-mail message entitled "YOU HAVE RECEIVED A REMOTE ASSISTANCE INVITATION" will show up in your inbox. The message will contain a link to click, which will look something like this: https://www.microsoft.com/remoteassistance/s.asp#1AjK8A2TD,4H8S QYYfvIpQF5prHYajrReyrAd2j6oHb4Qe/Eo1Ahs=,zb2.0RJ81UIfxb4Xfkp8thzdy8A=Z. When you click on the link, your browser will open to a page on Microsoft's Web site. The entire process of the two computers finding each other using this method takes place through the Microsoft's Web site. In addition, e-mail based Remote Assistance depends on a downloaded control.

When you visit the site, a Security Warning dialog box will appear and you will be prompted to specify whether you wish to install the Remote Assistance Server Control, as seen in Figure 3.16.

Figure 3.16 Downloading the Remote Assistance Server Control

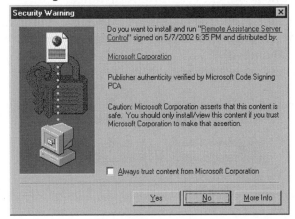

If you select **Yes**, the control will download and the page will load. If you are not accessing the page from a Windows XP or Windows Server 2003 computer, a message will display informing you that you must be running one of these operating systems to complete the connection. If you are accessing the Web page from a Windows XP or Windows Server 2003 computer, you will see a button entitled **Start Remote Assistance** in the middle of the Web page. When you click on this button, a small Remote Assistance dialog box appears, prompting you to enter the password associated with the invitation (if one was used). After you have typed in the password, click the **Yes** button to begin the connection.

Using a Saved File to Request Help

The third and final way of requesting assistance is to use a saved file. Obviously, if you use this method, you need to somehow transfer the file containing the invitation to the Expert. This can be done in one of several ways:

- The file can be e-mailed
- The file can be saved to a share on the network
- You can create a link to the file on a Web page (perhaps on the local Intranet)
- You can save the file on a floppy diskette and hand it to the person

To create a Remote Assistance invitation using a saved file, complete the steps discussed in Exercise 3.04.

EXERCISE 3.04

SENDING A FILE BASED REQUEST

1. Click **Start | Help and Support Center**.

2. On the right side of the Help and Support Center screen under the Support heading, click **Remote Assistance**.

3. In the next screen that is displayed, click the **Invite someone to help you** link. At the bottom of the next screen, click the **Save invitation as a file (Advanced)** link. This leads to a screen that contains two parts, as seen in Figure 3.17.

Figure 3.17 Creating an Remote Assistance Invitation Using a File

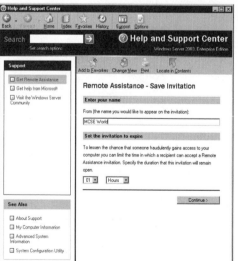

4. The first section is entitled Enter your name and contains a text box into which you can type your name. When you send someone a request using Windows Messenger or e-mail, the recipient can easily see who sent the request. This is not true with a file-based request, so this dialog box is used to embed that information into the request and make it readily available to the Expert.

5. The second portion of this screen is entitled Set the invitation to expire and contains a drop-down box that lets you specify a number between 0 and 99, and an interval drop-down box with selections for minutes, hours, or days. The possible range for the duration of a valid invitation is from 0 minutes to 99 days.

6. After you fill in the requested information, click on the **Continue** button at the bottom of the screen. On the next page verify that the option **Require the recipient to use a password** is selected. By default, the check box is selected and this requirement is enabled. Again, the intent is that if the invitation accidentally falls into the wrong hands, at least a password will be required to use it. The password must be entered twice, once in the **Type password** text box and again in the **Confirm password** text box.

7. After the password has been entered into each box, click the **Save Invitation** button at the bottom of the screen. This displays a Save As dialog box that allows you to specify a name and location for the file. The file will be saved with an .MSRCINCIDENT extension. After it is saved, the final screen is displayed. It confirms the file name and where it was saved. At the bottom of the screen, there are links to manage your outstanding invitation requests and create additional invitations. Figure 3.18 displays the file that is creating during this process.

Figure 3.18 Examining the Remote Assistance File

Responding to a Request for Help Using a Saved File

Responding to a Remote Assistance request that has been saved to a file is simply a matter of double clicking the file. When you do this, a small Remote Assistance dialog box appears, asking you to enter the password associated with the invitation if one was specified. After you type in the password, click the **Yes** button to initiate the connection. The following section shows how to complete the connection process for each of the methods described, and demonstrates what can be done when the connection has been established.

Completing the Remote Assistance Connection

After a request for assistance is accepted by the Expert user, a small Remote Assistance dialog box appears on the Expert's computer with a message indicating that a connection is being attempted. When the connection is established, the full Remote Assistance application opens, displaying a status message that says it is waiting for an answer from the Novice computer. When the connection is accepted by the Novice user, the status of the Remote Assistance application changes to Connected.

During this time, the Novice's system displays a small Remote Assistance dialog box that asks the user if they want to allow the Expert to view the computer's screen and chat with them. If the Novice clicks the **No** button, the connection is rejected. If the Novice clicks the **Yes** button, the connection is established. If too much time passes after the Expert attempts to establish the connection and before the Novice accepts it, a dialog box opens to inform the Novice that the invitation was accepted but has expired. This dialog box also states that a new invitation needs to be generated and offered. A dialog box is also displayed on the Expert's computer, indicating that the remote connection could not be established. When a connection is successfully established, a Remote Assistance application opens on the Novice's system.

Using the Completed Connection as the Expert

The Remote Assistance application on the Expert's computer consists of a tool bar across the top, a chat option on the left side, and a replica of the Novice's remote desktop on the right, as shown in Figure 3.19.

Figure 3.19 The Remote Assistance Utility on the Expert's Computer

The buttons on the tool bar across the top include the following:

- **Take Control** Initiates a request to allow the Expert to remotely control the cursor and keyboard input on the Novice's computer. When this button is clicked, a dialog box pops up on the Novice's computer, asking the Novice to allow or reject control by the Expert. Remote control is only possible if the **Allow this computer to be controlled remotely** box is checked on the **Remote** tab of the System applet in the Control Panel. If remote control is accepted by the Novice, a dialog box appears in the Remote Assistance application on the Expert's computer over the display of the Novice's desktop, stating that remote control has been accepted. Either party can end the remote control at any time by using the **Esc** key. After remote control is established, the Remote Control button changes to read **Release Control** and can be clicked to end the remote control of the session without ending the Remote Assistance session itself. Both the Novice and Expert can control the cursor and keyboard input for the Novice's system, so it is recommended that only one party be using the pointing device or typing at any given time. The Expert can use Remote control by clicking on the Novice desktop that is displayed in their Remote Assistance application.

- **Send a File** Allows the administrator to transmit a file from the Expert's to the Novice's computer.

- **Start Talking** Establishes an audio connection between the Novice's and Expert's computers for voice and/or video communication. When this button is clicked, the Audio and Video Tuning Wizard opens. The wizard allows the administrator to specify and test their microphone, audio card, and other related settings.

- **Settings** Opens the Remote Assistance Settings dialog box and allows adjustment of audio quality in accordance with the capacity of the underlying network. The Audio and Video Tuning Wizard, mentioned in the previous bullet point, can also be opened from this dialog box.

- **Disconnect** Terminates the connection between the Novice's and Expert's computers and ends the Remote Assistance session.

- **Help** Displays the About Remote Assistance help screen.

The left side of the Remote Assistance application on the Expert's computer contains a chat window. This allows the Novice and Expert to exchange text messages. In addition to chat communication, this portion of the application also contains status messages such as the names of users who are part of the connection, whether remote control is enabled, and how to stop remote control.

The right side of the Remote Assistance application on the Expert's computer displays the desktop of the Novice's system. When the connection is initially established, the desktop appears in View Only mode. This allows the Expert to view the desktop of the Novice, but the Expert cannot interact with it. The Expert can still exchange text messages or voice communications with the Novice in this mode, and can exchange files. If the Expert and Novice agree to switch from View Only to Remote Control, the Expert can then interact with the remote desktop and applications on the Novice's system. To do this, the Expert uses their pointing device and keyboard to select and input data into the desktop that is displayed on the right side of the Remote Assistance application.

Using the Completed Connection as the Novice

The Remote Assistance application on the Novice's computer consists of a chat window on the left side and a series of option buttons along the right, as shown in Figure 3.20.

Figure 3.20 The Remote Assistance Utility on the Novice's Computer

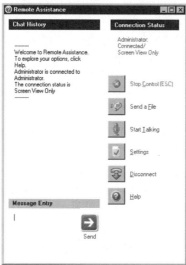

This application allows the Novice to send messages to and receive messages from the Expert. It also contains the following buttons:

- **Stop Control** Terminates the ability of the Expert to control the cursor and keyboard input on the Novice's computer.

- **Send a File** Allows for transmitting a file from the Novice's to the Expert's computer.

- **Start Talking** Establishes an audio connection between the Novice and Expert computers for voice and/or video communication. When clicked, the Audio and Video Tuning Wizard opens. The wizard allows the administrator to specify and test their microphone, speaker, and related settings.

- **Settings** Opens a dialog box that allows for the adjustment of audio quality in accordance with the capacity of the underlying network. The Audio and Video Tuning Wizard can also be opened from this dialog box.

- **Disconnect** Terminates the connection between the Novice's and Expert's computers and ends the Remote Assistance session.

- **Help** Brings up the About Remote Assistance help screen.

The left side of the Remote Assistance application on the Novice's computer contains a chat window. This allows the Novice and Expert to exchange text messages. In addition to chat communication, the left side of the application also displays status messages such as the names of users who are part of the connection, whether remote control is enabled, and how to stop remote control.

Managing Open Invitations

Sometimes the administrator might want to know the names of users with whom they have active Remote Assistance invitations open. They might want to cancel an invitation because they have solved the problem or because they want someone else to help them. The Help and Support Center provides a number of options for managing open invitations.

To manage your active invitations, follow these steps:

1. Click **Start | Help and Support**.

2. On the right side of the Help and Support Center screen, click **Remote Assistance** under the Support heading.

3. In the following screen, click the **View Invitation Status (x)** link. The **(x)** will be replaced on your screen by the number of invitations you have outstanding.

4. The next screen shows you a list of the invitations that are outstanding, as seen in Figure 3.21. The list consists of three columns: Sent To, Expiration Time, and Status. The Sent To column contains the name of the person to whom you sent the Windows Message or e-mail. If you saved the request to a file, this column will display the word Saved. The Expiration Time column will show the date and time that the invitation will expire. The Status column will show whether the invitation's status is Open or Expired. Now you can view or modify any of these invitations.

Figure 3.21 Viewing Remote Assistance Requests

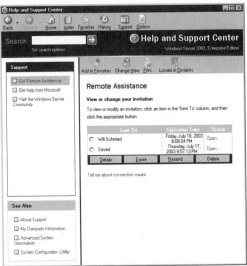

Each invitation has a radio button next to it, as seen in Figure 3.21. You can click a radio button to select one of the Invitations and then choose an action to perform using the buttons under the list box. The buttons include:

- **Details** Allows the administrator to view to whom the invitation was sent, when it was sent, when it expires, its current status, and whether it is password protected.

- **Expire** Allows the administrator to cause an invitation to expire immediately, regardless of the expiration time that was set when the invitation was originally created.

- **Resend** Can only be used with expired invitations. When selected, this option displays a screen that walks the administrator through the creation process for the invitation all over again. Remember that the request was originally saved to a file or sent via e-mail. Because of this, the screens and options presented are identical to those outlined earlier in the chapter.

- **Delete** Allows the administrator to permanently delete the invitation. If the invitation's status is Open when they select to delete it, a dialog box will pop up, informing them that the invitation will not be usable for connection. If the invitation's status is Expired, it is simply deleted and no pop-up box appears.

Remote Assistance Security Issues

Remote Assistance is a valuable tool, but it also contains serious security risks that must be planned for and managed. Remote Assistance makes it easy for any user to ask virtually anyone using a Windows XP or Windows Server 2003 computer to connect to their desktop—this person can be inside the company or a friend that is outside of the company. Although an outside person may be qualified to assist the user, in doing so they will likely receive full control of a client in the network.

This, of course, is unacceptable because they could place malicious software on the system while in control of it, view sensitive company information that normally is not allowed outside of the organization, and so forth. The best way to prevent this is to use the company's firewalls to prevent connection to Remote Assistance from outside the company's network. Remote Assistance uses the same port that all Terminal Services components do, TCP 3389. Simply blocking this port on the external firewalls prevents this type of unauthorized access.

Several other key security concerns should be addressed in a company's Remote Assistance policies. E-mail and file-based invitations allow the administrator to specify passwords. An invitation without password protection can be used by anyone that receives it by accident or intercepts it maliciously. Because of this, the use of these passwords should always be mandated.

A company may also want to protect traffic that contains Remote Assistance requests. E-mail is normally sent in unencrypted form on the network. This means that URL that is sent in the e-mail invitation is available for easy interception while it is in transit on the network. Likewise, a simple XML format is used for the invitation file. A simple pattern match could be used when monitoring the network to detect and automatically save this information to an unauthorized system while it is being sent across the network. If the e-mail or file invitations do not have passwords, they can be used immediately when they are captured in this way. Even if a password is specified, there is no limit to the number of times requests like these can be used for connection. A brute force attack could be used to attempt to break the password and successfully establish a session. For this reason, it is important that the Remote Assistance policy also specify a short expiration time for the invitation. Once expired, no connections are possible with it. A shorter time reduces the chances of successfully using a brute force attack. And, if no password is specified, at least the open window for misuse of the invitation is shorter.

Users should also be educated on when it is appropriate to accept Remote Assistance requests. As mentioned previously, a request saved to a file is stored in a standard XML file. These can easily be modified to perform malicious actions when run by a user on a local system. The e-mail request contains a URL to click on and can also be altered. In this case it may take the user to a page that performs malicious actions on their local system, or requires the download and installation of an unauthorized ActiveX control that is designed to appear legitimate to the user. Even an unsolicited request received through Windows messaging has security worries.

The best option is to maintain a tight policy that asks users to reject remote assistance invitations in all but a few instances. What is acceptable will relate specifically to a company. Some organizations allow acceptance only from immediate co-workers and known help desk staff. Others are more liberal and allow invitations to be accepted from any verifiable employee within the company. The most important rule is to not allow connections from outside of the organization. Again, this can be further prevented by the use of firewall rules.

NOTE

A Remote Desktop connection to computers running Windows XP is also possible, but only one connection is allowed (including a locally logged on user). This means that when you connect to the computer using Remote Desktop, if someone is already logged on at the computer, that user is logged off.

EXAM
70-292

OBJECTIVE
3.2
3.2.2

Using Terminal Services Client Tools

There are three primary tools that can be used to connect from a client system to Terminal Services for remote administration. These tools include:

- The Remote Desktop Connection utility
- The Remote Desktops console
- The Remote Desktop Web Connection utility

Each tool is designed to fill a very specific role, and it is important to be familiar with the capabilities and uses of each. The following sections examine how to install and use these utilities.

TEST DAY TIP

Be sure to familiarize yourself with the properties available for configuration in each of the client tools prior to taking the exam.

Using the Remote Desktop Connection Utility

The Remote Desktop Connection utility (formerly the Terminal Services Client Connection Manager) is the standard client for connecting to Terminal Services via Remote Desktop for Administration on a server or Terminal Services on a Terminal Server. It can be used for remote administration or full Terminal Server client use. It enables a user to connect to a single server running Terminal Services using the RDP over TCP/IP. The utility is installed with the operating system in Windows XP and Server 2003 and can be accessed by clicking **Start | Programs | Accessories | Communications** in those operating systems. If you use the client often, you might want to create a shortcut to it on your desktop. The Remote

Desktop Connection utility can also be installed and used on a number of older Windows operating systems, including Windows 2000, NT, ME, 98, and 95.

The older Terminal Services Client Connection Manager can still be used to connect to a Terminal Server from a Windows 3.11 computer with the 32-bit TCP/IP stack installed. There is also a 16-bit version of the Windows 2000 TS client for Windows for Workgroups 3.11 and a Macintosh client. If you need to connect MS-DOS, Linux or other client operating systems, you will need third party RDP or ICA client software. The Remote Desktop Connection utility is backward compatible and capable of communicating with Terminal Services in Windows XP, Windows 2000 and Windows NT 4.0, Terminal Server Edition. Let's take a look at how to install, configure, and use this critical utility.

 EXAM WARNING

The Remote Desktop Connection utility is the primary end user client connection tool for Terminal Services. Do not forget that it comes preinstalled on Windows XP and Windows Server 2003 and does not need to be installed separately.

Installing the Remote Desktop Connection Utility

If an administrator wants to use the Remote Desktop Connection utility on systems older than Windows XP, they need to install it first. The installation files can be retrieved from the Microsoft Web site, or if they have installed Windows Server 2003 they can share the client setup folder located at %systemroot%\system32\clients\tsclient. After they share this folder, computers on the network can connect to the share and run the setup.exe utility in the Win32 folder. If the administrator wants to deploy the client using Group Policy, Microsoft also includes an MSI installation file, msrdpcli.msi, in this directory.

Perform the following steps to install the Remote Desktop Connection client:

1. When you double click the **setup.exe** file, the installation wizard will launch. Read the initial welcome screen and then click the **Next** button.

2. Review the license agreement and then click the radio button next to **I accept the terms of the license agreement**, followed by the **Next** button.

3. On the Customer Information screen, enter your name for licensing purposes in the User Name text box, and your company for licensing purposes in the Organization text box.

4. In the Install this application for section, select the radio button next to **Anyone who uses this computer (all users)** if you want the utility to be available on the Windows Start menu for every user that logs on to the system. Select the radio button next to **Only for me (-)** if you only want the utility to appear in your Windows Start menu. When you have finished making your selection, click the **Next** button.

5. On the next screen, click the **Install** button to proceed with the installation or the **Back** button to review your choices. The application will remove any previously installed similar applications, and then complete its own installation.

6. Click the **Finish** button to close the wizard.

Launching and Using the Remote Desktop Connection Utility

After the application is installed, click **Start | Programs | Accessories | Communications | Remote Desktop Connection**. This opens the utility, as seen in Figure 3.22, with most of its configuration options hidden. To proceed with the connection, type the name or IP address of the Terminal Server, Windows Server 2003 computer, or Windows XP Professional computer to which you want to connect in the Computer drop-down box, or select it from the drop-down list if you have previously established a connection to it. By default, the name or IP address of the last computer to which you connected will be displayed. Finally, click on the **Connect** button.

Figure 3.22 Viewing Remote Assistance Requests

NOTE

Refer back to Chapter 2 for more discussion on the various components and configuration of Terminal Services in Terminal Server (Application) mode.

A Remote Desktop window will open. If the user name and password with which you are logged on to your current system are valid for connection to Terminal Services on the server, you will be automatically logged on and a session will appear. If not, you will be prompted to enter a valid user name and password. When you are connected, the remote desktop will appear in a window on your system by default, as seen in Figure 3.23. You can move your cursor over it, and then click on and use any item in the remote desktop just as you would if you were using your local system. You can also copy and paste between the remote and local computers.

Figure 3.23 The Remote Desktop Window

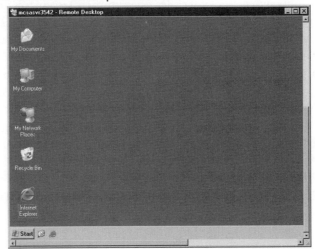

Connecting is a simple process; however, terminating a session requires a bit more explanation. There are two methods that can be used to end a session:

- **Logging off** To log off, simply click the **Start | Log Off** on the remote desktop. When you do this, it will completely log you out of the remote system in much the same way as if you logged out on your local system. Registry entries are properly written, programs are closed, and so forth. The session is completely removed from the Terminal Services computer, freeing up any system resources that were being used by your session. Make sure that you select **Log Off**, rather than **Shut Down**. If you select **Shut Down**, and you are logged onto the remote session with rights that allow your account to shut down the server, it will power down or reboot the server. This will affect everyone who is currently using the server.

- **Disconnecting** The second method of terminating your session is to use the process known as disconnection. When you disconnect from Terminal Services, your session remains on the server and is not removed. It continues to consume resources, although the video stream coming to your local computer and the input stream going from your local computer to the Terminal Services system are terminated. When you launch the Remote Desktop Connection utility again and connect to the same computer running Terminal Services, your session will still be there, exactly as you left it, and you can take up where you left off. This can be helpful in cases where an application is being run that requires lengthy processing. You do not have to remain connected for the application to run, and you can check back in later and obtain the result.

In general, it is best to properly log off and free up the resources being used by a session you no longer need. As will be seen a bit later, an administrator can cause a disconnected session to be reset if they do not return to it for a specified period of time. If they have left unsaved documents or other files open in their session, resetting will cause them to lose all work. Thus, it is usually safest to save your work before disconnecting. Disconnect from your session by clicking the close button (the **X**) in the top right corner of the Remote Desktop window.

You can also log off or disconnect using the Windows Security dialog box. This can be accessed by clicking **Start | Windows Security**, or by using the **Ctrl + Alt + End** key combination from within the session (this has the same effect as **Ctrl + Alt + Del** on the local machine). Once in the dialog, you can log off by clicking **Start | Log Off** button, or by selecting **Start | Shut Down** and then selecting **Log Off** from the drop-down box that appears. This same drop-down box also contains the **Disconnect** option.

Configuring the Remote Desktop Connection Utility

In the previous section, we simply launched the Remote Desktop Connection utility and established a connection. When the utility is initially launched, most of its configuration information is hidden. To display it before using it to establish a connection, click the **Options** button. This reveals a series of tabs and many additional settings that need to be configured.

The General Tab

The General tab, as seen in Figure 3.24, contains the Computer drop-down box, which contains names and IP addresses of computers to which the administrator previously connected, along with an option to browse the network for computers not listed. It also contains User name, Password, and Domain text boxes. Remember, by default the credentials with which you are logged on locally are used to establish your remote session. If you always want to ensure that a specific set of credentials is used to log onto Terminal Services, you can type the account information into these text boxes.

Figure 3.24 The Remote Desktop Connection General Tab

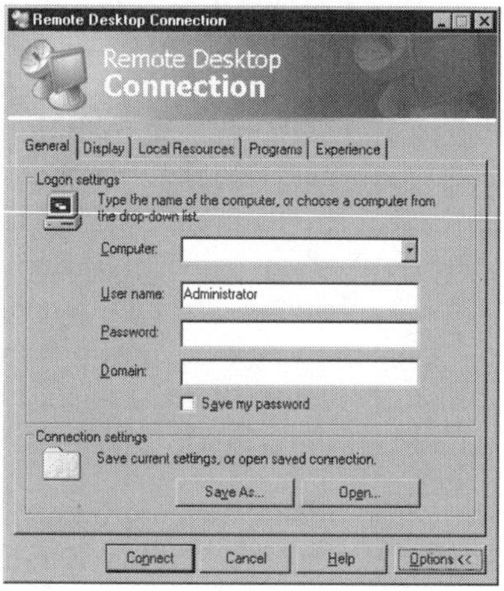

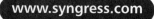

NOTE

In general, it is a poor security practice to leave the user name and password information saved in the utility. If you choose to do this, keep in mind that anyone with access to your computer can use the utility to establish a Terminal Services session.

This tab also allows you to save your connection settings. You might have several different systems to which you connect using Terminal Services. If so, it is helpful to not have to configure the utility each time you open it. When you click the **Save As** button, a Save As dialog box opens, asking you where you would like to save the file that contains your configuration information. The file will be saved with an .RDP extension, and can be double-clicked later to establish a Terminal Session. You can also use the **Open** button on this tab to specify that the settings from a previously saved RDP file be loaded into the utility.

The Display Tab

The Display tab, as seen in Figure 3.25, configures how the remote desktop appears on the client computer. The top portion of the screen contains a slider that controls the size of the remote desktop that will be displayed on the screen. The slider has four possible positions: 640x480, 800x600, 1024x768, and Full Screen. The default is 800x600.

Figure 3.25 The Remote Desktop Connection Display Tab

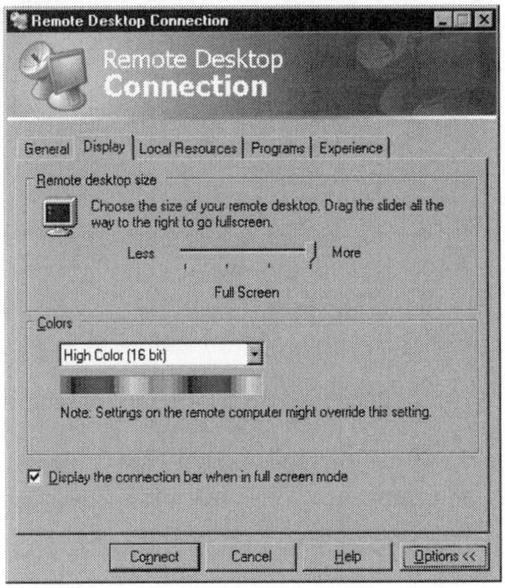

The next portion of this tab controls the color depth (in bits) of the remote desktop when it is displayed on the local computer. The drop-down list box contains the following options: 256 colors, High Color (15 bit), High Color (16 bit), and True Color (24 bit). Higher color depths require more resources. Note that the settings on the server itself may override your selection.

Finally, the bottom of the tab contains a check box entitled **Display the connection bar when in full screen mode.** When selected, this setting places a small bar, seen in Figure 3.26, at the top of a full screen remote desktop which makes it easier to size, minimize or maximize (to full screen), or close the Remote Desktop window.

Figure 3.26 The Full Screen Connection Bar

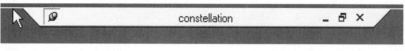

The Local Resources Tab

The Local Resources tab, as seen in Figure 3.27, allows you to control whether or not client resources are accessible in your remote session. Remember that when you are working in a session, you are actually working on the remote computer. This means that when you open Windows Explorer, the disk drives you see are the ones that are physically located on the Terminal Services computer, not the ones installed in your local computer. Selections on the Local Resources tab can be used to make your local disk drives, client-attached printers, and similar client side resources available for use within your remote desktop session.

Figure 3.27 The Remote Desktop Connection Local Resources Tab

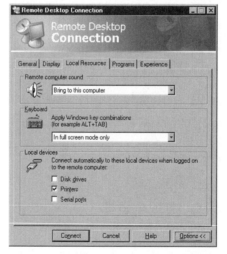

The first setting on the tab deals with whether audio will be used in the session. The default setting, **Bring to this Computer**, allows for any sounds played in the session to be transferred from the Terminal Services computer to the client. Audio transfer can be bandwidth-intensive in a thin client environment, so Microsoft also gives you the opportunity to not transfer this audio. The **Leave at Remote Computer** setting plays the audio in the session on the Terminal Services computer but does not transfer the audio to the client. The **Do not play** setting prevents audio in the session altogether.

> **NOTE**
>
> The ability to transfer audio is one of the important differences between the Remote Desktop Connection client and the older Windows 2000 Terminal Server client.

The next setting on the Local Resources tab relates to whether keyboard shortcut combinations are used by the local operating system or the Remote Desktop window. There are three possible settings for keyboard shortcut combinations:

- **In full screen mode only** In this mode (which is the default), when you use a shortcut combination, the system applies it to the local operating system, unless there is a full screen Remote Desktop window open.

- **On the local computer** This setting applies all shortcut combinations to the local operating system.

- **On the remote computer** This setting applies all shortcut combinations to the Remote Desktop window.

It is important to note that you cannot redirect the **Ctrl + Alt + Del** keyboard combination. This combination only works on the local operating system. An equivalent that can be used in the Remote Desktop window (mentioned earlier in the chapter) is **Ctrl + Alt + End**.

The final section of the tab contains a series of check boxes that can be selected to determine which devices from the client system are automatically made available to the user within the remote desktop session. By default, the following are selected: **Disk drives**, **Printers**, and **Smart cards** (if installed). An additional one, **Serial ports**, is not selected by default. When Disk drives, Serial ports, or Smart cards are selected, you may see a Remote Desktop Connection Security Warning box appear when you begin the connection process. This happens because opening up devices that allow input or may relate to the underlying security of your local machine can be risky. You should consider carefully whether these settings are actually needed, and configure the utility appropriately.

The Programs Tab

By default, when an administrator connects to a Terminal Services session, they will receive a Windows Server 2003 desktop. The selections on the Programs tab, as seen in Figure 3.28, allow them to receive only a specified application instead. If Terminal Services are being used to provide only a single application for each user, this setting can increase security by ensuring that users do not receive a full desktop upon connection. This prevents them from performing tasks on the server other than running the specified application. If the check box next to **Start the following program on connection** is selected, only that application will be available in the session. This option enables the Program path and file name text box. If the path to the application is already contained in one of the Windows path variables on the Terminal Services computer, the administrator can just type the name of the application's executable file in this box. If not, they must include the full path and file name of the executable. The check box also enables the Start in the following folder text box. If the application requires the specification of a working directory, enter it here. This is often the same directory in which the application itself is installed.

Figure 3.28 The Remote Desktop Connection Programs Tab

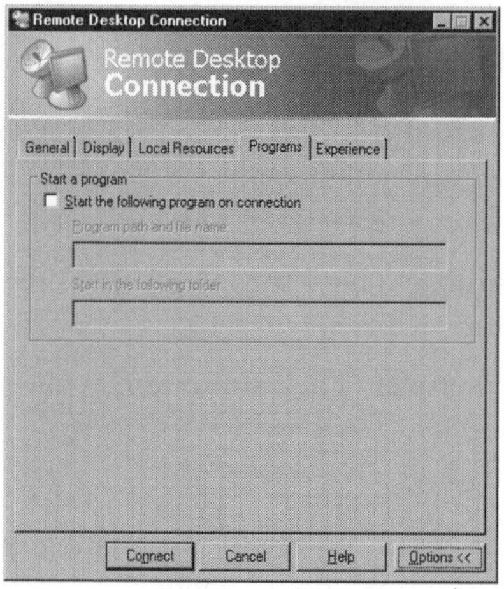

NOTE

Because the Programs tab on the Remote Desktop Connection utility can be configured by the user at the client computer, this is not the best way to control what the user can do on the Terminal Server. Administrators can use Group Policy to configure Terminal Server connection settings and user policies for better security.

After the connection is made with a specified program starting, the traditional methods of ending a session will not always be possible. Most programs have an Exit command on a menu, embedded in a button, or contained in a link. When you have specified an initial program, the Exit command is the equivalent of logging out. To disconnect, simply close the Remote Desktop Connection utility.

TEST DAY TIP

If you are connecting to the console session, the settings on this tab are ignored because a new session is not being created for you when you connect.

The Experience Tab

The Experience tab, as seen in Figure 3.29, allows the administrator to customize several performance features that control the overall feel of their session. All of these settings except Bitmap Caching can generate substantial amounts of additional bandwidth and should be used sparingly in low bandwidth environments.

Figure 3.29 The Remote Desktop Connection Experience Tab

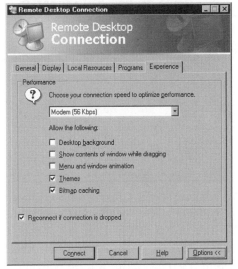

The check boxes on this page include the following:

- **Desktop background** Allows the background image of the desktop (wallpaper) in the remote session to be transferred to and displayed on the client.

- **Show contents of window while dragging** Rapidly refreshes a window so that its contents are visible as the user moves it around the screen in their Remote Desktop window.

- **Menu and window animation** Enables some sophisticated effects, such as the Windows Start menu fading in and out, to be displayed in the Remote Desktop window on the client computer.

- **Themes** Enables any themes used in the remote session to be enabled and transferred to the Remote Desktop window on the client.

- **Bitmap Caching** Enables bitmaps to be stored locally on the client system and called up from cache, rather than being transmitted multiple times across the network. Examples of bitmaps include desktop icons and icons on application toolbars. This setting improves performance, but not all thin client systems have a hard drive or other storage mechanism in which to store the bitmaps.

At the top of the Experience tab, there is a drop-down box that contains several predefined combinations of these settings that Microsoft has optimized for different levels of available bandwidth. Table 3.2 shows which bandwidth level corresponds to which settings:

Table 3.2 Preconfigured Bandwidth Settings

Connection speed selection	Desktop Background	Show contents of window while dragging	Menu and window animation	Themes	Bitmap caching
Modem (28.8Kbs)				X	
Modem (56Kbs) – default				X	X
Broadband (128 Kbps – 1.5 Mbps)		X	X	X	X
LAN (10Mbps or higher)	X	X	X	X	X
Custom				X	X

The Experience tab also contains a check box entitled **Reconnect if connection is dropped,** which is selected by default. The versions of Terminal Services included with Windows Server 2003 and Windows XP SP1 or later include the Automatic Reconnection feature. If dropped packets, network service interruptions, or other network errors cause a Terminal Services connection to disconnect, this feature will automatically attempt to reconnect to the session without requiring the administrator to reenter their logon credentials. By default, there will be a maximum of 20 reconnection attempts, which occur at 5-second intervals. Generally, a notification message will appear, informing the administrator that the connection has been lost and counting down the remaining connection attempts.

Using the Remote Desktops Console

The Remote Desktops console, as seen in Figure 3.30, is another utility that can be used to establish Terminal Services connections to Windows Server 2003 servers and Terminal Servers. The Remote Desktops console can safely be considered the primary Terminal Services client connection tool for administrators. It contains two outstanding features that are not found in the Remote Desktop Connection utility:

- **The Remote Desktops console can be used to connect to multiple Windows Server 2003 servers using Terminal Services** An administrator can configure and save the console with connection information for multiple servers. These connections can be used to establish and switch between sessions. For example, the administrator could configure the snap-in with connections for each of their servers and have a single tool that allows for remote administration of them. With the Remote Desktop Connection utility, they must open a new instance of the utility for each server to which they want to connect simultaneously. With the Remote Desktops console, they can quickly click between multiple running Terminal Service sessions.

- **The Remote Desktops console allows a remote connection to the console session** In the past, the inability to connect to the console session has prevented many administrators from being able to use Terminal Services for remote administration. In Windows 2000, this was not possible and as a result many administrators continued to use other remote administration utilities such as PC Anywhere and VNC. There are a number of server-based applications that send notification pop-up windows only to the console session on a server. Their messages cannot be redirected to another system, the Event Viewer, and so forth. If one or more of these applications is running on a server, the administrator needs to be able to view the actual console session to see these messages. With the Remote Desktop Connection utility and previous versions of Terminal Services and its clients, when an administrator connects to Terminal Services a new session is established. There is simply no way for the administrator to connect to the existing console session and see these messages.

Figure 3.30 The Remote Desktops Console

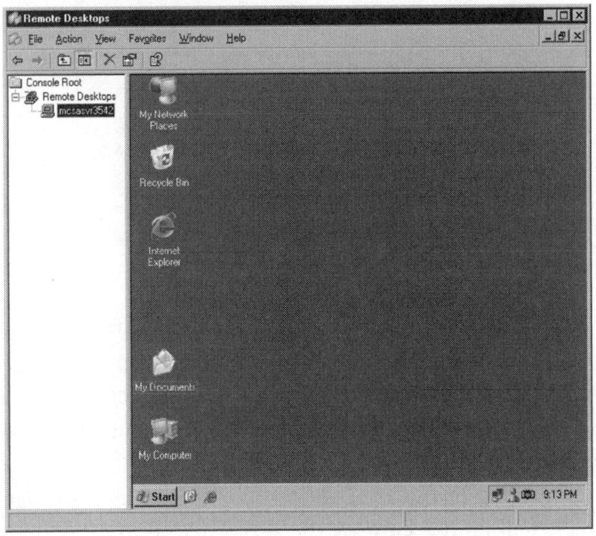

EXAM WARNING

Remember, the Remote Desktop console is designed to allow administrators to connect to multiple Terminal Servers, as well as the console session. The Remote Desktops console is *not* available on Windows XP Professional computers, only on

Windows Server 2003. However, you can use it on your Windows XP Professional computer to manage your servers by installing the Admin Pack (adminpak.msi, located in the i386 folder on the Windows Server 2003 installation CD).

Adding a New Connection

By default, no connections are configured. If you click on the Remote Desktops node at this point, nothing will appear to happen. Begin by right clicking the **Remote Desktops** node in the tree view on the left side of the utility. From the context menu that appears, select **Add new connection**. This will open the Add New Connection dialog box seen in Figure 3.31.

Figure 3.31 Creating a New Remote Desktop Connection

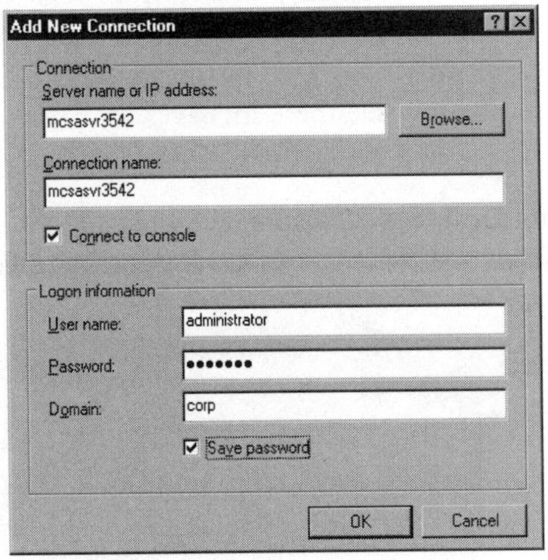

The top portion of the window contains the connection information. In the Server name or IP address text box, enter the fully qualified domain name (FQDN), NetBIOS name, or IP address of the server to which you wish to connect. If you use a FQDN or NetBIOS name, you must make sure that you have the necessary name resolution services running and properly configured on your network.

Next, enter a name to identify the connection in the Connection Name text box, or accept the default (which will be the same as the server name or IP address you entered in the previous field). This name will only be used to identify the connection within the utility.

Finally, leave the **Connect to console** check box selected if you want to connect to the server's console as mentioned earlier. Because this snap-in is intended for remote administration, this is the default setting. If you deselect the check box, Terminal Services will create a new session for you to use when you connect. If you leave it checked, you will be able to view and interact with the console session. Note that after you are authenticated, if someone else is connected to and using the console session (either locally or remotely) when you attempt your connection, you will be notified. The notification message will include the user name, whether the user is connected locally or remotely, and the session state. It is important to realize that only one user can be connected to and using the console session at any time. This means that if someone is using the console, whether remotely or locally, your new connection will force them out.

The lower half of the Add New Connection window allows you to store logon information to be used with the session. For security reasons, it is recommended that you *not* store user names and passwords in utilities such as this one. However, if you wish to do so, enter your logon name in the User name text box, followed by your password in the Password text box. Finally, in the Domain text box, type the name of your domain and select the **Save Password** check box if you wish to have your password information saved. When you are finished entering the information in the Add New Connection dialog box, click the **OK** button to save the connection. The connection should now appear under the Remote Desktops node in the tree view on the left of the MMC window.

Configuring a Saved Remote Connection's Properties

You can configure several properties for saved connections. Right-click the node in the left pane of the MMC that represents the connection you want to modify, and select **Properties** from the context menu. The Properties dialog box opens, as seen in Figure 3.32.

Figure 3.32 Configuring a Remote Desktop Connection

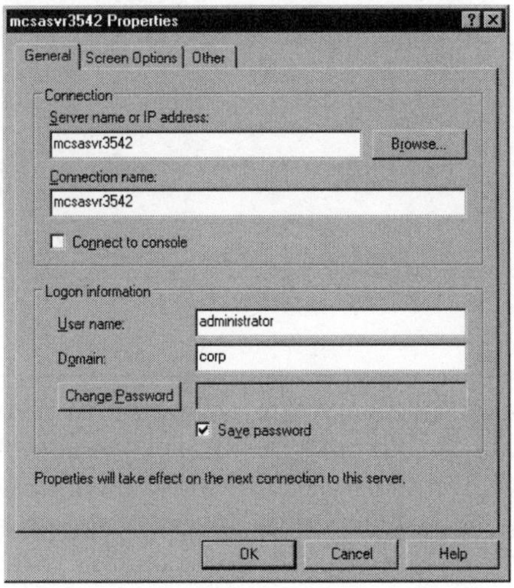

The General tab is essentially the same as the Add New Connection dialog box and contains the same fields for configuration. You can change any of the settings you made when you created the connection.

The Screen Options tab, as seen in Figure 3.33, allows you to choose the size of the remote desktop window that will appear in the snap-in. The desktop will appear in the currently blank space on the right side of the MMC window. You can select the size of the desktop that appears there. The default is for the desktop to fill all of the available space in the right pane of the MMC window. This default setting is called **Expand to fill MMC Result Pane** in Properties window. You can change this by selecting the radio button next to one of the other choices on the tab. The second choice is entitled **Choose desktop size**. When selected, it enables a drop-down box containing two standard resolutions: 640 x 480 and 800 x 600. The final option on the tab is **Enter custom desktop size**. When selected, it enables two text boxes: Width and Height. If the other available options do not provide you with the desired desktop size, you can manually enter the size you want into these text boxes.

Figure 3.33 The Screen Options Tab

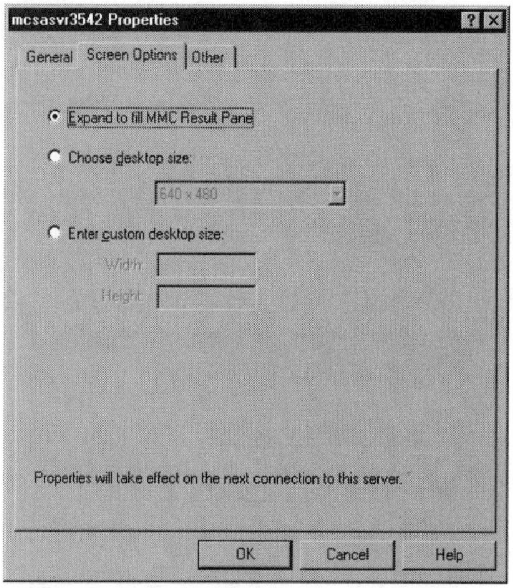

> **NOTE**
>
> It should be noted that the desktop size will be set at connection and will not change. If you start with the Remote Desktops console not maximized, connect to the remote server, and then maximize the console window, the desktop will not expand to fill the right side of the utility. If you change the properties to choose a specific desktop size or custom size while the session is running, you will not see any change. You can right click the connection name, select **Disconnect,** then right-click again and select **Connect** to see the size change.

Switch to the Other tab, as seen in Figure 3.34, to view the final set of options. You will see some settings that are familiar from your experience with the Remote Desktop Connection utility: the ability to start a program and/or redirect local drives.

Figure 3.34 The Other Tab

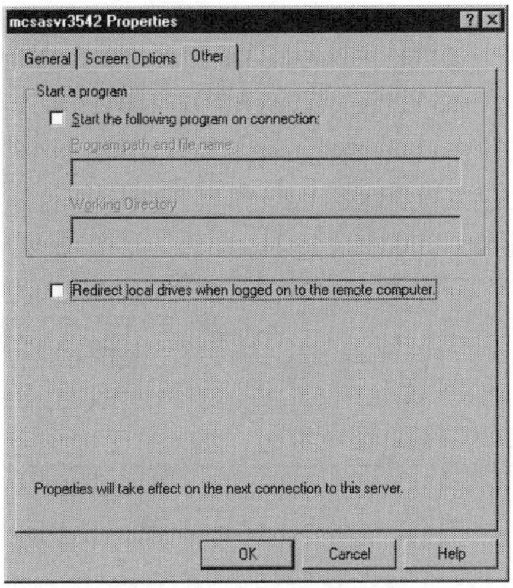

By default, you will receive a Windows Server 2003 desktop when you connect to a Terminal Services session. The first selection on this tab allows you to receive only a specified application instead. If the check box next to **Start the following program on connection** is selected, only that application will be available in the session. Selecting the box enables the Program path and file name text box. If the path to the application is already contained in one of the Windows path variables, you can type the file name of the application's executable file in this box. If not, you must include the full path and file name of the executable. The check box also enables the Working directory text box. If the application requires the specification of a working directory, enter it here. This is often the same directory into which the application itself is installed.

At the bottom of this tab is another check box entitled **Redirect local drives when logged on to the remote computer**. If this check box is selected, the drives on the client will be visible from within the session. This provides you with access to those local drives from Windows Explorer, as well as Open and Save As dialog boxes within applications. If it is not necessary to allow clients access to their local drives, you should leave this option disabled for security purposes. Note that there is no option to redirect local printers, serial ports, and smart cards as with the Remote Desktop Connection utility.

Connecting and Disconnecting

When you have your connection added and configured, connecting is a snap. To connect, simply right-click the node that represents your saved connection in the tree view in the left MMC pane and select **Connect** from the context menu. If you did not save your logon information in the Properties window for the connection, the information you provided was incorrect, or you want to log on with a different account, you will be required to enter a user name and password when the session appears in the right pane of the snap-in.

Disconnecting is just as simple. Right-click the node that represents your saved connection in the tree view in the left pane of the Remote Desktops console, and select **Disconnect** from the context menu. You can also use some of the other methods for logging off and disconnecting mentioned earlier in this chapter.

EXAM WARNING

Only the Remote Desktop MMC snap-in and the *mstsc /console* command can be used to connect to the console session of a Terminal Services computer. However, an administrator actually sitting at the server and using the console session can request help by using the Remote Assistance functionality in Terminal Services. It is important to note that, for security reasons, a console session cannot be viewed using Remote Desktop Control utility.

Using the Remote Desktop Web Connection Utility

The Remote Desktop Web Connection utility is designed to access a Terminal Services session through Microsoft Internet Explorer (MSIE) over TCP/IP. It consists of an ActiveX component that is downloaded to the client browser and sample Web pages with which that the client uses IE to connect. It replaces Windows 2000's Terminal Services Advanced Client (TSAC).

This utility depends on Internet Information Services 6 (IIS 6.0), which is not installed by default. Thus, in order to use the Remote Desktop Web Connection utility, you must begin by installing IIS 6.0 as discussed in Chapter 4.

Installing the Remote Desktop Web Connection Utility

The Remote Desktop Web Connection utility does not install automatically with IIS 6.0. It is not available for installation from the Configure Your Server Wizard, but must be added using the Add or Remove Programs utility from the Control Panel. To install it, perform the steps outlined in Exercise 3.05.

EXERCISE 3.05

INSTALLING THE REMOTE DESKTOP WEB CONNECTION

1. Open the Windows Components Wizard by clicking **Start | Settings | Control Panel | Add/Remove Programs** and then click the

Add/Remove Windows Components icon. After a few moments the Windows Component Wizard will open.

2. In the Components list, scroll down to select the check box next to **Application Server** and click the **Details** button.

3. In the Application Server dialog box that appears, select **Internet Information Services (IIS)** and click the **Details** button.

4. In the Internet Information Services (IIS) dialog box, select **World Wide Web Service** and click on the **Details** button.

5. In the World Wide Web Service dialog box, select the check box next to **Remote Desktop Web Connection**, as seen in Figure 3.35, and click the **OK** button. Also click the **OK** buttons on the Internet Information Services (IIS) and Application Server dialog boxes.

Figure 3.35 Installing the Remote Desktop Web Connection Utility

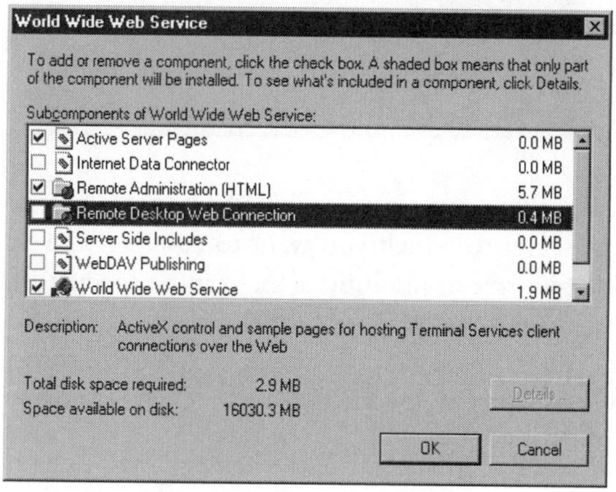

6. This will return you to the main screen of the Windows Components Wizard, where you should click the **Next** button. You may be prompted to supply the Windows Server 2003 installation files.

Using the Remote Desktop Web Connection Utility from a Client

To use the Remote Desktop Web Connection utility, open a version of Internet Explorer 5 or later on a client computer on the network, and connect to the following URL: http://*SERVER*/tsweb. When you do so, the Web page for the utility will appear and automatically detect whether you have the Remote Desktop ActiveX Control installed. If you do not, a Security Warning dialog box will appear, asking if you would like to install it, as seen in Figure 3.36. Click the **Yes** button to proceed with the installation. The control will then be downloaded and installed on your system.

Figure 3.36 Installing the Remote Desktop ActiveX Control

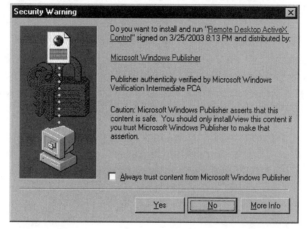

The default Web page contains two options. The Server text box is used to enter the name or IP address of the server to which you want to connect. The Size drop-down box contains a number of different screen resolutions that can be specified for the connection. The default is Full Screen, but other available options include: 640 x 480, 800 x 600, 1024 x 768, 1280 x 1224, and 1600 x 1200. There is also a check box entitled **Send logon information for this connection**. When selected, it adds two additional text boxes to the screen:

- **User name** Can be used to specify the account with which you want to connect
- **Domain** Can be used to specify the domain in which the account is located.

If you do not select this check box, you will be prompted for logon information when you attempt to connect. Once you have made your selections, click on the **Connect** button, as seen in Figure 3.37.

Figure 3.37 The Remote Desktop Web Connection Logon Page

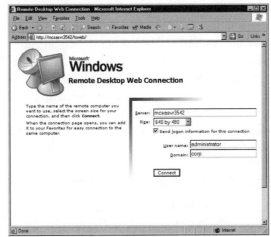

If you select any size setting less than Full Screen, the session will appear in the Web page itself, as shown in Figure 3.38.

Figure 3.38 Viewing a Session that is Embedded in a Browser Window

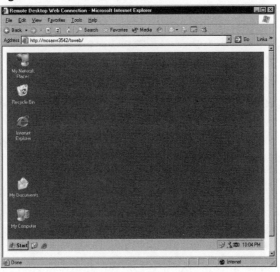

When you scroll through the Web page, the Terminal Services session will move with it. When you log off using the method described earlier in the chapter, the desktop disappears and the Web page displays the connection information and text boxes again. If you select **Full Screen**, a separate connection window is launched. The Web page changes to display a large blank box with text at the bottom of the page that indicates you are connected. The Remote Desktop can be minimized, sized, disconnected from, and logged off, in all of the ways mentioned earlier in the chapter.

Regardless of how you connect, a full session is established, which allows you to interact with a complete Windows Server 2003 desktop and all applications, as with the other clients. An important advantage of the Web client is that it does not require any client software to be installed. The ActiveX control that downloads to the browser upon connection to the default Web page is the only client software needed. In other words, if you are away from the computer you normally use for administration, this client can be used to administer one of your servers in an emergency from anywhere in the world. All that is needed on the client system is IE 5 or later.

Configuring & Implementing...

Configuring IE for Use with the Remote Desktop Web Connection utility

IE 6.0 is installed by default on a Windows Server 2003 system. During the installation, a special security configuration is applied to it that places significant restrictions on its use. The Internet Explorer Enhanced Security Configuration feature can significantly affect the way in which Web sites are displayed in the browser. Among other things, it prevents the download and installation of ActiveX components.

Because the Remote Desktop Web Connection utility relies on an ActiveX control, by default you cannot use the browser on a Windows Server 2003 server to establish a Terminal Services session. You can configure the Enhanced Security Configuration so it will not apply to administrators. This can be accomplished by performing the following steps:

1. Click **Start | Settings | Control Panel | Add/Remove Programs**.

2. Click the **Add/Remove Windows Components** button on the left side of the window.

3. In the Windows Component Wizard dialog box, scroll down and select **Internet Explorer Enhanced Security Configuration**.

4. Click on the **Details** button.

5. In the Internet Explorer Enhanced Security Configuration dialog box, clear the check box next to **For administrator groups** and click the **OK** button. It may take a few moments for the configuration changes to be made.

6. Click the **Next** button, followed by the **Finish** button on the final page of the wizard.

7. Close Add or Remove Programs.

Using Web Interface for Remote Administration

If you need to manage your servers from home or from another office, one option is to use a standard Web browser to administer your servers using the remote administration component of Windows Server 2003. You must configure your server first, but after you have done this, you can simply point the browser to your server's IP address and administer it from anywhere in the world. To access the server over the Internet, the following conditions must be met:

- The Remote Administration (Hypertext Markup Language [HTML]) component must be installed on the server. It is not installed by default with the exception of Windows Server 2003 Web Edition.

- Port 8098 on the server must be accessible through your Internet connection.

- Your server must have a valid external IP address.

If you want to access your servers only over your company network, an external IP address is not necessary, but you must still be able to communicate with port 8098 on the server. Microsoft recommends that the browser you use for remote administration be IE version 6.0 or later.

NOTE

Remote administration over the Web is not available for servers that are domain controllers.

To access your server over the Web, browse to https://*servername*:8098. You must use a secure connection. The :8098 in the URL directs the browser to connect to port 8098 on the server instead of the default port 80. You can change your server to work on a different port in IIS Manager. After you have connected to the server, you will see the Welcome page, as seen in Figure 3.39.

Through this Web site, you can carry out the more common administration tasks, such as configuring Web sites, managing network settings, and administering local user accounts. In Exercise 3.06, you will install Remote Administration (HTML) on a server.

Figure 3.39 Welcome Page for Server Web Administration

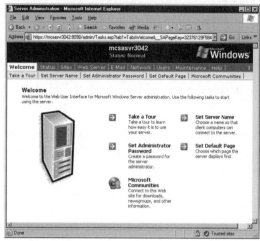

EXERCISE 3.06

INSTALL REMOTE ADMINISTRATION (HTML)

1. Open the Windows Components Wizard by clicking **Start | Settings | Control Panel | Add or Remove Programs** and then click the **Add/Remove Windows Components** icon. After a few moments the Windows Component Wizard will open.

2. In the Components list, scroll down to select the check box next to **Application Server** and click the **Details button**.

3. In the Application Server dialog box that appears, select **Internet Information Services (IIS)** and click the **Details** button.

4. In the Internet Information Services (IIS) dialog box, select **World Wide Web Service** and click on the **Details** button.

5. In the World Wide Web Service dialog box, select the check box next to **Remote Administration (HTML)**, as seen in Figure 3.40, and click the **OK** button. Also click the **OK** buttons in the Internet Information Services (IIS) and Application Server dialog boxes.

Figure 3.40 Installing the Remote Administration (HTML) Option

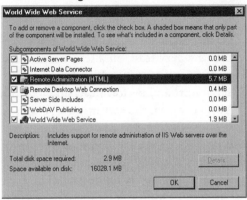

6. This will return you to the main screen of the Windows Components Wizard, where you should click the **Next** button. You may be prompted to supply the Windows Server 2003 installation files.

7. You can access the Remote Administration (HTML) Web page by opening your Web browser and typing **https://servername:8098**, where *servername* is the name of your server. Alternatively, you can use the Web Interface for Remote Administration option within the Administrative Tools folder.

Using Emergency Management Services

EXAM
70-292
OBJECTIVE
3.2.3

Emergency Management Services (EMS) is a new feature in Windows Server 2003 that enables the administrator to remotely manage a server when normal network connectivity has failed. Under normal conditions, the administrator uses the tools described in this and other chapters to manage their server either by being physically present at the server or over the network. However, what happens if the network crashes or the server does not boot properly?

Providing the server has the appropriate hardware and firmware, the administrator can remotely manage it without the presence of a local keyboard, mouse, or display. This is called out-of-band or "headless" operation. The key aim of out-of-band management is to get a server that is not working properly back to a normal operating state.

A number of situations might require an administrator to resort to out-of-band management:

- The server has stopped responding to normal network management commands.
- The network card in the server has failed.

- The server has not booted properly.
- The server has been shut down and you need to bring it up again.

The extent to which an administrator can use out-of-band management depends on the hardware of their server. At the very least, on a server with Windows Server 2003, a serial port, and EMS enabled, they can connect a VT100-type terminal or a computer with a terminal emulator to the serial port and perform certain tasks using the Special Administration Console (SAC). However, the server must be up and running to be able to manage it in this way.

If an administrator needs to be able to manage the server remotely when it has crashed or even been switched off, they need special hardware and firmware on the motherboard that provide features such as firmware console redirection. This means that they can monitor the server via the serial port right from the moment it starts up and even check out basic input/output system (BIOS) settings. EMS is not enabled by default, but can be enabled during an installation, an upgrade, or after setup has been completed.

New & Noteworthy...

Managing Several Windows Server 2003 Computers with EMS

EMS provides a useful service for managing your servers in an emergency situation. But what if you have a large number of computers running Windows Server 2003 in a computer room? What is the best way of hooking to EMS on all of them without having an array of terminals? A tidy way of providing access is to use a *terminal concentrator* (sometimes called a Terminal Server, not to be confused with Terminal Services).

A terminal concentrator has several serial ports (16 is a common number) and a network connection. You use a program like Telnet to connect to the terminal concentrator over the network, and then choose a particular port on the concentrator to connect to the device attached to that port. Connect each of the serial ports on the servers to the serial ports on the terminal concentrator and you can then connect to EMS over the network. Of course, if the terminal concentrator fails, then you will not be able to connect to any of the servers.

Exercise 3.07 outlines the process by which you can use Emergency Management Services. This exercise requires two computers—one with Windows Server 2003 and the other with any operating system and a terminal emulator—and a special serial cable with two female ends and a crossover, sometimes called a null-modem cable. Alternatively, you can use a single computer and a dumb terminal that connects to the serial port of the server computer.

EXERCISE 3.07

CONNECTING TO EMS

1. Connect the serial cable between the two computers using COM1 on both computers.

2. On the server to be managed, open a command window and type the command **bootcfg /ems on /id 1 /port COM1**. This enables EMS on serial port COM1. The *id* option specifies the operating system in the boot.ini list on which EMS is to be enabled. If you have more than one operating system on your computer, be sure to adjust the value of *id* accordingly.

3. On the second computer, start Hyperterminal or any other terminal emulator and connect to COM1 using a baud rate of 9600. You will not see anything in the terminal window yet.

4. Reboot the server computer. Watch the terminal window as the server computer restarts. You should see the normal server-starting messages, including the operating system loader where you can choose which operating system to boot. At this stage, you can interact with the boot process through the terminal window.

5. When the computer has finished booting, the SAC prompt appears, as shown in Figure 3.41.

Figure 3.41 The SAC

6. Type **cmd** to start a command-prompt channel.

7. To switch to the command-prompt channel type **ch si 1** and press the **spacebar** to view the channel.

8. Enter your logon name, domain, and password. Use the name of the computer for the domain if your computer is not part of a domain.

9. After you have successfully authenticated, you get the normal command prompt where you can navigate the directory tree and run commands.

Summary of Exam Objectives

Windows Server 2003 provides a wide range of management tools; some are graphical and others are command-line based. There are also many wizards to help less-experienced administrators through particular tasks.

Many of the graphical tools are built using the MMC and snap-ins. You can use snap-ins to configure your own customized administrative tools. It is important to realize that most tools (graphical and command-line) work over the network so that you can manage remote servers from your computer.

When you need to manage a server remotely, you can choose from a variety of tools, including a browser (for remote administration), Remote Desktop connection (using Terminal Services), snap-ins for the MMC, and the Administration Tools Pack. Some tasks, such as adding a user, can be carried out using any of the remote administration tools, whereas others require you to use a specific tool. End-users can use Remote Assistance to enable others access to their desktop to guide them through resolving a problem or show them how to do something.

Terminal Services contains two components for remote administration. The first, Remote Desktop for Administration, allows up to two administrators to simultaneously connect remotely to the server. Each receives their own session with a separate desktop. Using this mode, an administrator can also connect to the console session of the server. This option was not available in Windows 2000 and it allows the administrator to view the server's main desktop, just as if sitting at its keyboard. The second mode, Remote Assistance, allows a user, called the Novice, to request assistance from someone more knowledgeable, called the Expert. An invitation is sent from the Novice to the Expert, which enables the Expert to connect to and view the actual desktop of the Novice's computer. Only one of the Remote Assistance sessions can exist on a computer at any given time. The Novice can also allow the Expert to have cursor and keyboard input within the Novice's session. Both the Remote Desktop for Administration and Remote Access components must be enabled manually on the server.

There are three basic client tools that can be used to establish a Terminal Services connection. The Remote Desktop Connection utility is the primary tool designed for end users. It allows for connection to a single Terminal Server per instance of the utility and has a wide range of configuration options. The Remote Desktops MMC snap-in allows for connections to multiple Terminal Services computers within the same interface, and also allows you to connect to the console session. It is primarily designed for administrators. The Remote Desktop Web Connection utility is an IIS component that is installed from Add or Remove Programs in the Control Panel. IIS 6.0 must be installed on the Terminal Server to enable Wweb connections. It uses a client side ActiveX control as the client. When used in full screen mode, it launches a session window independent of the browser window. The Web client requires MSIE 5.0 or later, with security settings configured to allow ActiveX controls to be downloaded and installed.

Sometimes you will not be able to connect to a server over the network at all or it might have crashed completely. If the server is physically distant from you, consider using EMS. Provided that you have the appropriate hardware, you can establish access to the server even when the operating system is not running. Even with a server with no special hardware, you can still use EMS via the serial port to remotely manage the server using the SAC, but this will work only while the operating system is running.

Exam Objectives Fast Track

Recognizing Types of Management Tools

☑ Windows Server 2003 provides administrators with a variety of management tools including wizards, graphical administration tools, and command-line utilities.

☑ Most graphical administration tools can be found as pre-configured management consoles accessible via **Start | Programs | Administrative Tools**.

☑ Many graphical management tools are built using the MMC and snap-ins.

☑ You can create your own customized management tools by using snap-ins provided by the operating system or third-party products.

Using Terminal Services Components for Remote Administration

☑ Remote Desktop for Administration allows up to two administrators to remotely connect to the server simultaneously, each in their own session, to perform administrative tasks.

☑ Remote Assistance allows a user, called the Novice, to request help from someone more knowledgeable, called the Expert. The Expert is able to view and interact with the Novice's desktop remotely if permission is granted by the Novice.

☑ Though installed with the operating system, both Remote Desktop for Administration and Remote Assistance must be enabled manually after installation before they can be used.

Using Terminal Services Client Tools

☑ The Remote Desktop Connection utility is the primary Terminal Services client for end users. It comes with Windows Server 2003 and Windows XP, and can be installed on Windows 9x, NT, and 2000 computers.

☑ The Remote Desktop MMC snap-in is designed for administrators. It allows for connections to multiple servers within a single interface, as well as console session connections.

☑ The console session is the server's primary desktop, the one you would see if you were actually sitting at its physical keyboard.

☑ Only one administrator can be logged on to the console session at any given time. If another administrator attempts to log on, the current administrator will be logged off unless Group Policy prevents this.

☑ The Remote Desktop Web Connection utility can be used from client machines that do not have one of the other Terminal Services clients installed. It requires and is a subcomponent of IIS 6.0. When a user connects, an Active X control is downloaded to their system to serve as the local Terminal Services client. This utility is only supported by MSIE 5.0 and higher.

☑ End-users can use Remote Assistance to invite another person to view or take control of their desktops.

☑ The Web Interface for Remote Administration enables you to manage a server from anywhere in the world using a Web browser. However, the range of administration tasks is limited.

☑ Remote Desktop for Administration enables you to connect to a Windows 2000 Server or a Windows Server 2003 desktop via Terminal Services and act as if you were at the server. This enables you to perform any task on the server.

☑ You can install the Administration Tools Pack on a Windows XP computer to enable you to remotely manage servers.

☑ WMI provides a programming interface for developers to design management tools.

☑ Computer Management (a pre-configured MMC) and other MMC snap-ins provide local and remote management capability.

Using EMS

☑ EMS provides a means for managing a server even when network connectivity has failed.

☑ To manage a server even when the operating system is not running, special hardware is required.

☑ EMS provides a SAC that runs on the serial port and enables remote access via a serial cable or modem. The SAC runs when the operating system is running.

☑ EMS must be installed before it can be used.

Exam Objectives
Frequently Asked Questions

The following Frequently Asked Questions, answered by the authors of this book, are designed to both measure your understanding of the Exam Objectives presented in this chapter, and to assist you with real-life implementation of these concepts. You will also gain access to thousands of other FAQs at ITFAQnet.com.

Q: What type of administrative tools does Windows Server 2003 provide?

A: You can work with graphical tools, command-line utilities, or wizards.

Q: Which type of remote management tool would be most appropriate if you needed to manage your server from a customer's office?

A: The Web Interface for Remote Administration is generally best, assuming that your customer has Internet access.

Q: What management feature can users use to request help from someone else?

A: Computers running Windows XP or later include the Remote Assistance feature. This enables a user to send an invitation to another person to remotely view or take control of the user's desktop and provide assistance. Remote Assistance is enabled by default, but you can turn it off via the **Control Panel | System | Remote** tab.

Q: Can you manage Windows Server 2003 computers from your desktop computer?

A: Yes. There are several methods: Remote Desktop, Web Interface, Administration Tools Pack, and MMCs.

Q: What is the difference between Remote Desktop for Administration and the Terminal Server role?

A: Both are designed to allow remote Terminal Services connections. However, the Terminal Server role contains additional multi-user code that keeps user session and application settings separate. This allows for many users to connect using Terminal Services without having problems with the applications they are using. By default, Terminal Services allows only two connections for remote administration. When the Terminal Server role is installed, an unlimited number of users can connect simultaneously.

Q: How can I connect to, view, and interact with the console session using Terminal Services?

A: The Remote Desktop MMC snap-in is designed for administrator use. It allows for connection to multiple Terminal Services computers, in addition to defaulting to console session access. You can also connect to the console from the command-line by typing **mstsc /console**.

Q: Is Remote Assistance a part of Terminal Services or a separate component?

A: Like Remote Desktop for Administration, Remote Assistance exists in both Windows XP and Windows Server 2003 (Remote Desktop is only included in XP Professional, not XP Home, but Remote Assistance comes with both editions of XP). It is an additional service that uses the Terminal Services service to provide its core capabilities.

Q: There seem to be a number of different utilities that can be used to connect to Terminal Services and establish a session. Which one is the primary client tool for end users?

A: The Remote Desktop Connection utility is the primary end user connection tool. It comes pre-installed with Windows XP and Server 2003 and can be installed on Windows 9x, NT, and 2000 computers. It can be used to save connection settings to a file so that reconfiguration is not necessary when connecting to different servers. It also has a wide range of options that allow for optimization over almost any bandwidth. It includes several improvements over the Windows 2000 Terminal Services client, including the ability to redirect audio from the server to the client.

Q: I have enabled Remote Desktop connections. Why are administrators the only ones who can log on?

A: By default, only administrators can establish remote administration sessions. This makes sense when you think about it, since they are most likely to be the ones that will be connecting to the server remotely to do the work. However, if you need to allow others to connect, you can add them to the Remote Desktop Users group. This differs from Windows 2000 Terminal Services in remote administration mode, where there was no way to allow non-administrative users to connect.

Q: What does EMS provide?

A: The capability to manage a server, even when there is no network connectivity and sometimes even when the operating system has crashed (if you have the proper server hardware).

Q: What is the name of the management tool that EMS provides over the serial port?

A: SAC, the Special Administration Console. This enables you to run command-line programs in a terminal emulator.

Q: What is out-of-band management?

A: Out-of-band management refers to using a different set of tools from the standard ones; including tools that do not run over the network.

Self Test

A Quick Answer Key follows the Self Test questions. For complete questions, answers, and explanations to the Self Test questions in this chapter as well as the other chapters in this book, see the Self Test Appendix.

Recognizing Types of Management Tools

1. You are logged on to the server using an ordinary user account (i.e., without administrator privileges). You need to add several new printers on the server and you decided to use the prncnfg command-line utility. How do you do this without logging off?

   A. Select **Start | Run**, and then type **runas /user:administrator cmd**. In the command window run the **prncnfg** command.

   B. Select **Start | Programs | Administrative Tools | Prncnfg**, and then right-click and select **Run as**.

   C. Select **Start | Settings | Command**. In the command window type **runas /user:administrator cmd** and run the **prncnfg** command in the new command window that appears.

   D. Select **Start | Run** and then type **cmd**. In the command window run the **prncnfg** command.

2. You are creating a new MMC console for use by your help desk team that will be used to perform low level administrative functions in your network. You want the help desk team to be able to use the custom console, but not allow them to create any new windows or change the configuration of the console. What mode should you save this custom console in?

   A. Author mode

   B. User mode – full access

   C. User mode – limited access, multiple windows

   D. User mode – limited access, single window

Using Terminal Services
Components for Remote Administration

3. One of your users is having problems getting a productivity application to work correctly. You suspect that he is performing the steps involved in using the application incorrectly, but the application interface is complex and it is difficult for you to explain over the phone what he needs to do. The user is running Windows XP, and you want to connect to his PC and show him how to perform the task in question so that he can actually see you go through the steps. How would you arrange to do this?

   A. Send the user a Remote Assistance Request.

   B. Get the user to send a Remote Assistance Invitation.

   C. Connect to the user's PC using Remote Desktop.

   D. Connect to the user's PC using the Web Interface for Remote Administration.

4. You are at a branch office of your company assisting a user on her PC. While assisting the user, you receive a call that requires you to alter a DNS setting on the server back at the main office. The user has many applications open and you would prefer to not have to log her out if at all possible. What would be the best way to connect to the server?

   A. Install the Windows Administration Tool Pack on the user's PC.

   B. Connect to the server using the Web Interface for Administration.

   C. Use Computer Management on the PC and connect to the server.

   D. Connect to the server using Remote Desktop for Administration.

5. You are the network administrator for Joe's Crab Shack. While at a meeting in Redmond, Washington, you are informed that one of your newly installed Windows Server 2003 DNS servers has stopped performing name resolution. Your CEO has asked you to make a Remote Desktop connection to the server via your virtual private network (VPN) connection to the network. After you have connected to your internal network via VPN, you attempt to create a Remote Desktop connection to the server and cannot. The DNS server is located on the same IP subnet as the VPN server. What is the most likely reason for this problem?

   A. TCP port 3389 is being blocked at your firewall.

   B. Remote Desktop is not enabled on the server.

   C. You do not posses the required credentials.

   D. Your Internet connection does not support the RDP 5.1 protocol.

6. You have just installed Windows Server 2003 on one of your servers and would like to set up Remote Desktop for Administration so that you can connect to it remotely. Which of the following must you do? (Select all that apply.)

   A. Open the System properties in Control Panel

   B. On the Remote tab and select the check box next to **Turn on Remote Assistance and allow invitations to be sent from this computer**

   C. On the Remote tab, select the check box next to **Allow users to connect remotely to your computer**

   D. Do nothing

7. You are the network administrator for Joe's Crab Shack. While at a meeting in Redmond, Washington, you are informed that one of your Windows Server 2003 DHCP servers is not leasing any more DHCP leases to clients. Your assistant administrator has verified that there are plenty of unused leases in the current DHCP scope, but is unable to determine the cause of the problem. Company policy prohibits the use of any Instant Messaging clients within your internal network. How can your assistant get Remote Assistance from you to help troubleshoot the DHCP server?

   A. Use an e-mail-based request.

   B. Use MSN Messenger to make the request.

   C. Use Emergency Management Services to make the request.

   D. Use the Recovery Console to make the request.

8. No matter how hard you try, you just cannot seem to figure out how to access your e-mail using the new application that was installed over the weekend. You decide to use the Remote Assistance feature to ask an administrator to walk you through the process. Which of the following are valid methods that you can use to request assistance? (Select all that apply.)

   A. E-mail an administrator

   B. Use ICQ to contact an administrator

   C. Use Windows messaging to contact an administrator

   D. Save the request to a file and transfer it to an administrator

9. You are attempting to initiate a Remote Desktop for Administration session with one of your Windows Server 2003 servers over the Internet. The server has a publicly accessible IP address but it is located behind an external firewall and a screening router. You can ping the server and establish Telnet session to the server. You have verified with onsite personnel that Remote Desktop is enabled for this server and that your user account is allowed to make connections. What is the most likely reason for the inability to make the Remote Desktop for Administration connection?

A. Port 3389 is being blocked

B. Port 8088 is being blocked

C. IIS 6.0 is not installed

D. ASP.NET is not enabled on the server

10. You are configuring one of your Windows Server 2003 computers to allow Remote Desktop for Administration connections to it. What group do you need to add user accounts to in order to allow those users to create Remote Desktop for Administration connections?

A. Network Configuration Operators

B. Remote Desktop Users

C. Help Services Group

D. Telnet Clients

11. You are assisting a user with a configuration issue on his computer using a Remote Assistance session. You have tried unsuccessfully to take control of the user's computer. What possible reasons are there to explain why you have not been able to take control? (Select two correct answers.)

A. The Novice is not allowing you to take control of his computer.

B. A firewall is in place blocking the request.

C. The remote computer is not configured to allow it to be controlled remotely.

D. Your computer is not configured to allow it to initiate remote control sessions.

12. You have sent an e-mail request for Remote Assistance to your support desk but the request expired before they could answer it and assist you with your problem. Company policy only allows members of the support desk to create Remote Assistance connections. You want to allow the request to be answered. What is the easiest way to go about this?

A. Create a new request and send it to the support desk.

B. Delete the expired request, causing it to be recreated anew.

C. Resend the expired request to the support desk.

D. Initiate the Remote Assistance connection yourself.

13. You need to connect to your server's console remotely. Which graphical terminal services utility can you use to accomplish this?

A. The Remote Desktop Connection tool

B. The Remote Desktops console

    C. The Remote Desktop Connection Web utility

    D. The Terminal Services Client Configuration Manager utility

14. You are the network administrator for Joe's Crab Shack. You are creating the company policy for the usage of Remote Desktop for Administration. When discussing the differences between disconnecting and logging off from an RDA session, which of the following two statements are correct? (Select two correct answers.)

    A. Disconnected sessions do not remain on the server.

    B. Disconnected sessions remain on the server, often consuming resources.

    C. Logged off sessions do not remain on the server.

    D. Logged off sessions remain on the server, often consuming resources.

Using EMS

15. You have a computer that has Windows Server 2003 and Windows XP Professional installed on it. You have connected a terminal to the serial port of the computer so that you can manage it remotely using EMS. You reboot the server and see the list of available operating systems on the terminal. You select Windows XP Professional from the boot list and then find that there is no further response on the terminal. What has happened?

    A. The computer crashed while booting into Windows XP Professional.

    B. EMS was enabled on the wrong serial port in the Windows XP Professional installation.

    C. EMS was not enabled in the Windows XP Professional installation.

    D. Windows XP Professional does not support EMS.

Self Test Quick Answer Key

For complete questions, answers, and explanations to the Self Test questions in this chapter as well as the other chapters in this book, see the Self Test Appendix.

1. **A**
2. **D**
3. **B**
4. **D**
5. **B**
6. **A, C**
7. **A**
8. **A, C, D**

9. **A**
10. **B**
11. **A, C**
12. **C**
13. **B**
14. **B, C**
15. **D**

Chapter 4

MCSA/MCSE 70-292

Managing and Maintaining Web Servers

Exam Objectives in this Chapter:

3.3   Manage a Web server

3.3.1   Manage Internet Information Services (IIS)

3.3.2   Manage security for IIS

☑   Summary of Exam Objectives

☑   Exam Objectives Fast Track

☑   Exam Objectives Frequently Asked Questions

☑   Self Test

☑   Self Test Quick Answer Key

Introduction

Microsoft's Internet Information Services (IIS) is one of the most popular Web servers used on the Internet and in Intranets throughout the world. Windows Server 2003 includes the latest version, IIS 6.0. There have been changes, additions, and improvements to the software in the areas of core functionality and services, administration, security, and performance. IIS 6.0 has been redesigned to provide better reliability and more flexibility in configuring application environments.

In the past, Web servers have been a common vulnerability for hackers. It has been common for servers to be running rogue Web services without the knowledge of administrators. Thus, for security reasons, IIS 6.0 is not installed by default on Windows Server 2003 servers, with the exception of the Web Server Edition. When it is installed, it is initially configured in a high security mode.

Web servers are common targets due to their exposure to those outside the local network; therefore security is a priority in IIS 6.0. Consequently, a number of important Web services features—which worked automatically in previous versions—now need

to be explicitly enabled before they will work. This new focus on security means network administrators need to familiarize themselves with these changes in order to provide the Web server services needed on their networks.

This chapter examines the installation and configuration process for IIS 6.0 and introduces new security features, reliability features, and other new features. This chapter also shows how to use the Web Server Security Lockdown Wizard and how to manage security issues for Web servers. Lastly, this chapter discusses some common troubleshooting issues that may arise.

What is New in IIS 6.0?

Many of the new features in IIS 6.0 were designed to address technical and architectural issues found in IIS 5.0. The new features can be divided into several broad categories. The most important categories are security and reliability. Microsoft has invested a large number of resources on its new Trustworthy Computing initiative. IIS 6.0 is one of the first products to be developed under this security-focused strategy. Performance is also enhanced by key architectural modifications to the IIS 6.0 object model. The following sections investigate these changes in detail.

New Security Features

IIS 5.0 and earlier versions were constantly patched up by hot fixes from Microsoft. IIS was once considered one of the main security holes in the Windows platform, which was a major deterrent to using IIS as a commercial Web server. IIS 6.0 comes with an impressive list of new security features designed to win back commercial users. IIS 6.0 includes the following new security features:

- Advanced Digest authentication

- Server-Gated Cryptography

- Selectable Cryptographic Service Provider

- Configurable Worker Process Identity

- Default lockdown status

- New authorization framework

Advanced Digest Authentication

Advanced Digest authentication is an extension of *Digest security*. Digest security uses Message Digest 5 (MD5) hashing to encrypt user credentials such as the user name, password, and user role.

What is the purpose of MD5 hashing? Basic authentication sends the user name and password details over the network medium in base64 encoded format. These details can be easily "sniffed" (captured with a protocol analyzer) and decoded by an intruder, who can then use the credentials for nefarious purposes. The MD5 hash enhances security by applying more sophisticated and more difficult-to-crack cipher algorithms to deter these intruders. An MD5 hash is made up of binary data consisting of the user name, password, and *realm*. The realm is the name of the domain that authenticates the user. This means that Digest security is more secure than Basic authentication. These security features are explained in more detail in the "Managing IIS Security" section of this chapter.

⚠ EXAM WARNING

An MD5 hash is embedded into a Hyper Text Transfer Protocol (HTTP) 1.1 header, which is only supported by HTTP 1.1-enabled browsers. Digest or Advanced Digest authentication mechanisms cannot be enabled if the target browsers do not support HTTP 1.1. Internet Explorer 5.0 and above versions support HTTP 1.1, as well as recent versions of Netscape, Opera, Mozilla, and other popular browsers.

Advanced Digest authentication takes the Digest authentication model a bit further by storing the user credentials on a domain controller as an MD5 hash. The Active Directory database on the domain controller is used to store the user credentials. Thus, intruders need to get access to the Active Directory in order to steal the credentials. This adds another layer of security to protect access to Windows Server 2003 Web sites, and the network administrator does not need to modify the application code to accommodate this security feature.

TEST DAY TIP

Both Digest and Advanced Digest authentication only work on Web Distributed Authoring and Versioning (WebDAV)-enabled directories. WebDAV is a file sharing protocol commonly used in Windows Internet-related applications. WebDAV was previously referred to as *Web Folders*. It is a secure file transfer protocol over intranets and the Internet. Network administrators can download, upload, and manage files on remote computers across the Internet and intranets using WebDAV.

Server-Gated Cryptography

Communication between an IIS Web server and the Web client is completed using HTTP. These HTTP network transmissions can be easily compromised due to their text-based messaging formats. Therefore, HTTP calls must be encrypted between the client and the server. Secure Sockets Layer (SSL) and Transport Layer Security (TLS) are the most common encryption mechanisms used for Web sites. SSL and TLS enable a secure communication by encrypting the communication channel with a cipher algorithm. TLS is the later version of the SSL protocol and is more flexible because it can be used with any application layer protocol.

IIS 5.0 and earlier versions included SSL/TLS for secure communication between the Web client and the server. Server-Gated Cryptography (SGC) is an extension of SSL/TLS, which uses a strong 128-bit encryption algorithm to encode data. SGC does not require an application to run on the client machine, but does need a valid certificate at the client Web browser, which can be encoded and decoded. A special SGC certificate is needed to enable the SGC support built into IIS 6.0. Network administrators can obtain a certificate by contacting a certificate authority (CA) internally to the network or from a trusted third party such as VeriSign. Once the certificate has been acquired, it can be added to IIS like any other certificate. The "Configure Authentication Settings" section of this chapter discusses this in more detail. IIS 6.0 supports both 40-bit and 128-bit encryption sessions. This means that old 40-bit SGC certificates are still valid in IIS 6.0. SGC is commonly used to protect data for financial sector applications, such as banking and financial institutions.

EXAM WARNING

If you try to open an existing 40-bit SGC certificate, you may get a "The certificate has failed to verify for all of its intended purposes" warning. These certificates are targeted to Windows 2000 servers. Thus, you can have a valid certificate and can be misled by this warning. Windows 2000 only supports 40-bit encryption and Windows Server 2003 supports both 40-bit and 128-bit encryption.

Selectable Cryptographic Service Provider

SSL/TLS offers a secure environment in which to exchange data. The downside is performance—SSL/TLS is very CPU-intensive. IIS 6.0 comes with a new feature called *Selectable Cryptographic Service Provider (CSP)* that allows the user select from an optimized list of cryptography providers. A cryptographic service provider will provide an interface to encrypt communication between the server and the client. A CSP is not specific to IIS and can be used to handle cryptography and certificate management for all Windows applications.

Microsoft implements two default security providers: the *Microsoft DH SChannel Cryptographic provider* and the *Microsoft RSA SChannel Cryptographic provider*. The Microsoft implementations are optimized for IIS 6.0 to provide faster communication, and the private keys are stored in the Registry. The Microsoft Cryptographic API (Crypto API) contains an identical interface for all providers that enable developers to switch between providers without modifying the code. Each provider creates a public and a private key to enable data communication. The private key is stored on hardware devices (such as PCI cards, smart cards, and so forth) or in the Registry. The public CSP keys can also be stored in the Registry. The CSP can be configured using the IIS Certificate Wizard (discussed in Exercise 4.12).

Configurable Worker Process Identity

One of the most serious problems with previous IIS versions was the instability of the World Wide Web (WWW) Publishing Service. The failure of this service could result in the shutdown of a machine. IIS 6.0 runs each Web site in an isolated process environment called a *worker process*. If a Web site malfunctions, the problem is limited to its process environment and therefore does not cause the entire server to fail.

IIS 5.0 did not implement a worker process model, but instead had an isolated environment. IIS 6.0 can also run an IIS 5.0 isolated environment, if desired. With IIS 6.0, the network administrator can choose between a worker process model and an IIS 5.0 isolation model. The administrator can click the **Run WWW service in IIS 5.0 isolation mode** option box to run IIS in IIS 5.0 isolation mode. IIS will run in worker process model if this option is not selected. IIS can only run at one mode at a time; it is not possible to run worker process model Web sites and IIS 5.0 isolation mode Web sites simultaneously.

The worker process can be run with a lower permission level than the system account. The worker process shuts down the application if the IIS server is targeted with malicious code. IIS 6.0, which by default is run by the local system account, is not affected since the worker process can be configured to run under a less privileged account.

Default Lockdown Status

The default installation of IIS 6.0 results in a *lightweight* Web server. The only default feature available is the access to static content. This is to deter malicious access by intruders. This restricted functionality is referred to as *default locked down status*. This feature forces system administrators to manually enable and disable the necessary application features, thus preventing many of the attacks that have plagued IIS 5.0 implementations in the past.

New Authorization Framework

Authorization refers to the concept of confirming a user's access for a given resource. *Authentication* refers to obtaining access to the resource. When a user is authenticated, the system administrator must make sure that they are authorized to perform any tasks on the resource—this is the basis of authorization. There are two types of ASP.NET authorization options available for IIS 6.0:

- **File Authorization** The *FileAuthorizationModule* class is responsible for file authorization on Windows Server 2003. The module is activated by enabling **Windows Authentication** on a Web site. This module checks the Access Control List (ACL) on an ASP.NET file for a given user. If the ACL confirms that the user has access to the file, it is made available to the user.

- **URL Authorization** The *URLAuthorizationModule* class is responsible for URL authorization on Windows Server 2003. This mechanism uses the URL namespace to store user details and access roles. The URL authorization is available to use at any time. The authorization information is stored in a text file in a directory. The text file has an *<authorization>* tag to allow or deny access to the directory. A sample authorization file might look like this:

```
<authorization>
    <allow users="Chris"/>
    <allow roles="Admins"/>
    <deny users="kirby"/>
    <deny users="?"/>
</authorization>
```

This file enables *Chris* to access its content. It also allows any one with Admins user roles to access its content. The user *Kirby* is denied access to the content. No one else will be able to gain access to this directory as indicated by the *?* wildcard.

New & Noteworthy...

ASP versus ASP.NET...What's the Difference?

Active Server Pages (ASPs) are used to create Web-based applications combining HTTP, scripting, and ActiveX applets to provide dynamic Web sites. ASP uses a combination of VBScript, Jscript, and Component Object Model (COM) components. ASP is executed completely on the Web server and returns its output as standard Hypertext Markup Language (HTML) to the user's browser. In IIS, ASP is implemented as an Internet Server Application Programming Interface (ISAPI) filter named asp.dll that resides in the same memory space as IIS. When a user requests an ASP page, which has the extension. ASP, the request is processed by the filter which then loads the required DLLs to interpret the script on the page, executes the script on the server, and then returns the output to the user's browser.

Continued

ASP.NET is a more advanced platform for developing Web applications, services, and forms under the .NET platform. ASP.NET solution can be developing in Microsoft Visual Studio .NET and ASP.NET supports application creation using C#, VB.NET, and various other programming languages, which was not previously possible using ASP. ASP.NET is the successor to ASP and ASP+, and is backwards compatible with its earlier predecessors. ASP.NET offers a significant performance improvement because it is compiled instead of interpreted. Additionally, ASP.NET is more modular, allowing developers to piece together applications as required, resulting in a smaller footprint and overall improved performance. ASP.NET also supports a number of different authentication methods natively, including Basic authentication, Digest authentication, NT LAN Manager (NTLM) authentication, cookie-based authentication, and Microsoft .NET Passport authentication.

For more information about ASP and ASP.NET, see www.activeserverpages.com/learnasp/.

New Reliability Features

Microsoft has done a great job of redeveloping IIS to be more reliable and robust. Perhaps the most significant modification is the emphasis on the worker process model. IIS separates all user code from its World Wide Web Publishing service. The user application (different virtual sites) functions as a separate ISAPI application. The separate ISAPI workspace is referred to as a worker process. In IIS 5.0, each Web site ran within its own inetinfo.exe memory space—inetinfo.exe is the application that implements IIS 5.0. The IIS 6.0 worker process Web sites do not run within the inetinfo.exe memory space. Since the worker process runs in an isolated environment from the World Wide Web Publishing service, an error in the Web site application code (or malicious attack) will not cause the Web server to shut down. The worker process can also be configured to run on a specified central processing unit (CPU). The worker process model can store application-specific data on its own memory space; IIS 5.0 stored all the application data within the inetinfo.exe memory space.

The following reliability features are discussed next in this chapter:

- Health detection
- HTTP.sys kernel mode driver

Is the IIS 6.0 Worker Process Model Identical to IIS 5.0 Isolation Mode?

By default, IIS 6.0 runs using the worker process model. This mode of operation is more flexible and stable than the IIS 5.0 isolation model, providing the ability to isolate individual Web sites from each other. By isolating Web sites from one another, an attack on one Web site will not necessarily cause the entire IIS server to stop functioning or responding normally, as is often the case when using IIS 5.0.

With IIS 5.0 or IIS 6.0 in IIS 5.0 isolation mode, all Web site applications take place within the inetinfo.exe memory space, so an error or an attack on the application can result in the entire IIS server going down. IIS 5.0 uses ASP as its default scripting language, and IIS 6.0 uses ASP.NET which provides numerous security and performance enhancements over ASP. IIS 6.0 can run ASP, thus all of your IIS 5.0 ASP applications should run smoothly after an upgrade to IIS 6.0 in worker process model. If your ASP code does not function properly, you may have no choice but to consider using the IIS 5.0 isolation mode of IIS 6.0.

Health Detection

Health detection simplifies IIS Web site management. Health detection is performed by IIS over all its worker processes, which adds another level of reliability to the Web applications. The inetinfo.exe process (IIS) checks the availability of each worker process (different Web sites) periodically. This time limit can be configured by the IIS manager and is 240 seconds by default. Therefore, IIS will maintain a *heartbeat* between its worker processes—attempting to communicate with worker processes to make sure they are alive.

New Request Processing Architecture: HTTP.SYS Kernel Mode Driver

In Windows Server 2003, the HTTP stack is implemented as a kernel mode device driver called HTTP.sys. All incoming HTTP traffic goes through this kernel process, which is independent of the application process. IIS 6.0 is an application process and therefore external to HTTP.sys. HTTP.sys is responsible for the following tasks:

- **Connection Management** Managing the database connections from the ASP.NET pages to data bases
- **Caching** Reading from a static cache as opposed to recompiling the ASP.NET page
- **Bandwidth Throttling** Limiting the size of the Web requests to a Web site
- **Logging** Writing IIS information into a text log file

NOTE

Application processes run in user mode while operating system functions run in kernel mode.

In IIS 5.0, the HTTP request was consumed by IIS inetinfo.exe; in IIS 6.0, HTTP.sys relieves IIS of this responsibility. In doing so, it enhances IIS performance in the following ways:

- HTTP.sys enables caching, referred to as *flexible caching*, at the kernel level so that static data can be cached for faster response time. This is independent of, and much faster than user mode caching.

- HTTP.sys introduces a mapping concept called *application pooling*. Application pooling allows Web sites to run together in one or more processes, as long as they share the same pool designation. Web sites that are assigned different application pools never run in the same process. A central Web site (such as a credit card verification Web site) can be accessed by other miscellaneous sites (various eCommerce Web sites, and the like) by using this method. By using the correct application pool information, HTTP.sys can route the HTTP traffic to the correct Web site.

- HTTP.sys increases the number of Web sites that can be hosted using the application pool concept. This architecture also increases performance and more controlled access to valuable IIS resources.

Other New Features

The following sections examine some of the other new features in IIS 6.0. All of these changes are designed to improve IIS scalability. Some of these changes are a byproduct of the Microsoft .NET strategy, including:

- ASP.NET and IIS Integration
- Unicode Transformation Format-8
- XML Metabase

ASP.NET and IIS Integration

IIS is a Web server, and one of its functions is to accept HTTP requests. Thus, a scripting language is needed that can communicate with IIS in order to do this. Earlier versions of IIS (2.0 through 5.0) used ASP; IIS 6.0 uses ASP.NET for the same purpose. There are some significant changes to the ASP.NET architecture as compared to ASP. Some of the changes include the following:

- ASP.NET is based on Microsoft .NET framework, thus ASP.NET can be coded in multiple languages such as C#, VB.NET, JScript.NET, and so forth.

- There can be multiple language code in the same ASP.NET page. In other words, a VB.NET function can reside in a C# ASP.NET page.

- ASP code is interpreted, meaning that the code is complied line by line, not as the complete source file at once. ASP.NET code is compiled, meaning that the complete source file is complied once, not line-by-line compilation. This is a significant performance increase in IIS 6.0.

- ASP.NET allows for three levels of caching. The first option is to cache complete pages. The second option is to cache selected parts of the pages, which is referred to as *fragment caching*. The third option is to use *Caching API*. Developers can use this for control over caching behavior, and thus increase performance.

Unicode Transformation Format-8 (UTF-8)

Earlier versions of IIS log files were only available in English. This was a major issue for multilingual Web sites. Multilingual support is enabled by supporting Unicode Transformation Format 8 (UTF-8) characters codes. Computer applications do not understand human-readable characters; they only understand binary code. There are conversion tables available to convert a key value to a human readable character. These conversion tables are referred to as *Local Character Sets* or *Unicode formats* and are language specific, thus an English log file entry cannot be read in Japanese. UTF-8 format rectifies this problems. HTTP.sys can be configured to log details in a specific language format; therefore multiple log files can be maintained in multiple languages.

XML Metabase

The information store that contains IIS configuration settings is referred to as the *metabase*. The metabase is a hierarchical database in which all the information needed to configure IIS is stored.

In earlier IIS versions, the metabase data was in binary format, which made it difficult to edit or read the entries. The IIS 6.0 metabase, on the other hand, is in Extensible Markup Language (XML) format. These XML files are plaintext. A general text editor can be used to change the XML entries, and these changes can be performed when IIS 6.0 is running. Editing the XML metabase while IIS is running is referred to as *edit while running*. IIS does not need to be restarted to reflect the changes unless the schema file was completely overwritten with a new version.

This design change has also significantly increased the performance of IIS 6.0. It has considerably reduced the startup and shutdown time of IIS. Previously, in IIS 5.0, all of the IIS settings were kept in inetinfo.exe and the Registry. This resulted in multiple reads from the Registry and accessing of system resources during start-up. Now with all of this information contained in the XML metabase, this is not necessary; thus IIS 6.0 starts faster.

The metabase consists of the following two XML files:

- **metabase.xml** An XML document that contains IIS configuration values for the server such as Web site details and virtual directory details.

- **mbschema.xml** An XML document in which the metabase XML schema is stored, which acts as a validation tool to enter correct metabase values in metabase.xml.

The metabase files are located in the **%systemroot%\System32\Inetsrv** directory. You must possess administrator privileges to view the contents of the metabase entries.

Exam Warning

Be sure that you completely understand the structure of the new IIS 6.0 metabase including the files that make up the metabase.

Installing and Configuring IIS 6.0

Before a network administrator can use IIS, they must first install it unless they happen to be using Windows Server 2003 Web Edition. Remember that IIS is not installed by default in any of the other Windows Server 2003 family members. This is to minimize unauthorized access to the server.

If this IIS server is to act as a publicly accessible Internet Web server (as opposed to an intranet server), then the network administrator needs to register a domain name and obtain an IP address for the server. They will also need to obtain DNS services for the domain, from an ISP or another public DNS server. For more information on DNS, refer to Chapter 6.

The network administrator also needs to assign an Internet Protocol (IP) address or a unique machine name for references inside the enterprise. These details should be taken care of before any installations occur.

Note

Microsoft strongly recommends that IIS be installed on an NT File System (NTFS) formatted drive. The executable files and the virtual directories should reside on NTFS volumes. NTFS provides more secure file access than the FAT32 file system. It is recommended that the file system be converted if upgrading from an IIS 5.0 FAT32 system. A command-line utility called convert.exe can be used for this purpose.

Installation Methods

IIS is not installed by default in the Windows Server 2003 setup, except in the Web Server Edition. There are three different ways to install IIS:

- Use the Configure Your Server Wizard
- Use the Windows Component Wizard
- Use the Unattended Setup

Each option is examined in the following sections.

Head of the Class…

Default IIS Access Options

Each of the installation methods described in this chapter install IIS in *Locked Down* mode, which means you get access only to static Web material. All the ASP.NET scripts—Server Side Includes (SSI), WebDAV access, and Front Page Extensions—are disabled by default. If you try to access any of these facilities, you will get a "404 (Page not found)" error. These features must be enabled through the Web Services Extensions node in IIS Manager.

The details regarding how to enable dynamic features are discussed in the section titled "Common Administrative Tasks." If these features are enabled, they can be disabled later to increase security. Any Web service extension can be enabled or disabled individually as long as it is registered in the Web Service Extensions node, or all extensions can be prohibited from running. New extensions can be added and IIS can be configured so that a specific application can use the Web service extensions.

Using the Configure Your Server Wizard

In addition to its other possible roles (domain controller, file server, DNS server, and so forth), the Windows Server 2003 can act as an application server, and the components of the application server can be configured through the Configure Your Server Wizard. The application server components are COM+, ASP.NET, and IIS.

NOTE

In this context, the term *application server* has a different meaning from the one you may have used in the past. Here, we are not talking about a server that provides a network location on which productivity applications such as Microsoft Office are installed, nor or we talking about a server that you connect to and run applications from a thin client (a terminal server functioning as an application server). Instead, the "applications" we are referring to are Web-based applications such as Web-hosting services, as well as newsgroup services, File Transfer Protocol (FTP) services, and Simple Mail Transfer Protocol (SMTP) services.

Exercise 4.01 outlines the steps you will perform to install IIS 6.0 using the Configure Your Server Wizard.

EXERCISE 4.01

INSTALLING IIS 6.0 USING THE CONFIGURE YOUR SERVER WIZARD

1. Click **Start | Programs | Administrative Tools | Manage Your Server** to open the Manage Your Server utility, as seen in Figure 4.1. Click the **Add or remove a role** link to start the Configure Your Server Wizard.

Figure 4.1 Using the Manager Your Server Utility

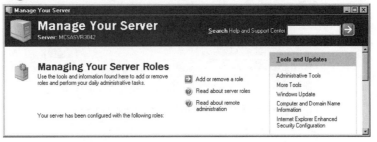

2. The Configure Your Server Wizard starts and displays the Preliminary Steps dialog box, as seen in Figure 4.2. After verifying that you are ready to continue, click **Next**.

Figure 4.2 Viewing Preliminary Steps for the Configure Your Server Wizard

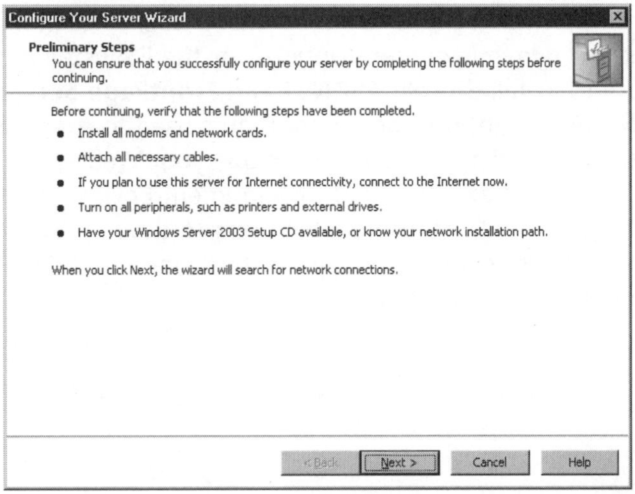

3. In the Configuration Options dialog box, you will be required to make a selection about how the configuration will proceed. The **Typical configuration for a first server** option enables the basic server communication options. It sets up a domain controller by installing Active Directory, DNS services, and dynamic host control protocol (DHCP) services. The **Custom configuration** option enables you to configure your server by selecting specific options from a list. Select the **Custom configuration** option and click **Next** to continue.

4. In the Server Role dialog box, as seen in Figure 4.3, you can select the new configuration for your Windows Server 2003. Several possible roles are shown on the Server Role dialog box. Select the **Application Server (IIS, ASP.NET)** option and click **Next** to continue.

Figure 4.3 The Server Role Dialog Box

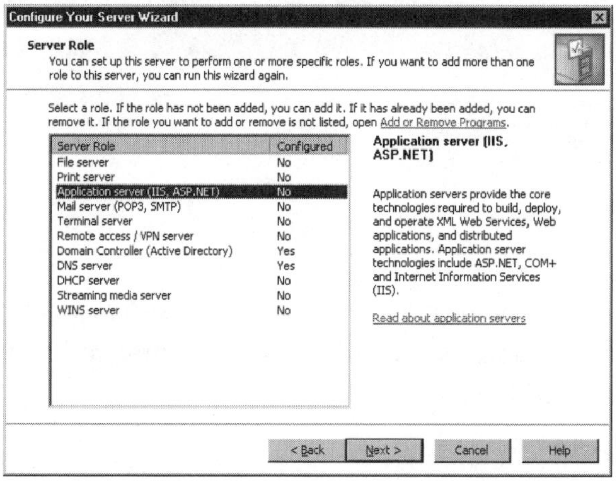

5. In the Application Server Options dialog box, as seen in Figure 4.4, you can select dynamic content options for the IIS installation. You can choose to install **Enable ASP.NET** and **FrontPage Server Extensions**. ASP.NET is a scripting framework that is used to execute IIS applications. The FrontPage extensions enable your Web application to be ported to another Integrated Development Environment (IDE). The FrontPage extensions also enable users to develop Web content and manage the Web site remotely. For this example, select both options and click **Next** to continue.

Figure 4.4 The Application Server Options Dialog Box

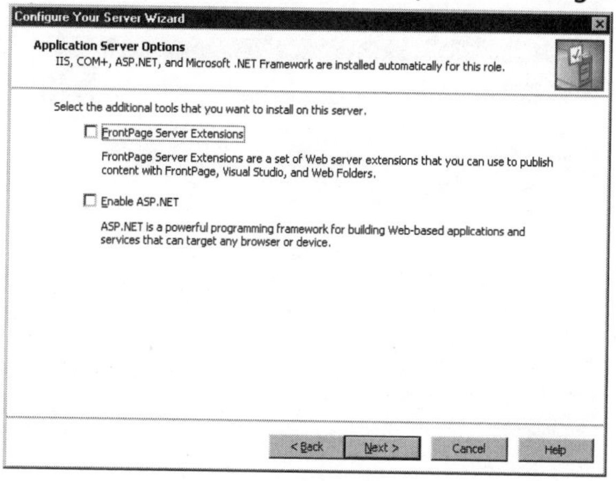

6. In the Summary of Selections dialog box, as seen in Figure 4.5, you can review the configuration that you have selected. Note that Windows may add options to be installed that you did not explicitly select, as they are required to support the options that you did select. Click the **Back** button if you need to change any of the settings. When you are ready to complete the installation, click **Next**.

Figure 4.5 The Summary of Selections Dialog Box

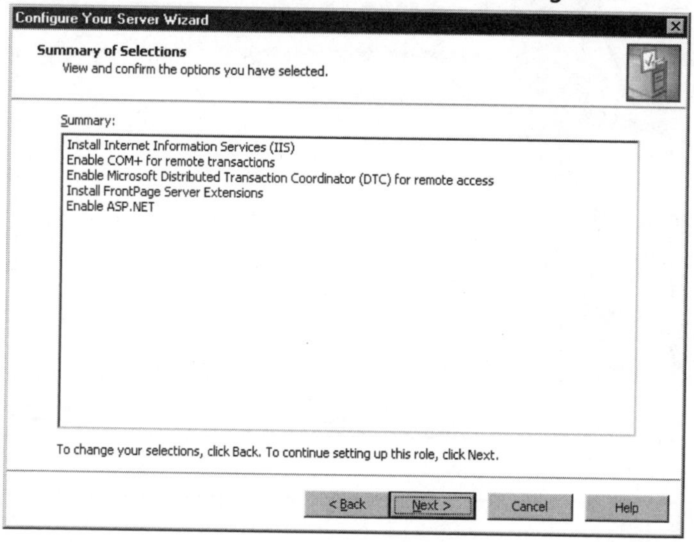

7. The Windows Component Wizard appears, as seen in Figure 4.6. You may be prompted to provide the location to the Windows Server 2003 installation files.

Figure 4.6 The Windows Components Wizard Performs the IIS Installation

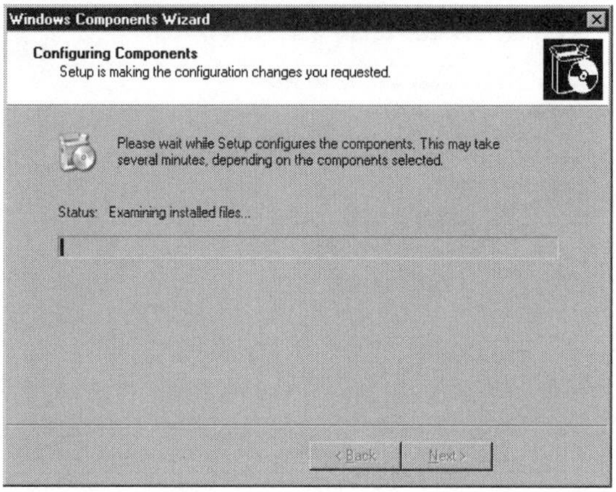

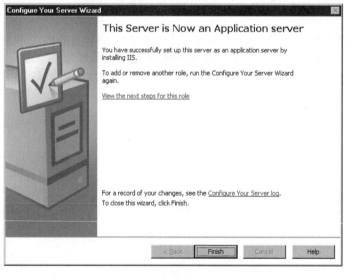

8. After some time, the Configure Your Server Wizard informs you that the installation of IIS has been completed, as seen in Figure 4.7. Click **Finish** to close the Wizard.

Figure 4.7 Completing the Configure Your Server Wizard

The next section examines how IIS 6.0 can be installed using the Windows Component Wizard directly.

Using the Windows Component Wizard to Install IIS 6.0

If you are more comfortable directly installing components onto your server, you can use the Windows Components Wizard to perform the installation of IIS 6.0 as outlined in Exercise 4.02.

EXERCISE 4.02

INSTALLING IIS 6.0 USING THE WINDOWS COMPONENT WIZARD

1. Click **Start | Settings | Control Panel | Add or Remove Programs** to open the Add or Remove Programs applet.

   Figure 4.8 The Add or Remove Programs Applet

   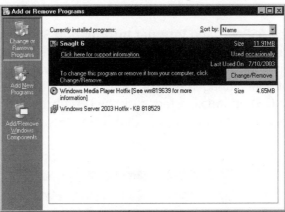

2. Click the **Add/Remove Windows Components** button to start the Windows Component Wizard, as seen in Figure 4.9.

   Figure 4.9 The Windows Components Wizard

   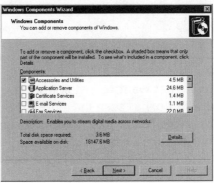

3. Select the **Application Server** option and click the **Details** button to open the Application Server dialog box, as seen in Figure 4.10.

Figure 4.10 Examining the Application Server Options

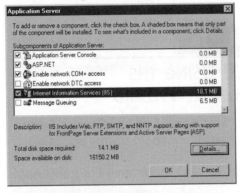

4. Select the **ASP.NET** and **Internet Information Services (IIS)** options. The **Enable network COM+ access** option is automatically selected for you. You do not need to select the **Application Server Console** option—this is an optional management component. With the **Internet Information Services (IIS)** option selected, click the **Details** button to open the **Internet Information Services (IIS)** dialog box seen in Figure 4.11.

Figure 4.11 Examining the Internet Information Services (IIS) Options

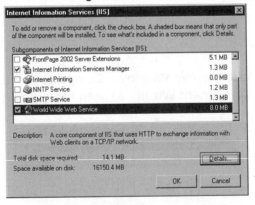

5. Select the options that want to install from the Internet Information Services (IIS) dialog box, as seen in Figure 4.11. By default, the **Internet Information Services Manager** and the **World Wide Web Service** are selected for you. You may wish to select additional options such as **File Transfer Protocol (FTP) Service**, **NNTP Service** or **SMTP Service** as well

at this time. Highlight the **World Wide Web Service** and select the **Details** button to open the World Wide Web Service dialog box, as seen in Figure 4.12.

Figure 4.12 The World Wide Web Service Dialog Box

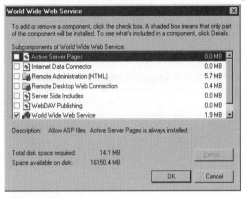

6. The **World Wide Web Service** is automatically selected for you. You can select other World Wide Web Services options as desired, such as **Server Side Includes** or **Active Server Pages**. After making your selections click **OK** to close the World Wide Web Service dialog box.

7. Click **OK** to close the Internet Information Services (IIS) dialog box.

8. Click **OK** to close the Application Server dialog box.

9. On the Windows Component Wizard dialog box, click **Next** to start the IIS installation.

10. The Configuring Windows dialog box appears, as seen previously in Figure 4.6. You may be prompted to provide the location to the Windows Server 2003 installation files.

11. After some time the Windows Component Wizard will inform you that the installation of IIS has been completed. Click **Finish** to close the Wizard.

Using Unattended Setup to Install IIS 6.0

The third option for installing IIS is using the unattended setup feature, which is commonly used by system administrators to install IIS 6.0 on multiple computers. When using this option, the setup program does not require manual intervention. The configuration settings—the selections that are made during an attended setup—are read from a text file and applied automatically by the operating system. The network administrator only needs to initiate the process, and IIS 6.0 will be installed according to the text file settings.

The script that provides the configuration settings is referred to as an *answer file* because it provides answers to the installation questions encountered in an attended setup. After creating the answer file, the administrator then runs winnt32.exe or the sysocmgr.exe command-line utility with the answer script as the parameter. The answer file has an .INF file extension. Some of the important options that are included in the answer file are shown in Table 4.1.

Table 4.1 Answer File Parameters for IIS Unattended Setup

Component	Answer File Parameter
ASP.NET	asp.net = on/off
FTP service	iis_ftp = on/off
IIS Manager	iis_inetmgr = on/off
NNTP Service	iis_nntp = on/off
SMTP Service	iis_smtp = on/off
WWW Service	iis_www = on/off
Active Server Pages	iis_asp = on/off
WebDAV Publishing (discussed later)	iis_webdav = on/off

Head of the Class...

Differences Between winnt32.exe and sysocmgr.exe

winnt32.exe is used by network administrators to install Windows Server 2003 and its components (including IIS 6.0). When a properly configured answer file is used with winnt32.exe, it installs Windows Server 2003 with IIS 6.0. In some cases, the administrator may need to install IIS 6.0 after the operating system is installed. The sysocmgr.exe utility is used to install IIS 6.0 with unattended setup after the operating system has been installed. Following are the steps for using sysocmgr.exe:

1. First, the answer file needs to be created. Open a text editor such as Notepad, and type the following:

```
[DefaultInstall]

Asp.net=on

Iis_inetmgr=on

Iis_www=on

Iis_asp=on
```

2. Save the file using a meaningful name, such as **c:\temp\iisSetup.inf**.

3. Click **Start | Run**.

Continued

> 4. Type **sysocmgr.exe /i:sysoc.inf /u:c:\temp\iisSetup.inf** and the installa-
> tion will begin. The *i:sysoc.inf* attribute is the Windows 2003 Server
> master initialization file for unattended setup.
>
> Installing IIS with unattended setup is very straightforward. The help files
> available for unattended setup can be found by using the *syscomgr.exe /?*
> syntax.

Managing IIS 6.0

The primary tool for managing IIS 6.0 is the Internet Information Services (IIS) Manager
console. Most of the management of IIS functions can be done using the IIS Manager, as
seen in Figure 4.13. In the left pane, there is a node for each instance of IIS that is installed.
Folders/subnodes underneath each node (identified by the server name) contain the FTP,
Application Pools, Web Sites, Web Service Extensions, Network News Transfer Protocol
(NNTP), and SMTP Server information.

Figure 4.13 The Internet Information Services (IIS) Manager Console

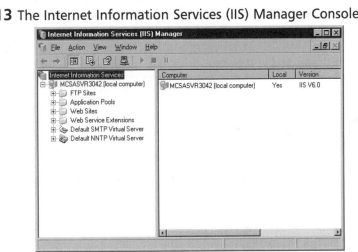

IIS Manager is the primary interface that handles all Internet-related functions. New
Web sites, FTP sites, SMTP virtual servers, and NNTP virtual servers can be set up using
this console. IIS servers can also be stopped and restarted from this interface. A very useful,
and often overlooked, feature of the IIS Manager is that it allows the network administrator
to manages the IIS servers running on several computers from a single location. The following sections explore some of the common uses for the IIS Manager.

Creating New Sites and Virtual Servers with IIS Manager

IIS Manager can be used to create new sites for any of the installed services: Web, FTP, SMTP, and NNTP. The creation of each site is made simple through an intuitive Wizard-driven interface. We will outline the process to create new sites and virtual servers as follows:

- Exercise 4.03 discusses creating new Web sites using the Web Site Creation Wizard.

- Exercise 4.04 discusses creating new FTP sites using the FTP Site Creation Wizard.

- Exercise 4.05 discusses creating new SMTP virtual servers using the New SMTP Virtual Server Wizard.

- Exercise 4.06 discusses creating new NNTP virtual servers using the New NNTP Virtual Server Wizard.

NOTE

It is common practice to remove the default installations created by IIS and create new Web sites, FTP sites, NNTP servers, and SMTP servers that are configured exactly as your organization requires.

Creating New Web Sites Using the Web Site Creation Wizard

The Web site is the most common implementation of IIS in Windows, thus we start our discussion with creating new Web sites.

EXERCISE 4.03

CREATING NEW WEB SITES USING THE WEB SITE CREATION WIZARD

1. Start the IIS Manager by clicking **Start | Programs | Administrative Tools | Internet Information Services (IIS) Manager**.

2. Navigate to the **Web Sites** node and right-click it. Select **New | Web Site** from the context menu, as seen in Figure 4.14.

Figure 4.14 Creating a New Web Site in IIS Manager

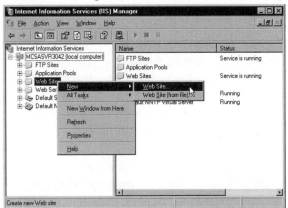

3. The Web Site Creation Wizard appears. Click **Next** to dismiss the opening dialog.

4. On the **Web Site Description** dialog box, as seen in Figure 4.15, you must enter a descriptive name for your new Web site. For our purposes, we will use **Internal Web site**. After entering the required information, click **Next** to continue.

Figure 4.15 Enter a Descriptive Web Site Name

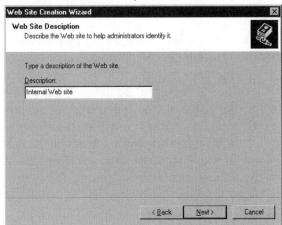

5. In the IP Address and Port settings dialog box, as seen in Figure 4.16, you must configure the IP addresses and port number that this new Web site will use. This dialog box is often one of the most confusing ones you will have to deal with during your administration of IIS. For example, suppose you have an intranet Web site that users will access by entering **intranet**

in their browsers. In this case, you would enter **intranet** into the Host Header area. If you wanted users to access the site on port 81, they would enter **Intranet:81** in their browser, and then you would enter **81** in the TCP port of this Web site. If you want the Web site to respond on all IP addresses assigned to the server, you can leave the default setting **All Unassigned** in the **Enter the IP address** to use for this web site area. (Using host headers to host multiple Web sites is discussed more in the "Hosting Multiple Web Sites" section of this chapter.) After making your configurations, click **Next** to continue.

Figure 4.16 Entering the IP Address and Port Settings for a Web Site

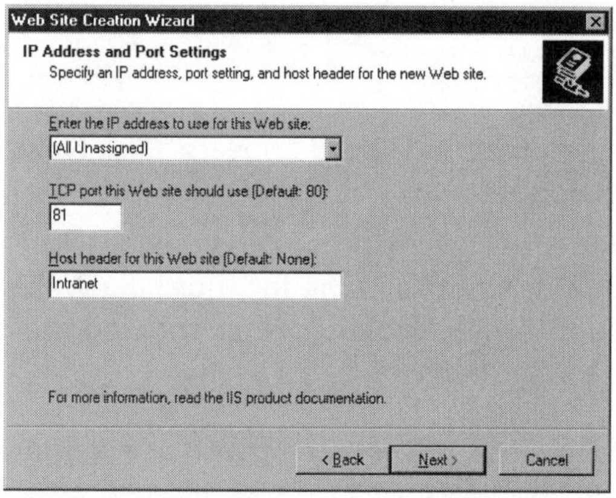

6. On the Web Site Home Directory dialog box, as seen in Figure 4.17, you must enter the location on the computer or network where the Web site's files are physically located. You can use the **Browse** button to locate this location, if required. By default, the **Allow anonymous access to this web site** option is selected; allowing anonymous access enables users to navigate the site without authenticating themselves. You may wish to disable anonymous access if you are hosting sensitive data on the Web site. For public Internet sites, you will most often want to allow anonymous access though, this setting can be changed later if needed. Click **Next** to continue.

Figure 4.17 Entering the Home Directory for a Web Site

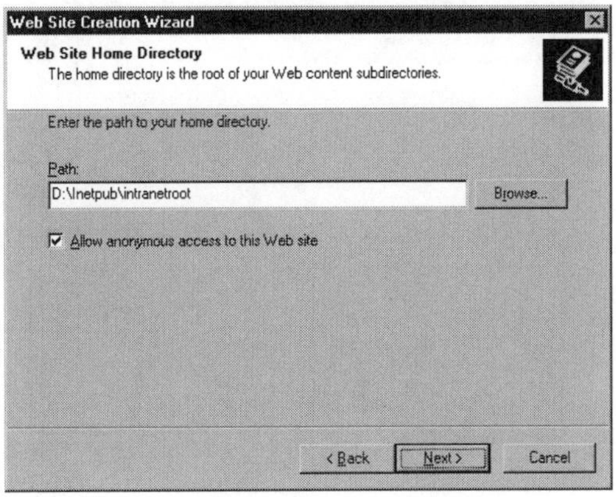

7. On the Web Site Access Permissions dialog box, as seen in Figure 4.18, you can configure the user access level to the new Web site. By default, the **Run** and **Read scripts** options are selected. Depending on the intended use of your new Web site, you may need to select additional user permissions.

   ■ Selecting the **Execute** option grants permission to execute Dynamic Link Libraries (DLLs) such as ISAPI DLLs or Common Gateway Interface (CGI) applications in the IIS space. Most of the business logic and interfaces to third party business models are stored as ISAPI DLLs or CGI applications, therefore you may need to enable the **Execute** permission to utilize these functions.

   ■ The **Write** option enables the user of the Web site to upload and write data into the Web site's home directory.

   ■ The **Browse** option enables *directory browsing* on the Web site— allowing the user to view a complete directory information list (files and their attributes: size, last modified time stamp, and so on) when navigating a directory. This is not widely recommended since it exposes all the files and interfaces to Web site users. If anony- mous access is also enabled, it can result in a large security problem for Internet Web sites.

   Click **Next** to finish the creation of the Web site after making your selections.

Figure 4.18 Entering Access Permissions for a Web Site

8. Click **Finish** to complete the Web Site Creation Wizard.

Creating New FTP Sites Using the FTP Site Creation Wizard

Creating a new FTP site is very similar to creating a new Web site. FTP sites enable the sharing of data with other users through the FTP, which is more efficient at moving large amounts of data than the Hyper Text Transfer Protocol (HTTP) is. Exercise 4.04 presents the steps required to create a new FTP site.

EXERCISE 4.04

CREATING NEW FTP SITES USING THE FTP SITE CREATION WIZARD

1. Start the IIS Manager by clicking **Start | Programs | Administrative Tools | Internet Information Services (IIS) Manager**.

2. Navigate to the **FTP Sites** node and right-click it. Select **New | FTP Site** from the context menu.

3. The FTP Site Creation Wizard appears. Click **Next** to dismiss the opening dialog.

4. In the FTP Site Description dialog box you must enter a descriptive name for your new FTP site. After entering the required information, click **Next** to continue.

5. In the IP Address and Port Settings dialog box, as seen in Figure 4.19, you must select an available IP address for the FTP site to use. Unlike Web sites, you do not have the option to use host headers to differentiate several Web sites using the same IP address and port number. The default port for FTP is 21 and should be used in most cases, although this can be changed as required. After making your configuration, click **Next** to continue.

Figure 4.19 Entering IP Address and Port Numbers for an FTP Site

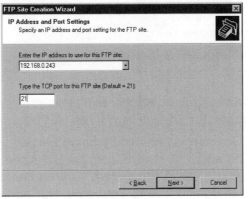

6. On the FTP User Isolation dialog box, as seen in Figure 4.20, you are presented with a critical decision—one that cannot be changed after you complete the creation of the FTP site. The user access for FTP server can be managed in several ways. The default setting is that every user has access to other user directories. This will not be a problem in many cases since a company FTP site distributes generic information regardless of the user (for example, enabling Beta product downloads to the test users). Users will have access to *all files* if the user is authenticated. In some cases, you may need to give different users access to different information. In this case, you need to *isolate* users to different directories. FTP user isolation prevents users from accessing the FTP home directory of another user on this FTP site. Select the **Isolate users** option to accomplish this scenario. This option uses NTFS directory authentication to perform this task. You can also go a step further and ask Active Directory to authenticate the user and assign an FTP home directory for the user. This is configured using the **Isolate the users using Active Directory** option. After making your selection, click **Next** to continue.

Figure 4.20 FTP Site User Isolation Options

Figure showing FTP Site Creation Wizard dialog box with FTP User Isolation options.

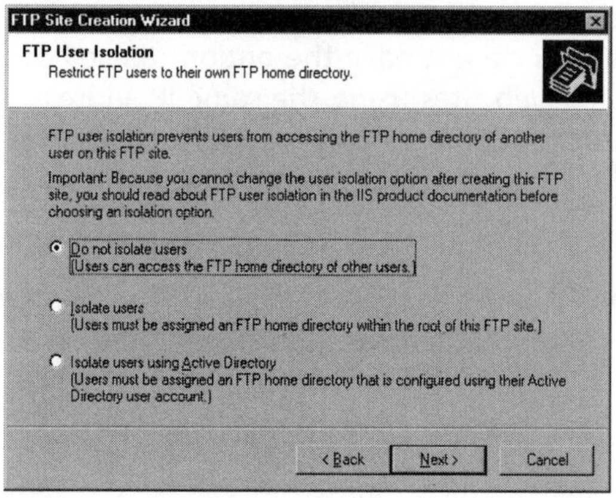

7. In the FTP Site Home Directory dialog box you must enter the physical path where the FTP site's files will reside. Click **Next** to continue.

8. In the FTP Site Access Permission dialog box, as seen in Figure 4.21, you are given the ability to control user access to the new FTP site. The default setting is **Read**. If required, you can also enable **Write** access if users need to upload files to the server. This option can be helpful in some cases; for example, your sales team needs to upload sales data to the FTP server for the weekly accounting purposes. However, this option can also be dangerous by allowing users to upload unauthorized content such as copyrighted materials. Therefore, it is not recommended that you enable **Write** access unless necessary. After making your selections, click **Next** to finish the creation of the FTP site.

Figure 4.21 FTP Site Access Permissions Dialog Box

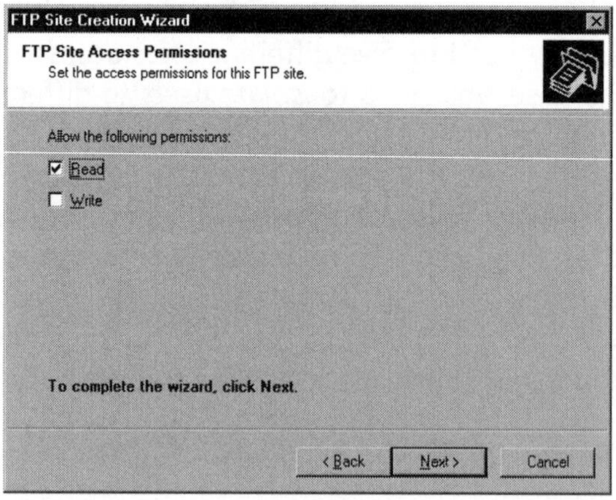

Figure showing FTP Site Creation Wizard dialog box with FTP Site Access Permissions.

9. Click **Finish** to complete the FTP Site Creation Wizard.

Creating New SMTP Virtual Servers
Using the New SMTP Virtual Server Wizard

SMTP virtual servers enable IIS to provide simple e-mail functionality to its Web sites. E-mail is used for transmitting a variety of business or administrative information, such as Web site errors that are sent to the Web site administrator. Therefore, Microsoft included the SMTP server with IIS 6.0. SMTP servers use TLS encryption to protect e-mail information and they communicate with DNS servers to validate the recipient's e-mail address. Sent e-mails are transferred to the *drop* directory; the SMTP server transmits all of the messages in the drop directory, allowing other non-IIS 6.0 applications to also send e-mail by putting their messages in the drop directory. The delivered e-mail is picked up from a *pickup* directory. Exercise 4.05 presents the required steps to create a new SMTP virtual server.

EXERCISE 4.05

CREATING NEW SMTP VIRTUAL SERVERS
USING THE NEW SMTP VIRTUAL SERVER WIZARD

1. Start the IIS Manager by clicking **Start | Programs | Administrative Tools | Internet Information Services (IIS) Manager**.

2. Navigate to the **Default SMTP server** node and right-click on it. Select **New | Virtual Server** from the context menu.

3. Unlike most other Wizards, the New SMTP Virtual Server Wizard starts immediately. Enter the name of the new SMTP virtual server you are creating, as seen in Figure 4.22. For this example, we will use **IntranetSMTPserver**. Click **Next** to continue.

Figure 4.22 Entering the Name of the SMTP Virtual Server

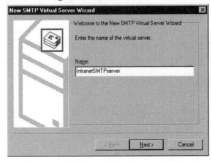

4. In the Select IP Address dialog box, as seen in Figure 4.23, you must select the IP address of the new SMTP virtual server. Click **Next** to continue.

Figure 4.23 Configuring the IP Address of the SMTP Virtual Server

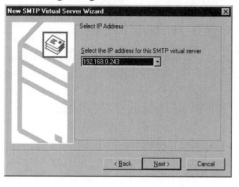

5. In the Select Home Directory dialog box, as seen in Figure 4.24, enter the location where the SMTP virtual server will physically store its files. Non-IIS 6.0 applications can also use the SMTP server to send e-mail; therefore it is a good practice to have general access to the home directory. Click **Next** to continue.

Figure 4.24 Configuring the Home Directory of the SMTP Virtual Server

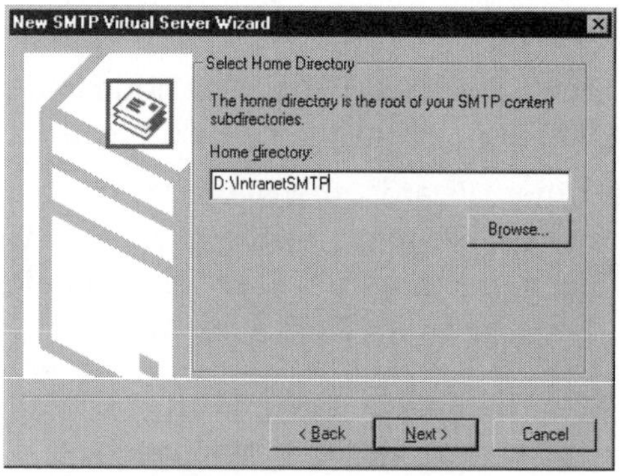

6. In the Default Domain dialog box, as seen in Figure 4.25, you must configure the default domain of the new SMTP virtual server. Click **Finish** to create the new SMTP virtual server.

Figure 4.25 Configuring the Default Domain of the SMTP Virtual Server

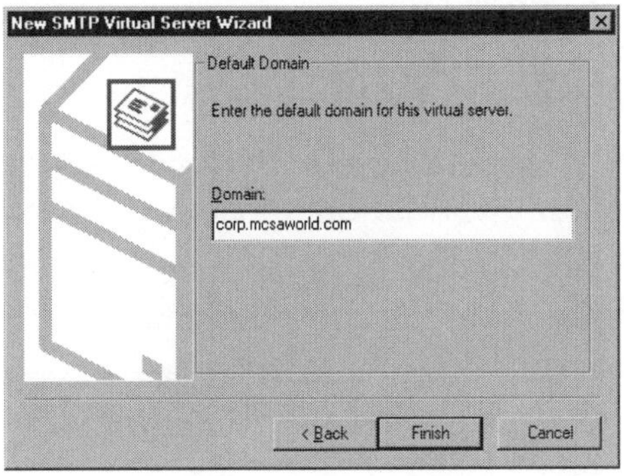

Entering IP Address Details SMTP Server

The IIS installation creates default SMTP and NNTP virtual servers, which are bound to the **(All Unassigned)** IP address. Therefore, if you try to select the default for the **IP Address and Port Settings** screen (that is, the **All Unassigned** option) the operation will fail. You can use the 127.0.0.1 IP address if you want to refer to the local machine. You can also use any other valid IP address available.

You can run multiple SMTP servers on a single IP address by using multiple port numbers. You can add these extra port numbers by opening the SMTP server properties dialog box, switching to the **General** tab, clicking the **Advanced** button, and entering IP and port number settings. You can also run multiple SMTP virtual servers on a single IIS 6.0 node. The best practice is to use multiple IP addresses for each virtual server. For example, run a single SMTP server for intranet use and dedicate another SMTP virtual server to Internet use.

Creating New NNTP Virtual Servers Using the New NNTP Virtual Server Wizard

The NNTP virtual server assists the IIS 6.0 server in facilitating discussion group functionality. The IIS setup creates one NNTP virtual server by default. Exercise 4.06 discusses the procedure for creating additional NNTP virtual servers.

EXERCISE 4.06

CREATING NEW NNTP VIRTUAL SERVERS USING THE NEW NNTP VIRTUAL SERVER WIZARD

1. Start the IIS Manager by clicking **Start | Programs | Administrative Tools | Internet Information Services (IIS) Manager**.

2. Navigate to **Default NNTP server** node and right-click on it. Select **New | Virtual Server** from the context menu.

3. Again, like the New SMTP Virtual Server Wizard, the New NNTP Virtual Server Wizard starts immediately. Enter the name for the new NNTP virtual server and click **Next** to continue.

4. In the Select IP Address and Port Number dialog box, as seen in Figure 4.26, you must select the IP address and port number to be used by this NNTP virtual server. By default, port 119 is assigned for NNTP, but you can change this if desired. You can host multiple NNTP virtual servers on a single server, however it is best practice to use a dedicated IP address for each NNTP virtual server. After making your configuration, click **Next** to continue.

Figure 4.26 Entering IP Address and Port Numbers for the NNTP Server

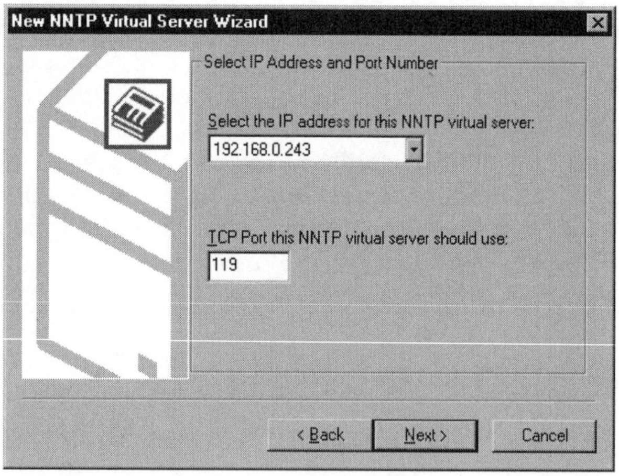

5. In the **Select Internal Files Path** dialog box, enter the location where the NNTP virtual server will store its internal operating files (this is not the location where the NNTP virtual server will store the NNTP related files). Click **Next** to continue.

6. In the Select Storage Medium dialog box, as seen in Figure 4.27, you can decide if the NNTP files should be stored locally (**File System**) or remotely (**Remote Share**). After making your selection, click **Next** to continue.

Figure 4.27 Selecting a Storage Medium for the NNTP Server

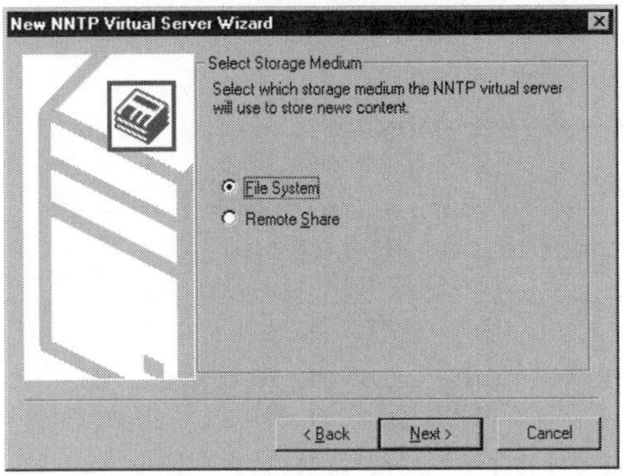

7. In the Select News Content Medium Info dialog box, as seen in Figure 4.28, you must enter the location where the NNTP files will be physically kept. You can use the Browse button to locate the folder you will use, if required. Click **Finish** to create the NNTP virtual server.

Figure 4.28 Selecting a News Content Path for the NNTP Server

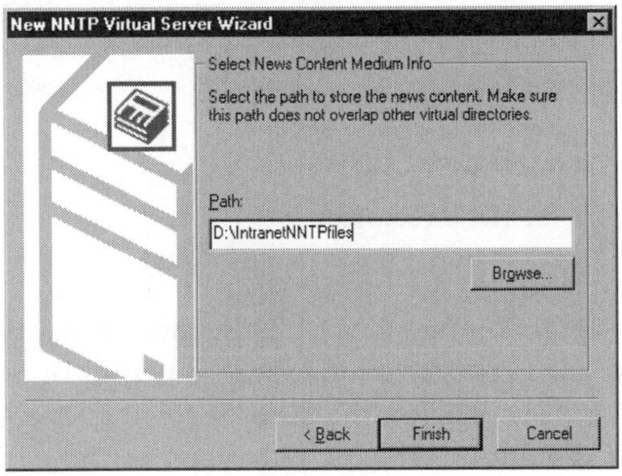

Common Administrative Tasks

IIS 6.0 networks administrators commonly find themselves performing the following administrative tasks:

- Enabling Web Service Extensions
- Creating virtual directories
- Hosting multiple Web sites
- Configuring Web site performance
- Working with ASP.NET
- Backing up and restoring the IIS metabase
- Enabling health detection

These topics are examined in the following sections.

Enabling Web Service Extensions

Web Service Extensions is a new feature in IIS 6.0 that provides network administrators with a Control Panel-like functionality for their IIS components. The Web Service Extensions allow the administrator to allow, prohibit, or change the component's properties. New IIS extensions (ISAPI applications and third-party IIS tools) can also be added to the IIS 6.0 server. By default, the following Web Service Extensions are available:

- ASP.NET extensions
- ASP extensions
- CGI and ISAPI applications
- Front Page Server extensions
- WebDAV support for IIS directories

The Web Service Extensions in the IIS Manager can be located by selecting the **Web Service Extensions node**, as seen in Figure 4.29. Right-clicking on any of the Web Service Extensions allows the network administrator to permit or prohibit it as well as examine its properties. Right-clicking on the **Web Service Extensions node** allows the administrator to add new extensions, prohibit extensions, or allow all extensions.

Figure 4.29 Viewing the Web Service Extensions

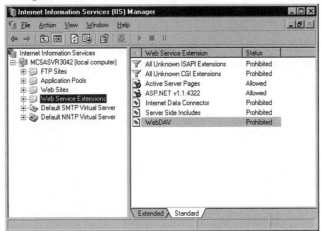

Creating Virtual Directories

A virtual directory is a *reference* to an existing directory on a Web or FTP site. Access can be obtained to the subdirectories from a root Web or FTP directory. And sometimes the network administrator needs to go beyond the root directory access information to process a Web request. Virtual directories can be used to remedy these scenarios. For example, suppose an administrator stores all image files for a large shopping catalogue in one directory. This allows them to point multiple Web servers to this single virtual directory, resulting in a low maintenance solution where they simply need to maintain one images directory instead of several. The Web or FTP site can refer to this directory as it exists within its directory structure, even if it physically exists outside of the Web server's directory structure.

The only real limitation to using virtual directories is that they are not a physical element—you cannot simply cut and paste its contents from one server to another. In addition, all virtual directories must be manually configured. The process for creating a virtual directory for a Web server is discussed in Exercise 4.07. The process for creating a virtual directory for an FTP server is very similar to that for a Web server.

EXERCISE 4.07

CREATING A NEW VIRTUAL DIRECTORY: WEB SERVER

1. Start the IIS Manager by clicking **Start** | **Programs** | **Administrative Tools** | **Internet Information Services (IIS) Manager**.

2. Select the Web site you are creating the virtual directory for. Right-click on it and select **New Virtual Directory** from the context menu.

3. The Virtual Directory Creation Wizard appears. Click **Next** to dismiss the opening page of the Wizard.

4. In the Virtual Directory Alias dialog box, as seen in Figure 4.30, you must enter a name for this new virtual directory. In this example the Alias is **ImageFiles**. Click **Next** to continue.

Figure 4.30 Entering the Virtual Directory Alias

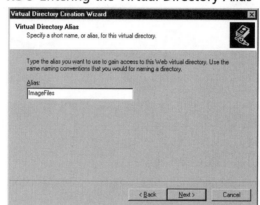

5. In the Web Site Content Directory dialog box, you must select the physical directory location that the virtual directory should point to. In our example, the virtual directory ImageFiles is pointing at D:\WWWImageFiles. Click **Next** to continue.

Figure 4.31 Entering the Web Site Content Directory

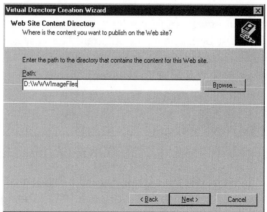

6. In the Virtual Directory Access Permissions dialog box, as seen in Figure 4.32, you must configure the permissions that will be allowed on the

new virtual directory. You will have the same options (**Read, Run scripts**) as you did when you previously created a new Web site. After making your selection, click **Next** to create the virtual directory.

Figure 4.32 Configuring the Virtual Directory Permissions

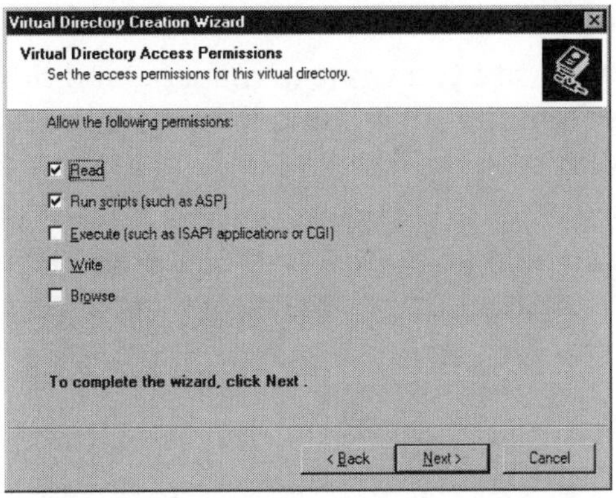

Hosting Multiple Web Sites

Hosting multiple Web sites can be done in one of three different ways:

- The most common is to assign an IP address to every new Web site. The obvious limitation is the number of IP addresses available for the organization, which is not a major issue for internal access within an enterprise. This practice can be an expensive one to manage depending on the number of public IP addresses that must be acquired.

- The second method is to use a single IP address, but different port numbers for each Web site.

- The third method of hosting multiple Web sites is to use host headers, as seen previously in the "Creating New Web Sites Using the Web Site Creation Wizard" section of this chapter.

Exercise 4.08 outlines the steps to change IP addresses and host headers for a Web site.

EXERCISE 4.08

CREATING A NEW VIRTUAL DIRECTORY: FTP SERVER

1. Start the IIS Manager by clicking **Start | Programs | Administrative Tools | Internet Information Services (IIS) Manager**.

2. Select the Web site you want to manage and right-click on it. Select **Properties** from the context menu to open the Web Site Properties dialog box, as seen in Figure 4.33.

Figure 4.33 Examining the Web Site Properties

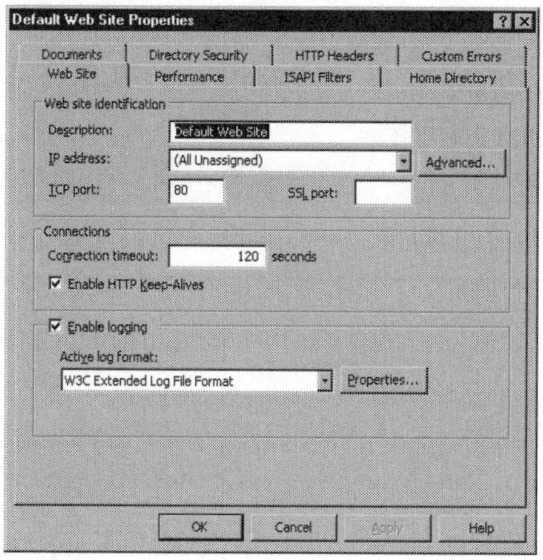

3. You can change the IP address that is assigned to the Web site by using the **IP address** drop-down menu.

4. Alternatively, you can change the port number that is assigned to the Web site by using the **TCP port** box.

5. If you want to change the host header that is assigned to the Web site, click the **Advanced** button to open the Advanced Web Site Identification dialog box, as seen in Figure 4.34. Host headers are unique DNS names that identify different Web sites. IIS receives all requests for a single IP address and filters them using the host header information, forwarding them to the correct Web site according to the header name. This is a good mechanism for implementing small to medium Web sites on a single machine. You should use a dedicated IP address for larger Web sites.

Figure 4.34 Examining the Header Information for a Web Site

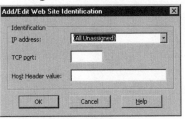

6. Click the **Add** button to add a new host header using the Add/Edit Web Identification dialog box, as seen in Figure 4.35. From this location, you can select the IP address of the Web site and its port number. You can also enter the host header information. After entering all of the information, click **OK** to save it.

Figure 4.35 Entering a Host Header for a Web Site

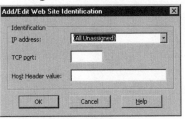

 NOTE

SSL certificates are issued for a Web site and are tied to an IP address or machine name. SSL Web sites should have a dedicated IP address for the Web site and not use host headers.

Configuring Web Site Performance

The performance of a Web site can be configured in two different ways:

- The bandwidth throttling option can be used to restrict resources for a given Web site. Bandwidth throttling limits the network bandwidth resources for a Web site. The maximum bandwidth value is 1024KB per second. This is also the default value. Bandwidth throttling can be enabled by selecting the **Limit the network bandwidth to this Web site** check box and specifying the maximum kilobytes per second value.

- The number of connections to the Web site can also be limited by selecting the **Unlimited** or **Connections limited to** option buttons and specifying a connection value.

Figure 4.36 illustrates the configuration for bandwidth throttling and connection limitations. The **Performance** tab can be accessed by right-clicking on a Web site and selecting **Properties** from the context menu.

Figure 4.36 Configuring Performance Options for a Web Site

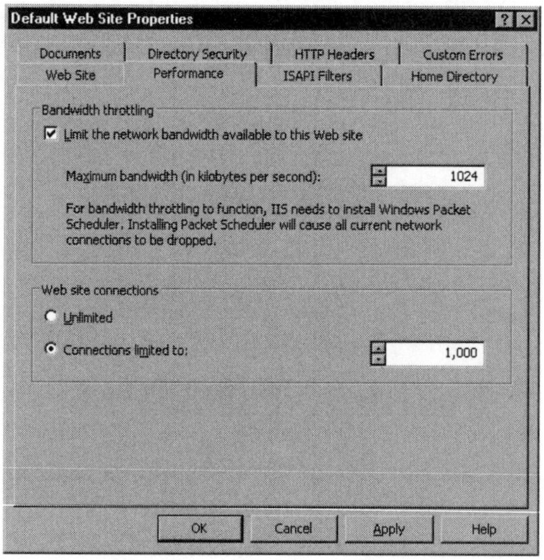

Working with ASP.NET

ASP.NET is an advanced version of Active Server Pages. IIS 6.0 allows the network administrator to run both ASP and ASP.NET applications. The ASP.NET scripts are built on the .NET model and the ASP scripts follow the old Windows COM. The ASP.NET model is scalable and performs better than the ASP model. ASP scripting can be used inside ASP.NET scripts. ASP.NET applications can be built on any .NET-compatible language (C#, VB.NET, JScript.NET, and so forth).

Before using ASP.NET, the administrator must first enable it as outlined in the following steps:

1. Start the IIS Manager by clicking **Start | Programs | Administrative Tools | Internet Information Services (IIS) Manager**.

2. Select the **Web Server Extensions node**.

3. Select the **ASP.NET object**, right-click on it, and select **Allow** from the context menu, as seen in Figure 4.37.

Figure 4.37 Enabling ASP.NET Support

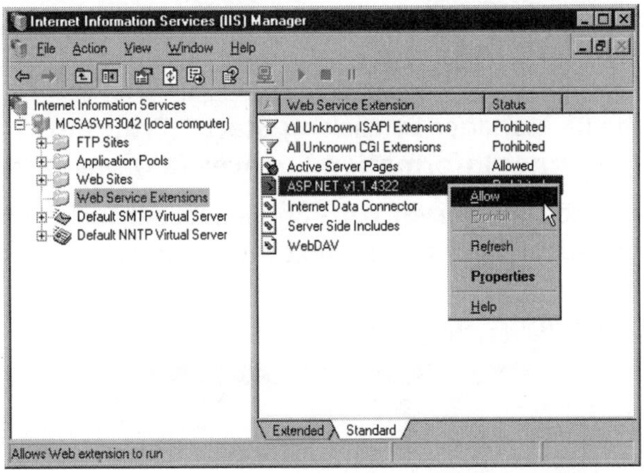

Backing Up and Restoring the IIS Metabase

The IIS metabase in IIS 6.0 uses two XML files to store its configuration information:

- metabase.xml
- mbschema.xml

It is a good practice to back up the metabase regularly in the event disaster strikes the IIS server. When the backup is performed, both the metabase itself and the metabase schema files are backed up. The metabase backup will back up both the metabase and metabase schema files. A file with the extension .md*VersionNumber* is created for the metabase, and a file with the extension .sc*VersionNumber* is created for the schema.

The metabase can be safely restored from the backup should disaster strike, however this process does not back up any IIS data such as Web site or FTP site content. The network administrator must back up and restore this content using the Windows Backup Utility, as discussed in Chapter 5.

When backing up the metabase, the administrator can encrypt it with a password to protect it. If the computer running IIS fails, the metabase can be restored from the backup on a new installation of Windows Server 2003 or on a different computer (if using secure backup). It is also possible to restore the metabase with a previous version of the metabase files that are saved in the history folder. However, the administrator cannot restore a backup from an earlier version of IIS. If they restore from the history files, they cannot restore to a different IIS installation or different computer.

IIS automatically makes regular backups of the metabase in addition to manual backups made by the administrator. History files are also created automatically, as long as the history feature is enabled (by default, it is). IIS Manager can be used to restore history files, as well as restoring from backup. Exercise 4.09 outlines the steps required to backup the IIS metabase.

EXERCISE 4.09

BACKING UP THE IIS METABASE

1. Start the IIS Manager by clicking **Start | Programs | Administrative Tools | Internet Information Services (IIS) Manager**.

2. Right-click on the **server root** and select **All Tasks | Backup/Restore Configuration** from the context menu, as seen in Figure 4.38.

Figure 4.38 Starting the Metabase Backup

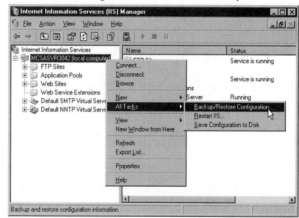

3. The Configuration Backup/Restore dialog box appears, as seen in Figure 4.39.

Figure 4.39 Performing a Backup or Restoration

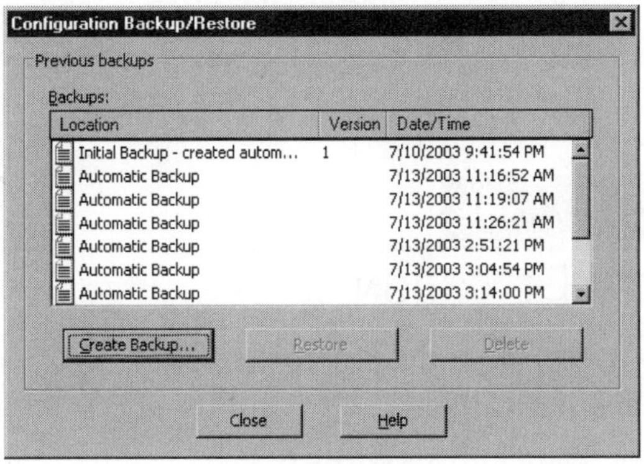

4. To create a new backup, click the **Create Backup** button. The Configuration Backup dialog box appears, as seen in Figure 4.40.

Figure 4.40 Configuring the Metabase Backup

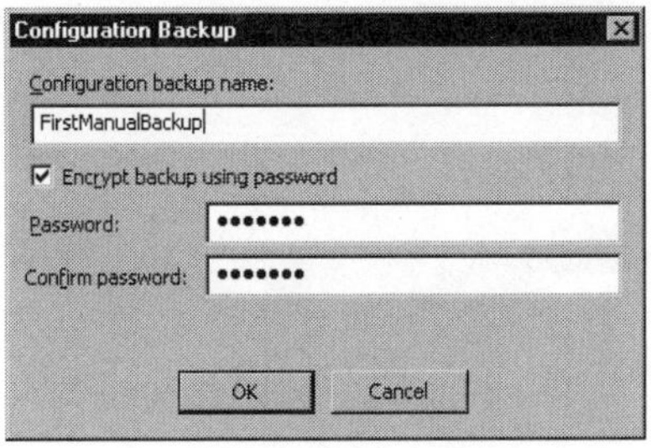

5. Enter a name for the configuration backup. For this example we use **FirstManualBackup**. You can also select to back up with a password by selecting the **Encrypt backup using password** checkbox. If you select this option, type and confirm the password. Click **OK** to create the backup.

6. Your new backup will appear in the list of backups. Restoring IIS from a backup is done through the same interface. Select the backup and click the **Restore** button if you wish to restore the backup.

7. Click **Close** to close the Configuration Backup/Restore dialog box.

Enabling Health Detection

Health detection enables IIS to monitor its worker process functionality. The network administrator can enable pinging and configure rapid application failover, discussed more in the "Troubleshooting IIS 6.0" section of this chapter. Administrators can also set the start up and shut down times for a worker process using the options discussed in Exercise 4.10. You can enable health detection by following the steps outlined in Exercise 4.10. Note that this process only works if you are running in worker process isolation mode—not in IIS 5.0 isolation mode.

EXERCISE 4.10

ENABLING HEALTH DETECTION

1. Start the IIS Manager by clicking **Start | Programs | Administrative Tools | Internet Information Services (IIS) Manager**.

2. Expand the **Application Pools** node.

3. Locate the application pool that contains the Web site you wish to enable health detection for. Right-click on it and select **Properties** from

Figure 4.41 Locating the Application Pool

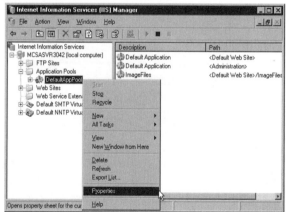

the context menu, as seen in Figure 4.41.

4. Switch to the **Health** tab of the Application Pool Properties dialog box, as seen in Figure 4.42.

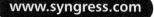

Figure 4.42 Examining the Health Detection Properties

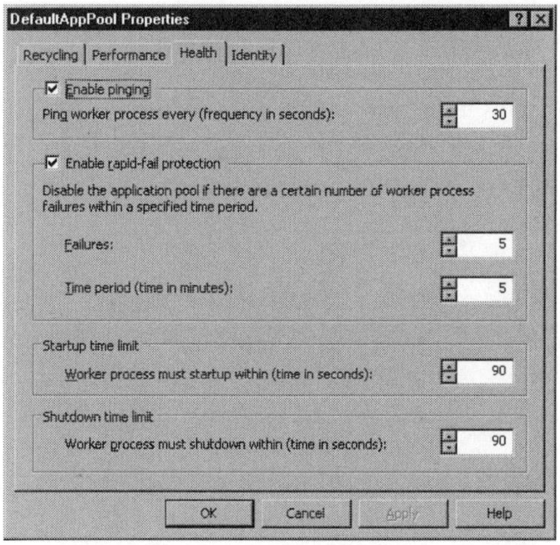

5. You can configure the ping interval using the **Enable pinging** option. This interval describes the timeframe to contact a worker process to make sure it is functioning accordingly. The default setting is 30 seconds. The **Enable rapid-fail protection** option is explained in the "503 error" section later in this chapter. You can also configure the worker process startup time (if the worker process restarts) with the Startup time limit option, and shutdown time (if the worker process gets into a deadlock position) using the Shutdown time limit option available on this tab.
6. Click **OK** to accept any changes you have made.

EXAM 70-292 OBJECTIVE 3.3.2

Managing IIS Security

Security in IIS revolves around three main areas:

- User authentication
- IP address/domain restrictions
- SSL secured connections

Overall, these concepts have not changed significantly since IIS 5.0, except that the Windows Server 2003 default installation extends more security features than the previous Windows server versions. The following sections examine each of these three areas in more detail. All security configurations are performed from the Directory Security tab of the Web/FTP site Properties dialog box, as seen in Figure 4.43.

Figure 4.43 Configuring Directory Security Properties

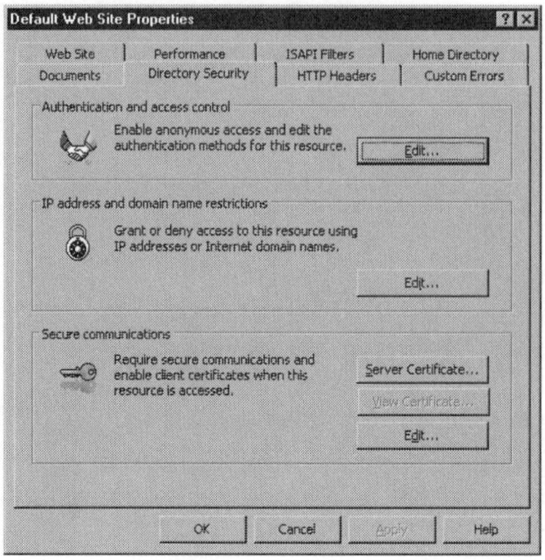

User Authentication Methods

Authentication is the process of validating a user's credentials. Since IIS 6.0 runs on Windows Server 2003, users cannot access IIS without being authenticated. IIS 6.0 supports the following types of authentication:

- Anonymous
- Basic
- Integrated Windows
- Digest
- .NET Passport
- Certificate mapping

Each of these authentication methods are examined in more detail in the following sections.

Anonymous Authentication

Anonymous authentication is the most commonly used method on the Internet. It is used for public Web sites that are not concerned with user-level authentication. Using anonymous access, companies do not have to maintain user accounts for everyone who will be accessing their sites. Anonymous access also works with browsers other than Internet Explorer.

IIS runs all HTTP and FTP requests in the security context of a Windows Server 2003 user account. Windows Server 2003 requires a logon. This means that for someone to log on or access files on a server, they must have a user account. For anonymous Web access to work, a Windows Server 2003 user account must exist. This account is used anytime someone connects to the server anonymously. IIS 6.0 creates a user account for this purpose when it is installed. The account is named IUSR_*computername*. *computername* is a variable that is replaced with your computer's name. This user account is a member of the Everyone group and the Guest group. It also has permission to logon locally to the Web server.

Basic Authentication

Basic authentication is used by almost every Web browser to pass usernames and passwords back to the server. It is widely supported in both Web browsers and Web servers. Basic authentication has several benefits:

- It works through firewalls and proxy servers.

- It is compatible with lower versions of Internet Explorer.

- It allows users to access resources that are not located on the IIS server.

- It allows the administrator to use NTFS permissions on a user-by-user basis to restrict access. Unlike anonymous access, each user has a unique username and password.

Basic authentication also has some drawbacks:

- Information is sent over the network as cleartext. The information is encoded with base64 encoding (see RFC 1521 for more information on base64 encoding), but it is sent in an unencrypted format. Someone could easily use a tool such as Network Monitor to view the information as it travels across the cable and use a base64 decoder to read it.

- By default, users must have the "Log on Locally" right to use basic authentication.

For Web requests, the network administrator can make basic authentication more secure using SSL to encrypt the session. SSL is a secure communication protocol invented by Netscape, used to encrypt communication between two computers. SSL is processor-intensive and will degrade the performance of a system. SSL must be used during the entire session because the browser sends the username and password to the server every time the user makes a request. Even if the administrator used SSL for only the initial logon, as soon as the user requested a different file, the user would be sending their username and password over the network as cleartext again. SSL should be used only on Web sites with sensitive data.

Users authenticating with basic authentication must provide a valid username and password. The user account can be a local account or a domain account. By default, the IIS server looks locally or in its local domain for the user account. If the user account is in another domain, the user must specify the domain name during logon. The syntax for this is *domain name\username,* where *domain name* is the name of the user's domain. For example, if you wanted to login as the user Bob in the Syngress domain, you would enter **Syngress\Bob** in the username field.

Integrated Windows Authentication

Integrated Windows Authentication (IWA) is a secure IIS authentication method because usernames and passwords are not transmitted across the network. IWA is convenient, because if a user is already logged on to the domain and if the user has the correct permissions for the site, they are not prompted for their username and password. Instead, IIS attempts to use the user's cached credentials for authentication. The cached credentials are hashed and sent to the IIS server for authentication. If the cached credentials do not have the correct permissions, the user is prompted to enter a different username and password.

IWA uses either NTLM or Kerberos for authentication. The Web browser and the IIS server negotiate which one to use. Both Kerberos and NTLM have their own advantages and disadvantages. Kerberos is less likely to be compromised because it is more secure than NTLM. Unlike NTLM, which authenticates only the client, Kerberos authenticates both the client and the server. This helps prevent spoofing. Kerberos allows users to access remote network resources not located on the IIS server. NTLM restricts users to the information located on the IIS server only.

Kerberos is the preferred authentication method. The following are requirements for Kerberos to be used instead of NTLM:

- The client machine must be in either the same domain as the IIS server or in a trusted domain.

- The client machine must be running Windows 2000.

- The client must be using Internet Explorer 5.0 or higher as its browser.

There are a few limitations of IWA:

- It works only with Internet Explorer 2.0 or higher (for NTLM authentication).

- While NTLM can generally get past firewalls, it is usually stopped by proxy servers.

- Kerberos can generally get past the proxy server, but is generally stopped by the firewall.

You must configure a *realm* when using Integrated Windows Authentication.

Digest Authentication

Digest authentication has many similarities to basic authentication, but it overcomes many of its associated problems. Digest authentication does not send usernames or passwords over the network. It is more secure than basic authentication, but requires more planning to make it work.

Some of the similarities with basic authentication are:

- Users must have the Log on Locally right.

- Both methods work through firewalls and proxy servers.

Like all authentication methods, digest authentication has some drawbacks:

- Users can only access resources on the IIS server. Their credentials cannot be passed to another computer.

- The IIS server must be a member of a domain.

- All user accounts must store passwords using reversible encryption.

- The method works only with Internet Explorer 5.0 or higher.

Digest authentication is secure due to the way it passes authentication information over the network. Usernames and passwords are never sent. Instead, IIS uses a message digest (also called a *hash*) to verify the user's credentials—hence the name Digest authentication. A hash works by applying a one-way mathematical formula to data. The data used here is the user's username and password. Because the hash is one-way, it cannot be reversed to recover a user's information.

In order for Digest authentication to work, all user accounts must be stored using reversible encryption. When an IIS server receives a Digest authentication request, it receives a hash value instead of a username and password. IIS sends the hash value to Active Directory to verify that the user's information is correct. Active Directory runs the same hashing formula against the user's information. If the hash value that Active Directory comes up with matches the hash it received from IIS, the user's information is correct. If Active Directory reaches a different value, the user's information is considered to be incorrect. Active Directory can only run the hashing formula against the user's information if it has a plaintext copy of the password. Choosing the **Store password using reversible encryption** option on a user account, as seen in Figure 4.44, stores a plaintext copy of the password in Active Directory. After enabling this setting for a user account, the user's password must be changed to create the plaintext copy.

Figure 4.44 Enabling Digest Authentication for a User Account

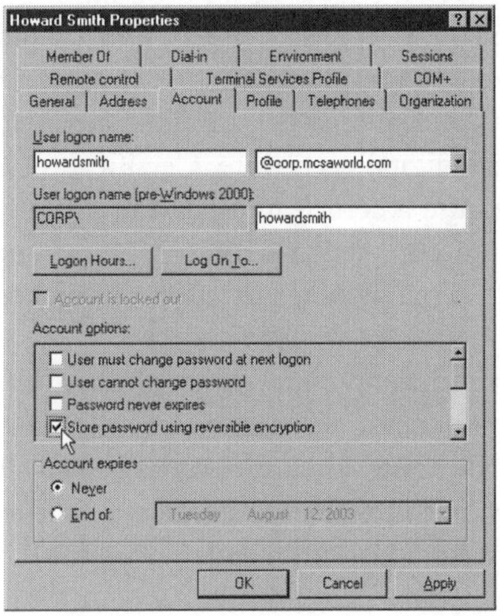

.NET Passport Authentication

The .NET Passport option uses .NET passports to authenticate Web users—a new feature in IIS 6.0. .NET Passport is a single sign-on mechanism. The incoming HTTP requests must have the passport credentials (user name and password) inside the query string or as a cookie value. As cookies can be compromised by attacks, it recommended that .NET Passport authentication be used over SSL. Network administrators must configure a default domain when using .NET Passport authentication.

EXAM WARNING

Support for .NET Passport authentication is a new feature to IIS 6.0. As such, make sure you have a complete understanding of it, including requirements to configure and implement it.

Using Client Certificate Mapping

Client certificate mapping is the process of mapping a certificate to a user account. There are two types of certificate mappings that are supported in IIS. Both methods require the use of SSL.

- One-to-one mapping
- Many-to-one mapping

Why is mapping beneficial? Normally, if an administrator wanted to give a user access to a site, they would create a user account. They would give the user a username and password and let them use one of the three authentication methods previously discussed—basic, digest, or Windows Integrated. This is done because the operating system requires the use of user accounts for controlling access. This takes a lot of administrative effort, because now the administrator has to maintain a large database of user accounts. They also have to worry about someone's password being compromised.

To provide better security and reduce the administrative workload, the network administrator could give their users a digital certificate. Certificates can be used to verify a user's identity. It is more efficient to use a certificate than a user account because certificates can be examined without having to connect to a database. It is generally safer to distribute certificates than user accounts. It is much easier to guess or crack someone's password than it is to forge a certificate.

Where does mapping fit into the picture? If certificates are more secure and easier to distribute than user accounts, but the operating system requires a user account to control access, what do we do? The administrator can create a *mapping* between the user account and the certificate. When the user presents the certificate to the operating system, the user is given whatever rights are assigned to the mapped account. The end result is identical to the user logging on with a username and password. This solution provides the best of both worlds. The administrator does not have to distribute usernames and passwords to all of their users, but they still employ user accounts to secure resources.

One-to-One Certificate Mapping

As the name indicates, one-to-one mappings map one user account to one certificate. The user presents their certificate, and IIS compares this certificate to the certificate that it contains for the user. If the certificates match, the user is authenticated with their mapped account. For this system to work, the server must contain a copy of all the client certificates. Generally, one-to-one mappings are used in smaller environments. One of the reasons mapping is used is to make the network easier to administer. Network administrators do not want to have to maintain a large database of user accounts. If one-to-one mappings are used in a large environment, a large database is created because every certificate is mapped to a unique account.

Many-to-One Certificate Mapping

Many-to-one mappings map many certificates to one user account and are usually processed differently than one-to-one mappings. Since there is not a one-to-one association between user accounts and certificates, the server does not have to maintain a copy of individual user certificates. The server uses rules to verify a client. Rules are configured to look for certain things in the client's certificate. If those things are correct, the user is mapped to the shared user account. For example, we could set up a rule to check which CA issued the certificate. If our company's CA issued the certificate, we would allow the mapping. If the certificate were issued by another CA, the user would be denied access.

TEST DAY TIP

You may find it helpful to write down the various methods of Web authentication on your scratch paper before beginning the exam. Be sure to write down the pros and cons of each method and any special considerations that must be taken into account when working with each method.

Configuring User Authentication

Clicking the **Edit** button on the Directory Security tab opens the Authentication Methods dialog box, as seen in Figure 4.45

Figure 4.45 Configuring Authentication Methods

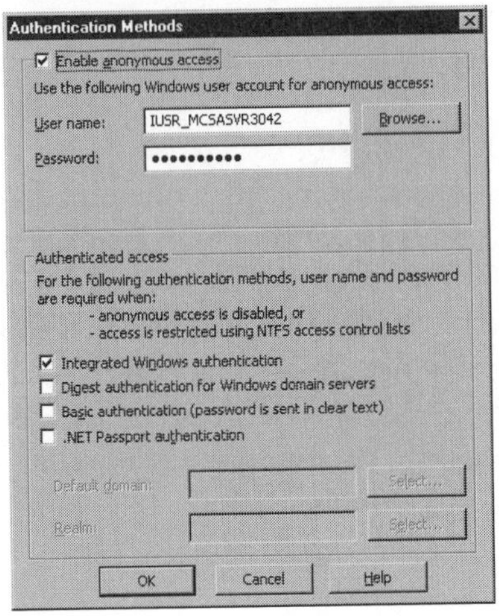

To configure the authentication methods to be used for a Web site, follow the steps outlined in Exercise 4.11.

EXERCISE 4.11

CONFIGURING WEB SITE AUTHENTICATION

1. Start the IIS Manager by clicking **Start | Programs | Administrative Tools | Internet Information Services (IIS) Manager**.

2. Select your Web site, and right-click and select **Properties** from the context menu.

3. Click the **Directory Security** tab.

4. Click **Edit** in the Authentication and Access control section of the **Directory Security** tab to open the Authentication Methods dialog box, as seen previously in Figure 4.45.

5. By default, the **Enable anonymous access** and **Integrated Windows authentication** options are enabled.

6. You can enable Digest authentication by selecting the **Digest authentication for Windows domain servers** option. You will be presented with a dialog box, as seen in Figure 4.46, warning you that Digest authentication can only be used for Active Directory domain user accounts. Click **Yes** to acknowledge the warning.

Figure 4.46 Configuring Authentication Methods

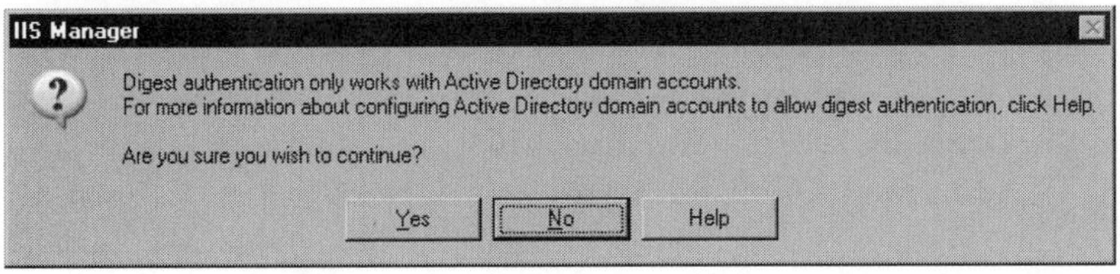

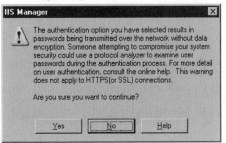

7. After you are returned to the Authentication Methods dialog box, ensure that you configure a realm so that digest authentication will function properly.

8. You can enable basic authentication by selecting the **Basic authentication** option. You will be presented with a warning dialog box, as seen in Figure 4.47, informing you that basic authentication transmits user credentials in clear text and recommends that you only use basic authentication over SSL-secured connections. Click **Yes** to acknowledge the warning.

Figure 4.47 Configuring Authentication Methods

9. You can enable .NET Passport authentication by selecting the **.NET Passport authentication** option. You must configure a default domain in order for .NET Passport authentication to function properly.

10. If you want to change the user account that is to be used for anonymous access, click the **Browse** button in the Enable anonymous access section of the dialog box. The standard Select User dialog box opens, as discussed in Chapter 1. You can also opt to disable anonymous access to your Web site by deselecting the **Enable anonymous access** option.

11. Click **OK** on the Authentication Methods dialog box to close it.

Configuring IP Address/Domain Restrictions

If desired, a network administrator can also opt to restrict users at the IP address or DNS domain level. This can be used to allow or block all but the configured IP addresses or domains. On the Directory Security tab, as seen previously in Figure 4.43, click the **Edit** button in the **IP address and domain name restrictions** section to open the IP Address and Domain Name Restrictions dialog box, as seen in Figure 4.48.

Figure 4.48 Assigning IP Address Restrictions on a Web Site

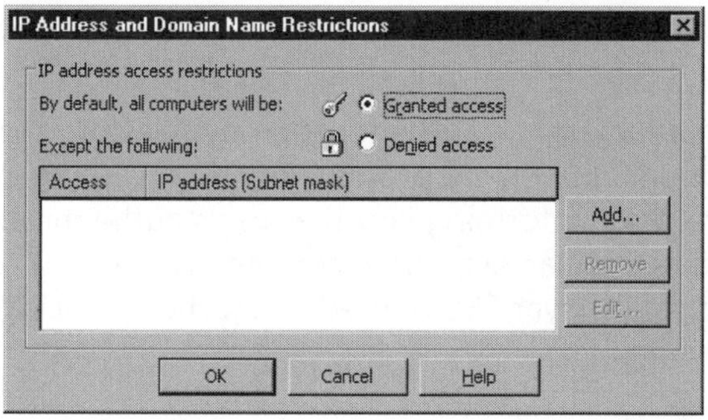

The administrator can choose to grant or deny access to all computers except those listed in the Except the following area of this dialog box. To add a new entry, click the **Add** button to open the dialog box, as seen in Figure 4.49. In this case an entry is being configured that will deny access to the specified IP address or domain name.

Figure 4.49 Assigning IP Address Restrictions on a Web Site

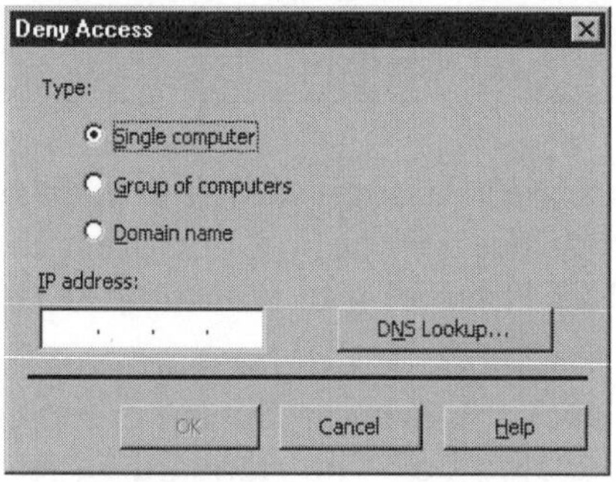

An entry can be configured using one of the following three methods:

- The IP address of a single computer
- An IP address range for a group of computers
- A domain name

Click **OK** after making your access control entry.

Configuring SSL-Secured Communications

SSL can be used to provide a digital certificate-based method of authenticating and securing communications that occur with the IIS server. Before a network administrator can use certificates on their Web servers for authentication, there are two server certificates that they must have. The first is for the CA, and the second is for the Web server. The administrator must have two different certificates for these two different functions, even if both reside on the same server.

It is assumed that you already have a Windows Server 2003 CA in place, if not you may want to review the concepts covered in *MCSE Planning and Maintaining a Windows Server 2003 Network Infrastructure: Exam 70-293 Study Guide and DVD Training System*, ISBN: 1931836930, 2003 by Syngress Publishing.

Exercise 4.12 outlines the process you must follow to obtain a server certificate for your IIS server.

EXERCISE 4.12

REQUESTING A SERVER CERTIFICATE FOR THE IIS SERVER

1. Start the IIS Manager by clicking **Start | Programs | Administrative Tools | Internet Information Services (IIS) Manager**.

2. Select your Web site, right-click and select **Properties** from the context menu.

3. Click the **Directory Security** tab.

4. Click **Server Certificate** in the Secure Communications section of the Directory Security tab to start the IIS Certificate Wizard. Click **Next** to dismiss the opening dialog box.

5. On the Server Certificate dialog box, as seen in Figure 4.50, you can select how you want to create the server SSL certificate. For this example, select the **Create a new certificate** option and click **Next** to continue.

6. In the Delayed or Immediate Request dialog box, as seen in Figure 4.51, you can decide when to send the certificate request. If you already have an online CA configured, you should select the **Send the request immediately to an online certification authority** option. Click **Next** to continue.

Figure 4.50 Selecting How to Create the Server SSL Certificate

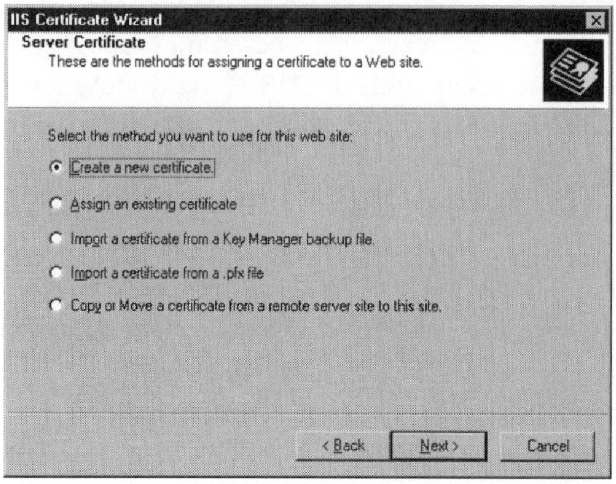

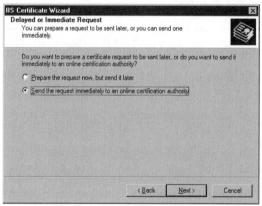

Figure 4.51 Selecting how to Transmit the Server SSL Certificate

7. In the Name and Security Settings dialog box, as seen in Figure 4.52, you must configure a descriptive name for the new certificate as well as the key length. In this example we have chosen to use **SSLSecurityforDefaultWebSite**. Click **Next** to continue.

Figure 4.52 Configuring the Certificate Name and Key Length

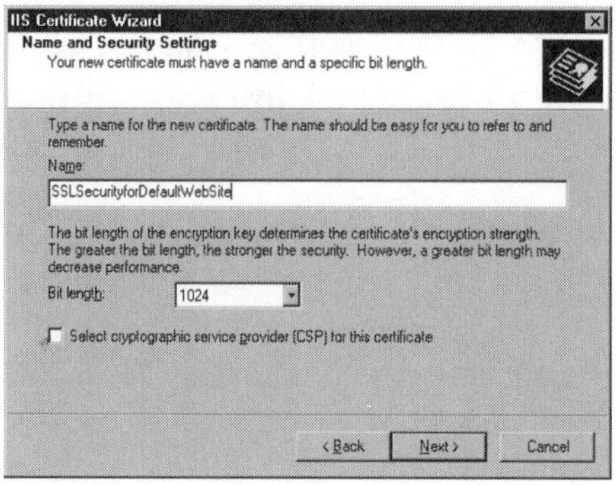

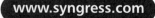

8. In the Organization Information dialog box enter or select the **Organization** and **Organizational unit** that the certificate is being issued for. Click **Next** to continue.

9. In the Your Site's Common Name dialog box, as seen in Figure 4.53, you must enter the IIS server's common name—its FQDN if on the Internet or its NetBIOS name if on an Intranet. This name is extremely critical and must be configured exactly the same as the name that users will use to connect to the site. Click **Next** to continue.

Figure 4.53 Configuring the Web Site's Common Name

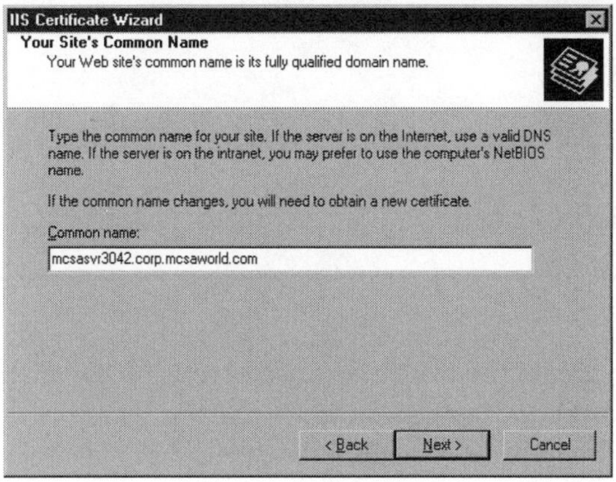

10. In the Geographical Information dialog box, enter the required geographical information and click **Next** to continue.

11. In the SSL Port dialog box, enter the TCP port that the Web site will use for SSL. The default is 443 and should not be changed in most cases. Click **Next** to continue.

12. In the Choose a Certification Authority dialog box, you must select the CA from the available listing that is be used to issue the new server SSL certificate. After making your selection, click **Next** to continue.

13. The Certificate Request Submission dialog box appears, as seen in Figure 4.54, allowing you a chance to review your settings before submitting the certificate request. If all is well, click **Next** to request the certificate.

Figure 4.54 Reviewing the Certificate Request Summary

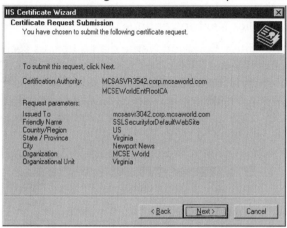

14.   Click **Finish** to close the IIS Certificate Wizard.

Now that you have gotten the server certificate, you must configure the server to use it. Exercise 4.13 outlines the process to configure SSL for secure communications and user authentication. User authentication via SSL uses certificate mapping.

NOTE

Remember that SSL uses port 443 by default, so make sure you have not blocked this at your firewall.

EXERCISE 4.13

CONFIGURING WEB SECURITY AND AUTHENTICATION USING SSL

1.   Start the IIS Manager by clicking **Start | Programs | Administrative Tools | Internet Information Services (IIS) Manager**.

2.   Select your Web site, right-click and select **Properties** from the context menu.

3.   Click the **Directory Security** tab.

4.   Click **Edit** in the Secure communications section of the Directory Security tab to open the Secure Communications dialog box, as seen in Figure 4.55.

Figure 4.55 Configuring SSL Properties for a Web Site

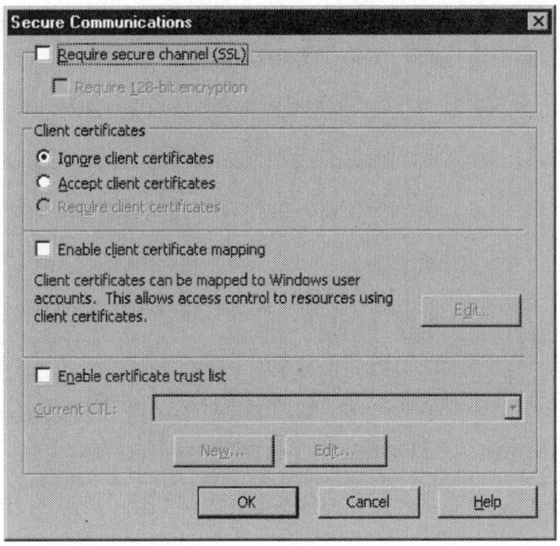

5. Configure your secure communication settings as desired:

   ■ Select the **Require secure channel (SSL)** check box to configure SSL-encrypted communication for visitors using a Web browser that supports secure communications—URLs starting with *https://*.

   ■ Select the **Require 128-bit encryption** check box to require a 128-bit encrypted communication link for a Web browser to connect with this Web site. This setting is only available once you have selected the **Require secure channel (SSL)** option.

   ■ Selecting the **Ignore client certificates** option allows users to have access without being prompted to present a client certificate. This is not a recommended setting as it degrades overall security.

   ■ Selecting the **Accept client certificates** option allows users with client certificates access, but does not require the certificate. A user that has a valid certificate can use certificate mapping, a user without a valid certificate will use one of the previously discussed authentication methods.

   ■ Selecting the **Require client certificates** allows only users with a valid client certificate to connect to the Web site. Users without a valid client certificate are denied access. This setting is only available once you have selected the **Require secure channel (SSL)** option.

6. If you want to use certificate mapping, select the **Enable client certificate mapping** check box and then click **Edit** to configure the mappings, as previously discussed.

7. To create or edit approved certificate trust lists (CTL) for the Web site, enable this option and click **New** or **Edit** to configure it. A CTL is a list of approved CAs for a particular Web site.

8. Click **OK** to close the Secure Communications dialog.

TEST DAY TIP

If you set the Require 128-bit encryption option and clients connect with a valid certificate but with a browser that cannot support 128-bit encryption, they will not be able to connect. Select this option with care!

Troubleshooting IIS 6.0

Let's examine some of the troubleshooting associated with IIS 6.0. Troubleshooting can be divided in three different areas:

- Content errors
- Connection errors
- Miscellaneous errors

Troubleshooting Content Errors

Content errors are often caused by ASP or ASP.NET application codes. These application codes or scripts are required to perform business intelligence tasks to manipulate data. Some of the more common content errors are discussed in the following sections.

Static Files Return 404 Errors

This is the most common IIS error and could be due to one of two main reasons:

- The user may have entered an incorrect URL
- The file extension is invalid

IIS is configured to only accept requests from files that have a valid extension. For example, IIS will understand the ".ASPX" extension, but it will not understand an ".ABC" file extension.

TEST DAY TIP

You can enable IIS 6.0 to accept all requests for any file extension by adding the **"*,application/octet-stream"** value to the MIME types list in IIS 6.0.

IIS checks for the file extension upon its receipt of a request. All of the valid file extensions are available as Multipurpose Internet Mail Extensions (MIME) formats in IIS. MIME types instruct the Web server how to process the incoming requests. For example, if an administrator requests an ".ASPX" file, the Web server knows to instruct ASP.NET to process the request. The MIME type does not have any effect on the returned data to the client.

EXAM WARNING

If you change the MIME settings, you need to restart the World Wide Web Publishing service. IIS 6.0 worker process needs to be recycled to detect the new MIME types. Therefore, a restart of the WWW service is necessary.

Dynamic Content Returns a 404 Error

IIS 6.0 default installation does not activate ASP.NET and CGI applications. These have to be manually enabled using the Web Service Extensions node of the IIS Manager, as previously discussed previously in the "Enabling Web Service Extensions" section. If the ASP.NET or CGI applications are not enabled, users will receive a 404 error on dynamic content.

Sessions Lost Due to Worker Process Recycling

A session could best be described as a data storage mechanism for a single user on a Web site. HTTP cookies are used to store information about the user activities; this information is referred to as session data. These ASP sessions were alive until the IIS server was restarted or they timed out. IIS 6.0 works on a worker process model, as previously discussed. Therefore, when the worker process stops, all session information is lost. The default installation configures IIS to recycle worker process every 120 minutes.

This session information is kept in RAM on the IIS server and can grow quite bulky in larger IIS implementations. This can result in adverse performance on the servers; therefore IIS 6.0 empties the session information by recycling the worker process every 1,740 minutes (or 29 hours) by default. The network administrator can either disable worker process recycling or extend the time settings if this creates problems. Worker process recycling can be configured by completing the steps outlined here:

1. Start the IIS Manager by clicking **Start** | **Programs** | **Administrative Tools** | **Internet Information Services (IIS) Manager**.

2. Expand the **Applications Pools** node and select the application pool that contains your Web site.

3. Right right-click on the selected application pool and select **Properties** from the context menu.

4. The Recycling tab, as seen in Figure 4.56, is shown by default and allows you to configure recycling as needed.

Figure 4.56 Configuring the Recycling Properties for an Application Pool

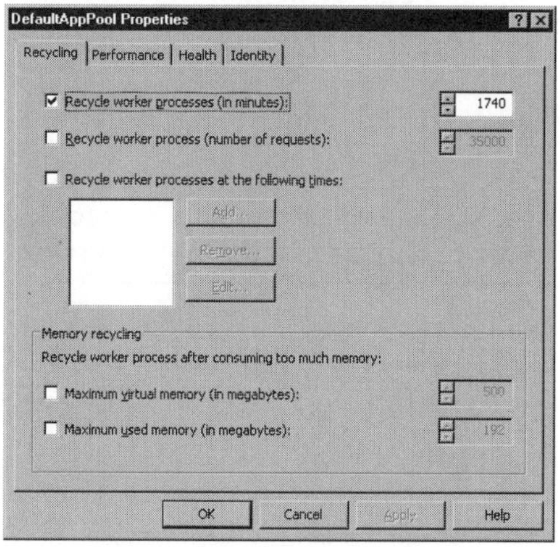

ASP.NET Pages are Returned as Static Files

ASP.NET files are processed at the server and the HTML is returned to the browser. In some cases this could be DHTML, depending on the complexity of the browser. If the IIS server does not recognize an ASP.NET file or the .ASPX file extension, the server returns the static text as the reply. This can happen if IIS is reinstalled without reregistering ASP.NET.

Troubleshooting Connection Errors

Typically, connection issues are related to the performance of IIS and ASP.NET. Some of the more common connection errors are discussed in the following sections:

503 Errors

This error is generally caused by HTTP.sys overload and is usually due to one of two reasons:

- The request queue length has exceeded the number of available application pool resources
- Rapid-fail protection has been initiated by IIS

Every application pool has a configurable queue length. If the request pool queue exceeds this amount, the HTTP.sys cannot process the requests. This results in a 503 error being sent to the client. The queue length of an application pool can be changed by performing the following steps:

1. Start the IIS Manager by clicking **Start | Programs | Administrative Tools | Internet Information Services (IIS) Manager**.

2. Expand the **Applications Pools** node and select the application pool that contains your Web site.

3. Right right-click on the selected application pool and select **Properties** from the context menu.

4. Switch to the **Performance** tab, as seen in Figure 4.57.

Figure 4.57 Configuring the Performance Properties of an Application

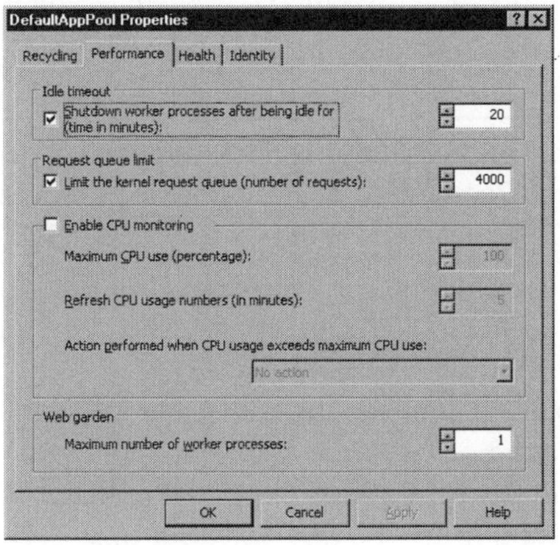

5. In the Request queue limit area, select the **Limit the kernel request queue** option and put a value in the text box.

6. Click **OK** to close the application pool Properties dialog box.

IIS initiates *rapid-fail protection* when too many application pool errors are generated for a specified time frame, which is usually the result of a memory leak in the application code. The default is five errors occurring in five minutes. This scenario triggers IIS to restart and issue a 503 error to the client. Alternatively, you can increase the error count and expand the timeframe by performing these steps:

1. Start the IIS Manager by clicking **Start | Programs | Administrative Tools | Internet Information Services (IIS) Manager**.

2. Expand the **Applications Pools** node and select the application pool that contains your Web site.

3. Right right-click on the selected application pool and select **Properties** from the context menu.

4. Switch to the **Health** tab, as seen previously in Figure 4.42.

5. In the Enable rapid-fail protection area, enter the value for **Failures** and **Time Period (in minutes)** spaces.

6. Click **OK** to close the application pool Properties dialog box.

401 Error – Sub-authentication Error

Anonymous access to Web sites is managed by the sub-authentication component (iissuba.dll). This DLL is not enabled by default in IIS 6.0, to avoid potential security risks due to anonymous access. The network administrator can enable the sub-authentication component by registering iissuba.dll and setting the *AnonymousPasswordSync* attribute in the metabase to **true**. The IIS administrator gets a warning when anonymous access is enabled.

TEST DAY TIP

The sub-authentication component for anonymous access is enabled by default in IIS 5.0 and lower. Remember, it is not enabled by default in IIS 6.0.

Client Requests Timing Out

There was less emphasis on connections timing out in IIS 5.0 and below; IIS 6.0 has made some considerable ground on this issue. IIS 6.0 has locked down and reduced the size of many client request properties, which has resulted in better efficiency and performance. Here are the new features in IIS 6.0 that deal with time outs:

- **Limits on response buffering** The network administrator can buffer all the process output at the server end and send the whole output to the client as a single entity, as opposed to processing some data, sending the information and starting to process the next bit of the initial request. This is referred to as *response buffering*. A timeout will result if the buffer exceeds the limit. This feature can be modified by using the *ASPBufferingLimit* metabase property.

- **Limits on posts** The maximum ASP post size is 204,800 bytes. A *post* refers to a HTTP POST response to the Web server. This is usually done as an HTML form submission. Sometimes these HTML form variables can be very lengthy. The maximum size allowed as HTTP POST request is referred to as Post limit/size. Each individual field can have up to 100k of data. If these fields are exceeded, a time out error is caused. This property can also be modified from the **AspMaxRequestEntityAllowed** property of the metabase.

- **Header size limitation** HTTP.sys only accepts a request that has less than 16K as the request header. HTTP.sys believes that anything larger is malicious and terminates the connection. The administrator can change this value by modifying the *MaxRequestBytes* registry key.

Troubleshooting Other Errors

The rest of the common errors you may experience do not clearly fall into content or connection categories, thus they are referred to as "other" errors.

File Not Found Errors for UNIX and Linux Files

IIS 6.0 can access and share information with UNIX and Linux systems. IIS 6.0, UNIX, and Linux all support mixed-case filenames. Unfortunately, the IIS *static file cache* stores filenames as upper case. UNIX and Linux systems are case sensitive whereas IIS is not. This results in the first file access occurring trouble-free; subsequent access to the same file will result in a *File Not Found* error because IIS 6.0 will try to extract it from the static file cache. The remedy is to disable static file cache if dealing with UNIX or Linux systems.

To disable static file cache on a Web site or a virtual directory, change the metabase property MD_VR_NO_CACHE to **1**. To disable static file cache for all sites, edit the DisableStaticFileCache=1 value in the registry. Changing these settings affect only ASP.NET files. ASP files are not affected by this change. The *static file cache* caches all of the static Web content for faster response times. Performance slips if this facility is disabled.

ISAPI Filters Are Not Automatically Visible as Properties of the Web Site

IIS 5.0 used to display all the ISAPI filters that are associated with a particular site. IIS 6.0 does not load an ISAPI DLL until it is actually invoked from a client request. Therefore, until the ISAPI DLL is loaded, it will not show up in the ISAPI tab of the Properties window. The network administrator must run IIS 6.0 in isolation mode if they want to get a complete list of ISAPI DLLs available for a site.

The Scripts and Msadc Virtual Directories Are Not Found in IIS 6.0

IIS 5.0 had executable permission on the Scripts and Msadc directories. This was one of the common security breaches of IIS 5.0. A malicious user could start to execute code in these virtual directories and take control of the IIS server. Therefore, IIS 6.0 is configured not to have these two directories to beef up security.

Summary of Exam Objectives

This chapter examined the installation, configuration, management, and troubleshooting of IIS 6.0 in Windows Server 2003. The objective was to get familiar with the new features and learn the main features of IIS. IIS 6.0 incorporates World Wide Web Service, FTP service, NNTP server, and SMTP server.

It investigated the new features in IIS 6.0. There are several new security features, including Advanced Digest authentication, SGC, SCP, and default lock down status. The new reliability features in IIS 6.0 are Health Detection and request processing architecture using HTTP.sys. Miscellaneous new features include XML Metabase, UTF-8 support and ASP.NET integration with IIS 6.0

We learned to create, start, stop, and delete all of these sites and virtual servers. The management of the IIS 6.0 functions is mainly done through the IIS Manager console. There are also command-line utilities available for these functions, as discussed in Appendix A. This chapter ended by examining security options available in IIS 6.0. Digest security, Basic Authentication, Windows Integrated Security, and .NET passport security models can be used to manage security. The new Web Service Extensions window can be used to conveniently enable or disable ASP, ASP.NET, FrontPage extensions, and WebDAV support on an IIS server.

Exam Objectives Fast Track

What is New in IIS 6.0?

- ☑ The new feature can be categorized into two main sections: security and reliability.

- ☑ Advance Digest authentication, Server-gated Cryptography, Selectable Cryptography Service Provider, separate Worker Process, and Default Lockdown Wizard are some of the new security features.

- ☑ IIS 6.0 runs on a separate worker process model. This means every Web site is a separate ISAPI application memory space, which is detached form IIS.

- ☑ There is Heath Detection system between IIS and the separate worker processes.

- ☑ HTTP.sys is the new kernel process that accepts all incoming IIS traffic. It uses application pools to assign resources to Web sites.

- ☑ ASP.NET is the default scripting mechanism available in IIS 6.0. It still supports the old ASP applications.

- ☑ IIS configuration settings are stored in a XML Metabase.

Installing and Configuring IIS 6.0

- ☑ IIS can be installed in three different ways. The first is by using Configure your Server Wizard. The second option is to use Add/Remove Programs from Control Panel. The final option is unattended setup.

- ☑ Systems administrators use the unattended setup to configure multiple computers.

Managing IIS 6.0

- ☑ Common management tasks that you should be familiar with include:

  - Creating new Web sites, FTP sites, NNTP virtual servers, and SMTP virtual servers
  - Enabling Web Service Extensions
  - Creating virtual directories
  - Hosting multiple Web sites
  - Configuring Web site performance
  - Working with ASP.NET
  - Backing up and restoring the IIS metabase
  - Enabling health detection

- ☑ The IIS Manager is the primary interface that you will use to perform all IIS functions.

- ☑ The IIS Manager can be used to manage multiple IIS servers from one location.

Managing IIS Security

- ☑ The network administrator can force the user to authenticate using Digest, Basic, Integrated Windows, and .NET Passport security.

- ☑ Anonymous access is not recommended for a Web site containing sensitive data.

- ☑ The safest authentication is the Digest Security option.

- ☑ The network administrator can also include IP restrictions to restrict known offenders and networks.

- ☑ Another security mechanism is to use SSL certificates to encrypt the communication between the server and the client.

Troubleshooting IIS 6.0

☑ Troubleshooting IIS can be categorized into two main sections: Content and Connection errors.

☑ A 404 error is due to a misspelled URL or an invalid file extension.

☑ Session data in IIS 6.0 can be lost because the worker process is recycled every two hours. (This is the default configurable setting.)

☑ 503 errors are due to an influx of HTTP requests to HTTP.sys. This can lead to Rapid-fail protection to restart the worker process.

☑ The time out parameters in IIS 6.0 are much more extensive than the IIS 5.0 settings.

Exam Objectives Frequently Asked Questions

The following Frequently Asked Questions, answered by the authors of this book, are designed to both measure your understanding of the Exam Objectives presented in this chapter, and to assist you with real-life implementation of these concepts. You will also gain access to thousands of other FAQs at ITFAQnet.com.

Q: How do I replicate Web content on multiple servers?

A: IIS 6.0 does not have a built-in content replication tool. Content replication is a major issue in managing large Web farms. Please use Microsoft Content Management Server (CMS) or Site Server tools for content replications.

Q: Can I remotely administer my IIS Server?

A: Yes. Both IIS Manager and the command-line tools provide tools to do this. IIS Manager lets you add remote computers as nodes to the IIS Manager console. All command-line utilities come with parameters to configure user name/password support for remote computers. All command-line utilities come with /s parameters for the remote computer name, /u parameters for the user name to logon to the remote machine, and /p parameters for the password for the user account. Appendix A covers a variety of the command-line utilities in additional detail.

Q: Can I give different access points to different users for a FTP site?

A: Yes. Using the FTP isolation utilities in IIS, you can point different FTP users to different physical FTP home directories.

Q: How can I convert a FAT system to an NTFS system?

A: There is a command-line utility called convert.exe for this purpose. The syntax is convert *DriveLetter: /FS:NTFS*. It is important to understand that a NTFS system cannot convert to a FAT system using this tool.

Q: How do I obtain SSL security access information?

A: This can be achieved by using the IIS Manager. Click on the Web site and select **Properties**. Then select the **Directory Security** tab. Chose the **View Certificate** button under the **Secure Communications** group box. The Certificate will have information on the version, serial number, signature algorithm (i.e. sha1RSA), Issuer, Valid From, Valid To, Subject, and Public Key.

Q: Can we have multiple SSL security certificates for a single Web site?

A: No. Only one security certificate is permitted for a single Web site.

Q: Can I reuse the same server certificate for multiple Web sites?

A: Yes. You can use the same SSL security certificate in multiple Web sites. Multiple sites have to be configured separately to use the same certificate.

Q: Can I attach SSL security certificates for FTP sites?

A: No. FTP sites do not support SSL without third party add-ons.

Q: Can I count my FTP users at a given point of time?

A: Yes. Click on the **Properties** of the FTP site. Click **Current Sessions** on the FTP Site tab. The FTP User Sessions message box will display the value.

Self Test

A Quick Answer Key follows the Self Test questions. For complete questions, answers, and explanations to the Self Test questions in this chapter as well as the other chapters in this book, see the Self Test Appendix.

What is New in IIS 6.0?

1. You have created a commercial Web site with sensitive business information. Your senior architect has advised you to use Advanced Digest authentication to maximize security benefits on IIS 6.0. You have been doing research on Advanced Digest authentication. What is an incorrect piece of information you came across in your research?

   A. It uses Active Directory to store user credentials

   B. It only works with HTTP 1.1 enabled browsers

   C. It will work with Internet Explorer 4.0 with JavaScript 1.3 support

   D. It only works with WebDAV enabled directories

2. IIS 6.0 introduces a worker process model concept. A worker process model is a separate ISAPI application (Web site) that runs in isolation. In previous IIS versions (version 5.0 and below) all applications ran in the same memory space as inetinfo.exe. IIS 6.0 does not let the applications run in the same space as inetinfo.exe. The IIS 6.0 concept of tracking its Web sites is referred as what?

   A. Using Health Detection

   B. Using HTTP.sys

   C. Using XML Metabase entries

   D. Using ASP.NET scripts that directly communicate to .NET Framework.

Installing and Configuring IIS 6.0

3. You have been instructed to install Windows Server 2003 on a Windows 2000 machine. The current Windows 2000 Server is running under a FAT32 system. The Windows Server 2003 installation will permit you to upgrade or perform a clean installation. When you are performing the upgrade you have an option between FAT32 and NTFS file systems. Which ones would you choose?

   A. FAT

   B. FAT32

    C. NTFS

    D. FAT64

4. You have installed the standard default installation of Windows Server 2003. You were disappointed to find out that the IIS 6.0 was not installed by default. You have read that you can install IIS in several ways. You pick the **Configure your Server Wizard** option. You have discovered that the Windows server acts like an Application Server while investigating this option. What technology is not included in the Windows Server 2003 application server technologies?

    A. COM+

    B. ASP.NET

    C. ASP

    D. IIS 6.0

5. You are employed as a Systems Administrator for a large Internet Server Provider. Your organization develops and hosts multiple Web sites for commercial users. Your organization is upgrading a Windows 2000 Web farm to Windows Server 2003 servers. There are ten production servers, two staging servers, and three development Web servers in the organization. You have been asked to perform the Windows Server 2003 installation on all of these servers. What is the best installation method for your organization?

    A. Use the Configure Your Server Wizard

    B. Use winnt32.exe with an answer file

    C. Use wyscomgr.exe with an answer file

    D. Use **Control Panel | Add/Remove Programs**

Managing IIS 6.0

6. You are creating a commercial Web site using IIS Manager 6.0. This Web site needs to communicate to the legacy payroll system of the organization. The communication is done using an ISAPI DLL from the Web site. Which permission right is important to read the payroll data with the help of the ISAPI DLL?

    A. Read

    B. Run Scripts

    C. Browse

    D. Execute

7. You are trying to create an SMTP virtual server using IIS Manager. You have entered the SMTP site name and are being asked to enter the IP address and the Port number for the SMTP server. You selected the default IP address option (All Unassigned) and Port 25. You click the **Next** button and get an error stating that the IP address and the port number is already in use. What is the cause of this error message?

   A. You must provide an IP address. (All Unassigned) is not acceptable

   B. You cannot use port number 25

   C. The default SMTP site used these settings already.

   D. You should use port number 80.

8. Web Services Extensions is a new feature in IIS 6.0. Using Web Services Extensions, we can configure IIS 6.0 components. We can enable and disable them from the IIS Manager console. You have been experimenting with enabling and disabling these components. You could not find some of the item(s) below. Which item(s) fall into this category?

   A. WebDAV

   B. ASP.NET

   C. File Sharing

   D. ASP

Managing IIS Security

9. There are several ways to apply security on Web sites. All of these can be configured by the Properties tab of a Web site. Which one of the following is not a security measure to prevent intruders from hacking into IIS 6.0 Web sites?

   A. Using SSL certificates

   B. Using WebDAV

   C. Using an authentication method to force the user to authenticate

   D. Apply IP restrictions on known offenders and networks

10. You have configured Digest authentication for your Web servers. Jon, one of your users who needs to authenticate to the Web servers, cannot do so. You have checked Jon's user account properties and found that the **Store Passwords Using Reversible Encryption** option has been checked, but Jon still cannot authenticate. What is the most likely reason for his troubles?

A. Jon's user account is disabled. You should enable it from Active Directory Users and Computers.

B. Jon did not change his password after the **Store Passwords Using Reversible Encryption** option was enabled for his account.

C. Jon changed his password after the **Store Passwords Using Reversible Encryption** option was enabled for his account, which disabled this setting.

D. Jon's computer that he is attempting to make the connection with does not have the 128-bit high encryption patch applied.

11. Andrew is the network administrator for a small Windows Server 2003 Active Directory domain. He has configured IWA for users attempting to authenticate to the Web server. Andrew's network is protected from the Internet by a Cisco PIX firewall. User's attempting to authenticate using IWA complain that they cannot authenticate. What is the most likely cause of the troubles?

A. Andrew has not configured the user's account properties with the **Store Passwords Using Reversible Encryption** option.

B. IWA fails when access is through a firewall due the fact that the firewall places its IP address in the hash, thus rendering the authentication request invalid.

C. Andrew has not configured for IWA in the Group Policy Object that covers the IIS server's computer account.

D. Andrew has not configured for IWA in the Group Policy Object that covers the user's accounts.

12. You have enabled SSL on your Web site but now users complain that they cannot establish secure connections on port 80. You know that port 80 is the standard HTTP port, not the secure HTTP port. What port should they be attempting to connect to?

A. 8080

B. 443

C. 25

D. 110

Troubleshooting IIS 6.0

13. You are hosting an ASP application that used session variables to store common data across the site. The ASP site was performing well in Windows 2000 server. Then you upgraded the server to Windows Server 2003 servers. After the upgrade your site seems to be losing session data regularly. It seems to be working fine after a reboot. As the day passes by it loses all of its session data. What could be the potential problem?

A. Session data is not supported in Windows Server 2003.

B. IIS 6.0 worker process is getting recycled every two hours

C. IIS 6.0 user isolation mode gets recycled every two hours.

D. You need to enable ASP.NET to handle sessions in Windows Server 2003 server.

14. Your Web server is running ASP.NET applications on IIS 6.0. An incorrect configuration setting has caused you to reinstall IIS 6.0 on this machine. Therefore, you have used the **Control Panel | Add Remove Programs** method to uninstall and reinstall IIS 6.0. Then you tried to load up your ASP.NET pages. Unfortunately, all ASP.NET pages are displayed as text. What could be the solution to this problem?

A. You need to reregister ASP.NET

B. You need to reformat the drive as NTFS and reinstall Windows Server 2003 with IIS.

C. You need to edit the Metabase XML file to recognize ASP.NET files.

D. You need to restart IIS from IIS Manager.

15. Your company's new MP3 player is getting very popular on the Internet. You are getting close to 2,500 requests per minute to download the product. Unfortunately your Web server is continuously getting 503 error for this product downloads. Your boss has asked you to look into this problem. What could be the issue?

A. Not enough bandwidth for the users.

B. HTTP.sys cannot handle the incoming traffic.

C. The worker process is getting recycled every five minutes.

D. The FTP Server needs to be run on isolation mode.

Self Test Quick Answer Key

For complete questions, answers, and explanations to the Self Test questions in this chapter as well as the other chapters in this book, see the Self Test Appendix.

1.	**C**		9.	**B**
2.	**A**		10.	**B**
3.	**C**		11.	**B**
4.	**C**		12.	**B**
5.	**B**		13.	**B**
6.	**D**		14.	**A**
7.	**C**		15.	**B**
8.	**C**			

Chapter 5

MCSA/MCSE 70-292

Managing and Implementing Disaster Recovery

Exam Objectives in this Chapter:

4.1 Perform system recovery for a server

4.1.1 Implement Automated System Recovery (ASR)

4.1.2 Restore data from shadow copy volumes

4.1.3 Back up files and System State data to media

4.1.4 Configure security for backup operations

☑ Summary of Exam Objectives

☑ Exam Objectives Fast Track

☑ Exam Objectives Frequently Asked Questions

☑ Self Test

☑ Self Test Quick Answer Key

Introduction

Regardless of how hard network administrators work to protect their networks and systems from disaster, sometimes the worst occurs. Servers are subject to hardware failure from age, overuse, or defects, data loss from hack attacks, and natural disasters such as fires or floods that can destroy both the data and the systems themselves. Planning for disaster is an important part of every network administrator's job.

Windows Server 2003 includes several tools to help network administrators prepare for a serious system failure or attack, ensure that mission-critical data will not be lost and that server downtime is minimized. A good disaster preparation plan starts with a strategy for regularly scheduled backups. The Windows Backup Utility provides an easy way to back up data with Backup and Restore Wizards. Also included is the Automated System Recovery (ASR) Utility. The ASR Wizard helps the network administrator create a two-part backup of the essential system components: a floppy disk containing system settings and a backup of the local system partition on other media.

Windows Server 2003 also supports other, more sophisticated approaches to recovering from server hardware failure. Fault tolerant disks (Redundant Array of Independent Devices [RAID]) can be an important part of a disaster preparation plan, and if a network administrator is running the Enterprise Edition of Windows Server 2003, they also have the option of using server clustering—the ultimate in fault tolerance.

This chapter shows how to create a basic backup plan for an organization's network and servers using the backup and recovery tools included with the Windows Server 2003 operating system.

Creating a Backup Plan

A backup allows data and system files to be archived to another location on the hard disk or to other media. Backups can be compared to making a photocopy of an original document, which creates a duplicate that can be stored safely in case the original is destroyed. As with a photocopy, a backup of data is a duplicate of the original data on a computer at the time the backup was taken. Unlike a photocopy, however, the quality of the backup data is equal to the quality of the original.

When problems occur, the backed up files can be restored to the location from which the data was originally copied, or to another location such as a different directory or a different machine. The ability to restore data is just as important as performing regular backups; if a backup cannot be restored, then the backed up data is lost as well as the original data.

Backing up and restoring data is a fundamental part of any disaster recovery plan. A backup plan provides procedures that detail which data should be backed up, how this data is to be backed up, and when it is to be backed up. The plan also provides information regarding the storage of backed up data and how it can be restored. Such information can be used during a disaster to restore system files and other data that may have been damaged or destroyed.

As discussed in the following sections, there are many different elements to a good backup plan. In addition to knowing how the Backup Utility can be used, the system administrator needs to make decisions about what data will be backed up, where it will be stored, and other issues. A good backup plan should be part of every network administrator's daily routine.

Backup Basics

Backing up data begins with deciding what information needs to be archived. Critical data such as trade secrets and other data crucial to business needs must be backed up. Other data, such as temporary files, applications, and so on may not need to be backed up, as they can easily be reinstalled or are simply not needed. Such decisions, however, vary from company to company and even from department to department.

In addition to data, it is important to back up the *System State*, which consists of the files that the operating system uses. These include the boot files, system files, the Registry, COM+ class registration database, and other files that Windows Server 2003 (depending on the server configuration) requires the network administrator to back up as a single unit. If the server fails at any point, these files can be used to restore the system to a functioning state.

Rather than simply backing up bits and pieces of a server, it is wise to back up everything on a server at the same time. This includes all data on the server and the System State. If the hard disk on the server fails or the entire server is lost in a disaster, then a full backup of everything can be used to restore the server quickly.

As seen later in the "Using Automated System Recovery" section of this chapter, the Backup Utility provided with Windows Server 2003 allows the network administrator to create an *ASR set*. An ASR set is a backup of system files that can be used to restore Windows Server 2003 if a major system failure occurs. When creating an ASR set, only system files are backed up, not data.

When creating a backup, the network administrator should always program the Backup Utility to create log files. Backup log files show which files were backed up, and can be saved or printed as a reference for restoring data. If a particular file or folder needs to be restored, the log file shows whether it was included in a particular backup.

When a backup is performed, the copied data is usually kept on media other than the local hard disk, because if the hard disk failed, both the original data on the disk and the backup would be lost. As discussed in the "Backup Media" section later in this chapter, other media such as tapes can be used to store backups safely. Microsoft recommends that three copies of the media be stored, with one copy kept offsite. Doing this ensures that if one or two of the copies are destroyed in a disaster, the third can be used to restore data and the system.

To prevent backups from being stolen and used to restore data to another machine, it is important that backup devices and media be kept physically secure. Backup media should be stored in a secure location such as a fire safe. The area in which it is stored should not be easily accessible. Likewise, the devices used to create backups should also be secured. Removable devices should be stored in secure environments, while servers with backup devices installed on them should be kept secure in locked server rooms. The physical security of devices and media should be as high as the security of data on the server.

It is important for personnel to be trained in how to perform backups and restores. Designated members of the Information Technology (IT) staff should be knowledgeable in the steps involved in creating backups and restoring data. They should know where media is stored, and should be aware of what data is to be backed up and when. If a disaster occurs, they should be able to follow the backup plan without incident.

It is important to test whether data can actually be restored. If a device seems to be backing up data properly but is actually failing to do so, the network administrator may not be aware of it until they need to restore the data. Rather than assuming everything is being backed up properly, the administrator should test their equipment by restoring data from a previous backup job. If files and folders are restored properly, the network administrator will be confident that the data can be restored during a disaster.

Backup Types

Before describing each of the backup types, it is important to understand that the type chosen affects how the *archive attribute* is handled. The archive attribute is a property of a file or folder that is used to indicate whether a file has changed since the last time it was backed up. Depending on the backup type used, the archive attributes of a file may or may not be cleared after it is backed up. When the file is modified, the archive attribute is reset to indicate it has changed and needs to be backed up again. Without the archive attribute, the Backup Utility is unable to tell whether files need to be backed up or not.

- **Normal** Normal backups are used when a network administrator wants to back up all of the files selected in a single backup job. When this type of backup is selected, the Backup Utility backs up the selected files to a file or tape, ignoring whether the archive attribute is set or cleared. In other words, it does not matter whether the file has been backed up before; it will be backed up again. After backing up a file, the archive attribute is changed to indicate that the file was backed up. Normal backups are commonly selected when performing full backups in which all files on a volume are backed up.

- **Incremental** Incremental backups are used to back up all files that have changed since the last normal or incremental backup. When each file is backed up, the archive attribute is cleared. Because only files that have changed are backed up, this type of backup takes the least amount of time to perform. However, it also takes the most amount of time to restore, because the last normal backup and every subsequent incremental backup must be restored to fully restore all data and make the contents of the computer as up-to-date as possible.

- **Differential** Differential backups are also used to back up all files that have changed since the last normal backup. However, when this type of backup is performed, the archive attribute is not cleared. This means that the data on one differential backup contains the same information as the previous differential backup, plus any additional files that have changed. Since unchanged data is continually being backed up with this method, differential backups take longer to perform than incremental backups. However, when restoring backed up data, only the last normal backup and the last differential backup need to be restored. This makes the time it takes to fully restore a system faster than with a combined normal and incremental backup method.

- **Copy** Copy backups are similar to normal backups in that they can both be restored from a single backup job, but differ because this type of backup does not change the archive attribute. Because the archive attribute is not modified, it will not affect any other backups that are performed afterwards. This is useful if the network administrator wants to make a copy of data on the computer, but does not want it to interfere with other backup operations involving normal and incremental backups.

- **Daily** Daily backups are used to back up all selected files that have been modified on a particular day. Files that have not been modified that day will not be backed up. As with a copy backup, daily backups can be restored from a single backup and do not affect the archive attribute. Because the archive attribute is not cleared, it will not interfere with other backup operations involving normal and incremental backups.

EXAM WARNING

Not all backups are the same. Remember that normal and incremental backups reset the archive attribute after backing up a file, but differential, copy, and daily backups do not. Normal, copy, and daily backups can be used to restore files from a single backup job. Incremental and differential backups are used in conjunction with normal backups. Differential backups back up all files that have changed since the last normal backup (even if backed up during a previous differential backup), and incremental backups only back up files that have changed since the last normal or incremental backup.

Backup Media

There are many different types of media to which backed up data can be stored. The media type you choose determines how much data can be stored on a single media target, and the speed at which backups can be performed. In choosing the type of media to use, the network administrator should estimate how much data will be copied during a backup job.

The Backup Utility that comes with Windows Server 2003 allows the network administrator to back up files to a tape or a file. The ability to back up to a file was introduced with the version of ntbackup.exe that came with Windows 2000. Prior to that, the Backup Utility for Windows NT 4.0 worked only with tape. If an administrator does not have a tape backup drive and wishes to use the Backup Utility, they can back up files to a file on the hard disk and then copy the file to a compact disk (CDR/CD-RW), digital video disk (DVD/DVD-R), or other media. While this requires an extra step in backing up data, it allows the administrator to use the Backup Utility if they do not have a tape unit or wish to store backup files on a server or in another location.

Media Types

Tapes are the most common media available on which backups can be stored. Tape backups use magnetic tapes to store data sequentially, which requires the tape to be cued up to the point where the data is located. This is similar to the tapes used in a cassette recorder, where you have to fast-forward or reverse the tape to find the information you want. The biggest advantage of tape backups is the relatively small expense of the media; more data can be stored on tape for a lesser cost than with other backup media types.

There are a number of different types of tape drives available, which support different sizes of data and allow an assorted number of tapes. Two of the most common types of tape drives are:

- Digital Audio Tape (DAT)
- Digital Linear Tape (DLT)

DAT stores data on 4mm tapes, while DLT stores it on a half-inch magnetic reel-to-reel tape, in which one reel is contained in the cartridge while the other is stored inside the DLT drive. DAT is not as fast as DLT, and does not provide as much storage capacity. However, it is less expensive than DLT, which makes DAT a popular method of tape backup.

DAT uses the Digital Data Storage (DDS) format, which uses a process similar to that used in VCRs to store data on the DAT tape. It performs a helical scan, in which read/write heads spin diagonally across a DAT tape. Two read heads and two write heads are used. When data is written, the read heads verify that data has been written correctly to the tape. If they detect any errors, the data is rewritten.

As shown in Table 5.1, there are different formats of DDS available for tape drives. These different versions of DDS provide different levels of storage capacity. The original DDS format only allowed storage for up to 1.3GB of data, but the next generation increased storage to 2GB of data on a 120-minute cartridge. The data on the original DDS format tapes was uncompressed, so less data could be stored on the tape than with the other methods. DDS-1 was the first format to use compression, and allows for storage of up to 4GB of data on a 120-minute cartridge. DDS-2 increased compression on a 120-minute cartridge to allow up to 8GB of data storage. DDS-3 uses a 125-minute cartridge and allows for storage of up to 24GB of compressed data. This format also introduced the use of Partial Response Maximum

Likelihood (PRML), which eliminates noise so that data is transferred to the tape cleaner and with fewer errors. Finally, DDS-4 allows 40GB of compressed data to be stored on a 125-minute cartridge. Each of these formats is backward compatible. This means that if an administrator has a DDS-3 device, they can use DDS-1 or DDS-2 cartridges.

Table 5.1 DDS Formats for DAT Drives

Type of Format	Storage Capacity (Uncompressed/Compressed)
DDS	2GB
DDS-1	2/4GB
DDS-2	4/8GB
DDS-3	12/24GB
DDS-4	20/40GB

As mentioned, DLT is faster than DDS and provides a higher storage capacity. Using this method, a network administrator can put more data on the tape, allowing them to use this media with larger hard disks, and/or relieving them from having to change tapes as often. As shown in Table 5.2, there are different generations of DLT that accommodate different levels of storage capacity.

Table 5.2 DLT Types and Capacities

DLT Type	Storage Capacity (Uncompressed/Compressed)
DLT2000	15/30GB
DLT4000	20/40GB
DLT7000	35/70GB
DLT8000	40/80GB

Unlike DDS, each version of DLT provides data compression. DLT2000 allows the network administrator to store up to 30GB of data, DLT4000 allows up to 40GB of data, DLT7000 allows up to 70GB of data, and DLT8000 allows up to 80GB of data storage. However, if compression is not used, then only half of this amount can be stored on the tape.

TEST DAY TIP

While the information included here about backup tapes is useful for understanding what type of backup drive and tapes your server needs, do not expect exam questions dealing with detailed information about backup media and equipment. Instead, remember that the Backup Utility is designed to store backups to a file or a tape. Backups cannot be stored directly to media such as a CD-R/RW or DVD.

Offsite Storage

It is not a good practice to keep all backup media in the same location or in the same area as the computers whose data was backed up. If all of the backups are together in the same location, they can all be destroyed simultaneously. For instance, if a fire or flood occurs and destroys the server room, all backup tapes stored in that room could also be destroyed. To protect the data, the network administrator should store the backups in different locations so that they will be safe until they are needed.

Offsite storage can be achieved in a number of ways. If a company has multiple buildings in different cities or different parts of a city, the backups from each site can be stored in one of the other buildings. Doing this makes it more likely that if one location experiences a disaster, the original data or backups will remain safe. If this is not possible, the network administrator can consider using a firm that provides offsite storage facilities. Some organizations store their offsite backups in a safety deposit box at a bank. The key is keeping the backups away from the physical location of the original data.

When deciding on an offsite storage facility, the network administrator should ensure that it is secure and has the environmental conditions necessary to keep the backups safe. They should ensure that the site has air conditioning and heating, as temperature changes may affect the integrity of data. It should also be protected from moisture and flooding, and have fire protection in case a disaster befalls the storage facility. The backups need to be locked up, and the network administrator's organization should have policies that dictate who can pick up the data when needed. Conversely, the network administrator will want the data to be quickly accessible, so that they can acquire the data from the facility if needed, without having to wait until the next time the building is open for business.

Media Rotation

Every good plan has an Achilles' heel. In the case of the backup plan, that weak point will most likely be the backup media itself. By implementing a well thought out and documented media rotation system, the network administrator can overcome the two largest issues that plague backup media:

- **Backup Media Lifetime** As already discussed, the most common type of backup media is some form of magnetic tape. While the tapes that are currently available are much more durable than their predecessors, they do not last forever. A backup plan must take steps to ensure that the backup jobs use a rotaion over several tapes to extend the lifetime of each tape as well as increase the reliability that each tape offers should the backup media be needed to perform a restoration. By using some form of documented rotation scheme, the network administrator can prevent one or a few tapes from being used repeatedly, thus reducing its lifetime and reliability. In short, the time to decide that a backup media needs to be retired is *not* after it has failed in a time of need.

- **Availability of Data History** In many small networks, it is feasible to simply perform a full backup every night. Unfortunately, this condition does not represent the reality that the vast majority of large networks experience. More often than not, time constraints limit the amount of data that can be backed up during the week, forcing the network administrator to perform full backups during non-peak hours, such as on a Saturday or Sunday morning. Another factor to consider is that larger networks may find themselves backing up data from multiple locations over the network. This can cause significant network traffic and performance issues during times when users are utilizing other network resources. The solution to these issues is to create a backup plan that includes a combination of available backup types, such as full, incremental, daily, and/or differential. To successfully perform the restoration, the network administrator will need to have all of the correct tapes available and restore the data from them in the correct order. As well, a good media rotation scheme can be used to provide the administrator with a history of data in the event that they need to recover an older version of a file. In all cases, having a well-documented media rotation system is a must for a backup plan.

There are an almost infinite amount of media rotation systems that can be created and used. The following sections examine three of the more common and popular ones' currently in use. Each of the three examples has its strengths and weaknesses—the one chosen depends on the network administrator's requirements and available budget.

The Five-tape Rotation System

The five-tape rotation system is the easiest to perform and the least expensive to initially implement. As the name implies, five backup tapes are required for this system, with one being used each day of the normal workweek. If required, this media rotation system can be easily modified to include six or seven days of backups, depending on when users create and modify files on the network. Backup tapes are normally labeled for each day of the week such as Monday, Tuesday, and so on, to ensure easy identification. The network administrator must perform a full backup on the first day they start using this media rotation system. Once the initial full backup is performed, the administrator can perform daily, differential, or incremental backups on the first four days of the week (assuming that only five backup tapes are being used), with a full backup being performed every Friday.

This media rotation system provides simplicity in that it only requires a limited number of backup tapes and can be easily implemented without requiring a complicated scheduling system. However, simplicity comes at a price: the five-tape rotation system only provides a week's worth of backup history, making recovery of files modified prior to this time impossible. Figure 5.1 illustrates a sample five-tape rotation system for a month containing 31 days. Note that an administrator can use any combination of daily, differential, or incremental backups for those days they are not performing a full backup.

Figure 5.1 The Five-tape Rotation System is the Simplest to Implement

Sunday	Monday	Tuesday	Wednesday	Thursday	Friday	Saturday
		1 Tuesday (differential)	2 Wednesday (differential)	3 Thursday (differential)	4 Friday (full)	5
6	7 Monday (differential)	8 Tuesday (differential)	9 Wednesday (differential)	10 Thursday (differential)	11 Friday (full)	12
13	14 Monday (differential)	15 Tuesday (differential)	16 Wednesday (differential)	17 Thursday (differential)	18 Friday (full)	19
20	21 Monday (differential)	22 Tuesday (differential)	23 Wednesday (differential)	24 Thursday (differential)	25 Friday (full)	26
27	28 Monday (differential)	29 Tuesday (differential)	30 Wednesday (differential)	31 Thursday (differential)		

The Grandfather, Father, Son System

The Grandfather, Father, Son (GFS) system is one of the most popular methods used today. The GFS system provides an entire year of backup history. However, this benefit comes at an increased price—it takes 20 backup tapes per year to implement the GFS system. There are three tape types that make up the GFS system:

- **Son** The son backup tapes are used Monday, Tuesday, Wednesday, and Thursday to perform daily, differential, or incremental backups as required by an organization. The network administrator needs four backup tapes for the son tapes.

- **Father** The father backup tapes are used each Friday except for the last Friday of the month. The father tapes are used to perform full backups, requiring four backup tapes. They provide an entire month of backup history.

- **Grandfather** The grandfather tapes are used only on the last Friday of the month to perform a full backup. Twelve backup tapes are required for the grandfather tapes, and they provide a full year of backup history.

When starting a new GFS rotation, the network administrator will need to perform a full backup on the first day, regardless of the day they are starting on. This ensures that they have the backup data needed in the event that disaster strikes before they use a father backup tape. Figure 5.2 illustrates a sample GFS rotation system for a month containing 31 days and four Fridays. Note that any combination of daily, differential, or incremental backups can be used for those days where a full backup is not being performed.

Figure 5.2 The GFS Rotation System is Easy to Implement and Provides a Year's Worth of Backup History

Sunday	Monday	Tuesday	Wednesday	Thursday	Friday	Saturday
		1 Son #2 (differential)	2 Son #3 (differential)	3 Son #4 (differential)	4 Father #1 (full)	5
6	7 Son #1 (differential)	8 Son #2 (differential)	9 Son #3 (differential)	10 Son #4 (differential)	11 Father #2 (full)	12
13	14 Son #1 (differential)	15 Son #2 (differential)	16 Son #3 (differential)	17 Son #4 (differential)	18 Father #3 (full)	19
20	21 Son #1 (differential)	22 Son #2 (differential)	23 Son #3 (differential)	24 Son #4 (differential)	25 Grandfather (full)	26
27	28 Son #1 (differential)	29 Son #2 (differential)	30 Son #3 (differential)	31 Son #4 (differential)		

The Tower of Hanoi System

The Tower of Hanoi method is based on a challenging disk and post game bearing the same name. The strengths of the Tower of Hanoi method are that it can be implemented with a minimum of five backup tapes and quickly scaled up to create backup histories for as long as a year and a half (or more) by adding additional tapes. When the basic configuration of five tapes is used, the Tower of Hanoi method provides a backup history stretching back 16 days, which is often adequate for the majority of organizations. Assuming that only five backup tapes are being used for the Tower of Hanoi method, they would be used as follows:

- **Tape #1** Used every other day for a full backup.
- **Tape #2** Used every fourth day for a full backup.
- **Tape #3** Used every eighth day for a full backup.
- **Tape #4** Used every sixteenth day for a full backup; alternates with Tape #5.
- **Tape #5** Used every sixteenth day for a full backup; alternates with Tape #4.

The primary disadvantage of the Tower of Hanoi method is that the network administrator must perform a full backup each night—something that larger organizations may not be able to accommodate. As well, managing the Tower of Hanoi method can be difficult unless adequately documented and scheduled. Figure 5.3 illustrates a sample Tower of Hanoi rotation system that uses five backup tapes.

Figure 5.3 The Tower of Hanoi Rotation System can be Difficult to Implement

Sunday	Monday	Tuesday	Wednesday	Thursday	Friday	Saturday
		1 Tape #1	2 Tape #2	3 Tape #1	4 Tape #3	5
6	7 Tape #1	8 Tape #2	9 Tape #1	10 Tape #4	11 Tape #1	12
13	14 Tape #2	15 Tape #1	16 Tape #3	17 Tape #1	18 Tape #2	19
20	21 Tape #1	22 Tape #4	23 Tape #1	24 Tape #2	25 Tape #1	26
27	28 Tape #3	29 Tape #1	30 Tape #2	31 Tape #1		

As seen in Figure 5.3, it can become difficult to maintain a Tower of Hanoi rotation system if careful planning and scheduling is not done beforehand. Creating and posting schedules at least two months in advanced helps alleviate this problem and make the Tower of Hanoi system more manageable. Should a network administrator desire to create a backup history longer than 16 days, they can easily do so by adding additional tapes. Consider the following:

- Adding a sixth tape (Tape #6) yields 32 days of backup history. Tape #6 is used every thirty-two days.

- Adding a seventh tape (Tape #7) yields 64 days of backup history. Tape #7 is used every sixty-four days.

- Adding an eighth tape (Tape #8) yields 128 days of backup history. Tape #8 is used every one-hundred and twenty-eight days.

The network administrator can continue to add tapes as required. Ten backup tapes provides a backup history of 512 days. However, there is an inherent flaw that exists with the Tower of Hanoi rotation method: Tapes #1 and #2 receive an extraordinary amount of wear and tear and will likely need to be replaced often, perhaps quarterly.

TEST DAY TIP

You are not likely to see any questions on the exam asking about specific media rotations. The discussion is included in this text as a reference for your backup planning and implementation.

EXAM
70-292
OBJECTIVE
4.1

Using the Windows Backup Utility

Windows Server 2003 provides a native Backup Utility that allows the network administrator to archive any files on the computer, regardless of whether the hard disk is formatted with File Allocation Table (FAT), FAT32, or New Technology File System (NTFS). When data is backed up, it is copied to an area of the hard disk or other media that can be stored in a separate location. If a user accidentally deletes a file, the data becomes corrupted, or a disaster occurs, the backup can then be used to copy this data back to the server.

NOTE

The Backup Utility in Windows Server 2003 uses the *Volume Shadow Copy* technique to create copies of data. This means that files that are open and being used by users or the system can be backed up. Volume shadow copies are discussed in more detail later in this chapter in the "Working with Volume Shadow Copies" section.

The Backup Utility has two modes:

- Backup and Restore Wizard
- Advanced Mode

When the Backup Utility is started for the first time after installing Windows Server 2003, the Backup or Restore Wizard appears, as seen in Figure 5.4. This Wizard takes the network administrator through the step-by-step process of backing up the server or restoring an existing backup from the hard disk or other media. From the initial welcome page of the wizard, the administrator can open the utility in Advanced Mode, which provides more features for those who are more comfortable with backing up and restoring data.

Figure 5.4 The Backup or Restore Wizard

NOTE

The Welcome page of the Backup Utility provides a checkbox to configure backup to always start in Advanced Mode. This disables the wizard.

The Backup Utility can be opened in one of two ways:

- Click **Start** | **Programs** | **Accessories** | **System Tools** | **Backup**.
- Click **Start** | **Run** and type **ntbackup**.

EXAM
70-292

OBJECTIVE
4.1.3

Understanding System State Data

Before moving further into a discussion about how to configure and use the Backup Utility, it is important to examine an often misunderstood item: the System State. The System State is the critical data stored on each computer that contains the information required for the proper startup and operation of the computer. Exactly what data this is varies from one computer to the next, depending on what function the computer is fulfilling. For example, domain controllers contain data pertinent to the Active Directory, while servers that are acting as Hyper Text Transfer Protocol (HTTP) or File Transfer Protocol (FTP) servers will have data that is specific to Internet Information Server (IIS). The following items are all part of the System State, but may not all be present on a single computer:

- Boot and system files (such as boot.ini, NTLDR, and so on)
- The Registry
- The COM+ class registration database
- The system files that are protected by Windows File Protection (located in %systemroot%\system32\dllcache)
- The Active Directory service if the server is a domain controller
- The SYSVOL directory if the server is a domain controller
- The cluster service information if the server is a member of a cluster
- The IIS metadirectory if IIS is installed on the server
- The Certificate Services database if the server is a Certificate Authority (CA)

Depending on the size of a network and the function of a specific server, the network administrator may need to back up the System State. For example, they should back up the System State data for domain controllers, cluster members, and IIS servers. On the other hand, they might also need to back up System State data for member servers providing file or print shares to the network.

It is important to understand that all of the files needed to completely restore a server are not included in the System State. Microsoft recommends that when backing up the System State, the network administrator also back up all of the files on the boot and system volumes of the server. This backs up all of the files used by the operating system and allows the administrator to restore a duplicate of the server (as it was when the backup was performed).

EXAM WARNING

When backing up the System State, you can only back up the System State of the local computer. You cannot back up the System State of a remote computer. System State files have dependencies that require you to back them up as a unit. You cannot back up individual components of the System State with the Backup Utility.

Head of the Class...

Special Backup Situations

Some types of data require that you follow special procedures to back them up. The System State data is one such special situation. Another special situation occurs when you want to back up files that are associated with Windows Media Services. To backup these files, you must follow the procedures that are outlined in the WMS Help files. You cannot use the normal backup procedures to back up and restore these files.

Microsoft recommends that if you want to back up database files on a Structured Query Language (SQL) server, you should use the backup and restore utilities that are included with SQL Server instead of the Windows Server 2003 Backup Utility. If your Windows Server 2003 computer is running cluster services (Enterprise or Datacenter editions), you need to perform an ASR backup for each cluster node, back up the cluster disks in each node, and then back up individual applications that run on the nodes.

EXAM 70-292
OBJECTIVE 4.1.3

4.1.3 Backup Configuration Options

Although the Backup Utility includes a very capable Wizard for configuring backup jobs, the network administrator should be aware of the various configuration options that are available, some of which cannot be accessed when the wizard is used. To access the options examined in the following sections, you will need to launch the Backup Utility in Advanced Mode as seen in Figure 5.5.

Figure 5.5 The Backup Utility Allows for Advanced Configuration

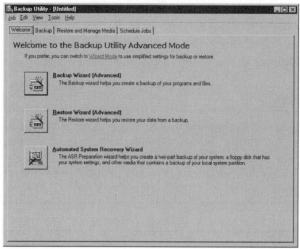

To begin the process of configuring the backup options available, click **Tools |
Options** to open the Options dialog box, as seen in Figure 5.6.

Configuring the General Options

From the General tab of the Options dialog box, as seen in Figure 5.6, you can configure
several options that define how the backup operation will be performed.

Figure 5.6 Configuring the General Backup Options

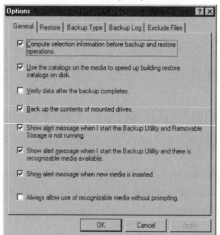

Table 5.4 explains each of the options available on the General tab of the backup
Options dialog box.

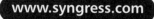

Table 5.4 Options Available on the General Tab of the Backup Options Dialog Box

Option	Description
Compute selection information before backup and restore operations.	When selected, information will be displayed on the number of files and bytes that will be needed to perform the backup or restore job. This information is shown prior to the start of a job.
Use the catalogs on the media to speed up building restore catalogs on disk.	Specifies whether to build an on-disk catalog from the on-media catalog when restoring data. This option is described in greater detail later in this chapter.
Verify data after the backup completes.	When the data is backed up, it is compared to the original data to ensure it is the same. This option is described in greater detail later in this chapter.
Back up the contents of mounted drives.	Backs up the contents of a mounted drive, which is a folder on an NTFS volume that functions as a drive. If not selected, only the path information for the mounted drive is backed up.
Show alert message when I start the Backup Utility and Removable Storage is not running.	Displays an alert when the Removable Storage service is not running, and will start this service automatically.
Show alert message when I start the Backup Utility and there is recognizable media available.	Displays an alert when the Removable Storage service detects that new media is available to which files can be backed up.
Show alert message when new media is inserted.	Alerts you when the Removable Storage service detects that new media has been inserted into a device.
Always allow use of recognizable media without prompting.	Allows the Removable Storage service to move any new media it detects to the Backup media pool, which is a collection of media used by the Backup Utility.

When looking at these options, you may notice that several of them deal with Removable Storage—a service that manages removable media such as tapes, and storage devices on Windows Server 2003. If this service is not running, backup will not be able to back up files to this media. Because of its importance, if you are backing up files to tape you should have the options relating to this service checked. As these options apply to backing up data to tape, you do not need to check these options if you are backing up data to files stored on a hard disk.

NOTE

By default, all options are checked on the General tab except two: "Verify data after the backup completes" and "Always allow use of recognizable media without prompting."

Configuring the Restore Options

From the Restore tab of the Options dialog box, as seen in Figure 5.7, you can configure several options that define how the restoration operation will be performed.

Figure 5.7 Configuring the Restore Backup Options

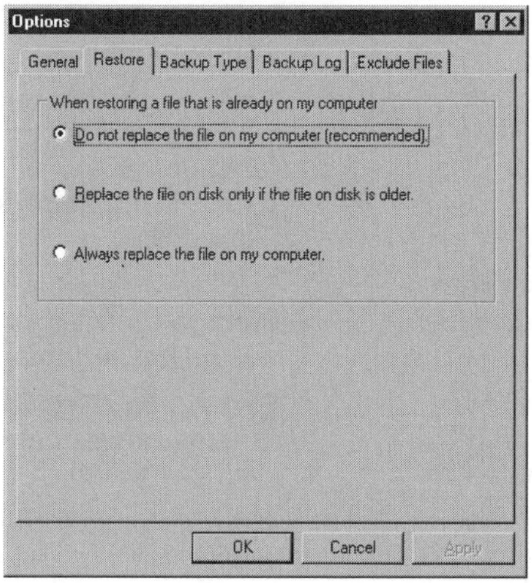

Selecting the **Do not replace the file on my computer (recommended)** option results in files being restored only when the file is not already present. This is the safest restoration option but leaves older files on the hard disk instead of replacing them with newer versions that may be contained in the backup file.

Selecting the **Replace the file on disk only if the file on disk is older** option results in files being restored only when the existing file is older than the file contained in the backup or is not present in the destination location. This option ensures that the most current files are restored.

Selecting the **Always replace the file on my computer** option results in files that already exist on the disk always being replaced, regardless of whether or not they are newer than the version contained in the backup file.

Configuring the Backup Type Options

From the Backup Types tab of the Options dialog box, as seen in Figure 5.8, you can select which type of backup will be performed. You can select from the five types of backups previously examined in the "Backup Types" section of this chapter.

Figure 5.8 Configuring the Backup Type Option

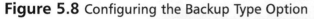

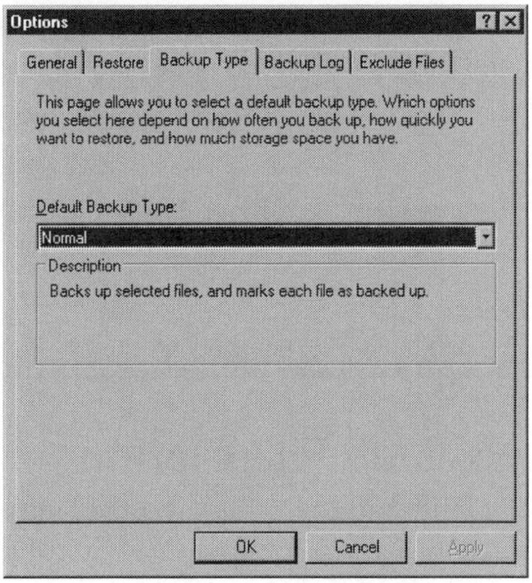

Configuring the Backup Log Options

From the Backup Log tab of the Options dialog box, as seen in Figure 5.9, you can specify how log files dealing with the backup process should be created. There are three options on this tab:

- Detailed
- Summary
- None (turns off logging of the backup job)

When the **Summary** option is selected, only key operations in the backup process are logged. The log shows when the backup process started and ended, errors, and other events. When the **Detailed** option is selected, all information about the backup is included in the log. The log not only includes information displayed in a summary log, but also has entries showing which files were backed up and their locations on the server. Although this can be handy for referencing what was backed up and when, a detailed log is also larger and uses more disk space.

Figure 5.9 Configuring the Backup Log Options

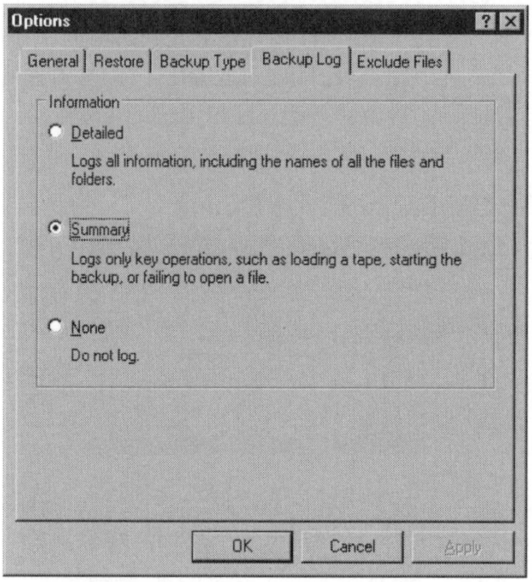

Configuring the Exclude File Options

From the Restore tab of the Options dialog box, as seen in Figure 5.10, you can identify the types of files you would like to exclude from your backup. This can be done for all users who own files on the machine, or only for the user currently logged in.

Figure 5.10 Configuring the Exclude File Backup Options

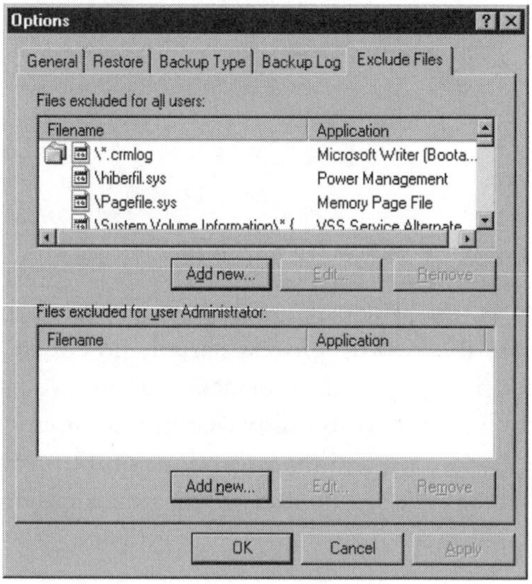

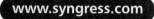

The top half of the Exclude Files tab shows files and file types that are excluded for all users. The bottom half of the Exclude Files tab shows files and file types that are excluded for the currently logged in user. You can click the **Add new** button to open the **Add Excluded Files** dialog box, as seen in Figure 5.11.

Figure 5.11 Configuring the Exclude File Backup Options

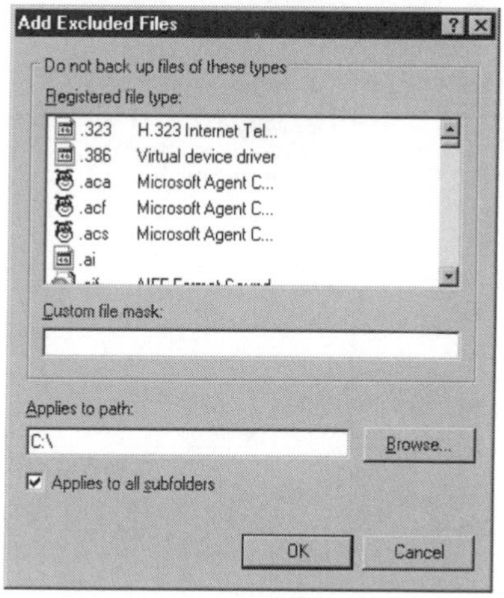

The file types listed in the Registered file type box are those that are tracked by Windows Server 2003 and included in the file associations of installed software on the machine. A custom file type can be entered using the **Custom file mask** field below this list. In this textbox, enter a **period (.)** followed by the **file extension** to indicate the types of files that should not be included in the backup. If you only want to exclude file types in a certain folder, type the path to that folder in the **Applies to path** textbox that appears below the custom file mask field. When this is done, only the specified file types that are located under that path are excluded. For example, you might exclude all text files with the extension .TXT under C:\WINDOWS. Excluding file types makes your backup set smaller and thereby faster to restore, because unneeded data is not included.

EXAM
70-292
OBJECTIVE
4.1.3
Using the Backup Utility in Advanced Mode

When you open the Backup Utility in Advanced Mode, you will be presented with the **Welcome to the Backup Utility Advanced Mode** page, as seen previously in Figure 5.5. There are three buttons, one to start the Backup Wizard (Advanced), one to start the Restore Wizard (Advanced), and one to start the ASR Wizard. The Backup Utility provides four tabs that provide the controls needed to perform various tasks, including configuring and starting backups, performing restorations, and creating backup schedules. Restoring data and using ASR are discussed in the "Using Automated System Recovery" section of this chapter.

When you switch to the **Backup** tab, the interface will look similar to that shown in Figure 5.12. If you do not want to use a wizard to control your backup, the Backup tab should be used to back up data files. Using the wizard is discussed in the next section.

Figure 5.12 The Backup Tab of the Backup Utility

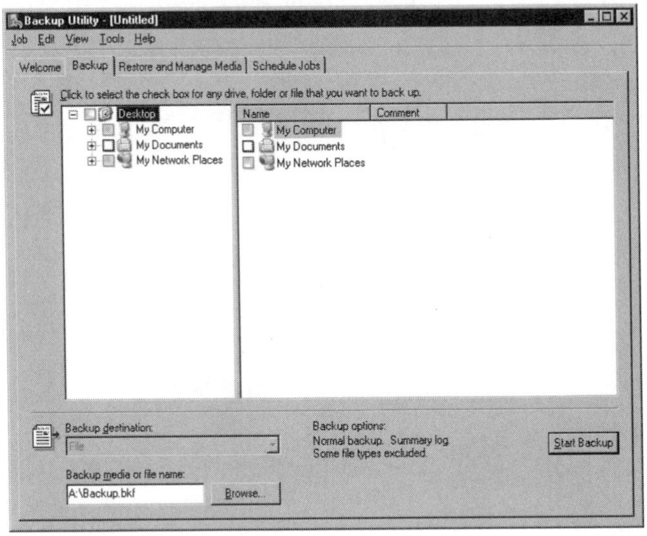

The Backup tab contains two panes that allow you to view the hierarchical listings of files and folders on the computer. The left tab allows you to navigate through the drives and can be expanded to show the various folders on those drives. When a drive or folder is selected, the right pane is used to view the files and folders within. In both panes, checkboxes appear beside the different drives, folders, and files. When these are checked or unchecked, the items are respectively selected or deselected for backup. As you can see, the Backup Utility makes it easy and straightforward to choose the files, folders, or entire drives that are to be included in your backup job.

Below the two panes are other controls that are used to provide information and start the backup process. The Backup destination field provides a context list of where the Backup Utility is to store the data (media type). You can choose to store the backup as a file, or back up to a tape device that is installed on the machine.

NOTE

If you do not have a tape device installed, the Backup destination field will be grayed out.

Underneath the Backup destination field is the Backup media or file name field where you can specify the path and filename of the location where the backup file will be stored, or (if you are backing up data to a tape) specify the tape you wish to use. If you plan to overwrite an existing backup file, you can click the **Browse** button to find the file. Finally, when you are ready to begin a backup job, simply click the **Start Backup** button to begin the process.

NOTE

You can name the backup whatever you want and use any file extension, but Microsoft recommends that you use the .BKF extension for backup files, as this will allow them to be recognized by the Backup Utility.

You can create a new backup job from the Backup tab by completing the steps discussed in Exercise 5.01. Using the Backup Wizard to create a backup job is examined in Exercise 5.02.

EXERCISE 5.01

CONFIGURING A BACKUP JOB USING THE BACKUP TAB

1. Start the Backup Utility by clicking **Start | Programs | Accessories | System Tools | Backup** or clicking **Start | Run** and typing **ntbackup**.

2. If the Backup or Restore Wizard opens, click the **Advanced Mode** link. This closes the Wizard and opens the Backup Utility.

3. Click the tab labeled **Backup**.

4. Click **Job | New** to create a new backup job.

5. The left pane of the Backup tab shows a directory tree, which can be used to view the drives and folders on the computer. The right pane can be used to view files and folders within the drive or folder you have selected in the left pane. In the left pane of the Backup tab, click on **Volume C**. This will change the display in the right pane to show the contents of the C: drive, as seen in Figure 5.13.

6. Scroll through the contents of Volume C and select the files you wish to back up by clicking on the checkbox beside each file or folder. Once checked, a file or folder is selected for backup.

7. In the **Backup Destination** dropdown menu, select whether you want to back up to a file (which is selected by default), or another medium (such as a tape device). For the purposes of this exercise, accept the

Figure 5.13 Locating Files to be Backed Up

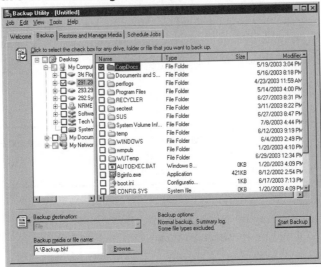

default choice of backing up to a file. (If you do not have a tape drive attached to your computer, this selection will be grayed out and your only choice is the default.)

8. In the **Backup Media or File Name** text box, enter the path and file-name for the backup file. This is where the backup file will be saved. Enter **C:\backup.bkf**.

9. Click **Tools | Options** to open the Options dialog box discussed previously in the "Backup Configuration Options" section of this chapter.

10. When the Options dialog appears, click the **General** tab. If the **Verify data after the backup completes** option is not selected, click on it so that a checkmark appears in the box.

11. Click the **Backup Type** tab and select **Normal** as the type of backup to perform.

12. Click the **Backup Log** tab, and click the option labeled **Detailed**. This provides a detailed log of the files being backed up.

13. Click **OK** to exit the Options dialog box.

14. Click the **Start Backup** button to start the backup process. The Backup Job Options dialog box opens, as seen in Figure 5.14.

Figure 5.14 The Backup Job Information Dialog Box

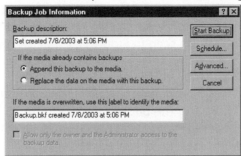

15. You can enter a more useful backup description and label in the pro-
     vided boxes—this will aid in identifying the backup later during a
     restore option. Also, you will need to select whether to append this
     backup to the existing backup data that is on the media, or to over-
     write the existing data. In most cases, you will want to select the
     Replace the data on the media with this backup option since you
     should already have your media rotation system in place.

16. You can configure additional options for the backup job by clicking the
     Advanced button to open the Advanced Backup Options dialog box, as
     seen in Figure 5.15. The options available are explained immediately
     following Exercise 5.01 in Table 5.5. Click **OK** after making your config-
     uration changes here.

Figure 5.15 Configuring Advanced Backup Options

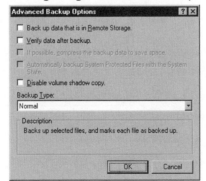

17. If you want to configure this backup job to run later or on a schedule,
     click the **Schedule** button; if you want to run the backup job immedi-
     ately, click the **Start Backup** button. If you are configuring a schedule,
     you will be prompted to save the backup configuration if you have not
     already done so. Click **Yes** when prompted by the warning dialog. By

default, Windows saves your backup configuration in the **\Local Settings\Application Data\Microsoft\Windows NT\NTBackup\data** folder in the user profile for the currently logged in user. The Save As dialog box opens, as seen in Figure 5.16, allowing you to select the location and file name to save the backup configuration as. Click **Save** after entering the desired file name.

Figure 5.16 Saving the Backup Configuration

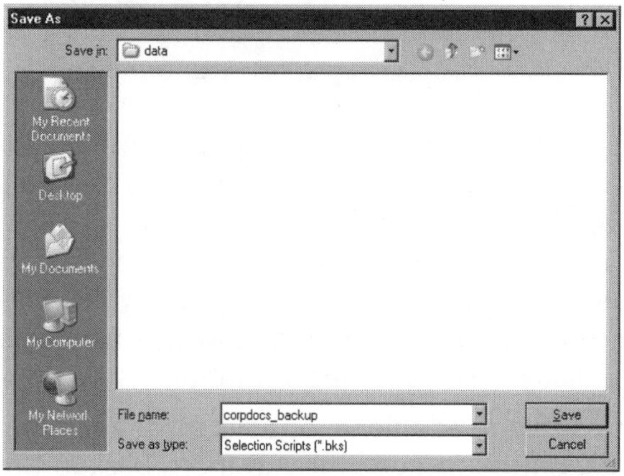

18. The Set Account Information dialog box opens, prompting you to enter the credentials of the user account that is to be used to run the scheduled back up. Enter the required information, as seen in Figure 5.17, and click **OK**.

Figure 5.17 Supplying a Set of Credentials with the Required Permissions

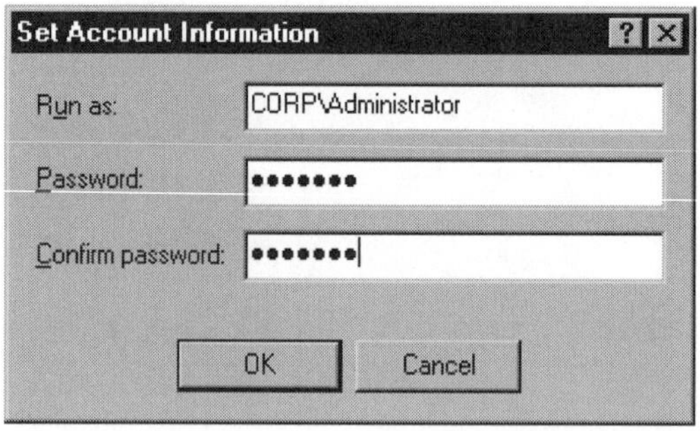

19. The Scheduled Job Options dialog box opens, as seen in Figure 5.18, allowing you to configure the backup job schedule.

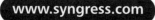

Figure 5.18 The Scheduled Job Options Dialog Box

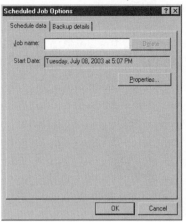

20. Enter a value for the job name and click the **Properties** button to begin the schedule configuration. The Schedule Job dialog box opens, allowing you to configure the backup schedule, as seen in Figure 5.19.

Figure 5.19 The Schedule Job Dialog to Configure the Backup Schedule

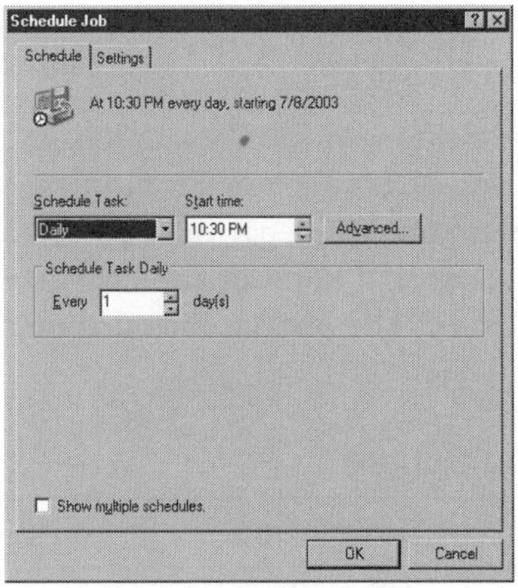

21. You can configure advanced scheduling options, such as only starting the backup when the computer has been idle for a specified amount of time, by using the **Settings** tab of the Schedule Job dialog box.

22. After you have finished creating your schedule, click **OK** to close the Schedule Job dialog box. You may be prompted to re-enter your network credentials again.

23. Click **OK** to close the Scheduled Job Options dialog box.

24. Your backup job will show up on the Schedule tab of the Backup Utility, as seen in Figure 5.20.

Figure 5.20 Examining the Backup Schedule

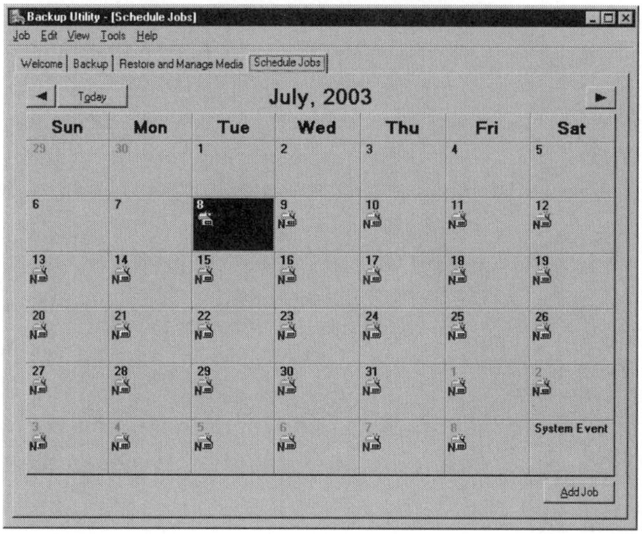

If you click the **Advanced** button on the Backup Job Information dialog box, the Advanced Backup Options dialog box will open. From this location, you can configure additional options that further control the behavior of the backup job being configured. By default, none of the options are selected. You can also change the type of backup being performed from this location if desired. The options included on this dialog box are detailed in Table 5.5.

Table 5.5 Advanced Backup Options

Option	Description
Back up data that is in Remote Storage.	If the "Back Up Data that is in Remote Storage" checkbox is checked, the job will also backup data that is included in Remote Storage. Remote Storage is a service that manages data that is infrequently used and migrates it from local storage to remote storage. When the user opens the file, it is automatically recalled without the user realizing that Remote Storage was used.
Verify data after backup.	Verifies that backed up data is identical to the original data.

Continued

Table 5.5 Advanced Backup Options

Option	Description
If possible, compress the backup data to save space.	If a tape backup is performed and compressed data is supported by the tape device, this option is enabled. Checking this box compresses the backed up data so that there is more room for storage on the tape. If no tape drive is installed, this box is grayed out.
Automatically backup System Protected Files with the System State.	If this option is selected, system files located in the system root (e.g. C:\WINDOWS) and boot files included with the System State are backed up.
Disable Volume Shadow Copy.	When performing a backup, the Windows Server 2003 Backup Utility by default creates a Volume Shadow Copy, which is a duplicate of the volume at the time the copy process began. This allows the Backup Utility to back up all selected files, including those that are currently open by users or the operating system. Because the Backup Utility uses a Volume Shadow Copy, it ensures that all selected data is backed up and any open files will not be corrupted during the process. If this checkbox is checked, files that are open or in use may be skipped when the backup is performed.

Using the Backup Utility in Wizard Mode

Should you decide that the Advanced Mode configuration is not what you need, or you simply want some guidance on getting the backup job configured correctly, you should consider using the Backup Wizard as discussed in Exercise 5.02.

EXERCISE 5.02

CONFIGURING A BACKUP JOB USING THE BACKUP WIZARD

1. Open the **Backup Wizard** by selecting **Start | Programs | Accessories | System Tools | Backup** or clicking **Start | Run** and typing **ntbackup**.

2. If the Backup or Restore Wizard opens, click the **Advanced Mode** link. This closes the wizard and opens the Backup Utility.

3. Click the **Backup Wizard (Advanced)** button to start the Backup Wizard.

4. Dismiss the opening page of the Wizard by clicking **Next**.

5. On the What to Back Up dialog box, seen in Figure 5.21, you need to select the scope of the backup that you wish to configure.

Figure 5.21 You can Back Up the Entire Computer, Selected Files or the System State

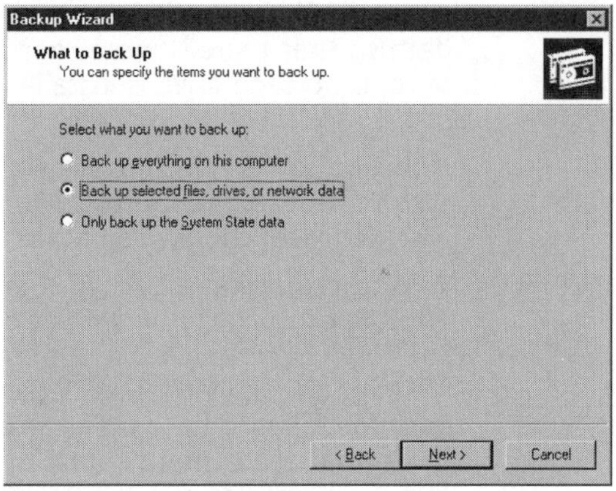

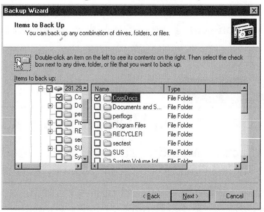

6. On the Items To Back Up dialog box, as seen in Figure 5.22, you can select exactly which files and folders you want to back up. This dialog box only appears if you select the **Back up selected files, drives or network data** option. Select the data that is to be backed up and click **Next** to continue.

Figure 5.22 Selecting Items for Back Up

7. On the Backup Type, Destination and Name dialog box, as seen in Figure 5.23, you need to select the location to save the backup file. You can use the **Browse** button to navigate to the location where the file will be saved and enter the file name for the backup file. Click **Next** to continue.

Figure 5.23 You Will Need to Select the Location to Place the Backup File

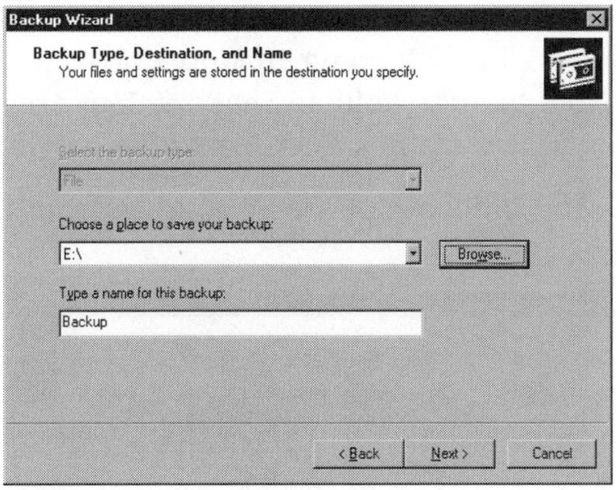

8. The Completing the Backup Wizard dialog box appears, as seen in Figure 5.24, informing you that you have completed the basic configuration of the backup job. To configure advanced options, including scheduling, click the **Advanced** button and continue to Step 9. If you want to perform this backup immediately, click **Finish**.

Figure 5.24 You can Configure a Schedule by Clicking the Advanced Button

9. On the Type of Backup dialog box, select the type of backup you want from the five available choices as previously discussed in the "Backup Types" section; the default selection is **Normal**. Click **Next** after making your selection.

10. On the How to Back Up dialog box, as seen in Figure 5.25, you have the option to select other advanced options such as data verification,

hardware compression (if supported by your backup devices) and disabling Volume Shadow Copy. Typically, you will opt to enable data verification and hardware compression. You should not, under normal circumstances, disable Volume Shadow Copy without a specific reason to do so. Note that the Volume Shadow Copy technology will be discussed later in this chapter. Click **Next** after making your selections.

Figure 5.25 Configuring Data Verification from the How to Back Up Dialog Box

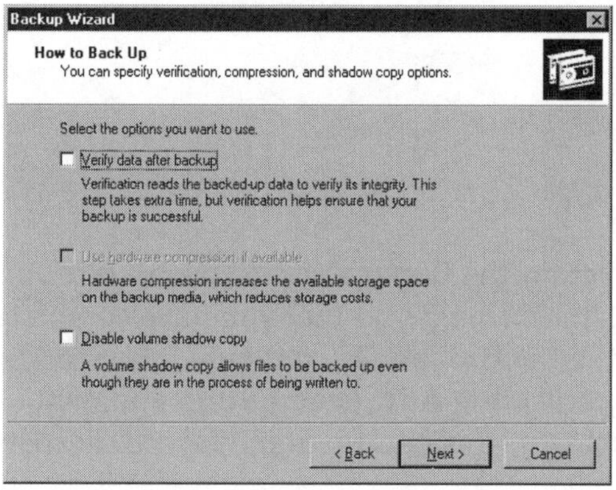

11. On the Backup Options dialog box, you will be given the option to overwrite existing backup data on your media or to append the backup job to the existing data on the media. In most cases, you will want to overwrite any existing data as you will be rotating backup media. Click **Next** after making your selection.

12. On the When to Back Up dialog box, as seen in Figure 5.26, you are given the option to start the backup immediately by selecting **Now** and clicking **Next**. If you want to configure it on a schedule, select **Later**, enter a job name, and click the **Set Schedule** button to configure a schedule. After configuring your schedule, click **Next** to continue.

Figure 5.26 Starting the Backup Now or Scheduling it for Later

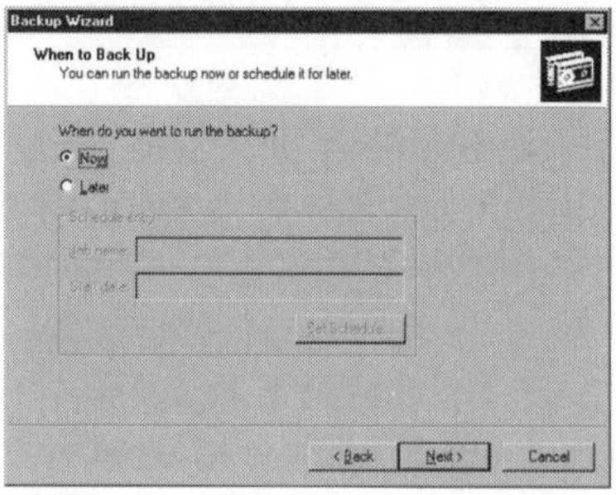

13. If you selected **Now**, clicking **Finish** will close the Backup Wizard and immediately start it. If you selected **Later**, you will be prompted again to supply your network credentials for an account authorized to perform backups. Click **Finish** to complete the Backup Wizard—you can find your backup job on the **Schedule** tab of the Backup Utility.

Configuring & Implementing...

Backing up System State Data

The System State is a set of files that the system uses to function, and must be backed up as a single unit. Windows Server 2003 requires these files to be backed up together, because the files included in the System State have dependencies, in which two or more files rely on one another to function. Because of this, you cannot choose individual System State files when performing a backup.

System State files are specific to each computer running Windows Server 2003, and cannot generally be swapped between servers. Since servers can have different hardware and software installed, swapping these files can result in devices, programs, or the operating system itself not functioning properly. Thus, when backing up System State files it is important to label the backup as belonging to a specific server so that you will not accidentally restore the wrong System State files to a server.

As discussed earlier in this chapter, the System State can be backed up using the Windows Server 2003 Backup Utility. The files that this utility considers to be part of the System State can vary between computers. On Windows Server 2003, it always includes the following:

- The Registry
- The COM+ class registration database
- System files
- Boot files

In addition to these, the Backup Utility might also include other files if the server is configured for a special purpose or has certain services installed. A domain controller has the Active Directory and the SYSVOL directory included in the System State, and a certificate server includes the Certificate Services database as part of the System State. If the server is part of a cluster, cluster service information is also included in the System State. If Windows Server 2003 is configured to be a Web server and has IIS installed, the IIS Metadirectory is also included. As can be seen, the role a server plays on a network and the services it has installed have a great impact on what is backed up as part of the System State.

Continued

The System State data can be backed up by checking the **System State** checkbox in the hierarchical list of volumes and folders in the left pane of the Backup tab with the Backup Utility running in Advanced Mode. Alternatively, you can use the command-line interface to back up the System State data by typing **ntbackup backup systemstate** at a command prompt.

TEST DAY TIP

There are a number of different items that can be included in a backup of System State data, and questions might appear on the exam asking which of these will be backed up for a particular server. Remember that the System State always includes the Registry, COM+ class registration database, system files, and boot files. Other elements that can be included depend on the role a server plays, and that role can be used to cue your memory. Certificate servers are the only servers that have the Certificate Services database included, just as domain controllers have elements exclusively relating to their role.

EXAM
70-292
OBJECTIVE
4.1.4

Configuring Security for Backup Operations

Being able to perform a backup requires the network administrator to have the proper permissions and rights. After all, if anyone could perform a backup, an unauthorized person could obtain a copy of the data stored on the computer. Note, however, that being able to back up data does not necessarily mean you are able to access and read it. Also note that a user who is authorized to back up data can back up and restore encrypted files without decrypting them.

The permissions and user rights needed to perform backup and restore operations in Windows Server 2003 are dependent on what is being backed up or restored, the permissions set on the files and folders, and the account being used to perform the backup and its group memberships.

Backup and restoration of files and folders on the local computer requires the network administrator to be a member of the Administrators or Backup Operators local group. A local group is a group that is created on the computer (in contrast to a group that is created on the domain controller and used throughout the domain). A local group is assigned rights and permissions that apply only to that computer. Because the rights and permissions are limited to that machine, accounts that are a part of these groups cannot perform backup or restoration of data on other machines.

To back up or restore files and folders on any computer in a domain, the network administrator must be a member of the Administrators or Backup Operators group on a domain controller. This also enables group members to back up or restore computers that are in a domain with which the administrator's domain has a two-way trust relationship.

NOTE

A two-way trust relationship allows authentication in one domain to be accepted in the other domain, so that the administrator does not have to create multiple accounts for a user in each domain. This allows an Administrator or Backup Operator in one domain to back up or restore files in the other domain.

If you are neither an Administrator nor a Backup Operator, there is still a chance that you might have the necessary permissions to perform a backup. The owner of a file or folder can generally back up their own files. If the owner has one or more of the following permissions to a file or folder, they can perform a backup:

- Read
- Read and execute
- Modify
- Full Control

In addition to these rights and permissions, it is important that a user to whom you want to give the ability to back up and restore files does not have any disk quota restrictions. Such restrictions make it impossible to perform backups of data.

When planning who should be able to perform backup and restoration on your network, keep the following points in mind:

- Files and folders can be backed from a local or remote computer as long as the user has the required access to the files and folders.
- When performing backups remotely, System State data cannot be saved.
- Members of the Administrators or Backup Operators groups do not explicitly need permissions to access the files being backed up—they have the ability to perform backups as a result of their group membership.

An administrator can also *delegate the authority* to perform backups to a user without placing that user in one of the authorized groups. Delegation of control can be done through the Delegation of Control Wizard or via Group Policy settings.

Restoring Backup Data

Should you ever need to put your backup plan to the ultimate test, its good to know how to perform a restoration. Performing a restoration should be a relatively smooth process, and Windows Server 2003 makes the restoration process fairly automatic. The basic restoration process is outlined in Exercise 5.03.

Configuring & Implementing...

Delegating Authority to Perform Backups via Group Policy

You can delegate the authority to perform backups by editing the Group Policy settings for a computer or a Windows Server 2003 domain. To do so, open the Group Policy Object (for a local computer, this is done by clicking **Start | All Programs | Administrative Tools | Local Security Policy**).

In a domain, it is done through the Active Directory Users and Computers administrative tool. Open the console and right-click the domain name, then select **Properties**. Click the **Group Policy tab** and select the **Default Domain Policy**. In the left pane, expand the **Computer Configuration | Windows Settings | Security Settings nodes**.

In either case, in the Group Policy Object Editor console, in the left pane under Security Settings, expand **Local Policies** and click **User Rights Assignment**. In the right pane, double-click **Back up files and directories**. Check the **Define these policy settings** checkbox if you are editing the domain policy. Click **Add User or Group**. You can select an individual user account or any group account to which you wish to delegate the authority to perform backups. The number of people who have the ability to back up and restore data varies from company to company. In some organizations, a higher level of security might be required, which limits the ability to perform backups to one person or group of Administrators. In other organizations, servers may be located in branch offices across the country. Since the Backup Utility can only be used to back up and restore the System State of the local computer, and cannot be used to back up another domain controller, this might require that people in each location be authorized to perform backups and restores. The choice of how security is configured will depend on the policies and needs of your organization.

EXERCISE 5.03

RESTORING BACKUP DATA

1. Open the Restore Wizard by selecting **Start | Programs | Accessories | System Tools | Backup** or clicking **Start | Run** and typing **ntbackup**.

2. If the Backup or Restore Wizard opens, click the **Advanced Mode** link. This closes the wizard and opens the Backup Utility.

3. Click the **Restore Wizard (Advanced)** button to start the Restore Wizard.

4. Dismiss the opening page of the Wizard by clicking **Next**.

5. On the What to Restore dialog box, as seen in Figure 5.27, you must locate and select the media containing the data that is to be backed up. Once you have located the correct backup set, expand the backup

file to enable selection of the files and folders you want to restore. If your backup file or backup media is not listed, you can use the **Browse** button to locate it. After you have selected the files and folders to be restored, click **Next** to continue with the restoration.

Figure 5.27 Selecting the Backup Set to Use and Files to be Restored

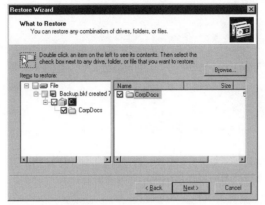

6. The Completing the Restore Wizard dialog box appears. If you need to configure additional advanced options, you can click the **Advanced** button to do so. If you are ready to start the restoration, click the **Finish** button.

7. On the Where to Restore dialog box, you are given the option to select the location to which the files and folders should be restored to. You can choose from the following options: **Original location**, **Alternate location**, or **Single folder**. After making your selection, click **Next** to continue.

8. On the How to Restore dialog box, you are given the option to determine what should occur if an existing file is found in the restoration location. You have options that are similar to those discussed previously in the "Backup Configuration Options" section of this chapter. After making your selection, click **Next** to continue.

9. On the Advanced Restore Options dialog box, as seen in Figure 5.28, you can select from several advanced restoration options that are available. The available options are determined by the type of backup you are restoring from, the type of backup hardware being used, and the role of the server that is being restored, and may not look exactly as seen in Figure 5.28. After making your selections, click **Next** to continue.

Figure 5.28 Configuring Additional Advanced Restoration Options

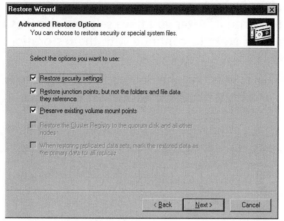

10. The Completing the Restore Wizard dialog box appears again. Click **Finish** to start the restoration process.

NOTE

Yu can use the ntbackup.exe command to create backups from the command-line, but you cannot perform restorations from the command-line. This can become a serious limitation should you need to restore a Windows Server 2003 computer that cannot be started normally—thus the reason for using ASR.

Using Automated System Recovery

Automated System Recovery (ASR) is a new feature in Windows Server 2003 that can be used to start a computer that cannot be started using any other means, such as Windows Backup, Safe Mode, the Recovery Console, and Last Known Good Configuration (LKGC). While implementing and using a backup plan to perform regular backups is a critical task that must be accomplished, the backups will be of little use in the event the server suffers a critical failure that prevents it from being started normally. ASR allows the network administrator to restore the operating system back to a previous state (current as of the time the ASR set was created), which then allows them to restart the Windows Server 2003 normally and continue repairing the computer as required.

The ASR process is actually made up of two key parts: a floppy disk that is used to start the Windows Server 2003 computer, and a backup file that contains the System State, system services, and disks associated with the operating system components. The startup disk also contains information about the configuration of the computer's disks, and information on how the ASR restoration is to be performed. Because an ASR set focuses on the files needed to restore the system, data files are not included in the backup.

An ASR set should be created each time a major hardware change or a change to the operating system is made on the computer running Windows Server 2003. For example, if the administrator installs a new hard disk or network card, or applies a security patch or Service Pack, an ASR set should be created. Then if a problem occurs after upgrading the system in such a way, the ASR set can be used to restore the system to its previous state after other methods of system recovery have been attempted.

ASR sets are easily created by using the Windows Server 2003 Backup Utility, as discussed in Exercise 5.04.

EXERCISE 5.04

CREATING AN ASR SET

1. Insert a blank 3-1/2 floppy disk into your server's floppy drive.

2. Open the **Backup Wizard** by selecting **Start | Programs | Accessories | System Tools | Backup** or clicking **Start | Run** and typing **ntbackup**.

3. If the Backup or Restore Wizard opens, click the **Advanced Mode** link. This closes the wizard and opens the Backup Utility.

4. Click the **Automated System Recovery Wizard** button to start the ASR Wizard.

5. Dismiss the opening page of the Wizard by clicking **Next**.

6. In the Backup Destination dialog box, enter the path and file name of the backup file to be used as part of the ASR set. Click **Next** to continue.

7. Click **Finish** to close the Wizard. This starts the ASR set creation process.

8. When prompted, click **OK** to confirm the floppy disk is inserted in the server's floppy drive.

9. Place the ASR floppy disk in a safe location until needed.

NOTE

You *must* have a floppy drive installed in the server that you will be performing the ASR restoration on.

Should you need to perform an ASR recovery, you can do so by performing the steps detailed in Exercise 5.05. Before starting the ASR recovery process, ensure that you have the following items readily available:

- The ASR floppy disk
- The ASR backup file
- The Windows Server 2003 CD
- Any special drivers required, such as RAID hardware or other mass storage device drivers—these will need to be available on floppy disk as well

EXERCISE 5.05

PERFORMING ASR RECOVERY

1. Start the server that is to be recovered using ASR.
2. Place the Windows Server 2003 CD in the CD drive.
3. Start from the CD when prompted to do so.
4. If you need to install special drivers, press **F6** when prompted to so.
5. Press **F2** when prompted to initiate the ASR recovery process.
6. Inset the ASR floppy disk in the server's floppy drive.
7. Follow the directions that are provided on screen.

EXAM
70-292

OBJECTIVE
4.1.2

Working with Volume Shadow Copy

Volume Shadow Copies are a new backup feature in Windows Server 2003 and are used to provide copies of data at a given point in time. Users can view the contents of shared folders and see previous versions of data. This allows them to use these copies as if they were restoring a backup of data from an earlier time.

When shadow copies are made of shared folders, there are a number of benefits. If a file was deleted or corrupted in some way, the network administrator can open the previous version and copy it to the original location or another location. This also allows the administrator to use previous versions to compare changes that have occurred between the versions.

The previous versions of files included in a shadow copy are read-only, preventing users from modifying the older version in any way. This maintains the integrity of the previous version, so that it remains a duplicate of the file at the time it was initially shadow copied. If users wish to make modifications to it, the older version can be copied to another location.

NOTE

Remember that by default, the Backup Utility makes shadow copies. In this section, we are talking about additional shadow copies that can be manually configured through the Computer Management console.

Making Shadow Copies of Shared Folders

Shadow copies are created and configured using the Computer Management console. From within the Computer Management console the network administrator can create multiple shadow copies for volumes and configure them individually. Configuration of shadow copies allows the administrator to control where they are stored, the amount of disk space they will take up, and schedule the frequency with which they will be created. You can control many details in making shadow copies of shared folders on a Windows Server 2003 computer.

Creating shadow copies has limitations, however. For example, an administrator cannot store an indefinite number of shadow copies on each volume that is enabled. For each volume that has shadow copies enabled, a maximum of 64 shadows copies can be created—this means the administrator can view up to 64 previous versions of data. Once this limit is reached, the oldest shadow copy is deleted and cannot be restored.

Enabling Shadow Copies on the Shared Resource

To enable shadow copies, open the Computer Management console by clicking **Start | Programs | Administrative Tools | Computer Management**. By default, the Volume Shadow Copy service is disabled and must be set for automatic startup. You will need to locate the Volume Shadow Copy service in the Services node of the Computer Management console, as seen in Figure 5.29, in order to configure it. Once you have located the Volume Shadow Copy service, double-click it to open its properties dialog box. Set the startup type for **Automatic** and click the **Start** button to start the service. Click **OK** to close the properties dialog box.

Figure 5.29 You Must Configure the Volume Shadow Copy Service

Locate the Shared Folders node of the Computer Management console and right-click on it, as seen in Figure 5.30. Select **All Tasks | Configure Shadow Copies**. The Shadow Copies dialog box opens, as seen in Figure 5.31.

Figure 5.30 Configuring Volume Shadow Copies

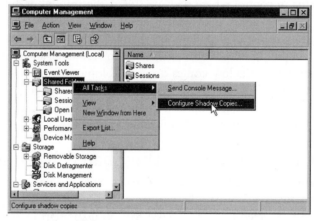

The Shadow Copies dialog box contains two areas: the upper area allows the network administrator to select a volume on the computer and click the **Enable** button to enable shadow copies on the selected volume. Note that by default, shadow copies are disabled on all volumes. To prevent a particular volume from using shadow copies, click the **Disable** button. The bottom area of the Shadow Copies dialog box displays the shadow copies that exist on a selected volume.

NOTE

When shadow copies are enabled on a volume, Windows presents a warning box that advises that the default settings are not appropriate if the server has a high Input/Output (I/O) load. If this is the case, you should manually configure the settings to put the storage area on a volume that will not be shadow copied. You must click **OK** to acknowledge the information presented in this dialog box before you can enable Volume Shadow Copies on that volume.

Figure 5.31 Shadow Copies are Disabled by Default

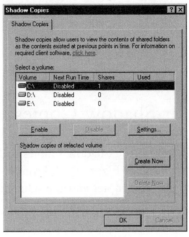

TEST DAY TIP

To enable shadow copies, you must be a member of the Administrators group on the local machine. If you are not a member of this group, you will not be able to make the necessary changes to the computer to enable, disable, or make modifications.

When shadow copies are enabled, Windows configures the feature with a default schedule and settings, although these settings can be modified. It can take some time after clicking **Enable** for Windows to do its work and enable the feature, so the network administrator must be patient. After shadow copies are enabled on a volume, the Shadow Copies dialog box reflects the change, as seen in Figure 5.32.

Figure 5.32 Shadow Copies Will be Shown After They Have Been Enabled

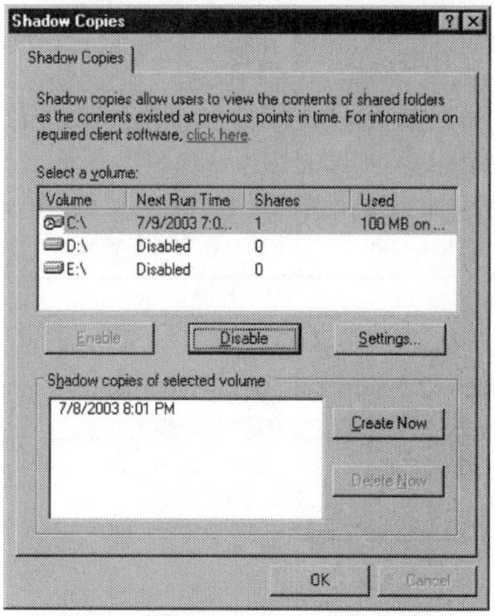

Changing Settings for Shadow Copies

After shadow copies have been enabled, the network administrator can modify the configuration by using the **Settings** button on the Shadow Copies dialog box. Clicking this button displays the Settings dialog box, as seen in Figure 5.33. From here the administrator can modify the storage area used for shadow copies and the schedule that controls how often they are created. The settings specified will only apply to the selected volume.

Figure 5.33 Configuring Shadow Copy settings

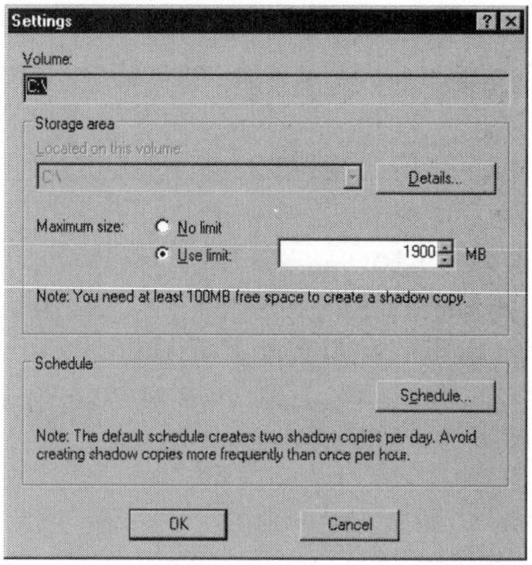

Defining Storage Options for Shadow Copies

The Storage Area frame of the Settings dialog box is used to modify where shadow copies are stored and how much space will be allocated to store them. Modifying these settings can improve system performance and allow shadow copies to be created more effectively.

The first field on this dialog box allows the network administrator to configure the volume on which shadow copies will be stored. The dropdown list allows the administrator to select different volumes on the server. However, if the computer only has one volume, the current volume will be the only choice and this dropdown list will be disabled. Even if there are additional volumes, by default the storage area will be on the same volume that is being shadow copied. Clicking the **Details** button beside the dropdown box allows the network administrator to view such information as available free space and total disk space.

The **Maximum Size** options below this dropdown list allows the network administrator to configure how much disk space will be used for storing shadow copies. The options available are **No Limit**, and **Use Limit**. If **No Limit** is selected, the system can use as much hard disk space as necessary to create shadow copies. If **Use Limit** is selected, the administrator can specify the maximum number of megabytes to be used for storage.

The amount of available hard disk space is important when using shadow copies. There must be a minimum of 100MB available for the system to create shadow copies. By default, Windows Server 2003 uses 10 percent of the total disk space of the volume containing files to be shadow copied. If there is an insignificant amount of free disk space available, the network administrator should use another volume on the server for storage.

The network administrator should carefully calculate the amount of hard disk space needed for shadow copies. If a limit is set that is too small, they might prohibit the system from making an adequate number of shadow copies. If this happens, and a version of an older file is needed, it might be unavailable because Windows Server 2003 needed to delete it to make room for newer shadow copies. It is also important to remember that the number of files in a shadow copy and the frequency with which shadow copies are created affects the amount of space used. If a network administrator is creating a daily shadow copy of ten files that are approximately the same size, it will take less space than a few dozen similar files that are copied hourly. After viewing the size, number of files, and frequency of several shadow copies, the administrator should decide whether there is enough room for the number of copies they want.

EXAM WARNING

Shadow copies only retain up to 64 previous versions. Once this limit is reached, the oldest shadow copy is permanently deleted. The number of previous versions is also affected by the amount of space available for shadow copies. There must be a minimum of 100MB available for the system to create shadow copies, but if this is not enough for 64 individual copies, there will be fewer created.

Scheduling Shadow Copies

The **Schedule** button opens the Schedule dialog box, as seen in Figure 5.34, and allows the network administrator to control when shadow copies are created. Using this tab, the administrator can configure Windows Server 2003 to create shadow copies at any of the following intervals:

- Daily
- Weekly
- Monthly
- Once
- At System startup
- At logon
- When idle

Figure 5.34 Configuring the Shadow Copy Schedule

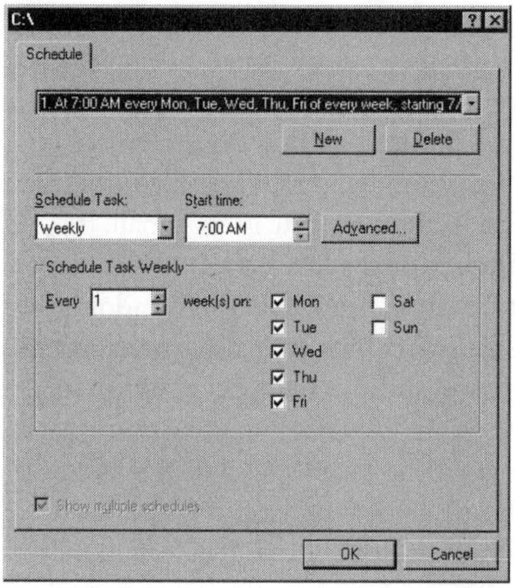

As with scheduling backups, each of these options provides the same additional configurable settings when selected. For example, if **Daily** is selected, the network administrator can control whether shadow copies are performed every day, every second day, every third day, and so on.

The Settings dialog box for shadow copies differs from that of the Backup Utility in that the administrator can create multiple scheduled tasks from this dialog box. By clicking the **New** button, they can create multiple scheduled tasks for creating shadow copies.

TEST DAY TIP

By default, two shadow copies per day are made. Although a greater or lesser number can be scheduled for creation, Microsoft recommends that the frequency at which they are created should not be greater than two per hour. Exceeding this recommendation limits how far back a user can access older versions of data.

Shadow copies can be configured for a volume by completing the steps outlined in Exercise 5.06.

EXERCISE 5.06

ENABLING AND CONFIGURING SHADOW COPIES

1. Click **Start | Programs | Administrative Tools | Computer Management** to open the **Computer Management** console.

2. In the left pane of the Computer Management console, expand the **System Tools** folder.

3. Right click **Shared Folders**. When the context menu appears, select **All Tasks | Configure Shadow Copies**.

4. When the Shadow Copies dialog box appears, a list of available volumes will be shown. Select the volume on which you want to enable shadow copies, and click the **Enable** button.

5. A dialog box appears asking for confirmation that you want to enable shadow copies for this volume. Click **Yes** to acknowledge the warning provided.

6. You can now configure the storage space used for shadow copies. Click the **Settings** button.

7. When the Settings dialog box appears, click the **Use limit** option in the **Storage Area** frame, and change the number of MB to **250**.

8. Click the **Schedule** button.

9. When the dialog box appears, click the **New** button to configure a new schedule.

10. Select **Daily** from the **Schedule Task** dropdown list, and set the **Start** time to **11:00** P.M.

11. Under **Schedule Task Daily**, change the number of days this is to run to **Every 2 days**.

12. Click **OK** to confirm these settings and exit the dialog box.

13. Click **OK** to exit the **Shadow Copies** dialog box, and confirm your changes.

Deploying the Client Software for Shadow Copies

To use shadow copies, client computers need special software installed. The Previous Versions client can be installed through a Windows Installer Package that is located on the Windows Server 2003 machine in **\system32\clinets\twclient** of the %systemroot% directory (typically named WINDOWS). After it is installed, this tool allows users to access previous versions of files that were included in a shadow copy.

Since the Previous Versions client is available as a Windows Installer Package, it can be deployed to client computers in a number of ways:

- The network administrator can copy the installation package to a shared folder on the server, and then notify users that it is available for those who wish to install it. Users can install it by right-clicking on the package, and then clicking **Install** on the menu that appears.

- It can also be installed by double-clicking on the package. This starts a wizard that asks the user if they want to install the software. The user clicks **Next** to begin the installation.

- The network administrator can also deploy the installation package through Group Policy. Software deployment. Group Policy allows the network administrator to offer software for installation or force it to be installed, by either publishing or assigning the software. By using Group Policy-based software deployment, the administrator ensures that the computers or users selected will have access to the Previous Versions Client.

Restoring Previous Versions of a File

Older versions of files included in a shadow copy are retained for a limited period. As mentioned earlier, a maximum of 64 shadow copies are retained, and fewer than 64 if there is a limited amount of disk space available. Because these previous versions of files might be permanently removed after a time, users may wish to keep a copy of an older version for future reference. Also, if a user accidentally deletes or overwrites the current copy of a file, it must be restored. Using the Previous Versions client, users can restore previous versions without having to ask the network administrator to restore data on their behalf.

To view previous versions of a file, access the shared folder on a volume using **My Network Places** (or **Network Neighborhood**, depending on the client operating system), as seen in Figure 5.35.

Figure 5.35 Locating a Shared Folder

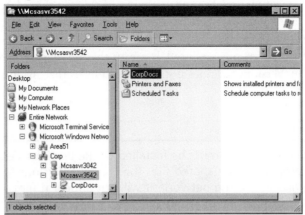

You can examine the shadow copies for the folder by right-clicking on it and selecting **Properties** from the context menu. From the Properties dialog box, click the **Previous Versions** tab. This displays a listing of previous versions of the folder, as seen in Figure 5.36. Select the version you want, and click the **View** button to open a read-only version of the folder.

Figure 5.36 Examining Previous Versions

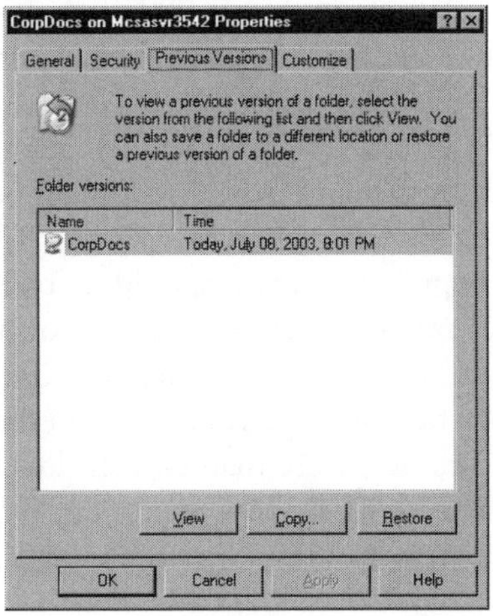

The entire previous version of a folder can be restored by selecting it and clicking **Restore**. When this button is clicked, a warning message appears, asking if you are sure you want to roll back the current version to the previous version of the file. If you click **Yes**, the current folder is overwritten with the older one.

Alternatively, the network administrator can restore specific individual files and sub-folders by copying or dragging them to the desired location. Copying a previous version of a file is also done through the **Previous Versions** tab. After selecting the previous version you want to copy, click the **Copy** button on this tab. This opens a **Copy Items** dialog box, which allows you to specify where the older version of this file should be copied.

Sometimes when using the Previous Versions tab, the network administrator may find that no previous versions of files are listed, or the Previous Versions tab itself does not appear. When no previous versions are listed, it means that no changes have been made to the file. If the Previous Versions tab does not appear, it means that shadow copying has not been enabled on that server.

EXAM WARNING

The Previous Versions Client must be installed or the Previous Versions tab will not appear in the properties of a shared file. The Previous Versions tab only appears when viewing files across the network. It will not appear if files are viewed on the local hard disk (for example, by using Windows Explorer to access a local shared folder).

Shadow Copies Best Practices

While shadow copies provide a useful tool for users to view, copy, and restore older versions of files, they should not be considered a substitute for regular backups. Shadow copies make copies of files stored on shared folders, but do not provide a duplicate of every file on the system that can be restored after Windows Server 2003 fails. In addition to enabling shadow copies, the network administrator should also routinely back up their system.

Shadow copies should not be created on dual boot systems. If a computer has Windows Server 2003 and Windows NT 4.0 installed on it in a dual boot configuration, shadow copies that persist when the older operating system is restarted might be corrupted. To avoid this, enable shadow copies only on computers that exclusively run Windows Server 2003.

Scheduling when shadow copies are created should be based on the work habits of users. If multiple shadow copies are created, the administrator does not want copies created when users have not made any changes. For example, if no one works on the weekend, there will not be any changes to files so there is no point in creating shadow copy files during that time. As mentioned earlier, more than two shadow copies per hour should not be scheduled, because a maximum of 64 shadow copies can be created on a volume. The more frequently shadow copies are made, the faster the older shadow copies will be removed from the system.

If the server is heavily used and there are a large number of disk reads and writes on the current volume, the network administrator should consider changing the volume where shadow copies are stored to a volume on a different physical disk. This allows the system to write shadow copies to a different hard disk, and improves performance. However, this change needs to be made before shadow copies are created. If shadow copies are already present on the volume, the administrator needs to delete all of the shadow copies on the volume before making the change.

Summary of Exam Objectives

Disasters can occur at any time, and can result from any number of causes. To prevent disasters from causing extensive damage, the network administrator needs to identify the types of disasters that can affect their business, and then implement plans and policies to deal with them effectively. Such plans include information on how to perform backups and restore data, recovering from server problems, and how to address other issues that can make the business unable to function.

Windows Server 2003 provides a number of tools that can be used when problems arise. The Backup Utility allows the network administrator to back up data, back up the system state, and create ASR sets. By implementing these measures, the network administrator can prevent data and system files from being permanently lost during a disaster.

ASR is a new feature in Windows Server 2003 that can be used to start a computer that cannot be started using any other means, such as Windows Backup, Safe Mode, the Recovery Console, or LKGC. While implementing and using a backup plan to perform regular backups is a critical task, the backups will be of little use should the server suffer a critical failure that prevents it from being started normally. ASR allows the network administrator to restore the operating system back to a previous state (current as of the time the ASR set was created), which then allows them to restart the Windows Server 2003 normally and continue repairing the computer as required.

The ASR process is made up of two key parts: a floppy disk that is used to start the Windows Server 2003 computer and a backup file that contains the system state, system services, and disks associated with the operating system components. The startup disk also contains information about the configuration of the computer's disks and information on how the ASR restoration is to be performed. Because an ASR set focuses on the files needed to restore the system, data files are not included in the backup.

Volume Shadow Copies are another new backup feature in Windows Server 2003 and are used to provide copies of data at a given point in time. Users can view the contents of shared folders and see previous versions of data. This allows them to use these copies as if they are restoring a backup of data from an earlier time.

When shadow copies are made of shared folders, there are a number of benefits. If a file was deleted or corrupted in some way, the network administrator can open the previous version and copy it to the original location or another location. This also allows the administrator to use previous versions to compare changes that have occurred between the versions.

The previous versions of files included in a shadow copy are read-only, preventing users from modifying the older version in any way. This maintains the integrity of the previous version, so that it remains a duplicate of the file at the time it was initially shadow copied. If users wish to make modifications to it, the older version can be copied to another location.

Exam Objectives Fast Track

Creating a Backup Plan

☑ Backup plans are used to protect data on a computer. When data is backed up, it is copied to an area of the hard disk or other media that can be stored in a separate location. If a user accidentally deletes a file, data becomes corrupted, or a disaster occurs, the backup can be used to copy this data back to the server.

☑ Windows Server 2003 provides a Backup Utility that allows the network administrator to back up files on the server, regardless of whether the hard disks are formatted as FAT, FAT32, or NTFS. This data can be backed up to a file or to a tape drive and kept until it needs to be restored.

☑ The Backup Utility provides five different types of backups that can be performed: Normal, Incremental, Differential, Copy, and Daily. The type of backup chosen will determine how much data is backed up, and the storage space required for the backup job.

☑ A good media rotation system should be part of every backup plan. By rotating the backup media in accordance with an approved procedure and schedule, the network administrator increases the reliability and lifetime of the backup media, thus enhancing their chances of performing a successful restoration. Having a solid media rotation system in place also provides an easy means to maintain a backup history.

Using the Windows Backup Utility

☑ The System State is that critical data stored on each computer that contains information that is required for the proper startup and operation of the computer. System State data includes these items:

- Boot and system files (such as boot.ini, NTLDR, etc.)

- The Registry

- The COM+ class registration database

- The system files that are protected by Windows File Protection (located in %systemroot%\system32\dllcache)

- The Active Directory service if the server is a domain controller

- The SYSVOL directory if the server is a domain controller

- The Cluster service information if the server is a member of a cluster

- The IIS metadirectory if IIS is installed on the server

- The Certificate Services database if the server is a CA

☑ The Backup Utility in Windows Server 2003 uses the Volume Shadow Copy technique to create copies of data. This means that even files that are open and being used by users or the system can be backed up.

☑ The Backup Utility has two modes of operation: Backup and Restore Wizard, and Advanced Mode.

☑ To back up or restore files and folders on any computer in a domain, a user needs to be a member of the Administrators or Backup Operators group on a domain controller.

☑ Files and folders can be backed up from a local or remote computer as long as the user has the required access to the files and folders.

☑ When performing backups remotely, system state data cannot be saved.

☑ An administrator can also delegate the authority to perform backups to a user without placing that user in one of the authorized groups. Delegation of control can be done through the Delegation of Control Wizard or via Group Policy settings.

Using Automated System Recovery

☑ The ASR process is made up of two key parts: a floppy disk that is used to start the Windows Server 2003 computer and a backup file that contains the system state, system services, and disks associated with the operating system components.

☑ The startup disk also contains information about the configuration of the computer's disks, and information on how the ASR restoration is to be performed. Because an ASR set focuses on the files needed to restore the system, data files are not included in the backup.

☑ An ASR set should be created each time a major hardware change or a change to the operating system is made on the computer running Windows Server 2003.

☑ The following items must be available when attempting to perform an ASR recovery:

- The ASR floppy disk

- The ASR backup file

- The Windows Server 2003 CD

- Any special drivers required, such as RAID hardware or other mass storage device drivers

    ☑   The target of an ASR recovery must have a working floppy drive installed.

Working with Volume Shadow Copy

    ☑   Volume shadow copies are used to provide copies of data as it is at a given point in time. Users can benefit from shared copies by being able to view, copy, or restore previous versions of data.

    ☑   The Previous Versions client allows users to access previous versions of files across the network. When the client software is installed, users can view, copy, and restore files from the Previous Versions tab of the file's properties.

    ☑   Shadow copies can be scheduled just as backups are scheduled. Windows Server 2003 can be scheduled to make shadow copies once, at system startup, at logon, when the computer is idle, or on a daily, weekly, or monthly basis.

Exam Objectives
Frequently Asked Questions

The following Frequently Asked Questions, answered by the authors of this book, are designed to both measure your understanding of the Exam Objectives presented in this chapter, and to assist you with real-life implementation of these concepts. You will also gain access to thousands of other FAQs at ITFAQnet.com.

Q: I have developed a disaster recovery plan, but I am not completely certain that the plans and procedures will be effective during a disaster. How can I be sure?

A: Perform "dry runs" of the disaster recovery plan to ensure that developed strategies work as expected, and revise any steps that are ineffective.

Q: I want users to be able to back up the files that they own. I have given them Full Control over the folders that belong to them on the server, but they still cannot back up files. What is the most likely reason for this?

A: If a user is not an Administrator or Backup Operator, they need read, read and execute, modify, or full control permissions over a file for which they have ownership. Since the users have Full Control, this is not the problem. The problem might reside in the fact that disk quotas have been set. Disk quota restrictions prevent users from being able to perform a backup.

Q: I have tried modifying a previous copy of a file included in shadow copy, but find I cannot. Why is this?

A: Previous versions of files included in a shadow copy are read-only, preventing users from modifying the older version in any way. This maintains the integrity of the previous version, so it remains a duplicate of the file at the time it was initially shadow copied. To modify a copy of the file, you would need to first copy it to another location.

Q: Our organization is very small, do we really need a difficult to use and complicated backup plan?

A: No, you certainly do not need to be using anything that is difficult or confusing. If your backup plan is difficult to use or confusing, then it is time for a new backup plan. Does this mean that you do not need any backup plan? Most definitely not. A backup plan is required for any size network that processes information that is important to it. A simple backup plan that says "We will backup using a five-tape rotation system with the tape from the previous night being taken offsite the next morning" might be a good solution for a small network. Tailor your backup plan to suit your needs, but whatever you do, have a backup plan of some kind!

Q: If I implement Volume Shadow Copies on the network data shares for our network, is there any reason I still need to perform normal backups?

A: Yes! Volume Shadow Copies were never intended to replace a normal, functional backup plan. The primary use for Volume Shadow Copies is to be able to quickly locate and use older versions of documents when required. You will still require a backup plan to ensure that all of your data is protected adequately in the event a disaster should occur.

Q: I need to perform an ASR recovery on a server that does not have a floppy drive, what can I do?

A: You must install a floppy drive into that server before you will be able to perform the ASR recovery. There is no way to get around this requirement.

Self Test

Creating a Backup Plan

1. You are creating a backup plan for your organization's network. Your plan calls for you to use the five-tape rotation system with all backup tapes being stored in the file cabinet in your office. You will be performing a differential backup Monday through Thursday and a full backup on Fridays. Your network consists of two Windows Server 2003 file servers that are to be backed up. You also have 40 Windows XP Professional client computers located on your network. What potential problem exists with your backup plan?

    A. The five-tape rotation system is not adequate for this size network.

    B. Differential backups should only be performed on Fridays, not daily.

    C. Backup media should be kept offsite.

    D. Full backups should not be performed once per week, they should occur monthly.

2. You are creating a backup plan for your organization's network. Your CIO wants you to use four backup tapes, one for each week of the month. You disagree with his plan and argue that it is not an effective media rotation system. What benefits can you present to your CIO to persuade him to allow you to use a more effective media rotation system such as the five-tape rotation? (Choose all that apply.)

    A. An effective media rotation system will increase the lifetime of the backup media in use.

    B. An effective media rotation system will reduce the cost spent on each backup tape.

    C. An effective media rotation system will provide a backup history.

    D. An effective media rotation system will reduce the lifetime of the backup media in use.

Using the Windows Backup Utility

3. You are the network administrator for the CVB Company. Your primary duty is to maintain and manage the disaster recovery operations for the network. On Thursday morning, one of your file servers crashes. You place a replacement server on the network but need to restore all files from the old file server before making it available to users. You performed a daily backup on Monday, a normal backup on Tuesday, and a differential backup on Wednesday. In what order do you need to restore data to the new server?

    A. Monday first, Tuesday second, Wednesday third

    B. Monday first, Wednesday second, Tuesday third

    C. Tuesday first, Wednesday second

    D. Wednesday first, Tuesday second

4. You have added a new server running Windows Server 2003 to your network. Although it is physically attached to the network, no one has access to the server yet, as you want to install some additional programs before making it available. Before installing third-party programs on the server, which will be needed by users of the network to perform certain jobs, you decide to back up the server. If there are any problems after installing the applications, you can then use the backup to restore the server to its previous state. When configuring the Backup Utility, you log in with the Administrator account and find that the "Backup destination" field is disabled, indicating that you can only back up to a file. What is the likely cause of this?

A. A tape device is not installed on the server, so the only backup destination the Backup Utility can use is a file.

B. The Windows Server 2003 computer is not available to network users yet, so nothing has changed on the server requiring a backup. The utility knows this, so this option is disabled.

C. You do not have the proper rights to perform a backup.

D. The "Backup destination" will always show that it is backing up to a file, regardless of where that file is stored.

5. Members of your organization store files on a Windows Server 2003 computer. Each department has its own folder, with subfolders inside for each employee within that department. A complaint has been made about an employee having non-work related files on the server that are considered offensive. Upon checking the contents of that person's folder, you find it to be true. You want to back up the entire contents of this folder, without affecting the backups that are performed daily. What will you do?

A. Perform a normal backup

B. Perform an incremental backup

C. Perform a copy backup

D. You cannot back up the files without affecting other backups that are performed

6. You are developing a backup plan that will be used to routinely back up data each night. There is a considerable amount of data on the Windows Server 2003 servers on the network, so you want backups to occur as quickly as possible. Due to the mission-critical nature of much of this data, you also want data to be restored as quickly as possible following a disaster. Based on these needs, which of the following backup types will you use in your plan?

A. Perform a normal backup each night

B. Perform a daily backup each night

C. Perform a normal backup, followed by nightly incremental backups

D. Perform a normal backup, followed by nightly differential backups

7. A user has ownership of files in a shared folder located on a Windows Server 2003 computer and wants to perform a backup of her files. She is a standard user, with no special rights or group memberships. Due to the amount of free disk space and the need of users to store sizable files, there are no restrictions on how much data a user can store on the server. The user has to temporarily perform the duties of another coworker who also uses this folder for his work. After modifying documents belonging to this person over the day, she tries to back up the files but finds she cannot. She calls and complains to you about the problem, hoping you can help. What is most likely the reason for this problem? (Choose all that apply.)

   A. She does not have the minimum permissions necessary to back up these files

   B. She is not an Administrator or Backup Operator.

   C. She does not have ownership of the files.

   D. Disk quota restrictions are preventing the backup.

8. You schedule a backup to run monthly on the 30th of each month, when you are using the Backup Utility to back up the system state of a Windows Server 2003 computer. This server contains data files used by users of the network. It also acts as a Web server for the local intranet and allows users to view information in HTML format on the network. Which of the following files will be included when the system state is backed up? (Choose all that apply.)

   A. IIS Metadirectory

   B. COM+ class registration database

   C. SYSVOL directory

   D. Certificate Services database

9. You are the network administrator for the CVB Company. Your primary duty is to maintain and manage the disaster recovery operations for the network. You are configuring a new backup job that will be used to perform nightly backups of a new file server recently placed on the network. You need to ensure that should a restoration be required, all files and folders contained in the backup file will be restored regardless of their age. What option should you configure for the backup job?

   A. Do not replace the file on my computer.

   B. Verify data after the backup completes.

   C. Back up the contents of mounted drives.

   D. Always replace the file on my computer.

10. You are the network administrator for the CVB Company. Your primary duty is to maintain and manage the disaster recovery operations for the network. You are configuring a new backup job that will be used to perform nightly backups of a new file server recently placed on the network. You need to ensure that only information such as loading a tape are included in the backup log. What option should you configure for the backup job?

    A. Always allow use of recognizable media without prompting

    B. Summary logging

    C. Information logging

    D. Show alert messages when new media is inserted

11. You are the network administrator for the CVB company. Your primary duty is to maintain and manage the disaster recovery operations for the network. You need to allow another user in your company, Catherine, to perform backup and restoration operations. You must not allow Catherine to have any more privileges than she requires. What two ways can you give Catherine only the required privileges? (Choose two correct answers.)

    A. Make Catherine a member of the Backup Operators group.

    B. Make Catherine a member of the Server Operators group.

    C. Make Catherine a member of the Domain Admins group.

    D. Run the Delegation of Control Wizard, targeting Catherine's user account.

Using Automated System Recovery

12. A disaster has occurred, requiring you to use an ASR set to restore the system. When using the ASR set to restore the system, you notice that certain files are not restored to the computer. What files are not included in the ASR set, and how will you remedy the problem?

    A. Data files are not included in the primary ASR set, and need to be restored from the data section of the ASR set. Information on the data set is found on the ASR floppy disk.

    B. Data files are not included in the ASR set, and need to be restored from a separate backup.

    C. System files are not included in an ASR set. They need to be restored from a system state backup.

    D. System services are not included in an ASR set, and need to be reinstalled from the installation CD.

13. You are the network administrator for the CVB Company. Your primary duty is to maintain and manage the disaster recovery operations for the network. You are preparing to create an ASR set for one of your critical print servers. After the ASR backup process has been completed, what will you have created? (Choose two correct answers.)

    A. A startup floppy disk that contains information about the ASR backup.

    B. A backup file that contains the System State, system services, and the disks associated with the server.

    C. A backup file that contains the System State, system services and data on the servers disks.

    D. A startup floppy disk that contains all third-party drivers you have installed on the server.

14. You are the network administrator for the CVB Company. Your primary duty is to maintain and manage the disaster recovery operations for the network. You are currently preparing a company policy outlining how an ASR recovery is to be performed for one of your critical print servers. What items should you list as being required in order to perform the ASR restoration? (Choose two correct answers.)

    A. The server that is being restored via ASR must have a DAT drive.

    B. The server that is being restored via ASR must have a floppy drive.

    C. You will need to have the Windows Server 2003 CD.

    D. You will need to have a DOS boot disk.

Working with Volume Shadow Copy

15. You are performing a backup of data stored in a folder of your Windows Server 2003 computer, using Volume Shadow Copies. Network users store their work in this folder, so you start the backup after most employees have gone home for the day. During the backup, you discover that an employee is working overtime, and has a document open that is in the folder being backed up. What will result from this situation?

    A. The backup will fail.

    B. The backup will corrupt the file, but succeed in backing up other files that are not open.

    C. The backup will back up the open file, and continue backing up any other files in the folder.

    D. The backup will restart, and keep doing so until the document is closed.

16. A user attempts to view the previous versions of a file that has been shadow copied on the server. When he tries to view the previous versions, he finds that he cannot although several other users can view the previous version. When he views the file's properties, there is no tab for previous versions. What is most likely the cause of this problem?

    A. Shadow copying is not enabled.

    B. There have been no modifications to the file since shadow copying was enabled.

    C. The Previous Versions client has not been installed on the server.

    D. The Previous Versions client has not been installed on the user's computer.

Self Test Quick Answer Key

For complete questions, answers, and explanations to the Self Test questions in this chapter as well as the other chapters in this book, see the Self Test Appendix.

1. **C**	9. **D**
2. **A, C**	10. **B**
3. **C**	11. **A, D**
4. **A**	12. **B**
5. **C**	13. **A, B**
6. **D**	14. **B, C**
7. **B, C**	15. **C**
8. **A, B**	16. **D**

Chapter 6

MCSA/MCSE 70-292

Implementing, Managing, and Maintaining Name Resolution

Exam Objectives in this Chapter:

5.1 Install and configure the DNS Server service

5.1.1 Configure DNS server options

5.1.2 Configure DNS zone options

5.1.3 Configure DNS forwarding

5.2 Manage DNS

5.2.1 Manage DNS zone settings

5.2.2 Manage DNS record settings

5.2.3 Manage DNS server options

☑ Summary of Exam Objectives

☑ Exam Objectives Fast Track

☑ Exam Objectives Frequently Asked Questions

☑ Self Test

☑ Self Test Quick Answer Key

Introduction

It was not too long ago that a network administrator could discuss networking computers on the same network segment and the words Domain Name System (DNS) would never surface during the conversation. It was also not so long ago that the NetBIOS Extended User Interface (NetBEUI) was the king of networking protocols in Windows NT networks. If an administrator needed to connect to a NetWare server they relied on the Internetwork Packet Exchange/Sequenced Packet Exchange (IPX/SPX) protocol.

One day, seemingly out of nowhere, the Internet happened. It had actually been around for quite some time courtesy of the Department of Defense and several large universities across the country, but organizations that wanted to connect their networks together either bought or leased dedicated lines between sites. This was not an altogether inexpensive proposition—especially before the wide spread use of fiber optics and satellite communications. With the introduction of the masses to the Internet, a crisis occurred: Transmission Control Protocol/Internet Protocol (TCP/IP) was not only needed within Windows networks, but demanded by administrators who began to see the power and flexibility that it promised. Microsoft, along with a host of other vendors, heard the demand and seemingly overnight TCP/IP support appeared in all operating systems. It was not until the introduction of Windows 2000, however, that TCP/IP became the de facto networking protocol in the Windows network arena. When Windows 2000 came out, TCP/IP and DNS were integral parts of the most powerful and flexible operating system made. Active Directory changed the way that Windows network administrators did their jobs. No longer would they be crippled by hard-to-manage system policies or have to resort to third-party solutions such as Novell's ZENWorks—Windows 2000 was a complete package, albeit with some problems, but a massive step in the right direction no less. But wait; how did DNS come into the picture all of a sudden?

DNS is a service that originated with the original Internet (Advanced Research Projects Agency Network [ARPANET] at the time) and is used to resolve a Fully Qualified Domain Name (FQDN) into an Internet Protocol (IP) address. It is important to remember that computers only care about two numbers: 0 and 1. Every operation any computer does is based solely on those two numbers. Everything else is added on to make things easier for the human beings that operate and interact with binary-speaking computers. Computers communicating with each other using TCP/IP do so by directing their traffic to an IP address, such as 216.238.8.44. This IP address is nothing more than a grouping of 32 0s or 1s in a specific order. For example, you are getting ready to take the latest Windows Server 2003 certification exam and you heard that Syngress Publishing has some study guides that might help you prepare for the exam. You want to check out the Syngress Publishing Web site so you can see for yourself. Without DNS you would need to know that the IP address for Syngress Publishing's Web site is 216.238.8.44. Thanks to DNS, you can simply type www.syngress.com into the browser and be connected. Think of DNS as a large phone book of sorts: you put in an easy-to-remember name and it returns a useful IP address that can be used to connect to a Web site.

Introducing and Planning the DNS Service

DNS is at the heart of Windows Server 2003. Therefore, this chapter begins with a discussion of how DNS works and what exactly it does for networks. Subsequent sections cover the installation and configuration of a Windows Server 2003 DNS server.

Back in the early days of connected computing, the Internet was known as the ARPANET. The total number of hosts on the entire ARPANET was less than 100, and a master list of server names and their respective IP addresses was maintained in a file called HOSTS.TXT. This worked great until more and more servers and computers began to connect to the ARPANET. In a short period of time a change had to be made. That change was the introduction of the DNS.

DNS is a large hierarchical database that contains the names and IP addresses for IP networks and hosts. In today's computing environment, DNS is used almost universally as the preferred means of name resolution. With Windows 2000, Microsoft migrated from their proprietary, less accepted Windows Internet Naming Service (WINS) to DNS, and has continued using DNS as the de facto standard for all Windows networks.

So what is a hierarchical database? In simple terms, it is a multilevel organization system. Consider the FQDN of mail.bigcorp.com. The MAIL portion of the FQDN represents the host (or computer). The BIGCORP portion of the FQDN represents what is known as a second level domain. The COM portion represents what is known as a top-level domain (TLD). Figure 6.1 illustrates this concept.

Figure 6.1 DNS Hierarchical Database System

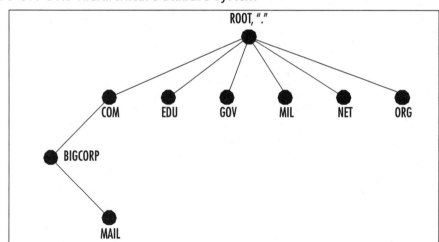

As seen in Figure 6.1, the top of the DNS hierarchy is called the *root*, which is symbolized by a single period ".". The DNS system is a distributed database that allows the entire database to be broken up into smaller segments, while maintaining an overall logical architecture to help provide required name resolution services on the Internet and private local networks. There are 13 root name servers that sit at the top of the hierarchical chain and perform top-level name resolution for Internet clients. These servers are located all over the globe, with the majority of them located in the United States.

DNS is designed to allow multiple name servers for redundancy and improved performance. For further performance improvement, the caching of resolution results is allowed on local DNS servers, thus preventing repetitive resolution requests. At each level of the DNS hierarchy, parts of the overall namespace are located on many computers, thus the data storage and query loads are distributed throughout thousands of DNS servers around the Internet. The hierarchical nature of DNS is designed in such a way that every computer on or off the Internet can be named as part of the DNS namespace.

The DNS Hierarchical Namespace

The simple and powerful DNS naming convention adds a layer of complexity to the planning process. The overall DNS namespace is a complex arrangement that consists of many different pieces, all arranged in a specific order. Similar to the way a file system is implemented on a computer to store files in folders, DNS names are created as part of a hierarchical database system. Hierarchies are very powerful storage systems because they can store large amounts of data while also making this data easily searchable.

Head of the Class...

Form of a Hierarchy...

Can you think of any other services in Windows Server 2003 that use a hierarchical arrangement? If you said Active Directory, you are correct! When Microsoft made the switch to DNS as the de facto name resolution standard for Windows networks, they designed Active Directory to mirror DNS. The Active Directory hierarchy is created directly on top of the existing rules that govern DNS hierarchies, thus the information in the DNS hierarchy of a Windows Server 2003 Active Directory network is directly related to that of the Active Directory hierarchy.

The Active Directory implementation is designed like a forest. At the top of the forest is a root domain; under this root domain are child domains. Each domain in the forest can have any number of child domains and any number of levels of domains below it, within the overall naming restrictions (discussed later in this chapter). Organizational units, containers, users, computers, and various other network objects are located within domains. Because Active Directory and DNS are so tightly interwoven, a TCP/IP network with DNS service is a requirement in order to create an Active Directory network.

The following list of key terms will be useful throughout the rest of this chapter.

- **FQDN** The domain name, which includes all domains at all levels between the host and root of DNS. As seen earlier, mail.bigcorp.com is a FQDN.

- **Leaf** The very last item in a hierarchical tree structure. Leaves do not contain any other objects and are commonly referred to as nodes in DNS.

- **Node** The point where two or more connecting lines in a hierarchical tree structure intersect at a common point. Nodes in DNS commonly refer to hosts, subdomains or even TLDs.

- **TLD** The suffix that is attached to all FQDN, such as COM. Some of the most common TLDs are detailed in Table 6.1.

- **Tree** A hierarchical data structure where each piece of data is connected to one or more pieces directly below it in the hierarchy. In the case of DNS, it is an inverted tree because the root appears at the top.

- **Zone** A file stored on a DNS server containing a logical grouping of host names within the DNS system that is used to perform name resolution.

Some common TLDs are presented in Table 6.1.

Table 6.1 Common TLDs

Top Level Domain	Description
COM	Originally intended for use by commercial entities, but has been used for many different reasons. An example of the COM TLD is mcsaworld.com.
EDU	Created for use by higher education institutions such as four-year colleges and universities. An example of the EDU TLD is stanford.edu.
GOV	Created for use by agencies of the United States federal government. An example of the GOV TLD is whitehouse.gov.
MIL	Created for use by agencies of the United States military. An example of the MIL TLD is army.mil.
NET	Originally intended for use by computer network providers and organizations dedicated to the Internet, but has been used for many different reasons. An example of the NET TLD is ibm.net.
ORG	Originally intended for use by nonprofit or noncommercial organizations, such as professional groups, churches, and other organizations, but has been used for many different reasons. An example of the ORG TLD is pbs.org.

TEST DAY TIP

There are over 100 country-specific TLDs currently in existence, such as CA for Canada, UK for the United Kingdom, and JP for Japan. For a complete listing of all country-specific TLDs, see www.iana.org/cctld/cctld-whois.htm.

Determining Namespace Requirements

Before installing a DNS server, it is important to do some planning. Because of the extensive integration of DNS and Active Directory in Windows Server 2003, an administrator must take great care to get their DNS implementation correct the first time around. This process can be started by realistically answering the following three questions.

1. **Will the DNS namespace being created be used for internal purposes only?** If the answer is no, the network administrator will need to ensure that they adhere to all requirements of RFC1123. If the answer is yes, they have much more flexibility. They might create a namespace such as mcsaworld.corp. This can be thought of as the *internal namespace*.

2. **Will the DNS namespace also be used on the Internet?** If yes, the network administrator should seriously consider registering a domain name for their organization with one of the many domain name registrars available. This will also impact their namespace naming system per the requirements of RFC1123. This can be thought of as the *external namespace*.

3. **Will the network administrator be implementing Active Directory on their network?** If yes, the network administrator should consider creating Active Directory integrated zones (discussed later in this chapter). The administrator will also need to ensure that any third-party DNS servers, such as Berkeley Internet Name Domain (BIND), meet the requirements of Active Directory.

NOTE

When planning DNS namespaces for an organization, it is important to pay particular attention to the internal and external namespaces. An internal namespace could be a Windows Server 2003 DNS infrastructure with the name mcsaworld.corp. Conversely, the external namespace could be reached via Internet-hosted DNS as mcsaworld.com so visitors could be directed to the Web server with that domain name. It is recommended that the internal namespace be kept private for security reasons.

Once these three questions are answered, the following three options need to be considered for creating the DNS namespace the network will be using.

- **Use an Existing DNS Namespace** This option is the easiest to start with, but requires additional administrative work (discussed later in this chapter). When a network administrator uses an existing DNS namespace, they are in effect using the same namespace for their external (Internet) and internal network segments. This method is fairly simple and provides easy access to both internal and external resources. The downside of this method is that it can leave an internal network wide open to attack and compromise. Administrators responsible for DNS must make sure that the appropriate records are stored on the internal and external DNS servers to maintain the security of the internal network.

■ **Use a Delegated Namespace** When an administrator uses a delegated namespace, they are opting to use a subdomain of their primary namespace. For example, suppose they are working for BigCorp Corporation and already own the bigcorp.com domain name. With a delegated namespace, the administrator might create the corp.bigcorp.com subdomain and use this as the root of their DNS and Active Directory implementation. Internal clients can easily be allowed to resolve external IP addresses through forwarding, while preventing external clients from resolving internal IP addresses. This option maintains the overall namespace and allows the network administrator to protect and isolate all internal data in its own forest. The only drawback to this option is that it adds additional length to the FQDN.

■ **Use a Completely Unique Namespace** When an administrator uses a completely unique namespace, they are using a separate but related domain name for their internal namespace. So, if they were already using the bigcorp.com domain name for their Internet namespace, they might consider using the bigcorp.net domain name for their internal namespace. This option is advantageous in two ways: no zone transfers are required between the internal and external namespaces, and the existing DNS namespace remains unchanged. This option also prevents internal clients from being exposed to the Internet by default.

NOTE

The method used most often by administrators is a delegated namespace, such as corp.bigcorp.com, if they already own the domain name bigcorp.com. This allows for a fairly contiguous and easy-to-remember namespace for all internal users. The internal namespace can be completely isolated for security reasons from the external namespace, yet still retain the familiar look of the existing external namespace.

Now that the questions are answered and the various options have been examined for creating a Windows Server 2003 DNS namespace, consider the following example of how it all comes together. ACME Rockets is a major manufacturer of rockets. They already own the domain name acmerockets.com and their corporate headquarters are located in Rockland, Massachusetts. ACME Rockets has field offices and manufacturing facilities located in the following countries: Canada, Mexico, England, France, Japan, and Australia. The corporate structure of ACME Rockets has the following major departments: Executive, Production, Sales, Information Technology, and Legal. Each department has several child divisions within it. Given this information, how would a network administrator design a namespace for ACME Rockets?

Starting with the namespace of acmerockets.com, let's delegate the namespace and create corp.acmerockets.com as the root of the internal DNS and Active Directory namespace. In this, corp becomes a third-level domain. From here, create fourth-level domains by country code. Each of these fourth-level domains can be subdivided further, if required, to create fifth-level domains for specific departments. In this example, we will stop at fourth level domains. Our solution is shown in Figure 6.2, but yours will vary depending on your methodology and specific requirements.

Figure 6.2 Delegated Namespace Configuration is Easily Implemented and Understood

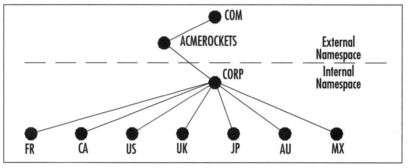

For example, if a server located in the United States is named ARDHCP0042, its FQDN would be ARDHCP0042.us.corp.acmerockets.com. As discussed previously, there are finite limitations on the total length of a FQDN as well as the characters that are allowed in a FQDN. These restrictions are outlined in Table 6.2.

Table 6.2 DNS Name Restrictions in Windows Server 2003 (per RFC1123)

Restriction	Standard DNS	DNS in Windows Server 2003 (Including Windows 2000)
Characters	Per the requirements of RFC 1123, only the standard characters are supported: "A" to "Z," "a" to "z," "0" to "9," and the hyphen, "-".	Provides standard support as specified in RFC1123. Also provides support for specifications RFC2181 and 2044.
FQDN length	The total length cannot exceed 255 bytes. Each label cannot exceed 63 bytes.	The same restrictions apply with the exception that domain controllers are limited to a FQDN that does not exceed 155 bytes in length.

Determining Zone Type Requirements

The next crucial pieces of the overall DNS puzzle are the concepts of *zones of authority* (*zones*) and *zone transfers*.

A zone of authority (zone) is a file that contains the complete information on a portion of a domain namespace—it is a subset of a domain. One name server (or multiple servers when DNS is Active Directory-integrated) is authoritative for every zone and will respond to any request that a client makes for name resolution against that zone. So, in looking at the DNS name www.syngress.com, syngress.com is a DNS zone within the com hierarchy. Remember that www is just the name or alias of a host within the syngress.com zone—typically that assigned to the Web server(s).

Zones store data in a *zone database file* (or *zone file*) located on the DNS server. Windows Server 2003 keeps its DNS zone files in the following location: %systemroot%\system32\dns. If Active Directory-integrated zones are implemented, the actual zone data is stored in the Active Directory database with the rest of the Active Directory data. Following is a list of the different types of zones that can be created when using the Windows Server 2003 DNS service.

- **Standard** The standard zone is supported by all versions of DNS server software and has been used since the introduction of DNS. There are two different roles that can be assigned when standard DNS zones are being used:

    - **Standard Primary** The standard primary zone holds the master copy of the zone file and will replicate it to all configured secondary zones using the standard zone file text format. All changes made to the zone file must be made by the primary zone server, as it holds the only writeable copy. Primary zones function similarly to the way Windows NT 4.0 Primary Domain Controllers (PDCs) operated in that only one server can write to the data.

    - **Standard Secondary** The standard secondary zone holds a read-only copy of the zone file in standard text format. Any number of secondary zone servers can be created to increase the performance and availability of the DNS implementation. Secondary zones function similarly to the way Windows NT 4.0 Backup Domain Controllers (BDCs) operated in that they possess a read-only copy of the data.

- **Active Directory-Integrated** All zone information is contained within the Active Directory database to provide for increased security and availability. When Active Directory-integrated zones are created, the DNS server runs on all domain controllers in the domain and any DNS server can modify the zone data. Active Directory-integrated zones do not perform zone transfers among themselves—they replicate data with the rest of the Active Directory data. Active Directory-integrated zones are only available on Windows 2000 Server and Windows Server 2003 DNS servers in an Active Directory domain.

- **Stub** Stub zones are new in Windows DNS, with support being introduced in Windows Server 2003. A stub zone contains only the specific resource records necessary to identify the authoritative DNS servers for the zone.

EXAM WARNING

What is the difference between a zone and a domain? A domain is a portion of the overall DNS namespace. A zone, however, can contain multiple contiguous domains.

Look at the corp.bigcorp.com domain. Inside of it is all of the information that is specific to that portion of the overall DNS namespace. us.corp.bigcorp.com is another example of a domain—one that is contiguous within the corp.bigcorp.com domain tree. While the two domains are related to each other and share a node, they are completely separate domains—each with their own resource records. A zone can be created on a DNS server that would contain records for both domains. A zone is a container that allows the network administrator to logically group and manage domains and their associated resource records as desired within their DNS implementation.

It is important not to overlook the importance of the zone type when planning a DNS implementation. The type of zone implemented will determine the placement and configuration of the DNS servers on the network. Consider the following points about standard zones and Active Directory-integrated zones:

- When using standard zones, the following items are important to remember:
  - Only one single DNS server holds the master (writeable) copy of the DNS zone file.
  - Zone transfers may be conducted using either incremental or full zone transfer as needed.
  - Full compatibility is provided with BIND DNS servers.

- When using Active Directory-integrated zones, the following items are important to remember:
  - DNS servers operate in a multimaster arrangement, allowing any DNS server to make changes to the zone data.
  - Zone transfers do not occur. Zone data is replicated with the Active Directory data.
  - DNS dynamic update has redundancy, as the failure of a single DNS server will not prevent updates from occurring.

- The Active Directory-integrated zones appear to BIND servers as standard primary zone servers.

- The security of zone data is increased due to being protected by Active Directory. Active Directory-integrated zones can be configured to use only secure dynamic updates, thus preventing rogue clients from populating the DNS zone file with bad information. As well, DACLs are used to control access to DNS.

- Zone data can be transferred to a standard secondary zone if desired for use in remote locations or DMZ environments.

Table 6.3 summarizes the key points to remember when choosing between standard and Active Directory-integrated zones.

Table 6.3 Standard and Active Directory-Integrated Zone Features

DNS Feature	Standard DNS Zones	Active Directory Integrated Zones
Meets the IETF specifications for DNS servers?	Yes	Yes
Uses Active Directory for replication?	No	Yes
Provides increased reliability and security?	No	Yes
Zone updates can occur after the failure of the master server?	No	Yes (all DNS servers operate in a multi-master arrangement)
Provides support for incremental zone transfers?	Yes	Yes (only changed zone data is replicated during the Active Directory replication cycle)

Standard secondary zones offer some very attractive benefits:

- When using standard zones, secondary zone servers provide availability and redundancy of the zone in the event that the primary zone server becomes unresponsive. Also, multiple secondary zone servers reduce the loading on the primary zone server.

- When using either standard or Active Directory-integrated zones, secondary zones can be used in remote offices to reduce wide area network (WAN) use and increase the speed of local name resolution at the remote site.

- When using either standard or Active Directory-integrated zones, secondary zones can be used in DMZs to provide a read-only copy of the zone data as required.

When using standard zones, it is important to ensure that only the desired DNS servers are allowed to perform zone transfers. Zone transfers conducted by attackers can provide a detailed "road map" of an entire network. Zone transfers occur only for standard zones. Active Directory-integrated zones use zone replication as part of the regular Active Directory replication schedule.

DNS, unlike WINS, always initiates zone transfers with the secondary zone server polling the primary server to determine what version the zone file is currently at. The zone version on the primary zone server is then compared to the version that the secondary zone server has to see if it has changed. If the zone version number has changed, the secondary zone server will initiate a zone transfer. Since a primary zone server will perform a zone transfer with any server requesting one, the network administrator must configure the servers that the primary zone server is authorized to perform zone transfers with.

Windows Server 2003 DNS supports both incremental (IXFR) and full (AXFR) zone transfers. If both DNS servers involved in a zone transfer support incremental zone transfers, the secondary zone server will pull from the primary zone server (standard or Active Directory-integrated) and only those changes that have been made to resource records for each incremental zone transfer version number. Using IXFR, a single resource record could potentially be updated multiple times during a zone transfer. By using IXFR, however, network traffic is greatly reduced and the overall zone transfer speed is increased.

When only Active Directory-integrated zones are used, zone transfer does not occur. Active Directory-integrated zones replicate data among all domain controllers, thus allowing all DNS servers (domain controllers) to change the zone data and have it replicated. Zone replication occurs on a per-property basis so that only the pertinent changes to a resource record are updated. Also, Active Directory-integrated zones only replicate the final result of multiple changes that are made to a resource record. Network administrators should always seek to implement Active Directory-integrated zones on their network.

Where do *forward lookup zones* and *reverse lookup zones* fit into the picture? A forward lookup zone is a specific zone file used to resolve an IP address from an FQDN. A reverse lookup zone does the exact opposite, resolving an FQDN from an IP address. Both types of lookup zones have their purposes, and for best results should always be configured and deployed within the DNS zones. While the DNS resolution process works perfectly without a reverse lookup zone configured, an administrator will not be able to get maximum power from the *nslookup* command, a command-line utility used to perform command-line name resolution and troubleshooting. The nslookup command is examined in more detail later in this chapter.

Determining Forwarding Requirements

To understand the operation of and need for DNS forwarding, it is important to understand how the name resolution sequence occurs. In a Windows TCP/IP network, all clients are DNS resolvers, meaning they have been configured with the IP address of one or more DNS servers and can perform name resolution queries against these DNS servers. The DNS resolver is part of the DNS Client service, which is automatically installed when Windows is installed. When a resolver performs a name resolution query against a DNS server, it is one of two types:

- **Recursive Query** A DNS query sent from the resolver or a DNS server to a DNS server, asking that DNS server to provide a complete answer to that query or reply with an error stating that it cannot provide the required information.

- **Iterative Query** A DNS query sent from the resolver or another DNS server in an effort to perform name resolution.

For DNS servers configured properly as forwarders, any recursive queries that cannot be answered by that DNS server are forwarded to another DNS server. If the query is for name resolution outside of that DNS server's zone of authority, it will perform an iterative query against a root DNS server and respond back to the resolver with the IP address of the DNS server responsible for the zone of authority, including the desired top-level name being queried. The DNS server then makes additional iterative queries as required to other DNS servers until the requested name resolution has been accomplished and the results returned to the resolver. This process is illustrated in Figure 6.3.

Consider an example where a client computer located in the bigcorp.com zone wants to contact a File Transfer Protocol (FTP) server located in the syngress.com zone. The process by which the client (the DNS resolver) obtains the requested IP address is explained in the following steps:

1. The client computer performs a recursive query against its local DNS server (hosting the bigcorp.com zone) for the IP address of the FTP server located in the syngress.com zone.

2. The local DNS server does not know this information, but is configured as a forwarder so it then issues an iterative query to one of the root DNS servers requesting the IP address of the FTP server located in the syngress.com zone.

3. The root DNS server does not know this IP address, but does know the IP address of the DNS server responsible for the syngress.com zone; therefore it provides this IP address to the bigcorp.com DNS server.

4. The local DNS server issues another iterative query, this time to the DNS server that is authoritative for the syngress.com zone, asking for the IP address of the FTP server.

5. The syngress.com DNS server is the authoritative server for the syngress.com zone so it can provide the requested name resolution service. Thus, it returns the requested IP address to the local DNS server.

6. The local DNS server passes this IP address information along to the client, completing the name resolution process.

7. The client uses this IP address to initiate a connection to FTP server ftp.syngress.com.

Figure 6.3 The Name Resolution Process may Involve Multiple Iterative Queries

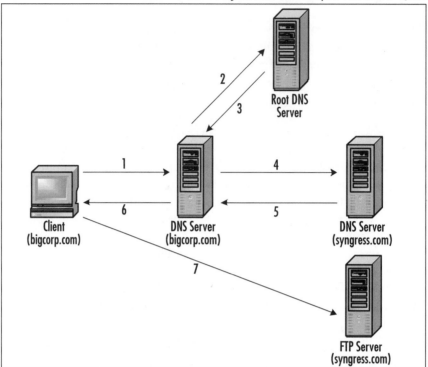

The local DNS server was able to provide the requested name resolution information to the client because it was configured as a *forwarder*—a DNS server allowed to take an incoming recursive query and pass it on to another DNS if it cannot answer the query. As seen in Figure 6.3, configuring forwarding can provide internal clients with an easy way to perform name resolution for computers not located on their internal network. Another application where DNS forwarders shine is when you have remote caching-only DNS servers (a DNS server that has no zone file, but instead only caches the results of queries in RAM) that forward name resolution queries to a centrally located DNS server if they do not have the answer in their cache. If a DNS forwarder does not receive a valid name resolution response from the server that it has forwarded the query to, it will attempt to perform the name resolution itself.

There are two other types of forwarding supported in Windows Server 2003. A *DNS slave server* is a DNS forwarder configured to not try to resolve a name resolution request if it does not receive a valid resolution response from its forwarded request. Slave servers are typically implemented in more secure situations where the network administrator wants to limit the number and types of connections crossing a specific connection. A new feature to DNS in Windows Server 2003 is *conditional forwarding*, in which an administrator can configure that DNS resolution requests should be forwarded to specific DNS servers based on the domain that the resolution is being requested for. Prior to Windows Server 2003, all forwarded requests were sent only to a single server. Consider the example in Figure 6.4 where name resolution requests for the internal network can be forwarded to one DNS server that contains information about internal DNS zones, but all other name resolutions (for Internet domains) can be forwarded to the Internet using standard forwarding procedures.

Figure 6.4 Name Resolution Requests are Forwarded to Specific DNS Servers Based on the Domain Name Being Requested

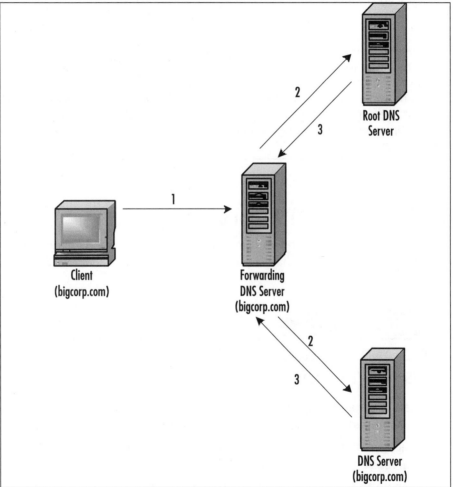

As seen in Figure 6.4, Step 1 remains the same; the client (DNS resolver) has issued a recursive query to a local DNS server. The local DNS server does not have authority for the requested zone information, but is configured as a conditional forwarder. The resolution request is forwarded to either an Internet DNS server or another local DNS server depending on the domain name contained in the name resolution request.

EXAM WARNING

If recursion is disabled for a DNS server, forwarding will also be disabled for that DNS server. For a DNS server to act as a forwarder, it must be able to issue recursive queries.

Now that the initial planning is done and the network administrator has a good idea of their requirements for their DNS implementation, it is time to install and configure Windows Server 2003 DNS server.

NOTE

To be a masterful MCSA on Windows Server 2003, it is important to know that planning a DNS infrastructure is critical prior to rolling out an Active Directory implementation in any sized enterprise. Planning the Active Directory infrastructure starts first with designing, installing, and configuring DNS. Active Directory needs DNS for implementation. Always install and lay out the DNS servers *before* setting up Active Directory.

Installing the DNS Service

Exercise 6.01 presents the process to install and perform the initial configuration for a DNS server and assumes that you already have an installed and functional Windows Server 2003 computer.

EXERCISE 6.01

INSTALLING AND CONFIGURING THE WINDOWS SERVER 2003 DNS SERVICE

1. Launch the Configure Your Server Wizard by clicking **Start | Programs | Administrative Tools | Configure Your Server Wizard**.

2. Click **Next** to dismiss the opening page of the Configure Your Server Wizard.

3. Ensure that you have completed all of the preliminary steps displayed in the Preliminary Steps dialog box, as seen in Figure 6.5, and click **Next** to continue.

Figure 6.5 Ensure that the Preliminary Steps Have Been Completed

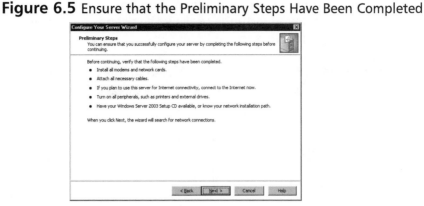

4. The Configure Your Server Wizard will briefly examine your network connections and operating system, as seen in Figure 6.6, before continuing. If necessary, you will be alerted to any problems that are found, such as misconfigured network adapters.

    Figure 6.6 Configure Your Server Wizard will Briefly Examine your Server Before Continuing

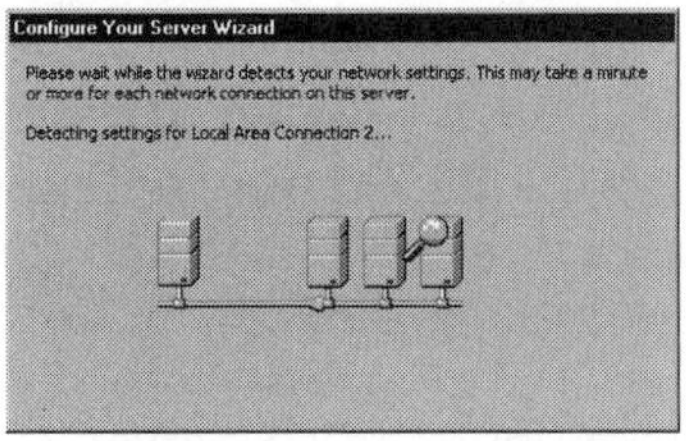

5. If no problems are found, you will be presented with the Server Role dialog box, as seen in Figure 6.7. Select the **DNS server** option and click **Next** to continue.

    Figure 6.7 Preconfigured Server Roles Selection Options

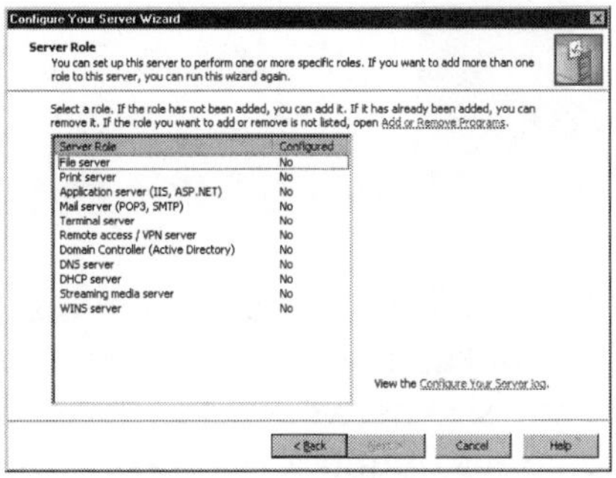

6. On the Summary of Selections dialog box, as seen in Figure 6.8, you will have the opportunity to view the actions the Wizard will perform for you. Click **Next** to continue.

Figure 6.8 Verify that the Selected Actions are Correct

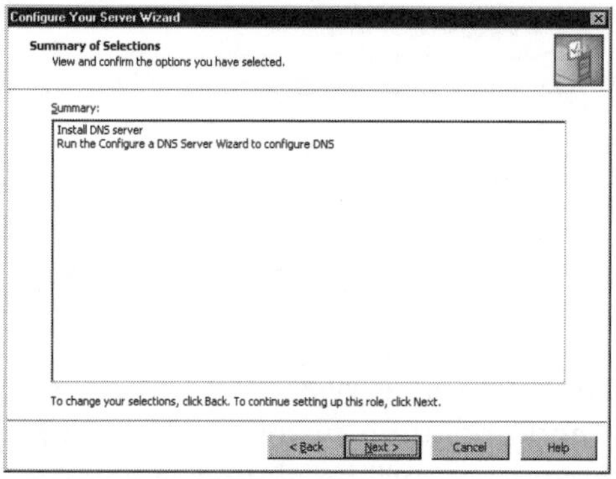

7. The Windows Component Wizard will briefly appear while it is installing the required files for the DNS service. You may be prompted to specify the location of your Windows Server 2003 CD-ROM or setup files during this step.

8. The Configure a DNS Server Wizard appears, as seen in Figure 6.9. You may wish to review the DNS server configuration checklist before continuing. When you are ready to start the configuration of your new DNS server, click **Next** to continue.

Figure 6.9 The Configure a DNS Server Wizard Offers to Let You Review Checklists Before Continuing

9. On the Select Configuration Action dialog box, as seen in Figure 6.10, select the type of lookup zones you want to configure. For the best performance in any size network select the **Create forward and reverse lookup zones** option. Click **Next** to continue.

Figure 6.10 Select the Type of Lookup Zones to be Created

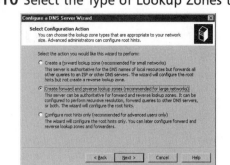

10. On the Forward Lookup Zone dialog box, as seen in Figure 6.11, select whether or not you want to create a forward lookup zone at this time. Select the **Yes, create a forward lookup zone now (recommended)** option. Click **Next** to continue.

Figure 6.11 Creating a Forward Lookup Zone

11. On the Zone Type dialog box, as seen in Figure 6.12, select the type of zone you are creating. As you can see, the Active Directory integrated option is not available—this DNS server is not a domain controller. Select the **Primary zone** option. Click **Next** to continue. (We will examine the process to convert primary zones into Active Directory integrated zones later in this chapter.)

Figure 6.12 Selecting the Type of Zone to Create

12. In the Zone Name dialog box, as seen in Figure 6.13, enter the name of the new forward lookup zone you are creating. In most cases, this will be same as the domain name you are using—in this instance it is corp.mcsaworld.com. Note that the zone name is not the name of the DNS server. Click **Next** to continue.

Figure 6.13 Selecting the Zone Name (Typically Synonymous with the Domain Name)

13. In the Zone File dialog box, as seen in Figure 6.14, enter the name of the zone file that is to be created. Note that you will only see this dialog box when you are not creating Active Directory-integrated zones. In the majority of cases, you should leave the default entry alone, as seen in Figure 6.14. Click **Next** to continue.

Figure 6.14 There is Usually No Reason to Change the
Default Zone File Name

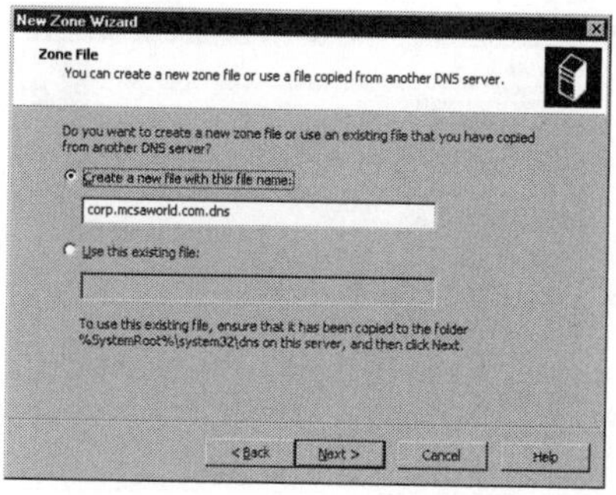

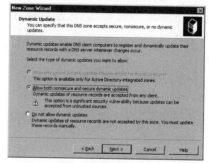

14. In the Dynamic Update dialog box, as seen in Figure 6.15, select
    whether or not you want to use dynamic update. Note that you cannot
    use secure dynamic updates unless you have created an Active
    Directory-integrated zone. Even though not completely secure, we are
    going to configure this zone for secure and nonsecure dynamic updates
    by selecting the **Allow both nonsecure and secure dynamic updates**
    option. Click **Next** to continue.

Figure 6.15 You Will Not Be Able to Use Secure
Dynamic Update with a Standard Zone

15. In the Reverse Lookup Zone dialog box, as seen in Figure 6.16, you
    have the option to create a reverse lookup zone. For optimal DNS per-
    formance, you should always create a reverse lookup zone. Select the
    Yes, create a reverse lookup zone now option. Click **Next** to con-
    tinue.

Figure 6.16 Reverse Lookup Zones Provide a Useful
Resolution Feature

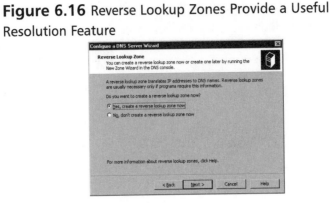

16. In the Zone Type dialog box, select the type of zone to be created—this
     time for the reverse lookup zone. Select the **Primary zone** option. Click
     Next to continue.

17. In the Reverse Lookup Zone Name dialog box, as seen in Figure 6.17,
     supply the name of the reverse lookup zone. In most cases, you would
     select the Network ID option and enter the first three octets of your IP
     subnet. Click **Next** to continue.

Figure 6.17 Creating the Reverse Lookup Zone Name using the First
Three Octets of the IP Subnet

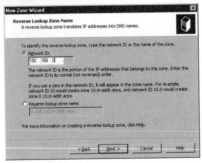

18. In the Zone File dialog box, as seen in Figure 6.18, enter the name for
     the reverse lookup zone. Leave the default value as is. Click **Next** to
     continue.

Figure 6.18 The Reverse Lookup Zone Name is a DNS Standard

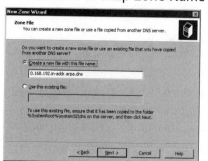

19. In the Dynamic Update dialog box select whether or not you want to use dynamic update. Note that you cannot use only secure dynamic updates unless you have created an Active Directory-integrated zone. Even though not completely secure, we are going to configure this zone for secure and nonsecure dynamic updates by selecting the **Allow both nonsecure and secure dynamic updates** option. Click **Next** to continue.

20. In the Forwarders dialog box, as seen in Figure 6.19, configure forwarders if desired. We will configure forwarding later in this chapter. Select the **No, it should not forward queries** option. Click **Next** to continue.

Figure 6.19 Configuring Forwarders (If Desired)

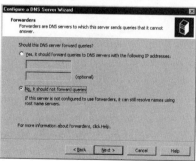

21. The Completing the Configure a DNS Server Wizard dialog box appears showing the results of your configuration. Click **Finish** to close the Configure a DNS Server Wizard.

22. Click **Finish** to close the Configure Your Server Wizard.

With the DNS server installed and basic configuration performed, it is time to configure the remaining DNS server options.

Configuring DNS Server Options

Once DNS is installed and configured, it is pretty much a "set-it and forget-it" service. However, there will be times when a network administrator will want or need to change the configuration options of the DNS server. Options that are configured at the server level apply to the entire server and all zones that it hosts. Open the DNS server properties dialog box, right-click on the DNS server in the DNS management console and select **Properties** from the context menu. The dialog box opens to the Interfaces tab, as seen in Figure 6.20.

The Interfaces Tab

The Interfaces tab, as shown in Figure 6.20, allows the network administrator to configure which network adapters will be used for the DNS service. As can be seen in Figure 6.20, this DNS server has two network adapters installed and both are listening for DNS queries. As many or as few of the properly installed and configure network adapters in the server for DNS can be configured.

Figure 6.20 The DNS Server Interfaces Tab

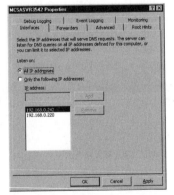

The Forwarders Tab

The default configuration of the Forwarders tab is seen in Figure 6.21. As discussed previously, Windows Server 2003 allows for the configuration of multiple forwarders. Each DNS domain entry can also have multiple forwarders. To create a new forwarder, perform the steps in Exercise 6.02.

Figure 6.21 The DNS Server Forwarders Tab

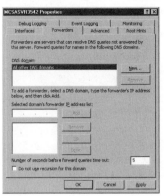

EXERCISE 6.02

CREATING A NEW DNS FORWARDER

1. Open the **DNS Management** console.

2. Open the DNS Server Properties dialog box and switch to the **Forwarders** tab.

3. Click the **New** button to open the New Forwarder dialog box, as seen in Figure 6.22.

Figure 6.22 Adding a New DNS Forwarder

4. Enter the DNS domain name. For example, if you want to configure a forwarder for all name resolution queries against the mcsaworld.com domain, you would enter that. Click **OK** to close the New Forwarder dialog box.

5. Click back to the Forwarders tab, and select the DNS domain you just entered.

6. In the **Selected domain's forwarder IP address list** box, enter the IP address of the DNS server that the resolution query is to be forwarded to and click the **Add** button. The IP address moves to the list as seen in Figure 6.23.

Figure 6.23 The Newly Configured DNS Forwarder

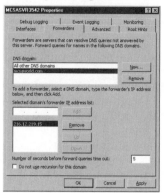

7. Add additional DNS server IP addresses for this forwarder or configure additional forwarders as desired.

8. Do not select the "Do not use recursion for this domain" option as it will disable the ability to forward resolution requests.

Head of the Class...

Putting Forwarding to Work!

A great way to implement a DNS forwarder is to configure all internal DNS servers as forwarders pointing toward another specific DNS server. Thus, this one specific DNS server is the only DNS server that will need to perform name resolution requests outside of the protected internal network—and the only DNS server that will need to initiate outbound DNS connections through the firewall.

By using this arrangement, a network administrator can configure the firewall to only allow outbound DNS traffic (TCP and User Datagram Protocol [UDP] port 53) from the IP address of the specified DNS server. Valid replies back to this DNS server will (in most cases) automatically be allowed back through the firewall in the inbound direction due to the firewall's ability to dynamically control access. When using this type of approach on a network, all other DNS traffic—both inbound and outbound at the firewall—will be automatically and safely dropped. This solution enhances the security of the DNS servers and adds security to the entire network.

The Advanced Tab

The Advanced tab, as seen in Figure 6.24, contains a collection of options that provide advanced configuration utilities.

Figure 6.24 The DNS Server Advanced Tab

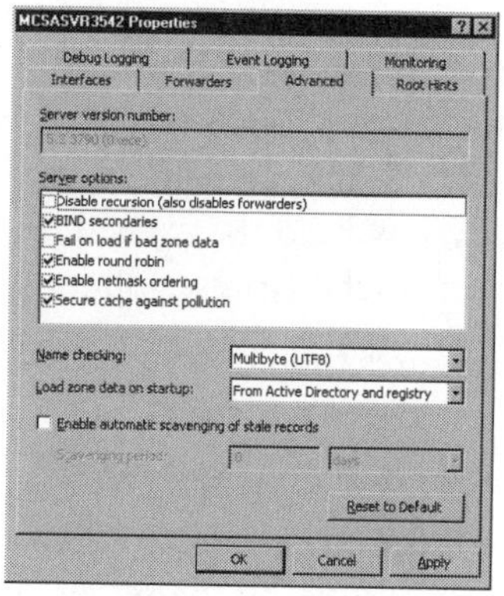

The following options can be configured from this tab:

- **Disable Recursion** Configures the DNS server to not use recursion for any zones hosted on the server. By default, this option is unchecked allowing the DNS server to use recursion.

- **BIND Secondaries** Configures the DNS server to not use fast zone transfer format when performing zone transfers to DNS servers using the BIND DNS service version 4.9.4 or earlier. All Windows-based DNS servers can take advantage of the fast zone transfer format, which uses compression and includes multiple records per TCP packet during a zone transfer. By default, this option is selected, disabling all fast zone transfers. The network administrator should deselect this option if they have only Windows DNS servers or have BIND DNS servers that are version 4.9.4 and later.

- **Fail On Load If Bad Zone Data** Configures the DNS service to fail to load the zone file if it contains records that have been determined to have errors. By default, this option is unchecked allowing the DNS service to log the data errors but otherwise ignore them and continue to load the zone file.

- **Enable Round Robin** Configures the DNS server to use a round robin rotation to rotate and reorder a list of resource records if multiple records are found of the same type during a query. By default, this option is selected, which enables round robin and increases overall network performance.

- **Enable Net Mask Ordering** Configures the DNS server to reorder its host (A) resource records in the response it sends to a resolution query, based on the IP address of the DNS resolver that sent the resolution query. By default, this option is selected, which allows the DNS server to use local subnet priority and increases overall network performance.

■ **Secure Cache Against Pollution** Configures the DNS server to use a secure response option that helps to prevent the adding of unrelated resource records that are included in a referral answer to their cache. The normal behavior of DNS is to cache all names in referral answers to speed up subsequent resolution requests. By using this feature, Windows Server 2003 DNS can determine if referred names are part of the exact related DNS domain name tree for which the original queried name was made. If not, they will not be cached. By default, this option is selected to protect the DNS server's cache against pollution.

■ **Name Checking** Configures the DNS server with one of three possible methods for checking the names it receives and processes during its operations. By default, the Multibyte (UTF8) option is enabled.

■ **Strict RFC (ANSI)** Strictly enforces RFC-compliant naming rules for all DNS names that are processed by the server. Any non-compliant names are treated as errors.

■ **Non-RFC (ANSI)** Allows names that are not RFC-compliant to be used with the DNS server, such as names that use ASCII characters.

■ **Multibyte (UTF8)** Allows names that use the Unicode 8-bit translation encoding scheme to be used with the DNS server.

■ **Load Zone Data on Startup** Configures the DNS server with one of three possible means by which to load the zone data during startup. By default, the **From Active Directory and Registry** option is enabled.

■ **From Registry** Configures the DNS service to load its data by reading parameters stored in the Registry.

■ **From File** Configures the DNS service to load its data from an optional boot file, such as those used by BIND DNS servers.

■ **From Active Directory and Registry** Configures the DNS service to load its data by reading parameters stored in the Active Directory database and the server Registry.

■ **Enable Automatic Scavenging of Stale Records** Specifies the time period at which scavenging is to occur for all zones on the server that are configured for aging and scavenging. In order for scavenging to occur, it must be configured at both the server and zone level. Configuring scavenging at the zone level is discussed in detail in the "Configuring Zone Options" section later in this chapter. Configuring scavenging at the server level is discussed in the "Configuring Aging and Scavenging for All Zones" section later in this chapter. By default, scavenging is disabled. When enabled, the default time period for scavenging actions to occur is every 7 days.

NOTE

In most cases, the default configuration options on the Advanced tab will be left as is. If there are no BIND DNS and all of the DNS servers support fast zone transfers, you will want to uncheck the **BIND Secondaries** option—this will increase the speed of the zone transfers.

The Root Hints Tab

The Root Hints tab, as seen in Figure 6.25, provides a list of the configured root DNS servers. By default, this information is provided during the installation of the DNS server for all 13 root DNS servers and should not be modified except for advanced configurations.

Figure 6.25 The Root Hints Tab

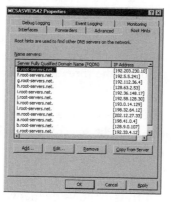

The Debug Logging Tab

The Debug Logging tab, as seen in Figure 6.26, provides advanced logging options that are disabled by default but can be used by a network administrator to troubleshoot and debug the DNS server's operation. The default configuration once Debug Logging has been enabled is also seen in Figure 6.26.

Figure 6.26 The Debug Logging Tab

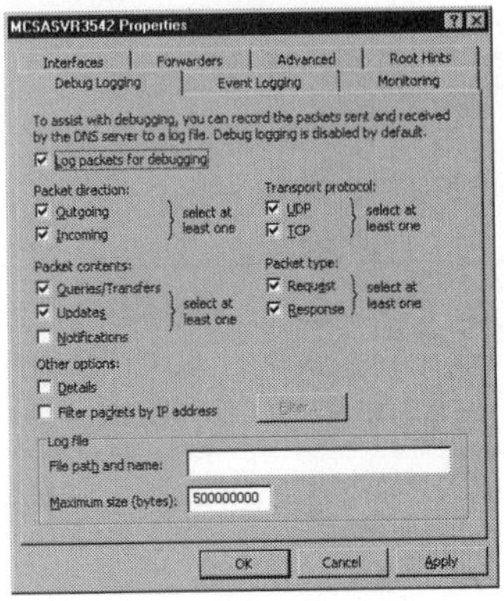

When configuring Debug Logging, the following options are available:

- **Packet Direction** Configures Outgoing (packets that are sent by the DNS server), Incoming (packets are that received by the DNS server), or both to be logged. At least one option must be selected under Packet direction.

- **Transport Protocol** Configures packets sent and received using UDP or TCP or both to be logged. At least one option must be selected under Transport protocol.

- **Packet Contents** Configures Queries/Transfers (packets containing standard RFC 1034 compliant queries), Updates (packets containing RFC 2136 compliant dynamic updates), Notifications (packets containing RFC 1996 compliant notifications), or any combination of the three to be logged. At least one option must be selected under Packet contents.

- **Packet Type** Configures Request packets or Response packets or both to be logged. At least one option must be selected under Packet type.

- **Details** Allows the network administrator to configure to have the entire packet contents logged.

- **Filter Packets by IP Address** Allows the network administrator to configure filtering for logging packets sent to or from a specific IP address to or from the DNS server.

- **File Path and Name** Allows the network administrator to configure the path location and file name of the DNS server debug log file. The default path is %systemroot%\system32\dns.

- **Maximum Size** Allows the network administrator to configure the maximum file size in bytes of the DNS server debug log file. When the maximum file size has been reached, the DNS server will overwrite the oldest information with new information. If this value is left blank, the log file will grow as required, which can quickly consume large amounts of hard drive space.

TEST DAY TIP

Debug Logging can be very resource intensive on a DNS server, possibly affecting the overall server performance and rapidly consuming disk space. Debug logging, therefore, should only be used for short durations of time when specific information is required to troubleshoot the performance of the DNS server. By selectively enabling debug logging options, the network administrator can perform detailed logging of selected events and actions occurring on the DNS server.

The Event Logging Tab

The Event Logging tab, as seen in Figure 6.27, configures what type of logging is to occur in the DNS event log. The default configuration is **All events** and is usually the best option. The level of logging by selecting another option can be reduced for a specific reason, such as only wanting to log errors or errors and warnings. The Event Viewer or the DNS management console can be used to view the DNS log.

Figure 6.27 The Event Logging Tab

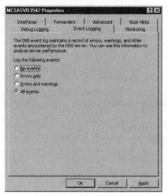

The Monitoring Tab

The Monitoring tab, as seen in Figure 6.28, allows for configuring the DNS server to perform periodic routing testing of its capability to perform simple and recursive DNS queries. By default, no tests are selected. For maximum reliability and performance, both types of tests should be configured to be performed by the DNS server on the desired schedule. The selected tests can also be manually initiated by clicking the **Test Now** button.

Figure 6.28 The Monitoring Tab

 # Configuring Zone Options

There are also configurable options available for both the forward and reverse lookup zones. The individual zones' properties dialog boxes are where critical items are configured, such as how dynamic updates are to occur, aging and scavenging options, and name servers that are allowed to perform zone transfers with the DNS server. As shown in Figure 6.29, the nodes of the DNS Management console need to be expanded in order to locate the forward and reverse lookup zones.

Figure 6.29 Locating the Forward and Reverse Lookup Zones

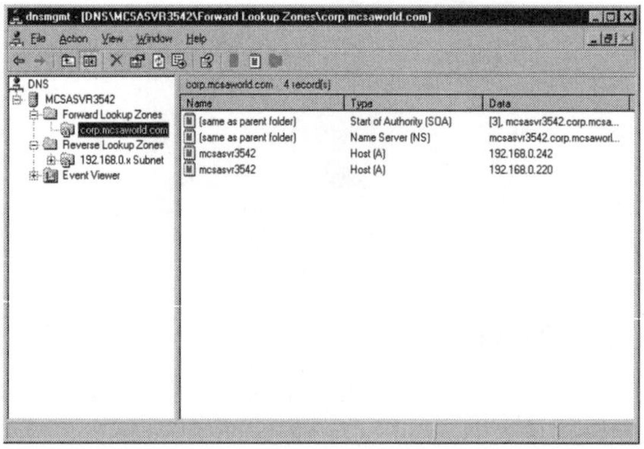

Configuring Forward Lookup Zone Options

After locating the correct forward lookup zone, its Properties dialog box can be opened by right-clicking on the zone and selecting **Properties** from the context menu. The **forward_lookup_zone_name** Properties box opens to the **General** tab, as seen in Figure 6.30.

The General Tab

The General tab, as seen in Figure 6.30, contains an assortment of basic options that a network administrator may wish to configure for their zones.

Figure 6.30 The Forward Lookup Zone General Tab

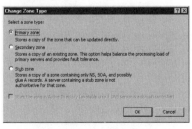

The following actions can be performed from the **General** tab:

- **Change the Zone Status** The zone can be paused or started depending on its current status.

- **Change the Zone Type** The Change Zone Type dialog box opens by clicking the **Change** button, as seen in Figure 6.31. If this zone were created on a domain controller, the network administrator would be able to change it to an Active Directory-integrated zone.

Figure 6.31 Changing the Zone Type

- **Configure Replication Properties** If the zone is Active Directory-integrated, the network administrator can configure how it should be replicated from the following options:

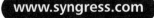

- **All DNS Servers in the Active Directory Forest** Configures the zone data to be replicated to all DNS servers running on domain controllers in the forest.

- **All DNS Servers in the Active Directory Domain** Configures the zone data to be replicated to all DNS servers running on domain controllers in the domain. This is default replication configuration for Active Directory-integrated zones.

- **All Domain Controllers in the Active Directory Domain** Configures the zone data to be replicated to all domain controllers in the domain. This option must be selected if a Windows 2000 DNS server is needed to load an Active Directory-integrated zone.

- **All Domain Controllers in a Specified Application Directory Partition** Configures the zone data to be replicated per the replication scope of the specified application directory partition.

- **Change the Zone File Name** The name of the zone data file can be changed, although normally there is no reason to do so.

- **Configure Dynamic Updates** Dynamic updates can be configured from the following options: None, Non-secure and Secure, and Secure (for Active Directory-integrated zones).

- **Set Zone Aging and Scavenging Options** Clicking the **Aging button** opens the Zone Aging/Scavenging Properties dialog box, as seen in Figure 6.32.

Figure 6.32 Configuring Zone Aging and Scavenging

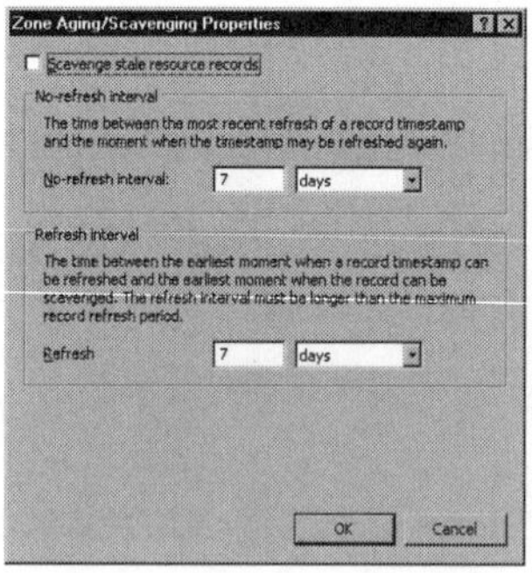

Aging and scavenging are available in Windows Server 2003 DNS to provide a way to remove stale resource records. Although dynamic update accurately and efficiently adds records to the zone file, it does not always do as thorough a job in removing them from the zone when they are no longer accurate—for example, when computers leave the network after an improper disconnection. In today's mobile computing world, this can be a huge problem for networks with large numbers of portable computers and Personal Digital Assistants (PDAs) that acquire DHCP leases and thus cause resource records to be created in the applicable DNS zones. The following problems can result from stale resource records that are left unattended over time:

- Stale resource records build up over time, causing larger zone files and longer zone transfers—both of which can cause reduced DNS server performance.

- Stale resource records might result in incorrect name resolution responses due to incorrect information in the zone file—this may potentially result in the inability to locate network resources.

- Stale resource records may prevent valid dynamic updates from being performed due to the domain names already being used.

Windows Server 2003 DNS implements the following features to alleviate the problems caused by stale resource records:

- **Resource Record Time Stamping** Resource records are time stamped with the date and time on the DNS server when records are dynamically added to the zone data. Resource records that are manually created (discussed in the "Managing DNS Record Settings" section later in this chapter), have their time stamp set to a zero value indicating that they are not subject to aging and scavenging.

- **Resource Record Aging** Resource records that are stored in local primary zones are aged depending on the configuring aging value and time stamp information.

- **Resource Record Scavenging** Resource records that remain in the zone data beyond the configured refresh period are scavenging from the zone data file. As mentioned previously, before scavenging can occur, it must be configured both at the server and the zone level. Also, only resource records that were added dynamically or manually and have a time stamp are subject to scavenging.

When referring to aging and scavenging, the following terms are important:

- **No-refresh Interval** The time interval configured for a zone that begins when the resource record was last refreshed (record refresh) and ends when the record next becomes eligible to have its time stamp refreshed again. This value is set to a default of seven days and should not be set unreasonably high as it will result in aging and scavenging not functioning properly.

- **Refresh Interval** The time interval configured for a zone that begins when the resource record first becomes eligible to have its time stamp reset during a record refresh and ends when the record becomes eligible to be scavenged from the zone data file. This value is set to a default of seven days and should not be set unreasonably high to avoid aging and scavenging from functioning improperly. Setting this value too low may prevent clients from being able to refresh their records.

- **Record Refresh** A dynamic update processed for a resource record that does not change any properties of the record other than the time stamp.

- **Record Update** A dynamic update processed for a resource record that changes other properties in the record in addition to the time stamp.

- **Scavenging Period** This value, configured at the server (using the **Enable automatic scavenging of stale records** option seen in Figure 6.24), specifies the time between scavenging actions for all zones that have scavenging configured. The default value is 7 days with the minimum allowed value being one hour to prevent server performance degradation.

TEST DAY TIP

It is not critical to memorize the definitions of these aging and scavenging terms as much as it important that you understand how aging and scavenging works and how the different time periods (no-refresh interval and refresh interval) affect aging and scavenging.

Scavenging of a record can begin as soon as the configured refresh interval has passed from the time stamp on the resource record. Record refresh cannot occur during the no-refresh interval period of time—any attempts to perform a refresh of a record are not accepted by the DNS server during this time period. Updates may be performed for resource records during the no-refresh interval, however, if the resource record has changed.

For example, if aging and scavenging are configured using the 7-day default value for both the no-refresh and refresh intervals as seen in Figure 6.32, a resource record would not be allowed to be refreshed during the first 7 days after its time stamp updates. However, it would be accepted by the DNS server. Over the next 7 days—days 8 through 14—the resource record is allowed to be both refreshed and updated if these updates are sent to the DNS server. Starting on day 15, this resource record would become eligible for scavenging and would be scavenged from the zone data sometime within the next 7 days (by default) when scavenging occurred again per its configured schedule.

The Start of Authority (SOA) Tab

The Start of Authority (SOA) tab, as seen in Figure 6.33, allows the network administrator to make changes to the SOA record for the zone file. The SOA and Name Server (NS) records are used when a zone file is loaded to determine what name servers are authoritative for the zone.

Figure 6.33 The Forward Lookup Zone SOA Tab

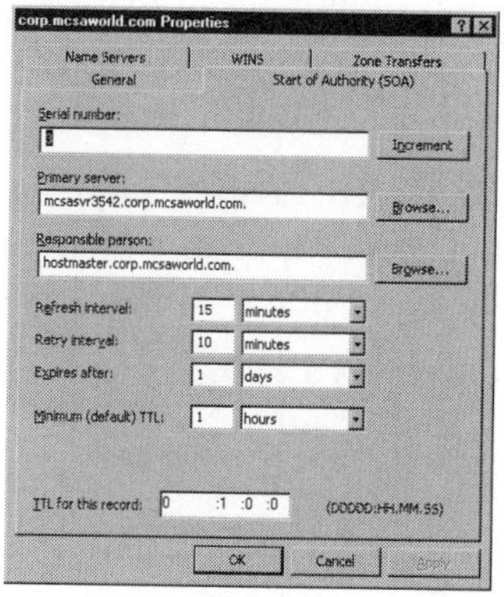

The SOA resource record is always the first record in any standard zone and indicates the server that is authoritative for the zone. The SOA record also contains other properties that provide information about the zone and affect how often zone transfers are conducted. The following fields are present in the SOA record and can be configured using the SOA tab:

- **Serial number** This value denotes the version number of the zone data file. The serial (zone version) number is incremented each time a resource record in that zone is changed, and is used to indicate to secondary servers that a zone transfer is required. The serial number can be manually incremented by clicking the **Increment** button.

- **Primary Server** This value indicates the DNS server that is authoritative for the zone. The primary server for the zone can be changed by clicking the **Browse** button and searching through the A and Canonical name (CNAME) records in the zone.

- **Responsible Person** The e-mail address of the administrator that is responsible for the zone. In DNS, periods "." are used instead of the "@" symbol so the value hostmaster.corp.mcsaworld.com. represents hostmaster@corp.mcsaworld.com.

- **Refresh Interval** Specifies the time interval that a secondary server is to wait before querying the primary server for the zone serial number. This value is configured for 15 minutes by default.

- **Retry Interval** Specifies the time interval that a secondary server is to wait before retrying a failed zone transfer. This value is configured for 10 minutes by default.

- **Expires After** Specifies the time before a secondary server will stop responding to queries after the refresh interval has passed and the zone has not been refreshed or updated. After this time period has passed, the secondary server no longer considers its local data to be reliable. This value is configured for 24 hours by default, which in most cases is a reasonable value. In environments where the DNS zone experiences a large number of changes in a day, the network administrator may consider decreasing this value to prevent secondary zones from using stale data should they be unable to perform a zone transfer.

- **Minimum (Default) Time To Live (TTL)** Specifies the TTL for the zone data and the maximum length of time in which negative caching of answers to name queries is to occur. This value is configured for 60 minutes by default.

- **TTL for this Record** Species a TTL for this specific resource record.

NOTE

Double-clicking the SOA or NS record from within the zone file itself opens the Zone Properties dialog box to the appropriate tab, as seen in Figures 6.33 and 6.34.

EXAM WARNING

TTL values can also be configured manually on any resource record in the zone. Any TTL that has been configured for a specific resource record will override the default TTL configured in the SOA resource record.

The Name Servers Tab

The Name Servers tab, as seen in Figure 6.34, lists all name servers that have been configured to be authoritative for a particular zone. The NS resource record causes the specified DNS server to be considered by other DNS servers and DNS resolvers to be authoritative for the zone, thus allowing it to provide definite answers to any name resolution queries made against that zone.

Figure 6.34 The Forward Lookup Zone Name Servers Tab

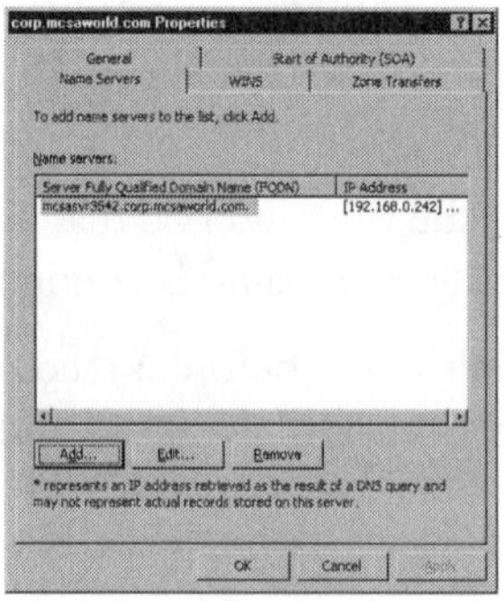

Additional NS records can be created by clicking the **Add** button to open the New Resource Record dialog box, as seen in Figure 6.35. The network administrator must enter the FQDN and at least one IP address of the DNS server that the new NS record is being created for. After providing this information, the administrator clicks **Add** to add the new NS record to the zone. They then click **OK** to close the New Resource Record dialog box when finished adding additional name servers to the domain.

Figure 6.35 Creating a New NS Resource Record

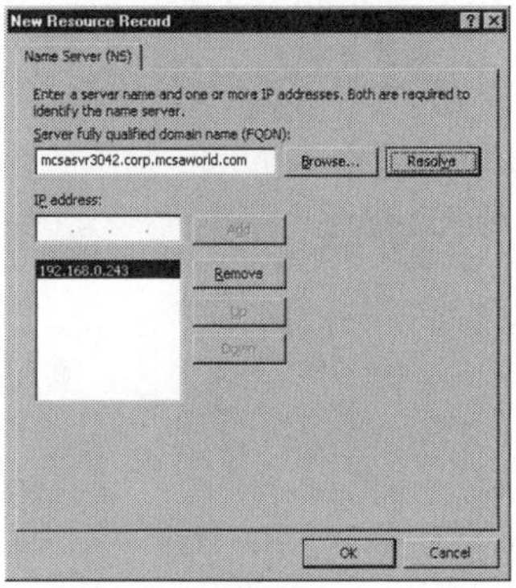

Looking back at the Name Servers tab, as seen in Figure 6.36, there are now two DNS servers that are authoritative for this zone, increasing resolution speed and reliability.

Figure 6.36 The New NS Resource Record is Displayed

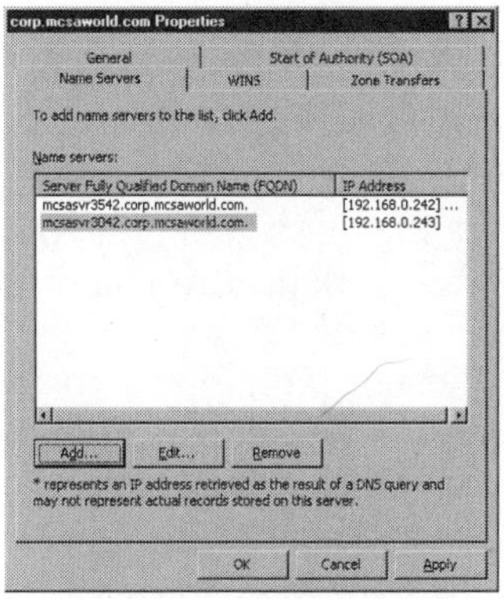

TEST DAY TIP

Although multiple NS records can be configured for a zone, there can only be one SOA record per zone.

The WINS Tab

The WINS tab, as seen in Figure 6.37, allows the network administrator to configure WINS integration with their DNS zones. Although not required in Windows networks that are purely Windows 2000 or later, WINS may be required in networks containing legacy Windows client computers that are using NetBIOS over TCP/IP (NBT) and require WINS for name resolution. If there are one or more WINS servers configured for a network, the network administrator can opt to enable WINS forward lookup for name resolution queries that are not located in the zone file. After enabling WINS forward lookups, they can then enter the IP addresses for their networks WINS servers.

Figure 6.37 The Forward Lookup Zone WINS Tab

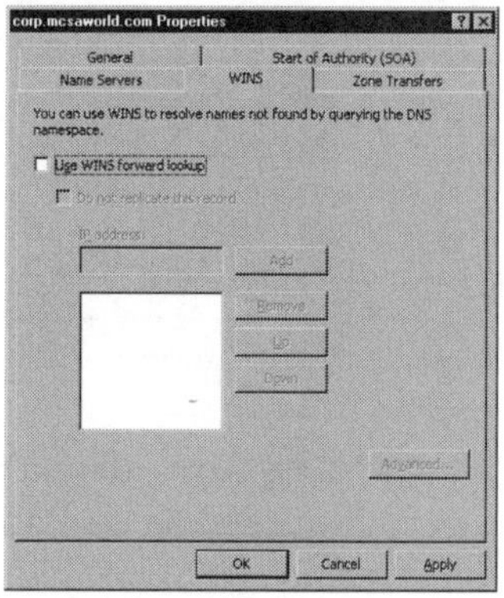

A Tale of Two Resolution Methods

TCP/IP was not always king in Microsoft Windows networks. While UNIX operating systems have used TCP/IP since their inception, Microsoft (and IBM) for a long time used the proprietary NetBEUI network protocol, and for good reason: NetBEUI was a great protocol for the networks of the time. It required no configuration past enabling support for it and did not require any complex addressing schemes like TCP/IP did. The only real downside—and the cause of the downfall of NetBEUI—was the fact that it relied on broadcasts for name resolution that in turn resulted in poor performance in larger networks and an inability to be used in routed environments. The message was clear: Windows had to provide support for DNS if it was to be considered a serious network operating system.

DNS was then added to Windows, but Microsoft discovered a problem: the NetBIOS names that Windows computers had been using did not function properly in a routed TCP/IP environment. NetBEUI relied heavily on broadcast messages to

Continued

advertise servers and network resources to clients. Routers, by default, do not forward broadcast messages, thus preventing NetBEUI from working in a large majority of the emerging corporate networks. (Note that one of the primary reasons for using routers within an internal network is to split up broadcast domains.) Microsoft needed to find a way to solve this problem so that TCP/IP could flourish in Windows networks. At first, the answer was thought to be an LMHOSTS file that would be used by each computer in a similar fashion to how the HOSTS file worked for DNS. In a short time, the difficulty of implementing this type of static solution became apparent to network administrators and Microsoft—a dynamic name resolution system was needed if Windows NetBEUI networks were to make use of TCP/IP. Thus WINS was born.

The Zone Transfers Tab

The Zone Transfers tab, as seen in Figure 6.38, allows the network administrator to configure to what other name servers zone transfers shall be performed. If zone transfers are enabled, the administrator can opt to perform them with any server that requests a zone transfer, with only those servers listed on the Name Servers tab (seen in Figure 6.36), or only to the name servers that they specify on the Zone Transfers tab. The default behavior is to conduct zone transfers only with servers listed on the Name Servers tab. This provides a fairly secure environment. However, for maximum DNS security, the administrator will want to configure zone transfers to occur only with those name servers they have configured on the Zone Transfers tab.

Figure 6.38 The Forward Lookup Zone Zone Transfers Tab

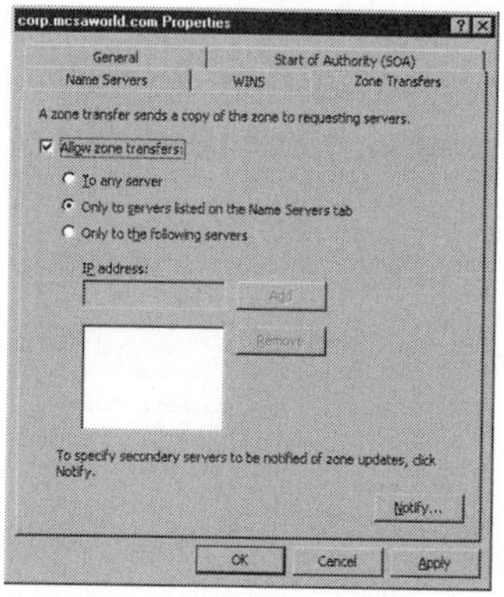

Administrator's also have the option to configure which name servers will be notified when the zone file has changed, by clicking the **Notify** button. The default behavior is to perform notifications only with servers listed on the Name Servers tab that provides an environment that is fairly secure. However, a network administrator can also configure only those servers specified on the Notify dialog box to be notified of changes to the zone file.

Figure 6.39 Configuring Name Servers to be Notified of Zone File Changes

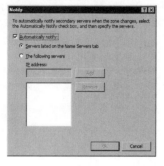

Configuring Reverse Lookup Zone Options

After locating the reverse lookup zone in question, its Properties dialog box can be opened by selecting the zone, right-clicking on it, and selecting **Properties** from the context menu. The **reverse_lookup_zone_name Properties** box opens to the **General** tab, as seen in Figure 6.40.

The General Tab

The General tab, as seen in Figure 6.40, contains an assortment of basic options that the network administrator may wish to configure for their zones. These options are the same as those discussed previously for forward lookup zones.

Figure 6.40 The Reverse Lookup Zone General Tab

NOTE

Allowing non-secure dynamic updates is a significant security risk because updates can be accepted from untrusted resources. Make sure this setting is configured correctly to increase security if needed.

The SOA Tab

The SOA tab, as seen in Figure 6.41, allows the network administrator to make changes to the SOA record for the zone file. The SOA and NS records are used when a zone file is loaded to determine what name servers are authoritative for the zone. These options are the same as those discussed previously for forward lookup zones.

Figure 6.41 The Reverse Lookup Zone SOA Tab

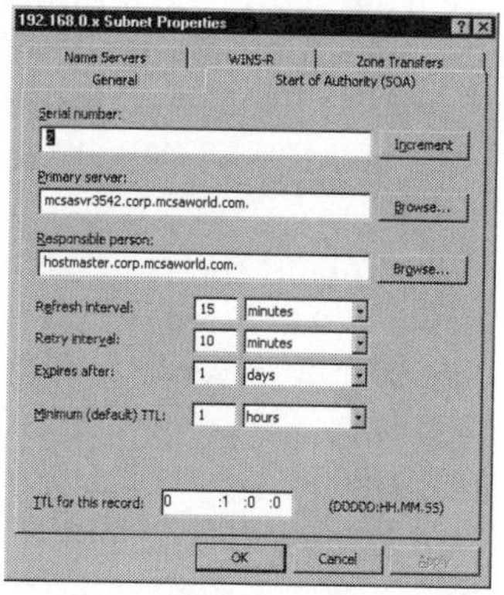

The Name Servers Tab

The SOA tab, as seen in Figure 6.42, allows the network administrator to make changes to the SOA record for the zone file. The SOA and NS records are used when a zone file is loaded to determine what name servers are authoritative for the zone. These options are the same as those discussed previously for forward lookup zones.

Figure 6.42 The Reverse Lookup Zone Name Servers Tab

The WINS-R Tab

The WINS-R tab, as seen in Figure 6.43, allows the network administrator to configure WINS integration with their DNS zones. After enabling WINS reverse lookups, they can also enter the domain name that should be appended to all names that are returned. For example, if the WINS-R query returned MCSAWXP042 and they had entered a domain name of corp.mcsaworld.com, the result that would be returned to the DNS resolver would be MCSAWXP042. corp.mcsaworld.com, just the same as if you had performed an actual reverse lookup using DNS. The WINS-R tab has no space to enter the IP addresses of WINS servers, and will use the same WINS servers that have been configured in the forward lookup zone's WINS tab.

Figure 6.43 The Reverse Lookup Zone WINS-R Tab

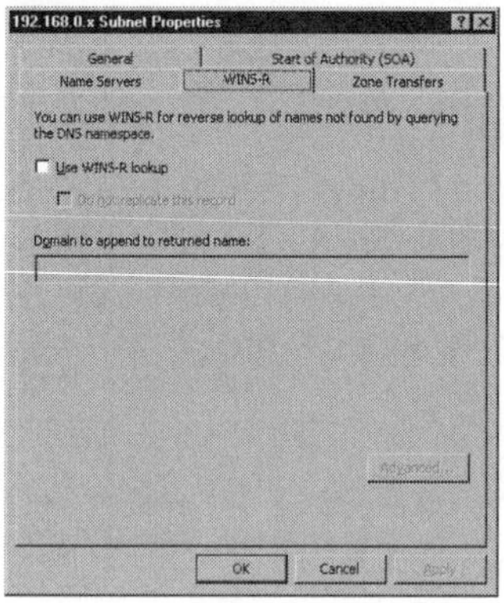

The Zone Transfers Tab

The Zone Transfers tab, as seen in Figure 6.38, allows the network administrator to configure to what other name servers zone transfers shall be performed. These options are the same as those discussed previously for forward lookup zones.

Figure 6.44 The Reverse Lookup Zone Zone Transfers Tab

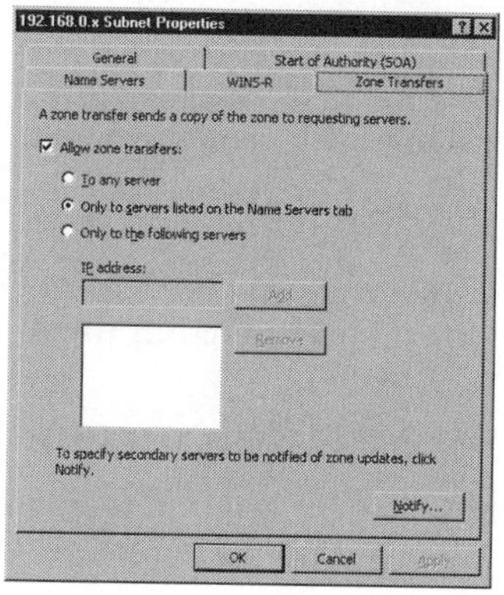

The following sections examine some management and maintenance tasks that a network administrator will routinely perform for zones, records, and servers.

Managing the DNS Service

EXAM 70-292
OBJECTIVE 5.2

The hardest part of administering DNS is installing and configuring it correctly. When it comes to the daily management of the DNS service and the DNS servers, there is not much to do. Some of the more common items might include managing or starting a scavenging cycle; creating, modifying, or deleting resource records; or reloading zones. The next sections examine some of the more common management tasks that a network administrator might find themselves performing for the DNS service.

Managing DNS Server Options

EXAM 70-292
OBJECTIVE 5.2.3

The DNS management console is the primary means by which the network administrator will perform management tasks for their DNS servers. The console is divided into two panes following the standard Microsoft Management Console (MMC) design. The left-hand pane displays servers and zones, while the right-hand pane displays the details and objects for the currently selected item in the left-hand pane. The following management options can be performed at the DNS server level:

- Connecting to remote DNS servers

- Removing servers from the DNS Management console

- Creating new DNS servers

- Creating new zones

- Configuring aging and scavenging for all zones

- Manually initiating record scavenging

- Updating the DNS server zone file

- Clearing the DNS server local cache

- Launching the nslookup command

- Starting, stopping, or pausing DNS servers

The process to create new DNS servers and new zones from the DNS Management console is functionally identical to the process outlined in Exercise 6.01. Each of the remaining management tasks are briefly examined in the following sections.

Connecting to Remote DNS Servers

As can be seen in Figure 6.45, there is only one management option available from the root of the DNS Management console: **Connect to DNS Server**.

Figure 6.45 Connecting to and Managing Multiple DNS Servers from One Location

By selecting this option from the context menu the **Connect to DNS Server** dialog box opens, as seen in Figure 6.46, allowing the network administrator to enter the name of the DNS server that they wish to add to their DNS management console. To do this, the administrator should select the **The following computer** option, enter the DNS server name, select the **Connect to the specified computer now** option, and click **OK** to add the DNS server to their DNS Management console.

Figure 6.46 Adding an Additional DNS Server to the Console

Removing Servers from the DNS Management Console

To remove to a DNS server from the DNS Management console, the network administrator needs only right-click on it and select **Delete** from the context menu, as seen in Figure 6.47. Deleting the DNS server from the console only removes management capability—it does not change the configuration or operation of the DNS server in any way.

Figure 6.47 Removing a DNS Server from the Console

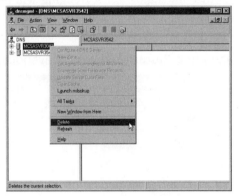

Configuring Aging and Scavenging for All Zones

As discussed previously, aging and scavenging must be enabled at both the server and the zone level for it to function. To configure aging and scavenging for the server, the administrator should right-click on the DNS server in the left-hand pane of the DNS management console and select **Set Aging/Scavenging for All Zones** from the context menu. The Server Aging/Scavenging Properties dialog box opens, as seen in Figure 6.48, allowing the administrator to configure aging and scavenging at the server level. The default values are 7 days for both the no-refresh interval and the refresh interval. The settings configured in this dialog box act as the default settings for all Active Directory-integrated zones. The network administrator will need to manually configure these values on any standard zones they have on their DNS servers. They will also be prompted to accept the changes they have made before they are actually applied to their zones.

Figure 6.48 Configuring Aging and Scavenging at the Server and Zone Levels

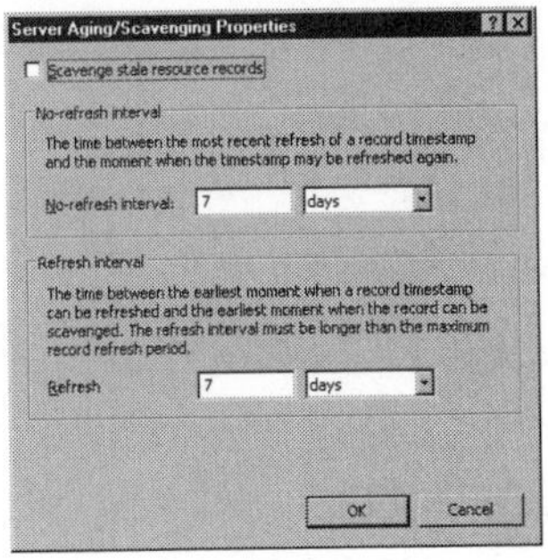

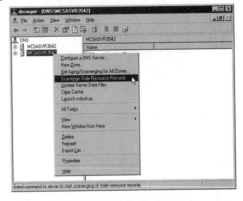

Manually Initiating Record Scavenging

If an administrator does not want to wait for the regularly scheduled scavenging option to occur, they can manually initiate a scavenging sequence by right-clicking on the DNS server and selecting **Scavenge Stale Resource Records** from the context menu, as seen in Figure 6.49. Only records that are eligible for scavenging will be scavenged. After selecting this option, the administrator will be prompted to start the scavenging sequence.

Figure 6.49 Manually Initiating Resource Record Scavenging

Updating the DNS Server Zone File

Typically, standard DNS servers only write the record changes stored in memory when they are shut down or at predefined update intervals. A network administrator can manually force a DNS server to commit all record changes in memory to the zone file by right-clicking the DNS server in the right-pane of the DNS Management console and selecting **Update Server Data Files** from the context menu, as seen previously in Figure 6.49. Active Directory-integrated zones cannot be updated using the DNS Management console and using the following command from the command-line:

```
dnscmd ServerName /ZoneUpdateFromDs ZoneName
```

The full syntax of the *dnscmd* command is beyond the scope of this discussion, and is examined in more detail in Appendix A.

Clearing the DNS Server Local Cache

The DNS server's local resolution cache can be cleared by right-clicking on the DNS server in the left-pane of the DNS management console and selecting **Clear Cache** from the context menu, as seen previously in Figure 6.49. Clearing the cache is useful as a routine maintenance task to get rid of stale data and may help in correcting name resolution difficulties due to stale data.

Launching the *nslookup* Command

The *nslookup* command is used to monitor and troubleshoot the performance of the DNS service. A new feature in Windows Server 2003 DNS provides a quick launch shortcut to start the *nslookup* command from within the DNS management console. Figure 6.50 shows the *nslookup* command being used to perform basic name resolution for an external and internal IP address. The full context and use of the *nslookup* command is discussed in Appendix A.

Figure 6.50 Using *nslookup* for Name Resolution and Troubleshooting

As can be seen, the first name query for www.syngress.com was returned and marked as being a "Non-authoritative answer" indicating that this local DNS server is not authoritative for the zone containing the host www.syngress.com. In the second name query, the local DNS server is authoritative for the information that was queried.

Starting, Stopping, or Pausing DNS Servers

If needed, the network administrator can start, stop, or pause the DNS server by right-clicking on the DNS server in the left-hand pane of the DNS Management console. From there select **All Tasks | Start**, **All Tasks | Stop**, or **All Tasks | Pause** from the context menu, as seen previously in Figure 6.49.

Managing DNS Zone Settings

EXAM 70-292 OBJECTIVE 5.2.1

The forward and reverse lookup zones also have a few management options available. From the context menu as seen in Figure 6.51, the network administrator can opt to update the server zone file for the specific zone, reload the zone from the zone file, create new zones, create new delegations, or create new records. They can also delete zones and refresh the window view. The creation of resource records is discussed in the next section "Managing DNS Record Settings."

Figure 6.51 Management of Zones is Fairly Limited

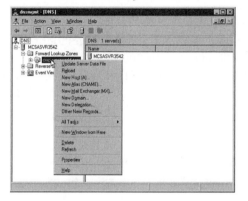

One of the ways that the DNS service provides for increased performance and reliability is through *delegated zones*. By dividing the total namespace that an organization is responsible for into multiple zones, they can be stored and replicated to other DNS servers, thereby increasing DNS availability. Delegating zones also provides an easy way to extend an existing namespace by adding subdomains to accommodate a new location or new requirements. When a delegated zone is created, the network administrator will need to create NS records in the parent zone pointing to the authoritative name servers for the newly created delegated zone. Without these NS records, the name servers in the delegated zone will not be considered authoritative for the zone and name resolution will not occur properly. Before the network administrator can delegate authority for a zone, they must first create the child zone in the parent zone.

Managing DNS Record Settings

A resource record is an entry in the DNS database that contains information that is used to process DNS queries received at the DNS server.

New resource records can be created in the forward or reverse lookup zones by selecting the record type from the context menu. If the record type the administrator wants to create is not listed on the context menus, they can create any of the supported types as listed in Table 6.4 by selecting the **Other New Records** option.

Figure 6.52 shows the dialog box the administrator will see if they select the **New Alias (CNAME)** record.

Figure 6.52 Creating a New CNAME Record

The *ping* command can be used to test the new CNAME record, as seen in Figure 6.53.

Figure 6.53 Testing the New CNAME Record

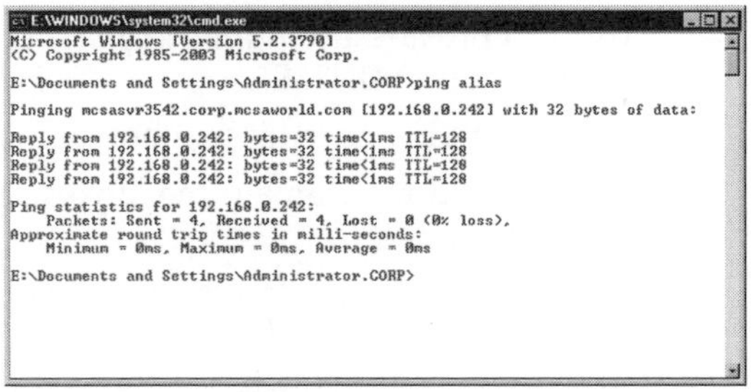

Figure 6.54 shows the dialog box the network administrator will see if they select the **Other New Records** option.

Figure 6.54 Selecting a Resource Record Type

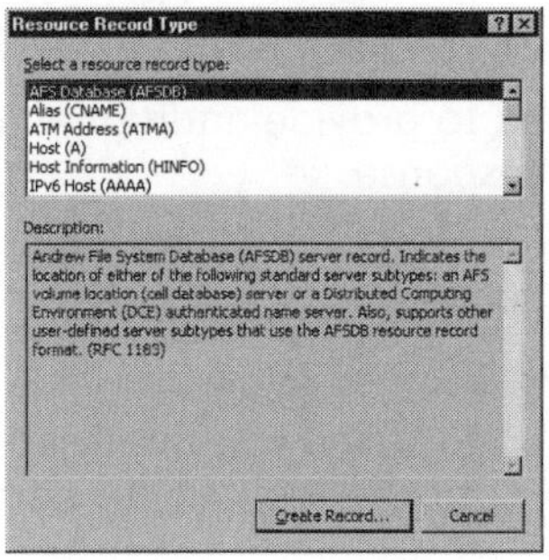

Table 6.4 outlines the resource record types supported by Windows Server 2003 DNS. The more commonly used records are denoted with an asterisk (★).

Table 6.4 Resource Record Types in Windows Server 2003 DNS

Record Type	Description
*A (IPv4 host)	Used to map a DNS domain name to an IP address for IPv4 32-bit IP addresses.
AAAA (IPv6 host)	Used to map a DNS domain name to an IP address for IPv6 128-bit IP addresses.
AFSDB (Andrew File System Database)	Used to map a DNS domain name to the host name for a server computer of a server subtype.
ATMA (Asynchronous Transfer Mode address)	Used to map a DNS domain name to an ATM address.
*CNAME (Canonical name)	Used to map an alias or alternate DNS name to a specified DNS domain name.
HINFO (Host information)	Used to specify the type of CPU and operating system in use on the DNS server.
ISDN (Integrated Services Digital Network)	Used to map a DNS domain name to an ITU-T E.163/E.164 ISDN telephone number.
KEY (Public key)	Used to provide the public key associated with the zone for (DNS Security) DNSSEC.
MB (Mailbox)	Used to map a domain mailbox name to a mailbox host.
MG (Mail group)	Used to add the domain mailboxes specified by the MB resource record to the zone.
MINFO (Mailbox mail list information)	Used to specify the domain mailbox name for the owner of a mailbox or mailing list.
MR (Mailbox renamed)	Used to specify the new name for an existing mailbox.
*MX (Mail exchanger)	Used to provide proper message routing to a mail exchanger host for mail that is sent to the domain name configured in the MX record.
*NS (Name Server)	Used to map a DNS domain name to the name of hosts operating DNS servers in the zone.
NXT (Next)	Used to indicate the nonexistence of a name in a zone.
OPT (Option)	Used to provide additional (optional) data in a DNS request or response.
*PTR (Pointer)	Used to map an IP address to a DNS domain name.
*RP (Responsible Person)	Used to specify the mailbox name of the person responsible for that zone.
RT (Route through)	Used to specify an intermediate host binding for hosts that do not have a direct connection to the external network.

Continued

Table 6.4 Resource Record Types in Windows Server 2003 DNS

Record Type	Description
SIG (Signature)	Used to encrypt a signer's resource record set when DNSSEC is implemented.
*SOA (Start of Authority)	Used to specify the name server that is authoritative for the zone and set forth basic properties relating to the zone.
*SRV (Service locator)	Used to allow servers providing TCP/IP based network services to be located using standard DNS queries. SRV records are extensively used in Active Directory-integrated zones such as for locating domain controllers using the Lightweight Directory Access Protocol (LDAP) service on TCP port 389.
TXT (Text)	Used to provide descriptive text about a resource record.
WKS (Well known service)	Used to specify the well known TCP/IP services that are supported by a particular protocol for a specific IP address.
X25 (X.25)	Used to map a DNS domain name to a Public Switched Data Network (PSDN) address number.

Exam Warning

You should be able to list several of the more common resource record types and their properties.

Summary of Exam Objectives

This chapter covered the DNS service from start to finish. The discussion began with the concept of hierarchical databases. DNS is a large hierarchical database that contains the names and IP addresses for IP networks and hosts. The use of hierarchical databases allows many records to be stored in the database in a very complex arrangement, while still allowing fast and easy retrieval of information stored in that database.

The top of the DNS namespace is referred to as the root, and is denoted by a single period, ".". Under the root are TLDs such as the familiar com and edu. Second-level domains, such as syngress.com and mcsaworld.com, are next in the hierarchy. The FQDN can contain as many child-level domains as desired provided that it does not exceed the maximum number of total characters in length or the allowable number of characters per label.

We next examined some of the planning requirements that a network administrator must fulfill to successfully implement the DNS service for their network. The three primary areas that they must carefully plan for include the namespace, the zone type, and the forwarding requirements. The namespace design will depend on whether the network administrator will be using a namespace for their internal network that is the same as, delegated from, or unique in comparison to the namespace used in their public network. They will need to determine what types of zones—standard or Active Directory-integrated—their implementation requires. In most cases, the network administrator should consider using Active Directory-integrated zones with standard secondary zones in remote and secure locations where having a local or read-only copy of the zone data will improve network performance or security. Finally, configuring forwarders for their DNS implementation should be seriously considered. A new feature in Windows Server 2003 DNS allows the network administrator to configure multiple forwarders depending on the domain name contained in the DNS query sent from the DNS resolver.

Once the network administrator has completed their planning, they are ready to move forward with the installation, configuration, and management of the DNS service. The DNS server service can be easily installed using the Configure Your Server wizard. Administrators can also perform the installation by using the DNS Management console directly. During installation and initial configuration of a new DNS server, the administrator will have the ability to configure the zone type (primary, secondary, or stub), whether or not the zone is to be Active Directory-integrated, the type of lookup zones to configure (forward, reverse, or both), and whether or not to configure the forwarders. They can create a reverse lookup zone after the server has been installed, if desired. They can also configure forwarding at a later time, which is usually more helpful due to the limited configuration allowed during the initial zone creation.

Managing DNS servers is a fairly simple task that can be accomplished from the DNS Management console. A network administrator can connect to remote DNS servers from a local DNS management console, negating the need to travel to each DNS server and locally administer it. Aging and scavenging options must be enabled and configured at both the server and the zone levels—configuration performed on a server hosting an Active

Directory-integrated zone automatically updates the zone configuration. Standard zones need to have their aging and scavenging options configured manually.

Administration of zones typically includes adding or removing additional name servers that are to be considered authoritative for the zone. A network administrator can also manually add resource records to their zones which may be required should they need specially created resource records, such as CNAME records that are not automatically created by dynamic update. They can only configure secure dynamic updates for their zones if they are Active Directory-integrated zones—non-secure dynamic updates are usually best avoided due to the strong potential for rogue clients to pollute the zone data.

Exam Objectives Fast Track

Introducing and Planning the DNS Service

- ☑ DNS is a very large hierarchical database that contains the names and IP addresses for IP networks and hosts.

- ☑ The top of the DNS hierarchy is actually called root, and is symbolized by a single period ".".

- ☑ The DNS system is actually a distributed database that allows the whole database to be broken up into smaller segments while maintaining an overall logical architecture to provide the required name resolution services anywhere on the Internet or a private local network.

- ☑ There are 13 root name servers that sit at the top of the hierarchical chain and perform top-level name resolution for all Internet clients.

- ☑ Because of the extensive integration of DNS and Active Directory in Windows Server 2003, the network administrator must take great care to get their DNS implementation correct the first time around.

- ☑ The network administrator has three choices when creating a DNS namespace: use an existing DNS namespace, use a delegated namespace, or use a unique namespace.

- ☑ Two types of name resolution queries can be performed: recursive and iterative.

- ☑ Windows Server 2003 DNS supports three zone types: Standard, Active Directory-integrated, and stub.

Installing the DNS Service

☑ The DNS service can be installed and configured by using the Configure Your Server Wizard or from within the DNS management console.

☑ Active Directory-integrated zones can only be created on DNS servers that are on domain controllers.

☑ Secure dynamic updates can only be configured for Active Directory-integrated zones.

☑ Forward lookups provide IP addresses for DNS names.

☑ Reverse lookups provide DNS names for IP addresses.

Configuring the DNS Server Options

☑ A new feature to DNS in Windows Server 2003 is conditional forwarding, in which an administrator can configure that DNS resolution requests should be forwarded to specific DNS servers based on the domain that the resolution is being requested for.

☑ Recursion must be enabled for forwarding to work.

☑ Windows Server 2003 DNS provides support for fast zone transfers. If an administrator has BIND DNS servers version 4.9.4 or earlier (or other third-party DNS servers), they can disable fast zone transfers by leaving the **BIND Secondaries** option selected. If all of their DNS servers support fast zone transfers, they should deselect this option.

☑ Windows Server 2003 DNS can protect its cache against pollution by resource records returned in name resolution queries that are not directly related to the original name resolution request domain.

☑ An administrator can use the options on the Debug Logging tab of the DNS server properties dialog box to monitor and troubleshoot a server that is not performing correctly. Debug logging can become resource intensive over time.

Configuring Zone Options

☑ Scavenging of a record can begin as soon as the configured refresh interval has passed from the time stamp on the resource record. Record refresh cannot occur during the no-refresh interval period of time—attempts to perform a refresh of a record are not accepted by the DNS server during this time period. Updates may be performed for resource records during the no-refresh interval, however, if the resource record has changed.

☑ The SOA resource record is always the first record in any standard zone and indicates the server that is authoritative for the zone. The SOA record also contains other properties that provide information about the zone and affect how often zone transfers are conducted.

☑ A network administrator can configure multiple NS records for a zone, however, they can have only one SOA record per zone.

☑ If a network administrator has enabled zone transfers, they can opt to perform them with any server that requests a zone transfer, only those servers listed on the Name Servers tab, or only to the name servers that you specify on the Zone Transfers tab.

☑ The zone serial number denotes the version number of the zone data file. The serial (zone version) number is incremented each time a resource record in that zone is changed, and is used to indicate to secondary servers that a zone transfer is required.

☑ The e-mail address of the administrator that is responsible for the zone (responsible person) uses periods "." instead of the "@" symbol.

☑ The refresh interval is the time interval configured for a zone that begins when the resource record first becomes eligible to have its time stamp reset during a record refresh and ends when the record becomes eligible to be scavenged from the zone data file.

☑ The no-refresh interval is the interval configured for a zone that begins when the resource record was last refreshed (record refresh) and ends when the record next becomes eligible to have its time stamp refreshed again.

Managing the DNS Service

☑ Aging and scavenging must be configured at the server and zone level to work.

☑ During the no-refresh interval, no refreshing is allowed for a resource record; however updates to the resource record are allowed.

☑ During the refresh interval, refreshes and updates are allowed for a resource record.

☑ Resource records become eligible for scavenging after the refresh interval has passed with no refresh or update to the record.

☑ Selecting the BIND secondaries option for a DNS server configures the DNS server to not use fast zone transfer format when performing zone transfers to DNS servers using the BIND DNS service version 4.9.4 or earlier.

☑ Only one SOA record may exist per zone; however, multiple NS records can exist in each zone.

☑ The SOA record contains the default properties for the zone and all records contained in the zone.

☑ A network administrator can configure zone transfers to occur only with specified name servers for increased security.

☑ A network administrator can connect to remote DNS servers from the DNS Management console to manage multiple DNS servers from a single location.

☑ The Windows Server 2003 DNS Management console now includes the ability to launch the *nslookup* command for command-line DNS verification and troubleshooting.

☑ A records are used to map a DNS domain name to an IP address for IPv4 32-bit IP addresses.

☑ CNAME records are used to map an alias or alternate DNS name to a specified DNS domain name.

☑ PTR records are used to map an IP address to a DNS domain name.

☑ SOA records are used to specify the name server that is authoritative for the zone and set forth basic properties relating to the zone.

Exam Objectives
Frequently Asked Questions

The following Frequently Asked Questions, answered by the authors of this book, are designed to both measure your understanding of the Exam Objectives presented in this chapter, and to assist you with real-life implementation of these concepts. You will also gain access to thousands of other FAQs at ITFAQnet.com.

Q: Why do I need to use DNS? Why can't I just assign IP addresses to all of my computers and have users remember them?

A: Aside from the fact that humans do not do well remembering large quantities of numbers, DNS is widely implemented and even required by many applications. Active Directory requires the DNS service to be available on the network. DNS is not perfect, but it is a good solution to the problem of locating network resources by using easy to remember and managable computer names.

Q: I plan on using Active Directory for my network, but I already have an existing BIND DNS server implementation. What do I need to do to ensure that I am ready for Active Directory?

A: To be fully compatible with Active Directory, your BIND servers should be version 8.2.2 or later. Version 4.9.6 provides support for Service Records (SRV), version 8.1.2 provides support for dynamic DNS (DDNS) and version 8.2.1 provides support for IXFR zone transfers.

Q: Why can't I use secure dynamic updates with a standard primary zone?

A: Secure dynamic updates can only be used with Active Directory-integrated zones where the identity of the DNS client can be absolutely confirmed. When Active Directory-integrated zones are used, the overall security and availability of the DNS implementation is increased exponentially.

Q: Why don't Active Directory-integrated zones perform zone transfers amongst the servers hosting them?

A: Active Directory-integrated zones replicate data during normal Active Directory replication events and thus do not need to perform zone transfers amongst the servers hosting them. Zone transfers can be performed to a secondary zone if it is in operation with Active Directory-integrated zones.

Q: Why do I need to use secondary zones if I am implementing an Active Directory-integrated zone solution?

A: Secondary zones can provide a variety of useful functions including increasing name resolution speed at remote locations), providing a read-only copy of the zone file for locations that cannot be kept as secure as desired (such as a DMZ), and decreasing the load on the primary or Active Directory-integrated zones by performing name resolution.

Q: Why don't DNS zones use a push-pull arrangement like WINS servers?

A: In a standard DNS implementation, only one server per zone maintains the master, writeable copy of the zone file—the primary zone server. All other secondary servers have a read-only copy of the zone data and thus will not have any reason to push their zone file to the primary zone server.

Self Test

A Quick Answer Key follows the Self Test questions. For complete questions, answers, and explanations to the Self Test questions in this chapter as well as the other chapters in this book, see the Self Test Appendix.

Introducing and Planning the DNS Service

1. You are the network administrator of the All Hands Life Rafts Company that is using an internal DNS namespace of corp.allhandsliferafts.com. You have a DHCP server located in the west domain of your internal network named DHCPSVR0442. What is the FQDN of this DHCP server?

   A. dhcpsvr0442.corp.allhandsliferafts.com

   B. dhcpsvr0442.west.corp.allhandsliferafts.com

   C. dhcpsvr0442.west.allhandsliferafts.com

   D. dhcpsvr0442.allhandsliferafts.com

2. You are interviewing Hannah for the position of assistant network administrator. You have been making preparations for a new DNS rollout for your new Windows Server 2003 network and asked Hannah what type of zones Windows Server 2003 DNS supports. Which of the following answers are correct? (Choose two answers.)

   A. Standard primary

   B. Forwarder

   C. Resolver

   D. Active Directory-integrated

3. Andrea is planning out a new DNS implementation for her company's network. Her company, Space Race Inc., is a major supplier of space travel-related items to several national governments and private organizations. The corporate network is extremely sensitive and all information contained within the network must be kept as secure as available without sacrificing availability. What type of zones should Andrea create in this new DNS implementation?

    A. Active Directory-integrated

    B. Standard primary

    C. Standard secondary

    D. Stub

4. You are creating a new standard primary forward lookup zone for your network. By default, what is the full path and file name of the zone file if it is being created for the domain sales.corp.mycompany.com?

    A. %systemroot%\dns\dns.sales.corp.mycompany.com

    B. %systemroot%\system32\dns\sales.corp.mycompany.com.dns

    C. %systemroot%\system32\dns\sales.corp.mycompany.com

    D. %systemroot%\system32\sales.corp.mycompany.com.dns

5. You have just completed the installation and initial configuration of a new Windows Server 2003 DNS server. While talking with another administrator in your company, you were told that you need to have a reverse lookup zone configured on the DNS server in order for the nslookup command to function completely. You know that you will most likely need to use nslookup at some time in the future to monitor and/or troubleshoot your DNS server, so you have decided to configure a reverse lookup zone. What does a reverse lookup zone actually do for you?

    A. A reverse lookup zone is used to provide resolution of host names to IP addresses.

    B. A reverse lookup zone maintains a read-only copy of the zone data file.

    C. A reverse lookup zone is used to provide increased security for DNS servers located in a DMZ.

    D. A reverse lookup zone is used to provide resolution of IP addresses from host names.

Installing the DNS Service

6. Robert is creating a new Windows Server 2003 DNS server on a member server that is part of his network's Active Directory domain. Robert is very concerned about the security of dynamic updates that are made to his zone file and wants to prevent rogue clients from being able to make entries via dynamic update. When Robert attempts to configure secure dynamic updates, he can only configure for nonsecure and secure dynamic updates. What has Robert done incorrectly that is preventing him from configuring only secure dynamic updates?

   A. Robert has not installed this DNS server on a domain controller.

   B. Robert has not logged into the network using an account that is a member of the DNS Admins group.

   C. Robert has not changed the domain functional mode to Windows Server 2003.

   D. Robert has not selected to create both a forward and reverse lookup zone during the server creation process.

7. You are network administrator for the ACME Rockets corporate network. You have already successfully installed and configured a core DNS implementation at the corporate headquarters that is using Active Directory-integrated zones for increased security and reliability. Presently, your remote offices and manufacturing plants are performing name resolution over your WAN links, which are almost completely saturated. You have been directed to correct this problem with the least amount of cost to the company and the least amount of administrative effort on your part, while at the same time ensuring that all remote locations can still resolve names at all other locations. What solution should you propose to reduce the traffic being sent over your WAN links due to name resolution?

   A. You should create additional delegated namespaces for each location and then create new Active Directory-integrated zones at each location. You should configure these new DNS servers to perform no zone replication outside of their child domains.

   B. You should create one or more standard secondary DNS servers in each remote location that is allowed to perform zone transfers with one or more of the Active Directory-integrated DNS servers located in the corporate headquarters.

   C. You should create one or more standard primary DNS servers in each remote location that is allowed to perform zone transfers with one or more of the Active Directory-integrated DNS servers located in the corporate headquarters.

   D. You should provision more WAN links to provide more bandwidth for your remote locations.

8. You are configuring a new Windows Server 2003 DNS server for your organization's internal network. This server will be authoritative for your internal namespace, but will not have any information configured in it for any part of the overall namespace outside of your internal network. What function will this DNS server be performing if it is allowed to assist in the resolution of IP addresses for computers that are located outside of your internal network?

   A. Aging

   B. Forwarding

   C. Zone transfer

   D. Scavenging

9. Chris is attempting to create a new primary zone for her network. When she runs the New Zone Wizard and gets to the dialog box allowing her to select what type of zone to create, she is not able to select the **Store the zone in Active Directory** option. What is the most likely reason for this problem?

   A. Chris is not a member of the Enterprise Admins group.

   B. Chris is not performing the procedure on a domain controller.

   C. Chris is not performing the procedure in the correct order.

   D. Chris is not a member of the Server Operators group.

Configuring the DNS Server Options

10. You are configuring your Windows Server 2003 DNS and want to prevent it from caching referral answers that are not directly related to the original name query that was sent. What option do you need to enable to ensure that this protection is configured properly on your DNS server?

    A. Enable round robin

    B. Enable netmask ordering

    C. Secure cache against pollution

    D. BIND secondaries

11. You have just completed the installation and basic configuration of a new Windows Server 2003 DNS server. You want to configure to which other name servers it will perform zone transfers to increase the security of your network and DNS infrastructure. By default, what other DNS servers will this new DNS server perform zone transfers with?

    A. Any DNS server that requests a zone transfer.

    B. Only the DNS servers that are listed on the Zone Transfers tab of the Zone Properties dialog box.

    C. Only the DNS servers that are listed on the Name Servers tab of the Zone Properties dialog box.

    D. Only the DNS servers that are listed on both the Zone Transfer and Name Servers tabs of the Zone Properties dialog box.

Configuring Zone Options

12. You have configured the aging and scavenging properties for your server and zones as follows:

    ■ No-refresh interval: 5 days

    ■ Refresh interval: 3 days

    ■ Enable automatic scavenging of stale records: 6 days

    After how many days from its time stamp date will a resource record be eligible to be scavenged from the zone data file if it does not receive a refresh or update?

    A. 3 days

    B. 5 days

    C. 8 days

    D. 11 days

13. Chris is the network administrator for Little Bots, Inc. She has recently completed the configuration of a new Windows Server 2003 DNS server using a standard primary forward lookup zone. After doing some additional reading, she has determined that it would be better to have this zone as an Active Directory- integrated zone using secure dynamic updates. Where will Chris need to make this configuration change from?

    A. From the Zone Transfers tab of the forward lookup zone Properties dialog box.

    B. From the General tab of the forward lookup zone Properties dialog box.

    C. From the Advanced tab of the DNS server Properties dialog box.

    D. From the root of the DNS Management console.

Managing the DNS Service

14. Jon wants to configure aging and scavenging for all of the zones located on his single DNS server. His zones are all Active Directory-integrated. Where can Jon go to configure the aging and scavenging values for his server and use the least amount of administrative effort?

    A. Jon will need to make his configuration on each zone hosted on the DNS server individually.

    B. Jon will need to make his configuration only once for any one forward lookup zone and only once for any one reverse lookup zone—the values will then become the default for the rest of the zones on the server.

    C. Jon will need to make his configuration during the initial installation of the DNS server and cannot change the values now.

    D. Jon will need to make his configuration from the DNS server's context menu, which will then become the default for all zones on the server.

15. You need to create a new resource record in your DNS zone file that will allow you to perform resolution of a host name given an IP address as input. Which of the following types of resource records do you need to create to allow this type of resolution to occur?

    A. PTR

    B. A

    C. CNAME

    D. SRV

16. You are attempting to verify basic network connectivity for one of your internal network servers. When you enter the *ping corp* command you get the following results:

    ```
    Pinging w3svr44543.internal.bigcorp.com [192.168.1.233]
    with 32 bytes of data:
    ```

    Why did the ping command not return the FQDN of corp.internal.bigcorp.com for the server?

    A. The A record for this server is configured incorrectly.

    B. The PTR record for this server is configured incorrectly.

    C. A CNAME record exists for this server.

    D. A NS record exists for this server.

Self Test Quick Answer Key

For complete questions, answers, and explanations to the Self Test questions in this chapter as well as the other chapters in this book, see the Self Test Appendix.

1.	**B**	9.	**B**
2.	**A, D**	10.	**C**
3.	**A**	11.	**C**
4.	**B**	12.	**C**
5.	**A**	13.	**B**
6.	**A**	14.	**D**
7.	**B**	15.	**A**
8.	**B**	16.	**C**

Chapter 7

MCSA/MCSE 70-292

Implementing, Managing, and Maintaining Network Security

Exam Objectives in this Chapter:

6.1   Implement secure network administration procedures

6.1.1   Implement security baseline settings and audit security settings by using security templates

6.1.2   Implement the principle of least privilege

☑   Summary of Exam Objectives

☑   Exam Objectives Fast Track

☑   Exam Objectives Frequently Asked Questions

☑   Self Test

☑   Self Test Quick Answer Key

Introduction

Network security is a popular topic. It seems that everywhere you look there is something in the news about a new exploit or vulnerability that has been exposed. Unfortunately, network security is not a quick, easy fix. To truly have a secure network, security must be implemented at several different layers. This is known as *defense-in-depth*. But where should a network administrator start when working towards increasing the security level of a network? One approach is to initially focus on the center of the network—the servers and client workstations—and then work outward towards the public Internet connection. Alternatively, you can start with the public connection—the routers, switches, and firewalls—and work towards the center of the network. The direction in which a network security plan is implemented depends on an organization's needs and requirements. However, in most cases, the network administrator will want to secure the Internet connection first and then focus on ensuring that the internal network is secure and, more importantly, stays secure.

A good security plan is one that realizes that network security is a daily, ongoing event that requires the administrator to not only implement an initial solution but also to monitor it and manage it over time to ensure that new threats and required changes are taken into account.

First and foremost, a network administrator should use the *principle of least privilege* for their user accounts. Next, they should configure and implement a solid security solution using security templates. After the security templates have been applied, the administrator should implement a well thought out auditing policy in order to track what users are doing on the network from a security standpoint.

EXAM 70-292

OBJECTIVE 6.1.2

Using the Principle of Least Privilege

The principle of least privilege is nothing more than a guideline for assigning user permissions to a network's users. There are no definitive guidelines to adhere to—each situation is different, each network is different. The basic premise of the principle of least privilege is that the network administrator should only give users the minimum privileges required to effectively and efficiently perform their specific jobs. Using the principle of least privilege, a compromised user account will have less impact on the overall security of a network, than if the network administrator were in the habit of assigning permissions to users that they did not explicitly require. For example, a user whose primary function is to manage a network's disaster recovery plan would typically only require Backup Operator privileges. Assigning this user Administrative permissions would open a security hole in the network's security plan. Should a user require additional privileges other than the privileges that their standard user account provides, they can have the administrator perform the task for them using their user account and the "Run As" command. Alternately, the user might have their own higher-level account that they can use with the Run As command or that can be used to log on to the network. Ideally, all normal user operations will be carried out in the context of a User account, not an Administrator account.

While it may seem that implementing the principle of least privilege is time consuming for the administrator, the opposite is true. By carefully planning and assigning groups the required privileges for each network function, the network administrator can quickly and accurately ensure that users have the privileges they require and nothing more. Users can be added to multiple groups where their privileges will be the cumulative total of the privileges applied to the groups they are members of. In all cases, the network administrator should avoid explicitly assigning permissions and user rights directly to users. By following the principle of least of privilege, the administrator will be able to make their network more secure.

EXAM WARNING

The principle of least privilege will be tested on the exam. As an administrator, you should know that you should only grant the permissions that are needed and nothing more. This means that you have to understand the following parts of access control: NT File System (NTFS) permissions, group assignments (default), and default permissions assigned to a user. Refer back to Chapter 1 for a refresher on using groups to assign permissions and user rights.

EXAM
70-292
OBJECTIVE
6.1
6.1.1

Implementing Security with Security Templates

In 2002, Microsoft stopped all new coding work on all products in order to find and correct security flaws in existing products. As a result of the Trustworthy Computing campaign, which also required all of Microsoft's programmers to take classes on writing secure code, Windows Server 2003 in its default installation is significantly more secure than any of its predecessors. This added security, however, does not relieve the network administrator of their administrative responsibilities to evaluate, implement, and monitor additional (customized) security configurations for their Windows Server 2003 computers and client workstations. The administrator also needs to understand how Windows XP, Windows 2000, and other legacy Windows clients interact with and affect the security of their Windows Server 2003 computers.

Microsoft provides a complete set of preconfigured security templates in Windows Server 2003 that the network administrator can use to quickly apply standardized security settings. Security templates can be used to apply a security configuration to a single computer, an organizational unit (OU), or a domain. While implementing the principle of least privilege is a policy-based action, using security templates is a hands-on activity requiring the attention and dedication of a very knowledgeable (and patient) network administrator. The following sections examine the preconfigured security templates that are provided with Windows Server 2003 as well as how they are used, customized, and implemented to increase security on a network.

Introduction to Security Templates

Although Windows Server 2003 is more secure than any previous version, network administrators are in no way relieved of the requirement to implement a security solution that is specific to the needs of and the threats faced by their network. Using security templates, the administrator can customize the security settings of their servers and workstations to meet these requirements. The preconfigured security templates provided with Windows Server 2003 can be thought of in one of two ways: they can either provide a great starting point for a customized security template solution, or they can be the final solution in and of themselves. Neither train of thought is more correct than the other—the choice made depends on the requirements of the network.

Security templates are nothing more than specially formatted text files that are coded to be read by the Security Configuration Manager tools. Security templates have the file extension *.INF and can be edited manually, if desired, in any standard text editing application. The preconfigured security templates can be found in the **%systemroot%\security\templates** folder on the Windows Server 2003 computer.

The Security Configuration Manager tools, discussed in more detail later in this section, consist of the following four items:

- The Security Configuration and Analysis snap-in
- The Security Templates snap-in
- Group Policy security extensions
- The secedit.exe command

Security templates can be broken down into two general categories: default and incremental. The default (or basic) templates are applied by the operating system when a clean install has been performed. They are not applied if an upgrade installation has been done. The incremental templates should be applied after the default security templates have been applied as they add additional security configuration settings to the existing configuration.

If a template ends in *ws*, it is for a standalone computer or member server (not a domain controller). If a template ends in *dc*, it is for a domain controller. Table 7.1 describes the function of these provided templates.

Administrators can save time and effort during an initial rollout by applying these templates to workstations, domain controllers, and member servers. Then, as time allows, they can customize and fine-tune security settings for local computers, OUs, or an entire domain.

Table 7.1 Windows Server 2003 Security Templates

Template (Filename)	Description
Default (Setup security.inf)	The Default security template is created during the installation of Windows Server 2003; thus it will vary from one computer to the next, depending on whether the installation was performed as a clean

Continued

Table 7.1 Windows Server 2003 Security Templates

Template (Filename)	Description
	installation or an upgrade. This security template represents the default security settings for the computer, and therefore can be used to reset the security settings for the entire computer or portions of the computer to the initial settings required. This template is created for member servers and workstations, but not for domain controllers. The default security template should never be applied to any computer other than the one it was created on. Additionally, this security template should never be applied via Group Policy due to the large amount of data it contains—it can result in performance degradation.
Default DC (DC security.inf)	The Default DC template is created when a member server is promoted to a domain controller and represents the default file, Registry, and system service security settings for that DC at that time. This security template can be used much like the Default security template to reset all or a portion of the specific domain controller's security settings at a later time if required.
Compatible (compatws.inf)	The Compatible security template provides a way for members of a Users group to run those applications that may be in use on the network that are not Windows logo compliant. Applications that are not Windows logo compliant often require users to have elevated privileges commonly associated with the Power Users group. By applying the Compatible security template, the network administrator can change the default file and registry permissions that are granted to the Users group, thus allowing them to run these non-compliant applications.
	Once the Compatible security template has been applied, all users will be removed from the Power Users group as they will no longer require this level of privilege to run the non-compliant applications. The Compatible template should never be applied to a domain controller, so the administrator must take care not to import it at the domain or domain controller level.
Secure (securews.inf, securedc.inf)	The Secure security templates start to actually secure the computers to which they have been applied. Two different Secure security templates

Continued

Table 7.1 Windows Server 2003 Security Templates

Template (Filename)	Description
	exist: securews.inf, which is for workstations and member servers, and securedc.inf, which is for domain controllers only.
	Secure security templates prevent the LAN Manager (LM) from being used on the network for authentication, thus preventing Windows 9x clients from being able to authenticate unless they have the Active Directory Client Extensions installed to enable NT LAN Manager (NTLMv2). The Secure security templates also implement Server Message Block (SMB) packet signing for servers. SMB packet signing is enabled by default for clients.
Highly Secure (hisecws.inf, hisecdc.inf)	The Highly Secure security templates continue to impose additional security restrictions on the computers that they have been applied to. The Highly Secure security templates allow only NTLMv2 authentication. Additionally, SMB packet signing is required when using the Highly Secure security templates.
	After applying the Highly Secure security templates, all members of the Power Users group are removed from this group. Additionally, only members of the Domain Admins group and the local administrative account are allowed to be members of the local Administrators group, further increasing security of the network by limiting who can have administrtive permissions on a computer.
	When the Highly Secure security templates are used, there are no provisions in place for applications that are not Windows logo compliant. Users will only be able to use logo compliant applications. Administrators will be able to use any application they desire.
System Root (rootsec.inf)	The System Root security template is used to define the permissions for the root of the system volume. Should these permissions have been changed, the network administrator can reapply them using this template. Should the administrator need to apply permissions, they can modify this template and use it to apply the same permissions to other volumes. Any existing explicitly configured permissions will not be overwritten on child objects when this security template is applied.

Continued

Table 7.1 Windows Server 2003 Security Templates

Template (Filename)	Description
No Terminal Server Use SID (notssid.inf)	The No Terminal Server Use SID security template is used to remove all unnecessary Terminal Services SIDs from the file system and Registry. This does not affect the security of the Terminal Server server in any way.

EXAM WARNING

You must have a solid grasp on the purpose and role of each security template that ships with Windows Server 2003. Key points to keep in mind when working with security templates are which ones are default, which ones are incremental, and the basic purpose of each, including the type of computer that it is to be deployed on. Know those security templates!

The Security Configuration Manager Tools

This section examines the Security Configuration Manager tools that the network administrator uses to design, test, and implement a security template solution. As mentioned previously, the Security Configuration Manager is actually comprised of four different tools that are used in various ways to achieve a complete solution. Two user interfaces are available to configure system security settings: the graphical interface and the secedit.exe command-line interface. You will do most of your work from the graphical interface and thus will you need to create a customized security management console. These tools *do not* already come in a preconfigured management console ready for usage. Exercise 7.01 presents the process by which you can make your customized security management console—a requirement to progress through the rest of this section.

EXERCISE 7.01

CREATING THE SECURITY CONSOLE

1. Choose **Start | Run**, enter **mmc** into the text box, and click **OK**. An empty MMC shell opens as seen in Figure 7.1

Figure 7.1 The Empty MMC Awaiting Customization

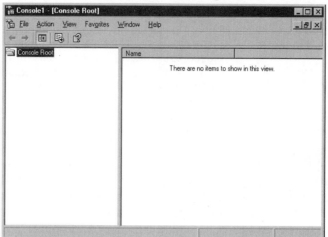

2. From the MMC menu, click **File | Add/Remove snap-in,** and then click the **Add** button.

3. Select and add the following snap-ins as seen in Figure 7.2:

   ■ Security Configuration and Analysis

   ■ Security Templates
   Note that you will need to add these snap-ins one at a time by selecting the first one and clicking the **Add** button. Next select the second snap-in and click the **Add** button again.

Figure 7.2 Selecting the Security Management Tools

4. Click **Close** in the Add Standalone Snap-in window.

5. Click **OK** in the Add/Remove Snap-in window.

6. Save your MMC by clicking **File | Save As**.

7. In the filename box, type **Security Management Console** or any other name you want. This will automatically save your MMC into the Administrative Tools folder of the currently logged in user. Your custom Security Management Console should look similar to the screen shown in Figure 7.3.

Figure 7.3 The Customized Console is Ready to Use

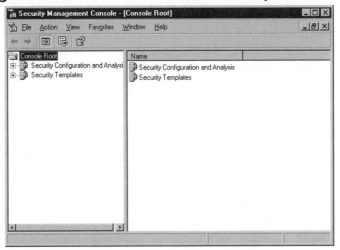

The Security Configuration and Analysis Snap-in

The Security Configuration and Analysis console snap-in can be used on a local computer to compare its current security configuration settings to those as defined by a template. The template being used for the analysis can either be one of the preconfigured templates supplied with Windows Server 2003 or a custom created template.

TEST DAY TIP

The key to working with the Security Configuration and Analysis snap-in is to never forget that it is used only on the *local* computer—never on a domain or OU scale. This limitation hampers its utility, but does not prevent developing and deploying robust security templates to an organization on a large scale. Importing templates into a domain or OU are discussed later in this chapter.

The Security Configuration and Analysis snap-in is used in one of two modes (as the name suggests): analysis or configuration.

When used in analysis mode, no changes are made to the existing security configuration of the computer. The administrator simply selects a security template to be used to compare the current computer security configuration against. The settings contained in this template are loaded into a temporary database and then compared to the settings in place on the computer. If desired, multiple templates can be loaded into the database, merging their settings and providing a conglomerate database. Additionally, the administrator can opt to clear the database settings before importing a security template to ensure that only the current security template is being used for the analysis. Once the database has been populated with the desired security template settings, the network administrator can perform any number of analysis routines using either the Security Configuration and Analysis snap-in or the secedit.exe command, which are discussed in more detail later.

When used in configuration mode, the current contents of the database are immediately applied to the local computer. It is always advisable to perform an analysis before performing a configuration operation using Security Configuration and Analysis snap-in, as there is no "undo" feature and thus no easy way to back out of changes just made without some preplanning having occurred.

After performing an analysis in Exercise 7.02, you will be presented with various icons identifying the result of the analysis as detailed in Table 7.2.

Table 7.2 The Windows Server 2003 Security Templates

Icon	Description
Red X	Indicates that this item was defined in both the database and on the computer, but that the settings do not match.
Green check mark	Indicates that this item was defined in both the database and on the computer and that the settings match.
Question mark	Indicates that this was not defined in the database and therefore was not examined on the computer.
Exclamation point	Indicates that this item was defined in the database but not on the computer and therefore was not examined.

Continued

Table 7.2 The Windows Server 2003 Security Templates

Icon	Description
No special icon	Indicates that this item was not defined in the analysis database or the computer and therefore was not examined.

It is difficult to completely comprehend the Security Configuration and Analysis snap-in, until you have used it at least once to perform an analysis and configuration of a computer. Exercise 7.02 discusses the process to perform an analysis of a Windows Server 2003 member server using the securews.inf template. Before doing that, however, it is important to discuss the database in more detail as well as the different areas that can be analyzed and configured using the Security Configuration and Analysis snap-in.

The database is central in the security analysis process. The administrator can initiate a security analysis after configuring the entries in the database to meet the organization's needs. The security analysis compares the settings in the database with the actual settings implemented on the local computer. Individual security settings are flagged by an icon that changes depending on whether the actual security settings are the same or different from those included in the database. The administrator will also be informed if there are settings that have not been configured at all and thus might require attention.

Prior to the security analysis, the administrator will configure the preferred security settings in the database by importing one or more desired security templates. After the database is populated with an ideal security scenario, it is tested against the current machine settings. As mentioned previously, once the database has been populated with the desired settings, it can be used multiple times to perform the same analysis or configuration action.

⚠ EXAM WARNING

Knowing and understanding the configurable areas and what role they play in the overall security process is important for this exam. Don't worry so much about memorizing each configurable item in these areas (we will discuss these items later in this chapter). You should just be aware that these different areas exist and what they are used for.

The following areas can be configured and analyzed using the Security Configuration and Analysis snap-in:

- **Account Policies** The Account Policies node includes those configuration variables that the network administrator formerly manipulated in the User Manager for Domains applet in Windows NT 4.0. The two subnodes of the Account Policies node include the Password Policy node and the Account Lockout Policy node. In the Password Policy node, the administrator can set the minimum and maximum password ages and password lengths. The Account Lockout Policy allows them to set lockout durations and reset options.

- **Local Policies** Local policies apply to the local machine. Subnodes of the Local Polices node include Audit Policy, Users Right Policy, and Security Options. Audit and User Rights policies look familiar to users of Windows NT 4.0. The Security Options node offers the administrator many options that formerly were available only by manipulating the Windows NT 4.0 Registry or through the Policy Editor (poledit). Examples include the ability to set the message text and message title during logon, restricting the use of floppy disks, and the Do not display last username at logon option.

- **Event Log** The Event Log node allows the administrator to configure security settings for the Event Log. These include maximum log sizes, configuring guest access to the Event Log, and whether or not the computer should shut down when the Security Log is full.

- **Restricted Groups** You can centrally control the members of groups. At times, an administrator will add someone temporarily to a group, such as the Backup Operators group, and then neglect to remove that user when they no longer need to be a member of that group. These lapses represent a potential hole in network security. The network administrator can configure a group membership list in the Restricted Groups node and then configure an approved list of members by reapplying the security template they created.

- **System Services** The network administrator can define the security parameters of all system services in the database via the System Services node. They can define whether a service startup should be automatic, manual, or disabled. The can also configure which user accounts have access to each service.

- **Registry** The Registry node allows you to set access restrictions on individual Registry keys. Note that you cannot create or otherwise edit the Registry from here—these actions will require the use of the Registry Editor.

- **File System** The File System node allows the network administrator to set folder and file permissions. This is a great aid to the administrator who might have been experimenting with access permissions on a large number of files or folders and then later cannot recall the original settings. They can apply a security template to restore all file and folder permissions to their original settings.

NOTE

The formulation of a well-planned security policy is a time-consuming process. To add a measure of fault tolerance, the database entries can be exported to a text file, which can be saved for later use on the same machine or applied to another machine, domain, or OU. The exported template is saved as an *.INF* file and can be imported to other computers, domains, and OUs. In this way, the security parameters can be reproduced exactly from one machine to another.

EXERCISE 7.02

ANALYZING SECURITY USING SECURITY CONFIGURATION AND ANALYIS

1. Open your custom security management console that was created in Exercise 7.01.

2. Right-click **Security Configuration and Analysis,** and select **Open Database.** The Open database dialog box, seen in Figure 7.4, opens.

Figure 7.4 The Open Database Dialog Box

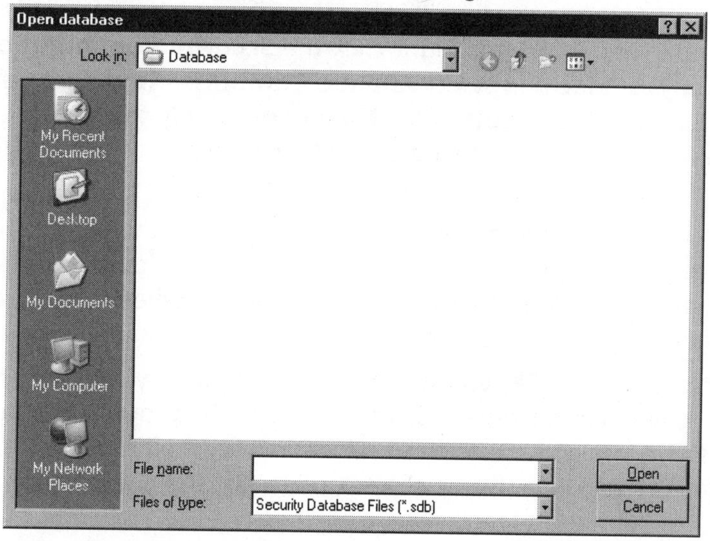

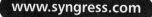

3. If there is already an existing database, you can open that one. If no databases are currently defined, you can create a new one by entering the name of the database in the filename box. Click **Open** to continue.

4. The Import Template dialog box appears, as seen in Figure 7.5. To populate the database with the security configuration entries you will need to select the security template that represents the level of security you are interested in. For this example, select the **securews.inf** template and click **Open** to continue.

Figure 7.5 The Import Template Dialog Box

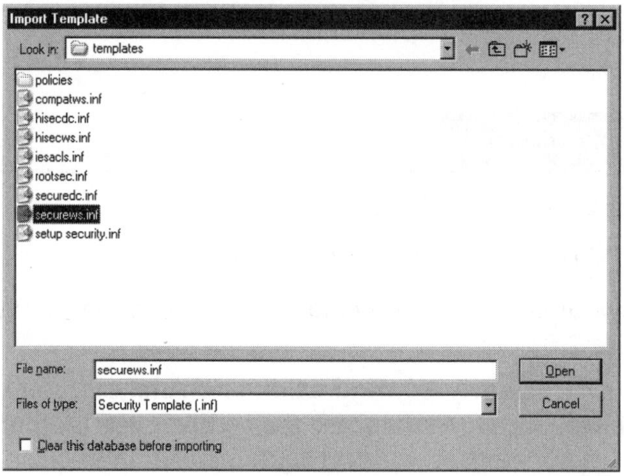

5. In the right pane, you will see instructions on how to analyze or configure your computer. Right-click the **Security Configuration and Analysis** node and select **Analyze Computer Now**. Be careful; if you select **Configure Computer Now**, it will apply the settings that you have imported into the database to the active security configuration of the computer.

6. You will next be prompted to give a location in which to store the log files. Use the Browse button to set the correct location. The default name for the log file is *database_name.log* (where *database_name* is the name of your database). Click **OK** to continue.

7. After you click **OK**, you will see the Analyzing System Security dialog box, as seen in Figure 7.6, which details the progress of the current security analysis. Once this process has finished running, you can see the differences between the template file and your local system.

Figure 7.6 Analyzing the System Security

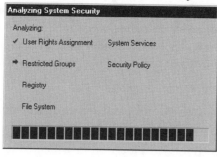

NOTE

Not all computers are created equal, thus it is perfectly normal (and expected) that some computers will have different initial security settings than are presented here. Your results may vary depending on the initial state of the computer being used for the analysis.

After the analysis is performed, the time consuming and critically important next step of inspecting the differences comes into play. The network administrator will need to look through each node of the analysis results and determine if the results agree with their desired settings for the computer. If the results are not agreeable, they can change the database setting by double-clicking on the configuration item to open its Properties dialog box, as seen in Figure 7.7. The change will then be implemented into the database for further analysis and configuration usage. The Configure option must be used to actually make the change to the computer itself.

Figure 7.7 Changing Settings from Within the Database

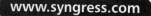

Once all of the database settings agree with how the administrator wants the computer to be configured, they can be applied by selecting **Configure Computer Now**. Additionally, the template can be exported for easy application to other computers in the same role (discussed later in this chapter). The steps needed to configure the computer with the settings contained in the database are as follows:

1. If not done already, complete Exercise 7.02.

2. Right-click the **Security Configuration and Analysis** node and select **Configure Computer Now**.

3. You will be prompted to give a location in which to store the log files. Use the Browse button to set the correct location. The default name for the log file is *database_name.log* (where *database_name* is the name of your database). Click **OK** to continue.

4. After the configuration is complete, you will need to perform another analysis to verify that the settings have been applied.

Configuring & Implementing…

Safety First!!

The Security Configuration and Analysis snap-in, the Security templates, the secedit.exe command-line tool, and the security extensions to the Group Policy Editor are powerful and efficient tools that allow you to manage and control your organization's security infrastructure. However, as with all the security configuration tools and capabilities of Windows Server 2003, you should use appropriate caution before employing these tools in a live environment. Before deployment, be sure to test your security configurations in a lab environment that resembles your live environment as closely as possible.

The secedit.exe command-line tool will allow you to schedule regular security audits of local policies on the machines in any domain and OU. By running scripts that call on the secedit.exe program, you can update each computer's personal database with the results of your security analysis. You can then later use the Security Configuration and Analysis snap-in to analyze the results of your automated analysis. Always watch for the effective policy, because this can differ from the policy that you applied to the local machine. Any existing domain or OU security policies that apply to the machine will overwrite local machine policy.

As mentioned previously, the weakness of the Security Configuration and Analysis snap-in is that it cannot be used to remotely configure computers. So what does a network administrator do with a customized security template that they have created and now need to deploy to other computers in the network? They can very easily export the settings from the database into a standard security template file that can be transferred to any computer desired.

To export the template, right-click on the **Security Configuration and Analysis node** and select **Export Template** from the context menu. Importing a template to the local computer that you have created elsewhere is just as easy: simply right-click on **Security Configuration and Analysis** and select **Import Template** from the context menu.

The Security Templates Snap-in

When first looking at the Security Templates snap-in (Figure 7.8), it might seem like it has no real purpose. However, this snap-in provides an ideal place to modify existing security templates or create entirely new ones from scratch, without any danger or possibility of accidentally applying the security template to the local computer (as with Security Configuration and Analysis) or to a larger range of computers (via Group Policy).

Figure 7.8 The Security Templates Snap-in

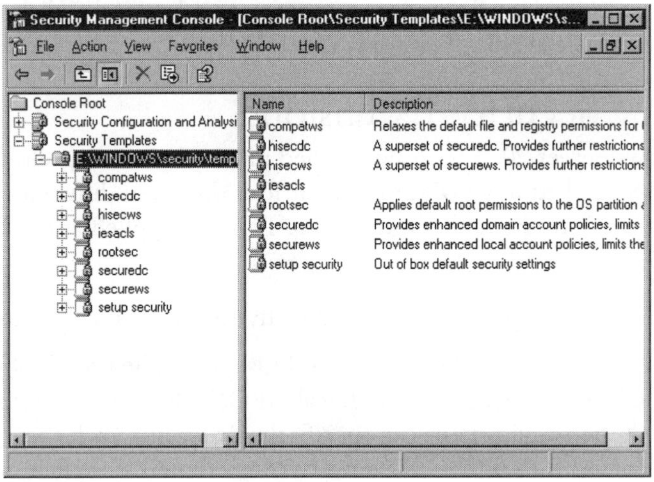

The network administrator can begin customizing an existing template simply by starting to make changes to it. When done editing an existing security template, the administrator should save it with a new name by right-clicking on it and selecting **Save As** from the context menu. This will prevent overwriting a preconfigured security template that may be needed at a later time.

If an administrator wants to start with a completely empty security template in which no settings have been preconfigured, they can do so by right-clicking on the template location node (such as E:\WINDOWS\security\templates) and selecting **New Template** from the context menu. The dialog box seen in Figure 7.9 will open prompting them to supply a name and description for the new template. The network administrator can now begin making security configurations in the new template.

Figure 7.9 Creating a New Security Template

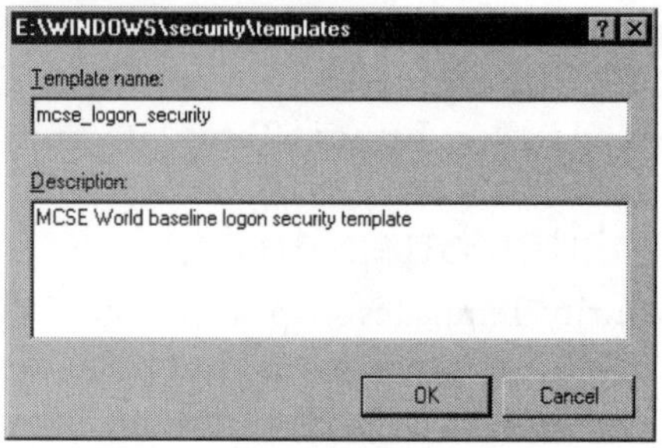

E:\WINDOWS\security\templates	? X

Template name:
mcse_logon_security

Description:
MCSE World baseline logon security template

OK   Cancel

After creating a customized security template, the network administrator can export it from the local computer, if required, by right-clicking on it and selecting **Save As** from the context menu. It is important to save the template with a descriptive name and in a location where it can be found later. To import a security template, right-click on the **Security Templates node** and select **New Template Search Path** from the context menu.

Group Policy Security Extensions

Security in Windows Server 2003 is ideally applied primarily by using Group Policies. Group Policy can be applied in an organization at four distinctly different levels, each inheriting the settings from the level above. Group Policy is applied at the following levels (and in this order):

- **Local** This is Group Policy applied directly to the local computer itself.

- **Site** Site level Group Policy objects (GPOs) are applied to all objects within that site. Site GPOs will overwrite the Local GPO. If there exists more than one Site level GPO, the administrator can specify the order in which they are applied, thus determining which GPOs will be overwritten should a conflict occur.

- **Domain** Domain level GPOs are applied to all objects within the domain and overwrite Site level GPOs. As with Site GPOs, the administrator can specify the order in which they are applied should more than one Domain level GPO exist.

- **OU** OU GPOs are processed last, with the GPO linked to the highest OU processed first, followed by the GPOs linked to each successive child OU. OU GPOs overwrite all GPOs that have come before them and therefore provide the most granular level of security configuration available out of all the levels of Group Policy. Again, should more than one OU level GPO exist, they are processed in the order specified by the administrator.

TEST DAY TIP

Make sure you have a complete understanding of the four levels at which Group Policy is applied and in the order in which they are applied.

Applying security through Group Policy is done using different tools for each level. At the Local level, using the Local Security Settings console as seen in Figure 7.10 allows you to configure and implement the Local GPO. Any changes made here will be implemented in the Local GPO. Note that these same changes can be made using a Local GPO console from the **Computer Configuration | Windows Settings | Security Settings** node.

Figure 7.10 Using the Local Security Settings Console

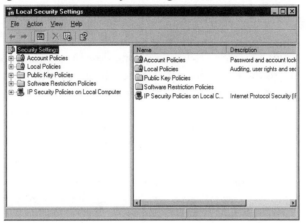

Applying security configurations to the Site level GPO is done by using the Active Directory Sites and Services console, as seen in Figure 7.11. The administrator can create or edit Group Policy to apply at the Site level by right-clicking on the site name, selecting **Properties**, and changing to the **Group Policy** tab of the Properties page. Security settings are not typically applied at the Site level, which may explain the lack of a tool specifically for this purpose.

Figure 7.11 Accessing Security Configuration Settings at the Site Level

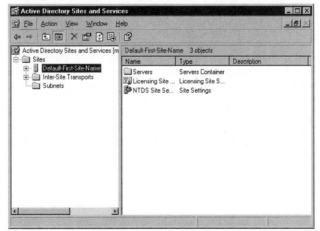

Applying security settings at the Domain level has been made fairly simple, thanks in part to the existence of the Domain Security Policy console seen in Figure 7.12. This console allows the network administrator to configure security settings for all objects in the domain, including child domains within that domain. Note that settings made using the Domain Security Policy console will be configured in the Default Domain GPO. Applying security at the domain is the most common method of Group Policy security application and will be discussed later in this chapter in the "Deploying Security Templates via Group Policy" section.

It is of interest that certain security configurations can only be made at the Domain level, such as those dealing with Account Policies and Registry security. This limitation is due to the fact that Active Directory only allows one domain account policy per domain. For more information, see the knowledge base article located at http://support. microsoft.com/default.aspx?scid=KB;en-us;255550.

Alternatively, the network administrator can work with domain level Group Policy from the Active Directory Users and Computers console by right-clicking the domain, selecting **Properties**, and then switching to the **Group Policy** tab.

Figure 7.12 Configuring the Domain Level Security Policy

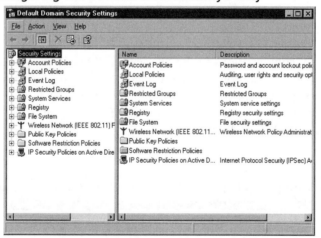

Configuring OU Group Policy and security settings requires the administrator to use the Active Directory Users and Computers console, as seen in Figure 7.13. To configure settings for a specific OU, the administrator should right-click on it and select **Properties** from the context menu. When the OU Properties dialog box opens, they then change to the **Group Policy** tab to start the OU GPO configuration. As mentioned previously, the administrator can work with Domain level Group Policy security settings by right-clicking on the domain and selecting **Properties** from the context menu.

Figure 7.13 Using the Active Directory Users and Computers Console to Configure Security Settings

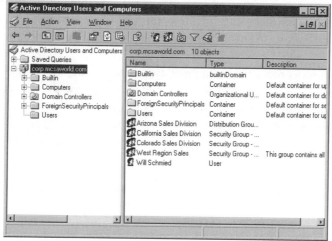

By applying one of the preconfigured templates and then performing customization tasks using the tools outlined here, the network administrator can quickly create custom security template solutions that meet their needs without the burden of starting completely from scratch. The "Configuring Security Templates" section examines each of the major areas that make up a security template.

Group Policy Security versus Security Templates

It may seem by now that using Group Policy to configure security settings and using security templates are two ways to accomplish the same task. This is indeed a true fact. The key difference comes in when you consider what each was designed for.

Security templates are designed to allow you to quickly apply a preconfigured security solution to a specific computer (or group of computers). These templates were designed to be a starting location for further customization—this is where Group Policy comes into play. Should you happen to apply a security template and then later decide you want to further enhance security in a specific area, you will most likely opt to use one of the aforementioned tools to edit the appropriate GPO. In short, look at security templates as a well-defined starting point that can be customized to meet the requirements of the situation by using Group Policy settings.

One key point to remember: any settings you configure directly in Group Policy cannot be exported into a template for use on another computer. By the same token, settings applied via templates can sometimes be very difficult to remove should you later change your mind about the template application.

The secedit.exe Command

The secedit.exe command line tool offers much of the functionality of the Security Configuration and Analysis snap-in from the command-line. This allows the administrator to script security analyses for many machines across the enterprise and save the results for later analysis.

The secedit.exe tool's reporting capabilities are limited. Although administrators can perform a security analysis from the command line, they cannot view the results of the analysis with secedit.exe. They must view the analysis results from the graphic Security Configuration and Analysis snap-in interface. Additionally, the secedit.exe tool can be used to configure, refresh, and export security settings as well as validate security configuration files.

TEST DAY TIP

For this exam, concentrate on understanding how secedit.exe can be used to analyze and configure system security.

The secedit.exe command has the following top-level syntax:

```
secedit [/analyze] [/configure] [/export] [/import] [/validate] [/GenerateRollback]
```

The functions of each top-level option are detailed here:

- **/analyze** Allows the network administrator to analyze the local computer by comparing its security settings against those contained in the database.

- **/configure** Allows the network administrator to configure the security settings of a local computer by applying the settings that are contained in the database.

- **/export** Allows the network administrator to export the security settings that are contained in the database into a security template *.INF* file.

- **/import** Allows the network administrator to import security templates into the database to be used for analysis and configuration of the local computer's security settings. You can use the */import* option to import multiple security templates into the database, if required.

- **/validate** Allows the network administrator to validate the syntax of a security template to ensure that it contains no errors before you import the security template into the database.

- **/GenerateRollback** Allows the network administrator to create a rollback security template that can be used to reset the security configuration to the state it was at before applying the security template.

The usage and specific switches that are associated with each top-level option of the secedit.exe command are explained in the following sections.

Head of the Class...

Viewing the Results of the secedit.exe Analysis

One of the primary weaknesses of the secedit.exe command is that it provides no means for you to view the results of the analysis directly. You will need to view the analysis results in the Security Configuration and Analysis snap-in by opening the database and log file that was created during the secedit.exe analysis. While you might at first be tempted to consider this method of analyzing the security settings, you will quickly see how the opposite is actually the case. By creating a script that runs the secedit.exe command on multiple computers, you can use the %*computername*% variable in the log file name to create a log file for each computer that has been scanned. Additionally, the log files can be saved to a centrally located file server to ensure they are all stored in one place. An administrator can then examine the log files from each computer's analysis from their desktop computer and determine where changes need to be made.

secedit /analyze

The *analyze* switch is used to initiate a security analysis and has the following syntax:

```
secedit /analyze /db FileName /cfg FileName /overwrite /log FileName /quiet
```

Table 7.3 details the function of each of the *analyze* switches.

Table 7.3 The *secedit* /*analyze* Parameters

Switch	Description
/db *FileName*	Used to specify the path and file name of the database that is to be used to perform the analysis.
/cfg *FileName*	Used to specify the path and file name of the security template that is to be imported into the database before the analysis is performed.
/overwrite	Used to specify that the database should be emptied of its current contents before importing the selected security template.
/log *FileName*	Used to specify the path and file name of the log file that is to be used during the analysis.
/quiet	Used to specify that the analysis process should occur with no further onscreen feedback.

As an example of how the *secedit /analyze* command is used, suppose that an administrator wanted to analyze the settings on a computer as compared to those contained in the securews.inf security template. Assuming that they are working from volume E, they would issue the following command (note that the sectest directory is one created especially for this purpose):

```
secedit /analyze /db e:\sectest\1.sdb /cfg
e:\windows\security\templates\securews.inf /log e:\sectest\1.log
```

Figure 7.14 shows the process in action.

Figure 7.14 Using the *secedit /analyze* Command

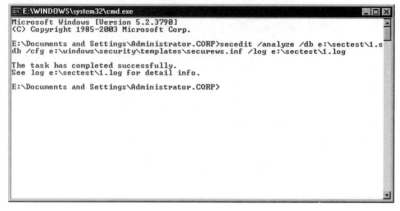

secedit /configure

The configure switch is used to deploy a security template to the local computer and has the following syntax:

```
secedit /configure /db FileName /cfg FileName /overwrite /areas Area1 Area2 ...
/log FileName /quiet
```

Table 7.4 details the function of each of the *analyze* switches.

Table 7.4 The *secedit /configure* Parameters

Switch	Description
/db FileName	Used to specify the path and file name of the database that is to be used to perform the configuration.
/cfg FileName	Used to specify the path and file name of the security template that is to be imported into the database before the configuration is performed.
/overwrite	Used to specify that the database should be emptied of its current contents before importing the selected security template.
/areas	Used to specify the security areas that are to be applied to the computer during the configuration process. If this parameter is not specified, all security areas are applied to the computer. The available options are: ■ **GROUP_MGMT** The Restricted Group settings ■ **USER_RIGHTS** The User Rights Assignment settings. ■ **REGKEYS** The Registry permissions settings.

Table 7.4 The *secedit* /*configure* Parameters

Switch	Description
	■ **FILESTORE** The File System permissions settings. ■ **SERVICES** The System Service settings.
/log *FileName*	Used to specify the path and file name of the log file that is to be used during the configuration.
/quiet	Used to specify that the configuration process should occur with no further onscreen feedback.

As an example of how the *secedit* /*configure* command is used, suppose a network administrator wanted to configure the settings on a computer with those contained in the securews.inf security template. Assuming they are working from volume E, they would issue the following command (note that the sectest directory is one created especially for this purpose:

```
secedit /configure /db e:\sectest\1.sdb /cfg
e:\windows\security\templates\securews.inf /log c:\sectest\1.log
```

Figure 7.15 shows the process in action.

Figure 7.15 Using the *secedit* /*configure* Command

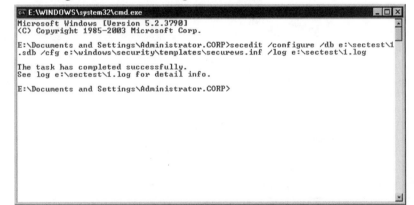

NOTE

The rest of the top-level options for the secedit.exe command are beyond the scope of the 70-292 exam and thus are not covered here. See Appendix A for a complete breakdown of the secedit.exe top-level options and their applicable switches.

Configuring Security Templates

The following sections look at using the security settings available in the security templates or the Group Policy security consoles.

Account Policies

Account policies define aspects of security relating primarily to passwords. The Password Policy node contains entries related to password aging and password length. Account Lockout Policy determines how many failed tries a person gets before the account is locked out. Kerberos Policy applies only to domain logons, since local logons do not use Kerberos. Entries include maximum lifetimes for various tickets, such as user tickets and user renewal. Figure 7.16 shows the Account Policies node expanded. Tables 7.5, 7.6, and 7.7 detail the configurable options available within the Account Policies node.

Figure 7.16 Account Policies

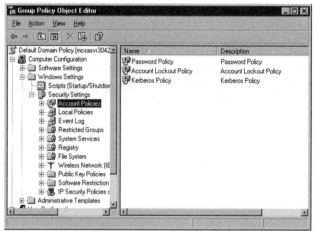

Table 7.5 Account Policies Options - Password Policy Node

Option	Description
Enforce password history	Remembers users' passwords. Requires that they cannot use the same password again until it has left the password history. Values range from 0 passwords remembered to 24 passwords remembered. The default is 0 passwords remembered.
Maximum password age	Defines the maximum amount of time that a user can keep a password without having to change it. Values

Continued

Table 7.5 Account Policies Options - Password Policy Node

Option	Description
	range from "the password never expires" to the "password" expires every 999 days. The default is 42 days.
Minimum password age	Defines the minimum amount of time that a user can keep a password without having to change it. Values range from the password can be changed immediately to the password can be changed after 998 days. The default is 0 days.
Minimum password length	Defines the minimum number of characters required for a user's password. Value ranges from no password required to at least 14 characters required. The default is 0 characters.
Passwords must meet complexity requirements	Requires that the user's password have a mix of uppercase, lowercase, and numbers. Value is either enabled or disabled. The default is disabled.
Store password using reversible encryption for all users in the domain	Stores a copy of the user's password in Active Directory using reversible encryption. This is required for the message digest authentication method to work. Value is either enabled or disabled. The default is disabled.

EXAM WARNING

Password policies can only be set at the domain level. Be attentive to questions that may suggest that they can be set at the Local, Site, or OU levels.

Head of the Class…

Password Age Policies

While setting a minimum password age is usually a good thing, there is at least one instance where it can actually provide a security breach in an organization. For example, say that a system administrator configured the minimum password age to be five days (before a user is allowed to change the password). If that password were comprised, the only way the security breach could be rectified would be through administrator intervention by resetting the password for the user from Active Directory Users and Computers.

Likewise, setting the minimum password age to 0 days and also configuring 0 passwords remembered allows users to circumvent the password rotation process by allowing them to use the same password over and over. The key to configuring effective policies, password or any other type, is to first analyze the

Continued

needs, then test the configuration, and finally to apply it once it has proved in testing that it meets or exceeds the requirements.

Table 7.6 Account Policies Options - Account Lockout Policy Node

Option	Description
Account lockout duration	Defines the time in minutes that an account will remain locked out. Value ranges from "account is locked out until administrator unlocks it" to 99,999 minutes (69 days, 10 hours, and 39 minutes). The default is not defined.
Account lockout threshold	Defines how many times a user can enter an incorrect password before the user's account is locked. Value ranges from "the account will not lock out" to 999 invalid logon attempts. The default is five attempts.
Reset account lockout counter after	Defines how long to keep track of unsuccessful logons. Value ranges from one minute to 99,999 minutes. The default is not defined.

Head of the Class…

Brute Force Hacking

One of the simplest means of gaining access to protected system resources is by "brute force hacking." Brute force hacking consists simply of trying to guess or crack passwords by trying all possible combinations. Brute force attacks can be performed by users themselves or by the use of specialized software utilities designed for this purpose. Brute force hacking differs from dictionary hacking in that dictionary hacking tries to guess passwords by comparing them to a large list of common words and phrases. By configuring for strong passwords, the network administrator can defeat dictionary hacking—protecting against brute force hacking is nearly impossible.

The only line of defense when it comes to brute force hacking (or even social hacking) comes down to configuring and implementing good auditing policies and also configuring account lockout policies with lockout durations that are appropriate for the sensitivity of the information contained within the network.

Table 7.7 Account Policies Options - Kerberos Policy Node

Option	Description
Enforce user logon restrictions	This forces the Key Distribution Center (KDC) to validate every request for a session ticket by examining the user rights policy on the target computer to make sure that the user has the right to either log on locally or access the computer across the network. This additionally checks to see that the requesting account is still valid. These checks are optional and may result in slower network access to services when enabled. The default setting is Enabled.
Maximum lifetime for service ticket	Defines the maximum amount of time in minutes that a service ticket is valid. Value ranges from tickets don't expire to 99,999 minutes. The default is 600 minutes (10 hours).
Maximum lifetime for user ticket	Defines the maximum amount of time in hours that a user ticket is valid. Value ranges from tickets don't expire to 99,999 hours. The default is 10 hours.
Maximum lifetime for user ticket renewal	Defines the maximum lifetime of a ticket (Ticket Granting Ticket or session ticket). No ticket can be renewed after this lifetime has passed. The default is 7 days.
Maximum tolerance for computer clock synchronization	Specifies the amount of time in minutes that computer clocks can be skewed. Value ranges from 0 minutes to 99,999 minutes. The default is 5 minutes.

Local Policies

Local policies include the Audit Policy, User Rights Assignment, and Security Options. Some Audit Policy selections include auditing log-on events, use of user privileges, systems events, and object access. The User Rights Assignment node includes the ability to grant or deny user rights such as the right to add workstations to the domain, change the system time, log on locally, and access the computer from the network.

The most profound improvements to the program are represented in the Security Options node, where an administrator can make changes that could only be made via direct Registry edits in Windows NT 4.0. Examples of such security options include clearing the pagefile when the system shuts down, messaging text during logon, keeping the number of previous logons in cache, and shutting down the system immediately if unable to log security audits.

Figure 7.17 shows the Local Policies node fully expanded. Tables 7.8, 7.9, and 7.10 detail the configurable options available within the Local Policies node. The improvements in local policy management are numerous with the addition of the configurable objects available in the Security Options node.

Figure 7.17 Account Policies

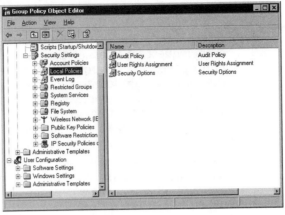

The audit policies outlined in Table 7.8 allow the network administrator to configure auditing to occur on their network as desired to assist in determining what exactly is occurring. Auditing is examined in more detail later in this chapter in the "Auditing Security Events" section.

Table 7.8 Local Policies Options - Audit Policy Node

Option	Description
Audit account logon events	Audits when an account is authenticated to the database. The default is not defined.
Audit account management	Audits when a user account or group is created, deleted, or modified. The default is not defined.
Audit directory service access	Audits when access is gained to an Active Directory object. The default is not defined.
Audit logon events	Audits when a user logs on or off a local computer and when a user makes a network connection to a machine. The default is not defined.
Audit object access	Audits when files, folders, or printers are accessed. The default is not defined.
Audit policy change	Audits when security options, user rights, or audit policies are modified. The default is not defined.
Audit privilege use	Audits when a user right is utilized. The default is not defined.
Audit process tracking	Audits when an application performs an action. The default is not defined.
Audit system events	Audits when a security-related event occurs, such as rebooting the computer. The default is not defined.

The user rights, as listed in Table 7.9, allow the network administrator to configure groups and users to have the ability to perform certain, specific actions on the network, or to be prevented from being able to perform specific actions. For example, configuring a group of users to connect to the Terminal Services servers with the "Allow logon through Terminal Services" user right, or configuring another group of users responsible for the organization's disaster recovery implementation using the "Back up files and directories" and "Restore files and directories" user rights.

Table 7.9 Local Policies Options - User Rights Assignments Node

Option	Description
Access this computer from the network	Allows a user or group to connect to the computer over the network. The default is not defined.
Act as part of the operating system	Allows a process to gain access to the resources operating system under any user identity. The default is not defined.
Add workstations to the domain	Allows a user or group to add a computer to the domain. The default is not defined.
Adjust memory quotas for a process	Allows a user to change the maximum memory that can be consumed by a process. The default is not defined.
Allow logon locally	Allows a user to log on interactively with the computer. The default is not defined.
Allow logon through Terminal Services	Allows users or groups to log on through Terminal Services. The default is not defined.
Back up files and directories	Allows a user or group to bypass file and directory permissions to back up the system. The default is not defined.
Bypass traverse checking	Allows a user or group to pass through directories without having access while navigating an object path in any Windows file system. The default is not defined.
Change the system time	Allows a user or group to set the time for the computer's internal clock. The default is not defined.
Create a pagefile	Allows a user or group to create and change the size of a pagefile. The default is not defined.
Create a token object	Allows a process to create a token to get access to any local resources. The default is not defined.
Create global objects	Allows a user to create a global object during a Terminal Services session. The default is not defined.
Create permanent shared objects	Allows a process to create a directory object in the object manager. The default is not defined.
Debug programs	Allows a user or group to attach a debugger to any process. The default is not defined.

Continued

Table 7.9 Local Policies Options - User Rights Assignments Node

Option	Description
Deny access to this computer from the network	Denies the ability to connect to the computer over the network. The default is not defined.
Deny logon as a batch job	Denies the ability to log on using a batch-queue facility. The default is not defined.
Deny logon as a service	Denies the ability to log on as a service. The default is not defined.
Deny logon locally	Denies a user or group the ability to log on the local machine. The default is not defined.
Deny logon through Terminal Services	Denies a user or group the ability to log on through Terminal Services. The default is not defined.
Enable computer and user accounts to be trusted for delegation	Allows a user or group to set the Trusted for Delegation setting on a user or computer object. The default is not defined.
Force shutdown from a remote system	Allows a user or group to shut down a remote system computer remotely. The default is not defined.
Generate security audits	Allows a process to make entries in the security log. The default is not defined.
Impersonate a client after authentication	Allows a program running on behalf of a client to impersonate that client. The default is not defined.
Increase scheduling priority	Allows a process to increase the execution priority for any processes to which it has Write property access. The default is not defined.
Load and unload device drivers	Allows a user or group to install and uninstall Plug-and-Play device drivers. The default is not defined.
Lock pages in memory	Allows a process to keep data in physical memory. The default is not defined.
Log on as a batch job	Allows a user or group to log on using a batch-queue facility. The default is not defined.
Log on as a service	Allows logging on as a service. The default is not defined.
Log on locally	Allows a user or group to log on the local machine. The default is not defined.
Manage auditing and security log	Allows a user or group to configure object access auditing. The default is not defined.
Modify firmware environment values	Allows changing the system environment values variables. The default is not defined.
Perform volume maintenance tasks	Allows a user or group to perform maintenance tasks on a volume, such as defragmentation. The default is not defined.

Continued

Table 7.9 Local Policies Options - User Rights Assignments Node

Option	Description
Profile single process	Allows a user or group to use performance-monitoring tools to monitor the performance of nonsystem processes. The default is not defined.
Profile system performance	Allows a user or group to use performance-monitoring tools to monitor the performance of system processes. The default is not defined.
Remove computer from docking station	Allows a user or group to undock a laptop within Windows 2000. The default is not defined.
Replace a process level token	Allows a process to replace the default token associated with a subprocess that has been started. The default is not defined.
Restore files and directories	Allows a user or group to bypass file and directory pe-missions when restoring backed up files and directories. The default is not defined.
Shut down the system	Allows a user or group to shut down the local computer. The default is not defined.
Synchronize directory service data	Allows a process to provide directory synchronization ser-vices. The default is not defined.
Take ownership of files or other objects	Allows a user or group to take ownership of any securable system object. The default is not defined.

The security options, as detailed in Table 7.10, allow the network administrator to configure extra and very granular security settings for their network and its computers. In the vast majority of cases, these options are not defined by default, thus providing the administrator with a baseline security configuration that can be configured either directly or through the use of security templates to further lock down the network as required.

TEST DAY TIP

While you should not be tested directly on your ability to remember all of these security options, you should at least be familiar with them and their general usage. You should also know where they are located.

Table 7.10 Local Policies Options - Security Options Node

Option	Description
Accounts: Administrator account status	Determines whether the local Administrative account is enabled or disabled. The default is not defined.
Accounts: Guest account status	Determines whether the local Guest account is enabled or disabled. The default is not defined.
Accounts: Limit local use of blank passwords to console logon only	Determines whether accounts with no passwords can be used to log on to the computer from any location other than locally. The default is not defined.
Accounts: Rename administrator account	Renames the administrator account to the name specified here. The default is not defined.
Accounts: Rename guest account	Renames the guest account to the name specified here. The default is not defined.
Audit: Audit the access of global system objects	Audits when a system object is accessed. The default is not defined.
Audit: Audit use of Backup and Restore privilege	Audits when the Backup and Restore privileges are used. The default is not defined.
Audit: Shut down system immediately if unable to log security audits	Shuts down the computer when the security log becomes full. The default is not defined.
Devices: Allow undock without having to log on	Determines if a portable computer can be undocked without first having to log on. The default is not defined.
Devices: Allowed to format and eject removable media	Defines which groups are allowed to format and eject removable media. The default is not defined.
Devices: Prevent users from installing printer drivers	Keeps users from installing printers. The default is not defined.
Devices: Restrict CD-ROM access to locally logged on user only	Restricts network access to the CD-ROM. The default is not defined.
Devices: Restrict floppy access to locally logged-on user only	Restricts network access to the floppy drive. The default is not defined.
Devices: Unsigned driver installation behavior	Controls what happens when the installation of an unsigned driver is attempted. Choices include: Silently succeed, Warn but allow installation, and Do not allow installation. The default is not defined.
Domain controller: Allow server operators to schedule tasks	Gives members of the Server Operators group the right to schedule tasks. The default is not defined.
Domain controller: LDAP server signing requirements	Determines whether the Lightweight Directory Access Protocol (LDAP) server requires signing to be negotiated with LDAP clients. The default is not defined.

Continued

Table 7.10 Local Policies Options - Security Options Node

Option	Description
Domain controller: Refuse machine account name changes	Determines whether domain controllers will refuse requests from member computers to change computer account passwords. The default is not defined.
Domain member: Digitally encrypt or sign secure channel data (always)	Requires the machine to encrypt or sign secure channel data. The default is not defined.
Domain member: Digitally encrypt secure channel data (when possible)	Configures the machine to encrypt secure channel data when communicating with a machine that supports digital encryption. The default is not defined.
Domain member: Digitally sign secure channel data (when possible)	Configures the machine to sign secure channel data when communicating with a machine that supports digital signing. The default is not defined.
Domain member: Disable machine account name changes	Determines whether a domain member periodically changes its computer account password. The default is not defined.
Domain member: Maximum machine account password age	Determines how often a domain member will attempt to change its computer account password. The default is not defined.
Domain member: Require strong (Windows 2000 or later) session key	Requires the use of a Windows 2000 session key. The default is not defined.
Interactive logon: Do not display last user name	Does not display the name of the last user to log on to the system. The default is not defined.
Interactive logon: Do not require Ctrl+Alt+Del	Configures the computer to not require a user to press **Ctrl+Alt+Del** to open the logon dialog box. The default is not defined.
Interactive logon: Message text for users attempting to log on	The text to be displayed in a window presented to all users logging on. The default is not defined.
Interactive logon: Message title for users attempting to log on	The title of the window presented to all users logging on. The default is not defined.
Interactive logon: Number of previous logons to cache (in case domain controller is not available)	Determines how many times users can log on with their cached credentials. The default is not defined.
Interactive logon: Prompt user to change password before expiration	Specifies how many days before password expiration the user is first prompted to change it. The default is not defined.

Continued

Table 7.10 Local Policies Options - Security Options Node

Option	Description
Interactive logon: Require Domain Controller authentication to unlock workstation	Specifies whether a domain controller must be contacted to unlock domain workstations. The default is not defined.
Interactive logon: Require smart card	Specifies that users must use a smart card to log on to the network. The default is not defined.
Interactive logon: Smart card removal behavior	Determines what will take place when a smart card is removed from the system. Choices include No Action, Lock Workstation, and Force Logoff. The default is not defined.
Microsoft network client: Digitally sign client communications (always)	Requires the computer to sign its communications when functioning as a client, whether or not the server supports signing. Unsigned communications are not allowed. The default is not defined.
Microsoft network client: Digitally sign client communications (when server agrees)	Configures the computer to request signed communications when functioning as a client to a server that supports signing. Unsigned communications will be allowed, but they are not preferred. The default is Enabled.
Microsoft network client: Send unencrypted password to connect to third-party SMB servers	Sends a clear text to password to SMB servers that don't support SMB signing. The default is not defined.
Microsoft network server: Amount of idle time before suspending session.	Defines how long a user can be connected in an idle state before the user's session is suspended. The default is not
Microsoft network server: Digitally sign communications (always)	Configures the server to require that all connecting clients sign their communications. Unsigned communications are not allowed. The default is not defined.
Microsoft network server: Digitally sign communications (if client agrees)	Configures the server to request signed communications when communicating with a client that supports signing. Unsigned communications will be allowed, but they are not preferred. The default is not defined.
Microsoft network server: Disconnect clients when logon hours expire	Determines whether to disconnect users connected to the local computer outside their user account's valid log-on hours. The default is not defined.
Network access: Allow anonymous SID/Name translation	Determines if an anonymous user can request SID attributes for another user. The default is not defined.
Network access: Do not allow anonymous enumeration of SAM accounts	Determines what additional permissions will be granted for anonymous connections to the computer. The default is not defined.

Continued

Table 7.10 Local Policies Options - Security Options Node

Option	Description
Network access: Do not allow anonymous enumeration of SAM accounts and shares	Determines whether anonymous enumeration of SAM accounts and shares is allowed. The default is not defined.
Network access: Do not allow storage of credentials or .NET Passports for network authentication	Determines whether Stored User Names and Passwords will save passwords, credentials, or .NET Passports for later use. The default is not defined.
Network access: Let Everyone permissions apply to anonymous users	Determines what additional permissions are granted for anonymous connections to the computer. The default is not defined.
Network access: Named Pipes that can be accessed anonymously	Determines which communication sessions will have attributes and permissions that allow anonymous access. The default is not defined.
Network access: Remotely accessible Registry paths	Determines which Registry paths can be accessed over the network. The default is not defined.
Network access: Remotely accessible Registry paths and subpaths	Determines which Registry paths and subpaths can be accessed over the network. The default is not defined.
Network access: Restrict anonymous access to Named Pipes and Shares	Specifies that anonymous access to shares and pipes is controlled by these settings: *Named pipes that can be accessed anonymously* and *Shares that can be accessed anonymously*. The default is not defined.
Network access: Shares that can be accessed anonymously	Determines which network shares can accessed by anonymous users. The default is not defined.
Network access: Sharing and security model for local accounts	Determines how network logons using local accounts are authenticated. The default is not defined.
Network security: Do not store LM hash value on next password change	Determines if the LM hash value for the new password is stored upon the next password change. The default is not defined.
Network security: Force logoff when logon hours expire	Determines whether to disconnect users who are connected to the local computer outside their user account's valid log-on hours. The default is disabled.
Network security: LM authentication level	Controls the level of authentication supported for down-level clients. The default is not defined.
Network security: LDAP client signing requirements	Determines the level of data signing that is requested on behalf of clients issuing LDAP Berkeley Internet Name Domain (BIND) requests. The default is not defined.

Continued

Table 7.10 Local Policies Options - Security Options Node

Option	Description
Network security: Minimum session security for NTLM SSP based (including secure RPC) clients	Allows a client to require the negotiation of message confidentiality, message integrity, 128-bit encryption, or NTLMv2 session security. The default is not defined.
Network security: Minimum session security for NTLM SSP based (including secure RPC) servers	Allows a server to require the negotiation of message confidentiality, message integrity, 128-bit encryption, or NTLMv2 session security. The default is not defined.
Recovery console: Allow automatic administrative logon	Automatically logs the administrator on with the recovery console administrator account when booting to recovery console. The default is not defined.
Recovery console: Allow floppy copy and access to all drives and all folders	Allows copying from a floppy when booted into recovery console. Also allows access to the entire hard drive in recovery mode. The default is not defined.
Shutdown: Allow system to be shut down without having to log on	Allows a user to shut down the computer without needing to be first logged in. The default is not defined.
Shutdown: Clear virtual memory pagefile	Empties the pagefile on shutdown. The default is not defined.
System cryptography: Force strong key protection for user keys stored on the computer	Determines if users' private keys require a password to be used. The default is not defined.
System cryptography: Use FIPS compliant algorithms for encryption, hashing, and signing	Determines if the Transport Layer Security/Secure Sockets Layer Security Provider supports only the TLS_RSA_WITH_3DES_EDE_CBC_SHA cipher suite. The default is not defined.
System objects: Default owner for objects created by members of the Administrators group	Determines which users and groups have the authority to run volume maintenance tasks such as Disk Defragmenter. The default is not defined.
System objects: Require case insensitivity for non-Windows subsystems	Determines whether case insensitivity is enforced for all subsystems. The default is not defined.
System objects: Strengthen default permissions of internal system objects (e.g. Symbolic Links)	Strengthens the default permissions of global system objects. The default is not defined.
System settings: Optional subsystems	Determines which subsystems are used to support your applications. The default is not defined.

Continued

Table 7.10 Local Policies Options - Security Options Node

Option	Description
System settings: Use Certificate Rules on Windows Executables for Software Restriction Policies	Determines if digital certificates are processed when a user or process attempts to run software with an .exe file name extension. The default is not defined.

New & Noteworthy...

Hardening Windows Server 2003

There are several additional Security Options that are not defined by default in Group Policy that can be used to perform system hardening. Chapter 10 of the *Threats and Countermeasures Guide*, available for download from http://go.microsoft.com/fwlink/?LinkId=15160, provides the procedure to modify the Registry to add the following Security Options:

- MSS: Number of connections to create when additional connections are necessary for Winsock applications
- MSS: Enable dynamic backlog for Winsock applications
- MSS: Maximum number of "quasi-free" connections for Winsock applications
- MSS: Minimum number of free connections for Winsock applications
- MSS: Allow automatic detection of dead network gateways
- MSS: Allow automatic detection of MTU size
- MSS: Allow ICMP redirects to override OSPF generated routes
- MSS: Allow IRDP to detect and configure Default Gateway addresses
- MSS: Allow the computer to ignore NetBIOS name release requests except from WINS servers
- MSS: Disable autorun for all drives
- MSS: Enable the computer to stop generating 8.3 style filenames
- MSS: How many dropped connect requests to initiate SYN attack protection
- MSS: How many times unacknowledged data is retransmitted
- MSS: How often keep-alive packets are sent in milliseconds
- MSS: IP source routing protection level
- MSS: Percentage threshold for the security event log at which the system will generate a warning
- MSS: SYN attack protection level

Continued

- MSS: SYN-ACK retransmissions when a connection request is not acknowledged
- MSS: The time in seconds before the screen saver grace period expires
- MSS: Enable Safe DLL search mode

Event Log

The Event Log node allows the administrator to configure settings specifically for event logs, as shown in Figure 7.18. Event Log Configuration settings allow the administrator to configure the length of time logs are retained as well as the size of the event logs. The administrator can also configure that the system should shut down if the security log becomes full. Table 7.11 presents the configurable options available within the Event Log Policies node.

Figure 7.18 Event Log Policies

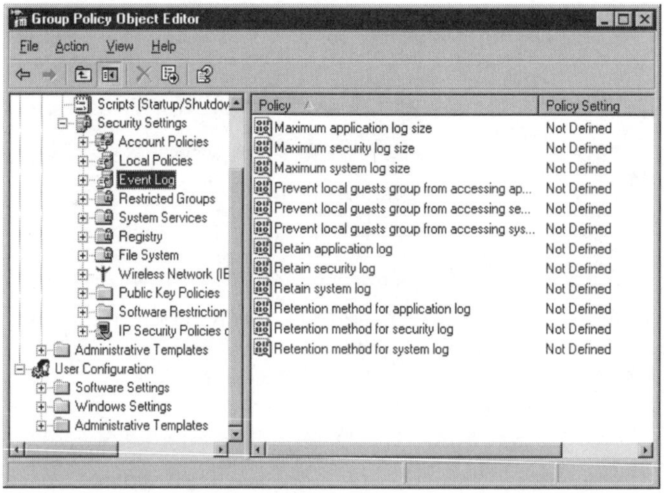

Table 7.11 Event Log Security Options

Option	Description
Maximum application log size	Controls how large the application log can grow. The default is 512 KB.
Maximum security log size	Controls how large the security log can grow. The default is 512 KB.

Continued

Table 7.11 Event Log Security Options

Option	Description
Maximum system log size	Controls how large the system log can grow. The default is 512 KB.
Restrict guest access to application log	Prevents guest access from reading the application log. The default is Disabled.
Restrict guest access to security log	Prevents guest access from reading the security log. The default is Disabled.
Restrict guest access to system log	Prevents guest access from reading the system log. The default is Disabled.
Retain application log	Tells the event log not to overwrite events in the application log that are older than the number of days defined. The default is 7 days.
Retain security log	Tells the event log not to overwrite events in the security log that are older than the number of days defined. The default is 7 days.
Retain system log	Tells the event log not to overwrite events in the system log that are older than the number of days defined. The default is 7 days.
Retention method for application log	Tells the event log what to do when the application log becomes full. Choices include "Overwrite events by days," "Overwrite events as needed," and "Do not overwrite events" (clear logs manually). The default is by days.
Retention method for security log	Tells the event log what to do when the security log becomes full. Choices include "Overwrite events by days," "Overwrite events as needed," and "Do not overwrite events (clear logs manually)." The default is by days.
Retention method for system log	Tells the event log what to do when the system log becomes full. Choices include "Overwrite events by days," "Overwrite events as needed," and "Do not overwrite events (clear logs manually)." The default is by days.

Restricted Groups

The Restricted Groups node lends something new to the security configuration options available in Windows Server 2003. A network administrator can define, as part of security policy, which users are allowed to be members of a group. At times, the administrator needs to temporarily add users to groups with a higher classification than the users' typical group membership. This might be the case when an administrator goes on vacation and another member of the team is assigned full administrative rights.

Configuring & Implementing...

To Shutdown or Not To Shutdown...

If you want to start a heated discussion between a group of experienced network administrators, throw out the following question: "Is it better to shut down a server automatically once its security logs are full?" You're likely to get quite a lively discussion after that. Let's examine the two trains of thought—after that you can decide for yourself which solution is better for your network.

The first group might say that yes, you should definitely configure servers to shut down automatically if the security log has been filled up. The argument goes like this: "If you implement auditing and pay careful attention to the log files, clearing them out every day as required, you can benefit from having Windows automatically shut down a server when its security log is full. Common sources of full security logs (when carefully tended to by the administrator) usually come from attempts to gain access to the server unsuccessfully or gained access to the server that is followed up by privilege use and abuse. Odds are that you have probably got enough information about the nature and source of the attack by the time the server shuts down. Why leave it exposed any more than you need to? Of course, this requires careful pruning and the daily attention of the administrator. Do not configure this setting if you plan on leaving the server to run unattended."

On the other hand, the second group might say that no, you should never configure a server to automatically shutdown if the security log is full. The argument is: "All it takes is one user on your local network to either figure this out (that you have automatic shutdown configured when the security log is full) or to just screw up and continue attempting to login with an incorrect password. You have, in effect, provided a convenient Denial of Service (DoS) means for attackers to use to take down your servers. Remember that a DoS is any action that prevents users from being able to utilize the normal network services, whether intentional or not. You could conceivably start forcing servers to shut down in about 15 minutes or so..."

So, which answer is right for you? That is a decision that you will have to make after weighing the cost of losing a server from the network, as compared to the benefit of protecting it from further attacks.

However, often the "temporary" promotion ends up being an inadvertently permanent one, and the user remains in the Administrators group. Groups can also become members of other groups when this is not part of the company security plan. By defining Restricted Group membership rules, an administrator can return group membership to that defined by security policy. Figure 7.19 shows the Restricted Groups node. Exercise 7.03 walks through configuring restricted groups.

Figure 7.19 The Restricted Groups Node

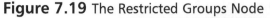

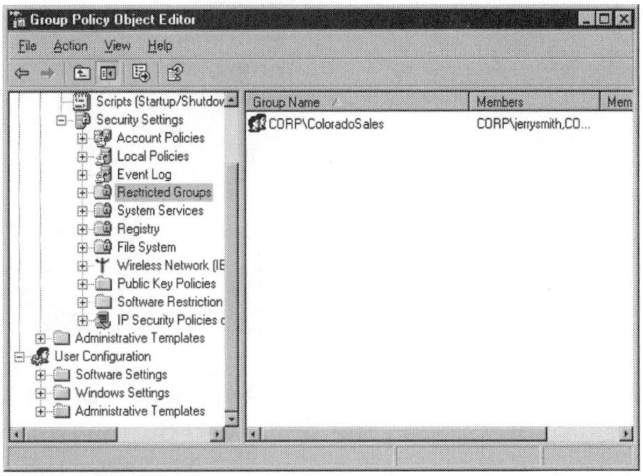

EXERCISE 7.03

CONFIGURING RESTRICTED GROUPS

1. Navigate to the **Restricted Groups** node of your Security Configuration and Analysis snap-in or the Restricted Groups node in the Group Policy Editor, Domain Security Policy console, or Local Security console.

2. Right-click **Restricted Groups** and choose **Add Group** from the context menu. The Add Groups dialog box opens, as seen in Figure 7.20.

Figure 7.20 The Add Groups Dialog Box

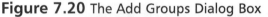

3. You can type the name of the group that you want to restrict, or click **Browse** to pick the group from a list. In this case, click **Browse**. The Select Groups dialog box opens, as seen in Figure 7.21.

Figure 7.21 The Select Groups Dialog Box

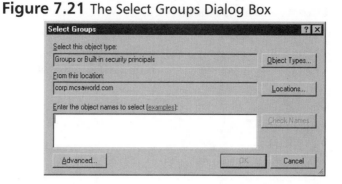

4. Enter the group name or click the **Advanced** button to search for all available groups. Clicking the **Advanced** button expands the Select Groups dialog box, as seen in Figure 7.22. Select the group or groups that you want to restrict and click **OK** three times.

Figure 7.22 The Expanded Select Groups Dialog Box

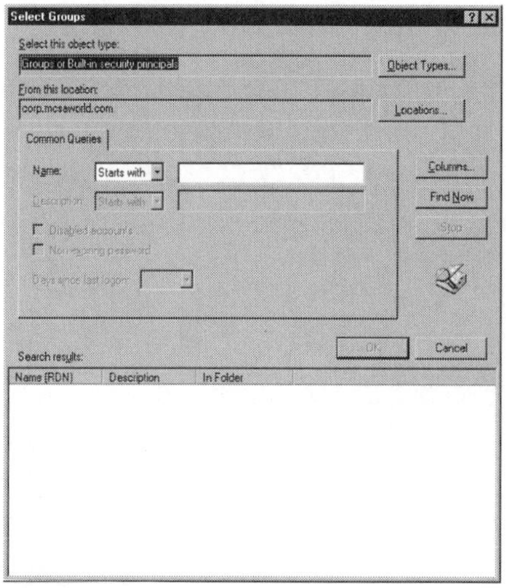

5. The group Properties dialog box will appear, as seen in Figure 7.23. Click the top **Add** button to add users and groups that are allowed to be a member of this group. Click the bottom **Add** button to add this group to other groups.

Figure 7.23 Adding Users to the Restricted Group

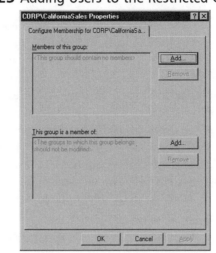

6. After you have added your allowed users, the group Properties dialog box will look similar to that seen in Figure 7.24.

Figure 7.24 The Completed Restricted Group

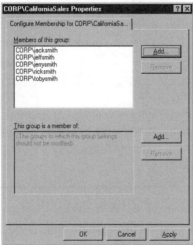

7. Click **OK** to close the group Properties dialog box and commit your changes.

System Services

The System Services node allows the network administrator to control security and startup policy on all the services defined in the template. Controlling the startup behavior of system services can save the administrator many headaches over time. Consider the situation of users starting up their own Remote Access Service (RAS) or Dynamic Host Control Protocol (DHCP) services haphazardly. This type of situation creates a large security risk for any network.

An administrator can set restrictive networking services startup properties and assign all computers that require certain services to an OU that has the right to start up particular networking services. Figure 7.25 shows some of the content of the Services node. Exercise 7.04 walks through configuring System Services Security.

Figure 7.25 The System Services Node

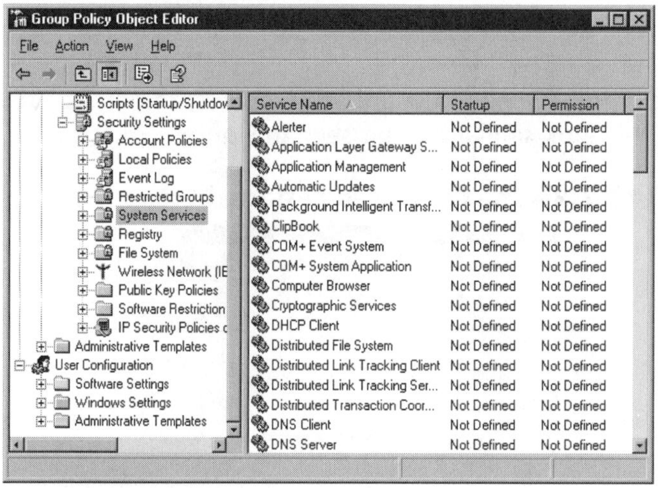

EXERCISE 7.04

CONFIGURING SYSTEM SERVICES SECURITY

1. Navigate to the **System Services** node of your **Security Configuration and Analysis** snap-in or the **Restricted Groups** node in the **Group Policy Editor, Domain Security Policy** console, or **Local Security** console.

2. Right-click the service that you want to secure and choose **Properties** from the context menu. You will see the Security Policy Setting dialog box, as seen in Figure 7.26.

Figure 7.26 The Security Policy Settings Dialog Box

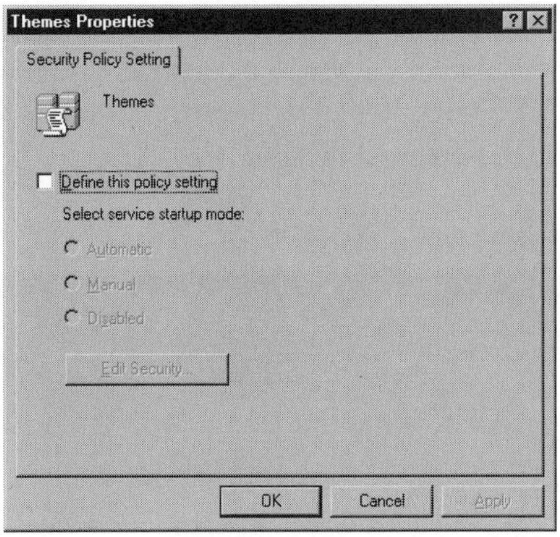

3. In the Security Policy Setting dialog box, check the box next to **Define this policy setting**. Select to have the service startup automatically, require a manual start, or be disabled.

4. Click the **Edit Security** button to open the Security dialog box, as seen in Figure 7.27. Configure the NTFS permissions for the service you require. Click **OK** twice to close the service Properties dialog box.

Figure 7.27 Configuring Security for a Service

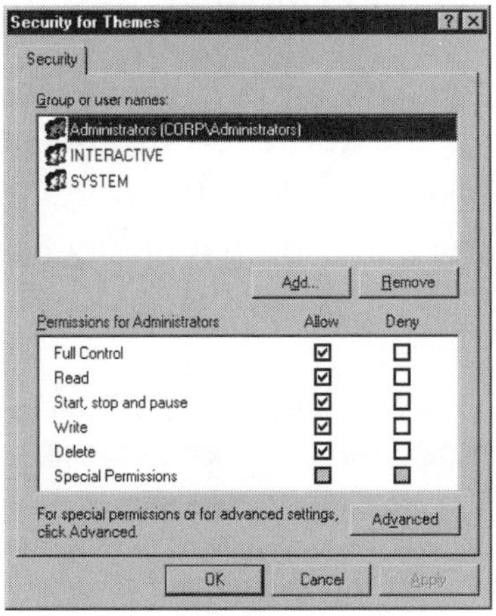

Registry

Registry keys can also be protected by policy. A network administrator can define a security policy for a Registry key or value in the database and then customize the propagation of the setting using the Key Properties dialog box. Figure 7.28 shows the Registry node. Exercise 7.05 walks through configuring Registry security.

Figure 7.28 The Registry Security Node

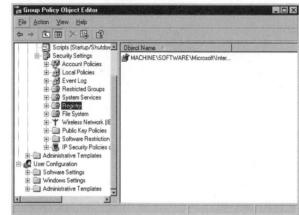

EXERCISE 7.05

CONFIGURING REGISTRY SECURITY

1. Navigate to the **Registry node** of your Security Configuration and Analysis snap-in or the **Restricted Groups** node in the Group Policy Editor, Domain Security Policy console, or Local Security console.

2. Right-click **Registry** and choose **Add Key** from the context menu. You will see the Select Registry Key dialog box shown in Figure 7.29.

Figure 7.29 The Select Registry Key Dialog Box

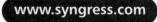

3. Navigate to the key that you want to secure. In this example, we are using the MACHINE\SOFTWARE key. Click **OK** to continue.

4. The Database Security dialog box, seen in Figure 7.30, opens. Use this window to choose the permissions that will be assigned to the secured Registry key. After customizing the permissions, click **OK**.

Figure 7.30 The Database Security Dialog Box

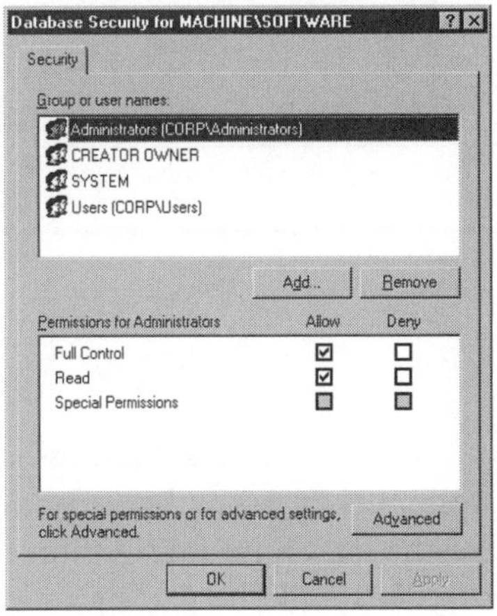

5. The Add Object dialog box, seen in Figure 7.31, opens. Use this window to tell Windows what to do with the permissions you set in Step 4. The choices are:

- **Configure this key then propagate inheritable permissions to all subkeys** This will set permissions at the selected key and all keys below it, merging these permissions with whatever permissions are already set at each subkey.

- **Configure this key then replace existing permissions on all subkeys with inheritable permissions** This will replace the permissions on each subkey with the permissions set at the selected key.

- **Do not allow permissions on this key to be replaced**

6. Choose one of the settings and click **OK**.

Figure 7.31 Configuring the Key Security Behavior

File System

The File System Security node allows the network administrator to configure NTFS permission for all local drives. It is common for a number of administrators to get into Windows Explorer and customize the NTFS permissions on files and folders throughout the file system. File and folder security should be part of a well-planned and well-implemented security plan.

This security plan can be implemented by setting File System Policy, as seen in Figure 7.32. The network administrator can then periodically audit the status of the file system to look for inconsistencies between the plan and the actual state of NTFS permissions in the local environment. Exercise 7.06 walks through the process of using file system security.

Figure 7.32 The File System Node

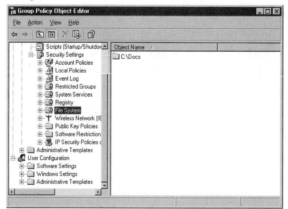

EXERCISE 7.06

CONFIGURING FILE SYSTEM SECURITY

1. Navigate to the **File System** node of your **Security Configuration and Analysis** snap-in or the **Restricted Groups** node in the **Group Policy Editor**, **Domain Security Policy** console, or **Local Security** console.

2. Right-click the **File System** node and select **Add File** from the context menu. The File or Folder dialog box, seen in Figure 7.33, opens.

Figure 7.33 Adding a File or Folder

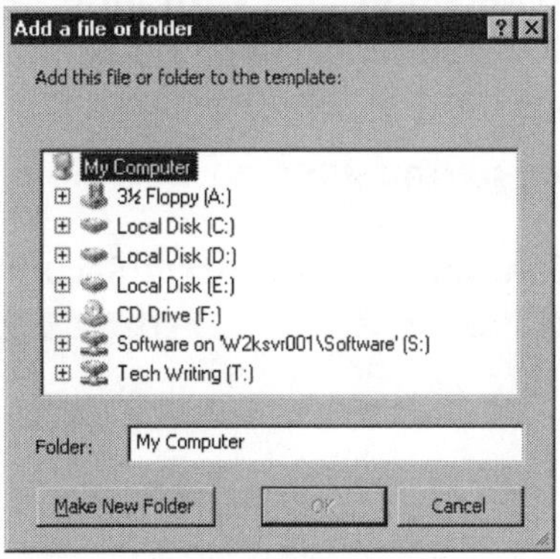

3. Navigate to the file or folder that you want to secure. In this example, we are going to use the root of the C: drive. Click **OK** to continue.

4. The Database Security dialog box, seen in Figure 7.34, opens. Use this window to choose the permissions that will be assigned to the secured file or folder. After customizing the permissions, click **OK**.

Figure 7.34 The Database Security Dialog Box

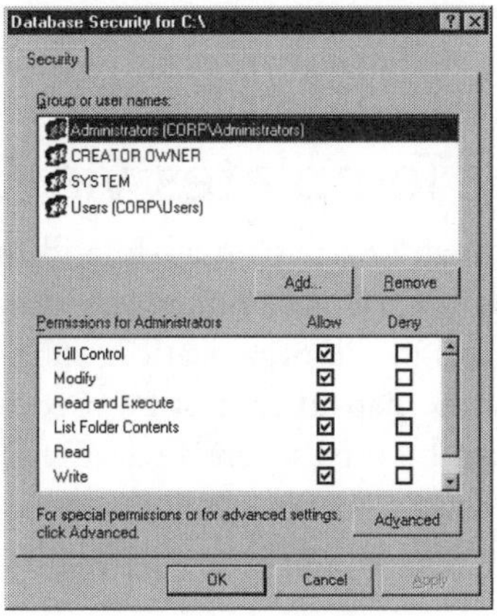

5. Now that you have set the permissions, you have to tell Windows how to propagate them. Figure 7.35 shows the Template Security Policy Setting window. Use this window to tell Windows what to do with the permissions you just configured. The choices are:

    ■   **Configure this file or folder then propagate inheritable permissions to all subfolders and files** This choice sets permissions at the selected file or folder and all subfolders and files below it, merging these permissions with whatever permissions are already set at each subfolder or file.

    ■   **Configure this file or folder then replace existing permissions on all subfolders and files with inheritable permissions** This choice replaces the permissions on each subfolder and file with the permissions set at the selected file or folder.

    ■   **Do not allow permissions on this file or folder to be replaced**

Figure 7.35 Configuring File System Security Inheritance Behavior

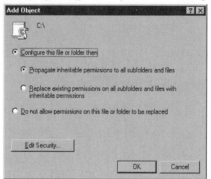

6. Choose the appropriate setting and click **OK**.

Deploying Security Templates via Group Policy

While the Security Configuration and Analysis snap-in and the secedit.exe command are useful for configuring local computer security policy, a major limitation exists for their use in applying security to higher levels in the organization, such as a domain or OU. The Security Configuration and Analysis snap-in cannot be used to directly apply security settings at these levels, however it can be used to create and test security templates at the local level for deployment at a higher level.

Security templates designed and tested using the Security Configuration and Analysis snap-in or the Security Templates snap-in can be exported, as discussed previously, and applied to a domain or OU using the Active Directory Users and Computers console. Security settings can also be configured directly in a GPO without using security templates; however, this is not recommended except at the lower levels of the OU structure as the administrator finds the need to apply a few specific settings to a specific group of users. Figure 7.36 illustrates the processing order of GPOs from the Local level (first) to the OU level (last).

Figure 7.36 Group Policy Application Order

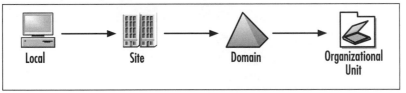

Local   Site   Domain   Organizational
Unit

Exercise 7.07 presents the process to import a security template into an OU level GPO. Exercise 7.08 presents the process to import a security template into a domain level GPO. You can, after you've imported a template, perform further customization if you desire by making edits directly in the Group Policy windows that you will have open while performing Exercise 7.07 and 7.08.

EXERCISE 7.07

IMPORTING SECURITY TEMPLATES AT THE OU LEVEL

1. Open the **Active Directory Users and Computers** console from the Administrative Tools menu. Right-click an OU and select **Properties** from the context menu.

2. The OUs Properties dialog box appears. Click the **Group Policy** tab, seen in Figure 7.37.

3. Click **New** to create a new GPO. Type a name for the GPO, such as **SecurityPolicy**. Make sure that the new object is selected then click **Edit**.

4. Expand **Computer Configuration**, and then expand **Windows Settings**. There are two subnodes of Windows Settings: Scripts and Security Settings.

5. Right-click the **Security Settings** node, seen in Figure 7.38, and select **Import Policy** from the context menu. The Import Policy From dialog box, seen in Figure 7.39, opens.

Figure 7.37 The Group Policy Tab of the OU Dialog Box

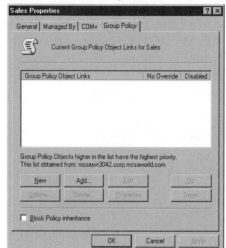

Figure 7.38 Group Policy Security Settings Node

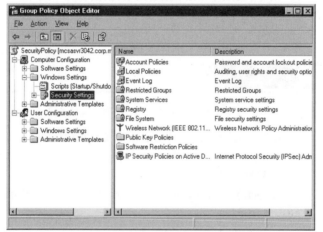

Figure 7.39 Locating the Security Policy to Import

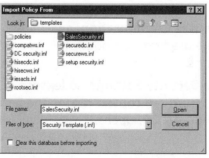

6. Notice that the policies are security template files with the .inf extension. You have the option of merging the template's entries into the present OUs security setup, or you can clear the present OUs security settings and have them replaced by the settings in the imported template. Select the security template desired and click **Open**. You are not given the option to test the template settings against the present OUs security configuration. The settings are enabled after you import the policy via the .inf file.

7. Close all windows back to the Active Directory Users and Computers console.

8. To immediately refresh Group Policy, run the **gpupdate /target:computer** command to force a Group Policy update.

Now let's look at applying a security template at the domain level. As seen in Exercise 7.08, the process is fairly similar between the two procedures, with the primary difference being the location at which the policy is imported. Additionally, the network administrator will (in most cases) need to allow a longer time for policy replication at the domain level as compared to policy replication for those computers in an OU.

EXERCISE 7.08

IMPORTING SECURITY TEMPLATES AT THE DOMAIN LEVEL

1. Open the **Active Directory Users and Computers** console from the Administrative Tools menu. Right-click the **domain** node and select **Properties** from the context menu.

2. The domain's properties dialog box appears. Click the **Group Policy** tab.

3. Click **New** to create a new GPO. Type a name for the GPO such as **DomainSecurityPolicy**. Make sure that the new object is selected then click **Edit**.

4. Expand **Computer Configuration**, and then expand **Windows Settings**. There are two subnodes of Windows Settings: Scripts and Security Settings.

5. Right-click the **Security Settings** node and select **Import Policy** from the context menu. The Import Policy From dialog box opens.

6. Notice that the policies are security template files with the .inf extension. You have the option of merging the template's entries into the

present OUs security setup, or you can clear the present OUs security settings and have them replaced by the settings in the imported template. Select the security template desired and click **Open**. You are not given the option to test the template settings against the present OUs security configuration. The settings are enabled after you import the policy via the .inf file.

7. Close all windows back to the Active Directory Users and Computers console.

8. To immediately refresh Group Policy, run the **gpupdate /target:computer** command to force a Group Policy update.

Of course, configuring and implementing a security solution is only the first part of maintaining security for a network. The network administrator must now monitor and maintain network security—auditing can play a vital role in this process. Auditing in Windows Server 2003 is examined in the next section.

EXAM
70-292

OBJECTIVE
6.1
6.1.1

Auditing Security Events

Implementing a security solution is only the first step in maintaining security for a network. The network administrator will next need to perform auditing on the network to determine exactly what is occurring on a daily basis. Auditing in Windows Server 2003 is, for the most part, a fairly easy thing to configure; however, it does require appropriate planning to ensure that the administrator's intentions and end results are in agreement.

Auditing can be a one- or two-part process, depending on what is being audited. To audit system events such as user logins and privilege use, the administrator only needs to configure the appropriate auditing categories. To audit object access, the administrator needs to first enable this setting and then configure auditing specifically on the object. Both types of auditing are examined in the following sections. However, auditing is not something to jump into without proper research and planning. A network administrator must first understand that they can configure auditing to occur at the same levels as they can apply a GPO to. This is an important point to remember when creating an auditing plan.

Auditing Areas

It is important to understand the different areas that Windows Server 2003 provides for auditing network events before an auditing solution can be successfully planned or implemented. The following auditing options are available, as seen in Figure 7.40:

- Audit account logon events
- Audit account management

- Audit directory service access

- Audit logon events

- Audit object access

- Audit policy change

- Audit privilege use

- Audit process tracking

- Audit system events

Figure 7.40 Audit Policy Options

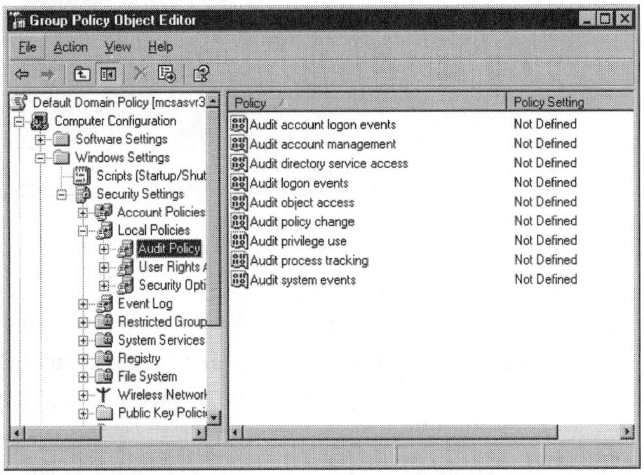

Each of these auditing areas are examined in more detail in the following sections.

TEST DAY TIP

The following lists of auditing events are, for the most part, all inclusive and are designed to serve more as a resource for the administrator than something that you should be overly worried about committing to memory for test day.

Audit Account Logon Events

The *Audit account logon events* option allows the network administrator to configure auditing to occur upon each instance of a user logging on or off the network. A success audit generates an audit entry when a user successfully logs in, and a failure audit generates an entry when a user unsuccessfully attempts to log in.

Typical events that might occur as a result of configuring account logon event auditing include:

- **672** An authentication service (AS) ticket was successfully issued and validated

- **673** A ticket granting service (TGS) ticket was granted

- **674** A security principal renewed an AS ticket or TGS ticket

- **675** Pre-authentication failed

- **676** Authentication Ticket Request Failed

- **677** A TGS ticket was not granted

- **678** An account was successfully mapped to a domain account

- **680** Identifies the account used for the successful logon attempt

- **681** A domain account log on was attempted

- **682** A user has reconnected to a disconnected Terminal Services session

- **683** A user disconnected a Terminal Services session without logging off

Audit Account Management

The *Audit account management* option allows the administrator to configure auditing to occur for each account management event on a computer. Some typical account management events might include actions such as creating a new user account, creating a new group, renaming a user account, disabling a user account, and setting or changing a password. A success audit generates an audit entry when any account management event is successful, and a failure audit generates an entry when any account management event fails.

Typical events that might occur as a result of configuring account management event auditing include:

- **624** User account created

- **627** Password change attempted

- **628** User account password set

- **630** User account deleted

- **631** Security-enabled global group created

- **632** Security-enabled global group member added

- **633** Security-enabled global group member removed

- **634** Security-enabled global group deleted

- **635** Security-disabled local group created

- **636** Security-disabled local group member added

- **637** Security-enabled local group member removed

- **638** Security-enabled local group deleted

- **639** Security-enabled local group changed

- **641** Security-enabled global group changed

- **642** User account changed

- **643** Domain policy changed

- **644** User account locked out

- **645** Computer account created

- **646** Computer account changed

- **647** Computer account deleted

- **648** Local security group with security disabled was created

- **649** Local security group with security disabled was changed

- **650** Member added to a security-disabled local security group

- **651** Member removed from a security-disabled local security group

- **652** Security-disabled local group deleted

- **653** Security-disabled global group created

- **654** Security-disabled global group changed

- **655** Member added to security-disabled global group

- **656** Member removed from security-disabled global group

- **657** Security-disabled global group deleted

- **658** Security-enabled universal group created

- **659** Security-enabled universal group changed

- **660** Member added to security-enabled universal group

- **661** Member removed from security-enabled universal group

- **662** Security-enabled universal group deleted

- **663** Security-disabled universal group created

- **664** Security-disabled universal group changed

- **665** Member added to security-disabled universal group

- **666** Member removed from security-disabled universal group

- **667** Security-disabled universal group deleted

- **668** Group type was changed
- **684** Set security descriptor of members of administrative groups
- **685** Name of account was changed

Audit Directory Service Access

The *Audit directory service access* option allows the network administrator to configure auditing to occur when a user accesses an Active Directory object that has its own system access control list (SACL). Only Active Directory objects, such as GPOs will be audited by this option. A success audit generates an audit entry when a user successfully accesses an Active Directory object that has a SACL specified, and a failure audit generates an entry when an unsuccessful access attempt occurs.

Typical events that might occur as a result of configuring directory service access auditing include:

- **566** A generic object operation took place

Audit Logon Events

The *Audit logon events* option allows the network administrator to configure auditing to occur upon each instance of a user logging on or off a computer. Audit events will be generated on domain controllers for domain accounts and on the local computer for local accounts. If both the Audit Logon Events and the Audit Account Logon Events options are configured, logons and logoffs that use a domain account generate logon or logoff audit events on the local computer as well as the DC. A success audit generates an audit entry when a logon attempt succeeds, and a failure audit generates an audit entry when a logon attempt fails.

Typical events that might occur as a result of configuring logon event auditing include:

- **528** A user successfully logged on to a computer
- **529** A logon attempt was made with an unknown user name or bad password
- **530** The user account tried to log on outside of the allowed time
- **531** A logon attempt was made using a disabled account
- **532** A logon attempt was made using an expired account
- **533** The user is not allowed to log on at this computer
- **534** A user attempted to log on with a logon type that is not allowed for the account
- **535** The password for the specified account has expired
- **536** The Net Logon service is not active

- **537** The log-on attempt failed for other reasons

- **538** A user logged off

- **539** The account was locked out at the time the logon attempt was made

- **540** Successful Network Logon

- **541** Main mode Internet Key Exchange (IKE) authentication completed

- **542** A data channel was terminated

- **543** Main mode was terminated

- **544** Main mode authentication failed because of an invalid certificate

- **545** Main mode authentication failed because of a Kerberos failure or an invalid password

- **546** IKE security association establishment failed because of an invalid proposal

- **547** Failure occurred during an IKE handshake

- **548** Logon failure – SID from trusted domain does not match the client's account domain SID

- **549** Logon failure – untrusted namespace SIDs were filtered out during cross-forest authentication

- **550** Possible Denial of Service (DoS) attack in progress

- **551** User initiated the logoff process

- **552** User successfully logged on to a computer while already logged on as a different user

- **682** User has reconnected to a disconnected Terminal Services session

- **683** User disconnected a Terminal Services session without logging off

Audit Object Access

The *Audit object access* option allows the network administrator to configure auditing to occur upon each instance of user access to an object, such as a file, folder, printer, or registry key that has its own SACL configured. To configure auditing for object access, the administrator also needs to configure auditing specifically on each object they want to perform auditing on. A success audit generates an audit entry when a user successfully accesses an object, and a failure audit generates an audit entry when a user unsuccessfully attempts to access an object.

Typical events that might occur as a result of configuring object access auditing include:

- **560** Access granted to an existing object

- **562** Handle to an object was closed

- **563** Attempt made to open an object to delete it
- **564** Protected object deleted
- **565** Access granted to an existing object type
- **567** Permission associated with a handle used
- **568** Attempt made to create a hard link to a file that is being audited
- **569** Resource manager in Authorization Manager attempted to create a client context
- **570** Client attempted to access an object
- **571** Client context deleted by the Authorization Manager application
- **572** Administrator manager initialized the application
- **772** Certificate manager denied a pending certificate request
- **773** Certificate Services received a resubmitted certificate request
- **774** Certificate Services revoked a certificate
- **775** Certificate Services received a request to publish the certificate revocation list
- **776** Certificate Services published the certificate revocation list
- **777** Certificate request extension was made
- **778** One or more certificate request attributes changed
- **779** Certificate Services received a request to shutdown
- **780** Certificate Services backup started
- **781** Certificate Services backup completed
- **782** Certificate Services restore started
- **783** Certificate Services restore completed
- **784** Certificate Services started
- **785** Certificate Services stopped
- **786** Security permissions for Certificate Services changed
- **787** Certificate Services retrieved an archived key
- **788** Certificate Services imported a certificate
- **789** Audit filter for Certificate Services changed
- **790** Certificate Services received a certificate request
- **791** Certificate Services approved a certificate request and issued a certificate
- **792** Certificate Services denied a certificate request

- **793** Certificate Services set the status of a certificate request to pending

- **794** Certificate manager settings for Certificate Services changed

- **795** Configuration entry changed in Certificate Services

- **796** Property of Certificate Services changed

- **797** Certificate Services archived a key

- **798** Certificate Services imported and archived a key

- **799** Certificate Services published the CA certificate to Active Directory

- **800** One or more rows have been deleted from the certificate database

- **801** Role separation enabled for Certificate Services

Audit Policy Change

The *Audit policy change* option allows the network administrator to configure auditing to occur upon every occurrence of changing a user rights assignment policy, audit policy, IPSec policy, or trust policy. A success audit generates an audit entry when a change to one of these policies is successful, and a failure audit generates an audit entry when a change to one of these policies fails.

Typical events that might occur as a result of configuring audit policy change auditing include:

- **610** Trust relationship with another domain created

- **611** Trust relationship with another domain was removed

- **612** Audit policy was changed

- **613** Internet Protocol security (IPSec) policy agent started

- **614** IPSec policy agent was disabled

- **615** IPSec policy agent changed

- **616** IPSec policy agent encountered a potentially serious failure

- **617** Kerberos policy changed

- **618** Encrypted Data Recovery policy changed

- **620** Trust relationship with another domain was modified

- **621** System access was granted to an account

- **622** System access was removed from an account

- **623** Per user auditing policy was set for a user

- **625** Per user auditing policy was refreshed

- **768** Collision detected between a namespace element in one forest and a namespace element in another forest

- **769** Trusted forest information was added

- **770** Trusted forest information was deleted

- **771** Trusted forest information was modified

- **805** Event log service read the security log configuration for a session

Audit Privilege Use

The *Audit privilege use* option allows the network administrator to configure auditing to occur upon every occurrence of a user exercising a user right. A success audit generates an audit entry when the exercise of a user right succeeds, and a failure audit generates an audit entry when the exercise of a user right fails.

Typical events that might occur as a result of configuring audit privilege use auditing include:

- **576** Specified privileges were added to a user's access token

- **577** A user attempted to perform a privileged system service operation

- **578** Privileges were used on an already open handle to a protected object

Audit Process Tracking

The *Audit process tracking* option allows the network administrator to configure auditing to occur upon every occurrence of events such as program activation, process exit, handle duplication, and indirect object access. A success audit generates an audit entry when the process being tracked succeeds, and a failure audit generates an audit entry when the process being tracked fails.

Typical events that might occur as a result of configuring audit process tracking auditing include:

- **592** A new process was created

- **593** A process existed

- **594** A handle to an object was duplicated

- **595** Indirect access to an object was obtained

- **596** A data protection master key was backed up

- **597** A data protection master key was recovered from a recovery server

- **598** Auditable data was protected

- **599** Auditable data was unprotected

- **600** A process was assigned a primary token
- **601** A user attempted to install a service
- **602** A scheduler job was created

Audit System Events

The *Audit system events* option allows the network administrator to configure auditing to occur upon every occurrence of certain system events occur such as computer restarts and shutdowns. A successful audit generates an audit entry when a system event is executed successfully, and a failure audit generates an audit entry when a system event is attempted unsuccessfully.

Typical events that might occur as a result of configuring audit system events auditing include:

- **512** Windows is starting up
- **513** Windows is shutting down
- **514** An authentication package was loaded by the Local Security Authority
- **515** A trusted logon process has registered with the Local Security Authority
- **516** Internal resources allocated for the queuing of security event messages have been exhausted
- **517** The audit log was cleared
- **518** A notification package was loaded by the Security Accounts Manager
- **519** A process is using an invalid local procedure call port in an attempt to impersonate a client
- **520** The system time was changed

TEST DAY TIP

While you do not need to memorize all of the auditing event IDs presented here, you should become familiar with them. You may be presented with some general auditing questions dealing with types of entries that can be written to the security log.

Planning for Auditing

While auditing is actually a simple thing to implement, it does require a fair amount of planning in order to perform as intended. Microsoft provides some basic auditing best practices as recommended considerations for any administrator preparing to configure auditing for their network.

- **Create a detailed auditing plan *before* you start to plan an auditing solution** What exactly are you trying to audit for? Are you auditing for unsuccessful user access to unauthorized resources? Perhaps you are auditing for unauthorized network access attempts that might indicate a network attack is under way? You may have an entirely different goal in mind for your auditing plan. No matter what you are trying to audit for, you need to first well define it before you can plan to audit for it.

- **Audit for success and failure events in system events** Auditing of system events will allow a network administrator to quickly track any unusual activity that could be indicative of an attacker trying to gain access to a network or compromise computers on a network.

- **Audit for success events on domain controllers in account logon events** By auditing successful account logon events the network administrator will be able to determine when users are logging on and off the network. This can be useful to determine if users are accessing the network at odd hours, which might indicate illicit activities on their part or by an attacker who has gained a set of network credentials.

- **Audit for success events in policy change events** By auditing successful policy change events you will be able to track whom is changing items—and thereby determine if unauthorized users are making policy changes.

- **Audit for success events in account management events** By auditing successful account management events a network administrator can verify that the changes they made were successful. Failure auditing can be done for short periods of time without degrading system performance to look for specific activity, but should not normally be done for a long duration.

- **Audit object access on specific objects of interest** Configure object access auditing on only the objects you are concerned with. If you only need to audit access to a specific file, do not audit access to the entire folder. If you only want to audit for read access, do not audit for full control. Configuring object access auditing in this way will greatly cut down on extraneous audit entries you will have to filter through to locate what you are concerned with.

- **Examine logs from a single location** It is impractical to visit computers locally and examine their audit logs except in the smallest of networks. Several third-party applications exist that can examine all logs on the network from a single computer. Microsoft also provides two freely available applications. EventCombMT, a graphical log analysis tool, can be downloaded from www.microsoft.com/technet/security/prodtech/windows/secwin2k. DumpEL, a command line log analysis tool, can best be found by searching for it at the Microsoft Downloads Center located at www.microsoft.com/downloads.

Configuring and Implementing Auditing

You are now ready to configure and implement an auditing solution. You may want to create a completely new security template for the purpose of implementing auditing or you may want to directly configure auditing in an existing GPO. Exercise 7.09 outlines the process to configure auditing by using a new security template created expressly for this purpose.

EXERCISE 7.09

CONFIGURING AND IMPLEMENTING AN AUDITING SOLUTION

1. Open the custom security management console that was created in Exercise 7.01.

2. Create a new security template by right-clicking the storage location node (i.e. E:\windows\security\templates) and selecting **New Template** from the context menu.

3. Enter a name for the new security template.

4. Expand the nodes in the new security template to the Audit Policy node, as seen in Figure 7.41.

Figure 7.41 Locating the Auditing Options

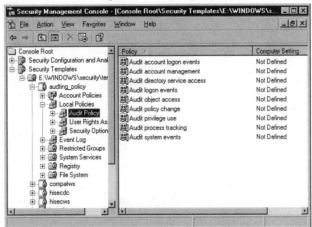

5. Open the auditing options that you wish to configure auditing for by double-clicking them. For example, if you want to configure Audit account logon events, open its Properties dialog box and select the **Define These Policy Settings** in the **Template** option as well as **Success and Failure**, as seen in Figure 7.42. Click **OK** to accept your configuration.

Figure 7.42 Configuring Account Logon Event Auditing

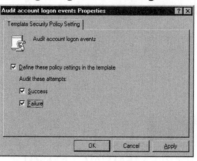

6. After you have completed configuring your desired auditing options, save the template by right-clicking it in the left pane and selecting **Save** from the context menu.

7. Open the **Active Directory Users and Computers** console and select a new or existing GPO to import this security template into.

8. Import the security policy as discussed previously in Exercise 7.07 for an OU or Exercise 7.08 for a domain.

9. If you will be auditing object access, right-click on the object (files, folders, printers, etc.) and select **Properties** from the context menu.

10. Switch to the **Security** tab, as seen in Figure 7.43, and click the **Advanced** button to open the Advanced Security Settings dialog box.

Figure 7.43 Configuring the Security Properties of an Object

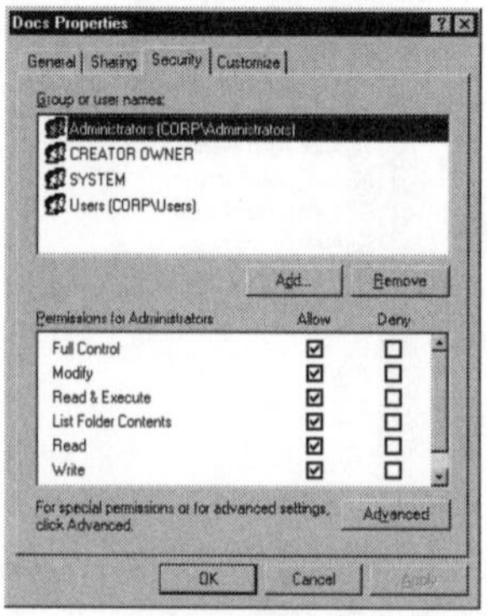

11. Switch to the **Auditing tab,** as seen in Figure 7.44.

Figure 7.44 Configuring Object Access Auditing

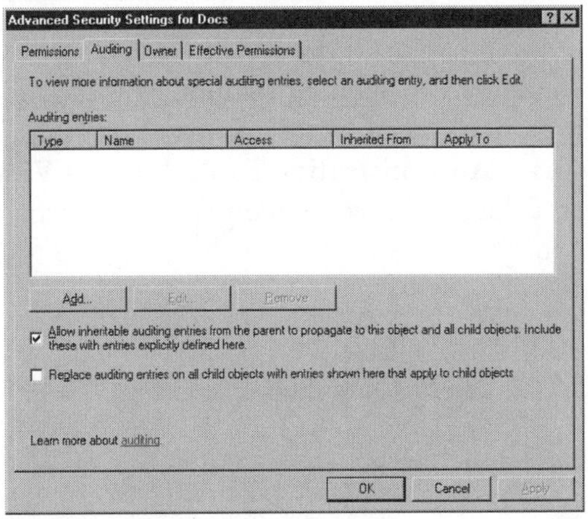

12. Click the **Add** button to open the Select User or Group dialog box from which you can select the users and groups that you want to audit object access for. If you need to audit multiple users or groups, you should configure them in as few auditing entries as possible. Also, if you need to audit the actions of all users, you should configure auditing for the Everyone group for best performance. After you have configured the desired users and groups, click **OK** to continue.

13. When the Auditing Entry dialog box appears, seen in Figure 7.45, select what success or failure events you want to audit for on the selected object. Make your selections and then click **OK** to confirm them.

Figure 7.45 Configuring Object Access Auditing

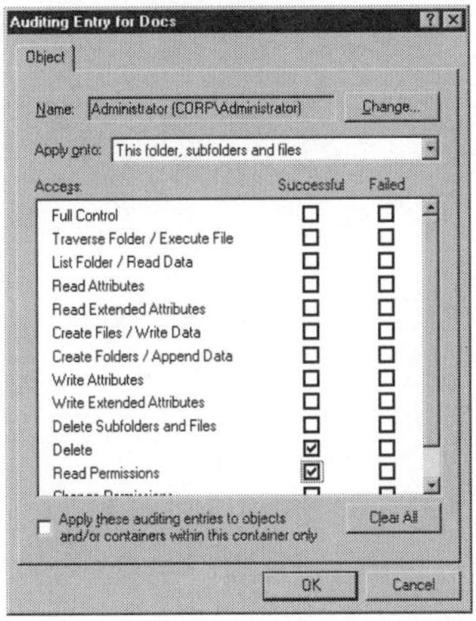

14. Close the remaining dialog boxes, and you are done configuring auditing.

Now that you have configured an auditing solution, you should test it to see how it works. You will find audit entries located in the Security Log of the Event Viewer by clicking **Start | Programs | Administrative Tools | Event Viewer**. Items with a closed lock icon indicate a failure audit while items with a key icon indicate a success audit, as seen in Figure 7.46.

Figure 7.46 Examining the Security Logs

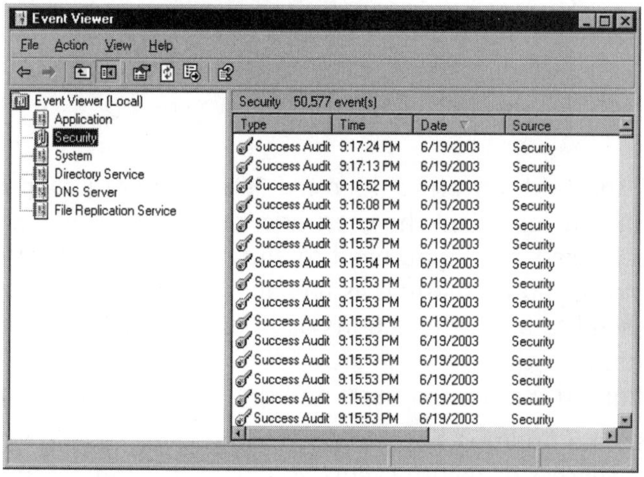

Summary of Exam Objectives

The Security Configuration Manager tool set introduces a new and more efficient way to manage security parameters in Windows Server 2003. Using this new set of configuration and management tools, the administrator can configure and manage the security policies for a single machine or an entire domain or OU. The tool set includes the Security Configuration and Analysis snap-in, the Security Templates snap-in, the secedit.exe command line tool, and the security settings extensions to the Group Policy Editor. Together, these tools can be used to create and configure security policies for local machines, domains, or OUs.

The Security Configuration and Analysis snap-in allows the administrator to create a database with security configuration entries. These security configuration entries can be used to test against the existing security configuration of a local machine. After the security analysis is complete, the network manager can save the database entries into a text file with the .inf extension. This text file, which is a template consisting of security configuration entries, can be saved or imported in order to define the security definition of another local machine, a domain, or an OU. The security variables in the database can also be applied to the local machine, replacing the current security configuration. The new configuration is applied after the analysis is complete.

Security configurations can be saved as templates, which are text files that contain security configuration information. These templates are imported into the Security Configuration and Analysis snap-in database for analysis and application. The Security Configuration and Analysis snap-in cannot be used to configure or analyze security configurations of a domain or OU. At present, there is no way to export extant domain or OU security configurations. However, you can configure the security of a domain or OU via the security settings Group Policy extensions.

The secedit.exe command line tool allows the administrator to script security analyses, security configurations, security updates, and export of templates. Its functionality is almost equal to that of the Security Configuration and Analysis snap-in, except that the administrator must use the graphical interface to review the results of a security analysis performed by secedit.exe.

An administrator can use the security settings Group Policy extensions to configure domain or OU security policy. In addition, they can import security templates directly into the domain or OU. The network administrator should do this with great caution if they have already customized the security settings for a domain or OU. At present, an administrator cannot export the previous settings into a template that might be restored later. However, if the administrator always reconfigures the security parameters of a domain or OU by using templates, such templates can always be restored in the future.

Even after all of the work to configure and implement a solid security solution is done, no solution is perfect or all-inclusive. Auditing is a required part of maintaining network security that cannot be overlooked and can help detect unauthorized or abnormal network activities early before they have a chance to become a successful attack that could have catastrophic effects on the network. A careful balance must be maintained between too much and too little auditing, however, or else the network administrator will have too many audit entries to search through or too few audit entries to provide any useful information.

Exam Objectives Fast Track

Implementing Security with Security Templates

☑ The key components of the Security Configuration Manager tool set are: the Security Configuration and Analysis snap-in, the Security Templates snap-in, the Group Policy security extensions, and the secedit.exe command.

☑ The Security Configuration and Analysis snap-in creates, configures, and tests security scenarios. You can create text-based .INF files that contain security settings. You can apply these files to the computer or save them for later use.

☑ Microsoft provides templates for configuring security. Default and incremental templates are available. Default templates are applied during a fresh install only. The incremental templates provide additional security above the defaults.

☑ Secedit.exe allows us to configure security from the command prompt.

☑ The Security Templates snap-in allows us to view and customize the template files stored in **%windir%\security\templates**.

☑ Account policies define password policy, account lockout policy, and Kerberos policy.

☑ Local policies include the audit policy, user rights assignment, and security options.

☑ Event Log configuration settings allow you to configure the length of time logs are retained as well as the size of the event logs.

☑ The Restricted Groups setting configures group membership and group nesting.

☑ Registry Policy sets permissions on Registry keys.

☑ The File System Security setting configures NTFS permission for all local drives.

☑ The System Services setting controls the startup policy for all local services.

☑ The Security Configuration and Analysis snap-in can be used to deploy a security template to a local machine.

☑ Security settings can be deployed to a domain or OU by using the security settings in a GPO.

☑ You can deploy security templates across the network by making use of the secedit.exe tool in a script or batch file.

☑ Compare security policies in the template with the actual state of the local machine. This practice allows you to see the differences before they apply the policy.

☑ Use Security Configuration and Analysis to view the results of an analysis in a graphical format.

☑ Use the secedit.exe tool to analyze security settings from the command prompt. This can be useful if combined with a script or batch file to automatically scan large numbers of computers.

☑ After differences in settings have been identified you can determine the next course of action.

Auditing Security Events

☑ Auditing is the process of analyzing gathered data for the purpose of determining a possible problem, or in the security arena, an attack or exploit. Auditing is best used on any system that can generate some type of log file that can be saved, referred to, and analyzed. Auditing is the process of logging and analyzing events that occur to proactively find and eliminate problems like attacks, hacking, or mischief.

☑ An audit can either be for success or failure of a specific event. The network administrator must plan accordingly for what they are hoping to learn about the network in order to determine what type of auditing to configure.

☑ The Audit account management option allows the network administrator to configure auditing to occur for each account management event on a computer. Some typical account management events might include actions such as creating a new user account, creating a new group, renaming a user account, disabling a user account, and setting or changing a password.

☑ The Audit directory service access option allows the network administrator to configure auditing to occur when a user accesses an Active Directory object that has its own SACL. Only Active Directory objects such as GPOs will be audited by this option.

☑ The Audit logon events option allows the network administrator to configure auditing to occur upon each instance of a user logging on or off a computer. Audit events will be generated on domain controllers for domain accounts and on the local computer for local accounts. If both the Audit Logon Events and the Audit Account Logon Events options are configured, logons and logoffs that use a domain account generate logon or logoff audit events on the local computer as well as the domain controller.

☑ The Audit logon events option allows the network administrator to configure auditing to occur upon each instance of user access to an object, such as a file, folder, printer, or registry key that has its own SACL configured. To configure auditing for object access, the network administrator also needs to configure auditing specifically on each object they want to perform auditing on.

☑ The Audit policy change option allows the network administrator to configure auditing to occur upon every occurrence of changing a user rights assignment policy, audit policy, IPSec policy, or trust policy.

☑ The Audit privilege use option allows the network administrator to configure auditing to occur upon every occurrence of a user exercising a user right.

☑ The Audit process tracking option allows the network administrator to configure auditing to occur upon every occurrence of events such as program activation, process exit, handle duplication, and indirect object access.

☑ The Audit process tracking option allows the network administrator to configure auditing to occur upon every occurrence of certain system events such as computer restarts and shutdowns.

Exam Objectives Frequently Asked Questions

The following Frequently Asked Questions, answered by the authors of this book, are designed to both measure your understanding of the Exam Objectives presented in this chapter, and to assist you with real-life implementation of these concepts. You will also gain access to thousands of other FAQs at ITFAQnet.com.

Q: Can I use the Security Configuration and Analysis snap-in to analyze the security configuration of a domain or OU?

A: Not at this time. This capability should be added in the future. However, at present, you can test scenarios against the current configuration for the local machine.

Q: I would like to use scripts to analyze a number of computers in my domain. What tool would I use to accomplish this task?

A: The secedit.exe command line tool allows the administrator to analyze a number of machines by creating scripts that can be automated. You can then view the results of the analysis by opening the database file against which the analysis was run.

Q: Why have the changes I made to the security policy on the local computer not taken effect?

A: Effective policy depends on whether a computer is a member of a domain or an OU. Policy precedence flows in the order in which policies are applied. First the local policy is applied, then site policy is applied, then domain policy is applied, and finally OU policy is applied. If there are conflicts among the policies, the last policy applied prevails.

Q: Can I migrate my existing Windows NT 4.0 policies to Windows Server 2003?

A: No. The NT policies were stored in a .POL file, which included things such as group memberships. There is no way for the Windows Server 2003 Group Policy model, which is centered on Active Directory, to interpret the entries in the .POL file. Microsoft recommends configuring the settings in the old .POL files in Active Directory. You can do this easily using the security settings extension to the Group Policy Editor. The Windows NT 4.0 .POL files were created by the System Policy Editor, which used .adm files as templates for the options configured in system policy. These files are compatible with Windows Server 2003 .ADM files. However, you should not import these templates, because you might damage the registries of client machines. This means that after a Registry setting is set using Windows NT 4.0 .ADM files, the setting will persist until the specified policy is reversed or the Registry itself is directly edited.

Q: How do I reverse the changes I made after applying a security policy?

A: There is no direct mechanism, such as an Undo button, that will allow you to reverse the changes. Before you enact any changes to the local computer policy, back up the present configuration by exporting the current settings to an .INF file. Then you can restore your system to its previous state by importing the .inf file into the database and reapplying the changes.

Q: It seems like an awful lot of trouble to go through to configure a template, then analyze it, and then finally deploy it. Wouldn't it just be easier to make the changes directly to the target machine if I know what I am doing and skip the other steps?

A: Yes it would be easier to make the changes directly—until you make a mistake. At that time you may find yourself out of luck and unable to undo the changes you have made. Even though the process seems overly long or complicated, it's really not. In reality, the process of configuring, analyzing, and deploying templates is the best way to go about rolling out even and appropriate security settings for any sized organization.

Q: I need to parse my event logs. I would like to parse my default Event Viewer logs (Security, Application, and System) as well as my DNS logs. I have the dumpel.exe command-line tool but I can't seem to get it to work right. What am I doing wrong?

A: The only thing you are doing wrong is trying to get the DNS log with a tool that will only parse the Security, Application, and System logs. You may want to use the EventCombMT tool instead. It will do all the logs you need to parse.

Q: When performing an Audit, I would like to log when someone on a server uses the command prompt program successfully. This is known as cmd.exe. How would I audit this and get it to show up in the Event Viewer Security log?

A: You would want to Audit process tracking. Process tracking events will provide you with detailed tracking information for events such as program activation, process exit, handle duplication, and indirect object access. If you turn on success-based auditing for process tracking, when someone uses the command prompt, you will get an event in the Event Viewer Security log.

Self Test

A Quick Answer Key follows the Self Test questions. For complete questions, answers, and explanations to the Self Test questions in this chapter as well as the other chapters in this book, see the Self Test Appendix.

Implementing Security with Security Templates

1. You are the security administrator for Catherine's Crab Shack, Inc. You are responsible for analyzing and configuring the security of all Windows XP Professional client computers within the network. You are considering the various tools that are available for you to use. When considering the secedit.exe tool for this task, what specifically can you use it to perform? (Choose all that apply.)

   A. It can be used to list the current Group Policy in effect for a specific user and computer.

   B. It can be used to analyze the security settings of a system.

   C. It can be used to validate the syntax of chosen security template.

   D. It can be used to edit group membership and permissions for a user or group.

   E. It can be used to remotely monitor privilege use.

   F. It can be used to configure system security settings.

   G. It can be used to export the values stored in a database to an .inf file.

2. Andrew must increase the security on the workstations in his network at any cost, preferably achieving the most secure configuration possible. What would be the best template to apply to his workstations to provide the maximum amount of security and what negative side effects can he expect to see from the application of the chosen template? (Choose two correct answers.)

A. hisecdc.inf

B. securews.inf

C. basicsv.inf

D. securedc.inf

E. hisecws.inf

F. He should expect no adverse effects to occur except for potentially increased login and logoff times due to extra policy processing invoked by the more secure template.

G. He should expect to lose network connectivity with all other computers that do not support IPSec.

H. He should expect to have to configure Active Directory integrated zones for his DNS servers to support the newly configured workstations.

3. You are preparing to deploy some custom security templates across your organization in an effort to increase the overall security of the network. You plan on deploying your security templates via Group Policy. What is the correct processing order for Group Policy in Windows Server 2003?

A. Local, Domain, Site, OU

B. Local, Site, Domain, OU

C. Site, Domain, OU, Local

D. Domain, Site, OU, Local

4. You are the security administrator for Catherine's Crab Shack, Inc. You are responsible for analyzing and configuring the security of all Windows XP Professional client computers within the network. You have recently had some problems where computers on your network have failed to start properly due to users making modifications to certain areas of their computer's Registry. You need to secure these areas of the Registry to prevent these occurrences in the future. What can you do to protect these specific areas of the Registry from modification by unauthorized users?

A. Use the secedit.exe utility with the validate switch to set security settings on the Registry keys of concern.

B. Use the regedit application to set security settings on the Registry keys of concern.

C. Use the Security Templates and Security Configuration and Analysis snap-ins to configure, analyze, and implement security settings on the Registry keys of concern.

D. Use Windows Explorer to mark the Registry files as Read Only.

E. Use Windows Explorer to set NTFS permissions on the Registry files so that only authorized users may access them.

5. You want to configure auditing for the workstations in a specific OU in your network. You have opened Security Configuration and Analysis and selected the basicwk.inf template. What section of the template contains the options that you need to configure to enable auditing?

    A. Local Policies

    B. Account Policies

    C. Event Log

    D. Registry

6. You are the security administrator for your company's network. You have 100 Windows Server 2003 and approximately 1,700 Windows XP Professional computers in your organization that you are responsible for that are spread across multiple sites (North America, South America, Europe, Asia) and OUs. You use EventCombMT to collect Event Log data from every computer once a week for analysis by your assistant administrators. You have found that some computers often have less than one week of events in their Event Logs and want to ensure that events are not getting overwritten when the logs have reached their maximum allowed size. You propose to enlarge the maximum log size from the default value of 512kb for the Application Log, System Log and Security Log. How will you go about performing this change and use the least amount of administrative effort?

    A. Instruct each of your assistants to visit each and every computer and make the changes locally.

    B. Configure and test the settings in a security template that is then deployed to the North American site.

    C. Configure and test the settings in a security template that is then deployed at the domain level.

    D. Send an e-mail message to your users instructing them how to make the changes.

7. Austin has been delegated administrative responsibility for several OUs in his department. How can Austin most easily make the same changes to the security settings applied to his OUs?

    A. Austin should configure and test a template on a local machine using Security Configuration and Analysis. When he gets the configuration established that he requires, he should export the template and then import it into the specific OU GPOs he is responsible for.

    B. Austin should use the Security Configuration and Analysis snap-in and target it at the specific OU he wants to work with to make the changes.

    C. Austin should edit the GPOs directly for each of the OUs he is responsible for.

    D. Austin should ask a Domain Administrator to apply the desired settings at the domain level and let them propagate down to his OUs.

8. You have configured and tested two custom security templates for use on your corpo-
    rate network, corpserver.inf and corpdesktop.inf. Your network is running all Windows
    Server 2003 servers and Windows XP Professional workstations and is fragmented into
    three distinct sections due to the extremely high cost of establishing WAN links
    between your three geographical locations. You do have dial-up connectivity between
    the sites using standard POTS lines, but these have proven to be unreliable at best. How
    can you deploy these templates to the other two sites in your network?

    A. You will need to deploy them to two extra domain controllers and then ship one
        each to your other two sites.

    B. You will need to export them from Security Configuration and Analysis and send
        the .inf files to your other two remote sites. Once there, the other two sites can
        import them into the required GPO.

    C. You will need to establish a Frame Relay connection between all three sites at the
        same time and push the templates across the WAN link.

    D. You will need to make a RDP connection to each Domain Controller in the
        remote sites and apply the template to them.

9. You have customized the securews.inf template to include Account Policy settings spe-
    cific to your organizations requirements. At what level should you deploy this cus-
    tomized template to achieve the maximum result? Your network consists of one
    Windows Server 2003 Active Directory domain, spread out over three sites. You have
    approximately 18 OUs in use at the present time.

    A. Domain

    B. Site

    C. Local computer

    D. OU

10. Andrea is the network administrator of 55 Windows XP Professional workstations, 10
    Windows Server 2003 member servers and four Windows Server 2003 domain con-
    trollers. She would like to perform a security analysis on all of her computers without
    having to physically visit each one. How can Andrea accomplish this task?

    A. This cannot be done at the current time. Andrea will need to sit in front of each machine and use the Security Configuration and Analysis snap-in to perform the analysis.

    B. Andrea can target a remote computer by right-clicking on **Security Configuration and Analysis** and selecting **Connect to another computer**.

    C. Andrea can create a script or batch file using the secedit.exe utility with the analyze switch that has an entry for each computer that she wants to analyze.

    D. Andrea can create a script or batch file using the secedit.exe utility with the analyze switch that calls on a pre-populated text file containing the list of computers to be analyzed.

11. Chris is attempting to use the Security Configuration and Analysis snap-in to perform an analysis of one of her member servers. The member server is currently configured with the default settings. She wants to compare its settings with those in the securewk.inf security template. What is the correct order of steps that she needs to perform in order to perform the analysis?

    Step 1: Right-click on **Security Configuration and Analysis** and select **Analyze computer now**.

    Step 2: Right-click on **Security Configuration and Analysis** and select **Open database**.

    Step 3: Select the security template to be used in the analysis.

    Step 4: Select the log file to be used in the analysis.

    Step 5: Right-click on **Security Configuration and Analysis** and select **Configure computer now**.

    Step 6: Select the database to be used in the analysis.

    A. 2, 1, 3, 6, 4

    B. 1, 6, 4, 5, 3

    C. 2, 6, 4, 3, 1

    D. 2, 6, 3, 1, 4

    E. 1, 6, 3, 2, 4

12. You have just completed an analysis of your local computer using Security Configuration and Analysis. When looking at the analysis results, you notice several icons have a green check mark on them. You are concerned that your settings do not match those of the template you compared your computer to. What do icons with green check marks mean?

A. A discrepancy exists between the database settings and the computer setting.

B. No analysis was performed for this item because it was not configured in the database.

C. The database setting and the computer setting match.

D. No analysis was performed for this item because it is not applicable to the computer.

Auditing Security Events

13. Jake is responsible for six Windows Server 2003 computers in his organization. He has noticed that lately there are multiple login attempts on the main file server. What can Jake do to find out if in fact his system is trying to be exploited by a possible attacker? (Choose all that apply.)

A. Use DumpEL to find the attack IDs numbered 200–600 in the System Event Log. This will indicate a possible attack.

B. Turn on success and failure auditing for Logon events. Check the Application Log daily for possible password cracking attacks

C. Set up a Windows Server 2003 security template that will only allow for registered IP's to connect to and communicate with the file server.

D. Configure your router to only let the file server NetBIOS name be authenticated for communication

14. Stan is the network administrator responsible for 10 Windows Server 2003 computers and 400 Windows XP Professional workstations that are separated geographically across four sites: NY, LA, ATL and CHI. Stan is tasked with auditing two of the Windows XP Professional Workstations because the owners of these two workstations are complaining that each time they work on their workstations, they think someone has tried to log in to them. From the list below, what is the most logical way to audit the two workstations so that you can analyze if an attack is actually trying to be performed?

A. Use the Local Security policy on each local workstation and Audit Logon events (success and failure).

B. Use the GPO Security policy on the NY OU and Audit Logon events (success and failure).

C. Use the Local Security policy on the Domain Controller and Audit Logon events (success and failure).

D. Use the Local Security policy on the Domain and Audit Logon events (success and failure).

15. Chris is the administrator of a large Windows Server 2003 network. The company that he works for is a leading provider of state-of-the-art rocket propulsion systems that are used by several countries in their space-going rockets. Company policy states that the network access attempts of all temporary employees are to be tracked, regardless of what workstation they logon to. What auditing options does Chris need to configure to ensure that he can track the access of all temporary employees? (Choose two correct options.)

    A. Audit logon events

    B. Audit privilege use

    C. Audit system events

    D. Audit account logon events

16. Jon is the administrator for a large Windows Server 2003 network for a company that is involved in high-level genetics research. All data transmissions within the company are secured by using IPSec. Recently IPSec communications have intermittently begun to fail as a result of the configured IPSec policies having been changed. Jon needs to determine who is changing the IPSec policies on his network. What should Jon configure auditing for?

    A. Audit privilege use

    B. Audit system events

    C. Audit policy change

    D. Audit process tracking

Self Test Quick Answer Key

For complete questions, answers, and explanations to the Self Test questions in this chapter as well as the other chapters in this book, see the Self Test Appendix.

1.	**B, C, F, G**	9.	**A**
2.	**E, G**	10.	**C**
3.	**B**	11.	**D**
4.	**C**	12.	**C**
5.	**A**	13.	**B**
6.	**C**	14.	**A**
7.	**A**	15.	**A, D**
8.	**B**	16.	**C**

Chapter 8

MCSA/MCSE 70-292

Managing and Implementing Software Updates

Exam Objectives in this Chapter:

3.1 Manage software update infrastructure

6.2 Install and configure software update infrastructure

6.2.1 Install and configure software update services

6.2.2 Install and configure automatic client update settings

6.2.3 Configure software updates on earlier operating systems

☑ Summary of Exam Objectives

☑ Exam Objectives Fast Track

☑ Exam Objectives Frequently Asked Questions

☑ Self Test

☑ Self Test Quick Answer Key

Introduction

An important part of the daily job of a Windows Server 2003 network administrator is to keep the network's servers and client computers up-to-date with required security updates and other patches. Not long ago, this required the use of a third-party solution or Microsoft's own Systems Management Server (SMS) 2.0. However, times have changed for the better; if an entire network is composed of Windows 2000 or higher computers the network administrator can quickly and easily implement Software Update Services (SUS) to keep their computers up-to-date.

SUS is one part of a two-part solution. When paired with the required version of the Automatic Updates client software, SUS acts like a local Windows Update Web server by providing required updates and patches to clients from inside the network. It is not by accident that SUS looks and feels almost identical to Windows Update—Microsoft relied on the Windows Update code extensively when it created and released SUS to the public in 2002. This chapter examines the installation, configuring, and usage of SUS and Automatic Updates both on the server side and on the client side of a network. This chapter also discusses the choices available to keep the legacy network clients up-to-date with required patches and updates.

EXAM 70-292
OBJECTIVE 6.2
Installing, Configuring, and Managing the Software Update Infrastructure

Windows Server 2003 provides native support for SUS, however, it does not include SUS by default. Therefore the network administrator will need to download and install SUS on their server before they can get started. Is it worth the trouble and effort to implement an SUS server? Why not just continue to use the existing methods already in place? The answer to this question varies depending on the size, complexity, and operating system makeup of the organization. If an administrator already has a complex solution utilizing a third-party product or SMS in place, they might not want to make the move to SUS. If they do not have a high-quality solution or have no solution at all, then SUS is most likely what they have been waiting for.

SUS provides the ability to centralize the deployment of all *approved* updates to Windows 2000 or better clients. The network administrator has full control over which of the available updates actually become approved updates and therefore can be downloaded and installed on the client computers. Now instead of the client computers directly contacting the Windows Update Web servers either manually or via the Automatic Updates client, they can be pointed to the internal SUS server. The ability to house their own internal Windows Update servers can be a tremendous benefit to network administrators in terms of decreased bandwidth usage, if the majority of their clients are in one location. Even if the administrator has network clients spread all over the globe, they can still use

SUS to provide a framework in which their clients will still only download and install those updates that they have approved beforehand. SUS can also be configured to not download any updates locally and instead point clients to the Windows Update Web servers to acquire those updates that were previously approved for installation on the network.

EXAM WARNING

It is important to understand that SUS can scale to any size Windows Server 2003 network. Options such as the ability to leave updates on the Windows Update Web servers and the ability to have SUS server synchronizing available updates from other SUS servers allow for a greater amount of flexibility and control over the final design. Don't get trapped in the mindset that every SUS server is its own island—when implemented properly, they can be used to create a large area solution.

EXAM 70-292
OBJECTIVE 6.2.1

Installing Software Update Services

Before a network administrator can use SUS with the Automatic Updates client, they need to download and install the required files. The SUS installer, the updated Automatic Updates client, and several useful whitepapers on SUS and Automatic Updates can be found at www.microsoft.com/windows2000/windowsupdate/sus/default.asp. The SUS application must be installed regardless of which operating system the server is running. For this instance we will assume that a Windows Server 2003 is being used. Depending on the Service Pack level installed on the client computers, the administrator may or may not need to install an updated Automatic Updates client. They will need to have their clients at the following Service Pack level to avoid installing the Automatic Updates client:

- Windows 2000 Service Pack 3 (or higher)
- Windows XP Service Pack 1 (or higher)
- Windows Server 2003 RTM (no Service Pack required)

The server that SUS will be installed on must meet the following requirements:

- Pentium III 700MHz or higher CPU
- 512MB RAM
- 6GB free disk space on an NT File System (NTFS) formatted partition
- System partition must be formatted with NTFS
- IIS 6.0 must be installed and operational

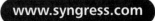

New & Noteworthy...

SUS Fits Your Network!

On many of the Windows administrator's discussion lists I monitor, a common complaint is about the Automatic Updates feature of Windows. It seems that a large number of administrators do not like Automatic Updates and, in fact, consider it to be about as useful as the Windows Licensing Service (a topic for another discussion on another day). Why so many people dislike Automatic Updates is not a mystery to me; however, they have most likely never properly installed and configured SUS within their network to make the Automatic Updates client useful.

In its default configuration, Automatic Updates is indeed a pain in the neck. It is enabled by default, and while it does not automatically download and install any updates, it does notify users about updates that are available to be downloaded and installed by using an icon in the system tray next to the clock. In addition to this, many administrators do not approve of the extra (and uncontrolled) traffic out of the network that the Automatic Updates client initiates. The typical solution that most administrators implement is to disable the Automatic Updates client. A better solution is to install and properly configure an SUS-based solution that not only eliminates the undesirable parts of Automatic Updates in its default form, but also provides an efficient and easy-to-manage means of keeping the network clients up to date.

SUS is currently at Service Pack 1, which now allows it to be installed on domain controllers—a feature missing in the initial release of SUS. This allows SUS to be installed in any network, even one that is using Small Business Server (SBS) instead of a full-featured version of Windows Server 2003. You do not have to have a dedicated IIS server for SUS; however, depending on the size and complexity of your internal network, you may experience better performance by creating one or more dedicated SUS servers. You can save money by purchasing licenses for Windows Server 2003 Web Edition and using these servers for your SUS solution.

Exercise 8.01 outlines the process to install and configure the SUS server for a network.

EXERCISE 8.01

INSTALLING AND CONFIGURING SUS

1. Ensure that IIS 6.0 is installed and operational. Refer to Chapter 4 for information on IIS.

2. Double-click the **SUS installation file** to begin the installation on your new SUS server.

3. The Microsoft Software Update Services Setup Wizard opens. Click **Next** to dismiss the opening page of the Wizard.

4. After reading the End-User License Agreement, select **I accept the terms in the License Agreement** and click **Next** to continue. You must agree to the terms in order to continue the installation of SUS.

5. In the Choose Setup Type dialog box, click the **Custom** button to allow you to configure the location to which the update files will be saved on the local network.

6. In the Choose file locations dialog box, as seen in Figure 8.1, you have the opportunity to select a local network location for the SUS files or to leave them on the Windows Update Web servers and simply direct Automatic Updates clients towards the Windows Update servers. The default location of C:\SUS\content (depending on the volume that you have Windows Server 2003 installed on) is sufficient in most cases. Click **Next** after making your selection.

Figure 8.1 Selecting the Location to Store the SUS Update Files

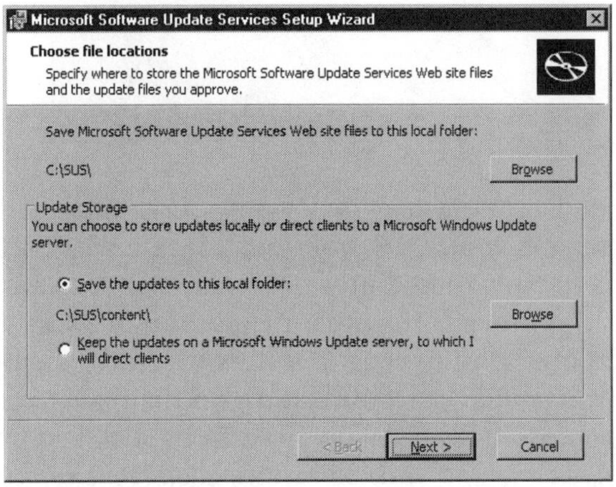

![Microsoft Software Update Services Setup Wizard - Choose file locations dialog box showing options to save Web site files to C:\SUS\ and update storage options with "Save the updates to this local folder: C:\SUS\content\" selected]

 EXAM WARNING

Remember that you can point your Automatic Updates clients directly to the Microsoft Windows Update Web servers or to another internal SUS server if desired. This may be a useful configuration in cases where you have a large, geographically dispersed network and need to reduce loading on a specific portion of the network.

7. In the Language Settings dialog box, as seen in Figure 8.2, select the languages that you want SUS to download updates for. The default **All available languages** download updates for all language versions of Windows is not the recommended selection as it will cause all updates for all languages of Windows 2000, Windows XP, and Windows Server 2003 to be downloaded to your local SUS server. Select either **English only** or **Specific languages** to ensure you download only the updates you specifically require. After making your selection, click **Next** to continue.

Figure 8.2 Selecting the Languages for which SUS will Provide Updates

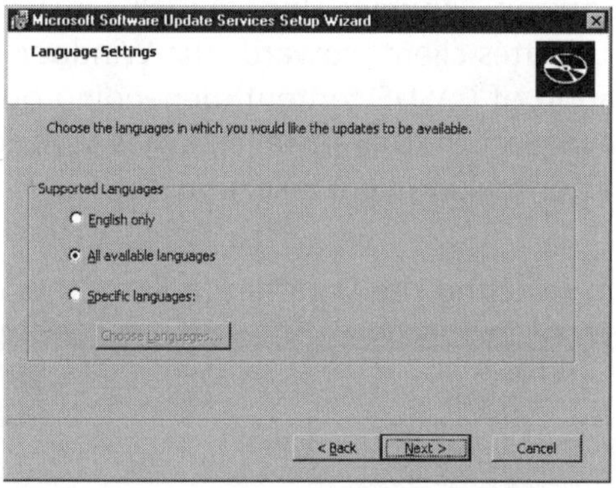

8. In the Handling new versions of previously approved updates dialog box, as seen in Figure 8.3, you must decide what is to occur when an update is downloaded that is a newer version of an update that you previously approved. The default selection of **I will manually approve new versions of approved updates** is usually the best (and safest) option. You should perform testing on the newer version of the update before approving it and allowing it to be installed on your network clients. After making your selection, click **Next** to continue.

9. In the Ready to install dialog box, as seen in Figure 8.4, you will be shown the URL that your network clients will need to be pointed towards to connect to the SUS server. This is the URL that you will use when configuring the Automatic Updates Group Policy options. When you are ready to start the actual installation of SUS, click **Install** to continue.

10. When the Wizard has completed the installation process, click **Finish** to close it.

Figure 8.3 Configuring SUS to Require Approval of Updated Versions of Approved Updates

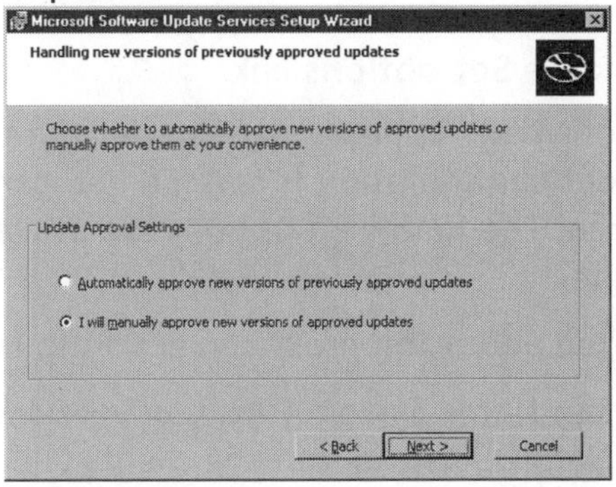

Figure 8.4 The URL of Your SUS Server for Later Configuration

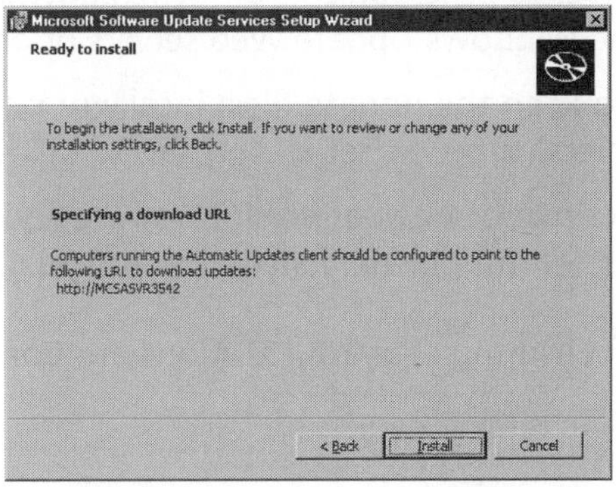

11. The SUS administration page, as seen in Figure 8.5, should automatically open in Internet Explorer. If it does not open, you can open it by entering **http://servername/SUSAdmin** in your browser or by clicking the **Microsoft Software Update Services** icon which is located in the Administrative Tools folder accessible from the Start menu.

Figure 8.5 Using Your Web Browser to Configure and Manage the SUS Server

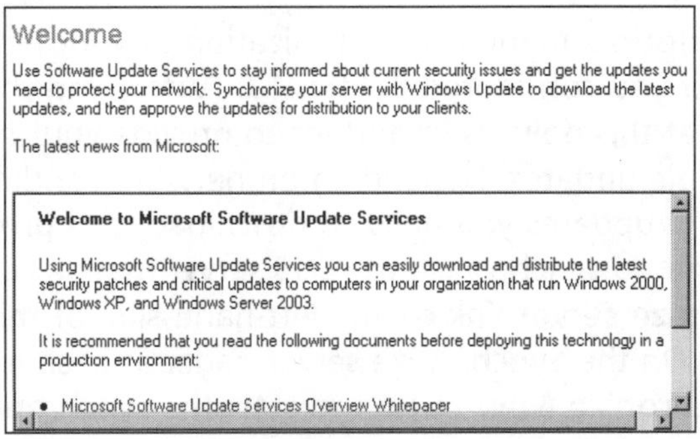

12. Before beginning any other configuration or management tasks for your newly installed SUS server, you must ensure that its options are configured properly. On the left-hand side of the SUS administration window, click the **Set options** link.

13. The Set options page appears, as seen in Figure 8.6, allowing you to verify that your configuration is correct. You can change the configuration if required. The following options are available for configuration from this page:

  ■   Information about the proxy server configuration (if required).

  ■   The Domain Name System (DNS) or Network Basic Input/Output System (NetBIOS) name that the clients will be using to contact the SUS server.

  ■   What server to synchronize from when downloading new updates—either the Windows Update Web servers or another SUS server.

  ■   Where to keep the update files: locally or on the Windows Update Web servers (this was set during the installation process).

  ■   What to do about newer versions of previously approved updates (this was set during the installation process).

Figure 8.6 Ensuring that Your Options are Configured Correctly

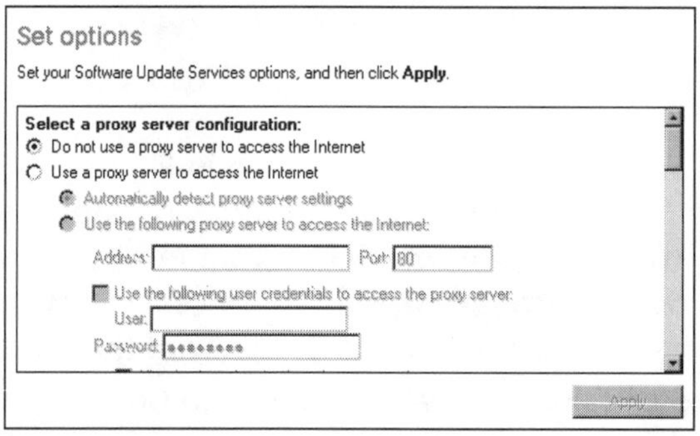

14. Next, perform a manual synchronization of your new SUS server against the server you configured in Step 13. Performing the manual synchronization at this point is important to provide your new SUS server with all available updates. Depending on network conditions and the amount of updates you need to download, this process might take some time. To synchronize the SUS server manually, click the **Synchronize server** link on the left-hand side of the SUS administration window. On the Synchronize server page, as seen in Figure 8.7, click the **Synchronize Now** button to start the synchronization process.

Figure 8.7 Starting the Manual Synchronization Process

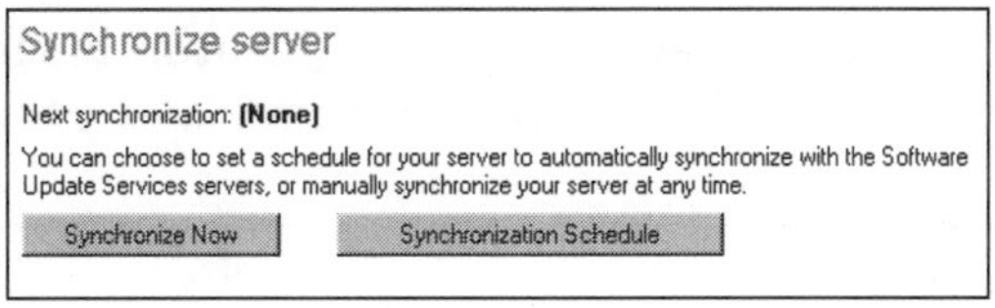

Synchronize server

Next synchronization: **[None]**

You can choose to set a schedule for your server to automatically synchronize with the Software
Update Services servers, or manually synchronize your server at any time.

[Synchronize Now]   [Synchronization Schedule]

15. After the manual synchronization has started, click the
Synchronization Schedule button to configure a schedule for the SUS
server to synchronize content. The Schedule Synchronization Web Page
dialog, as seen in Figure 8.8, opens allowing you to configure a
schedule that suits your needs (typically one week between events).
Click **OK** to close the dialog box after configuring your schedule.

Figure 8.8 Scheduling the SUS Content Synchronization Schedule

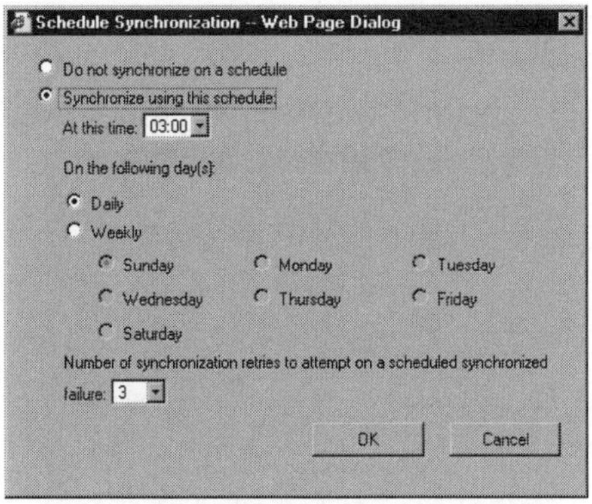

16. Once all available updates have been synchronized to your SUS server,
you will be presented with a VBScript dialog box for confirmation. Click
OK to acknowledge that synchronization has completed. You will be
prompted to approve updates that will be made available for
Automatic Updates clients on your network, as seen in Figure 8.9.

Figure 8.9 Manually Approving All Updates Before They Can be
Issued

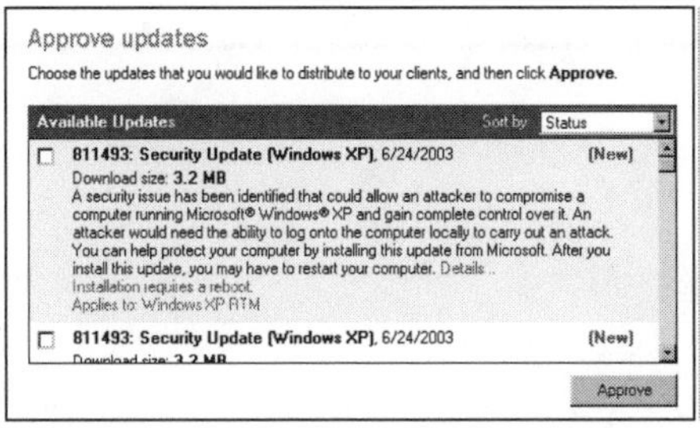

NOTE

Remember that you should not approve any of the available updates until you have aggressively tested them in a test lab that simulates your actual production network.

17. When you are ready to approve an update, you need only to place a check mark in the selection box next to it. When you have approved all updates you want at this time, click the **Approve** button.

18. When prompted by the VBScript dialog box, click **Yes** to approve the list of updates you have selected.

19. You will be presented with a Supplemental EULA, as seen in Figure 8.10, which you need to accept in order to make the selected updates available for installation. Click **Accept** to complete the approval process.

Figure 8.10 Accepting the Supplemental EULA

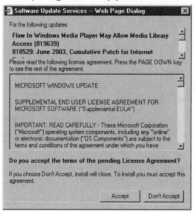

20. You will be prompted once again by a VBScript dialog box, informing you that your updates are ready for distribution. Click **OK** to close the dialog box and complete the approval process.

Configuring & Implementing…

Take Care of Those Servers…

When you stop to think about it, servers are the lifeblood of your network. True, the network exists to provide clients with information and services they need in order to be useful to users, but servers are perhaps one of the most important infrastructure solutions that exist, as well as the most widely used. The importance of testing any update to be deployed to your servers cannot be emphasized enough. You must test all updates, no matter how small or seemingly trivial, that will be applied to your servers before they are deployed. After all, you don't want to be known as the administrator that brought the entire company's business to a grinding halt because you failed to adequately test an update before deploying it.

Of course, after testing has been completed to your satisfaction, you are still not ready to deploy updates to your servers. You need a well-documented (and approved) upgrade plan that includes a back out plan in the event that things do not occur as you intended. Only proceed to install updates after you have been granted approval from your supervisor and the back out plan is well documented. You must also ensure that you have a well-tested disaster recovery plan in place. Other solutions such as disk imaging or hot standby systems can also provide some amount of redundancy for recovery purposes.

The last precaution that you should take when updating servers is to only apply the required updates to the required servers—blindly applying all updates to all servers is not only a waste of time and bandwidth, it can also lead to problems. Your update plan should be carefully prepared to specify exactly which updates will be applied to which servers in order to prevent this sort of issue. On that note, you may want to apply updates incrementally over a week or two in order to observe how production servers respond to the update—no matter how much testing you do in the lab, you will never be able to truly recreate the real network conditions that exist in your organization.

With SUS installed and configured on your server, you should next install and configure Automatic Updates on your clients so that they can begin to download and install approved updates.

Installing and Configuring the Automatic Update Client

As mentioned previously, your clients may or may not need to have an updated Automatic Updates client installed on them. Your computers will need to be at the following Service Pack levels to avoid requiring an updated version of the Automatic Updates client:

- Windows 2000 Service Pack 3 (or higher)
- Windows XP Service Pack 1 (or higher)
- Windows Server 2003 RTM (no Service Pack required)

If needed, you can download the Automatic Updates client from www.microsoft.com/windows2000/windowsupdate/sus/default.asp.

Depending on the size and configuration of your network, you will either be configuring Automatic Updates through Group Policy for a domain environment or through the System applet for a local computer. Exercise 8.02 examines the process to configure Automatic Updates via Group Policy. Exercise 8.03 examines the process to configure Automatic Updates via the System applet.

EXERCISE 8.02

CONFIGURING AUTOMATIC UPDATES VIA GROUP POLICY

1. Click **Start** | **Programs** | **Administrative Tools** | **Active Directory Users and Computers** to open the Active Directory Users and Computers console.

2. Depending on the size and organization of your network, you may want to apply the Automatic Updates settings at the domain level or to one or more specific OUs. For this example, we will be configuring the settings at the domain level.

3. Right-click on the domain node and select **Properties** to open the domain Properties dialog box. Switch to the **Group Policy** tab, as seen in Figure 8.11.

Figure 8.11 Locating the Group Policy Objects

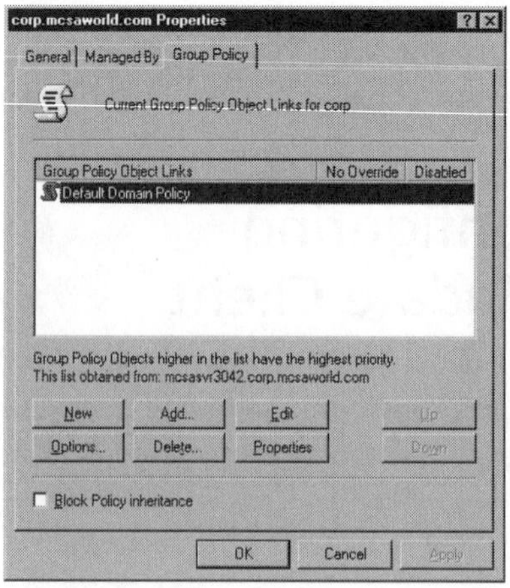

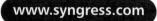

4. Click the **New** button to create a new GPO. Name the new GPO some-
    thing meaningful, such as **Domain Automatic Updates Policy** and
    then click the **Edit** button to open the Group Policy Object Editor.

5. In the Group Policy Object Editor, expand the following nodes to locate
    the Automatic Updates configuration options: **Computer Configuration
    | Administrative Templates | Windows Components | Windows
    Update**. You should see the options presented in Figure 8.12.

Figure 8.12 Locating the Automatic Updates Options

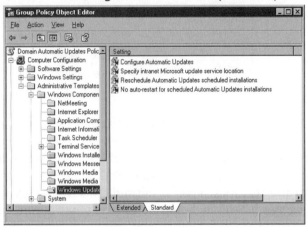

6. Double-click the **Configure Automatic Updates** option, as seen in
    Figure 8.13, to open its configuration options. Select the **Enabled**
    option. Select from the following installation options:

    ■ **2** - Notify before downloading any updates and notify again before
       installing them

    ■ **3** - Download the updates automatically and notify when they are
       ready to be installed

    ■ **4** - Automatically download updates and install them on the
       schedule specified
       If you've selected **4**, you need to configure an installation schedule
    by configuring it using the other two drop-down boxes. Be sure to
    allow adequate time after your SUS server's configured synchronization
    time. Note that you must enable the Configure Automatic Updates
    option in order for SUS to function properly. Click **OK** to accept the
    configuration.

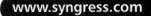

Figure 8.13 Configuring the Configure Automatic Updates Properties

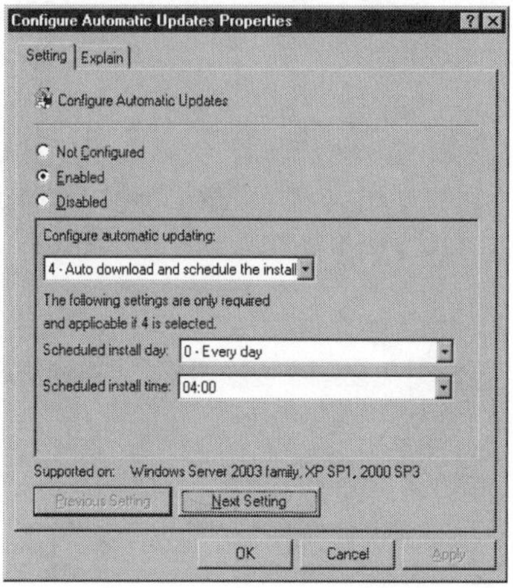

7. Double-click the **Specify intranet Microsoft update service location** option, as seen in Figure 8.14, to open its configuration options. Select the **Enabled** option. Enter the URL of your SUS server in both the SUS and statistics server boxes as seen. You can enter another IIS server's URL for the statistics server if desired. This is where you will be able to examine the SUS IIS logs and determine what updates have been applied to what clients. Note that you must enable the **Specify intranet Microsoft update service location** option and specify the correct URL in order for SUS to function properly. Click **OK** to accept the configuration.

Figure 8.14 Specifying the SUS Server for Automatic Updates Clients to Use

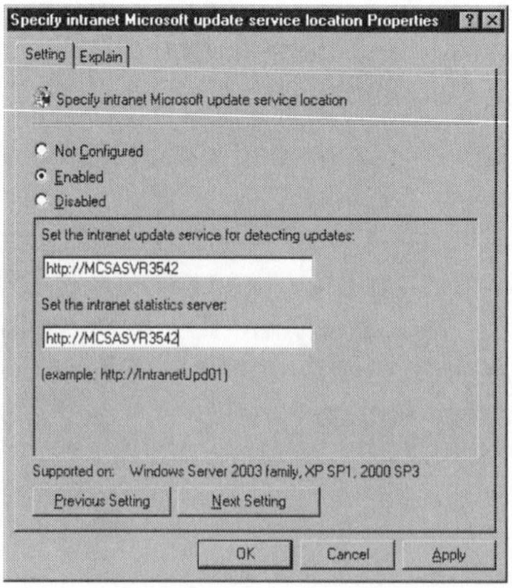

EXAM WARNING

You can have multiple or independent (or even synchronized) SUS servers within your network; therefore, you can point groups of clients at different SUS servers by geographic location, department, or other system if desired. For example, you might configure the Automatic Updates Group Policy settings at the organizational unit (OU) level and point each OU towards a different SUS server.

8. Double-click the **Reschedule Automatic Updates scheduled installations Properties** options, as seen in Figure 8.15, to open its configuration options. Select the **Enabled** option and configure a time to allow clients that missed an Automatic Updates cycle to download and install available updates after startup. Click **OK** to accept the configuration.

Figure 8.15 Specifying the Behavior for Missed Automatic Updates Cycles

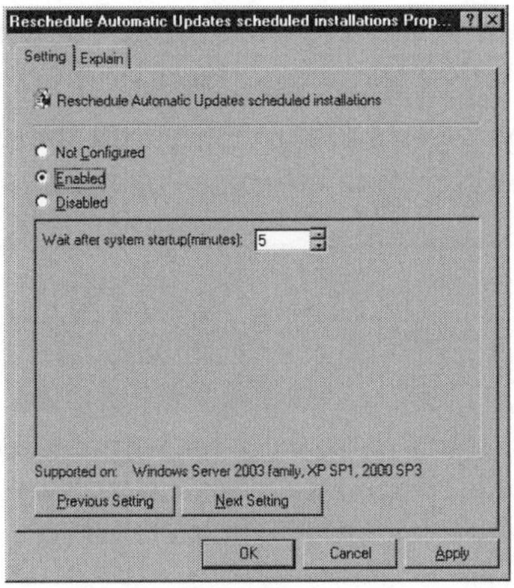

9. Double-click the **No auto-restart for scheduled Automatic Updates installations** option, as seen in Figure 8.16, to open its configuration options. Select the **Disabled** option to allow clients to automatically restart after updates have been installed. Note that clients will not be able to apply any future updates until the client has been restarted at some time in the future. Click **OK** to accept the configuration.

Figure 8.16 Allowing Clients to Automatically Restart After Applying Updates

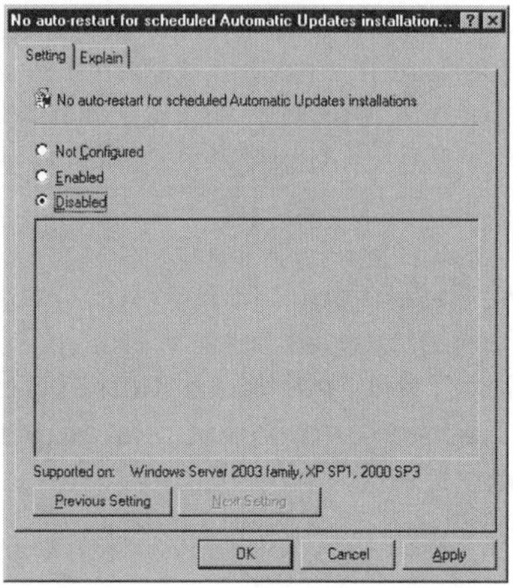

10. Close the **Group Policy Object Editor,** the **Domain Properties** dialog box, and the **Active Directory Users and Computers** console.

11. To immediately refresh Group Policy, run the **gpupdate /target:computer** command to force a Group Policy update.

If you will not be configuring the Automatic Updates options via Group Policy, you will either need to allow your clients to download any available applicable updates from the Windows Update Web servers (the default behavior without SUS installed) or you can manually edit the Registry to direct clients towards an SUS server of your choosing. Once you have successfully created the required Registry entries, you can export them for easy importing into other computers.

Figure 8.17 shows the Automatic Updates tab of the System Properties applet, which can be accessed by clicking **Start | Settings | Control Panel | System** and switching to the **Automatic Updates** tab. You will be able to configure whether or not Automatic Updates are to be performed as well as how and when updates should be installed.

If you want to manually edit the Registry to create the required entries, perform the process detailed in Exercise 8.03.

NOTE

Directly editing the Registry is an advanced administrative task and should not be performed by those unfamiliar or uncomfortable with this action. Errors left in the Registry due to incorrect editing actions can cause the computer to fail to start or operate properly. Always proceed with caution when manually editing the Registry.

Figure 8.17 Configuring Automatic Updates via the System Applet

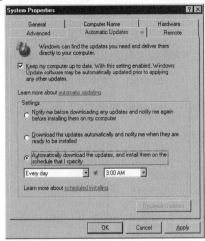

Exercise 8.03

Configuring Automatic Updates in the Registry

1. Open the Registry Editor by clicking **Start | Run**, typing **regedt32**, and clicking **OK**. The Registry Editor, as seen in Figure 8.18, opens.

Figure 8.18 The Registry Editor Window

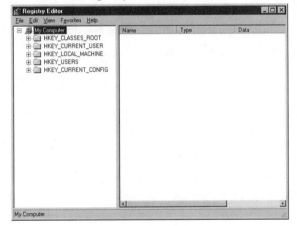

2. Expand the keys to reach the following key: **HKEY_LOCAL_MACHINE\SOFTWARE\Policies\Microsoft\Windows\WindowsUpdate**, as seen in Figure 8.19. If the **WindowsUpdate** key does not exist, you must create it by right-clicking on the Windows key and

selecting **New | Key** from the context menu. Name the key **WindowsUpdate**.

Figure 8.19 Locating the Windows Update Settings

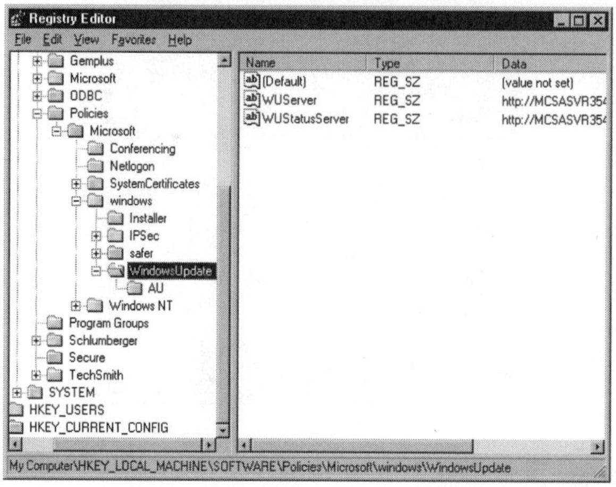

3. If your SUS server is not listed in Figure 8.19, you need to create two new string entries. Right-click in the **WindowsUpdate** key and select **New | String** to create a new string value. Name the first string **WUServer**. Double-click on the **WUServer** string to open its configuration, as seen in Figure 8.20. Enter the URL to the SUS server and click **OK**.

Figure 8.20 Locating the Windows Update Settings

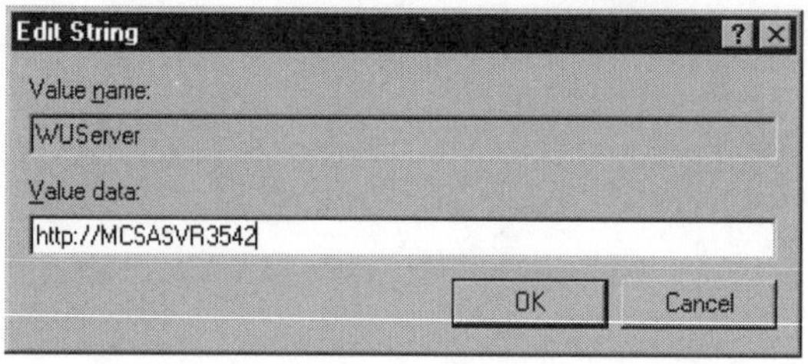

4. Create another string value named **WUStatusServer**. Double-click on the **WUStatusServer** string to open its configuration. Enter the URL to the SUS server or IIS server that will be hosting the SUS IIS logs and click **OK**.

5. If the AU key does not exist within the WindowsUpdate key, you must create it by right-clicking on the **WindowsUpdate** key and selecting **New | Key** from the context menu. Name the key **AU**.

6. Within the AU key, you need to create new DWORD values to configure the Automatic Updates options. To create a new DWORD value, right-click the **AU** key and select **New | DWORD** Value from the context menu. You need to create the DWORD values detailed in Table 8.1 to completely configure Automatic Updates. When done, you should have something similar to that seen in Figure 8.21.

Table 8.1 AU Key Values

Value Name	Value Data	Value Base
RescheduleWaitTime	Between 1 – 60 (minutes)	Hexadecimal
NoAutoRebootWithLoggedOnUsers	0 – Automatically restarts clients 1 – Does not automatically restart clients	Hexadecimal
NoAutoUpdate	0 – Automatic Updates is enabled 1 – Automatic Updates is disabled	Hexadecimal
AUOptions	2 – Notify before down-loading any updates and notify again before installing them 3 – Download the updates automatically and notify when they are ready to be installed 4 – Automatically download updates and install them on the schedule specified	Hexadecimal
ScheduledInstallDay	0 – Everyday 1 (Sunday) – 7 (Saturday)	Hexadecimal
ScheduledInstallTime	0 – 23 (Midnight to 11 PM)	Hexadecimal
UseWUServer	1 – Automatic Updates uses server specified by the WUServer string.	Hexadecimal

7. If you want to export your new settings to a Registry file, right-click in the **WindowsUpdate k**ey and select **Export** from the context menu to open the Export Registry File dialog box, as seen in Figure 8.22.

Figure 8.21 Examining the Results of Your Registry Editing

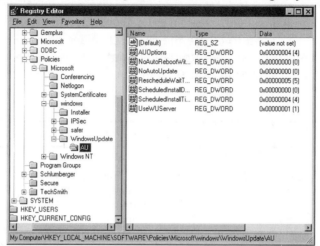

Figure 8.22 Easily Exporting the Keys and Values You Have Just Created

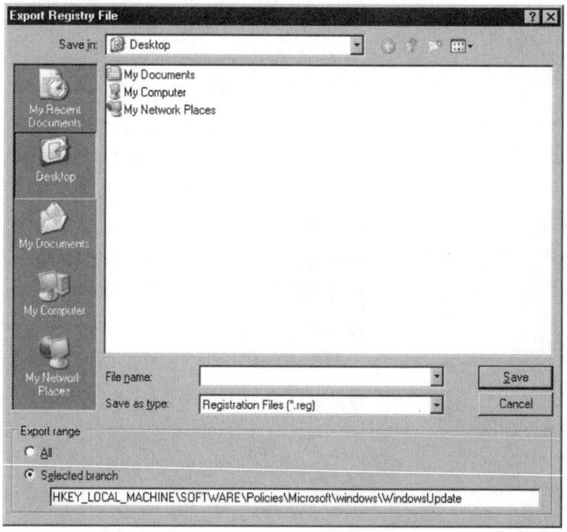

8. Enter the location and file name of the file, select the **.REG** file type, and click the **Save** button.

9. To close the Registry Editor and save your configuration changes, click **File | Exit**.

Once you have gotten SUS and Automatic Updates installed and configured properly, it should (in most cases) run without requiring much management outside of testing and approving updates. You should, however, be aware of the various management actions that you can perform for SUS and Automatic Updates.

EXAM WARNING

Pay special attention to any scenarios dealing with performing updates on "critical" or "production" servers.

Managing Software Update Services

After installing and configuring SUS, the most common administrative task that you will be responsible for is approving the updates that are to be issued to clients. However, there are several other administrative tasks that you should be familiar with. These actions include:

- Viewing the synchronization log

- Viewing the approval log

- Monitoring the SUS server

- Examining the event logs

- Viewing the SUS IIS logs

Each of these tasks are examined in the following sections.

Viewing the Synchronization Logs

Synchronization logs detail synchronization events that have occurred on your SUS server. They can be viewed from within the SUS administrative page by clicking the **View synchronization log** link in the left-hand side of the window or directly by opening the file from Windows Explorer. Viewing the synchronization logs from within SUS will yield output similar to that seen in Figure 8.23.

Figure 8.23 Viewing the Synchronization Logs

Synchronization Log

This log includes information about synchronizations that have occurred between your local server and the Software Update Services servers.

Automatic Sync Started- Saturday, June 28, 2003 3:00:00 AM
   Software Update Services is up to date. No changes were required during synchronization.
Sync Finished-Saturday, June 28, 2003 3:00:01 AM

Automatic Sync Started- Saturday, June 28, 2003 2:59:57 AM
   Software Update Services is up to date. No changes were required during synchronization.
Sync Finished-Saturday, June 28, 2003 2:59:59 AM

Manual Sync Started- Friday, June 27, 2003 9:11:29 PM Successful

Clear Log   Print Log...

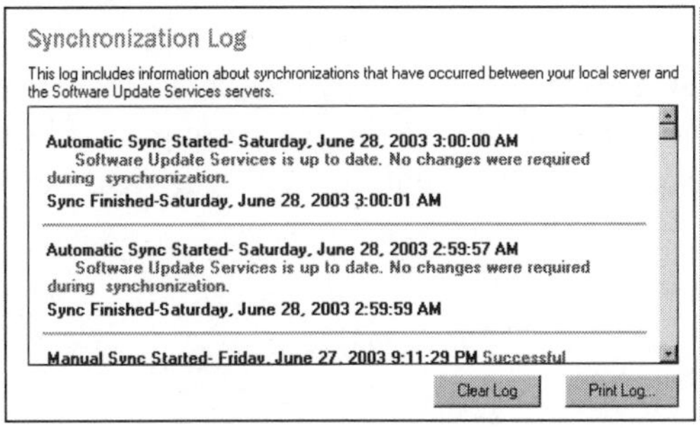

From this screen you can determine information about the following items from the synchronization logs:

- When the last synchronization event was performed.
- Whether or not each synchronization event was successful or failed.
- The next scheduled synchronization time, if scheduled synchronizations are configured.
- What updates have been downloaded and/or updated since the last synchronization was performed.
- What updates failed to properly synchronize during the synchronization event.
- Whether the synchronization event was an automatic or manual synchronization.

To view the file directly you can go to *x*:\Inetpub\wwwroot\autoupdate\administration\history-sync.xml, where *x* is the volume that your IIS content is located on. Viewing the synchronization logs directly yields an output similar to that seen in Figure 8.24.

Figure 8.24 The Synchronization Log File

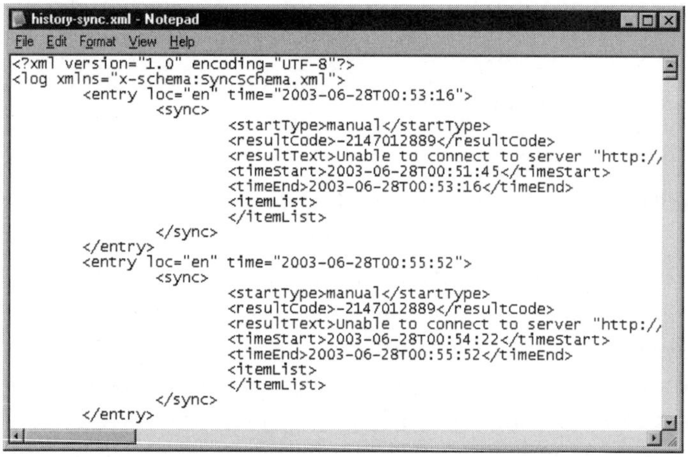

```
history-sync.xml - Notepad
File Edit Format View Help
<?xml version="1.0" encoding="UTF-8"?>
<log xmlns="x-schema:SyncSchema.xml">
        <entry loc="en" time="2003-06-28T00:53:16">
                <sync>
                        <startType>manual</startType>
                        <resultCode>-2147012889</resultCode>
                        <resultText>Unable to connect to server "http:/
                        <timeStart>2003-06-28T00:51:45</timeStart>
                        <timeEnd>2003-06-28T00:53:16</timeEnd>
                        <itemList>
                        </itemList>
                </sync>
        </entry>
        <entry loc="en" time="2003-06-28T00:55:52">
                <sync>
                        <startType>manual</startType>
                        <resultCode>-2147012889</resultCode>
                        <resultText>Unable to connect to server "http:/
                        <timeStart>2003-06-28T00:54:22</timeStart>
                        <timeEnd>2003-06-28T00:55:52</timeEnd>
                        <itemList>
                        </itemList>
                </sync>
        </entry>
```

Viewing the Approval Logs

Approval logs detail which updates have been approved on your SUS server. They can be viewed from within the SUS administrative page by clicking the **View approval log** link in the left-hand side of the window, or directly by opening the file from Windows Explorer. Viewing the approval logs from within SUS will yield output similar to that seen in Figure 8.25.

Figure 8.25 Viewing the Approval Logs

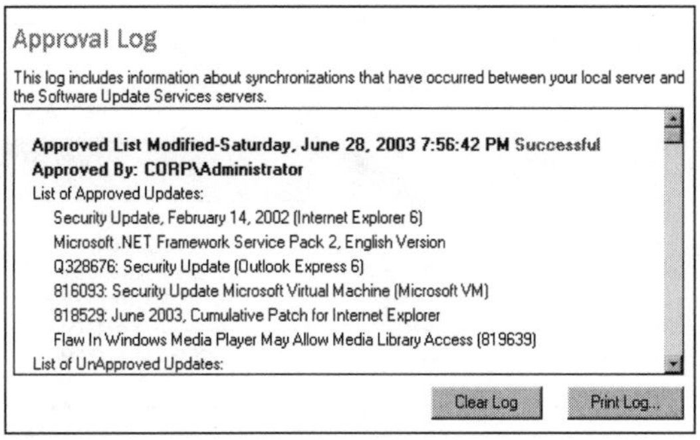

From this screen you can determine information about the following items from the approval logs:

- Updates that have been approved for client installation.

- Updates that have not been approved for client installation.

- Who made the approval change.

- The date and time the approval change occurred.

To view the file directly, go to x:\Inetpub\wwwroot\autoupdate\administration\history-approve.xml, where x is the volume that your IIS content is located on.

Monitoring the SUS Server

The SUS server keeps a current listing of all available updates in its metadata cache—a database that is kept in volatile (random access memory [RAM]). This cache includes metadata that identifies and categorizes updates including information relating to the applicability of each update. Clicking the **Monitor server** link in the left-hand side of the SUS administrative window allows you to view the status of available updates for all supported products.

The data that is contained in this cache is refreshed during every synchronization event and represents the total number of updates that apply to a specific product—not how many updates have been approved by you or subsequently installed by your clients. The data in the cache is current as of the last server synchronization event and can be refreshed at any time by clicking the **Refresh** button. Figure 8.26 details a typical server monitor listing.

Figure 8.26 Viewing the Number of Available Updates

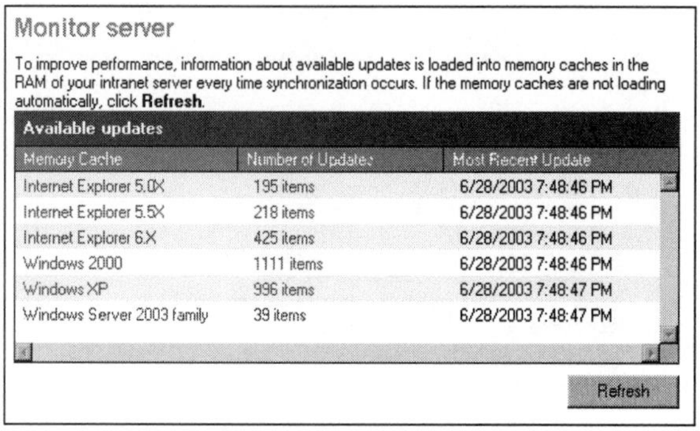

Examining the Event Logs

The SUS server creates various SUS-specific Event Log entries that can be useful when monitoring and troubleshooting the SUS server. The Automatic Updates client also creates various Event Log entries detailing its operation. Log entries are written into the System Log and can be accessed by clicking **Start | Programs | Administrative Tools | Event Viewer** and selecting the **System** log, as seen in Figure 8.27.

Figure 8.27 Locating the System Logs

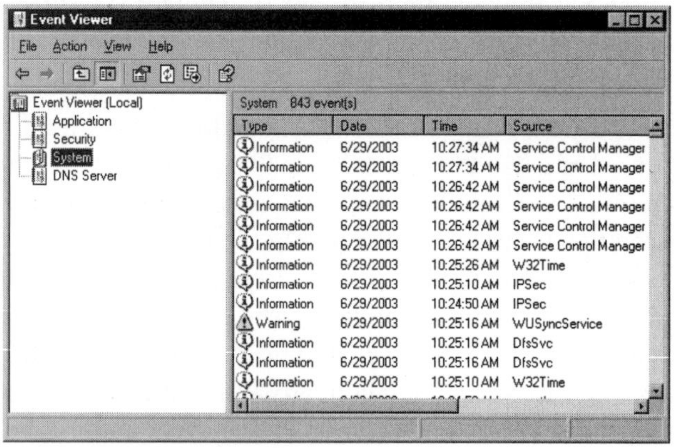

From this window you can determine the following entries relating to SUS in your Event Logs:

- **101** Software Update Services encountered a failure during synchronization

- **102** Software Update Services did not complete synchronization. An administrator cancelled the synchronization

- **103** Software Update Services did not complete synchronization. During the synchronization, a file was downloaded that was not correctly signed by Microsoft

- **104** Software Update Services successfully synchronized all content

- **105** Software Update Services successfully synchronized some content during this synchronization. However, not all items were downloaded successfully

- **106** Software Update Services has encountered a problem

- **107** Software Update Services failed to load some configuration information

- **108** Software Update Services failed to save some configuration information

- **109** Not all temporary files were successfully deleted during the last content synchronization

- **110** The catalog was not successfully deleted after the last synchronization

- **111** The list of Software Update Services updates that are available on this server has been successfully changed

- **112** The list of Software Update Services updates that are available on this server failed to be updated

Figure 8.28 illustrates an example of a typical entry you might see relating to SUS.

Figure 8.28 Examining Event ID 111

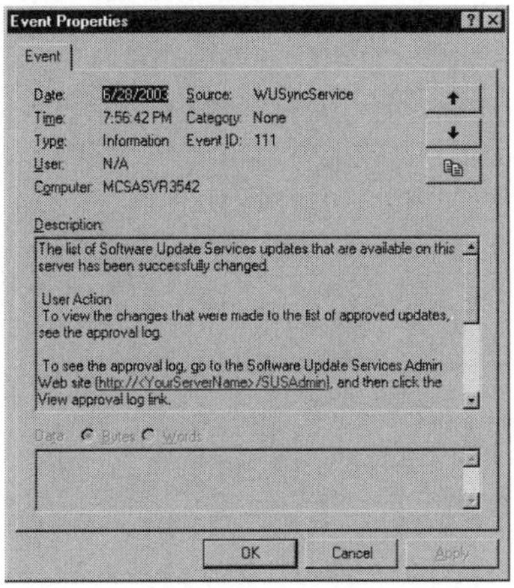

Automatic Updates also creates event log entries in the System log as it installs updates. Some of the more typical entries that you might see for Automatic Updates include:

- **18** Installation ready

- **19** Installation successful

- **22** Restart required
- **1074** The process winlogon.exe has initiated the restart of computer

Viewing the SUS IIS Logs

The IIS logs can also be viewed directly from the SUS server to determine the status of client updates. By default, the SUS logs can be viewed at the following location: %WINDOWS%/system32/LogFiles/W3SVC*x* where *x* is a random integer and %WINDOWS% represents the installation path of your Windows Server 2003 installation. Log files will be created on a daily basis using the standard W3C logging format (by default) and will use a naming convention of *exyymmdd.log*. For example, the log for June 28, 2003 would be named ex030628.log. Logging options can be managed from the IIS Manager console (refer back to Chapter 4 for additional information on IIS). Direct examination of the IIS logs is a task usually left for advanced administrators, although a number of tools are available, both as freeware and commercial software, that can be used to make the examination easier. Figure 8.29 illustrates a typical SUS IIS server log.

Figure 8.29 The IIS Logs can be Very Difficult to Interpret for the Uninitiated

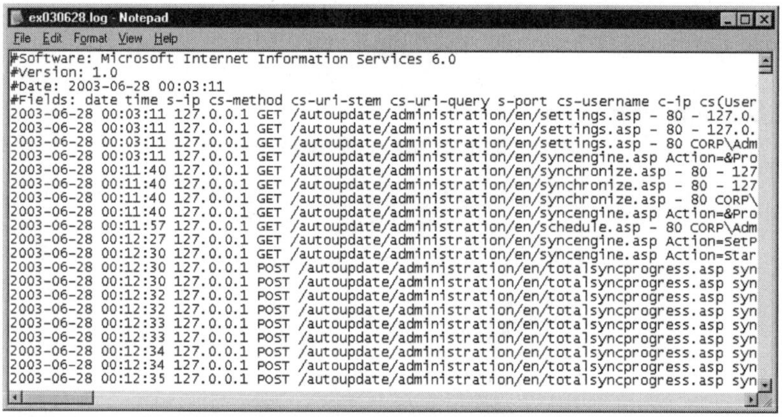


```
#Software: Microsoft Internet Information Services 6.0
#Version: 1.0
#Date: 2003-06-28 00:03:11
#Fields: date time s-ip cs-method cs-uri-stem cs-uri-query s-port cs-username c-ip cs(User
2003-06-28 00:03:11 127.0.0.1 GET /autoupdate/administration/en/settings.asp - 80 - 127.0.
2003-06-28 00:03:11 127.0.0.1 GET /autoupdate/administration/en/settings.asp - 80 - 127.0.
2003-06-28 00:03:11 127.0.0.1 GET /autoupdate/administration/en/settings.asp - 80 CORP\Adm
2003-06-28 00:03:11 127.0.0.1 GET /autoupdate/administration/en/syncengine.asp Action=&Pro
2003-06-28 00:11:40 127.0.0.1 GET /autoupdate/administration/en/synchronize.asp - 80 - 127
2003-06-28 00:11:40 127.0.0.1 GET /autoupdate/administration/en/synchronize.asp - 80 - 127
2003-06-28 00:11:40 127.0.0.1 GET /autoupdate/administration/en/synchronize.asp - 80 CORP\
2003-06-28 00:11:40 127.0.0.1 GET /autoupdate/administration/en/syncengine.asp Action=&Pro
2003-06-28 00:11:57 127.0.0.1 GET /autoupdate/administration/en/schedule.asp - 80 CORP\Adm
2003-06-28 00:12:27 127.0.0.1 GET /autoupdate/administration/en/syncengine.asp Action=SetP
2003-06-28 00:12:30 127.0.0.1 GET /autoupdate/administration/en/syncengine.asp Action=Star
2003-06-28 00:12:30 127.0.0.1 POST /autoupdate/administration/en/totalsyncprogress.asp syn
2003-06-28 00:12:30 127.0.0.1 POST /autoupdate/administration/en/totalsyncprogress.asp syn
2003-06-28 00:12:32 127.0.0.1 POST /autoupdate/administration/en/totalsyncprogress.asp syn
2003-06-28 00:12:32 127.0.0.1 POST /autoupdate/administration/en/totalsyncprogress.asp syn
2003-06-28 00:12:33 127.0.0.1 POST /autoupdate/administration/en/totalsyncprogress.asp syn
2003-06-28 00:12:33 127.0.0.1 POST /autoupdate/administration/en/totalsyncprogress.asp syn
2003-06-28 00:12:34 127.0.0.1 POST /autoupdate/administration/en/totalsyncprogress.asp syn
2003-06-28 00:12:34 127.0.0.1 POST /autoupdate/administration/en/totalsyncprogress.asp syn
2003-06-28 00:12:35 127.0.0.1 POST /autoupdate/administration/en/totalsyncprogress.asp syn
```

The following sections examine some typical problems and troubleshooting actions involved with SUS and Automatic Updates.

Troubleshooting SUS and Automatic Updates

SUS and Automatic Updates, once installed, will typically run with little or no difficulties. Some of the more common problems that may occur are detailed in Table 8.2.

Table 8.2 Common SUS and Automatic Updates Problems

Problem	Solution
The SUS administration page is not functioning properly	This problem can be manifested in several ways, from partial functionality loss in the SUS administration page to a failure for synchronization to occur properly. To remedy this problem, you should restart the **Software Update Services Synchronization Service** from the Services console.
The SUS administration page cannot be accessed. Automatic Updates clients cannot connect to the SUS server.	The SUS server has stopped running or responding to client requests. To remedy this problem, you should restart the **World Wide Web Publishing Service** from the Services console. You may also need to perform further troubleshooting to determine if a larger problem is causing the WWW service to fail to function properly.
The Automatic Updates clients are not downloading and installing updates.	The correct SUS server may not be configured in the Automatic Updates options. Check and correct the configuration as required.

Managing Updates for Legacy Clients

Up to this point, we have been focused on solutions that can be used to keep Windows 2000, Windows XP, and Windows Server 2003 clients up to date. But what can be done for legacy clients that cannot participate in Active Directory? These clients still require updates as new security flaws are discovered in these operating systems and their components, including Internet Explorer and Media Player.

When it comes to keeping these computers up to date, there are a handful of choices to choose from:

- Windows Update
- Windows Update Catalog
- SMS and third-party applications

It is important to note that these solutions can be used for clients that are geographically distant, that will not utilize Automatic Updates, or otherwise cannot participate in any other form of software updating discussed previously.

TEST DAY TIP

Upgrading legacy clients to Windows 2000 Professional or Windows XP Professional is an alternative to implementing any of the legacy client update methods examined here.

Windows Update

Windows Update is a simple and easy-to-use method of updating one specific computer at a time. Windows Update can be used to update a local computer and requires that updates be downloaded from Microsoft. Using Windows Update is a good choice if the number of computers to be updated is relatively small, or if Active Directory is not implemented in the network. Recall that SUS works best when the Automatic Updates clients are configured via Group Policy. As the number of computers and sites increases, so does the workload involved in using Windows Update. The exact number of computers where this breaking point occurs is not a fixed number, and can vary from organization to organization. A good guideline is ten computers. If there are ten computers or less in an organization, in most cases it is feasible to use Windows Update without exerting excessive administrative effort. Anything more than ten computers and another means of keeping your computers up to date should be considered. Another concern with using Windows Update is that each computer will download the files it requires independently of what any other computer has previously downloaded, which can put quite a hit on the network bandwidth.

If there is a need to use Windows Update, the process to scan download updates is presented in Exercise 8.04.

TEST DAY TIP

Do not expect to be tested on a large amount of Windows Update knowledge during your exam. Most likely, you will only see it lightly referenced. What you need to take away from the discussion in this chapter is what it does, how it works, and why it is a limited solution not suitable for enterprise usage.

EXERCISE 8.04

UPDATING A SINGLE COMPUTER USING WINDOWS UPDATE

1. Click **Start | Windows Update** to open an Internet Explorer window pointed at Windows Update. If the shortcut is missing, enter **http://windowsupdate.microsoft.com** into your browser. The Internet Explorer window, as seen in Figure 8.30, will appear. If you are asked to

download and install anything from Microsoft, accept the download—this is a critical part of the process.

Figure 8.30 The Windows Update Web Site

2. Click **Scan for updates** to start analysis of your computer. After the analysis has completed, you can navigate through the three categories of updates to determine what Windows Update has found that your computer needs. The categories are arranged from most important to least important with regards to computer security and safety. Available updates can be seen in Figure 8.31.

Figure 8.31 Examining Available Updates

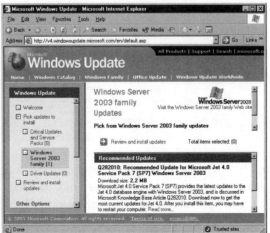

By default, Windows Update automatically places into your download basket any items that it finds that fall into the Critical Updates and Service Packs category. This does not mean that they should be installed all at once, or that they must be installed at all. To see what has been identified and selected as Critical Updates or Service Packs, click on **Critical Updates and Service Packs**. Some items may be mutually exclusive and must be downloaded and installed separately from the rest of the selected items. In this case, you would need to either remove all other items from your download list or remove the one specific item. We recommend checking the entire list to make sure that other items are not mutually exclusive, and also that it contains only the items you want to download. You can read more about any item by clicking the **Read more** link at the end of each update's description.

3. Another useful tool to help determine what has been previously applied using Windows Update is the View installation option. Clicking **View installation history** changes the display to that seen in Figure 8.32. The installed items will likely differ from the details shown in Figure 8.32.

Figure 8.32 Checking Previously Installed Updates

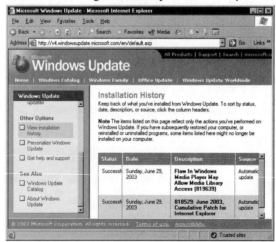

4. Once all of the updates that you want have been added to the list , click the **Review and install updates** links to progress to the next step of the Windows Update process, as shown in Figure 8.33.

Figure 8.33 Reviewing Selected Updates

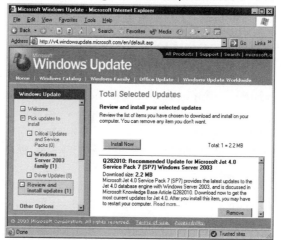

5. Once again the option to examine the chosen selected updates is provided. At this point it is also possible to remove them from the list if required. Once satisfied with the selections, click the **Install Now** button.

6. A supplemental licensing agreement, as shown in Figure 8.34, will appear. Click **Accept** to complete the process.

Figure 8.34 Accepting the Licensing Agreement

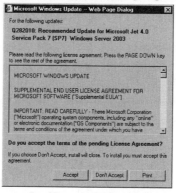

7. Windows Update now downloads and installs the selected updates. More often than not a restart will be required after the installation to complete the process. This allows files that were in use to be updated on startup.

TEST DAY TIP

If you are updating a Windows 2000, Windows XP, or Windows Server 2003 computer using Windows Update, you must have local administrative privileges on the computer in order for the process to be successful.

Using Windows Update is a simple, easy-to-use method for updating a single computer or a few computers. If you have more than a few computers to update or want to control when and how the updates are applied to your computers, you may wish to consider using the Windows Update Catalog and a deployment application, such as SMS.

Windows Update Catalog

The Windows Update Catalog and the SUS have replaced what was once known as Corporate Windows Update. Corporate Windows Update allowed network administrators to browse through all of the available updates for an operating system, download the required updates, and then deploy them using any available means such as scripting or SMS.

For the most part, Windows Update Catalog performs the same function as the now defunct Corporate Windows Update site. SUS takes the concept a step further by automatically downloading the updates to the SUS server and staging them until it is time to deploy them. The process of using the Windows Update Catalog to locate, select, and download updates is detailed in Exercise 8.05.

EXERCISE 8.05

GETTING UPDATES USING THE WINDOWS UPDATE CATALOG

1. Open **Internet Explorer** and enter **http://windowsupdate. microsoft.com/catalog** into the Address bar. The Windows Update Catalog will open, as shown in Figure 8.35.

2. Click **Find updates for Microsoft Windows operating systems** to start the process of finding updates for your legacy computers.

3. Choose the operating system and desired language from the choices given, as seen in Figure 8.36, to locate available downloads. To perform an advanced search to only locate specific items such as Service Packs or Recommended Updates, click **Advanced search options**. Once the search parameters have been configured, click **Search** to continue.

4. Available updates will be enumerated by search category. Clicking **Critical Updates and Service Packs** in this case yields the output shown in Figure 8.37.

Figure 8.35 The Windows Update Catalog

Figure 8.36 Selecting the Search Criteria

5. Browse through the list of updates to determine what is needed. It is possible to gain additional information about a specific update by clicking the **Read more** link within the update's descriptive text. Click **Add** to place an update into the download basket. When the update selection process is complete, click **Go to Download Basket**.

6. The Download Basket, as seen in Figure 8.38, shows all chosen updates and allows you to configure a location to download the files to. When ready to download the chosen files, click **Download Now**.

Figure 8.37 Listing the Updates for the Chosen Operating System and Language

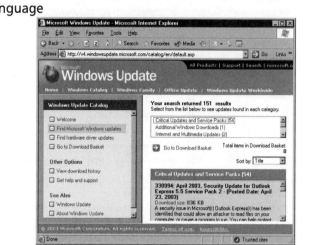

Figure 8.38 Preparing to Download the Selected Update Items

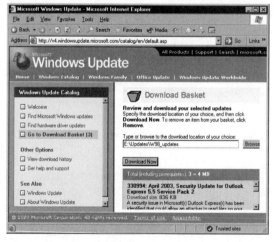

7. When prompted to accept the licensing agreement, do so in order to complete the download.

8. Downloaded files can be tracked in the Download History, as seen in Figure 8.39. Now that the updates have been downloaded, you can deploy them using your choice of methods as discussed previously.

Figure 8.39 Keeping Track of Downloaded Updates

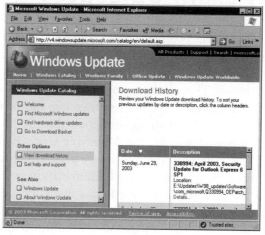

Systems Management Server and Third-party Applications

If the updates are acquired via the Windows Update Catalog or another means, such as directly downloading them from the applicable TechNet pages, then the deployment process to clients requires the use of an additional product such as SMS or a third-party application expressly designed for this purpose.

Microsoft's SMS is an extremely powerful and popular management application that can be used to administer many of the later versions of the Windows operating system. SMS can be used to perform the following tasks:

- Maintain a hardware inventory of computers on the network.

- Maintain a software inventory of software installed on computers on the network.

- Install and update software and other files to computers on the network.

- Remotely manage applications over the network.

- Remotely monitor network traffic by using an advanced data capture and analysis utility.

- Take control of computers on the network for the purpose of maintaining or troubleshooting them.

SMS can also be used for many other purposes, and although they are beyond the scope of this book, a wealth of information on using SMS to administer your network can be found at www.microsoft.com/smserver/techinfo/default.asp. SMS 2003 is in beta testing at the time of this publication and promises to provide more robust Active Directory integration and several other new enhancements. For more information on SMS 2003, see www.microsoft.com/smserver/evaluation/future/default.asp.

Summary of Exam Objectives

This chapter examined SUS, the newest technology available to keep Windows 2000, Windows XP, and Windows Server 2003 networks updated with the latest required updates and patches. SUS is part of a two-part system that also includes the Automatic Updates client.

SUS provides the ability to centralize the deployment of all approved updates to Windows 2000 or better clients. The administrator has full control over which of the available updates actually become approved updates and therefore can be downloaded by and installed on client computers. Instead of client computers directly contacting the Windows Update Web servers (either manually or via the Automatic Updates client), they can be pointed to an internal SUS server. The ability to host a private internal Windows Update server can be a tremendous benefit to network administrators in terms of decreased bandwidth usage if all (or the majority) of clients reside in a single location. However, even if network clients are in multiple locations, it is still possible to use SUS to provide a framework within which the clients will still only download and install approved updates. SUS can be configured to not download any updates locally and instead point clients to the Windows Update Web servers to acquire those previously approved updates for installation on the network. Whatever the size or design of a network, it is a good bet that SUS can be used to increase the security of clients by providing them with the required updates and patches in a safe and efficient manner.

But what about those clients that cannot participate in Group Policy and thus cannot use SUS? What about legacy Windows 98 and older clients? These clients need to be updated using one of several other available means, including the Windows Update Web site or using an additional product such as SMS. Windows Update has been around for awhile and the basic premise and operation of it has not changed much: clients connect to it and an analysis is made of the client to determine what, if any, updates are missing from the client's current installation. After the analysis, the user has the option to select desired updates for automatic download and installation. While Windows Update is not a bad choice for a few computers, it can quickly become an administrative and network burden as the number of computers to be updated increases. In these situations, acquiring updates using the Windows Update Catalog or directly from the TechNet pages of concern and then pushing the updates out to legacy clients should be considered using a product such as SMS or any one of a number of third-party applications that have been designed for this purpose.

Exam Objectives Fast Track

Installing, Configuring, and Managing the Software Update Infrastructure

☑ The SUS and the Automatic Updates client work together to allow network administrators to automatically download updates from the Windows Update servers. No downloaded updates can be installed on a client computer until an administrator has approved them for release. Automatic Updates, configured from Group Policy, can then either silently install any approved updates or prompt the computer user for action.

☑ SUS can be installed on any Windows 2000 Server or Windows Server 2003 computer that meets the hardware and configuration requirements.

☑ You must have the correct version of the Automatic Updates client to be able to configure Automatic Updates to connect to a local SUS server instead of the Windows Update Web servers.

☑ SUS can be configured to download updates locally or to leave them on a Windows Update Web server.

☑ SUS can be configured to acquire updates from synchronizing against another SUS server.

☑ You can create a global SUS solution using a distributed network of SUS servers that service local clients only.

☑ All administration of SUS is performed from your Web browser, and can be secured using Secure Sockets Layer (SSL) by installing a server SSL certificate through the IIS Manager console.

☑ Take great care when applying updates to servers. Ensure that you have thoroughly tested the update and have a solid back out plan in place before starting to update any server. Update servers in waves to allow for time to observe their performance (in small groups) after being updated.

Managing Updates for Legacy Clients

☑ Use the Windows Update Web site to update small groups of computers or computers that are not connected to the main organizational network.

☑ Using the Windows Update Catalog, you can select and download updates of your choosing. You can later deploy them in any means desired, including scripting or manual installation.

☑ Dedicated software management packages, such as SMS, can also be used to deploy updates to client computers.

☑ Legacy clients should be upgraded to Windows 2000 Professional or Windows XP Professional if possible, if they must participate in a SUS environment.

Exam Objectives Frequently Asked Questions

The following Frequently Asked Questions, answered by the authors of this book, are designed to both measure your understanding of the Exam Objectives presented in this chapter, and to assist you with real-life implementation of these concepts. You will also gain access to thousands of other FAQs at ITFAQnet.com.

Q: What happened to the Corporate Windows Update Web site? How am I going to download updates in bulk now?

A: The Corporate Windows Update Web site was replaced in early 2002 by two new services from Microsoft: SUS and the Windows Update Catalog. Of these, the Windows Update Catalog functions in roughly the same manner that the old Corporate Windows Update Web site used to. You can select updates by operating system and download them to your servers for testing and deployment.

Q: I have installed the SUS on a member server in my company but my Automatic Updates clients are getting updates that I have not approved. What is wrong?

A: The most likely cause of this issue is that you have most likely not installed the newest version of Automatic Updates (required to function with SUS) and you have not configured the Automatic Updates client behavior in Group Policy to pull updates from your internal servers. Until you configure Automatic Updates from Group Policy, it can (and will) continue to pull downloads from the Windows Update servers.

Q: I thought that SUS could not run on a domain controller. When did this change?

A: The original release of SUS, although very useful, could not run on a domain controller. This excluded many smaller networks, such as those using SBS, from being able to use SUS to manage their client updates. The newest version (1.0 SP1 as of this writing) supports installation on domain controllers as long as all other requirements have been met.

Q: It seems like an awful lot of trouble to install and configure SUS. Why shouldn't I just leave my Windows XP Professional clients to download and install updates on their own using Automatic Updates?

A: While this solution may work fine in some environments, you are playing with fire the majority of the time. The largest advantage to SUS is that you, the administrator, control exactly what updates are allowed to be installed onto client computers. This prevents compatibility and usability problems the vast majority of the time. Another large advantage to SUS is that it can dramatically cut down on bandwidth usage at your gateway, which in many cases can translate into dollars saved off the bottom line.

Q: I tried to configure Automatic Updates from the System applet, but all of the options were grayed out. Do I have the wrong version installed?

A: No. In the case where all options are grayed out, this indicates that Group Policy is controlling Automatic Updates options automatically.

Q: Do I have to have Automatic Updates automatically restart my clients after updates have been installed?

A: No, but you are best off by doing so for two reasons. First, many updates cannot be completely installed until the subsequent restart of the computer due to locked files that might currently be in use. Second, the client will not be able to detect any new updates until the next restart after updates have been installed.

Self Test

A Quick Answer Key follows the Self Test questions. For complete questions, answers, and explanations to the Self Test questions in this chapter as well as the other chapters in this book, see the Self Test Appendix.

Installing, Configuring and Managing the Software Update Infrastructure

1. Chris is the sole desktop administrator for a Windows 2003 Server Active Directory network, and is responsible for 200 Windows XP Professional computers in her organization. All of the computers are on one campus, however, they are scattered among four different buildings. What is the easiest way for Chris to keep all of her clients updated with the patches and updates they need, but not to allow any updates or patches to be issued until she is satisfied that the patch is stable?

   A. Chris should use Windows Update on each computer locally to download and install the updates her computers need.

   B. Chris should use the Windows Update Catalog to download and install the updates her computers need.

   C. Chris should use SUS and the Automatic Updates client to download and install the updates her computers need.

    D. Chris should download all of the updates she needs and create an integrated installation CD-ROM to distribute to each of the four buildings to install the updates on her computers.

2. You are the network administrator for a corporate network. You recently completed the installation and initial configuration of SUS on an internal Windows Server 2003 computer. All of the client computers use Windows XP Professional SP1. All of the servers on the network are Windows Server 2003 computers. The internal network operates in an Active Directory domain. You want all client computers to automatically download from your SUS server and install any required updates each night at 10 P.M. You want all clients that have installed updates to then restart themselves automatically so that they will be ready to use again in the morning when employees return to work. Which of the following actions should you perform that will help you to achieve the desired results? (Choose two correct answers)

    A. Configure Automatic Updates on each of your local client computers to download and install updates nightly.

    B. Configure the Group Policy settings for Automatic Updates to automatically download and install available updates nightly at 10P.M.

    C. Configure the Group Policy settings for Automatic Updates to not automatically restart client computers.

    D. Configure the Group Policy settings for Automatic Updates to specify the local URL of your SUS server.

3. The CIO of Robert's Rockets has instructed you, the network administrator, to install and configure a SUS-based solution that is to be used to keep all internal client computers up to date with the latest required patches and updates. Robert's Rockets has its world headquarters in Massachusetts with regional offices worldwide. You are concerned about the possible saturation of your wide area network (WAN) links by remote clients downloading and installing updates from the SUS servers you have planned for placement in the headquarters server room. The CIO has informed you that you must perform all approval of updates from the corporate headquarters, but that it does not matter where the updates are downloaded from. What two solutions could you implement that will allow you to approve all updates locally but not overburden your WAN links? (Choose two correct answers.)

    A. Install multiple SUS servers on your network worldwide. Allow administrators in remote locations to have administrative control over the SUS servers located in their locations.

    B. Install multiple SUS servers on your network worldwide. Configure the servers in remote locations to keep updates locally on the SUS server. Configure the servers in remote locations to synchronize against the SUS server located in your corporate headquarters. Configure clients in remote locations to use the SUS server that is located closest to them geographically.

C. Install multiple SUS servers on your network worldwide. Configure the servers in remote locations to not download updates but instead to point clients to the Windows Update Web servers. Configure the servers in remote locations to synchronize against the SUS server located in your corporate headquarters. Configure clients in remote locations to use the SUS server that is located closest to them geographically.

D. Install a Network Load Balanced SUS server cluster in your corporate headquarters. Configure clients in remote locations to download all updates directly from the Windows Update Web servers.

4. You are the network administrator with a global SUS solution in place. Currently, all remote sites have dedicated WAN links that connect to your global headquarters in Massachusetts that are used for SUS only. You have been directed by your CIO to reduce costs and improve the performance of the SUS solution in use on your network. Each of your remote locations also currently has an ISDN connection through a local ISP for Internet connectivity. The corporate headquarters has a full T-1 connection to the Internet. Any solution that you come up with must still allow for only local approval of all available updates. How can you eliminate the need for the WAN links and improve the speed and performance of the SUS solution your network has in place?

A. Install and configure SUS servers in each remote location. Configure virtual private network (VPN) links through the Internet from each remote location to the corporate headquarters. Configure the SUS servers in each remote location to synchronize their content from the local SUS server.

B. Install and configure SUS servers in each remote location. Configure the SUS servers in each remote location to be managed by a local administrator.

C. Install and configure SUS servers in each remote location. Configure the SUS server in each location to synchronize their content from the local SUS server using Simple Mail Transfer Protocol (SMTP).

D. Install and configure SUS servers in each remote location. Configure VPN links through the Internet from each remote location to the corporate headquarters. Configure the SUS servers in each remote location to be managed by a local administrator.

5. You are the network administrator for Area 51 Networks, and have just completed a default installation of Windows Server 2003 Enterprise Edition on a new server. You are now preparing to install and configure SUS. What additional step must you first complete before you can successfully install and configure SUS on this server?

    A. You must join this server to a Windows Server 2003 Active Directory domain.

    B. You must install and configure the Routing and Remote Access Service (RRAS) on this server.

    C. You must install and configure IIS on this server.

    D. You must create and configure a shared folder on this server.

6. You are the network administrator and have just completed a default installation of Windows Server 2003 Enterprise Edition on a new server. You are now preparing to install and configure SUS. The server has three hard drives installed, configured as follows:

- Drive-0: Volume C, NTFS, 4 GB free space, Windows operating system files
- Drive-1: Volume D, FAT32, 12 GB free space, shared network storage folder
- Drive-2: Volume E, unformatted, 20 GB free space.

Which two of the following additional steps should you complete before installing the SUS server to ensure that it is installed correctly? (Choose two correct answers)

    A. Format Volume E with the NTFS file system.

    B. Create and configure a shared folder on this server.

    C. Convert Volume D to the NTFS file system.

    D. Format Volume C with the NTFS file system.

7. Your network is operating in Windows Server 2003 functional mode at both the domain and forest level. A four-node NLB cluster running ISA Server 2000 has been placed between your internal network and your Internet connection. You have recently installed and configured an SUS server on your internal network; however, it cannot establish a connection to the Windows Update Web servers. What must you do to ensure that your SUS solution functions properly?

    A. Place the SUS server on the screened subnet that has direct access to the Internet.

    B. Configure the proxy server properties in the SUS server options.

    C. Create a VPN tunnel through the ISA server cluster to the Internet.

    D. Open port 3389 on your router to allow SUS traffic through.

8. Tom has configured Automatic Updates via Group Policy to download updates from an internal SUS server named GREEN42. All client computers on Tom's network are running Windows 2000 Professional SP4. Automatic Updates was configured to download and install, automatically, any available updates from GREEN42 on a daily basis. After several weeks, Tom notices that no updates have been applied to his client computer. Given what you know so far, what could be the possible reasons why no updates have been received on Tom's computer?

    A. Tom has not configured synchronization to occur on the SUS server.

    B. Tom has not approved any updates on the SUS server for client installation.

    C. Tom does not have the required version of the Automatic Updates client on his computer.

    D. Tom does not have the required version of the SUS application installed on his server.

9. Your global network is operating in Windows Server 2003 functional mode at both the domain and forest level and is geographically dispersed over 25 locations in North America and Western Europe. You have installed and configured SUS servers that have subsequently been placed in all remote locations on your network. All Group Policy configuration is performed at the corporate headquarters in Massachusetts. You have OUs corresponding to each remote location on your network. How should you configure the *Specify intranet Microsoft update service location* option for each of your OUs?

    A. You should point the clients in all OUs towards the SUS server that is located in your corporate headquarters.

    B. You should point the clients in North American OUs to Western European SUS servers for redundancy. Likewise, you should point the clients in the Western European OUs to North American SUS servers.

    C. You should point the clients in each OU towards the local SUS server located at that location.

    D. You should point the clients in all OUs towards all available SUS servers for maximum reliability.

10. Your global network is operating in Windows Server 2003 functional mode at both the domain and forest level. Your network is geographically dispersed over 25 locations in North America and Western Europe. You have installed and configured SUS servers that have subsequently been placed in all remote locations on your network. All Group Policy configuration is performed at the corporate headquarters in Massachusetts. You have 1,500 Windows XP Professional SP1 desktop clients and 700 Windows 2000 Professional SP4 portable computer clients on your network. The portable computers are often not attached to the network during the scheduled update installation time of 3A.M. What can you do to ensure that these portable computer clients will automatically download and install available approved updates the next time they are started while connected to the network?

A. Enable the **Configure Automatic Updates** option and select an installation time of 1 P.M. daily.

B. Enable the **Specify intranet Microsoft update service location** option and enter the URL of your SUS server.

C. Enable the **Reschedule Automatic Updates scheduled installations** option and configure a time delay of 10 minutes.

D. Enable the **No auto-restart for scheduled Automatic Updates installations** option.

11. You have recently installed and configured a SUS server for your 5,000 Windows XP Professional SP1 clients to use to download and install approved updates from. All clients are located in one of the ten OUs that correspond to the various departments within the company, with approximately 500 computers per department. You have also configured Automatic Updates in Group Policy at the domain level to point all of your clients towards the SUS server. After a week has gone by, you have determined through performance monitoring that your single SUS server is being slightly over-loaded. You decide to configure a second SUS server that your clients can connect to. How should you configure your clients so that half of them connect to the first SUS server and half of them connect to the second SUS server without disrupting any of the other existing Group Policies you have in place and without any any extra admin-istrative effort on your part?

A. Create two new OUs and move half of the client computers into each of the OUs. Configure a new GPO for each OU that points the Automatic Updates clients towards one of the two SUS servers. Remove the Automatic Updates GPO that is linked to the domain.

B. Create two new GPOs, with one of them pointing Automatic Updates clients towards the first SUS server and the other pointing clients towards the second SUS server. Link each of the GPOs to five of the ten departmental OUs you have. Remove the Automatic Updates GPO that is linked to the domain.

C. Create a new GPO for each of the ten OUs. Configure five of the new GPOs to point at the first SUS server and the other five new GPOs to point at the second SUS server. Remove the Automatic Updates GPO that is linked to the domain.

D. Create two new OUs within each of the 10 existing OUs. Create two new GPOs, with one of them pointing Automatic Updates clients towards the first SUS server and the other pointing clients towards the second SUS server. Link one of the new GPOs to one of the new OUs and link the other new GPO to the other new OU in each of the departmental OUs. Move half of the client computers in each departmental OU to each of the new OUs created within the departmental OU. Remove the Automatic Updates GPO that is linked to the domain.

12. You have recently installed and configured an SUS server for your 5,000 Windows XP Professional SP1 clients to use to download and install approved updates from. Automatic Updates works fine the first day after you configure it, but after that time, no updates have been downloaded and installed by your clients even though you have approved several new updates. You have accessed the SUS server and can find nothing wrong with the server's operation. What is the most likely cause for this problem?

    A. Your clients are pointing at the wrong SUS server.

    B. You have not configured rescheduling of missed scheduled updates.

    C. You have not configured clients to automatically restart after installation of updates.

    D. You have not enabled Automatic Updates to occur with a scheduled installation day and time.

13. Your network is operating in Windows Server 2003 functional mode at both the domain and forest level. You have recently installed and configured a SUS server for your 3,500 Windows XP Professional SP1 clients to use to download and install approved updates from. All of your Windows XP Professional clients can successfully download and install updates from the SUS server. You have just hired three temporary contractors who require network access so that they can reach the Internet to check their e-mail and browse Web pages. You want the Windows XP Professional SP1 portable computers these contractors are using to also contact your SUS server to ensure that they are not the cause of a security breach on your network. You do not want to join these computers to your domain; however they must still be allowed to contact your SUS server. How will you configure these three portable computers to enable Automatic Updates from your SUS server?

    A. Install the updated version of the Automatic Updates client.

    B. Manually create and configure the *HKEY_LOCAL_MACHINE\SOFTWARE\ Policies\Microsoft\Windows\WindowsUpdate* Registry key.

    C. Manually create and configure the *HKEY_CURRENT_CONFIG\SOFT- WARE\Policies\Microsoft\Windows\WindowsUpdate* Registry key.

    D. You cannot accomplish this without joining the three portable computers to your Active Directory network.

14. You are the assistant network administrator; the regular administrator is on vacation for the next two months. Your network is operating in Windows Server 2003 functional mode at both the domain and forest level. Before going on vacation, the regular administrator installed and configured an SUS server for your 3,500 Windows XP Professional SP1 clients to use to download and install approved updates from. Where can you quickly determine what updates the regular administrator had approved before she left on her vacation?

A. You should view the approval log on the SUS server.

B. You should view the SUS IIS logs.

C. You should view the synchronization log on the SUS server.

D. You should view the SUS server options.

15. You have installed and configured an SUS server and configured the Automatic
Updates to automatically download and install updates on a daily basis. After three
days, you determine that your clients have installed no updates. When you attempt to
access your SUS administration page, you cannot access the page and receive the following error from IIS: "The page you are looking for is currently unavailable. The
Web site might be experiencing technical difficulties, or you may need to adjust your
browser settings." What is the most likely cause for this problem?

A. The Software Update Synchronization Service has stopped functioning normally.

B. The World Wide Web Publishing Service has stopped functioning normally.

C. The WebClient Service has stopped functioning properly.

D. The SUS server is not properly identified in the Automatic Updates options.

Managing Updates for Legacy Clients

16. You have a Windows Server 2003 network that is operating in Windows Server 2003
functional mode at both the domain and forest level. All of your Windows 2000
Professional and Windows XP Professional clients are using an SUS server to download and install required updates. You also have an assortment of Windows 98 and
Windows Millennium Edition computers that you are responsible for supporting.
Using Windows Update locally on each of the legacy computers is not an option as
they are distributed over six locations up and down the East Coast. You have network
connectivity will all remote locations through VPN connections that have been created over the Internet and link each remote location with the home office. Each
remote location has an ISDN connection to the Internet using a local ISP. You need
to be able to keep all of your legacy clients up to date with required security patches
and updates. You also are the only person authorized in your companies IT policy to
distribute security updates. How can you accomplish the required goal? (Choose two
correct answers)

A. Create computer accounts for the Windows 98 and Windows Millennium Edition computers in Active Directory Users and Computers.

B. Use the Windows Update Catalog to locate and download required updates. Create a script that will install the updates remotely over your VPNs on the required computers.

C. Use the Windows Update Catalog to locate and download required updates. Use SMS to install the updates remotely over your VPNs on the required computers.

D. Instruct users at each location on how to use Windows Update to download and install required updates locally.

Self Test Quick Answer Key

For complete questions, answers, and explanations to the Self Test questions in this chapter as well as the other chapters in this book, see the Self Test Appendix.

1.	**C**	9.	**C**
2.	**B, D**	10.	**C**
3.	**B**	11.	**B**
4.	**A**	12.	**C**
5.	**C**	13.	**B**
6.	**A, C**	14.	**A**
7.	**B**	15.	**B**
8.	**A, B**	16.	**B, C**

MCSA/MCSE 70-292

MCSA Command-Line Reference

Introduction

Appendix A provides additional information and can be used as a reference for the command-line utilities we have discussed in the book. Appendix A should not be considered an exhaustive reference by any means, but rather a convenient and more detailed resource for the command-line utilities.

Some of the largest improvements for administrators from Windows 2000 Server to Windows Server 2003 are the significant enhancements that have been made in command-line utility functionality.

The commands discussed in Appendix A are arranged by their usage. For example, you will find commands relating to Active Directory and DNS management, rather than commands for Chapter 1, Chapter 2, and so forth. If you require additional information on a command that is included in Appendix A, we recommend you use the built-in help system of Windows Server 2003 to locate the required information.

> **NOTE**
>
> Anytime you have blank spaces in an entry, such as *West Region Sales*, you must place the entire entry in quotation marks such as *"CN=West Region Sales,DC=corp, DC=mcsaworld,DC=com"*. This is done to ensure that Windows properly parses the command and produces the desired output.

Active Directory Management

The following new command-line tools have been added to make Active Directory management easier:

- *dsadd*
- *dsmod*
- *dsrm*
- *dsmove*
- *dsquery*
- *dsget*
- *gpresult*
- *whoami*

The following parameters are identical across all usages of the *dsadd, dsmod, dsrm, dsmove, dsquery, and dsget* commands and will only be explained the first time in Table A.1: {*-s Server | -d Domain*}, *-u UserName, -p* {*Password | **}, *-q,* {*-uc | -uco | -uci*}.

The following commands are not new to Windows Server 2003, but are still highly valuable to an Administrator:

- *csvde*
- *ldifde*

dsadd

The *dsadd* command can be used to add new objects into Active Directory such as contacts, computers, groups, organizational units (OUs) and users. *dsadd* has the following top-level options:

- *dsadd computer*
- *dsadd contact*
- *dsadd group*
- *dsadd ou*
- *dsadd user*
- *dsadd quota*

dsadd computer

The *dsadd computer* command is used to add a single computer account object to Active Directory and uses the following syntax:

```
dsadd computer ComputerDN [-samid SAMName] [-desc Description]
[-loc Location] [-memberof GroupDN] [{-s Server | -d Domain}]
[-u UserName] [-p {Password | *}] [-q] [{-uc | -uco | -uci}]
```

Table A.1 details the parameters associated with the *dsadd computer* command.

Table A.1 *dsadd computer* Parameters

Switch	Function
ComputerDN	Specifies the distinguished name of the object to add.
-samid *SAMName*	Specifies the Security Accounts Manager (SAM) name to use for the created object—this will become the pre-Windows 2000 group name. If not specified, this name is derived from the distinguished name.
-desc *Description*	Specifies the description of the created object.
-loc *Location*	Specifies the location of the added object.
-memberof *GroupDN*	Specifies the group memberships of the new object.
-s *Server*	Specifies which computer to connect to in order to perform the operation.
-d *Domain*	Specifies which domain to connect to in order to perform the operation.
-u *UserName*	Specifies the remote server login user name to use.
-p {*Password* | *}	Specifies the remote server login password. * will prompt for the password.
-q	Specifies that all standard output is suppressed.
-uc	Specifies to use Unicode format for input from or output to a pipe.
-uco	Specifies to use Unicode format for output to a pipe or file.
-uci	Specifies to use Unicode format for input from a pipe or file.

dsadd contact

The *dsadd contact* command is used to add a single contact object to Active Directory and uses the following syntax:

```
dsadd contact ContactDN [-fn FirstName] [-mi Initial] [-ln LastName]
[-display DisplayName] [-desc Description] [-office Office]
[-tel PhoneNumber] [-email E-mail] [-hometel HomePhoneNumber]
[-pager PagerNumber] [-mobile CellPhoneNumber] [-fax FaxNumber]
[-iptel IPPhoneNumber] [-title Title] [-dept Department] [-company Company]
[{-s Server | -d Domain}] [-u UserName] [-p {Password | *}] [-q]
[{-uc | -uco | -uci}]
```

Table A.2 details the parameters associated with the *dsadd contact* command.

Table A.2 *dsadd contact* Parameters

Switch	Function
ContactDN	Specifies the distinguished name of the object to add.
-fn *FirstName*	Specifies the first name of the new contact.
-mi *Initial*	Specifies the middle initial of the new contact.
-ln *LastName*	Specifies the last name of the new contact.
-display *DisplayName*	Specifies the display name of the new contact.
-desc *Description*	Specifies the description of the object being created.
-office *Office*	Specifies the office location of the new contact.
-tel *PhoneNumber*	Specifies the telephone number of the new contact.
-email *E-mail*	Specifies the e-mail address of the new contact.
-hometel *HomePhoneNumber*	Specifies the home telephone number of the new contact.
-pager *PagerNumber*	Specifies the pager phone number of the new contact.
-mobile *CellPhoneNumber*	Specifies the mobile phone number of the new contact.
-fax *FaxNumber*	Specifies the fax phone number of the new contact.
-iptel *IPPhoneNumber*	Specifies the IP phone number of the new contact.
-title *Title*	Specifies the title of the new contact.
-dept *Department*	Specifies the department of the new contact.
-company *Company*	Specifies the company name of the new contact.

dsadd group

The *dsadd group* command is used to add a single group object to Active Directory and uses the following syntax:

```
dsadd group GroupDN [-secgrp {yes | no}] [-scope {l | g | u}]
[-samid SAMName] [-desc Description] [-memberof Group]
[-members Member ...] [{-s Server | -d Domain}] [-u UserName]
[-p {Password | *}] [-q] [{-uc | -uco | -uci}]
```

Table A.3 details the parameters associated with the *dsadd group* command.

Table A.3 *dsadd group* Parameters

Switch	Function
GroupDN	Specifies the distinguished name of the object to add.
-secgrp {yes	no}	Specifies the group type. A *yes* answer (the default) indicates a security group and a *no* answer indicates a distribution group.
-scope {l	g	u}	Specifies the scope of the group: *Domain Local, Global* or *Universal*.

Continued

Table A.3 *dsadd group* Parameters

Switch	Function
-samid *SAMName*	Specifies the SAM name to use for the created object—this will become the pre-Windows 2000 group name. If not specified, this name is derived from the distinguished name.
-desc *Description*	Specifies the description of the created object.
memberof *Group*	Specifies the group memberships of the new object.
-members *Member*	Specifies the objects that should be added to the new group.

dsadd ou

The *dsadd ou* command is used to add a single OU to Active Directory and uses the following syntax:

```
dsadd ou OrganizationalUnitDN [-desc Description] [{-s Server | -d Domain}]
[-u UserName] [-p {Password | *}] [-q] [{-uc | -uco | -uci}]
```

Table A.4 details the parameters associated with the *dsadd ou* command.

Table A.4 *dsadd ou* Parameters

Switch	Function
OrganizationalUnitDN	Specifies the distinguished name of the object to add.
-desc *Description*	Specifies the description of the created object.

dsadd user

The *dsadd user* command is used to add a single user object to Active Directory and uses the following syntax:

```
dsadd user UserDN [-samid SAMName] [-upn UPN] [-fn FirstName] [-mi Initial]
[-ln LastName] [-display DisplayName] [-empid EmployeeID]
[-pwd {Password | *}] [-desc Description] [-memberof Group]
[-office Office] [-tel PhoneNumber] [-email E-mail]
[-hometel HomePhoneNumber] [-pager PagerNumber] [-mobile CellPhoneNumber]
[-fax FaxNumber] [-iptel IPPhoneNumber] [-webpg WebPage] [-title Title]
[-dept Department] [-company Company] [-mgr Manager] [-hmdir HomeDirectory]
[-hmdrv DriveLetter:] [-profile ProfilePath] [-loscr ScriptPath]
[-mustchpwd {yes | no}] [-canchpwd {yes | no}] [-reversiblepwd {yes | no}]
[-pwdneverexpires {yes | no}] [-acctexpires NumberOfDays]
[-disabled {yes | no}] [{-s Server | -d Domain}] [-u UserName]
[-p {Password | *}] [-q] [{-uc | -uco | -uci}]
```

Table A.5 details the parameters associated with the *dsadd user* command.

Table A.5 *dsadd user* Parameters

Switch	Function
UserDN	Specifies the distinguished name of the object to add.
-samid *SAMName*	Specifies the SAM name to use for the created object—this will become the pre-Windows 2000 group name. If not specified, this name is derived from the distinguished name.
-upn *UPN*	Specifies the user principal name of the new user object.
-fn *FirstName*	Specifies the first name of the new user object.
-mi *Initial*	Specifies the middle initial of the new user object.
-ln *LastName*	Specifies the last name of the new user object.
-display *DisplayName*	Specifies the display name of the new user object.
-empid *EmployeeID*	Specifies the employee ID number of the new user object.
-pwd {*Password* | *}	Specifies the new user object password. * will prompt for the password.
-desc *Description*	Specifies the description of the object being created.
-memberof *Group*	Specifies the group memberships s for the new object.
-office *Office*	Specifies the office location of the new user object.
-tel *PhoneNumber*	Specifies the telephone number of the new user object.
-email *E-mail*	Specifies the e-mail address of the new user object.
-hometel *HomePhoneNumber*	Specifies the home telephone number of the new user object.
-pager *PagerNumber*	Specifies the pager phone number of the new user object.
-mobile *CellPhoneNumber*	Specifies the mobile phone number of the new user object.
-fax *FaxNumber*	Specifies the fax phone number of the new user object.
-iptel *IPPhoneNumber*	Specifies the IP phone number of the new user object.
-webpg *WebPage*	Specifies the Web site location for the new user.
-title *Title*	Specifies the title of the new user object.
-dept *Department*	Specifies the department of the new user object.
-company *Company*	Specifies the company name of the new user object.
-mgr *Manager*	Specifies the manager of the new user.
-hmdir *HomeDirectory*	Specifies the home directory for the new user object.
-hmdrv *DriveLetter*:	Specifies the home directory drive letter for the new user object.
-profile *ProfilePath*	Specifies the profile path for the new user object.
-loscr *ScriptPath*	Specifies the script path for the new user object.

Continued

Table A.5 *dsadd user* Parameters

Switch	Function
-mustchpwd {yes | no }	Specifies whether or not the new user account must change its password upon next login.
-canchpwd {yes | no}	Specifies whether or not the user can change the new user object password.
-reversiblepwd {yes | no	Specifies whether or not to store the password for the new user object using reversible encryption.
-pwdneverexpires {yes | no}	Specified whether or not the new user object password expires.
-acctexpires *NumberOfDays*	Specifies the expiration of the new user object.
-disabled {yes | no}	Specifies whether or not the new user object is disabled upon creation.

dsadd quota

The *dsadd quota* command is used to add a quota specification to a directory partition and uses the following syntax:

```
dsadd quota -part PartitionDN [-rdn RelativeDistinguishedName] -acct Name
-qlimit Value [-desc Description] [{-s Server | -d Domain}] [-u UserName]
[-p {Password | *}] [-q] [{-uc | -uco | -uci}]
```

NOTE

A *quota* specification determines the maximum number of directory objects a given security principal can own in a specified directory partition.

Table A.6 details the parameters associated with the *dsadd quota* command.

Table A.6 *dsadd quota* Parameters

Switch	Function
-part *PartitionDN*	Specifies the distinguished name of the directory partition that you are creating a quota for.
-rdn *Relative DistinguishedName*	Specifies the relative distinguished name of the quota specification being created.
-acct *Name*	Specifies the security principal that the quota applies to.
-qlimit *Value*	Specifies the number of objects in the directory partition that can be owned by the specified security principal.
-desc *Description*	Specifies the description of the quota restriction being created.

dsmod

The *dsmod* command can be used to modify existing objects Active Directory such as contacts, computers, groups, OUs and users. *dsmod* has the following top level options:

- *dsmod computer*
- *dsmod contact*
- *dsmod group*
- *dsmod ou*
- *dsmod server*
- *dsmod user*
- *dsmod quota*
- *dsmod partition*

dsmod computer

The *dsmod computer* command is used modify the properties of one or more existing computers in Active Directory and uses the following syntax:

```
dsmod computer ComputerDN [-desc Description] [-loc Location]
[-disabled {yes | no}] [-reset] [{-s Server | -d Domain}] [-u UserName]
[-p {Password | *}] [-c] [-q] [{-uc | -uco | -uci}]
```

Table A.7 details the parameters associated with the *dsmod computer* command.

Table A.7 *dsmod computer* Parameters

Switch	Function
ComputerDN	Specifies the distinguished name of the modified object or objects.
-desc Description	Specifies the description of the modified object.
-loc Location	Specifies the location of the modified object.
-disabled {yes	no }	Specifies whether or not the computer account is disabled.
-reset	Specifies the computer account is to be reset.
-c	Specifies the command is to continue processing in the event of an error.

dsmod contact

The *dsmod contact* command is used modify the properties of one or more existing contacts in Active Directory and uses the following syntax:

```
dsmod contact ContactDN [-fn FirstName] [-mi Initial] [-ln LastName]
[-display DisplayName] [-desc Description] [-office Office]
[-tel PhoneNumber] [-email E-mail] [-hometel HomePhoneNumber]
[-pager PagerNumber] [-mobile CellPhoneNumber] [-fax FaxNumber]
[-iptel IPPhoneNumber] [-title Title] [-dept Department] [-company Company]
[{-s Server | -d Domain}] [-u UserName] [-p {Password | *}] [-c] [-q]
[{-uc | -uco | -uci}]
```

Table A.8 details the parameters associated with the *dsmod contact* command.

Table A.8 *dsmod contact* Parameters

Switch	Function
ContactDN	Specifies the distinguished name of the modified object or objects.
-fn *FirstName*	Specifies the first name of the modified contact.
-mi *Initial*	Specifies the middle initial of the modified contact.
-ln *LastName*	Specifies the last name of the modified contact.
-display *DisplayName*	Specifies the display name of the modified contact.
-desc *Description*	Specifies the description of the modified contact.
-office *Office*	Specifies the office location of the modified contact.
-tel *PhoneNumber*	Specifies the telephone number of the modified contact.
-email *E-mail*	Specifies the e-mail address of the modified contact.
-hometel *HomePhoneNumber*	Specifies the home telephone number of the modified contact.
-pager *PagerNumber*	Specifies the pager phone number of the modified contact.
-mobile *CellPhoneNumber*	Specifies the mobile phone number of the modified contact.
-fax *FaxNumber*	Specifies the fax phone number of the modified contact.
-iptel *IPPhoneNumber*	Specifies the IP phone number of the modified contact.
-title *Title*	Specifies the title of the modified contact.
-dept *Department*	Specifies the department of the modified contact.
-company *Company*	Specifies the company name of the modified contact.
-c	Specifies the command is to continue processing in the event of an error.

dsmod group

The *dsmod group* command is used modify the properties of one or more existing groups in Active Directory and uses the following syntax:

```
dsmod group GroupDN [-samid SAMName] [-desc Description]
```

```
[-secgrp {yes | no}] [-scope {l | g | u}]
[{-addmbr | -rmmbr | -chmbr} MemberDN ...] [{-s Server | -d Domain}]
[-u UserName] [-p {Password | *}] [-c] [-q] [{-uc | -uco | -uci}]
```

Table A.9 details the parameters associated with the *dsmod group* command.

Table A.9 *dsmod group* parameters

Switch	Function
GroupDN	Specifies the distinguished name of the modified object.
-samid *SAMName*	Specifies the SAM name to use for the modified object—this will become the pre-Windows 2000 group name. If not specified, this name is derived from the distinguished name.
-desc *Description*	Specifies the description of the modified object.
-secgrp {yes | no}	Specifies the group type. A *yes* answer (the default) indicates a security group and a *no* answer indicates a distribution group.
-scope {l | g | u}	Specifies the scope of the group: *Domain Local*, *Global* or *Universal*.
-addmbr *MemberDN*	Specifies the members that are added to the group.
-rmmbr *MemberDN*	Specifies the members that are removed from the group.
-chmbr *MemberDN*	Specifies the members that are replaced in the group.
-c	Specifies the command is to continue processing in the event of an error.

dsmod ou

The *dsmod ou* command is used modify the properties of one or more existing OUs in Active Directory and uses the following syntax:

```
dsmod ou OrganizationalUnitDN [-desc Description]
[{-s Server | -d Domain}] [-u UserName] [-p {Password | *}]
[-c] [-q] [{-uc | -uco | -uci}]
```

Table A.10 details the parameters associated with the *dsmod ou* command.

Table A.10 *dsmod ou* Parameters

Switch	Function
OrganizationalUnitDN	Specifies the distinguished name of the object to modify.
-desc *Description*	Specifies the description of the modified object.
-c	Specifies the command is to continue processing in the event of an error.

dsmod server

The *dsmod server* command is used modify the properties of a domain controller and uses the following syntax:

```
dsmod server ServerDN [-desc Description] [-isgc {yes | no}]
[{-s Server | -d Domain}] [-u UserName] [-p {Password | *}]
[-c] [-q] [{-uc | -uco | -uci}]
```

Table A.11 details the parameters associated with the *dsmod server* command.

Table A.11 *dsmod server* Parameters

Switch	Function
ServerDN	Specifies the distinguished name of the object to modify.
-desc *Description*	Specifies the description of the modified object.
-isgc {yes | no }	Specifies whether or not this server is a Global Catalog server.
-c	Specifies the command is to continue processing in the event of an error.

dsmod user

The *dsmod user* command is used modify the properties of one or more existing users in Active Directory and uses the following syntax:

```
dsmod user UserDN [-upn UPN] [-fn FirstName] [-mi Initial]
[-ln LastName] [-display DisplayName] [-empid EmployeeID]
[-pwd (Password | *)] [-desc Description] [-office Office]
[-tel PhoneNumber] [-email E-mailAddress] [-hometel HomePhoneNumber]
[-pager PagerNumber] [-mobile CellPhoneNumber] [-fax FaxNumber]
[-iptel IPPhoneNumber] [-webpg WebPage] [-title Title] [-dept Department]
[-company Company] [-mgr Manager] [-hmdir HomeDirectory]
[-hmdrv DriveLetter:] [-profile ProfilePath] [-loscr ScriptPath]
[-mustchpwd {yes | no}] [-canchpwd {yes | no}] [-reversiblepwd {yes | no}]
[-pwdneverexpires {yes | no}] [-acctexpires NumberOfDays]
[-disabled {yes | no}] [{-s Server | -d Domain}] [-u UserName]
[-p {Password | *}] [-c] [-q] [{-uc | -uco | -uci}]
```

Table A.12 details the parameters associated with the *dsmod user* command.

Table A.12 *dsmod user* Parameters

Switch	Function
UserDN	Specifies the distinguished name of the object to modify.
-upn *UPN*	Specifies the user principal name of the modified user object.
-fn *FirstName*	Specifies the first name of the modified user object.
-mi *Initial*	Specifies the middle initial of the modified user object.
-ln *LastName*	Specifies the last name of the modified user object.
-display *DisplayName*	Specifies the display name of the modified user object.
-empid *EmployeeID*	Specifies the employee ID number of the modified user object.
-pwd {*Password* | *}	Specifies the modified user object password. * will prompt for the password.
-desc *Description*	Specifies the description of the modified object.
-office *Office*	Specifies the office location of the modified user object.
-tel *PhoneNumber*	Specifies the telephone number of the modified user object.
-email *E-mailAddress*	Specifies the e-mail address of the modified user object.
-hometel *HomePhoneNumber*	Specifies the home telephone number of the modified user object.
-pager *PagerNumber*	Specifies the pager phone number of the modified user object.
-mobile *CellPhoneNumber*	Specifies the mobile phone number of the modified user object.
-fax *FaxNumber*	Specifies the fax phone number of the modified user object.
-iptel *IPPhoneNumber*	Specifies the IP phone number of the modified user object.
-webpg *WebPage*	Specifies the Web site location of the modified user object.
-title *Title*	Specifies the title of the modified user object.
-dept *Department*	Specifies the department of the modified user object.
-company *Company*	Specifies the company name of the modified user object.
-mgr *Manager*	Specifies the manager of the modified user object.
-hmdir *HomeDirectory*	Specifies the home directory for the modified user object.
-hmdrv *DriveLetter*:	Specifies the home directory drive letter for modified user object.
-profile *ProfilePath*	Specifies the profile path for the modified user object.
-loscr *ScriptPath*	Specifies the script path for the modified user object.
-mustchpwd {yes | no }	Specifies whether or not the new user account must have its password changed upon next login.
-canchpwd {yes | no}	Specifies whether or not the user can change the password of the user object being modified.

Continued

Table A.12 *dsmod user* Parameters

Switch	Function
-reversiblepwd {yes | no	Specifies whether or not the modified user object password is to be stored using reversible encryption.
-pwdneverexpires {yes | no}	Specified whether or not the modified user object password expires.
-acctexpires *NumberOfDays*	Specifies the expiration of the modified user object.
-disabled {yes | no}	Specifies whether or not the modified user object is disabled.
-c	Specifies the command is to continue processing in the event of an error.

dsmod quota

The *dsmod quota* command is used modify the properties of one or more quota specifications in Active Directory and uses the following syntax:

```
dsmod quota QuotaDN [-qlimit Value] [-desc Description]
[{-s Server | -d Domain}] [-u UserName] [-p {Password | *}]
[-c] [-q] [{-uc | -uco | -uci}]
```

Table A.13 details the parameters associated with the *dsmod quota* command.

Table A.13 *dsmod quota* Parameters

Switch	Function
QuotaDN	Specifies the distinguished name of the quota you are modifying.
-qlimit *Value*	Specifies the number of objects in the directory partition that can be owned by the specified security principal.
-desc *Description*	Specifies the description of the modified quota restriction.
-c	Specifies the command is to continue processing in the event of an error.

dsmod partition

The *dsmod partition* command is used modify the properties of one or more existing partitions in Active Directory and uses the following syntax:

```
dsmod partition PartitionDN [-qdefault Value] [-qtmbstnwt Percent]
[{-s Server | -d Domain}] [-u UserName] [-p {Password | *}]
[-c] [-q] [{-uc | -uco | -uci}]
```

Table A.14 details the parameters associated with the *dsmod quota* command.

Table A.14 *dsmod partition* Parameters

Switch	Function
PartitionDN	Specifies the distinguished name of the directory partition that you are modifying.
-qdefault *Value*	Specifies the default quota to setting for the modified partition.
-qtmbstnwt *Percent*	Specifies the percentage that the tombstone object count should be reduced when calculating quota usage.
-c	Specifies the command is to continue processing in the event of an error.

dsrm

The *dsrm* command can be used to remove existing objects from Active Directory such as contacts, computers, groups, OUs and users. *dsrm* has the following syntax:

```
dsrm ObjectDN [-subtree [-exclude]] [-noprompt]
[{-s Server | -d Domain}] [-u UserName] [-p {Password | *}]
[-c] [-q] [{-uc | -uco | -uci}]
```

Table A.15 details the parameters associated with the *dsrm* command.

Table A.15 *dsrm* Parameters

Switch	Function
ObjectDN	Specifies the distinguished name of the objects to delete.
-subtree [-exclude]	Specifies the object and all objects contained in the subtree under that object are deleted. The *–exclude* parameter indicates that the base object is to remain and all objects in the subtree under that object are deleted.
-noprompt	Specifies no prompts are displayed to confirm the deletion of each object.
-c	Specifies the command is to continue processing in the event of an error.

dsmove

The *dsmove* command can be used to a single existing object in Active Directory within the same domain from one location to another. *dsmove* can also be used to rename an object and uses the following syntax:

```
dsmove ObjectDN [-newname NewName] [-newparent ParentDN]
[{-s Server | -d Domain}] [-u UserName] [-p {Password | *}]
[-q] [{-uc | -uco | -uci}]
```

Table A.16 details the parameters associated with the *dsmove* command.

Table A.16 *dsmove* Parameters

Switch	Function
ObjectDN	Specifies the distinguished name of the objects to move.
-newname *NewName*	Specifies the new name of the object.
-newparent *ParentDN*	Specifies the new location of the object that you are moving.

dsquery

The *dsquery* command can be used to query Active Directory per the criteria specified to locate a specific object or type of object. *dsquery* has the following top-level options:

- *dsquery computer*

- *dsquery contact*

- *dsquery group*

- *dsquery ou*

- *dsquery site*

- *dsquery server*

- *dsquery user*

- *dsquery quota*

- *dsquery partition*

- *dsquery ★*

dsquery computer

The *dsquery computer* command is used query Active Directory for information about a computer and uses the following syntax:

```
dsquery computer [{StartNode | forestroot | domainroot}]
[-o {dn | rdn | samid}] [-scope {subtree | onelevel | base}]
[-name Name] [-desc Description] [-samid SAMName] [-inactive NumberOfWeeks]
[-stalepwd NumberOfDays] [-disabled] [{-s Server | -d Domain}] [-u UserName]
[-p {Password | *}] [-q] [-r] [-gc] [-limit NumberOfObjects]
[{-uc | -uco | -uci}]
```

Table A.17 details the parameters associated with the *dsquery computer* command.

Table A.17 *dsquery computer* Parameters

Switch	Function
StartNode | forestroot | domainroot	Specifies where the search should start.
-o {dn | rdn | samid}	Specifies the output format for the search results.
-scope {subtree | onelevel | base}	Specifies the scope of the search.
-name *Name*	Searches for objects whose common name (CN) attributes match the specified value.
-desc *Description*	Searches for objects whose descriptions match the specified value.
-samid *SAMName*	Searches for objects whose SAM names match the specified value.
-inactive *NumberOfWeeks*	Searches for computers that have been inactive for a specified time value.
stalepwd *NumberOfDays*	Searches for computers that have not changed their password for a specified time value.
-disabled	Searches for computers whose accounts are disabled.
-r	Specifies the search will use recursion or follow referrals during the search process.
-gc	Specifies that the search is to use the Global Catalog.
-limit *NumberOfObjects*	Specifies a limit to the number of matches that are returned for the search.

dsquery contact

The *dsquery contact* command is used query Active Directory for information about a contact and uses the following syntax:

```
dsquery contact [{StartNode | forestroot | domainroot}] [-o {dn | rdn}]
[-scope {subtree | onelevel | base}] [-name Name] [-desc Description]
[{-s Server | -d Domain}] [-u UserName] [-p {Password | *}] [-q] [-r]
[-gc] [-limit NumberOfObjects] [{-uc | -uco | -uci}]
```

Table A.18 details the parameters associated with the *dsquery contact* command.

Table A.18 *dsquery contact* Parameters

Switch	Function
StartNode | forestroot | domainroot	Specifies where the search should start.
-o {dn | rdn }	Specifies the output format for the search results.
-scope {subtree | onelevel | base}	Specifies the scope of the search.

Continued

Table A.18 *dsquery contact* Parameters

Switch	Function
-desc *Description*	Searches for objects whose descriptions match the specified value.
-r	Specifies the search to use recursion or follow referrals during the search process.
-gc	Specifies that the search is to use the Global Catalog.
-limit *NumberOfObjects*	Specifies a limit to the number of matches that are returned for the search.

dsquery group

The *dsquery group* command is used query Active Directory for information about groups and uses the following syntax:

```
dsquery group [{StartNode | forestroot | domainroot}]
[-o {dn | rdn | samid}] [-scope {subtree | onelevel | base}]
[-name Filter] [-desc Description] [-samid SAMName]
[{-s Server | -d Domain}] [-u UserName] [-p {Password | *}]
[-q] [-r] [-gc] [-limit NumberOfObjects] [{-uc | -uco | -uci}]
```

Table A.19 details the parameters associated with the *dsquery group* command.

Table A.19 *dsquery group* Parameters

Switch	Function
StartNode | forestroot | domainroot	Specifies where the search should start.
-o {dn | rdn | samid }	Specifies the output format for the search results.
-scope {subtree | onelevel | base}	Specifies the scope of the search.
-name *Name*	Searches for objects whose CN attributes match the specified value.
-desc *Description*	Searches for objects whose descriptions match the specified value.
-samid *SAMName*	Searches for objects whose SAM names match the specified value.
-r	Specifies the search to use recursion or follow referrals during the search process.
-gc	Specifies that the search is to use the Global Catalog.
-limit *NumberOfObjects*	Specifies a limit to the number of matches that are returned for the search.

dsquery ou

The *dsquery ou* command is used query Active Directory for information about OUs and uses the following syntax:

```
dsquery ou [{StartNode | forestroot | domainroot}] [-o {dn | rdn}]
[-scope {subtree | onelevel | base}] [-name Name] [-desc Description]
[{-s Server | -d Domain}] [-u UserName] [-p {Password | *}] [-q] [-r]
[-gc] [-limit NumberOfObjects] [{-uc | -uco | -uci}]
```

Table A.20 details the parameters associated with the *dsquery ou* command.

Table A.20 *dsquery ou* Parameters

Switch	Function
StartNode | forestroot | domainroot	Specifies where the search should start.
-o {dn | rdn }	Specifies the output format for the search results.
-scope {subtree | onelevel | base}	Specifies the scope of the search.
-name Name	Searches for objects whose CN attributes match the specified value.
-desc Description	Searches for objects whose descriptions match the specified value.
-r	Specifies the search to use recursion or follow referrals during the search process.
-gc	Specifies that the search is to use the Global Catalog.
-limit NumberOfObjects	Specifies a limit to the number of matches that are returned for the search.

dsquery site

The *dsquery site* command is used query Active Directory for information about sites and uses the following syntax:

```
dsquery site [-o {dn | rdn}] [-name Name] [-desc Description]
[{-s Server | -d Domain}] [-u UserName] [-p {Password | *}]
[-q] [-r] [-gc] [-limit NumberOfObjects] [{-uc | -uco | -uci}]
```

Table A.21 details the parameters associated with the *dsquery site* command.

Table A.21 *dsquery site* Parameters

Switch	Function
-o {dn | rdn }	Specifies the output format for the search results.
-name *Name*	Searches for objects whose CN attributes match the specified value.
-desc *Description*	Searches for objects whose descriptions match the specified value.
-r	Specifies the search to use recursion or follow referrals during the search process.
-gc	Specifies that the search is to use the Global Catalog.
-limit *NumberOfObjects*	Specifies a limit to the number of matches that are returned for the search.

dsquery server

The *dsquery server* command is used query Active Directory for information about domain controllers and uses the following syntax:

```
dsquery server [-o {dn | rdn}] [-forest] [-domain DomainName]
[-site SiteName] [-name Name] [-desc Description]
[-hasfsmo {schema | name | infr | pdc | rid}] [-isgc]
[{-s Server | -d Domain}] [-u UserName] [-p {Password | *}]
[-q] [-r] [-gc] [-limit NumberOfObjects] [{-uc | -uco | -uci}]
```

Table A.22 details the parameters associated with the *dsquery server* command.

Table A.22 *dsquery server* Parameters

Switch	Function
-o {dn | rdn }	Specifies the output format for the search results.
-forest	Searches for all domain controllers in the current forest.
-domain *DomainName*	Searches for all domain controllers in the specified domain.
-site *SiteName*	Searches for all domain controllers in the specified site.
-name *Name*	Searches for objects whose CN attributes match the specified value.
-desc *Description*	Searches for objects whose descriptions match the specified value.
-hasfsmo {schema | name | infr | pdc | rid}	Searches for the domain controller(s) that hold the specified operations master role.
-isgc	Searches for all domain controllers specified in the scope that are Global Catalog servers.
-r	Specifies the search to use recursion or follow referrals during the search process.

Continued

Table A.22 *dsquery server* Parameters

Switch	Function
-gc	Specifies that the search is to use the Global Catalog.
-limit *NumberOfObjects*	Specifies a limit to the number of matches that are returned for the search.

dsquery user

The *dsquery user* command is used query Active Directory for information about users and uses the following syntax:

```
dsquery user [{StartNode | forestroot | domainroot}]
[-o {dn | rdn | upn | samid}] [-scope {subtree | onelevel | base}]
[-name Name] [-desc Description] [-upn UPN] [-samid SAMName]
[-inactive NumberOfWeeks] [-stalepwd NumberOfDays] [-disabled]
[{-s Server | -d Domain}] [-u UserName] [-p {Password | *}]
[-q] [-r] [-gc] [-limit NumberOfObjects] [{-uc | -uco | -uci}]
```

Table A.23 details the parameters associated with the *dsquery user* command.

Table A.23 *dsquery user* Parameters

Switch	Function
StartNode | forestroot | domainroot	Specifies where the search should start.
-o {dn | rdn | upn | samid }	Specifies the output format for the search results.
-scope {subtree | onelevel | base}	Specifies the scope of the search.
-name *Name*	Searches for objects whose CN attributes match the specified value.
-desc *Description*	Searches for objects whose descriptions match the specified value.
-upn *UPN*	Searches for objects whose UPN matches the specified value.
-samid *SAMName*	Searches for objects whose SAM names match the specified value.
-inactive *NumberOfWeeks*	Searches for inactive users for the specified time value.
stalepwd *NumberOfDays*	Searches for users that have not changed their password for the specified time value.
-disabled	Searches for users with disabled accounts.
-r	Specifies the search to use recursion or follow referrals during the search process.

Continued

Table A.23 *dsquery user* Parameters

Switch	Function
-gc	Specifies that the search is to use the Global Catalog.
-limit *NumberOfObjects*	Specifies a limit to the number of matches that are returned for the search.

dsquery quota

The *dsquery quota* command is used query Active Directory for information about quota specifications and uses the following syntax:

```
dsquery quota {domainroot | ObjectDN} [-o {dn | rdn}] [-acct Name]
[-qlimit Filter] [-desc Description] [{-s Server | -d Domain}]
[-u UserName] [-p {Password | *}] [-q] [-r] [-gc] [-limit NumberOfObjects]
[{-uc | -uco | -uci}]
```

Table A.24 details the parameters associated with the *dsquery quota* command.

Table A.24 *dsquery quota* Parameters

Switch	Function
domainroot | ObjectDN	Specifies where the search should start.
-o {dn | rdn }	Specifies the output format for the search results.
-acct *Name*	Specifies the search to locate quota specifications assigned to the specified security principal.
-qlimit *Filter*	Searches for quota limits that match a specified value.
-desc *Description*	Searches for objects whose descriptions match a specified value.
-r	Specifies the search to use recursion or follow referrals during the search process.
-gc	Specifies that the search is to use the Global Catalog.
-limit *NumberOfObjects*	Specifies a limit to the number of matches that are returned for the search.

dsquery partition

The *dsquery partition* command is used query Active Directory for information about partition objects and uses the following syntax:

```
dsquery partition [-o {dn | rdn}] [-part Filter] [{-s Server | -d Domain}]
[-u UserName] [-p {Password | *}] [-q] [-r] [-gc] [-limit NumberOfObjects]
[{-uc | -uco | -uci}]
```

Table A.25 details the parameters associated with the *dsquery partition* command.

Table A.25 *dsquery partition* Parameters

Switch	Function
-o {dn	rdn }	Specifies the output format for the search results.
-part *Filter*	Searches for partition objects whose common name matches the specified value.
-r	Specifies the search to use recursion or follow referrals during the search process.
-gc	Specifies that the search is to use the Global Catalog.
-limit *NumberOfObjects*	Specifies a limit to the number of matches that are returned for the search.

dsquery ★

The *dsquery* ★ command is used query Active Directory for information about objects using the specified criteria for an LDAP query and uses the following syntax:

```
dsquery * [{ObjectDN | forestroot | domainroot}]
[-scope {subtree | onelevel | base}] [-filter LDAPFilter]
[-attr {AttributeList | *}] [-attrsonly] [-l] [{-s Server | -d Domain}]
[-u UserName] [-p {Password | *}] [-q] [-r] [-gc] [-limit NumberOfObjects]
[{-uc | -uco | -uci}]
```

Table A.26 details the parameters associated with the *dsquery* ★ command.

Table A.26 *dsquery* * Parameters

Switch	Function
ObjectDN	forestroot	domainroot	Specifies where the search should start.
-scope {subtree	onelevel	base}	Specifies the scope of the search.
-filter *LDAPFilter*	Specifies an explicit LDAP search filter.
-attr {*AttributeList*	*}	Specifies the attributes to display in the search output.
-attrsonly	Specifies the attribute types to display in the search output.
-l	Specifies search output to be displayed in a list instead of table format.
-r	Specifies that the search is to use recursion or follow referrals during the search process.
-gc	Specifies that the search is to use the Global Catalog.
-limit *NumberOfObjects*	Specifies a limit to the number of matches that are returned for the search.

dsget

The *dsget* command can be used to display the selected properties of Active Directory objects. *dsget* has the following top-level options:

- *dsget computer*
- *dsget contact*
- *dsget group*
- *dsget ou*
- *dsget site*
- *dsget server*
- *dsget user*
- *dsget subnet*
- *dsget site*
- *dsget quota*
- *dsget partition*

dsget computer

The *dsget computer* command is used display the properties of a specified computer in Active Directory and has two possible usage variations. The first allows you to view the properties for multiple computers, while the second allows you to view the membership information for a single computer. The *dsget computer* command uses the following syntax:

```
dsget computer ComputerDN ... [-dn] [-samid] [-sid] [-desc] [-loc]
[-disabled] [{-s Server | -d Domain}] [-u UserName] [-p {Password | *}]
[-c] [-q] [-l] [{-uc | -uco | -uci}] [-part PartitionDN [-qlimit] [-qused]]


dsget computer ComputerDN [-memberof [-expand]] [{-s Server | -d Domain}]
[-u UserName] [-p {Password | *}] [-c] [-q] [-l] [{-uc | -uco | -uci}]
```

Table A.27 details the parameters associated with the *dsget computer* command.

Table A.27 *dsget computer* Parameters

Switch	Function
ComputerDN	Specifies the distinguished name of the computer information you want to view.
-dn	Displays the distinguished name of the computer.

Continued

Table A.27 *dsget computer* Parameters

Switch	Function
-samid	Displays the SAM account name of the computer.
-sid	Displays the SID of the computer.
-desc	Searches for objects whose description matches the specified value.
-loc	Displays the location of the computer.
-disabled	Searches for computers with disabled accounts.
-l	Specifies search output to be displayed in a list instead of a table format.
-c	Specifies the command is to continue processing in the event of an error.
-part *PartitionDN*	Connects to the specified directory partition.
-qlimit	Displays the quota limit in place on the object.
-qused	Displays the quota used by the object.
-memberof	Displays the group memberships of the computer.
-expand	Specifies that group recursion is to occur when locating groups the computer is a member of.

dsget contact

The *dsget contact* command is used display the properties of a specified contact in Active Directory and uses the following syntax:

```
dsget contact ContactDN [-dn] [-fn] [-mi] [-ln] [-display] [-desc]
[-office] [-tel] [-email] [-hometel] [-pager] [-mobile] [-fax] [-iptel]
[-title] [-dept] [-company] [{-s Server | -d Domain}] [-u UserName]
[-p {Password | *}] [-c] [-q] [-l] [{-uc | -uco | -uci}]
```

Table A.28 details the parameters associated with the *dsget contact* command.

Table A.28 *dsget contact* Parameters

Switch	Function
ContactDN	Specifies the distinguished name of the contact information you want to view.
-dn	Displays the distinguished name of the contact.
-fn	Displays the first name of the contact.
-mi	Displays the middle initial of the contact.
-ln	Displays the last name of the contact.
-display	Displays the display name of the contact.
-desc	Displays the description of the contact.

Continued

Table A.28 *dsget contact* Parameters

Switch	Function
-office	Displays the office location of the contact.
-tel	Displays the telephone number of the contact.
-email	Displays the e-mail address of the contact.
-hometel	Displays the home telephone number of the contact.
-pager	Displays the pager phone number of the contact.
-mobile	Displays the mobile phone number of the contact.
-fax	Displays the fax phone number of the contact.
-iptel	Displays the IP phone number of the contact.
-title	Displays the title of the contact.
-dept	Displays the department of the contact.
-company	Displays the company name of the contact.
-c	Specifies the command is to continue processing in the event of an error.
-l	Specifies search output to be displayed in a list instead of a table format.

dsget group

The *dsget grouip* command is used to display the properties of a specified group in Active Directory and has two possible variations in usage. The first allows you to view the properties for multiple groups, while the second allows you to view the membership information for a single group. The *dsget group* command uses the following syntax:

```
dsget group GroupDN [-dn] [-samid] [-sid] [-desc] [-secgrp] [-scope]
[{-s Server | -d Domain}] [-u UserName] [-p {Password | *}] [-c] [-q]
[-l] [{-uc | -uco | -uci}] [-part PartitionDN [-qlimit] [-qused]]
```

```
dsget group GroupDN [{-memberof | -members}] [-expand]
[{-s Server | -d Domain}] [-u UserName] [-p {Password | *}] [-c]
[-q] [-l] [{-uc | -uco | -uci}]
```

Table A.29 details the parameters associated with the *dsget group* command.

Table A.29 *dsget group* Parameters

Switch	Function
GroupDN	Specifies the distinguished name of the group information you want to view.
-dn	Displays the distinguished name of the group.
-samid	Displays the SAM account name of the group.

Continued

Table A.29 *dsget group* Parameters

Switch	Function
-sid	Displays the SID of the group.
-desc	Searches for objects whose description matches the specified value.
-secgrp	Displays whether or not the group is a security group.
-scope	Displays information about the scope of the group.
-l	Specifies search output to be displayed in a list instead of a table format.
-part *PartitionDN*	Connects to the specified directory partition.
-qlimit	Displays the object quota limit.
-qused	Displays the quota used by the object.
-memberof	Displays the group memberships of the group.
-members	Displays the objects that are members of the group.
-expand	Specifies that group recursion occurs when locating groups the group is a member of.
-c	Specifies the command is to continue processing in the event of an error.

dsget ou

The *dsget ou* command is used display the properties of a specified OU in Active Directory and uses the following syntax:

```
dsget ou OrganizationalUnitDN [-dn] [-desc] [{-s Server | -d Domain}]
[-u UserName] [-p {Password | *}] [-c] [-q] [-l] [{-uc | -uco | -uci}]
```

Table A.30 details the parameters associated with the *dsget ou* command.

Table A.30 *dsget ou* Parameters

Switch	Function
OrganizationalUnitDN	Specifies the distinguished name of the OU information you want to view.
-dn	Displays the distinguished name of the OU.
-desc	Displays the description of the OU.
-c	Specifies the command is to continue processing in the event of an error.
-l	Specifies the search output is displayed in a list instead of a table format.

dsget server

The *dsget server* command is used display the properties of a specified domain controller in Active Directory and has three possible usage variations. The first allows you to view the general properties for the specified domain controller, the second allows you to display a listing of security principals who own the largest number of objects in the directory, and the third allows you to display a listing of the directory partitions on the specified domain controller. The *dsget server* command uses the following syntax:

```
dsget server ServerDN ... [-dn] [-desc] [-dnsname] [-site] [-isgc]
[{-s Server | -d Domain}] [-u UserName] [-p {Password | *}] [-c] [-q]
[-l] [{-uc | -uco | -uci}]


dsget server ServerDN [{-s Server | -d Domain}] [-u UserName]
[-p {Password | *}] [-c] [-q] [-l] [{-uc | -uco | -uci}]
[-topobjowner Display]


dsget server ServerDN [{-s Server | -d Domain}] [-u UserName]
[-p {Password | *}] [-c] [-q] [-l] [{-uc | -uco | -uci}] [-part PartitionDN]
```

Table A.31 details the parameters associated with the *dsget server* command.

Table A.31 *dsget server* Parameters

Switch	Function
ServerDN	Specifies the distinguished name of the domain controller information you want to view.
-dn	Displays the distinguished name of the domain controller.
-desc	Displays the description of the domain controller.
-dnsname	Displays the DNS host name of the domain controller.
-site	Displays the site in which the domain controller is located.
-isgc	Displays whether or not the domain controller is a Global Catalog server.
-l	Specifies the search output is displayed in a list instead of a table format.
-topobjowner Display	Displays a listing of the security principals that own the largest number of directory objects on the server.
-part PartitionDN	Connects to the specified directory partition.
-c	Specifies the command is to continue processing in the event of an error.

dsget user

The *dsget user* command is used display the properties of a specified group in Active Directory and has two possible variations in usage. The first allows you to view the properties for multiple users, while the second allows you to view the group membership information for a single user. The *dsget user* command uses the following syntax:

```
dsget user UserDN [-dn] [-samid] [-sid] [-upn] [-fn] [-mi] [-ln]

[-display] [-empid] [-desc] [-office] [-tel] [-email] [-hometel] [-pager]

[-mobile] [-fax] [-iptel] [-webpg] [-title] [-dept] [-company] [-mgr]

[-hmdir] [-hmdrv] [-profile] [-loscr] [-mustchpwd] [-canchpwd]

[-pwdneverexpires] [-disabled] [-acctexpires] [-reversiblepwd]

[{-uc | -uco | -uci}] [-part PartitionDN [-qlimit] [-qused]]


dsget user UserDN [-memberof] [-expand] [{-uc | -uco | -uci}]
```

Table A.32 details the parameters associated with the *dsget user* command.

Table A.32 *dsget user* Parameters

Switch	Function
UserDN	Specifies the distinguished name of the user information you want to view.
-dn	Displays the distinguished name of the user.
-samid	Displays the SAM name of the user.
-upn	Displays the user principal name of the user.
-sid	Displays the SIDs of the user.
-fn	Displays the first name of the user.
-mi	Displays the middle initial of the user.
-ln	Displays the last name of the user.
-display	Displays the display name of the user.
-empid	Displays the employee ID of the user.
-desc	Displays the description of the user.
-office	Displays the office location of the user.
-tel	Displays the telephone number of the user.
-email	Displays the e-mail address of the user.
-hometel	Displays the home telephone number of the user.
-pager	Displays the pager phone number of the user.
-mobile	Displays the mobile phone number of the user.
-fax	Displays the fax phone number of the user.

Continued

Table A.32 *dsget user* Parameters

Switch	Function
-iptel	Displays the IP phone number of the user.
-webpg	Displays the Web page of the user.
-title	Displays the title of the user.
-dept	Displays the department of the user.
-company	Displays the company name of the user.
-mgr	Displays the manager of the user.
-hmdir	Displays the home directory of the user.
-hmdrv	Displays the home drive of the user.
-profile	Displays the profile path of the user.
-loscr	Displays the logon script path of the user.
-mustchpwd	Displays whether or not the user must change their password upon next logon.
-canchpwd	Displays whether or not the user can change their password.
-pwdneverexpires	Displays whether or not the user account password expires.
-disabled	Displays whether or not the user account is disabled.
-acctexpires	Displays when the user account expires.
-reversiblepwd reversible	Displays whether or not the user account password is stored used encryption.
-part PartitionDN	Connects to the specified directory partition.
-qlimit	Displays the quota limit set for the user.
-qused	Displays the quota used by the user.
-memberof	Displays the groups the user is a member of.
-expand	Specifies that group recursion occurs when locating groups that the user is a member of.

dsget subnet

The *dsget subnet* command is used display the properties of a specified subnet in Active Directory and uses the following syntax:

```
dsget subnet SubnetDN [-dn] [-desc] [-loc] [-site]
[{-s Server | -d Domain}] [-u UserName] [-p {Password | *}]
[-c] [-q] [-l] [{-uc | -uco | -uci}]
```

Table A.33 details the parameters associated with the *dsget subnet* command.

Table A.33 *dsget subnet* Parameters

Switch	Function
SubnetDN	Specifies the distinguished name of the subnet information you want to view.
-dn	Displays the distinguished name of the subnet.
-desc	Displays the description of the subnet.
-loc	Displays the subnet location.
-site	Displays the site name of the subnet.
-l	Specifies search output is displayed in a list instead of a table format.
-c	Specifies the command is to continue processing in the event of an error.

dsget site

The *dsget site* command is used display the properties of a specified site in Active Directory and uses the following syntax:

```
dsget site SiteCN [-dn] [-desc] [-autotopology] [-cachegroups]
[-prefGCsite] [{-s Server | -d Domain}] [-u UserName] [-p {Password | *}]
[-c] [-q] [-l] [{-uc | -uco | -uci}]
```

Table A.34 details the parameters associated with the *dsget site* command.

Table A.34 *dsget site* Parameters

Switch	Function
SiteCN	Specifies the common name of the site information you want to view.
-dn	Displays the distinguished name of the site.
-desc	Displays the description of the site.
-autotopology	Displays whether or not the automatic intersite topology generation feature is enabled.
-cachegroups	Displays whether or not the caching of universal group memberships is cached.
-prefGCsite	Displays the name of the preferred Global Catalog site for this site's domain controllers.
-l	Specifies search output is displayed in a list instead of a table format.
-c	Specifies the command is to continue processing in the event of an error.

dsget quota

The *dsget quota* command is used display the properties of a specified quota specification in Active Directory and uses the following syntax:

```
dsget quota ObjectDN [-dn] [-acct] [-qlimit] [{-s Server | -d Domain}]
[-u UserName] [-p {Password | *}] [-c] [-q] [-l] [{-uc | -uco | -uci}]
```

Table A.35 details the parameters associated with the *dsget quota* command.

Table A.35 *dsget quota* Parameters

Switch	Function
ObjectDN	Specifies the distinguished name of the quota information you want to view.
-dn	Displays the distinguished name of the quota.
-acct	Displays the distinguished names for the accounts that the quota is assigned to.
-qlimit	Displays the quota limit for the specified quota.
-qused	Displays the quota used for the specified quota.
-l	Specifies search output is displayed in a list instead of a table format.
-c	Specifies the command is to continue processing in the event of an error.

dsget partition

The *dsget partition* command is used display the properties of a specified partition in Active Directory and uses the following syntax:

```
dsget partition ObjectDN ... [-dn] [-qdefault] [-qtmbstnwt]
[-topobjowner Display] [{-s Server | -d Domain}] [-u UserName]
[-p {Password | *}] [-c] [-q] [-l] [{-uc | -uco | -uci}]
```

Table A.36 details the parameters associated with the *dsget partition* command.

Table A.36 *dsget partition* Parameters

Switch	Function
ObjectDN	Specifies the distinguished name of the partition information you want to view.
-dn	Displays the distinguished name of the partition.
-qdefault	Displays the default quota that is applied all security principals.
-qtmbstnwt	Displays the percent that the tombstone object count should be reduced.
-topobjowner *Display*	Displays a listing of the security principals that own the largest number of directory objects in the partition.
-l	Specifies search output is displayed in a list instead of a table format.
-c	Specifies the command is to continue processing in the event of an error.

gpresult

The *gpresult* command can be used to display Group Policy settings and the Resultant Set of Policy (RSoP) applied to a user and uses the following syntax:

```
gpresult [/s Computer [/u Domain\User /p Password]] [/user TargetUserName]
[/scope {user | computer}] [{/v | /z}]
```

Table A.37 details the parameters associated with the *gpresult* command.

Table A.37 *gpresult* Parameters

Switch	Function
/s *Computer*	Specifies the name or IP address of a remote computer.
/u *Domain\User*	Specifies a user account whose permissions are to be used to run the command.
/p *Password*	Specifies the password for the provided user account.
/user *TargetUserName*	Specifies the user name of user whose RSoP is to be displayed.
/scope {user | computer}	Displays either computer or user settings.
/v	Specifies to provide verbose output.
/z	Specifies that output should display all available information. You can direct the output to a text file by using */z file.txt*.

whoami

The *whoami* command returns information about the currently logged in user including domain name, computer name, user name, group names, logon identifier, and privileges and uses the following possible syntaxes:

```
whoami {/upn | /fqdn | /logonid}
whoami [{/user | /groups | /priv}] [/fo Format]
whoami /all [/fo Format]
```

Table A.38 details the parameters associated with the *whoami* command.

Table A.38 *whoami* Parameters

Switch	Function
/upn	Displays the user name in User Principal Name (UPN) format.
/fqdn	Displays the user name in FQDN format.
/logonid	Displays the logon ID.
/user	Displays the current user name.
/groups	Displays group names.

Continued

Table A.38 *whoami* Parameters

Switch	Function
/priv	Displays privileges.
/fo Format	Specifies the output display format. Options include:
	■ table Displays output in a table. This is the default value
	■ list Displays output in a list
	■ csv Displays output in comma-delimited (.CSV) format
/all	Displays the user name and groups, SID and privileges in the current access token.

csvde and ldifde

Realizing that administrators may have the need to import and export data into and out of Active Directory and other Lightweight Directory Access Protocol (LDAP) directory services, Microsoft has provided two utilities to accomplish that task.

- ***csvde* (CSV Directory Exchange)** *csvde* uses files formatted in the Microsoft comma-separated value (CSV) format. The advantage of the CSV format is that it is supported by many other applications such as Microsoft Excel and Microsoft Access, thus allowing you to manipulate data in these applications before importing it. The downside to using *csvde* is that it only allows the addition of new objects—*ldifde* allows the modification of existing objects.

- ***ldifde* (LDAP Data Interchange Format Directory Exchange)** *ldifde* can be used to extend the Active Directory schema, export data from Active Directory into other LDAP applications and services and to populate the Active Directory database with LDAP data from other directory services. LDIF is an Internet standard file format for performing batch import and export operations that conform to LDAP standards.

The full syntax of the *csvde* command is as follows:

```
csvde [-i] [-f FileName] [-s ServerName] [-c String1 String2] [-v]
[-j Path] [-t PortNumber] [-d BaseDN] [-r LDAPFilter] [-p Scope]
[-l LDAPAttributeList] [-o LDAPAttributeList] [-g] [-m] [-n] [-k]
[-a UserDistinguishedName Password] [-b UserName Domain Password]
```

The *ldifde* command also follows the same syntax:

```
ldifde [-i] [-f FileName] [-s ServerName] [-c String1 String2] [-v]
[-j Path] [-t PortNumber] [-d BaseDN] [-r LDAPFilter] [-p Scope]
[-l LDAPAttributeList] [-o LDAPAttributeList] [-g] [-m] [-n] [-k]
[-a UserDistinguishedName Password] [-b UserName Domain Password]
```

Table A.39 details the parameters associated with the *csvde* and *ldifde* commands.

Table A.39 *csvde/ldifde* Parameters

Switch	Function
Basic Global Parameters	
-i	Specifies to use import mode, if not specified export mode is used.
-f *FileName*	Specifies the file name for the import or export operation.
-s *ServerName*	Specifies the domain controller that is used for the import or export operation.
-c *String1 String2*	Specifies that all instances of *String1* are to be replaced with *String2*.
-v	Sets verbose mode.
-t *PortNumber*	Specifies port number connections. The default port is 389 for LDAP and 3268 for Global Catalog servers.
Export Related Parameters	
-d *BaseDN*	Specifies the distinguished name of the search base for data export.
-r *LDAPFilter*	Specifies an LDAP search filter for data export.
-p *Scope*	Specifies the search scope, the scope options are *Base*, *OneLevel*, or *SubTree*.
-l *LDAPAttributeList*	Specifies the list of attributes to return for the export query results.
-o *LDAPAttributeList*	Specifies the list of attributes to omit from the export query results.
-g	Specifies that paged searches are omitted.
-m	Specifies to omit attributes that only apply to Active Directory objects such as the *ObjectGUID*, *objectSID*, *pwdLastSet* and *samAccountType* attributes.
-n	Specifies that the export of binary values it to be omitted.
-j *Path*	Specifies the log file path and name.
Import Related Parameters	
-k	Specifies to ignore errors during the import operation and continue processing.

Continued

Table A.39 *csvde/ldifde* Parameters

Switch	Function
Credentials Parameters	
-a *UserDistinguishedName Password*	Specifies the command to run using *UserDistinguishedName* and *Password*. By default, the credentials of the user currently logged on are used.
-b *UserName Domain Password*	Specifies the command to be run using *Username Domain* and *Password*. By default, the credentials of the user currently logged on are used.

DNS Management

Microsoft has provided two new DNS management tools for Windows Server 2003: *dnscmd* and *dnslint*. As well, the ever-reliable *nslookup* command is still an important part of any DNS administrator's tool kit.

dnscmd

This *dnscmd* command can be used to display and change the properties of DNS servers, zones and resource records. The *dnscmd* is an enhanced version of the *dnsstat* command. *dnscmd* has the following general syntax:

```
dnscmd ServerName Command [Command Parameters]
```

The *ServerName* placeholder is used to specify the DNS server that you wish to manage by IP address, FQDN or host name. If the *ServerName* is not supplied, the command will be processed on the local server. The following commands are available for use with the *dnscmd* command:

- *dnscmd /ageallrecords*
- *dnscmd /clearcache*
- *dnscmd /config*
- *dnscmd /createbuiltindirectorypartitions*
- *dnscmd /createdirectorypartition*
- *dnscmd /deletedirectorypartition*
- *dnscmd /directorypartitioninfo*
- *dnscmd /enlistdirectorypartition*
- *dnscmd /enumdirectorypartitions*
- *dnscmd /enumrecords*
- *dnscmd /enumzones*
- *dnscmd /info*

- *dnscmd /nodedelete*
- *dnscmd /recordadd*
- *dnscmd /recorddelete*
- *dnscmd /resetforwarders*
- *dnscmd /resetlistenaddresses*
- *dnscmd /startscavenging*
- *dnscmd /statistics*
- *dnscmd /unenlistdirectorypartition*
- *dnscmd /writebackfiles*
- *dnscmd /zoneadd*
- *dnscmd /zonechangedirectorypartition*
- *dnscmd /zonedelete*
- *dnscmd /zoneexport*
- *dnscmd /zoneinfo*
- *dnscmd /zonepause*
- *dnscmd /zoneprint*
- *dnscmd /zoneresettype*
- *dnscmd /zonerefresh*
- *dnscmd /zonereload*
- *dnscmd /zoneresetmasters*
- *dnscmd /zoneresetscavengeservers*
- *dnscmd /zoneresetsecondaries*
- *dnscmd /zoneresume*
- *dnscmd /zoneupdatefromds*
- *dnscmd /zonewriteback*

dnscmd /ageallrecords

The *dnscmd /ageallrecords* command is used to set the time stamp on all resource records to the current time and uses the following syntax:

```
dnscmd [ServerName] /ageallrecords ZoneName NodeName [/tree]|[/f]
```

Table A.39 details the parameters associated with the *dnscmd /ageallrecords* command.

Table A.39 *dnscmd /ageallrecords* Parameters

Switch	Function
ZoneName	Specifies the zone FQDN.
/NodeName	Specifies the node to age.
/tree	Specifies that all child nodes should also be aged.
/f	Specifies that confirmation is not required to age the records.

dnscmd /clearcache

The *dnscmd /clearcache* command is used to clear the DNS cache of resource records and uses the following syntax:

```
dnscmd [ServerName] /clearcache
```

dnscmd /config

The *dnscmd /config* command is used to change values in the registry for a DNS server and its zones and uses the following syntax:

```
dnscmd [ServerName] /config ServerOption [Value] ZoneOption [Value]
```

WARNING

Experienced administrators should only perform direct editing of the Registry. Before editing, always backup the Registry.

Table A.40 details the parameters associated with the *dnscmd /config* command at the server level. While Table A.41 details the parameters associated with the *dnscmd /config* command at the zone level.

Table A.40 *dnscmd /config* Server Level Parameters

Server Option Switch	Function
/addressanswerlimit [0|5-28]	Specifies the maximum number of host records that a DNS server can send in response to a query. The default value is 0; other possible values can be between 5 and 28.
/bindsecondaries [0|1]	Specifies whether or not to use fast zone transfers. The default setting of 1 disables this option.
/bootmethod [0|1|2|3]	Specifies where the DNS server loads its configuration information from at startup. The default setting is 3.

Continued

Table A.40 *dnscmd* /*config* Server Level Parameters

Server Option Switch	Function
	■ 0 No source
	■ 1 Loads from the BIND file that is located in the DNS directory
	■ 2 Loads from the registry
	■ 3 Loads from Active Directory and the registry
/defaultagingstate [0|1]	Specifies whether or not scavenging is enabled on newly created zones. The default setting of 1 disables this option.
/defaultnorefreshinterval [0x1-0xFFFFFFFF|0xA8]	Specifies a period of time during which refreshes are not accepted for dynamically updated records. The default value is 0xA8.
/defaultrefreshinterval [0x1-0xFFFFFFFF|0xA8]	Specifies a period of time during which refreshes are accepted for dynamically updated records. The default value is 0xA8.
/disableautoreversezones [0|1]	Specifies whether or not reverse lookup zones are to be automatically created. The default setting of 0 enables this option.
/disablensrecordsautocreation [0|1]	Specifies whether or not the DNS server automatically creates NS records for the zones that it hosts.
/dspollinginterval 0-30	Specifies how often the DNS server will poll Active Directory for changes in Active Directory integrated zones.
/dstombstoneinterval [1-30]	Specifies the amount of time in seconds that tombstoned records should be kept alive in Active Directory.
/ednscachetimeout [3600-15724800]	Specifies the number of seconds that Extension Methods for DNS (EDNS) information is cached. The default is 604,800 seconds.
/enableednsprobes [0|1]	Specifies whether or not EDNS probes are enabled.
/enablednssec [0|1]	Specifies whether or not the DNS Security Extensions (DNSSEC) are enabled.
/eventloglevel [0|1|2|4]	Specifies the level of logging that is to occur in the DNS log. The default value is 4.
	■ 0 Logs no events
	■ 1 Logs only errors
	■ 2 Logs only errors and warnings
	■ 4 Logs errors, warnings, and informational events
/forwarddelegations [0|1]	Specifies how a query for a delegated zone is to be handled by the DNS server. The default value is 0.

Continued

Table A.40 *dnscmd /config* Server Level Parameters

Server Option Switch	Function
	■ 0 Automatically sends queries referring to delegated subzones to the appropriate subzone ■ 1 Forwards queries referring to the delegated subzone to the existing forwarders
/forwardingtimeout [0x1-0xFFFFFFFF|0x5]	Specifies how many seconds that a DNS will wait for a forwarder to respond before querying another one. The default value is 0x5 (5 seconds).
/isslave [0|1]	Specifies how the DNS server will respond when a forwarded query receives no response. The default value is 0. ■ 0 If the forwarder does not respond, the server attempts to resolve the query itself ■ 1 If the forwarder does not respond, the server terminates the search and sends a failure to the resolver
/localnetpriority [0|1]	Specifies the order in which the host records are returned when the DNS server has multiple host records for the same name. The default value is 1. ■ 0 Returns the records in the order in which they are listed in the DNS database ■ 1 Returns the records that have similar IP network addresses first
/logfilemaxsize [0x10000-0xFFFFFFFF|0x400000]	Specifies the maximum size in bytes that the DNS.log file can grow to. The default size is 0x400000 (4MB).
/logfilepath [Path+LogFileName]	Specifies the path of the DNS.log file.
/logipfilterlist IPAddress [, IPAddress...]	Specifies the packets that are to be logged into the debug log file by IP address.
/loglevel [EventType]	Specifies the types of events that are to be logged in the DNS.log file. The default value is 0x0. ■ 0x0 The DNS server does not create a log ■ 0x10 Logs queries ■ 0x10 Logs notifications ■ 0x20 Logs updates ■ 0xFE Logs non-query ■ 0x100 Logs question transactions

Continued

Table A.40 *dnscmd* /config Server Level Parameters

Server Option Switch	Function
	■ 0x200 Logs answers
	■ 0x1000 Logs send packets
	■ 0x2000 Logs receive packets
	■ 0x4000 Logs UDP packets
	■ 0x8000 Logs TCP packets
	■ 0xFFFF Logs all packets
	■ 0x10000 Logs Active Directory write transactions
	■ 0x20000 Logs Active Directory update transactions
	■ 0x1000000 Logs full packets
	■ 0x80000000 Logs write-through transactions
/maxcachesize	Specifies the maximum allowable size of the DNS server's cache.
/maxcachettl [0x0-0xFFFFFFFF| 0x15180]	Specifies the time in seconds that a record is maintained in the cache. The default setting is 0x15180 (86,400 seconds).
/maxnegativecachettl [0x1-0xFFFFFFFF|0x384]	Specifies the time in seconds that an entry causing a negative answer to a query remains in the cache. The default setting is 0x384 (900 seconds).
/namecheckflag [0|1|2|3]	Specifies which character standard is to be used for allowing DNS names. The default value is 3.
	■ 0 Uses ANSI characters that comply with IETF Requests For Comment (RFCs)
	■ 1 Uses ANSI characters that do not necessarily comply with IETF RFCs
	■ 2 Uses multibyte UTF8 characters
	■ 3 Uses all characters
/norecursion [0|1]	Specifies whether or not a DNS server will perform recursive name resolution. The default value is 0.
/recursionretry [0x1-0xFFFFFFFF|0x3]	Specifies the time in seconds that the server will wait before trying again to contact a remote server. The default value is 0x3 (3 seconds).
/recursiontimeout [0x1-0xFFFFFFFF|0xF]	Specifies the time in seconds that a DNS server will wait before discontinuing attempts to contact a remote server. The default value is 0xF (15 seconds).

Continued

Table A.40 *dnscmd* /*config* Server Level Parameters

Server Option Switch	Function
/roundrobin [0|1]	Specifies how host records are retuned when multiple host records exist for the same name. The default value is 1.
/rpcprotocol [0x0|0x1|0x2|0x4|0xFFFFFFFF]	Specifies the protocol that RPC will use when making a new connection from the DNS server. The default value is 0xFFFFFFFF.
	■ 0x0 Disables RPC for DNS
	■ 0x1 Uses TCP/IP
	■ 0x2 Uses named pipes
	■ 0x4 Uses LPC
	■ 0xFFFFFFFF All protocols
/scavenginginterval [0x0-0xFFFFFFFF|0x0]	Specifies whether or not scavenging is enabled and the number of hours between scavenging cycles. The default value is 0x0, which will disable scavenging.
/secureresponses [0|1]	Specifies whether or not DNS filters the records that are in the cache. The default value is 0.
	■ 0 Saves all responses to name queries to a cache
	■ 1 Saves only the records that belong to the same DNS subtree to a cache
/sendport [0x0-0xFFFFFFFF|0x0]	Specifies the port number that DNS will use to send recursive queries. The default value of 0x0 specifies a random port.
/strictfileparsing [0|1]	Specifies the behavior of the DNS server when it encounters an error while loading the zone data. The default value is 0.
	■ 0 Continues to load even if the server encounters an erroneous record, the error is recorded in the DNS log.
	■ 1 Stops loading and records the error in the DNS log
/updateoptions RecordValue	Specifies that dynamic updates are prohibited for specific record types. Multiple records can be prohibited by using the hexadecimal sum of their individual values.
	■ 0x0 Does not restrict any record types
	■ 0x1 Excludes Start of Authority (SOA) records
	■ 0x2 Excludes name server (NS) records
	■ 0x4 Excludes delegation NS records

Table A.40 *dnscmd* /*config* Server Level Parameters

Server Option Switch	Function
	■ 0x8 Excludes server host records
	■ 0x100 On secure dynamic update, excludes SOA records
	■ 0x200 On secure dynamic update, excludes root NS records
	■ 0x30F On standard dynamic update, excludes NS, SOA, and server host records; for secure dynamic update, excludes root NS and SOA records
	■ 0x400 On secure dynamic update, excludes delegation NS records.
	■ 0x800 On secure dynamic update, excludes server host records
	■ 0x1000000 Excludes DS records
	■ 0x80000000 Disables DNS dynamic update
/writeauthorityns [0|1]	Specifies when the DNS server will write NS records in the authority section of a response. The default value is 0.
	■ 0 Writes NS records in the Authority section of referrals only
	■ 1 Writes NS records in the Authority section of all successful authoritative responses
/xfrconnecttimeout [0x0-0xFFFFFFFF|0x1E]	Specifies the time in seconds that a primary DNS server will wait for a zone transfer response from a secondary. The default value is 0x1E (30 seconds).

Table A.41 *dnscmd* /*config* Zone Level Parameters

Zone Option Switch	Function
/aging	Specifies whether or not scavenging is enabled for the specified zone.
/allownsrecordsautocreation	Forces an override on the DNS server's NS record autocreation setting for the specified zone.
/allowupdate	Specifies whether or not the specified zone will accept dynamic updates for the specified zone.
/forwarderslave	Forces an override on the DNS server /*isslave* setting for the specified zone.

Continued

Table A.41 *dnscmd /config* Zone Level Parameters

Zone Option Switch	Function
/forwardertimeout	Specifies how many seconds the specified zone waits for a forwarder to respond before contacting another for the specified zone.
/norefreshinterval	Specifies the time interval during which no refreshes can be made to dynamically created records for the specified zone.
/refreshinterval	Specifies the time interval during which refreshes are allowed to dynamically created records for the specified zone.
/securesecondaries	Specifies which secondary servers are allowed to receive updates from the master for the specified zone.

dnscmd /createbuiltindirectorypartitions

The *dnscmd /createbuiltindirectorypartitions* command is used to create a DNS application directory partition and uses the following syntax:

```
dnscmd [ServerName] /createbuiltindirectorypartitions [/forest]
[/alldomains]
```

Table A.42 details the parameters associated with the *dnscmd /createbuiltindirectorypartitions* command.

Table A.42 *dnscmd /createbuiltindirectorypartitions* Parameters

Switch	Function
/forest	Creates a DNS directory partition in the specified forest.
/alldomains	Creates a DNS directory partition in all domains in the forest.

dnscmd /createdirectorypartition

The *dnscmd /createdirectorypartition* command is used to create an additional DNS application directory partition and uses the following syntax:

```
dnscmd [ServerName] /createdirectorypartition FQDNofDP
```

The *FQDNofDP* placeholder specifies the FQDN of the DNS application partition.

dnscmd /deletedirectorypartition

The *dnscmd /deletedirectorypartition* command is used to delete a DNS application directory partition and uses the following syntax:

```
dnscmd [ServerName] /deletedirectorypartition FQDNofDP
```

The *FQDNofDP* placeholder specifies the FQDN of the DNS application partition.

dnscmd /directorypartitioninfo

The *dnscmd /directorypartitioninfo* command is used to display information about a DNS application directory partition and uses the following syntax:

```
dnscmd [ServerName] /directorypartitioninfo FQDNofDP [/detail]
```

Table A.43 details the parameters associated with the *dnscmd /directorypartitioninfo* command.

Table A.43 *dnscmd /directorypartitioninfo* Parameters

Switch	Function
FQDNofDP	Specifies the DNS application partition FQDN.
/detail	Displays all information about the partition.

dnscmd /enlistdirectorypartition

The *dnscmd /enlistdirectorypartition* command is used to add the specified DNS server to a DNS application directory partition replica set and uses the following syntax:

```
dnscmd [ServerName] /enlistdirectorypartition FQDNofDP
```

The *FQDNofDP* placeholder specifies the FQDN of the DNS application partition.

dnscmd /enumdirectorypartitions

The *dnscmd /enumdirectorypartitions* command is used to list information about the DNS application partitions on a specified server and uses theand uses the following syntax:

```
dnscmd [ServerName] /enumdirectorypartitions [/custom]
```

The */custom* parameter specifies that only user created application partitions are to be listed.

dnscmd /enumrecords

The *dnscmd /enumrecords* command is used to list resource records in a specified DNS zone and uses the following syntax:

```
dnscmd [ServerName] /enumrecords ZoneName NodeName [/type RRType RRData]
[/authority] [/glue] [/additional] [/node |/child |/startchild ChildName]
[/continue |/detail]
```

Table A.44 details the parameters associated with the *dnscmd /enumrecords* command.

Table A.44 *dnscmd /enumrecords* Parameters

Switch	Function
ZoneName	Specifies the zone name.
NodeName	Specifies the node name.
/type *RRType RRData*	Specifies the type of record and type of data.
/authority	Specifies to include authoritative data.
/glue	Specifies to include glue data.
/additional	Specifies to include all information is to be included in the output.
/node	Lists only records of the specified node.
/child	Lists only records of the specified child.
/startchild *ChildName*	Lists records starting at the specified child.
/continue	Specifies to display only the record and data type.
/detail	Specifies to display all information about a record.

dnscmd /enumzones

The *dnscmd /enumzones* command is used to list zones that exist on a specified server and uses the following syntax:

```
dnscmd [ServerName] /enumzones
[/primary| /secondary| /forwarder| /stub| /cache| /auto-created]
[/forward|/reverse|/ds|/file]
[/domaindirectorypartition| /forestdirectorypartition|
/customdirectorypartition| /legacydirectorypartition| /directorypartition
DPFQDN]
```

Table A.45 details the parameters associated with the *dnscmd /enumzones* command.

Table A.45 *dnscmd /enumzones* Parameters

Switch	Function
/primary	Lists all standard primary or Active Directory integrated zones.
/secondary	Lists all standard secondary zones.
/forwarder	Lists all zones that forward queries to another DNS server.
/stub	Lists all stub zones.
/cache	Lists all zones that are loaded into the cache.
/auto-created	Lists all zones that were automatically created during the DNS server installation.
/forward	Lists all forward lookup zones.
/reverse	Lists all reverse lookup zones.

Continued

Table A.45 *dnscmd /enumzones* Parameters

Switch	Function
/ds	Lists all Active Directory integrated zones.
/file	Lists all zones that are not Active Directory integrated.
/domaindirectorypartition	Lists all zones that are stored in the domain directory partition.
/forestdirectorypartition	Lists all zones that are stored in the forest DNS application directory partitions.
/customdirectorypartition	Lists all zones that are stored in user created application directory partitions.
/legacydirectorypartition	Lists all zones that are stored in the domain directory partition.
/directorypartition *DPFQDN*	Lists all zones that are stored in the specified directory partition.

dnscmd /info

The *dnscmd /info* command is used to display the registry settings in the **HKEY_LOCAL_MACHINE\SYSTEM\CurrentControlSet\Services\DNS\ Parameters** key and uses the following syntax:

```
dnscmd [ServerName] /info [Setting]
```

The settings that can be displayed are those listed under the *dnscmd /config* command in Table A.40.

dnscmd /nodedelete

The *dnscmd /nodelete* command is used to delete all records on a specified server and uses the following syntax:

```
dnscmd [ServerName] /nodedelete ZoneName NodeName [/tree] [/f]
```

Table A.46 details the parameters associated with the *dnscmd /nodelete* command.

Table A.46 *dnscmd /nodelete* Parameters

Switch	Function
ZoneName	Specifies the name of the zone.
NodeName	Specifies the name of the node.
/tree	Specifies to delete all child records.
/f	Specifies to not display confirmation during the process.

dnscmd /recordadd

The *dnscmd /recordadd* command is used to add a record to the specified zone has the following syntax:

```
dnscmd [ServerName] /recordadd ZoneName NodeName RRType RRData
```

Table A.47 details the parameters associated with the *dnscmd /recordadd* command.

Table A.47 *dnscmd /recordadd* Parameters

Switch	Function
ZoneName	Specifies the name of the zone.
NodeName	Specifies the name of the node.
RRType	Specifies the type of record to add.
RRData	Specifies the record data.

dnscmd /recorddelete

The *dnscmd /recorddelete* command is used to add a delete a record from the specified zone has the following syntax:

```
dnscmd ServerName /recorddelete ZoneName NodeName RRType RRData [/f]
```

Table A.48 details the parameters associated with the *dnscmd /recorddelete* command.

Table A.48 *dnscmd /recorddelete* Parameters

Switch	Function
ZoneName	Specifies the name of the zone.
NodeName	Specifies the name of the node.
RRType	Specifies the type of record to delete.
RRData	Specifies the record data that is expected.
/f	Specifies to not display confirmation during the process.

dnscmd /resetforwarders

The *dnscmd /resetforwarders* command is used to set the IP addresses to which the specified DNS server will forward DNS queries and uses the following syntax:

```
dnscmd [ServerName] /resetforwarders [IPAddress]
[/timeout TimeOut] [/slave|/noslave]
```

Table A.49 details the parameters associated with the *dnscmd /resetforwarders* command.

Table A.49 *dnscmd /resetforwarders* Parameters

Switch	Function
IPAddress	Specifies the list of IP addresses that the DNS server will forward unresolved queries.

Continued

Table A.49 *dnscmd /resetforwarders* Parameters

Switch	Function
/timeout *TimeOut*	Specifies the time (seconds) that the DNS server waits for a response from the forwarder.
/slave	Specifies that the DNS server to not perform its own iterative queries if the forwarder fails to resolve the query.
/noslave	Specifies that the DNS server to perform its own iterative queries if the forwarder fails to resolve the query.

dnscmd /resetlistenaddresses

The *dnscmd /resetlistenaddresses* command is used to set the IP addresses on the specified server that listens for DNS requests and uses the following syntax:

```
dnscmd [ServerName] /resetlistenaddresses [ListenAddress]
```

The *ListenAddress* placeholder specifies the IP address to listen to for DNS client requests.

dnscmd /startscavenging

The *dnscmd /startscavenging* command is used to immediately start scavenging on the specified server and uses the following syntax:

```
dnscmd [ServerName] /startscavenging
```

dnscmd /statistics

The *dnscmd /statistics* command is used to display or clear statistics on the specified server and uses the following syntax:

```
dnscmd [ServerName] /statistics [StatID] [/clear]
```

Table A.50 details the parameters associated with the *dnscmd /statistics* command.

Table A.50 *dnscmd /statistics* Parameters

Switch	Function
StatID	Specifies the statistic or combination of statistics that is to be displayed. Options include: ■ 00000001 Time ■ 00000002 Query ■ 00000004 Query2 ■ 00000008 Recurse ■ 00000010 Master

Continued

Table A.50 *dnscmd /statistics* Parameters

Switch	Function
	<ul><li>00000020 Secondary</li><li>00000040 WINS</li><li>00000100 Update</li><li>00000200 SkwanSec</li><li>00000400 Ds</li><li>00010000 Memory</li><li>00100000 PacketMem</li><li>00040000 Dbase</li><li>00080000 Records</li><li>00200000 NbstatMem</li></ul>
/clear	Specifies to reset the specified statistic.

dnscmd /unenlistdirectorypartition

The *dnscmd /unenlistdirectorypartition* command is used to remove the specified server from the specified directory partition replica set and uses the following syntax:

```
dnscmd [ServerName] /unenlistdirectorypartition FQDNofDP
```

The *FQDNofDP* placeholder specifies the FQDN of the DNS application partition.

dnscmd /writebackfiles

The *dnscmd /writebackfiles* command is used to commit any changes being held in memory to the zone file and uses theand uses the following syntax:

```
dnscmd [ServerName] /writebackfiles [ZoneName]
```

The *ZoneName* parameter specifies the zone to work with.

dnscmd /zoneadd

The *dnscmd /zoneadd* command is used to add a zone to the specified server and uses the following syntax:

```
dnscmd [ServerName] /zoneadd ZoneName ZoneType
[/dp FQDN| {/domain|/enterprise|/legacy}]
```

Table A.51 details the parameters associated with the *dnscmd /zoneadd* command.

Table A.51 *dnscmd /zoneadd* Parameters

Switch	Function
ZoneName	Specifies the zone that to create.
ZoneType	Specifies the type of zone to create.
/dp *FQDN*	Specifies the FQDN of the directory partition that the zone is to be created in.
/domain	Specifies to create the zone on the domain directory partition.
/enterprise	Specifies to create the zone is on the enterprise directory partition.
/legacy	Specifies to create the zone on a legacy directory partition.

dnscmd /zonechangedirectorypartition

The *dnscmd /zonechangedirectorypartition* command is used to change the directory partition the specified zone resides on and uses the following syntax:

```
dnscmd [ServerName] /zonechangedirectorypartition [ZoneName]
{ [NewPartitionName] | [ZoneType] }
```

Table A.52 details the parameters associated with the *dnscmd /zonechangedirectorypartition* command.

Table A.52 *dnscmd /zonechangedirectorypartition* Parameters

Switch	Function
ZoneName	Specifies the current FQDN of the partition the zone resides in.
NewPartitionName	Specifies the FQDN of the partition to move the zone to.
ZoneType	Specifies the type of zone to move.

dnscmd /zonedelete

The *dnscmd /zonedelete* command is used to delete the specified zone and uses the following syntax:

```
dnscmd [ServerName] /zonedelete ZoneName [/dsdel] [/f]
```

Table A.53 details the parameters associated with the *dnscmd /zonedelete* command.

Table A.53 *dnscmd /zonedelete* Parameters

Switch	Function
ZoneName	Specifies the FQDN of the zone to delete.
/dsdel	Specifies that the zone is to be deleted from Active Directory.
/f	Specifies the command to proceed without prompting.

dnscmd /zoneexport

The *dnscmd /zoneexport* command is used to create a text file listing the resource records of the specified zone and uses the following syntax:

```
dnscmd [ServerName] /zoneexport ZoneName ZoneExportFile
```

Table A.54 details the parameters associated with the *dnscmd /zoneexport* command.

Table A.54 *dnscmd /zoneexport* Parameters

Switch	Function
ZoneName	Specifies the FQDN of the zone to list.
ZoneExportFile	Specifies the name of the file to create.

dnscmd /zoneinfo

The *dnscmd /zoneinfo* command is used to display settings from the **HKEY_LOCAL _MACHINE\SYSTEM\CurrentControlSet\Services\DNS\Parameters\Zones\Zone Name** Registry key and uses the following syntax:

```
dnscmd [ServerName] /zoneinfo ZoneName [Setting]
```

The settings that can be displayed are those listed under the *dnscmd /config* command in Table A.41.

dnscmd /zonepause

The *dnscmd /zonepause* command is used to pause the specified zone and uses the following syntax:

```
dnscmd [ServerName] /zonepause ZoneName
```

The *ZoneName* parameter specifies the zone to pause.

dnscmd /zoneprint

The *dnscmd /zoneprint* command is used to list the records in the specified zone and uses the following syntax:

```
dnscmd [ServerName] /zoneprint ZoneName
```

The *ZoneName* parameter specifies the zone to list.

dnscmd /zoneresettype

The *dnscmd /zoneresettype* command is used to change the zone type of the specified zone and uses the following syntax:

```
dnscmd [ServerName] /zoneresettype ZoneName ZoneType
[/overwrite_mem|/overwrite_ds]
```

Table A.55 details the parameters associated with the *dnscmd /zoneresettype* command.

Table A.55 *dnscmd /zoneresettype* Parameters

Switch	Function
ZoneName	Specifies the FQDN of the zone to change.
ZoneType	Specifies the zone type to create.
/overwrite_mem	Specifies that existing data is to be overwritten with data from Active Directory.
/overwrite_ds	Specifies that existing Active Directory data is to be overwritten.

dnscmd /zonerefresh

The *dnscmd /zonerefresh* command is used to force a secondary zone to update from its master and uses the following syntax:

```
dnscmd ServerName /zonerefresh ZoneName
```

The *ZoneName* parameter specifies the FQDN of the zone to refresh.

dnscmd /zonereload

The *dnscmd /zonereload* command is used reload a zone from its source and uses the following syntax:

```
dnscmd ServerName /zonereload ZoneName
```

The *ZoneName* parameter specifies the FQDN of the zone to reload.

dnscmd /zoneresetmasters

The *dnscmd /zoneresetmasters* command is used to reset the IP address of the master server that provides zone transfers for a secondary zone and uses the following syntax:

```
dnscmd ServerName /zoneresetmasters ZoneName [/local] [ServerIPs]
```

Table A.56 details the parameters associated with the *dnscmd /zoneresetmasters* command.

Table A.56 *dnscmd /zoneresetmasters* Parameters

Switch	Function
ZoneName	Specifies the FQDN of the zone to be reset.
/local	Specifies a lost master list for Active Directory integrated zones.
ServerIPs	Specifies the IP address of the master servers for the secondary zone.

dnscmd /zoneresetscavengeservers

The *dnscmd /zoneresetscavengeservers* command is used to change the IP addresses of the servers that are allowed to scavenge the specified zone and uses the following syntax:

```
dnscmd [ServerName] /zoneresetscavengeservers ZoneName[ServerIPs]
```

Table A.57 details the parameters associated with the *dnscmd /zoneresetscavengeservers* command.

Table A.57 *dnscmd /zoneresetscavengeservers* Parameters

Switch	Function
ZoneName	Specifies the FQDN of the zone to scavenge.
ServerIPs	Specifies the IP address of servers that are allowed to scavenge.

dnscmd /zoneresetsecondaries

The *dnscmd /zoneresetsecondaries* command is used to specify the IP addresses to which the master server will respond when asked for a zone transfer and uses the following syntax:

```
dnscmd [ServerName] /zoneresetsecondaries ZoneName
{/noxfr|/nonsecure|/securens|/securelist SecurityIPAddresses}
{/nonotify|/notify|/notifylist NotifyIPAddresses}
```

Table A.58 details the parameters associated with the *dnscmd /zoneresetsecondaries* command.

Table A.58 *dnscmd /zoneresetsecondaries* Parameters

Switch	Function
ZoneName	Specifies the FQDN of the zone that is to have its secondaries configured.
/noxfr	Specifies no zone transfers are allowed.
/nonsecure	Specifies all zone transfers are allowed.
/securens	Specifies only the servers listed in the NS records are allowed to perform zone transfers.
/securelist	Specifies only the servers listed are allowed to perform zone transfers.
SecurityIPAddresses	Specifies the list of IP addresses that are allowed to receive zone transfers. Used with the */securelist* parameter.
/nonotify	Specifies no zone change notifications are sent to secondary servers.
/notify	Specifies zone change notifications are sent to all secondary servers.
/notifylist	Specifies zone change notifications are sent only to a specified list of servers.
NotifyIPAddresses	Specifies the list of IP addresses that are receive zone change notifications.

dnscmd /zoneresume

The *dnscmd /zoneresume* command is used to start a paused zone and uses the following syntax:

```
dnscmd ServerName /zoneresume ZoneName
```

The *ZoneName* parameter specifies the FQDN of the zone to resume.

dnscmd /zoneupdatefromds

The *dnscmd /zoneupdatefromds* command is used to update the specified Active Directory integrated zone and uses the following syntax:

```
dnscmd ServerName /zoneupdatefromds ZoneName
```

The *ZoneName* parameter specifies the FQDN of the zone to update.

dnscmd /zonewriteback

The *dnscmd /zonewriteback* command is used to write changes stored in memory to the zone file and uses the following syntax:

```
dnscmd ServerName /zonewriteback ZoneName
```

The *ZoneName* parameter specifies the FQDN of the zone to update.

dnslint

The *dnslint* command allows you to verify and troubleshoot DNS records for a specified domain name and uses the following syntax:

```
dnslint /d domain_name | /ad | /ql {text_file | autocreate} [/v]
[/r report_name] [/y] [/no_open] [/s alternate_DNS_server_ip_address]
[/c SMTP|POP|IMAP] [/t] [/test_tcp]
```

Table A.59 details the parameters associated with the *dnslint* command.

Table A.59 *dnslint* Parameters

Switch	Function
/d domain_name	Specifies the domain to test.
/ad	Specifies the DNS records used by Active Directory for replication to test.
/ql {text_file | autocreate}	Specifies to use a query list that contains a list of DNS names.
/v	Specifies to use verbose output.
/r report_name	Specifies to create a report with the command output.
/y	Specifies that any existing report files are to be overwritten.

Continued

Table A.59 *dnslint* Parameters

Switch	Function
/no_open	Specifies that the command is not to open the report after it is created.
/s alternate_DNS_server_ip_address	Specifies the IP address for the DNS server, allowing the testing of internal domain structures.
/c SMTP|POP|IMAP	Specifies to perform connectivity testing on well-known e-mail ports.
/t	Specifies to create a plaintext file with the command output.
/test_tcp	Specifies to test TCP port 53 and UDP port 53.

NOTE

You must always specify one of the following parameters: */d*, */ad*, or */ql*, but you cannot use any of these parameters together.

nslookup

The nslookup command is used to display DNS information and troubleshoot DNS servers and uses the following general syntax:

```
nslookup [-SubCommand] [{ComputerToFind | -Server}]
```

The *SubCommand* placeholder specifies one or more nslookup subcommands that are to be issued. The *ComputerToFind* placeholder specifies a computer to lookup information for using the current DNS server. The *Server* placeholder specifies the DNS server to use.

Table A.60 details the subcommands associated with the *nslookup* command.

Table A.60 *nslookup* Subcommands

Subcommand	Function
-exit	Quits *nslookup*.
-finger	Specifies that *nslookup* is to connect to the specified finger server. Uses the syntax *finger [UserName] [{[>] FileName|[>>] FileName}]*.
-help	Displays help for the *nslookup* subcommands.
-ls	Specifies that *nslookup* to list information for a DNS domain. Uses the syntax *ls [Option] DNSDomain [{[>] FileName|[>>] FileName}]*.
-lserver	Specifies a new default server using the specified DNS domain. Uses the syntax *lserver DNSDomain*.
-root	Specifies a new default server using the root sever of the DNS domain.
-server	Specifies a new default server using the specific DNS domain. Uses the syntax *server DNSDomain*.
-set	Specifies a configuration change for how *nslookup* functions. Uses the syntax *set KeyWord[=Value]*.

Continued

Table A.60 *nslookup* Subcommands

Subcommand	Function
-set all	Displays the current configuration of all subcommands.
-set class	Specifies the query class to be used. Options include: ■ *IN* Internet class ■ *CHAOS* Chaos class ■ *HESIOD* MIT Athena Hesiod class ■ *ANY*
-set d2	Specifies whether or not exhaustive debugging is to occur. The default option is *nod2*. Options include: ■ *nod2* Turns off exhaustive debugging mode ■ *d2* Turns on exhaustive debugging mode
-set debug	Specified whether or not debugging mode is to be used. The default option is *nodebug*. Options include: ■ *nodebug* Turns off debugging mode. ■ *debug* Turns on debugging mode.
-set defname	Specifies that the default DNS name is to be appended to a single component lookup request. The default option is defname. Options include: ■ *nodefname* Stops appending the default DNS domain name to a single component lookup request ■ *defname* Appends the default DNS domain name to a single component lookup request
-set domain	Specifies the default DNS domain name. Uses the syntax *set domain=DomainName*.
-set ignore	Specifies to ignore packet truncation. The default option is noignore. Options include: ■ *noignore* Does not ignore packet truncation errors. ■ *ignore* Ignores packet truncation errors
-set port	Specifies the default port use. Uses the syntax *set port=Port.*
-set querytype	Specifies the resource record type for the query. Uses the syntax *set query type=ResourceRecordType*.
-set recurse	Specifies that the DNS server is to query other servers if it does not have the requested information. The default option is *recurse*. Options include: ■ *norecurse* Stops the DNS name server from querying other servers

Continued

Table A.60 *nslookup* subcommands

Subcommand	Function
	■ *recurse* Tells the DNS name server to query other servers if it does not have the information
-set retry	Specifies the number of retries to perform. Uses the syntax *set retry=number*.
-set root	Specifies the root server to use for queries. Uses the syntax *set root=RootServer*.
-set search	Specifies that the DNS domain names in the DNS search list are to be appended to the request until an answer is received. The default option is *search*. Options include:
	■ *nosearch* Stops appending the DNS domain names in the DNS domain search list to the request
	■ *search* Appends the DNS domain names in the DNS domain search list to the request until an answer is received
-set srchlist	Specifies the default DNS domain name and search list. Uses the syntax *set srchlist=DomainName[/...].*
-set timeout	Specifies the number of seconds to wait for a reply to a request. Uses the syntax *set timeout=Number*.
-set type	Specifies the resource record type for the query. Uses the syntax *set type=ResourceRecordType*.
-set vc	Specifies whether or not to use a virtual circuit when sending requests to the server. The default option is *novc*. Options include:
	■ *novc* Specifies to never use a virtual circuit when sending requests
	■ *vc* Specifies to always use a virtual circuit when sending requests
-view	Specifies to sort the list output of the *ls* command. Uses the syntax *view FileName*.

NOTE

nslookup can be used in one of two different modes: interactive and noninteractive. When you only want to lookup a single item of information, you would normally use the noninteractive mode by issuing a command similar to *nslookup my_computer my_server*. If you do not supply the server information, the default DNS server will be used.

When you need to lookup multiple items, you would normally use the interactive mode by issuing the command *nslookup*. When in interactive mode, you can modify the behavior of *nslookup* using any of the available subcommands.

IIS 6.0 Management

The IIS Manager is the GUI interface for all IIS management functions, and the primary means for performing all IIS related management. However, command-line tools can also accomplish the same tasks that can be completed using the IIS Manager. These command-line tools are actually VBScript functions with *.VBS file extensions. The new IIS management commands include:

- *iisweb.vbs*
- *iisftp.vbs*
- *iisvdir.vbs*
- *iisftpdr.vbs*
- *iisback.vbs*
- *iiscnfg.vbs*

NOTE
You will need to allow Windows Server 2003 to register *cscript* as the default script host for .VBS files to use these IIS management scripts.

NOTE
The following parameters are identical across all usages of the *iis***.vbs* utilities and will only be explained the first time in Table A.61: */s Computer, /u [Domain\]User, /p Password*.

iisweb.vbs

The *iisweb.vbs* utility is used to manage Web sites in IIS 6.0 and uses the following top-level options:

- *iisweb /create*
- *iisweb /delete*
- *iisweb /start*
- *iisweb /stop*
- *iisweb /pause*
- *iisweb /query*

iisweb /create

The *iisweb /create* command is used to create new IIS 6.0 Web sites and uses the following syntax:

```
iisweb /create Path SiteName [/b Port] [/i IPAddress]
[/d HostHeader] [/dontstart] [/s Computer [/u [Domain\]User [/p Password]]
```

Table A.61 details the parameters associated with the *iisweb /create* command.

Table A.61 *iisweb /create* Parameters

Switch	Function
Path	Specifies the path to the Web site files.
SiteName	Specifies the name of the Web site.
/b Port	Specifies the port number that the Web site will answer requests on.
/l IPAddress	Specifies the IP address of the Web site.
/d HostHeader	Specifies the host header for the new Web site.
/dontstart	Specifies that the new Web site will not start after creation.

iisweb /delete, /start, /stop, /pause

The *iisweb /delete, /start, /stop* and */pause* commands are used to perform the specified action to the specified Web site and have the following general syntax:

```
iisweb {/delete | /start | /stop | /pause} WebSite
[/s Computer [/u [Domain\]User [/p Password]]
```

Table A.62 details the parameters associated with the *iisweb /delete, /start, /stop, /pause* commands.

Table A.62 *iisweb /delete, /start, /stop, /pause* Parameters

Parameter	Description
{/delete	/start	/stop	/pause}	Performs the specified action on the specified Web site.
WebSite	Specifies the name of the Web site to perform the command on.

 EXAM WARNING

In IIS 6.0 you can have multiple Web sites with the same name as long as they have different metabase entries. To delete them you need to give the exact metabase entry name (as apposed to site name).

iisweb /query

The *iisweb /query* command is used to display information about IIS 6.0 Web sites and uses the following syntax:

```
iisweb /query WebSite [/s Computer [/u [Domain\]User
[/p Password]]
```

The parameters for the *iisweb* */query* command are the same as those for the *iisweb* */create* command as detailed in Table A.61.

iisvdir.vbs

The *iisvdir.vbs* utility is used to manage virtual directories for Web sites in IIS 6.0 and uses the following top-level options:

- *iisvdir* */create*
- *iisvdir* */delete*
- *iisvdir* */query*

iisvdir /create

The *iisvdir* */create* command is used to create new virtual directories for Web sites and uses the following syntax:

```
Iisvdir /create WebSite [/VirtualPath] Name PhysicalPath
[/s Computer [/u [Domain\]User [/p Password]]
```

Table A.62 details the parameters associated with the *iisvdir* */create* command.

Table A.62 *iisvdir* /create Parameters

Switch	Function
WebSite	Specifies the name of the Web site to perform the command on.
/VirtualPath	Specifies the virtual path of the new virtual directory.
Name	Specifies the name of the new virtual directory.
PhysicalPath	Specifies the physical path the new virtual directory points to.

iisvdir /delete

The *iisvdir* */delete* command is used to delete an existing virtual directory for a Web site and uses the following syntax:

```
iisvdir /delete WebSite [/VirtualPath] Name
[/s Computer [/u [Domain\]User [/p Password]]
```

Table A.63 details the parameters associated with the *iisvdir/ delete* command.

Table A.63 *iisvdir* /*delete* Parameters

Parameter	Description
WebSite	Specifies the name of the Web site to perform the command on.
/VirtualPath	Specifies the virtual path to be deleted.
Name	Specifies the name of the virtual directory to be deleted.

iisvdir /query

The *iisvdir* /*query* command is used to display information about a virtual directory for a Web site uses the following syntax:

```
iisvdir /query WebSite [/VirtualPath]
[/s Computer [/u [Domain\]User [/p Password]]
```

Table A.64 details the parameters associated with the *iisvdir* /*query* command.

Table A.64 *iisvdir* /*query* Parameters

Parameter	Description
WebSite	Specifies the name of the Web site to perform the command on.
/VirtualPath	Specifies the virtual path to be display information about.

iisftp.vbs

The *iisftp.vbs* utility is used to manage FTP sites in IIS 6.0 and uses the following top-level options:

- *iisftp* /*create*
- *iisftp* /*delete*
- *iisftp* /*start*
- *iisftp* /*stop*
- *iisftp* /*pause*
- *iisftp* /*setadprop*
- *iisftp* /*getadprop*
- *iisftp* /*query*

iisftp /create

The *iisftp* /*create* command is used to create new IIS 6.0 FTP sites and uses the following syntax:

```
iisftp /create Path SiteName [/b Port] [/i IPAddress] [/dontstart]
```

```
[/isolation {ActiveDirectory | Local}
[/domain DomainName /Admin [Domain\]User /AdminPwd Password]]
[/s Computer [/u [Domain\]User /p [Password]]
```

Table A.65 details the parameters associated with the *iisftp /create* command.

Table A.65 *iisftp /create* Parameters

Switch	Function
Path	Specifies the path to the FTP site files.
SiteName	Specifies the name of the FTP site.
/b *Port*	Specifies the port number that the FTP site will answer requests on.
/l *IPAddress*	Specifies the IP address of the FTP site.
/dontstart	Specifies that the new FTP site will not start after creation.
/isolation {Active Directory	Local}	Specifies the isolation mode (Active Directory or Local) that the FTP site operates in.
/domain *DomainName*	Specifies the Active Directory domain when the isolation mode is set for Active Directory.
/Admin [Domain\]User	Specifies the administrator's account name when the isolation mode is set for Active Directory.
/AdminPwd *Password*	Specifies the administrator's password when the isolation mode is set for Active Directory.

iisftp /delete, /start, /stop, /pause

The *iisftp /delete, /start, /stop* and */pause* commands are used to perform the specified action to the specified FTP site and uses the following general syntax:

```
iisftp {/delete | /start | /stop | /pause} FTPSite
[/s Computer [/u [Domain\]User [/p Password]]
```

Table A.66 details the parameters associated with the *iisftp /delete, /start, /stop, /pause* commands.

Table A.66 *iisftp /delete, /start, /stop, /pause* Parameters

Parameter	Description
{/delete	/start	/stop	/pause}	Performs the specified action on the specified FTP site.
FTPSite	Specifies the name of the FTP site to perform the command on.

iisftp /query

The *iisftp /query* command is used to display information about IIS 6.0 FTP sites and uses the following syntax:

```
iisftp /query FTPSite [/s Computer [/u [Domain\]User [/p Password]]
```

The *FTPSite* parameter specifies the FTP site to perform the command on.

iisftp /setadprop

The *iisftp /setadprop* command is used to set FTP properties in Active Directory for a specified and uses the following syntax:

```
iisftp /setadprop UserID {FTPDir | FTPRoot} PropertyID
[/s Computer [/u [Domain\]User [/p Password]]
```

Table A.67 details the parameters associated with the *iisftp /setadprop* command.

Table A.67 *iisftp /setadprop* Parameters

Parameter	Description
UserID	Specifies the user logon ID.
FTPDir	FTPRoot	Specifies FTP isolation at either directory or root level.
PropertyID	Specifies the value of the directory or root isolation.

iisftp /getadprop

The *iisftp /getadprop* command is used to view FTP properties in Active Directory for a specified and uses the following syntax:

```
iisftp /getadprop UserID [/s Computer [/u [Domain\]User [/p Password]]
```

The *UserID* parameter specifies the user logon ID to examine.

iisftpdr.vbs

The *iisftpdr.vbs* utility is used to manage virtual directories for FTP sites in IIS 6.0 and uses the following top-level options:

- *iisftpdr /create*
- *iisftpdr /delete*
- *iisftpdr /query*

iisftpdr /create

The *iisftpdr /create* command is used to delete an existing virtual directory for a FTP site and uses the following syntax:

```
iisftpdr /create FTPSite [/VirtualPath] Name PhysicalPath
[/s Computer [/u [Domain\]User [/p Password]]
```

Table A.68 details the parameters associated with the *iisftpdr /create* command.

Table A.68 *iiftpdr /create* Parameters

Parameter	Description
FTPSite	Specifies the name of the FTP site to perform the command on.
/VirtualPath	Specifies the virtual path to create.
Name	Specifies the name of the virtual directory to create.
PhysicalPath	Specifies the physical path to point to the new virtual directory.

iisftpdr /delete

The *iisftpdr /delete* command is used to delete an existing virtual directory for an FTP site and uses the following syntax:

```
iisftpdr /delete FTPSite [/VirtualPath] Name

[/s Computer [/u [Domain\]User [/p Password]]
```

Table A.69 details the parameters associated with the *iisftpdr /delete* command.

Table A.69 *iisftpdr /delete* Parameters

Parameter	Description
FTPSite	Specifies the name of the FTP site to perform the command on.
/VirtualPath	Specifies the virtual path to delete.
Name	Specifies the name of the virtual directory to delete.

iisftpdr /query

The *iisftpdr /query* command is used to display information about a virtual directory for a Web site and uses the following syntax:

```
iisftpdr /query FTPSite [/VirtualPath]

[/s Computer [/u [Domain\]User [/p Password]]
```

Table A.70 details the parameters associated with the *iisftpd /query* command.

Table A.70 *iisftpdr /query* Parameters

Parameter	Description
FTPSite	Specifies the name of the FTP site to perform the command on.
/VirtualPath	Specifies the virtual path to display information about.

iisback.vbs

The iisback.vbs utility is used to backup and restore the IIS configuration, including the IIS metabase and metabase XML and uses the following top-level options:

- *iisback /backup*
- *iisback /restore*
- *iisback /delete*
- *iisback /list*

EXAM WARNING

iisback.vbs only creates backups. It does not copy the IIS configuration details, therefore you cannot copy a backup from one machine to another and expect the IIS server inherit the information. Use *iiscnfg.vbs* if want to replicate the IIS configuration settings.

TEST DAY TIP

IIS 6.0 backups are encrypted with a session key. The session key is only validated when you try to restore the backup. You will be able to read and delete the backups. You will not be able to modify the encrypted session key details of the backup.

iisback /backup

The *iisback /backup* command is used to backup the IIS metabase and schema and uses the following syntax:

```
iisback /backup [/b BackupName]
[/v {Integer | NEXT_VERSION | HIGHEST_VERSION}] [/overwrite]
[/e EncryptionPassword] [/s Computer [/u [Domain\]User [/p Password]]]
```

Table A.71 details the parameters associated with the *iisback /backup* command.

Table A.71 *iisback /backup* Parameters

Parameter	Description
/b BackupName	Name of the backup.
/v {Integer | NEXT_VERSION | HIGHEST_VERSION}	Specifies the version number of the backup copy. *NEXT_VERSION* will increment the current version number by 1. *HIGHEST_VERSION* can only be used with the */overwrite* parameter. It will create a backup of the last (highest) version number. (This will overwrite the highest version backup). The default is *NEXT_VERSION*.
/overwrite	Specifies that the existing backup is to be overwritten.
/e EncryptionPassword	Specifies the encrypted session key password associated with the backup.

iisback /restore

The *iisback /restore* command is used to restore the IIS metabase and schema and uses the following syntax:

```
iisback /restore /b BackupName [/v {Integer | HIGHEST_VERSION}]

[/e EncryptionPassword] [/s Computer [/u [Domain\]User [/p Password]]
```

Table A.72 details the parameters associated with the *iisback /restore* command.

Table A.72 *iisback /restore* Parameters

Parameter	Description
/b BackupName	Name of the backup.
/v {Integer | HIGHEST_VERSION}	Specifies the version number of the backup copy to be used for the restoration.
/e EncryptionPassword	Specifies the encrypted session key password associated with the backup.

iisback /delete

The *iisback /delete* command is used to delete a backup copy of the IIS metabase and schema and uses the following syntax:

```
iisback /delete /b BackupName /v {Integer | HIGHEST_VERSION}

[/s Computer [/u [Domain\]User [/p Password]]
```

Table A.73 details the parameters associated with the *iisback /delete* command.

Table A.73 *iisback /delete* Parameters

Parameter	Description
/b BackupName	Name of the backup.
/v {Integer | HIGHEST_VERSION}	Specifies the version number of the backup copy to delete.

iisback /list

The *iisback /list* command is used to display backup copies of the IIS metabase and schema and uses the following syntax:

```
iisback /list [/s Computer [/u [Domain\]User [/p Password]]
```

iiscnfg.vbs

The *iiscnfg.vbs* utility is used to manage the configuration settings of IIS 6.0 and uses the following top-level options:

- *iiscnfg /export*
- *iiscnfg /import*
- *iiscnfg /copy*
- *iiscnfg /save*

iiscnfg /export

The *iiscnfg /export* command is used to copy all or part of the IIS metabase to an XML file and uses the following syntax:

```
iiscnfg /export /f [Path\] FileName.xml /sp MetabasePath
[/d EncryptingPassword] [/inherited] [/children]
[/s Computer [/u [Domain\]User [/p Password]]
```

Table A.74 details the parameters associated with the *iiscnfg /export* command.

Table A.74 *iiscnfg /export* Parameters

Parameter	Description
/f [Path\] FileName.xml	Specifies the path and file name for the export file.
/sp MetabasePath	Specifies the metabase keys to export.
/d EncryptingPassword	Specifies the encrypted session key password associated with the export.
/inherited	Specifies that inherited properties of the exported keys are to be exported to the file as well.
/children	Specifies to recursively add the subkeys of the specified key to the export file.

iiscnfg /import

The *iiscnfg /import* command is used to add configuration settings from an XML file to the IIS metabase and uses the following syntax:

```
iiscnfg /import /f [Path\]FileName /sp SourcePath /dp DestinationPath
[/d EncryptingPassword] [/children] [/inherited] [/merge]
[/s Computer [/u [Domain\]User [/p Password]]
```

Table A.75 details the parameters associated with the *iiscnfg /import* command.

Table A.75 *iiscnfg /import* Parameters

Parameter	Description
/f [Path\] FileName.xml	Specifies the path and file name for the import file.
/sp SourcePath	Specifies the metabase keys to export.

Continued

Table A.75 *iiscnfg /import* Parameters

Parameter	Description
/dp *DestinationPath*	Specifies where in the metabase to place the imported keys.
/d *EncryptingPassword*	Specifies the encrypted session key password associated with the export.
/children	Specifies to recursively add the subkeys of the specified key to the export file.
/inherited	Specifies that inherited properties of the exported keys are to be exported to the file.
/merge	Specifies that the keys in the XML are to be merged with the existing metabase keys.

iiscnfg /copy

The *iiscnfg /copy* command is used to copy the IIS metabase and schema from one computer to another and uses the following syntax:

```
iiscnfg /copy /ts TargetComputer /tu TargetUser /tp TargetPassword

[/s Computer [/u [Domain\]User [/p Password]]
```

Table A.76 details the parameters associated with the *iiscnfg /copy* command.

Table A.76 *iiscnfg /copy* Parameters

Parameter	Description
/ts *TargetComputer*	Specifies the target computer.
/tu *TargetUser*	Specifies the user account to use to contact the remote server.
/tp *TargetPassword*	Specifies the account password for the specified with the /tu parameter.

iiscnfg /save

The *iiscnfg /save* command is used to save the IIS metabase and schema to a disk and uses the following syntax:

```
iiscnfg /save [/s Computer [/u [Domain\]User [/p Password]]
```

Security Template Management

Your primary interface for creating, testing and implementing security templates in Windows Server 2003 will be the Security Configuration and Analysis and the Security Templates MMC snap-ins. The weakness, however, of Security Configuration and Analysis is that it can only be used to analyze and configure security for a local computer. If you need to perform an analysis across a network, you will need to use the *secedit* command.

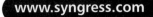
www.syngress.com

secedit

The *secedit* command-line tool offers much of the functionality of the Security Configuration and Analysis snap-in from the command-line. This allows the administrator to script security analyses for many machines across the enterprise and save the results for later analysis.

The reporting abilities of *secedit* are limited. Although you can perform a security analysis from the command-line, you cannot view the results of the analysis with *secedit*. You must view the analysis results from the graphic Security Configuration and Analysis snap-in interface. Additionally, the *secedit* tool can be used to configure, refresh and export security settings as well as validate security configuration files.

The *secedit* command uses the following top-level options:

- *secedit /analyze*
- *secedit /configure*
- *secedit /export*
- *secedit /import*
- *secedit /validate*
- *secedit /GenerateRollback*

secedit /analyze

The *secedit /anaylze* command is used to initiate a security analysis and uses the following syntax:

```
secedit /analyze /db FileName [/cfg FileName] [/overwrite]
[/log FileName] [/quiet]
```

Table A.77 details the parameters associated with the *secedit /analyze* command.

Table A.77 *secedit /analyze* Parameters

Parameter	Description
/db *FileName*	Specifies the path and file name of the database to use.
/cfg *FileName*	Specifies the path and file name of the security template that is to import into the database before the analysis is performed.
/overwrite	Specifies that the database should be emptied of its current contents before importing the selected security template.
/log *FileName*	Specifies the path and file name of the log file to use.
/quiet	Specifies that the process occurs with no further onscreen feedback.

secedit /configure

The *secedit /configure* command is used to deploy a security template and uses the following syntax:

```
secedit /configure /db FileName [/cfg FileName ] [/overwrite]
[/areas Area1 Area2 ...] [/log FileName] [/quiet]
```

Table A.78 details the parameters associated with the *secedit /configure* command.

Table A.78 *secedit /configure* Parameters

Parameter	Description
/db *FileName*	Specifies the path and file name of the database that to use.
/cfg *FileName*	Specifies the path and file name of the security template that to import into the database before performing the configuration.
/overwrite	Specifies that the database should be emptied of its current contents before importing the selected security template.
/areas	Specifies the security areas that are to be applied to the computer during the configuration process. If this parameter is not specified, all security areas are applied to the computer. The available options are: ■ *GROUP_MGMT* The Restricted Group settings ■ *USER_RIGHTS* The User Rights Assignment settings ■ *REGKEYS* The Registry permissions settings ■ *FILESTORE* The File System permissions settings ■ *SERVICES* The System Service settings
/log *FileName*	Specifies the path and file name of the log file to use.
/quiet	Specifies that the process occurs with no further onscreen feedback.

secedit /export

The *secedit /export* command is used to export a security template from a database and uses the following syntax:

```
secedit /export [/DB FileName] [/mergedpolicy] [/cfg FileName]
[/areas Area1 Area2] [/log FileName] [/quiet]
```

Table A.79 details the parameters associated with the *secedit /export* command.

Table A.79 *secedit /export* Parameters

Parameter	Description
/db *FileName*	Specifies the path and file name of the database to use.
/mergedpolicy	Used to merge and export domain and local policy security settings.
/cfg *FileName*	Specifies the path and file name of the security template to use.
/areas	Specifies the security areas to export. If this parameter is not specified, all security areas are applied to the computer. The available options are as follows and are defined in Table A.78: <ul><li>*GROUP_MGMT*</li><li>*USER_RIGHTS*</li><li>*REGKEYS*</li><li>*FILESTORE*</li><li>*SERVICES*</li></ul>
/log *FileName*	Specifies the path and file name of the log file to use.
/quiet	Specifies that the process occurs with no further onscreen feedback.

secedit /import

The *secedit /import* command is used to import a security template into a database and uses the following syntax:

```
secedit /import /db FileName /cfg FileName [/overwrite]
[/areas Area1 Area2] [/log FileName] [/quiet]
```

Table A.80 details the parameters associated with the *secedit /import* command.

Table A.80 *secedit /import* Parameters

Parameter	Description
/db *FileName*	Specifies the path and file name of the database to use.
/cfg *FileName*	Specifies the path and file name of the security template to use.
/overwrite	Specifies that the database should be emptied of its current contents before importing the selected security template.
/areas	Specifies the security areas that are to be imported. If this parameter is not specified, all security areas are applied to the computer. The available options are as follows and are defined in Table A.78: <ul><li>GROUP_MGMT</li><li>USER_RIGHTS</li><li>REGKEYS</li></ul>

Continued

Table A.80 *secedit /import* Parameters

Parameter	Description
	■ FILESTORE
	■ SERVICES
/log *FileName*	Specifies the path and file name of the log file to use.
/quiet	Specifies that the process occurs with no further onscreen feedback.

secedit /validate

The *secedit /validate* command is used to validate the syntax of a security template and uses the following syntax:

```
secedit /validate FileName
```

secedit /GenerateRollback

The *secedit /GenerateRollback* command is used to generate a rollback template and uses the following syntax:

```
secedit /GenerateRollback /CFG FileName

/RBK SecurityTemplatefilename [/log RollbackFileName] [/quiet]
```

Table A.81 details the parameters associated with the *secedit /GenerateRollback* command.

Table A.81 *secedit /GenerateRollback* Parameters

Parameter	Description
/cfg *FileName*	Specifies the name of the security template that you want to create a rollback template for.
/RBK *Security Templatefilename*	Specifies the file name of the security template that will be created as the rollback template.
/log *RollbackFile Name*	Specifies the path and file name of the log file to use.
/quiet	Specifies that the process occurs with no further onscreen feedback.

Windows Backup Management

Although you will perform the majority of your backup operations from within the GUI by using the Windows Backup Utility, you may wish to use the *ntbackup* command at times, such as for scripting backups to be performed. Recall that you can only perform backups using the *ntbackup* command—restoration is not supported.

ntbackup

The *ntbackup* command is used to perform backup operations at the command prompt and uses the following syntax:

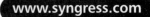

```
ntbackup backup [systemstate] "@FileName.bks" /J {"JobName"}
[/P {"PoolName"}] [/G {"GUIDName"}] [/T {"TapeName"}] [/N {"MediaName"}]
[/F {"FileName"}] [/D {"SetDescription"}] [/DS {"ServerName"}]
[/IS {"ServerName"}] [/A] [/V:{yes | no}] [/R:{yes | no}] [/L:{f | s | n}]
[/M {BackupType}] [/RS:{yes | no}] [/HC:{on | off}] [/SNAP:{on | off}]
```

Table A.82 details the parameters associated with the *ntbackup* command.

Table A.82 *ntbackup* Parameters

Parameter	Description
systemstate	Specifies that the system state data is to be backed up.
@FileName.bks	Specifies the name of the backup file to be created.
/J {"JobName"}	Specifies the job name assigned to the backup job.
/P {"PoolName}	Specifies the media pool that you want to use media for the backup.
G {"GUIDName"}	Specifies this tape is to be overwritten or appended to.
/T {"TapeName"}	Specifies this tape is to be overwritten or appended to.
/N {"MediaName"}	Specifies a new tape name.
/F {"FileName"}	Specifies the logical disk path and file name.
/D {"SetDescription"}	Specifies a label for each backup set.
/DS {"ServerName"}	Specifies that the directory service file for the specified Exchange Server to be backed up.
/IS {"ServerName"}	Specifies that the information store file for the specified Exchange Server to be backed up.
/A	Specified that the data is to be appended. Must be used in conjunction with the /G or /T switch, but not the /P switch.
/V:{yes	no}	Specifies whether or not the data is verified after the backup.
/R:{yes	no}	Specifies whether or not access to the backup set is restricted to the owner and members of the Administrators group.
/L:{f	s	n}	Specifies the type of log file to create. Options include: ■ *F* = Full ■ *S* = Summary ■ *N* = None
/M {BackupType}	Specifies the backup type from the available options: *normal, copy, differential, incremental*, or *daily*.
/RS:{yes	no}	Specifies that the backed up data is to be migrated to Remote Storage.
/HC:{on	off}	Specifies whether or not to use hardware compression.
/SNAP:{on	off}	Specifies whether or not the backup should use volume shadow copy.

MCSA/MCSE 70-292

Self Test Questions, Answers, and Explanations

This appendix provides complete Self Test Questions, Answers, and Explanations for each chapter.

Chapter 1 Overview of Windows Server 2003

Creating and Managing Groups

1. You are an assistant network administrator for Billy's Jeans, Inc. You have been tasked with creating three new groups, one for each of the following divisions: Sales, Marketing, and Production. The Sales group is to be configured with permissions required to access a shared network folder named Sales. The Marketing group is to be configured only for e-mail distribution to its members. The Production group is to be configured for both e-mail distribution and with the required permissions to access the Sales folder. Which of the following set of actions presents the correct steps to accomplish the requirement you have been tasked with?

    A. Create a security group named Sales and configure the Sales folder with the required permissions for this group. Create a security group named Marketing and configure the Sales folder with the required permissions for this group. Create a distribution group named Production and configure the Sales folder with the required permissions for this group. Additionally, configure an e-mail address for the Production group.

    B. Create a distribution group named Sales and configure the Sales folder with the required permissions for this group. Create a distribution group named Marketing and configure an e-mail address for this group. Create a security group named Production and configure the Sales folder with the required permissions for this group. Additionally, configure an e-mail address for the Production group.

    C. Create a security group named Sales and configure the Sales folder with the required permissions for this group. Create a distribution group named Production and configure an e-mail address for this group. Create a security group named Marketing and configure an e-mail address for this group.

    D. Create a security group named Sales and configure the Sales folder with the required permissions for this group. Create a distribution group named Marketing and configure an e-mail address for this group. Create a security group named Production and configure an e-mail address for this group. Additionally, configure the Sales folder with the required permissions for the Production group.

    ☑ **D.** The correct steps to be performed are to create security groups for both the Sales and Production divisions and configure the required permissions for both groups on the Sales folder. Additionally, the Production group should be configured with an e-mail address to allow message distribution. Lastly, a distribution group for the Marketing division should be created and configured with an e-mail address to allow message distribution.

☒ **A, B, C.** The Marketing division requires a distribution group and the Production division sion requires a security group configured additionally with an e-mail address, therefore Answer **A** is incorrect. A distribution group cannot be used to configure security settings, as in the case of the Sales group, therefore Answer **B** is incorrect. The Marketing security group was not correctly configured with the required permissions to the Sales folder, therefore Answer **C** is incorrect.

2. Hannah is preparing to configure user rights and permissions for 1,600 users that are spread out over five different departments: Sales, Marketing, Production, Engineering, and Administration. Each department is composed of two divisions: East and West. The network is also composed of two child domains under the root domain: East and West. The network has a total of ten divisions. How can Hannah create groups to use in assigning user rights and permissions without causing excessive directory replication between the two child domains? (Choose two correct answers.)

   A. Hannah should create Universal groups for all ten divisions.

   B. Hannah should create two Universal groups, UEast and Uwest, and place the five respective departmental groups in them.

   C. Hannah should create Global groups for all ten divisions.

   D. Hannah should create two Global groups, GEast and Gwest, and place the five respective departmental groups in them.

   ☑ **B, C.** The most efficient way to accomplish this task is for Hannah to create ten Global groups (such as GWSales, GWMarketing, GWProduction, GWEngineering, GWAdministration, GESales, GEMarking, GEProduction, GEEngineering, and GEAdministration). She should also create two Universal groups, UEast and UWest. Into the UEast group she should place the five eastern divisional groups; into the UWest group she should place the five western divisional groups. By placing the user accounts into the Global groups, Hannah can prevent replication of these objects (which typically require frequent maintenance) from being replicated to other domain Global Catalog servers. Membership changes in these Global groups will have no affect on the Universal groups and thus will not cause replication traffic to increase.

   ☒ **A, D.** The creation of Universal groups for each of the ten divisions would not be the best solution as the user account would be placed directly in these Universal groups, resulting in excessive amounts of replication traffic, therefore Answer **A** is incorrect. Also, creating Global groups to hold the divisional groups would not achieve the desired effect, therefore Answer **D** is incorrect.

3. You are preparing to assign user rights and permissions to 150 users on your network. Which of the following reasons explain why assigning the rights and permissions to a group and then placing the users into the group is the best course of action? (Choose three correct answers.)

A. Configuring user rights and permissions on groups is more accurate than configuring user rights and permissions on individual user accounts.

B. Configuring user rights and permissions on groups requires less administrative time and labor to perform.

C. Configuring user rights and permissions on groups allows you to quickly manage which users get these rights and permissions by adding or removing them from the group.

D. Configuring user rights and permissions ·on groups prevents attackers from using the user accounts in an unauthorized fashion.

☑ **A, B, C.** Answer **A** is correct because by configuring the user rights and permissions on one group instead of 150 users, you have much less chance for error—as well, all users will be configured in the same way. Answer **B** can be considered correct since you are only making the configuration on one object instead of 150 objects, the amount of time required drops dramatically. Lastly Answer **C** is correct, because by configuring the group with the required rights and permissions, you can quickly and efficiently effect changes to individual user accounts by adding or removing them from the group.

☒ **D.** The process of configuring user rights and permissions on a group instead of directly on a user account does not directly prevent attackers from using the account in unauthorized fashion. It does, however, lesson the chance for a misconfiguration, therefore, Answer **D** is incorrect.

4. Austin is attempting to create a new group for his network that he wants to place several Global groups into. When he tries to create the new group as a Universal group, the option to do so is not available. What is the most likely reason for this problem?

A. Austin's domain is operating in the Windows NT 4.0 native functional mode.

B. Austin's domain is operating in the Windows 2000 mixed functional mode.

C. Austin's domain is operating in the Windows Server 2003 functional mode.

D. Austin's domain is operating in the Windows 2000 native functional mode.

☑ **B.** The most likely reason for not having the option to create a Universal group is that the domain is not operating at a high enough functional level, which means that Answer **B** is the most likely cause of the problem. The domain must be at least at Windows 2000 native or better in order to create Universal groups.

☒ **A, C, D.** There is not a functional mode called Windows NT 4.0, therefore Answer **A** is incorrect. If the domain functional mode was Windows Server 2003 or Windows 2000 native, Austin would be able to create Universal groups, therefore Answers **C** and **D** are incorrect.

5. Andrea has created a new security group for several help desk staff in her company. She has configured the required user rights and permissions on this security group and placed the help desk staff user accounts into the group. When Andrea tries to send an e-mail message to the security group, she gets a bounce back informing her that no such user was found. What is the most likely reason for this problem?

   A. One of the users in the group is not mailbox enabled.

   B. The group does not have an e-mail address configured for it.

   C. The group is not a distribution group.

   D. None of the users in the group are mailbox enabled.

   ☑ **B.** The most likely reason for this problem is that the group itself is not configured with an e-mail address. When a security group (or distribution group) is configured with an e-mail address, e-mail messages sent to that address will be forwarded to all members that are mailbox enabled.

   ☒ **A, C, D.** The e-mail status of individual users has no affect on e-mail sent to the entire group, therefore Answers **A** and **D** are incorrect. Security groups can also be used to distribute e-mail to group members, therefore Answer **C** is incorrect.

6. Jon is creating several dozen new Domain Local security groups for his network. What command line utility could Jon use to create these groups for him?

   A. dsadd group *GroupDN* –secgrp yes –scope l –samid *SAMName* –desc *Description*

   B. dsadd group *GroupDN* –secgrp yes –scope g –samid *SAMName* –desc *Description*

   C. dsadd group *GroupDN* –secgrp no –scope l –samid *SAMName* –desc *Description*

   D. dsadd group *GroupDN* –secgrp yes –scope u –samid *SAMName* –desc *Description*

   ☑ **A.** The command used to add a Domain Local security group is dsadd group *GroupDN* –secgrp yes –scope l –samid *SAMName* –desc *Description*.

   ☒ **B, C, D.** The –scope g modifier denotes that a Global group is to be created, therefore Answer **B** is incorrect. The –secgrp no modifier denotes that a distribution group is to be created, therefore Answer **C** is incorrect. The –scope u modifier denotes that a Universal group is to be created, therefore Answer **D** is incorrect.

7. You have been tasked with determining the group membership status of several hundred employees within your organization. You have determined that it would be more efficient to perform this task from the command line. Which command line utility can be used to determine which groups a specified user is a member of?

   A. *dsquery*

   B. *dsget*

   C. *dsmod*

   D. *dsrm*

☑ **B.** The *dsget* command in the syntax of *dsget user UserDN -memberof* can be used to determine which groups the user is a member of.

☒ **A, C, D.** The *dsquery* command is used to query Active Directory to locate a specific object or object type, therefore Answer **A** is incorrect. The *dsmod* command is used to modify an existing object in Active Directory, therefore Answer **C** is incorrect. The *dsrm* command is used to remove an existing object from Active Directory, therefore Answer **D** is incorrect.

8. Andrew is a member of the help desk staff for Tim's Tents, Inc. Where can Andrew look to determine what groups a user is a member of from within the Windows GUI?

   A. The Member Of tab in the group Properties dialog box.

   B. The Member Of tab in the user Properties dialog box.

   C. The Account tab in the user Properties dialog box.

   D. The Managed By tab in the group Properties tab.

   ☑ **B.** From within the Windows GUI, Andrew will need to open the user's Properties dialog box and switch to the Member Of tab.

   ☒ **A, C, D.** The Member Of tab in the group Properties dialog box lists which groups that group is a member of, therefore Answer **A** is incorrect. The Account tab in the user Properties dialog box will not show what groups the user is a member of, therefore Answer **C** is incorrect. The Managed By tab of the group Properties dialog box shows the contact information for the user responsible for managing the group, therefore Answer **D** is incorrect.

Creating and Managing User Accounts

9. Which of the following user accounts is used to provide anonymous access to IIS resources and is a member of the Domain Users and Guests groups?

   A. IWAM_*computername*

   B. SUPPORT_*xxxxxxxx*

   C. IUSR_*computername*

   D. krbtgt

   ☑ **C.** The IUSR_*computername* user account is created upon the installation of IIS on a server and is used to provide anonymous access to IIS resources.

   ☒ **A, B, D.** The IWAM_*computername* account is used by IIS to start out of process applications, therefore Answer **A** is incorrect. The SUPPORT_*xxxxxxxx* account is used for the Help and Support Service and is disabled by default, therefore Answer **B** is incorrect. The krbtgt account is used by the Kerberos KDC as its service account, therefore Answer **D** is incorrect.

10. You have just completed a clean installation of Windows Server 2003 on a new server in your organization. Several default user accounts are created by the installation process. Which of the following default users are disabled by default? (Choose two correct answers.)

    A. Administrator

    B. Guest

    C. IUSR_*computername*

    D. SUPPORT_*xxxxxxxx*

    ☑ **B, D.** The Guest and SUPPORT_*xxxxxxxx* user accounts are disabled by default. Although the krbtgt user account appears to be disabled, it is not truly disabled. You will not be able to manually enable it either.

    ☒ **A, C.** The Administrator and IUSR_*computername* user accounts are not disabled by default, therefore Answers **A** and **C** are incorrect.

11. You are in the process of creating new user accounts from the command line using the *dsadd* command. If the *–pwd* ★ modifier is specified, what is the net result?

    A. The password is to be randomly assigned.

    B. The password is to be left blank.

    C. The password is to be taken from another list.

    D. The password is to be supplied during the creation process.

    ☑ **D.** The *–pwd* ★ modifier specifies that the password is to be supplied during the creation process by the administrator.

    ☒ **A, B, C.** Passwords are not randomly assigned during account creation, therefore Answer **A** is incorrect. If a blank password is desired, the *–pwd* modifier can be omitted entirely, making Answer **B** incorrect. The *dsadd* command does not support importing passwords from another list, therefore Answer **C** is incorrect.

12. You are a help desk staff member for your organization. A member of the Advertising department has requested that her password be changed. Which of the following items of information will you need to know in order to reset the password for her?

    A. The user's current password.

    B. The user's e-mail address.

    C. The user's account name

    D. The user's supervisor's name.

    ☑ **C.** In order to reset a user's password, the only thing you absolutely must know is that account name so that you can locate it within Active Directory Users and Computers.

Additional security measures might be in place within your organization that require the user to supply a security code word or some other means to aid in verifying the user request is authentic and not a form of social engineering.

☒ **A, B, D.** You will not need to know the current password in order to reset it, therefore Answer **A** is incorrect. You will not need to know the user's e-mail address to reset their password, therefore Answer **B** is incorrect. You will also not need to know the user's supervisor's name to reset their password, therefore Answer **D** is incorrect.

Creating and Managing Computer Accounts

13. Which of the following computers can have computer accounts in Active Directory? (Choose all correct answers.)

    A. Windows 2000 Professional

    B. Windows XP Professional

    C. Windows 98

    D. Windows 95

    ☑ **A, B, C, D.** Computer accounts can be created for all Windows computers in Active Directory, although only Windows 2000 or better computers will be able to fully participate in Active Directory and use Group Policy. Pre-Windows 2000 computers will need to use System Policies in order to have security and management options configured on them.

    ☒ All of the answers are correct.

14. In what two ways can computer accounts be created in Active Directory? (Choose two correct answers.)

    A. By joining a Windows 95 computer to the domain.

    B. By joining a Windows 2000 Professional computer to the domain.

    C. Through manual creation from Active Directory Sites and Services.

    D. Through manual creation from Active Directory Users and Computers.

    ☑ **B, D.** When Windows 2000 or better computers are joined to the domain, computer accounts are automatically created for them in Active Directory in the computers container (by default). You can also manually create computer accounts from Active Directory Users and Computers or from the command line through the usage of the *dsadd* command.

    ☒ **A, C.** Windows 95 computers cannot be joined to the domain, therefore Answer **A** is incorrect. The Active Directory Sites and Services console is not used to create computer accounts, therefore Answer **C** is incorrect.

Importing and Exporting Active Directory Data

15. Chris is preparing to import a CSV file containing data from another LDAP-compliant directory service into the Active Directory of her domain. What is the minimum command that she will need to issue to perform the importation of the data in the file named userlist.csv?

    A. csvde –f *filename*

    B. ldifde –i –f *filename*

    C. csvde –i –f *filename*

    D. csvde –i

    ☑ **C.** The minimum command that Chris will need to issue is *csvde –I –f filename.*

    ☒ **A**, **B**, **D.** To perform an import event, the *–i* switch must be specified, therefore Answer **A** is incorrect. The *ldifde* command is not used to work with CSV files, therefore Answer **B** is incorrect. The *–f* switch must be specified to denote the path and filename being imported, therefore Answer **D** is incorrect.

Chapter 2 Managing and Maintaining Terminal Server Access

The Need for Terminal Services: A Survey of Computing Environments

1. Jim is the systems administrator for NVC Corporation, the makers of world famous widgets. NVC Corporation has 20 Windows Server 2003 servers and 200 Windows XP Professional and Windows 2000 Professional client workstations. Management would like to deploy services to three new remotes sites. The need is to deploy a single application to five remote users at each site. Jim has been tasked with designing a brand new Terminal Services infrastructure. Jim needs to choose a computing model. Which model does Jim require?

    A. Centralized Computing Model

    B. Distributed Computing Model

    C. Mixed Environment

    D. Terminal Services should not be used here

☑ **A.** When using centralized computing all your resources are located on a central server or mainframe. Clients access resources remotely. The clients have very little intelligence and little if any processing power. All processing of data and its storage are done on the centralized CPU, server, terminal server, or mainframe and only screenshots of the outcome are sent to the client. Clients are generally thin clients or dumb terminals

☒ **B, C, D.** Answer **B** is incorrect, because the distributed model is quite the opposite of the centralized model. Answer **C** is incorrect, because although mixed could work, there really is no need for CPU strength on the desktop if only one single application is needed. Answer **D** is incorrect, because given the fact that such small sites have such small needs, Terminal Services would be the perfect fit for this solution.

2. Jake is the systems engineer for Runners Inc. Runners Inc. has 30 Windows Server 2003 servers, 500 Windows XP Professional and Windows 2000 Professional client workstations. Jake's boss has asked him to help in the development of a new solution for two small branch offices that will be used to deploy two applications to approximately 10 users at each office. Jim has been asked to explain what the most cost would be associated with. What is the best answer Jim could offer??

A. The clients

B. The Terminal Server

C. A PC workstation at each site

D. You should not use a Terminal Server solution

☑ **B.** Using a centralized computing environment will mean that most of the costs associated with running this solution are placed on the Terminal Server, where all the intelligence and computing strength is. Since the hardware used to run the Terminal Server is fairly inexpensive it will be a cheaper solution

☒ **A, C, D.** Answer **A** is incorrect, because the clients will be thin clients and very little cost is associated with deploying thin clients. Answer **C** is incorrect, because you would not use PC's in this location if you can deploy thin clients to save money. Answer **D** is incorrect, because since is has to be a cost effective solution you would need to deploy a Terminal Server with a thin client solution.

Introduction to Windows Server 2003 Terminal Services

3. Several components use the Terminal Services service in Windows Server 2003. Which of the following are used primarily for remote administration? (Select all that apply.)

A. Remote Desktop for Administration

B. Remote Assistance

C. The Terminal Server Role

D. The RDP protocol

☑ **A, B.** Remote Desktop for Administration and Remote Assistance are designed to allow for remote administration, therefore Answer **A** is correct. Remote Desktop for Administration allows an administrator to connect using Terminal Services and obtain a remote server desktop, or connect to the console session of the server. Remote Assistance is used when requesting assistance from an administrator or other helper, therefore Answer **B** is correct. It allows the remote administrator to view and interact with the local desktop of the system from which the request for assistance came.

☒ **C, D.** Answer **C** is incorrect, because the Terminal Server role makes the Terminal Services computer a Terminal Server (multi-user application server). In this mode, the server is primarily designed to make applications and Windows Server 2003 remote desktops available to a large number of remote users. It contains extra code for keeping the application settings separate and uses significant additional resources on the Terminal Server computer. Thus, its principle use is not remote administration. Answer **D** is incorrect, because the RDP is used for all Terminal Services connections through Microsoft client software, not just the ones involving remote administration.

4. One of your co-workers asks how to install Terminal Services on his newly installed Windows Server 2003 server so he can perform administrative tasks on the server. Which of the following is the correct advice to give him?

A. Add the Terminal Server role from the Manage Your Server utility.

B. Add the Terminal Server role from the Add or Remove Programs utility.

C. The Terminal Server role is installed by default.

D. Do nothing.

☑ **D.** Terminal Services is installed by default for remote administration purposes when you install Windows Server 2003.

☒ **A, B, C.** Answer **C** is incorrect, because in Windows 2000, Terminal Services was a separate component requiring installation in either Remote Administration or Application Server mode. As mentioned earlier, in Windows Server 2003, Terminal Services for Remote Administration is installed automatically with the operating system. However, Application Server mode is now called the Terminal Server role and is an additional component requiring separate installation,. Answers **A** and **B** are incorrect, because, even though both can be used to install the Terminal Server role, the question specified that Terminal Services was to be used to perform administrative tasks, and did not mention a need for the Terminal Server role.

5. A co-worker asks you what type of system can be used as a thin client to a Windows Server 2003 Terminal Server. Which of the following answers would you give her? (Select all that apply.)

A. A PDA running Windows CE

B. A PDA running Windows Pocket PC

C. A desktop computer running Macintosh OS X

D. A desktop computer running Windows 95

☑ **A, B, C, D.** To use a Microsoft Terminal Services client, a thin client device can be a wide range of computers including a PDA running the Windows CE or Pocket PC operating system or a full desktop computer running Windows 3.11 (with the 32-bit network stack installed), 95, 98, ME, 2000, XP, or Server 2003, therefore Answers **A, B, C,** and **D** are correct. It can also be a special thin client device, which contains a processor, memory, video card, and network card, but no hard drive. These systems often store a Windows-based operating system in memory and when booted enable the user to launch a Terminal Services client and establish a session to a Terminal Server. Microsoft has also released a Terminal Services client for the Apple MAC OS X.

☒ All answers are correct.

Installing and Configuring a Terminal Server

6. Will is the systems administrator for Wiley's, the makers of world famous pretzels. Wiley's has 20 Windows Server 2003 servers, 200 Windows XP Professional and Windows 2000 Professional client workstations. Will needs to ensure that clients can connect to his Terminal Servers using only 128-bit encryption. What encryption option should he select?

A. High

B. FIPS Compliant

C. Low

D. Client Compatible

☑ **A.** The High encryption setting provides 128-bit data encryption.

☒ **B, C, D.** Answer **B** is incorrect, because FIPS Compliant encryption provides greater than 128-bit encryption. Answer **C** is incorrect, because Low encryption provides only 56-bits of encryption. Answer **D** is incorrect, because the Client Compatible setting provides an encryption setting that is supported by the client.

7. Andrew is the systems administrator for NVC Corporation, the makers of widgets. NVC Corporation has 20 Windows Server 2003 servers and 200 Windows XP Professional and Windows 2000 Professional client workstations. Andrew needs to configure a Server Role. Where in the Windows Server 2003 interface can Andrew configure a Server Role?

A. He can use the Control Panel.

B. He can use the Administrative Tools MMC.

C. He can use the Local Security MMC.

D. He can use the Manage Your Server utility.

☑ **D.** With Windows Server 2003, you can now use the Manage Your Server utility to configure your system. This utility will is helpful when you want to set up an Application Server. It simplifies the process and lets you use Wizards to help you set up the server, which is quicker and easier.

☒ **A, B, C.** Answer **A** is incorrect, because the Control Panel will not help you to configure a server role, the Manage Your Server utility will. Answer **B** is incorrect, because there is no such thing as the Administrative Tools MMC. Answer **C** is incorrect, because you would not configure a server role in the local security MMC.

8. Barbara is the systems engineer for Runners, Inc. Runners, Inc. has 30 Windows Server 2003 servers and 500 Windows XP Professional and Windows 2000 Professional client workstations. Barbara needs to deploy two new Windows Server 2003 systems to two remote offices, one in each. She is sending the servers to the remote sites and has hired Jimmy, a MCSE certified consultant to set up and configure the two servers. Jimmy needs to set up one as a File and Print Server and the other as a Terminal Server. From which utility can Jimmy quickly set up and deploy the two servers using Server Roles?

A. He can use the Active Directory Sites and Services console.

B. He can use the Active Directory Users and Computers console.

C. He can use the Manage Your Server utility.

D. Barbara needs to do it remotely; she can use the Maintain Your Server console.

☑ **C.** With Windows Server 2003, you can now use the Manage Your Server utility to quickly configure your system. This utility will be helpful to you when you want to set up an Application Server. You need to know how to set up a Server Role with the Manage Your Server tool.

☒ **A, B, D.** Answer **A** is incorrect, because the Active Directory Sites and Services console is not where you would set a server role. Answer **B** is incorrect, because the Active Directory Users and Computers console is not where you would set a server role. Answer **D** is incorrect, because there is no such thing as the Maintain your Server console.

9. You have been asked to create and configure a new Terminal Services connection that will allow users to connect only with 128-bit encryption. Which of the following utilities will you use to accomplish this task?

A. Terminal Services Manager

B. Terminal Services Configuration

C. Terminal Server Licensing

D. Remote Desktops MMC

☑ **B**. In the Terminal Services Configuration utility the High encryption setting can be used to create a listener connection that allows only 128-bit encryption for sessions. When set at the connection level, it will require all clients that attempt to connect to the server be capable of this level of encryption. Clients that do not support 128-bit encryption will not be allowed to establish a session.

☒ **A, C, D**. Answer **A** is incorrect, because Terminal Services Manager is used to monitor, connect to, disconnect from, log off, remote control, and reset sessions. It cannot be used to specify encryption requirements. Answer **C** is incorrect, because Terminal Server Licensing also cannot be used to specify encryption settings. It is used to properly license clients for use with the Terminal Server role, therefore Answer **D** is incorrect, because the Remote Desktops MMC is used to connect simultaneously to multiple Terminal Servers; it does not allow you to set encryption levels.

10. You recently implemented a Terminal Server at your company. Right from the start, you notice that performance is slow. You carefully benchmarked and stress tested your beta system, and you thought you had planned for any amount of capacity that would be required. Upon further investigation, you notice that most of the resources are being taken up by disconnected sessions, some of which are days old. You decide to set a timeout for the termination of disconnected sessions. Which of the following could you use to set the timeout? (Select all that apply.)

A. The properties of user accounts

B. The properties of connections in the Terminal Services Configuration utility

C. Group Policy

D. The server properties in the Terminals Services Manager utility

☑ **A, B, C**. User account extensions for Terminal Services extend the standard property tabs in a user's account by default, there Answer **A** is correct. Sessions is one of several tabs provided by these extensions. It contains a disconnected session setting that can be used to terminate disconnected sessions on a server after a specified period of time. However, you would need to configure this in the Properties of every user account that connects to the Terminal Server, so it probably is not the best way to accomplish your purpose. A similar setting exists in the properties of a connection within the Terminal Services Configuration utility on the Settings tab, therefore Answer **B** also correct. This is a better choice, as these settings apply to all users who use that connection. Finally, the setting also appears in Group Policy under the **Computer Configuration | Administrative Template | Windows Settings | Terminal Services | Sessions**, therefore Answer **C** is correct. Microsoft recommends that you use Group Policy to control Terminal Services settings that will apply to all users, instead of the Configuration utility whenever possible, so this is the best option.

☒ **D**. Answer **D** is incorrect, because disconnected timeout settings cannot be configured in the properties of a server using the Terminal Services Manager utility. This utility is used to monitor, connect to, disconnect from, log off, remotely control, and reset sessions.

11. One of your co-workers has been reading up on Terminal Services and asks if she can run a few questions by you to see if she understands the concepts. Which of the following statements will you tell her are accurate? (Select all that apply.)

    A. Many Terminal Services settings have a corresponding setting in Group Policy.

    B. In Group Policy, Terminal Services settings can be found under both the User and Computer Configuration nodes.

    C. When different Terminal Services settings are specified at the user properties, connection properties and Group Policy levels, the connection properties are the effective settings.

    D. Group Policy can be used to prevent an administrator from being forcibly logged off from a console session when another administrator is attempting to connect.

    ☑ **A, B, D**. Many, if not most, configuration settings that can be specified in a user account's properties or at the connection level can also be specified using Group Policy settings, therefore Answer **A** is correct. Within the GPO Editor, Terminal Services configuration items can be found under both the User and Computer Configuration nodes, therefore Answer **B** is correct. The Deny log off of an administrator logged in to the console session setting enables the behavior it describes, therefore Answer **D** is correct.

    ☒ **C**. Answer **C** is incorrect, because the Group Policy settings always override any conflicting configurations in the user account or connection properties.

12. Jess is the systems engineer for Runners, Inc. the makers of really fast sneakers. Runners, Inc. has 30 Windows Server 2003 servers, 30 Windows 98 PCs, 500 Windows XP Professional and Windows 2000 Professional client workstations. Jess needs to configure 56-bit encryption for his clients. What encryption option should Jess select?

    A. FIPS Compliant

    B. Client Compatible

    C. High

    D. Low

    ☑ **D**. The Low setting configures 56-bit encryption.

    ☒ **A, B, C**. Answer **A** is incorrect, because FIPS compliant encryption is much stronger than 56-bit. Answer **B** is incorrect, because client compatible will not be used, as you have no need to use anything other than 56-bit encryption. Answer **C** is incorrect, because since 56-bit is needed, encryption at 128-bit is not required.

Terminal Server Licensing

13. Another administrator in a different region of the country is installing the Terminal Server role. Knowing that you recently did this, the administrator asks for your advice. You mention to him that he must also be sure to install the Terminal Server License component. What will you tell him about installing this component?

    A. That the License Server role must be installed from the Manage Your Server utility.

    B. That Terminal Server License must be selected and installed from Add or Remove Programs.

    C. That the License Server is automatically installed with Terminal Services.

    D. That the License Server does not come with Windows Server 2003 and must be purchased separately.

    ☑ **B.** The Terminal Server License component must be installed from Add or Remove Programs in Control Panel. After it is installed, you must add valid client licenses to it so that they can be handed out for clients. If this is not done, Terminal Services clients will not be able to connect 120 days after the first client connects to the Terminal Server. Microsoft recommends installing the Terminal Server License component on a separate computer from the one on which you have the Terminal Server role installed.

    ☒ **A, C, D.** Answer **A** is incorrect, because there is no License server role, although the computer on which the license component is installed is often called a license server. In addition, Terminal Services License component does not appear in the list of components that can be installed from Manage Your Server. You can, however, open the Add or Remove Programs utility from the Manage Your Server utility. Answer **C** is incorrect, because the Terminal Server License utility is not automatically installed when you install the Terminal Server role. Answer **D** is incorrect, because the Terminal Server License component comes with Windows Server 2003, but the individual licenses it holds must be purchased separately.

Troubleshooting Terminal Services

14. Several months ago, you installed the Terminal Server role on one of the servers at your company. This morning, clients are having difficulty connecting to Terminal Services but are still able to use file and print services on the server. The error message says it is a licensing issue but you are sure that you properly licensed your Windows Server 2003 server, as well as all of your client systems. What might be causing this? (Select all that apply.)

    A. The temporary evaluation period has expired.

    B. You failed to properly configure Terminal Services client licenses on the license server.

    C. The server was installed with a temporary license code, which has expired.

    D. You did not properly install a license server.

☑ **A, B, D.** In addition to installing the Terminal Server role, you must also install the Terminal Server Licensing component and properly install Terminal Services client licenses on it. These are different from the CALs for the operating systems on your client computers. If you fail to complete any of these steps, your Terminal Services clients will be unable to connect when the evaluation period expires, which is 120 days after the first client connection occurs.

☒ **C.** Answer **C** is incorrect, because clients can still connect to file and print services on the Windows Server 2003 server hosting the Terminal Server role; it is clear that the server itself is licensed and functioning properly.

15. Your network uses Windows NT clients running the Terminal Services Client Connection Manager utility. The user working next to you notices that when you connect to a Terminal Server, you are automatically logged in, while she is always prompted for a password. She asks if you can help to configure her system to automatically logon as well. Which of the following will you recommend?

A. Configure **Automatic logon** on the **General** tab in the **Properties** of the connection, and enter the appropriate logon credentials in the **User name**, **Password**, and **Domain** text boxes.

B. Logon to her Windows 2000 client using your user name and password.

C. Configure **Always use the following logon information:** on the Logon Settings tab in the connection properties of the Terminal Services Configuration utility.

D. Configure the **User name**, **Domain**, **Password**, and **Confirm password** text boxes on the Logon Settings tab for the connection in the Terminal Services Configuration utility.

☑ **A.** In this case, the Terminal Services Client Connection Manager cannot pass the user's system logon credentials directly to Terminal Services running on the server. A quick fix for this is to enter them into the Client Connection Manager on the General properties tab. The only danger here is that if the user leaves the machine unattended, someone else could sit down and connect to a session without being prompted for credentials.

☒ **B, C, D.** Answer **B** is incorrect, because the problem is not with the credential being used, but with the configuration of the client utility. In addition, you should never give your logon credentials to another user. Answers **C** and **D** are also incorrect, because the Terminal Services Configuration utility is for administrators, not users. Settings made in this tool will affect all users.

Chapter 3 Managing and Maintaining Remote Servers

Recognizing Types of Management Tools

1. You are logged on to the server using an ordinary user account (i.e., without administrator privileges). You need to add several new printers on the server and you decided to use the prncnfg command-line utility. How do you do this without logging off?

   A. Select **Start | Run**, and then type **runas /user:administrator cmd**. In the command window run the **prncnfg** command.

   B. Select **Start | Programs | Administrative Tools | Prncnfg**, and then right-click and select **Run as**.

   C. Select **Start | Settings | Command**. In the command window type **runas /user:administrator cmd** and run the **prncnfg** command in the new command window that appears.

   D. Select **Start | Run** and then type **cmd**. In the command window run the **prncnfg** command.

   ☑ **A.** To run the **prncnfg** command-line utility, you need to have administrator privileges. The **runas** command enables you to run a command with the credentials of a different user, in this case the administrator.

   ☒ **B, C, D.** Answer **B** is incorrect, because **prncnfg** does not appear in Administrative Tools. Answer **C** is incorrect, because there is no such menu combination. Command does not appear under **Start | Settings**. Answer **D** is incorrect, because the command prompt is running using the unprivileged user credentials and administrator privileges are required to add a printer.

2. You are creating a new MMC console for use by your help desk team that will be used to perform low level administrative functions in your network. You want the help desk team to be able to use the custom console, but not allow them to create any new windows or change the configuration of the console. What mode should you save this custom console in?

   A. Author mode

   B. User mode - full access

   C. User mode - limited access, multiple window

   D. User mode - limited access, single window

   ☑ **D.** You will need to save the custom console using the User mode—limited access, single window option in order to prevent users from changing the console or opening new windows.

☒ **A**, **B**, **C**. Answer **A** is incorrect, because by saving the console in Author mode users will be allowed to change the configuration of the console and change any part of it. Answer **B** is incorrect, because by saving the console in User mode - full access mode allows a user to have full access to the windowing command without being able to change the configuration of the console. Answer **C** is incorrect, because by saving the console in User mode limited access, multiple window allows a user to create new windows without being able to change the configuration of the console.

Using Terminal Services Components for Remote Administration

3. One of your users is having problems getting a productivity application to work correctly. You suspect that he is performing the steps involved in using the application incorrectly, but the application interface is complex and it is difficult for you to explain over the phone what he needs to do. The user is running Windows XP, and you want to connect to his PC and show him how to perform the task in question so that he can actually see you go through the steps. How would you arrange to do this?

A. Send the user a Remote Assistance Request.

B. Get the user to send a Remote Assistance Invitation.

C. Connect to the user's PC using Remote Desktop.

D. Connect to the user's PC using the Web Interface for Remote Administration.

☑ **B**. By getting the user to send you a Remote Assistance Invitation, you can connect to the user's desktop and the user can follow what you are doing, therefore Answer **B** is correct.

☒ **A**, **C**, **D**. Answer **A** is incorrect, because sending the user a Remote Assistance Request is the incorrect terminology when working with Remote Assistance. Answer **C** is incorrect, because connecting to a user's PC using Remote Desktop logs off anyone at the PC and he will not be able to see what you are doing. Answer **D** is incorrect, because Remote Administration is not available on Windows XP computers.

4. You are at a branch office of your company assisting a user on her PC. While assisting the user, you receive a call that requires you to alter a DNS setting on the server back at the main office. The user has many applications open and you would prefer to not have to log her out if at all possible. What would be the best way to connect to the server?

A. Install the Windows Administration Tool Pack on the user's PC.

B. Connect to the server using the Web Interface for Administration.

C. Use Computer Management on the PC and connect to the server.

D. Connect to the server using Remote Desktop for Administration.

☑ **D.** The simplest way to configure DNS on the server is to connect to the server using a Remote Desktop connection and then run the DNS Manager in the Remote Desktop session. You do not even have to log the user off her PC.

☒ **A, B, C.** Answer **A** is incorrect, because installing the Windows Administration Tool Pack would install DNS Manager on the user's PC. But you would have to log the user off, locate the source file for the Administration Tool Pack, and run the DNS Manager as an administrator. Answer **B** is incorrect, because the Web Interface for Administration does not include a DNS management tool. Answer **C** is incorrect, because Computer Management does not include the DNS snap-in.

5. You are the network administrator for Joe's Crab Shack. While at a meeting in Redmond, Washington, you are informed that one of your newly installed Windows Server 2003 DNS servers has stopped performing name resolution. Your CEO has asked you to make a Remote Desktop connection to the server via your virtual private network (VPN) connection to the network. After you have connected to your internal network via VPN, you attempt to create a Remote Desktop connection to the server and cannot. The DNS server is located on the same IP subnet as the VPN server. What is the most likely reason for this problem?

A. TCP port 3389 is being blocked at your firewall.

B. Remote Desktop is not enabled on the server.

C. You do not posses the required credentials.

D. Your Internet connection does not support the RDP 5.1 protocol.

☑ **B.** The most likely problem is that you have not enabled Remote Desktop connections for this new server.

☒ **A, C, D.** Answer **A** is incorrect, because since you have already connected to your internal network using a VPN, and both the VPN server and the DNS server are on the same IP subnet, the status of firewall ports is not an issue. Answer **C** is incorrect, because by default, when Remote Desktop for Administration is enabled, all administrative accounts can make connections. Answer **D** is incorrect, because no special support is required to use RDP over TCP/IP.

6. You have just installed Windows Server 2003 on one of your servers and would like to set up Remote Desktop for Administration so that you can connect to it remotely. Which of the following must you do? (Select all that apply.)

A. Open the System properties in Control Panel

B. On the Remote tab and select the check box next to **Turn on Remote Assistance and allow invitations to be sent from this computer**

C. On the Remote tab, select the check box next to **Allow users to connect remotely to your computer**

D. Do nothing

☑ **A, C**. Although installed by default with the Windows Server 2003 operating system, Remote Desktop for Administration must still be enabled before you can use it. To accomplish this, go to the **Remote** tab in the **System** properties located in **Control Panel** and select the check box next to **Allow users to connect remotely to your computer** located in the Remote Desktop section of the tab. After it is enabled, you should specify which users may connect by clicking on the **Select remote users** button on this tab or adding them to the Remote Desktop Users group.

☒ **B, D**. Answer **B** is incorrect, because this check box turns on the Remote Assistance feature, not Remote Desktop for Administration. Answer **D** is incorrect, because although installed by default, Remote Desktop for Administration must still be enabled.

7. You are the network administrator for Joe's Crab Shack. While at a meeting in Redmond, Washington, you are informed that one of your Windows Server 2003 DHCP servers is not leasing any more DHCP leases to clients. Your assistant administrator has verified that there are plenty of unused leases in the current DHCP scope, but is unable to determine the cause of the problem. Company policy prohibits the use of any Instant Messaging clients within your internal network. How can your assistant get Remote Assistance from you to help troubleshoot the DHCP server?

A. Use an e-mail-based request.

B. Use MSN Messenger to make the request.

C. Use Emergency Management Services to make the request.

D. Use the Recovery Console to make the request.

☑ **A**. In this case, the only valid answer is to create and send an e-mail based request asking for Remote Assistance.

☒ **B, C, D**. Answer **B** is incorrect, because MSN Messenger cannot be used to send Remote Assistance requests. Answer **C** is incorrect, because EMS is not used for Remote Assistance. Answer **D** is incorrect, because the Recovery Console cannot be used for Remote Assistance.

8. No matter how hard you try, you just cannot seem to figure out how to access your e-mail using the new application that was installed over the weekend. You decide to use the Remote Assistance feature to ask an administrator to walk you through the process. Which of the following are valid methods that you can use to request assistance? (Select all that apply.)

A. E-mail an administrator

B. Use ICQ to contact an administrator

C. Use Windows messaging to contact an administrator

D. Save the request to a file and transfer it to an administrator

☑ **A, C, D.** There are three methods that a Novice can use to request help from an Expert. First, the Novice can have Remote Assistance generate an e-mail request that contains a link on which the Expert can click to begin the session, therefore Answer **A** is correct. Second, the Novice can initiate a Remote Assistance request using Windows Messaging, therefore Answer **C** is correct. Finally, the Novice can save the Remote Assistance request to a file and give it to the Expert on a floppy or transfer it to the Expert across a network, therefore Answer **D** is correct.

☒ **B.** Answer **B** is incorrect, because although similar to Windows Messaging, the ICQ messaging client was not created by Microsoft and does not contain the necessary code to request a Remote Assistance session.

9. You are attempting to initiate a Remote Desktop for Administration session with one of your Windows Server 2003 servers over the Internet. The server has a publicly accessible IP address but it is located behind an external firewall and a screening router. You can ping the server and establish Telnet session to the server. You have verified with onsite personnel that Remote Desktop is enabled for this server and that your user account is allowed to make connections. What is the most likely reason for the inability to make the Remote Desktop for Administration connection?

A. Port 3389 is being blocked

B. Port 8088 is being blocked

C. IIS 6.0 is not installed

D. ASP.NET is not enabled on the server

☑ **A.** All RDP connections use port 3389, thus if this port is not passing traffic a connection will not be successful.

☒ **B, C, D.** Answer **B** is incorrect, because Port 8088 and 8089 are used by the Web Interface for Remote Administration, not for RDP. Answers **C** and **D** are incorrect, because IIS 6.0 and ASP.NET are not required to initiate a Remote Desktop connection.

10. You are configuring one of your Windows Server 2003 computers to allow Remote Desktop for Administration connections to it. What group do you need to add user accounts to in order to allow those users to create Remote Desktop for Administration connections?

A. Network Configuration Operators

B. Remote Desktop Users

C. Help Services Group

D. Telnet Clients

☑ **B.** You must add the users who will be creating Remote Desktop for Administration connections to this server to the local Remote Desktop Users group on the computer.

☒ **A, C, D**. Answer **A** is incorrect, because the Network Configuration Operators group is allowed to manage some of the networking properties of a server, but not to create Remote Desktop for Administration connections. Answer **C** is incorrect, because the Help Services Group is used by Remote Assistance connections. Answer **D** is incorrect, because the Telnet Clients group is populated with users who are allowed to create Telnet connections to the server.

11. You are assisting a user with a configuration issue on his computer using a Remote Assistance session. You have tried unsuccessfully to take control of the user's computer. What possible reasons are there to explain why you have not been able to take control? (Select two correct answers.)

    A. The Novice is not allowing you to take control of his computer.

    B. A firewall is in place blocking the request.

    C. The remote computer is not configured to allow it to be controlled remotely.

    D. Your computer is not configured to allow it to initiate remote control sessions.

    ☑ **A, C**. Either the Novice is not allowing you to take control or the remote computer is not configured to allow you to take remote control, therefore Answers **A** and **C** are correct.

    ☒ **B, D**. Answer **B** is incorrect, because if you have an existing Remote Assistance session, a firewall would not likely be the cause of your inability to take control of the remote computer. Firewall and router issues typically prevent connections from being created in the first place. Answer **D** is incorrect, because your local computer requires no special configuration to allow you to take remote control of a remote computer.

12. You have sent an e-mail request for Remote Assistance to your support desk but the request expired before they could answer it and assist you with your problem. Company policy only allows members of the support desk to create Remote Assistance connections. You want to allow the request to be answered. What is the easiest way to go about this?

    A. Create a new request and send it to the support desk.

    B. Delete the expired request, causing it to be recreated anew.

    C. Resend the expired request to the support desk.

    D. Initiate the Remote Assistance connection yourself.

    ☑ **C**. The easiest way to allow an expired request to be answered is to resend it as some of the required information will be retained from the previously expired request.

    ☒ **A, B, D**. Answer **A** is incorrect, because creating a new request from scratch is not the most efficient solution as you will have to reenter all required information. Answer **B** is incorrect, because deleting the request does not cause it to be automatically recreated. Answer **D** is incorrect, because initiating the Remote Assistance request yourself is not an option per company policy.

13. You need to connect to your server's console remotely. Which graphical terminal services utility can you use to accomplish this?

    A. The Remote Desktop Connection tool

    B. The Remote Desktop console

    C. The Remote Desktop Connection Web utility

    D. The Terminal Services Client Configuration Manager utility

    ☑ **B.** The Remote Desktop console can be used to connect to the console session. On the Add New Connection window, select the check box next to **Connect to console**. It is important to note that a console connection can also be started from the command line, by using the **mstsc** command with the **/console** switch.

    ☒ **A, C, D.** Each of these utilities is primarily designed to allow users to establish a single connection to a terminal services computer. By contrast, the Remote Desktop MMC console is a tool that is intended for administrators to use in establishing connections to one or more terminal services sessions within a single interface. Because the console should be accessed only by an administrator, this tool is the only one with that option.

14. You are the network administrator for Joe's Crab Shack. You are creating the company policy for the usage of Remote Desktop for Administration. When discussing the differences between disconnecting and logging off from an RDA session, which of the following two statements are correct? (Choose two correct answers.)

    A. Disconnected sessions do not remain on the server.

    B. Disconnected sessions remain on the server, often consuming resources.

    C. Logged off sessions do not remain on the server.

    D. Logged off sessions remain on the server, often consuming resources.

    ☑ **B, C.** Answer **B** is correct, because disconnected sessions remain on the server, waiting for reconnection by the user. They are still full sessions and continue to consume resources. For this reason, many administrators prefer to terminate these sessions after a period of time, to free up the resources they are using. Answer **C** is correct, because when a user logs off from a session, the session is fully removed from the terminal services computer and the resources it was consuming become available to the other clients.

    ☒ **A, D.** Answer **A** is incorrect, because disconnected sessions remain on the server. Answer **D** is incorrect, because logged off sessions do not remain on the server.

Using EMS

15. You have a computer that has Windows Server 2003 and Windows XP Professional installed on it. You have connected a terminal to the serial port of the computer so that you can manage it remotely using EMS. You reboot the server and see the list of available operating systems on the terminal. You select Windows XP Professional from the boot list and then find that there is no further response on the terminal. What has happened?

    A. The computer crashed while booting into Windows XP Professional.

    B. EMS was enabled on the wrong serial port in the Windows XP Professional installation.

    C. EMS was not enabled in the Windows XP Professional installation.

    D. Windows XP Professional does not support EMS.

    ☑ **D**. Only Windows Server 2003 supports EMS, so as soon as Windows XP starts up there is no further communication on the serial port.

    ☒ **A**, **B**, **C**. Answers **A**, **B**, and **C** are all incorrect because Windows XP does not support EMS.

Chapter 4 Managing and Maintaining Web Servers

What is New in IIS 6.0?

1. You have created a commercial Web site with sensitive business information. Your senior architect has advised you to use Advanced Digest authentication to maximize security benefits on IIS 6.0. You have been doing research on Advanced Digest authentication. What is an incorrect piece of information you came across in your research?

    A. It uses Active Directory to store user credentials

    B. It only works with HTTP 1.1 enabled browsers

    C. It will work with Internet Explorer 4.0 with JavaScript 1.3 support

    D. It only works with WebDAV enabled directories

    ☑ **C**. Advance Digest authentication only works with HTTP 1.1 enabled browsers. Internet Explorer 4.0 implements HTTP 1.0. The HTTP 1.1 support was enabled after Internet Explorer version 5.0. The JavaScript 1.3 support is irrelevant.

    ☒ **A**, **B**, **D**. Answer **A** is incorrect, because Advance Digest authentication uses Active Directory for user credentials storage. Answers **B** and **D** are incorrect, because they are also features of Advance Digest authentication.

2. IIS 6.0 introduces a worker process model concept. A worker process model is a separate ISAPI application (Web site) that runs in isolation. In previous IIS versions (version 5.0 and below) all applications ran in the same memory space as inetinfo.exe. IIS 6.0 does not let the applications run in the same space as inetinfo.exe. The IIS 6.0 concept of tracking its Web sites is referred as what?

    A. Using Health Detection

    B. Using HTTP.sys

    C. Using XML Metabase entries

    D. Using ASP.NET scripts that directly communicate to .NET Framework.

    ☑ **A.** Heath Detection is the technology that IIS uses to make sure they are running smoothly.

    ☒ **B, C, D.** Answer **B** is incorrect, because HTTP.sys is the new kernel mode driver to accept all incoming HTTP traffic. The Metabase holds all the configuration settings for IIS, therefore Answer **C** is incorrect, because ASP.NET is a scripting language to perform business intelligence tasks. Answer **D** is incorrect, because it does not assist IIS in synchronizing its worker process. .

Installing and Configuring IIS 6.0

3. You have been instructed to install Windows Server 2003 on a Windows 2000 machine. The current Windows 2000 Server is running under a FAT32 system. The Windows Server 2003 installation will permit you to upgrade or perform a clean installation. When you are performing the upgrade you have an option between FAT32 and NTFS file systems. Which ones would you choose?

    A. FAT

    B. FAT32

    C. NTFS

    D. FAT64

    ☑ **C.** The preferred file system is NTFS. IIS 6.0 and other servers rely on NTFS security permissions to authenticate users.

    ☒ **A, B, D.** Answer **A** is incorrect, because FAT is an old DOS file system that does not provide file security. This was superceded by FAT32. Answer **B** is also incorrect, because FAT32 was a 32-bit file allocation system that optimized the file system by utilizing a 4K cluster size over the 16 or 32K cluster sizes used by the original version of FAT, but still did not provide for file or folder security. Answer **D** is incorrect, because the FAT64 system was a proposed 64-bit file allocation system that follows the FAT format. This option is not implemented yet.

4. You have installed the standard default installation of Windows Server 2003. You were disappointed to find out that the IIS 6.0 was not installed by default. You have read that you can install IIS in several ways. You pick the **Configure your Server Wizard** option. You have discovered that the Windows server acts like an Application Server while investigating this option. What technology is not included in the Windows Server 2003 application server technologies?

   A. COM+

   B. ASP.NET

   C. ASP

   D. IIS 6.0

   ☑ **C.** ASP is not an application server technology.

   ☒ **A, B, D.** Answers **A, B** and **D** are incorrect, because all COM+, ASP.NET, and IIS 6.0 are application server technologies in Windows Server 2003. These components can be configured from the Manage Your Server option from the Start menu.

5. You are employed as a Systems Administrator for a large Internet Server Provider. Your organization develops and hosts multiple Web sites for commercial users. Your organization is upgrading Windows 2000 Web farm to Windows Server 2003 servers. There are ten production servers, two staging servers, and three development Web servers in the organization. You have been asked to perform the Windows Server 2003 installation on all of these servers. What is the best installation method for your organization?

   A. Use the Configure Your Server Wizard

   B. Use winnt32.exe with an answer file

   C. Use syscomgr.exe with an answer file

   D. Use **Control Panel | Add/Remove Programs**

   ☑ **B.** This is complete Windows Server 2003 upgrade with IIS as an additional component. Therefore we should be using winnt32.exe not syscomgr.exe.

   ☒ **A, C, D.** The upgrading from Windows 2000 to Windows Server 2003 server is the main catch with the question. Answers **A, C,** and **D** are all used as different options to install II6 6.0 after the operating system is been installed. The only command that can install IIS in parallel to Windows Server 2003 operating system is winnt32.exe.

Managing IIS 6.0

6. You are creating a commercial Web site using IIS Manager 6.0. This Web site need to communicate to the legacy payroll system of the organization. The communication is done using an ISAPI DLL from the Web site. Which permission right is important to read the payroll data with the help of the ISAPI DLL?

A. Read

B. Run Scripts

C. Browse

D. Execute

☑ **D.** You need Execute rights to perform ISAPI and CGI application interaction.

☒ **A, B, C.** Answer **A** is incorrect, because it is there to confuse the user with the "read the payroll data" explanation. Answer **B** is incorrect, because Run Scripts only enable ASP and ASP.NET scripts to execute on a Web site. Answer **C** is incorrect, because the Browse option enables directory browsing on a Web site.

7. You are trying to create an SMTP virtual server using IIS Manager. You have entered the SMTP site name and are being asked to enter the IP address and the Port number for the SMTP server. You selected the default IP address option (All Unassigned) and Port 25. You click the **Next** button and get an error stating that the IP address and the port number is already in use. What is the cause of this error message?

A. You must provide an IP address. (All Unassigned) is not acceptable

B. You cannot use port number 25

C. The default SMTP site used these settings already.

D. You should use port number 80.

☑ **C.** The default SMTP site already uses these settings. The IIS installation creates the Default SMTP site on (All Unassigned) IP address.

☒ **A, B, D.** Answer **A** is incorrect, because you can use (IP Unassigned) to run a SMTP site. Answer **B** is incorrect, because it is common convention that people associate port number 25 with SMTP. However, there is nothing stopping the users from running a SMTP site from a different port number. Answer **D** is also incorrect, because Port number 80 is commonly used for HTTP traffic. Therefore we should not use port 80 in any SMTP communications.

8. Web Services Extensions is a new feature in IIS 6.0. Using Web Services Extensions, we can configure IIS 6.0 components. We can enable and disable them from the IIS Manager console. You have been experimenting with enabling and disabling these components. You could not find some of the item(s) below. Which item(s) fall into this category?

A. WebDAV

B. ASP.NET

C. File Sharing

D. ASP

☑ **C.** File sharing is an Application Server component. It does not have any relationship with Web Service Extensions.

☒ **A, B, D.** Answer **A** is incorrect, because WebDAV access can be enabled and disabled from the Web Service Extension window. Answer **B** is incorrect, because ASP.NET is also under the control of the Web Service Extensions. Answer **D** is also incorrect, because ASP.NET is under the control of the Web Service Extensions.

Managing IIS Security

9. There are several ways to apply security on Web sites. All of these can be configured by the Properties tab of a Web site. Which one of the following is not a security measure to prevent intruders from hacking into IIS 6.0 Web sites?

   A. Using SSL certificates

   B. Using WebDAV

   C. Using an authentication method to force the user to authenticate

   D. Apply IP restrictions on known offenders and networks

   ☑ **B.** WebDAV is a file sharing mechanism and does not have any implications on Web site security.

   ☒ **A, C, D.** Answer **A** is incorrect, because SSL has been used for years to encrypt communication to preserve sensitive information. Answer **C** is incorrect, because by forcing the users to authenticate we can check their credentials and keep a log of their activity. Answer **D** is incorrect, because we can also restrict the user by entering IP address restrictions on a Web site.

10. You have configured Digest authentication for your Web servers. Jon, one of your users who needs to authenticate to the Web servers, cannot do so. You have checked Jon's user account properties and found that the **Store Passwords Using Reversible Encryption** option has been checked, but Jon still cannot authenticate. What is the most likely reason for his troubles?

   A. Jon's user account is disabled. You should enable it from Active Directory Users and Computers.

   B. Jon did not change his password after the **Store Passwords Using Reversible Encryption** option was enabled for his account.

   C. Jon changed his password after the **Store Passwords Using Reversible Encryption** option was enabled for his account, which disabled this setting.

   D. Jon's computer that he is attempting to make the connection with does not have the 128-bit high encryption patch applied.

☑ **B.** If the **Store Passwords Using Reversible Encryption** option is selected and Jon still cannot use Digest authentication, it is highly likely that he has not changed his password since it was enabled. Changing his password will correct this situation.

☒ **A, C, D.** Answer **A** is incorrect, because if Jon's account were disabled, he would not be able to use it at all, which is not the case here. Answer **C** is incorrect, because changing Jon's password after enabling reversible encryption is just the fix needed for this situation. Answer **D** is incorrect, because applying the high encryption patch is not a factor in this situation.

11. Andrew is the network administrator for a small Windows Server 2003 Active Directory domain. He has configured IWA for users attempting to authenticate to the Web server. Andrew's network is protected from the Internet by a Cisco PIX firewall. User's attempting to authenticate using IWA complain that they cannot authenticate. What is the most likely cause of the troubles?

   A. Andrew has not configured the user's account properties with the **Store Passwords Using Reversible Encryption** option.

   B. IWA fails when access is through a firewall due the fact that the firewall places its IP address in the hash, thus rendering the authentication request invalid.

   C. Andrew has not configured for IWA in the Group Policy Object that covers the IIS server's computer account.

   D. Andrew has not configured for IWA in the Group Policy Object that covers the user's accounts.

   ☑ **B.** One of the weaknesses with IWA is that it does not work through a firewall. The firewall places its IP address in the IWA hash, thus making the authentication request invalid.

   ☒ **A, C, D.** Answer **A** is incorrect, because configuring reversible encryption is for Digest authentication, not Integrated Windows authentication. Answers **C** and **D** are incorrect, because IWA is not configured via Group Policy, but instead via the Web site Properties page.

12. You have enabled SSL on your Web site but now users complain that they cannot establish secure connections on port 80. You know that port 80 is the standard HTTP port, not the secure HTTP port. What port should they be attempting to connect to?

   A. 8080

   B. 443

   C. 25

   D. 110

   ☑ **B.** SSL makes connections on port 443 using URLs starting with https://.

☒ **A, C, D**. Answer **A** is incorrect, because Port 8080 is typically used by proxy servers. Answer **C** is incorrect, because Port 25 is used for SMTP. Answer **D** is incorrect, because Port 110 is used by POP3.

Troubleshooting IIS 6.0

13. You are hosting an ASP application that used session variables to store common data across the site. The ASP site was performing well in Windows 2000 server. Then you upgraded the server to Windows Server 2003 servers. After the upgrade your site seems to be losing session data regularly. It seems to be working fine after a reboot. As the day passes by it loses all of its session data. What could be the potential problem?

A. Session data is not supported in Windows Server 2003.

B. IIS 6.0 worker process is getting recycled every two hours

C. IIS 6.0 user isolation mode gets recycled every two hours.

D. You need to enable ASP.NET to handle sessions in Windows Server 2003 server.

☑ **B**. The worker process is being recycled every two hours by default. (The time span is configurable.) Thus, we lose all ASP session information with each recycle.

☒ **A, C, D**. Answer **A** is incorrect, because Windows Server 2003 does support Sessions. Answer **C** is incorrect, because the user isolation mode does not get recycled every two hours. It was there to confuse the user between Answers **B** and **C**. Answer **D** is incorrect, because we do not need ASP.NET to enable Session support in Windows Server 2003.

14. Your Web server is running ASP.NET applications on IIS 6.0. An incorrect configuration setting has caused you to reinstall IIS 6.0 on this machine. Therefore, you have used the **Control Panel | Add Remove Programs** method to uninstall and reinstall IIS 6.0. Then you tried to load up your ASP.NET pages. Unfortunately, all ASP.NET pages are displayed as text. What could be the solution to this problem?

A. You need to reregister ASP.NET

B. You need to reformat the drive as NTFS and reinstall Windows Server 2003 with IIS.

C. You need to edit the Metabase XML file to recognize ASP.NET files.

D. You need to restart IIS from IIS Manager.

☑ **A**. You need to reregister ASP.NET when you reinstall IIS 6.0.

☒ **B, C, D**. Answer **B** is incorrect, because we do not need to reformat the machine to reinstall IIS. We only need to make IIS remember where to find ASP.NET in this case. Answer **C** is incorrect, because you can enable ASP.NET setting using the Metabase XML file. But it does not solve this particular problem. Answer **D** is incorrect, because restarting IIS will not make difference either.

15. Your company's new MP3 player is getting very popular on the Internet. You are getting close to 2,500 requests per minute to download the product. Unfortunately your Web server is continuously getting 503 error for this product downloads. Your boss has asked you to look into this problem. What could be the issue?

   A. Not enough bandwidth for the users.

   B. HTTP.sys cannot handle the incoming traffic.

   C. The worker process is getting recycled every five minutes.

   D. The FTP Server needs to be run on isolation mode.

   ☑ **B**. Error 503 occurs when the incoming HTTP requests cannot be handled by HTTP.sys. The default queue length is 2,000 requests for a minute. When this limit is exceeded we start getting 503 errors.

   ☒ **A, C, D**. Answer **A** is incorrect, because error 503 is a server error and bandwidth is not a major concern for this error. Answer **C** is incorrect, because the worker process recycles every two hours, not five minutes. Answer **D** is incorrect, because FTP sever cannot be run in isolation mode. IIS as a whole can be run in isolation mode.

Chapter 5 Managing and Implementing Disaster Recovery

Creating a Backup Plan

1. You are creating a backup plan for your organization's network. Your plan calls for you to use the five-tape rotation system with all backup tapes being stored in the file cabinet in your office. You will be performing a differential backup Monday through Thursday and a full backup on Fridays. Your network consists of two Windows Server 2003 file servers that are to be backed up. You also have 40 Windows XP Professional client computers located on your network. What potential problem exists with your backup plan?

   A. The five-tape rotation system is not adequate for this size network.

   B. Differential backups should only be performed on Fridays, not daily.

   C. Backup media should be kept offsite.

   D. Full backups should not be performed once per week, they should occur monthly.

   ☑ **C**. The problem with this plan is that backup media is being kept onsite. A better solution would be to move backup media offsite the morning following its creation.

   ☒ **A, B, D**. The five-tape rotation system is adequate for most any size network, and especially so for this small network that has only two servers to be backed up, therefore Answer **A** is incorrect. Differential backups are best performed on a daily basis as they back up data that has changed since the last full or incremental backup, therefore Answer **B** is incorrect. Full backups are best performed at least once a week, not once per month, therefore Answer **D** is incorrect.

2. You are creating a backup plan for your organization's network. Your CIO wants you to use four backup tapes, one for each week of the month. You disagree with his plan and argue that it is not an effective media rotation system. What benefits can you present to your CIO to persuade him to allow you to use a more effective media rotation system such as the five-tape rotation? (Choose all that apply.)

   A. An effective media rotation system will increase the lifetime of the backup media in use.

   B. An effective media rotation system will reduce the cost spent on each backup tape.

   C. An effective media rotation system will provide a backup history.

   D. An effective media rotation system will reduce the lifetime of the backup media in use.

   ☑ **A, C.** Answers **A** and **C** are the best answers. Implementing a media rotation system as a part of your backup plan will increase the lifetime of the backup media by evenly distributing wear and tear amongst all backup tapes. As well, a media rotation system can provide a backup history by allowing multiple days worth to be maintained.

   ☒ **B, D.** The cost per tape is not affected by implementing a media rotation system, although you may be able to buy tapes less often, therefore Answer **B** is incorrect. Answer **D** is incorrect, because implementing a media rotation system as a part of your backup plan will increase the lifetime of the backup media by evenly distributing wear and tear amongst all backup tapes, therefore Answer **D** is incorrect.

Using the Windows Backup Utility

3. You are the network administrator for the CVB Company. Your primary duty is to maintain and manage the disaster recovery operations for the network. On Thursday morning, one of your file servers crashes. You place a replacement server on the network but need to restore all files from the old file server before making it available to users. You performed a daily backup on Monday, a normal backup on Tuesday, and a differential backup on Wednesday. In what order do you need to restore data to the new server?

   A. Monday first, Tuesday second, Wednesday third

   B. Monday first, Wednesday second, Tuesday third

   C. Tuesday first, Wednesday second

   D. Wednesday first, Tuesday second

☑ **C.** Since you performed a normal backup on Tuesday, you can begin your restoration process with that tape. After the Tuesday tape has been restored, you will need to restore the differential backup from Wednesday in order to fully restore all data to the new server.

☒ **A, B, D.** The Monday tape is not required since a normal backup was performed on Tuesday, therefore Answers **A** and **B** are incorrect. Data is always restored from oldest to newest, therefore Answer **D** is incorrect.

4. You have added a new server running Windows Server 2003 to your network. Although it is physically attached to the network, no one has access to the server yet, as you want to install some additional programs before making it available. Before installing third-party programs on the server that will be needed by users of the network to perform certain jobs, you decide to back up the server. If there are any problems after installing the applications, you can then use the backup to restore the server to its previous state. When configuring the Backup Utility, you log in with the Administrator account and find that the "Backup destination" field is disabled, indicating that you can only back up to a file. What is the likely cause of this?

A. A tape device is not installed on the server, so the only backup destination the Backup Utility can use is a file.

B. The Windows Server 2003 computer is not available to network users yet, so nothing has changed on the server requiring a backup. The utility knows this, so this option is disabled.

C. You do not have the proper rights to perform a backup.

D. The "Backup destination" will always show that it is backing up to a file, regardless of where that file is stored.

☑ **A.** A tape device is not installed on the server, so the only backup destination the Backup Utility can use is a file. The Backup destination field has a dropdown list that allows you to specify where the utility should store the backup. This allows you to choose whether to store the backup as a file or to a tape device that is installed on the machine. If you do not have a tape device installed, this field will be disabled.

☒ **B, C, D.** Answer **B** is incorrect, because you can run a backup and store it on tape, regardless of whether users have modified data. Also, even though users do not have access to it, the server would have modified files as it started and ran, meaning that some files used by the system would have their archive attribute set anyway. Answer **C** is incorrect, because Administrators and Backup Operators have the necessary rights to perform backups. Answer **D** is incorrect, because when a tape device and media is available for Backup to use, it will allow you to select to use it from the Backup destination dropdown list.

5. Members of your organization store files on a Windows Server 2003 computer. Each department has its own folder, with subfolders inside for each employee within that department. A complaint has been made about an employee having non-work related files on the server that are considered offensive. Upon checking the contents of that person's folder, you find it to be true. You want to back up the entire contents of this folder, without affecting the backups that are performed daily. What will you do?

A. Perform a normal backup

B. Perform an incremental backup

C. Perform a copy backup

D. You cannot back up the files without affecting other backups that are performed

☑ **C.** A copy backup will back up the entire contents of the folder without changing the archive attribute of backed up files. Because the archive attribute is not modified, it will not affect any incremental or differential backups that are performed. This is useful if you want to make a copy of data on the computer, but do not want it to interfere with other backup operations involving normal and incremental backups.

☒ **A, B, D.** Answer **A** is incorrect, because a normal backup will change the archive attribute of files that are backed up, which will affect other backups that are performed daily. Answer **B** is incorrect, because incremental backups will also affect the other backups. This answer is also incorrect because it will only back up files that have changed since the last normal or incremental backup (not the entire contents of the folder). Answer **D** is incorrect, because a copy backup will back up the entire contents of the folder, without affecting the archive attribute of the files.

6. You are developing a backup plan that will be used to routinely back up data each night. There is a considerable amount of data on the Windows Server 2003 servers on the network, so you want backups to occur as quickly as possible. Due to the mission-critical nature of much of this data, you also want data to be restored as quickly as possible following a disaster. Based on these needs, which of the following backup types will you use in your plan?

A. Perform a normal backup each night

B. Perform a daily backup each night

C. Perform a normal backup, followed by nightly incremental backups

D. Perform a normal backup, followed by nightly differential backups

☑ **D.** Perform a normal backup, followed by nightly differential backups. A normal backup will back up all of the selected files, while subsequent differential backups will back up all data that has changed since the last normal (or incremental backup). When this type of backup is performed, the archive attribute is not cleared, so data on one differential backup will contain the same information as the previous differential backup plus any additional files that have changed. When restoring backed up data, the last normal backup and last differential backup need to be restored.

☒ **A, B, C.** Answer **A** is incorrect, because a normal backup backs up all the files you select in a single backup job. This means that all files selected for backup will be backed up, regardless of whether they have changed or not. This will take a considerable amount of time each night to back up data. Answer **B** is incorrect, because a daily backup backs up all of the files you select that have been modified on that particular day. Any data before the first backup is performed will not be backed up. This means that if a disaster occurs, all of the data will not be available to be restored. Answer **C** is incorrect, because a normal backup with nightly incremental backups will take longer to restore than a differential backup. An incremental backup backs up all data that was changed since the normal or incremental backup. Because the normal backup and every subsequent incremental backup needs to be restored to fully restore all data, it will take longer to restore than a combined normal and differential backup.

7. A user has ownership of files in a shared folder located on a Windows Server 2003 computer and wants to perform a backup of her files. She is a standard user, with no special rights or group memberships. Due to the amount of free disk space and the need of users to store sizable files, there are no restrictions on how much data a user can store on the server. The user has to temporarily perform the duties of another coworker who also uses this folder for his work. After modifying documents belonging to this person over the day, she tries to back up the files but finds she cannot. She calls and complains to you about the problem, hoping you can help. What is most likely the reason for this problem? (Choose all that apply.)

A. She does not have the minimum permissions necessary to back up these files

B. She is not an Administrator or Backup Operator.

C. She does not have ownership of the files.

D. Disk quota restrictions are preventing the backup.

☑ **B, C.** Answers **B** and **C** are the best answers. She is not an Administrator or Backup Operator, and does not have ownership of the files. If this user was an Administrator or Backup Operator, she could back up these files. However, giving her this level of security is overkill if the only reason is to enable her to back up someone else's files. While the user has the necessary permissions to the files, she must also have ownership of the file.

☒ **A, D.** Answer **A** is incorrect, because the permissions needed to back up a file that you own is Read Read and Execute, Modify, or Full Control. Since she is able to modify the documents she's attempting to back up, she has the minimum permissions needed. Answer **D** is incorrect, because the scenario states that disk quotas are not used on the server.

8. You schedule a backup to run monthly on the 30th of each month, when you are using the Backup Utility to back up the system state of a Windows Server 2003 computer. This server contains data files used by users of the network. It also acts as a Web server for the local intranet and allows users to view information in HTML format on the network. Which of the following files will be included when the system state is backed up? (Choose all that apply.)

   A. IIS Metadirectory

   B. COM+ class registration database

   C. SYSVOL directory

   D. Certificate Services database

   ☑ **A, B.** The IIS Metadirectory, COM+ Class registration database and Registry will be backed up. On Windows Server 2003, the System State will always include the Registry, COM+ Class registration database, system files, and boot files. Because this server is configured to be a Web server and has IIS installed, the IIS Metadirectory will also be included.

   ☒ **C, D.** Answer **C** is incorrect, because Active Directory and the SYSVOL directory are included in the System State only on domain controllers. The scenario does not state that the server is a domain controller. Answer **D** is incorrect, because only certificate servers include the Certificate Services database as part of the System State. The scenario does not state that the server is a certificate server.

9. You are the network administrator for the CVB Company. Your primary duty is to maintain and manage the disaster recovery operations for the network. You are configuring a new backup job that will be used to perform nightly backups of a new file server recently placed on the network. You need to ensure that should a restoration be required, all files and folders contained in the backup file will be restored regardless of their age. What option should you configure for the backup job?

   A. Do not replace the file on my computer.

   B. Verify data after the backup completes.

   C. Back up the contents of mounted drives.

   D. Always replace the file on my computer.

   ☑ **D.** By selecting the "Always replace the file on my computer" option, you will ensure that the restoration process always restores all files, even in a newer version already exists in the target location.

   ☒ **A, B, C.** Answer **A** is incorrect, because the "Do not replace the file on my computer" option configures the restoration process to never replace any existing files during the restoration process. Answer **B** is incorrect, because the "Verify data after the backup completes" option configures the backup process to verify data integrity as part of the backup process. Answer **C** is incorrect, because the "Back up contents of mounted drives" option configures the backup process to backup the contents of the mounted drive.

10. You are the network administrator for the CVB Company. Your primary duty is to maintain and manage the disaster recovery operations for the network. You are configuring a new backup job that will be used to perform nightly backups of a new file server recently placed on the network. You need to ensure that only information such as loading a tape are included in the backup log. What option should you configure for the backup job?

A. Always allow use of recognizable media without prompting

B. Summary logging

C. Information logging

D. Show alert messages when new media is inserted

☑ **B.** Selecting the summary logging option will configure logging to only occur when key operations such as loading tapes or starting backups occur.

☒ **A, C, D.** Answer **A** is incorrect, because the "Allow use of recognizable media without prompting" option will not affect how logging is performed. Answer **C** is incorrect, because "Information logging" is not a logging option. The valid logging options are: Detailed, Summary, and None. Answer **D** is incorrect, because the "Show alert message when new media is inserted" option will not affect how logging is performed.

11. You are the network administrator for the CVB company. Your primary duty is to maintain and manage the disaster recovery operations for the network. You need to allow another user in your company, Catherine, to perform backup and restoration operations. You must not allow Catherine to have any more privileges than she requires. What two ways can you give Catherine only the required privileges? (Choose two correct answers.)

A. Make Catherine a member of the Backup Operators group.

B. Make Catherine a member of the Server Operators group.

C. Make Catherine a member of the Domain Admins group.

D. Run the Delegation of Control Wizard, targeting Catherine's user account.

☑ **A, D.** You can easily allow Catherine to perform backup and restoration operations without giving her any extra privileges, by either making her user account a member of the Backup Operators group or by delegating permission to her user account by using the Delegation of Control Wizard.

☒ **B, C.** Answers **B** and **C** are incorrect, because making Catherine a member of the Server Operators or Domain Admins groups will result in her having privileges that she does not require.

Using Automated System Recovery

12. A disaster has occurred, requiring you to use an ASR set to restore the system. When using the ASR set to restore the system, you notice that certain files are not restored to the computer. What files are not included in the ASR set, and how will you remedy the problem?

    A. Data files are not included in the primary ASR set, and need to be restored from the data section of the ASR set. Information on the data set is found on the ASR floppy disk.

    B. Data files are not included in the ASR set, and need to be restored from a separate backup.

    C. System files are not included in an ASR set. They need to be restored from a system state backup.

    D. System services are not included in an ASR set, and need to be reinstalled from the installation CD.

    ☑ **B**. Data files are not included in the ASR set, and need to be restored from a separate backup. When you create an ASR set, the System State, system services, and disks associated with operating system components are backed up. A floppy disk is created that contains information about the backup, disk configurations, and how to restore these to the system. Because an ASR set focuses on files needed to restore the system, data files are not included in the backup.

    ☒ **A, C, D**. Answer **A** is incorrect, because the ASR set only includes files needed to restore the system, and not data files. There is not a primary versus data ASR set that can be used to restore data. Answer **C** is incorrect, because the ASR set consists of files needed to restore the system, and includes System State data. Answer **D** is incorrect, because the ASR set includes system services.

13. You are the network administrator for the CVB Company. Your primary duty is to maintain and manage the disaster recovery operations for the network. You are preparing to create an ASR set for one of your critical print servers. After the ASR backup process has been completed, what will you have created? (Choose two correct answers.)

    A. A startup floppy disk that contains information about the ASR backup.

    B. A backup file that contains the System State, system services, and the disks associated with the server.

    C. A backup file that contains the System State, system services and data on the servers disks.

    D. A startup floppy disk that contains all third-party drivers you have installed on the server.

☑ **A, B.** Answers **A** and **B** are the best answers. The ASR backup process creates two things: a startup floppy disk that contains information about the ASR backup including the configuration of the server's disk and how the restoration process is to be performed, and a backup file that contains the System State, system services, and the disks associated with the server.

☒ **C, D.** Answer **C** is incorrect, because the ASR backup file does not contain any data. Answer **D** is incorrect, because the startup floppy disk does not automatically contain the third-party drivers you need for mass storage devices. You will need to place these drivers on a separate floppy disk yourself.

14. You are the network administrator for the CVB Company. Your primary duty is to maintain and manage the disaster recovery operations for the network. You are currently preparing a company policy outlining how an ASR recovery is to be performed for one of your critical print servers. What items should you list as being required in order to perform the ASR restoration? (Choose two correct answers.)

    A. The server that is being restored via ASR must have a DAT drive.

    B. The server that is being restored via ASR must have a floppy drive.

    C. You will need to have the Windows Server 2003 CD.

    D. You will need to have a DOS boot disk.

    ☑ **B, C.** The server that is to be restored via ASR must have a floppy drive installed—there is no workaround for this. You must also have the following items readily available to you: the ASR floppy disk, the ASR backup file, the Windows Server 2003 CD, and a floppy disk containing any additional third-party mass storage drivers that your server requires, therefore Answers **B** and **C** are correct.

    ☒ **A, D.** Answer **A** is incorrect, because a DAT drive is not required unless that is the location where your ASR backup file is located. Answer **D** is incorrect, because a DOS boot disk is not required in order to perform ASR restoration.

Working with Volume Shadow Copy

15. You are performing a backup of data stored in a folder of your Windows Server 2003 computer, using Volume Shadow Copies. Network users store their work in this folder, so you start the backup after most employees have gone home for the day. During the backup, you discover that an employee is working overtime, and has a document open that is in the folder being backed up. What will result from this situation?

    A. The backup will fail.

    B. The backup will corrupt the file, but succeed in backing up other files that are not open.

C. The backup will back up the open file, and continue backing up any other files in the folder.

D. The backup will restart, and keep doing so until the document is closed.

☑ **C.** The backup will back up the open file, and continue backing up any other files in the folder. The backup will succeed because the Windows Server 2003 Backup Utility creates a Volume Shadow Copy, which is a duplicate of the volume at the time the copy process began. This allows the Backup Utility to back up all selected files, including those that are currently open and in use by users or the operating system. Because the Backup Utility uses a Volume Shadow Copy, it ensures that all selected data is backed up and open files are not corrupted in the process.

☒ **A, B, D.** Answer **A** is incorrect, because an open document will not cause a backup job to fail. Answer **B** is incorrect, because the Backup Utility is working from a Volume Shadow Copy, the document will not be corrupted by the backup process. Answer **D** is incorrect, because the backup job will not restart due to an open document when Volume Shadow Copies are used.

16. A user attempts to view the previous versions of a file that has been shadow copied on the server. When he tries to view the previous versions, he finds that he cannot although several other users can view the previous version. When he views the file's properties, there is no tab for previous versions. What is most likely the cause of this problem?

A. Shadow copying is not enabled.

B. There have been no modifications to the file since shadow copying was enabled.

C. The Previous Versions client has not been installed on the server.

D. The Previous Versions client has not been installed on the user's computer.

☑ **D.** The Previous Versions client has not been installed on the user's computer. Until this client software is installed, the Previous Versions tab will not appear on the properties of files he views.

☒ **A, B, C.** Answer **A** is incorrect, because other users are able to view previous versions. Answer **B** is incorrect, because if no modifications have been made to the file since shadow copying was enabled, the user would be able to see the Previous Versions tab of the file's properties, but would not see any previous versions. Answer **C** is incorrect, because the Previous Versions Client needs to be installed on the user's machine, not on the server.

Chapter 6 Implementing, Managing, and Maintaining Name Resolution

Introducing and Planning the DNS Service

1. You are the network administrator of the All Hands Life Rafts Company that is using an internal DNS namespace of corp.allhandsliferafts.com. You have a DHCP server located in the west domain of your internal network named DHCPSVR0442. What is the FQDN of this DHCP server?

   A. dhcpsvr0442.corp.allhandsliferafts.com

   B. dhcpsvr0442.west.corp.allhandsliferafts.com

   C. dhcpsvr0442.west.allhandsliferafts.com

   D. dhcpsvr0442.allhandsliferafts.com

   ☑ **B.** The FQDN of a computer includes all names from the computer's name to the TLD name. In this example, only the option dhcpsvr0442.west.corp.allhandsliferafts.com is a FQDN.

   ☒ **A, C, D.** dhcpsvr0442.corp.allhandsliferafts.com does not represent the FQDN because it is missing the domain "west," therefore Answer **A** is incorrect. dhcpsvr0442.west.all-handsliferafts.com does not represent the FQDN because the domain "corp" is missing, therefore Answer **C** is incorrect. dhcpsvr0442.allhandsliferafts.com does represent the FQDN because the domains "west" and "corp" are missing, therefore Answer **D** is incorrect.

2. You are interviewing Hannah for the position of assistant network administrator. You have been making preparations for a new DNS rollout for your new Windows Server 2003 network and asked Hannah what type of zones Windows Server 2003 DNS supports. Which of the following answers are correct? (Choose two answers.)

   A. Standard primary

   B. Forwarder

   C. Resolver

   D. Active Directory-integrated

   ☑ **A, D.** Answers **A** and **D** are correct. Windows Server 2003 DNS supports the following types of zones: standard (primary and secondary), Active Directory-integrated, and stub.

   ☒ **B, C.** Forwarders are DNS servers that have been configured to forward name resolution queries they cannot answer to another DNS server, therefore Answer **B** is incorrect. Resolvers are DNS clients that submit name resolution queries to DNS servers, therefore Answer **C** is incorrect.

3. Andrea is planning out a new DNS implementation for her company's network. Her company, Space Race Inc., is a major supplier of space travel-related items to several national governments and private organizations. The corporate network is extremely sensitive and all information contained within the network must be kept as secure as available without sacrificing availability. What type of zones should Andrea create in this new DNS implementation?

   A.   Active Directory-integrated

   B.   Standard primary

   C.   Standard secondary

   D.   Stub

   ☑ **A**. For maximum security and reliability, Andrea must implement Active Directory-integrated zones which store zone data in Active Directory and use standard Active Directory permissions and user rights to control various levels of access to this data and the DNS service itself.

   ☒ **B, C, D**. Standard primary, standard secondary, and stub zones do not provide a high level of security compared to that offered by Active Directory-integrated zones. As well, Active Directory-integrated zones offer increased reliability and redundancy because they operate in a multimaster arrangement where any DNS server (domain controller) can update the zone data. Lastly, the failure of one Active Directory-integrated DNS server will not result in the zone becoming unavailable for update, therefore Answers **B**, **C** and **D** are all incorrect.

4. You are creating a new standard primary forward lookup zone for your network. By default, what is the full path and file name of the zone file if it is being created for the domain sales.corp.mycompany.com?

   A.   %systemroot%\dns\dns.sales.corp.mycompany.com

   B.   %systemroot%\system32\dns\sales.corp.mycompany.com.dns

   C.   %systemroot%\system32\dns\sales.corp.mycompany.com

   D.   %systemroot%\system32\sales.corp.mycompany.com.dns

   ☑ **B**. The default path for new standard zones is %systemroot%\system32\dns. The default file name for this new standard forward lookup zone will be sales.corp.mycompany.com.dns.

   ☒ **A, C, D**. The default path for new standard zones is %systemroot%\system32\dns, therefore Answers **A** and **D** are incorrect. The default file name for this new standard forward lookup zone will be sales.corp.mycompany.com.dns, therefore Answer **C** is incorrect.

5. You have just completed the installation and initial configuration of a new Windows Server 2003 DNS server. While talking with another administrator in your company, you were told that you need to have a reverse lookup zone configured on the DNS server in order for the nslookup command to function completely. You know that you will most likely need to use nslookup at some time in the future to monitor and/or troubleshoot your DNS server, so you have decided to configure a reverse lookup zone. What does a reverse lookup zone actually do for you?

    A. A reverse lookup zone is used to provide resolution of host names to IP addresses.

    B. A reverse lookup zone maintains a read-only copy of the zone data file.

    C. A reverse lookup zone is used to provide increased security for DNS servers located in a DMZ.

    D. A reverse lookup zone is used to provide resolution of IP addresses from host names.

    ☑ **A.** A reverse lookup zone provides resolution of host names from given IP addresses.

    ☒ **B, C, D.** A secondary zone server holds a read-only copy of the zone data file, therefore Answer **B** is incorrect. A reverse lookup zone is not used to secure a DNS server that is located in a DMZ, therefore Answer **C** is incorrect. A forward lookup zone is used to provide resolution of IP addresses from given host names or fully qualified domain names, therefore Answer **D** is incorrect.

Installing the DNS Service

6. Robert is creating a new Windows Server 2003 DNS server on a member server that is part of his network's Active Directory domain. Robert is very concerned about the security of dynamic updates that are made to his zone file and wants to prevent rogue clients from being able to make entries via dynamic update. When Robert attempts to configure secure dynamic updates, he can only configure for nonsecure and secure dynamic updates. What has Robert done incorrectly that is preventing him from configuring only secure dynamic updates?

    A. Robert has not installed this DNS server on a domain controller.

    B. Robert has not logged into the network using an account that is a member of the DNS Admins group.

    C. Robert has not changed the domain functional mode to Windows Server 2003.

    D. Robert has not selected to create both a forward and reverse lookup zone during the server creation process.

    ☑ **A.** To configure secure dynamic updates, the zone must be an Active Directory integrated zone. Active Directory integrated zones can only be created on DNS servers that are running on domain controllers.

☒ **B, C, D**. Robert does not need to be a member of the DNS Admins group to install the new DNS server and configure it for secure dynamic updates, therefore Answer **B** is incorrect. The domain functional mode has no bearing on Robert being able to configure secure dynamic updates, therefore Answer **C** is incorrect. Robert does not need to create both forward and reverse lookup zones to use secure dynamic updates at this time, he only needs to house his DNS server on a domain controller. Therefore Answer **D** is incorrect.

7. You are network administrator for the ACME Rockets corporate network. You have already successfully installed and configured a core DNS implementation at the corporate headquarters that is using Active Directory-integrated zones for increased security and reliability. Presently, your remote offices and manufacturing plants are performing name resolution over your WAN links, which are almost completely saturated. You have been directed to correct this problem with the least amount of cost to the company and the least amount of administrative effort on your part, while at the same time ensuring that all remote locations can still resolve names at all other locations. What solution should you propose to reduce the traffic being sent over your WAN links due to name resolution?

   A. You should create additional delegated namespaces for each location and then create new Active Directory-integrated zones at each location. You should configure these new DNS servers to perform no zone replication outside of their child domains.

   B. You should create one or more standard secondary DNS servers in each remote location that is allowed to perform zone transfers with one or more of the Active Directory-integrated DNS servers located in the corporate headquarters.

   C. You should create one or more standard primary DNS servers in each remote location that is allowed to perform zone transfers with one or more of the Active Directory-integrated DNS servers located in the corporate headquarters.

   D. You should provision more WAN links to provide more bandwidth for your remote locations.

   ☑ **B**. Only by creating standard secondary zone servers can you meet the requirements of reducing WAN link traffic and ensuring that complete name resolution is supported in the most administratively efficient manner.

   ☒ **A, C, D**. Creating additional delegated namespaces using Active Directory-integrated zones may prevent name resolution from occurring across the entire network without additional configuration and is certainly not the cheapest or most administratively efficient solution, therefore Answer **A** is incorrect. Creating standard primary zones will not allow them to perform zone transfers with the corporate headquarters, thus name resolution will be impacted, therefore Answer **C** is incorrect. Provisioning more WAN links is most certainly not the most cost effective solution, therefore Answer **D** is incorrect.

8. You are configuring a new Windows Server 2003 DNS server for your organization's internal network. This server will be authoritative for your internal namespace, but will not have any information configured in it for any part of the overall namespace outside of your internal network. What function will this DNS server be performing if it is allowed to assist in the resolution of IP addresses for computers that are located outside of your internal network?

   A. Aging

   B. Forwarding

   C. Zone transfer

   D. Scavenging

   ☑ **B.** A DNS forwarder is a DNS server that has been configured to pass name resolution requests that it cannot answer along to another DNS server in an effort to provide the requested resolution information.

   ☒ **A, C, D.** Aging refers to the process by which resource records are first passed through the no-refresh interval and then through the refresh interval during which they are not subject to scavenging from the zone file as stale records, therefore Answer **A** is incorrect. A zone transfer occurs when a secondary zone server determines that its zone file version number is not incremented as high as the zone file on the primary server, therefore Answer **C** is incorrect. Scavenging occurs after a resource record has lived past the refresh interval without a refresh or update having been performed for it, therefore Answer **D** is incorrect.

9. Chris is attempting to create a new primary zone for her network. When she runs the New Zone Wizard and gets to the dialog box allowing her to select what type of zone to create, she is not able to select the **Store the zone in Active Directory** option. What is the most likely reason for this problem?

   A. Chris is not a member of the Enterprise Admins group.

   B. Chris is not performing the procedure on a domain controller.

   C. Chris is not performing the procedure in the correct order.

   D. Chris is not a member of the Server Operators group.

   ☑ **B.** The most likely reason for this problem is that the server Chris is creating the new zone on is not a domain controller—only domain controllers running the DNS service can host Active Directory-integrated zones.

   ☒ **A, C, D.** Chris does not need to be a member of the Enterprise Admins or Server Operators group to perform this procedure, therefore Answers **A** and **D** are incorrect. The New Zone Wizard controls the order in which the configuration is performed, thus not allowing any way for Chris to perform the procedure in the wrong order, therefore Answer **C** is incorrect.

Configuring the DNS Server Options

10. You are configuring your Windows Server 2003 DNS and want to prevent it from caching referral answers that are not directly related to the original name query that was sent. What option do you need to enable to ensure that this protection is configured properly on your DNS server?

    A. Enable round robin

    B. Enable netmask ordering

    C. Secure cache against pollution

    D. BIND secondaries

    ☑ **C.** You will need to enable the **Secure cache against pollution** option in order to prevent the caching of unrelated referral answers.

    ☒ **A, B, D.** The "Enable round robin" option configures the DNS server to use a round robin rotation to rotate and reorder a list of resource records if multiple records are found of the same type during a query, therefore Answer **A** is incorrect. The "Enable network ordering" option configures the DNS server to reorder its host (A) resource records in the response it sends to a resolution query based on the IP address of the DNS resolver that sent the resolution query, therefore Answer **C** is incorrect. The BIND secondaries option configures the DNS server to not use fast zone transfer format when performing zone transfers to DNS servers using the BIND DNS service version 4.9.4 or earlier, therefore Answer **D** is incorrect.

11. You have just completed the installation and basic configuration of a new Windows Server 2003 DNS server. You want to configure to which other name servers it will perform zone transfers to increase the security of your network and DNS infrastructure. By default, what other DNS servers will this new DNS server perform zone transfers with?

    A. Any DNS server that requests a zone transfer.

    B. Only the DNS servers that are listed on the Zone Transfers tab of the Zone Properties dialog box.

    C. Only the DNS servers that are listed on the Name Servers tab of the Zone Properties dialog box.

    D. Only the DNS servers that are listed on both the Zone Transfer and Name Servers tabs of the Zone Properties dialog box.

    ☑ **C.** By default, a Windows Server 2003 DNS serve will perform zone transfers only with the DNS serves that are listed on the Name Servers tab of the Zone Properties dialog box.

    ☒ **A, B, D.** DNS servers will not perform zone transfers with all other DNS servers unless the To any server option is selected, which it is not by default, therefore Answer **A** is incorrect. By default, a Windows Server 2003 DNS serve will perform zone transfers only with the DNS servers that are listed on the Name Servers tab of the Zone Properties dialog box, therefore Answers **B** and **D** are incorrect.

Configuring Zone Options

12. You have configured the aging and scavenging properties for your server and zones as follows:

   ■ No-refresh interval: 5 days

   ■ Refresh interval: 3 days

   ■ Enable automatic scavenging of stale records: 6 days

   After how many days from its time stamp date will a resource record be eligible to be scavenged from the zone data file if it does not receive a refresh or update?

   A. 3 days

   B. 5 days

   C. 8 days

   D. 11 days

   ☑ **C.** Assuming that the resource record does not receive any updates during the no-refresh interval and no refreshes or updates during the refresh interval, the record would then become eligible after eight days—the sum of the no-refresh interval and the refresh interval.

   ☒ **A, B, D.** The time period of three days represents the refresh interval during which the resource record is allowed to be refreshed or updated to have its time stamp changed, this Answer **A** is incorrect. The time period of five days represents the no-refresh interval during which the resource record is not allowed to be refresh but can be updated, which then will update the time stamp, therefore Answer **B** is incorrect. The time period of 11 days has no bearing when aging and scavenging is configured as detailed, therefore Answer **D** is incorrect.

13. Chris is the network administrator for Little Bots, Inc. She has recently completed the configuration of a new Windows Server 2003 DNS server using a standard primary forward lookup zone. After doing some additional reading, she has determined that it would be better to have this zone as an Active Directory-integrated zone using secure dynamic updates. Where will Chris need to make this configuration change from?

   A. From the Zone Transfers tab of the forward lookup zone Properties dialog box.

   B. From the General tab of the forward lookup zone Properties dialog box.

   C. From the Advanced tab of the DNS server Properties dialog box.

D.   From the root of the DNS Management console.

☑ **B.** Assuming that the DNS server is actually running on a domain controller, Chris will be able to change the zone type to Active Directory-integrated and also configure it to use secure dynamic updates from the General tab of the forward lookup zone Properties dialog box. She can perform the same configuration change for a reverse lookup zone from the General tab of its Properties dialog box.

☒ **A, C, D.** The Zone Transfer tab of the forward lookup zone Properties dialog box is used to configure what other name servers the server will perform name transfers with, therefore Answer **A** is incorrect. The Advanced tab of the DNS server Properties dialog box does not contain the options that Chris requires, therefore Answer **C** is incorrect. The root of the DNS management console also does not contain the options that Chris requires, therefore Answer **D** is incorrect.

Managing the DNS Service

14. Jon wants to configure aging and scavenging for all of the zones located on his single DNS server. His zones are all Active Directory-integrated. Where can Jon go to configure the aging and scavenging values for his server and use the least amount of administrative effort?

A.   Jon will need to make his configuration on each zone hosted on the DNS server individually.

B.   Jon will need to make his configuration only once for any one forward lookup zone and only once for any one reverse lookup zone—the values will then become the default for the rest of the zones on the server.

C.   Jon will need to make his configuration during the initial installation of the DNS server and cannot change the values now.

D.   Jon will need to make his configuration from the DNS server's context menu, which will then become the default for all zones on the server.

☑ **D.** When Active Directory-integrated zones are used, configuring aging and scavenging from the server by selecting Set Aging/Scavenging for All Zones on the server context menu configures the selected values as the defaults for all zones. Standard zones will still require manual configuration to enable the aging and scavenging values.

☒ **A, B, C.** Jon does not need to make the configuration on each zone, therefore Answer **A** is incorrect. Jon does not need to make the configuration one time on one forward and one reverse lookup zone, therefore Answer **B** is incorrect. The configuration of aging and scavenging is not done during the installation of the DNS server, therefore Answer **C** is incorrect.

15. You need to create a new resource record in your DNS zone file that will allow you to perform resolution of a host name given an IP address as input. Which of the following types of resource records do you need to create to allow this type of resolution to occur?

    A. PTR

    B. A

    C. CNAME

    D. SRV

    ☑ **A.** The PTR (Pointer) record is used for reverse lookups and maps an IP address to a host name.

    ☒ **B, C, D.** A (host) records are used to map a DNS domain name to an IP address, therefore Answer **B** is incorrect. CNAME records are used to configure an alias for a DNS domain name, therefore Answer **C** is incorrect. SRV (Service locator) records are used to allow servers providing TCP/IP based network services to be located using standard DNS queries, therefore Answer **D** is incorrect.

16. You are attempting to verify basic network connectivity for one of your internal network servers. When you enter the *ping corp* command you get the following results:

    ```
    Pinging w3svr44543.internal.bigcorp.com [192.168.1.233]
          with 32 bytes of data:
    ```

    Why did the *ping* command not return the FQDN of corp.internal.bigcorp.com for the server?

    A. The A record for this server is configured incorrectly.

    B. The PTR record for this server is configured incorrectly.

    C. A CNAME record exists for this server.

    D. A NS record exists for this server.

    ☑ **C.** In this case, the host name CORP is an alias for a server with a FQDN of w3svr44543.internal.bigcorp.com. There appears to be nothing wrong with the configuration of any zone resource records.

    ☒ **A, B, D.** If any an A record was configured incorrectly, the display would most likely return an error indicating that the host could not be found, therefore Answer **A** is incorrect. The PTR record would not be used during this operation since the lookup is being performed against the forward lookup zone, therefore Answer **B** is incorrect. The existence of an NS record has no bearing on the results displayed after the ping command, therefore Answer **D** is incorrect.

Chapter 7 Implementing, Managing, and Maintaining Network Security

Implementing Security with Security Templates

1. You are the security administrator for Catherine's Crab Shack, Inc. You are responsible for analyzing and configuring the security of all Windows XP Professional client computers within the network. You are considering the various tools that are available for you to use. When considering the secedit.exe tool for this task, what specifically can you use it to perform? (Choose all that apply.)

   A. It can be used to list the current Group Policy in effect for a specific user and computer.

   B. It can be used to analyze the security settings of a system.

   C. It can be used to validate the syntax of chosen security template.

   D. It can be used to edit group membership and permissions for a user or group.

   E. It can be used to remotely monitor privilege use.

   F. It can be used to configure system security settings.

   G. It can be used to export the values stored in a database to an .inf file.

   ☑ **B, C, F, G.** The secedit.exe utility can be used to analyze system security, configure system security, export security settings, and to validate the syntax of a security template, therefore Answers **B, C, F,** and **G** are correct. Refer back to the "Using Secedit.exe" section in Chapter 7 for a thorough review of the functions and switches of the secedit.exe tool.

   ☒ **A, D, E.** The secedit.exe utility does not list current Group Policy settings that have been applied to a user or computer, that can be done using the gpresult.exe tool, therefore Answer **A** is incorrect. Group membership and permissions for users and groups is not done using the secedit.exe utility, therefore Answer **D** is incorrect. Finally, secedit does not perform remote monitoring of privilege usage; therefore Answer **E** is also incorrect.

2. Andrew must increase the security on the workstations in his network at any cost, preferably achieving the most secure configuration possible. What would be the best template to apply to his workstations to provide the maximum amount of security and what negative side effects can he expect to see from the application of the chosen template? (Chose two correct answers.)

   A. hisecdc.inf

   B. securews.inf

   C. basicsv.inf

   D. securedc.inf

   E. hisecws.inf

   F. He should expect no adverse effects to occur except for potentially increased login and logoff times due to extra policy processing invoked by the more secure template.

   G. He should expect to lose network connectivity with all other computers that do not support IPSec.

   H. He should expect to have to configure Active Directory integrated zones for his DNS servers to support the newly configured workstations.

   ☑ **E, G**. Highly Secure configurations add security to network communications. IPSec will be configured for these machines and will be required for communications. Two highly secure templates are provided: hisecdc.inf for domain controllers and hisecws.inf for workstations and member servers. The highly secure templates provide the highest level of pre-configured security available, but will cause communications problems with legacy clients due to the requirement of IPSec for network communications. Therefore Answer **E** and **G** are correct.

   ☒ **A, B, C, D, F, H**. The hisecdc.inf security template is for Domain Controllers, therefore Answer **A** is incorrect. The securews.inf security template is for workstations and member servers, therefore Answer **B** is incorrect. The basicsv.inf security template is the default template for member servers, therefore Answer **C** is incorrect. The securedc.inf security template is for applying the Secure settings to domain controllers, therefore Answer **D** is incorrect. As noted, the primary effect of applying Highly Secure templates will be a loss of network connectivity to computers that are not running IPSec, so it is essential that all computers requiring communications be configured for IPSec; such as domain controllers and member servers that the IPSec configured workstations will be contacting, therefore Answers **F** and **H** are also incorrect.

3. You are preparing to deploy some custom security templates across your organization in an effort to increase the overall security of the network. You plan on deploying your security templates via Group Policy. What is the correct processing order for Group Policy in Windows Server 2003?

   A. Local, Domain, Site, OU

   B. Local, Site, Domain, OU

   C. Site, Domain, OU, Local

   D. Domain, Site, OU, Local

   ☑ **B**. The correct Group Policy application order in Windows Server 2003 is Local, Site, Domain, OU. Remember that later GPOs overwrite ones that have been applied earlier.

   ☒ **A, C, D**. The correct Group Policy application order in Windows Server 2003 is Local, Site, Domain, OU, therefore Answers **A**, **C** and **D** are incorrect.

4. You are the security administrator for Catherine's Crab Shack, Inc. You are responsible for analyzing and configuring the security of all Windows XP Professional client computers within the network. You have recently had some problems where computers on your network have failed to start properly due to users making modifications to certain areas of their computer's Registry. You need to secure these areas of the Registry to prevent these occurrences in the future. What can you do to protect these specific areas of the Registry from modification by unauthorized users?

   A. Use the secedit.exe utility with the validate switch to set security settings on the Registry keys of concern.

   B. Use the regedit application to set security settings on the Registry keys of concern.

   C. Use the Security Templates and Security Configuration and Analysis snap-ins to configure, analyze, and implement security settings on the Registry keys of concern.

   D. Use Windows Explorer to mark the Registry files as Read Only.

   E. Use Windows Explorer to set NTFS permissions on the Registry files so that only authorized users may access them.

   ☑ **C.** You use the Security Templates snap-in to edit the settings of a template and configure the security settings you require. You can then use the Security Configuration and Analysis snap-in to analyze and deploy the settings.

   ☒ **A, B, D, E.** Using secedit with the validate switch instructs secedit to perform a validation of a template before importing it onto a computer, therefore Answer **A** is incorrect. Using the regedit application will not allow you to protect the keys from modification, therefore Answer **B** is incorrect. Marking the Registry files as Read Only or changing their NTFS permissions will most likely cause your computer to operate erratically or stop functioning properly altogether and is not recommended, therefore Answers **D** and **E** are also incorrect.

5. You want to configure auditing for the workstations in a specific OU in your network. You have opened Security Configuration and Analysis and selected the basicwk.inf template. What section of the template contains the options that you need to configure to enable auditing?

   A. Local Policies

   B. Account Policies

   C. Event Log

   D. Registry

   ☑ **A.** The Local Policies node contains three areas, one of which is the Audit Policies area. Inside of the Audit Policies area is where you will configure what to audit for in this template.

   ☒ **B, C, D.** The Account Policies node pertains to account issues such as password aging and length, therefore Answer **B** is incorrect. The Event Log node contains settings that allow you to configure the Event Log, therefore Answer **C** is incorrect. The Registry node contains settings that allow you set key level security settings in the Registry, therefore Answer **D** is incorrect.

6. You are the security administrator for your company's network. You have 100 Windows Server 2003 and approximately 1,700 Windows XP Professional computers in your organization that you are responsible for that are spread across multiple sites (North America, South America, Europe, Asia) and OUs. You use EventCombMT to collect Event Log data from every computer once a week for analysis by your assistant administrators. You have found that some computers often have less than one week of events in their Event Logs and want to ensure that events are not getting overwritten when the logs have reached their maximum allowed size. You propose to enlarge the maximum log size from the default value of 512kb for the Application Log, System Log and Security Log. How will you go about performing this change and use the least amount of administrative effort?

   A. Instruct each of your assistants to visit each and every computer and make the changes locally.

   B. Configure and test the settings in a security template that is then deployed to the North American site.

   C. Configure and test the settings in a security template that is then deployed at the domain level.

   D. Send an e-mail message to your users instructing them how to make the changes.

   ☑ **C.** The only viable option is to create and test the required settings in a security template that is then deployed at the domain level. You will then have affected the changes on all computers in your network.

   ☒ **A, B, D.** Having your assistant administrators make the changes locally would consume vast amounts of time—a waste of money and resources, therefore Answer **A** is incorrect. Deploying the settings at the North American site level will not result in the settings being deployed to all of your network clients, therefore Answer **B** is incorrect. Your users will not be able to make the changes required as they do not have the required permissions, therefore Answer **D** is incorrect.

7. Austin has been delegated administrative responsibility for several OUs in his department. How can Austin most easily make the same changes to the security settings applied to his OUs?

   A. Austin should configure and test a template on a local machine using Security Configuration and Analysis. When he gets the configuration established that he requires, he should export the template and then import it into the specific OU GPOs he is responsible for.

B. Austin should use the Security Configuration and Analysis snap-in and target it at the specific OU he wants to work with to make the changes.

C. Austin should edit the GPOs directly for each of the OUs he is responsible for.

D. Austin should ask a Domain Administrator to apply the desired settings at the domain level and let them propagate down to his OUs.

☑ **A.** The best way to ensure that the changes Austin makes are identical on all of his OUs is for him to configure and analyze an incremental security template using the Security Configuration and Analysis snap-in . Once he has gotten the required settings configured to his liking he can then export the security template and subsequently import it into a GPO in each of the OUs he is responsible for.

☒ **B, C, D.** The Security Configuration and Analysis snap-in cannot be targeted at any level other than the local machine, so using it and targeting it towards an OU is not possible, therefore Answer **B** is incorrect. While editing the GPO for each OU he is responsible for is a viable solution, this introduces the possibility of making different configuration settings in the various OUs, thus making this a bad choice for Austin, therefore Answer **C** is incorrect. Applying the settings at the domain level is unnecessary since Austin only needs the settings applied to his specific OUs. Additionally, settings applied at the domain level may be overwritten by GPOs that are at the OU level, therefore Answer **D** is also incorrect.

8. You have configured and tested two custom security templates for use on your corporate network, corpserver.inf and corpdesktop.inf. Your network is running all Windows Server 2003 servers and Windows XP Professional workstations and is fragmented into three distinct sections due to the extremely high cost of establishing WAN links between your three geographical locations. You do have dial-up connectivity between the sites using standard POTS lines, but these have proven to be unreliable at best. How can you deploy these templates to the other two sites in your network?

A. You will need to deploy them to two extra domain controllers and then ship one each to your other two sites.

B. You will need to export them from Security Configuration and Analysis and send the .INF files to your other two remote sites. Once there, the other two sites can import them into the required GPO.

C. You will need to establish a Frame Relay connection between all three sites at the same time and push the templates across the WAN link.

D. You will need to make a RDP connection to each domain controller in the remote sites and apply the template to them.

☑ **B.** By exporting the templates from Security Configuration and Analysis, you can send them by any available means to a remote location for application on the network.

☒ **A, C, D**. Shipping fully functional domain controllers is not a very good idea for a number of reasons, not limited to damage or theft, therefore Answer **A** is incorrect. Establishing a Frame Relay wide area network (WAN) link just for the purpose of applying a couple of extremely small security templates is an extremely large waste of resources that can be avoided. Additionally, you will still need to apply the templates to the other sites in the same fashion regardless of how you get them there, so Answer **C** is incorrect. Making an Remote Desktop Protocol (RDP) connection to each remote site does not seem likely since we were never told about having this capability as well as the fact that connectivity does not appear to exist, therefore Answer **D** is incorrect.

9. You have customized the securews.inf template to include Account Policy settings specific to your organizations requirements. At what level should you deploy this customized template to achieve the maximum result? Your network consists of one Windows Server 2003 Active Directory domain, spread out over three sites. You have approximately 18 OUs in use at the present time.

A. Domain

B. Site

C. Local computer

D. OU

☑ **A.** You will need to deploy this template at the domain level as Windows Server 2003 Active Directory only allows for one domain account policy.

☒ **B, C, D.** You will need to deploy this template at the domain level as Windows Server 2003 Active Directory only allows for one domain account policy, therefore Answers **B, C** and **D** are incorrect.

10. Andrea is the network administrator of 55 Windows XP Professional workstations, 10 Windows Server 2003 member servers and four Windows Server 2003 domain controllers. She would like to perform a security analysis on all of her computers without having to physically visit each one. How can Andrea accomplish this task?

A. This cannot be done at the current time. Andrea will need to sit in front of each machine and use the Security Configuration and Analysis snap-in to perform the analysis.

B. Andrea can target a remote computer by right-clicking on **Security Configuration and Analysis** and selecting **Connect to another computer**.

C. Andrea can create a script or batch file using the secedit.exe utility with the analyze switch that has an entry for each computer that she wants to analyze.

D. Andrea can create a script or batch file using the secedit.exe utility with the analyze switch that calls on a pre-populated text file containing the list of computers to be analyzed.

☑ **C.** The easiest way to perform the analysis on a large number of remote computers is to create a custom script or batch file using *secedit /analyze*. There should be an entry in the file for each computer that is to be configured, including the database to use or create, the template to use, and the log file to use or create. Each entry should specify an absolute location using UNC file locations; it is recommended to create the database and log files in a central location for easier viewing later.

Incorrect Answers & Explanations. **A, B, D.** Andrea will be able to perform the required security analysis easily by using the secedit tool, therefore Answer **A** is incorrect. The **Connect to another computer** option, available in tools such as the Computer Management console, is not available for use in the Security Configuration and Analysis snap-in, therefore Answer **B** is incorrect. secedit cannot make use of an external text file that contains the scan parameters, therefore Answer **D** is incorrect.

11. Chris is attempting to use the Security Configuration and Analysis snap-in to perform an analysis of one of her member servers. The member server is currently configured with the default settings. She wants to compare its settings with those in the securewk.inf security template. What is the correct order of steps that she needs to perform in order to perform the analysis? Step 1: Right-click on **Security Configuration and Analysis** and select **Analyze computer now**. Step 2: Right-click on **Security Configuration and Analysis** and select **Open database**. Step 3: Select the security template to be used in the analysis. Step 4: Select the log file to be used in the analysis. Step 5: Right-click on **Security Configuration and Analysis** and select **Configure computer now**. Step 6: Select the database to be used in the analysis.

   A. 2, 1, 3, 6, 4

   B. 1, 6, 4, 5, 3

   C. 2, 6, 4, 3, 1

   D. 2, 6, 3, 1, 4

   E. 1, 6, 3, 2, 4

   ☑ **D.** The correct order to perform a security analysis using the Security Configuration and Analysis snap-in is: Select Open Database, select the database to be used, select the security template to be used, select Analyze computer now, and lastly to select the log file to be used. You would not need to select Configure computer now until you are ready to apply the database settings to the computer.

   ☒ **A, B, C, E.** The correct order to perform a security analysis using the Security Configuration and Analysis snap-in is: Select Open Database, select the database to be used, select the security template to be used, select Analyze computer now, and lastly select the log file to be used. You would not need to select Configure computer now until you are ready to apply the database settings to the computer. Therefore, Answers **A, B, C** and **E** are incorrect.

12. You have just completed an analysis of your local computer using Security Configuration and Analysis. When looking at the analysis results, you notice several icons have a green check mark on them. You are concerned that your settings do not match those of the template you compared your computer to. What do icons with green check marks mean?

   A. A discrepancy exists between the database settings and the computer setting.

   B. No analysis was performed for this item because it was not configured in the database.

   C. The database setting and the computer setting match.

   D. No analysis was performed for this item because it is not applicable to the computer.

   ☑ **C.** A green check mark indicates the database setting and the computer setting match.

   ☒ **A, B, D.** A discrepancy between the database and the computer settings is marked with a red X, therefore Answer **A** is incorrect. When an analysis is not performed because no settings were configured in the database, a generic icon is displayed, therefore Answer **B** is incorrect. When an analysis is not performed because the setting is not applicable to the computer, an exclamation point or question mark will be seen, therefore Answer **D** is incorrect.

Auditing Security Events

13. Jake is responsible for six Windows Server 2003 computers in his organization. He has noticed that lately there are multiple login attempts on the main file server. What can Jake do to find out if in fact his system is trying to be exploited by a possible attacker? (Choose all that apply.)

   A. Use DumpEL to find the attack IDs numbered 200–600 in the System Event Log. This will indicate a possible attack.

   B. Turn on success and failure auditing for Logon events. Check the Application Log daily for possible password cracking attacks

   C. Set up a Windows Server 2003 security template that will only allow for registered IP's to connect to and communicate with the file server.

   D. Configure your router to only let the file server NetBIOS name be authenticated for communication

   ☑ **B.** Auditing for success and failure logon events will help you to determine if you are possibly being targeted by an attacker.

   ☒ **A, C, D.** DumpEL is used to parse Event Viewer logs and the security related events will be logged in the Security log, not the system log, therefore Answer **A** is incorrect. A security template will not work in this fashion, therefore Answer **C** is incorrect. Security templates have nothing to do with looking for registered IP's. Routers cannot be configured to authenticate Windows based NetBIOS names, therefore Answer **D** is incorrect.

14. Stan is the network administrator responsible for 10 Windows Server 2003 computers and 400 Windows XP Professional workstations that are separated geographically across 4 sites: NY, LA, ATL and CHI. Stan is tasked with auditing two of the Windows XP Professional Workstations because the owners of these two workstations are complaining that each time they work on their workstations, they think someone has tried to log in to them. From the list below, what is the most logical way to audit the two workstations so that you can analyze if an attack is actually trying to be performed?

   A. Use the Local Security policy on each local workstation and Audit Logon events (success and failure).

   B. Use the GPO Security policy on the NY OU and Audit Logon events (success and failure).

   C. Use the Local Security policy on the Domain Controller and Audit Logon events (success and failure).

   D. Use the Local Security policy on the Domain and Audit Logon events (success and failure).

   ☑ **A.** The most logical way to audit this issue is to use the Local Security policy on each local workstation and Audit Logon events (success and failure).

   ☒ **B, C, D.** From the available options, the only way you can configure auditing on only the two workstations of concern is to configure it on the workstations locally. Answers **B, C** and **D** all implement too much auditing and therefore are incorrect.

15. Chris is the administrator of a large Windows Server 2003 network. The company that he works for is a leading provider of state-of-the-art rocket propulsion systems that are used by several countries in their space-going rockets. Company policy states that the network access attempts of all temporary employees are to be tracked, regardless of what workstation they logon to. What auditing options does Chris need to configure to ensure that he can track the access of all temporary employees? (Choose two correct options.)

   A. Audit logon events

   B. Audit privilege use

   C. Audit system events

   D. Audit account logon events

   ☑ **A, D.** By configuring auditing for both the Audit logon events option and the Audit account logon events option, all user logons and logoffs that use a domain account generate logon or logoff audit events on the local computer as well as the domain controller.

   ☒ **B, C.** The Audit privilege use option will configure an auditing entry to be written upon each instance of a user exercising a user right, therefore Answer **B** is incorrect. The Audit system events option swill configure an auditing entry to be written each time a system event such as starting up or shutting down a computer occurs, therefore Answer **C** is incorrect.

16. Jon is the administrator for a large Windows Server 2003 network for a company that is involved in high-level genetics research. All data transmissions within the company are secured by using IPSec. Recently IPSec communications have intermittently begun to fail as a result of the configured IPSec policies having been changed. Jon needs to determine who is changing the IPSec policies on his network. What should Jon configure auditing for?

   A. Audit privilege use

   B. Audit system events

   C. Audit policy change

   D. Audit process tracking

   ☑ **C.** The Audit policy change option will configure an auditing entry to be written upon each occurrence of changing a user rights assignment policy, audit policy, IPSec policy, or trust policy.

   ☒ **A, B, D.** The Audit privilege use option will configure an auditing entry to be written upon each instance of a user exercising a user right, therefore Answer **A** is incorrect. The Audit system events options will configure an auditing entry to be written each time a system event such as starting up or shutting down a computer occurs, therefore Answer **B** is incorrect. The audit process tracking option will configure an audit entry to be written upon each occurrence of events such as program activation, process exit, handle duplication, and indirect object access, therefore Answer **D** is incorrect.

Chapter 8 Managing and Implementing Software Updates

1. Chris is the sole desktop administrator for a Windows 2003 Server Active Directory network, and is responsible for 200 Windows XP Professional computers in her organization. All of the computers are on one campus, however, they are scattered among four different buildings. What is the easiest way for Chris to keep all of her clients updated with the patches and updates they need, but not to allow any updates or patches to be issued until she is satisfied that the patch is stable?

   A. Chris should use Windows Update on each computer locally to download and install the updates her computers need.

   B. Chris should use the Windows Update Catalog to download and install the updates her computers need.

C. Chris should use SUS and the Automatic Updates client to download and install the updates her computers need.

D. Chris should download all of the updates she needs and create an integrated installation CD-ROM to distribute to each of the four buildings to install the updates on her computers.

☑ **C.** By using the SUS to download updates to the local computer, Chris can examine each one for applicability (not all updates that are downloaded will be applicable to her network) and test them for stability and compatibility. When she is satisfied with an update, she can add it to the list of approved updates in SUS. Automatic Updates clients, when configured properly in Group Policy to look toward an internal SUS server, will only make available those updates that have been placed on the approved list within SUS.

☒ **A, B, D.** Visiting each computer and using Windows Update would be a waste of time and network resources for Chris, especially considering that her 200 computers are spread out over four different buildings, therefore Answer **A** is incorrect. Using the Windows Update Catalog would enable Chris to selectively download the updates she wanted; however, this does not provide any automatic means of update deployment and installation like that offered by the combination of SUS and Automatic Updates, therefore Answer **B** is incorrect. Creating an integrated installation CD-ROM is a fantastic solution for deploying new clients, but not a realistic one in this case as the computers are already in place, therefore Answer **D** is incorrect.

2. You are the network administrator for a corporate network. You recently completed the installation and initial configuration of SUS on an internal Windows Server 2003 computer. All of the client computers use Windows XP Professional SP1. All of the servers on the network are Windows Server 2003 computers. The internal network operates in an Active Directory domain. You want all client computers to automatically download from your SUS server and install any required updates each night at 10 p.m. You want all clients that have installed updates to then restart themselves automatically so that they will be ready to use again in the morning when employees return to work. Which of the following actions should you perform that will help you to achieve the desired results? (Choose two correct answers.)

A. Configure Automatic Updates on each of your local client computers to download and install updates nightly.

B. Configure the Group Policy settings for Automatic Updates to automatically download and install available updates nightly at 10P.M.

C. Configure the Group Policy settings for Automatic Updates to not automatically restart client computers.

D. Configure the Group Policy settings for Automatic Updates to specify the local URL of your SUS server.

☑ **B, D.** In order for SUS to provide updates to clients, you will need to enable it and then configure a schedule for clients to download and install available updates. As well, you will need to provide the correct local URL for the SUS server so that your clients can successfully make connections to it. You will also need to configure the clients to automatically restart after the installation has been completed, which is not listed here as an action to be performed.

☒ **A, C.** In an Active Directory environment, you would not configure the Automatic Updates settings locally on each computer, therefore Answer **A** is incorrect. Your goal is to have the client computers automatically restart after the installations have been performed, therefore Answer **C** is incorrect.

3. The CIO of Robert's Rockets has instructed you, the network administrator, to install and configure a SUS-based solution that is to be used to keep all internal client computers up to date with the latest required patches and updates. Robert's Rockets has its world headquarters in Massachusetts with regional offices worldwide. You are concerned about the possible saturation of your wide area network (WAN) links by remote clients downloading and installing updates from the SUS servers you have planned for placement in the headquarters server room. The CIO has informed you that you must perform all approval of updates from the corporate headquarters, but that it does not matter where the updates are downloaded from. What two solutions could you implement that will allow you to approve all updates locally but not overburden your WAN links? (Choose two correct answers.)

A. Install multiple SUS servers on your network worldwide. Allow administrators in remote locations to have administrative control over the SUS servers located in their locations.

B. Install multiple SUS servers on your network worldwide. Configure the servers in remote locations to keep updates locally on the SUS server. Configure the servers in remote locations to synchronize against the SUS server located in your corporate headquarters. Configure clients in remote locations to use the SUS server that is located closest to them geographically.

C. Install multiple SUS servers on your network worldwide. Configure the servers in remote locations to not download updates but instead to point clients to the Windows Update Web servers. Configure the servers in remote locations to synchronize against the SUS server located in your corporate headquarters. Configure clients in remote locations to use the SUS server that is located closest to them geographically.

D. Install a Network Load Balanced SUS server cluster in your corporate headquarters. Configure clients in remote locations to download all updates directly from the Windows Update Web servers.

☑ **B, C.** Answers **B** and **C** provide a distributed SUS solution in which local approval control is maintained and remote clients download their updates from locations that are geographically close to them.

☒ **A, D.** Allowing administrators in remote locations to have control over the SUS servers violates the requirement that all administrative control is to be maintained locally, therefore Answer **A** is incorrect. Installing a NLB cluster of SUS servers in the corporate headquarters is not a bad idea, but having remote clients download directly from the Windows Update Web servers prevents you from being able to control which updates are installed on clients, therefore Answer **D** is incorrect.

4. You are the network administrator with a Global SUS solution in place. Currently, all remote sites have dedicated WAN links that connect to your Global headquarters in Massachusetts that are used for SUS only. You have been directed by your CIO to reduce costs and improve the performance of the SUS solution in use on your network. Each of your remote locations also currently has an ISDN connection through a local ISP for Internet connectivity. The corporate headquarters has a full T-1 connection to the Internet. Any solution that you come up with must still allow for only local approval of all available updates. How can you eliminate the need for the WAN links and improve the speed and performance of the SUS solution your network has in place?

A. Install and configure SUS servers in each remote location. Configure virtual private network (VPN) links through the Internet from each remote location to the corporate headquarters. Configure the SUS servers in each remote location to synchronize their content from the local SUS server.

B. Install and configure SUS servers in each remote location. Configure the SUS servers in each remote location to be managed by a local administrator.

C. Install and configure SUS servers in each remote location. Configure the SUS server in each location to synchronize their content from the local SUS server using Simple Mail Transfer Protocol (SMTP).

D. Install and configure SUS servers in each remote location. Configure VPN links through the Internet from each remote location to the corporate headquarters. Configure the SUS servers in each remote location to be managed by a local administrator.

☑ **A.** By installing and configuring SUS servers in each remote location that synchronize content from the local SUS server via a VPN tunnel, you can eliminate the cost of the WAN links, maintain local administrative control, and increase performance of the SUS solution as each SUS server can download content from the Windows Update Web servers using its own Internet connection.

☒ **B, C, D.** Allowing remote SUS servers to be administered by the administrator in their location violates the requirement that all update approval must be performed locally, therefore Answers **B** and **D** are incorrect. SUS does not synchronize content via SMTP, although Active Directory can perform replication over SMTP if required, therefore Answer **C** is incorrect.

5. You are the network administrator for Area 51 Networks, and have just completed a default installation of Windows Server 2003 Enterprise Edition on a new server. You are now preparing to install and configure SUS. What additional step must you first complete before you can successfully install and configure SUS on this server?

   A. You must join this server to a Windows Server 2003 Active Directory domain.

   B. You must install and configure the Routing and Remote Access Service (RRAS) on this server.

   C. You must install and configure IIS on this server.

   D. You must create and configure a shared folder on this server.

   ☑ **C.** IIS 6.0 must be installed and functioning properly on this server before you can successfully install and configure SUS on it.

   ☒ **A, B, D.** The SUS server does not need to be a part of the domain, although making the server part of the domain will increase its security and manageability, therefore Answer **A** is incorrect. The RRAS service does not need to be present on the SUS server, therefore Answer **B** is incorrect. You will not need to create a shared folder on the server before installing SUS, therefore Answer **D** is incorrect.

6. You are the network administrator and have just completed a default installation of Windows Server 2003 Enterprise Edition on a new server. You are now preparing to install and configure SUS. The server has three hard drives installed, configured as follows:

   ■ Drive-0: Volume C, NTFS, 4GB free space, Windows operating system files

   ■ Drive-1: Volume D, FAT32, 12GB free space, shared network storage folder

   ■ Drive-2: Volume E, unformatted, 20GB free space.

   Which two of the following additional steps should you complete before installing the SUS server to ensure that it is installed correctly? (Choose two correct answers)

   A. Format Volume E with the NTFS file system.

   B. Create and configure a shared folder on this server.

   C. Convert Volume D to the NTFS file system.

   D. Format Volume C with the NTFS file system.

   ☑ **A, C.** You could either format the unformatted Volume E with NTFS or convert the existing Volume D from FAT32 to NTFS in order to meet the requirement that SUS has of needing at least 6GB of free space on an NTFS partition in order to store its download updates.

☒ **B**, **D**. There is no need to create another shared folder on the server before installing SUS, therefore Answer **B** is incorrect. Formatting Volume C is not a good idea as it is currently housing your Windows operating system files, therefore Answer **D** is incorrect.

7. Your network is operating in Windows Server 2003 functional mode at both the domain and forest level. A four-node NLB cluster running ISA Server 2000 has been placed between your internal network and your Internet connection. You have recently installed and configured an SUS server on your internal network; however, it cannot establish a connection to the Windows Update Web servers. What must you do to ensure that your SUS solution functions properly?

A. Place the SUS server on the screened subnet that has direct access to the Internet.

B. Configure the proxy server properties in the SUS server options.

C. Create a VPN tunnel through the ISA server cluster to the Internet.

D. Open port 3389 on your router to allow SUS traffic through.

☑ **B**. You will need to configure the SUS server with the required properties to connect to the proxy server, in this case ISA Server 2000.

☒ **A**, **C**, **D**. Placing the SUS server on the screened subnet is not required and will most likely only result in it being subjected to various unwanted connection attempts and attacks, therefore Answer **A** is incorrect. You do not need to create a VPN tunnel through the ISA Serer to the Internet, therefore Answer **C** is incorrect. Port 3389 is used for Remote Desktop and Terminal Services, not SUS, therefore Answer **D** is incorrect.

8. Tom has configured Automatic Updates via Group Policy to download updates from an internal SUS server named GREEN42. All client computers on Tom's network are running Windows 2000 Professional SP4. Automatic Updates was configured to download and install, automatically, any available updates from GREEN42 on a daily basis. After several weeks, Tom notices that no updates have been applied to his client computer. Given what you know so far, what could be the possible reasons why no updates have been received on Tom's computer?

A. Tom has not configured synchronization to occur on the SUS server.

B. Tom has not approved any updates on the SUS server for client installation.

C. Tom does not have the required version of the Automatic Updates client on his computer.

D. Tom does not have the required version of the SUS application installed on his server.

☑ **A**, **B**. The most likely reasons presented are that Tom has not configured synchronization to occur, thus no updates are available or that Tom has not approved any updates, thus no updates are available to install on clients.

☒ **C, D**. Since Tom has Windows 2000 SP4 installed on all of his clients, he has a version of Automatic Updates that is compatible with SUS, therefore Answer **C** is incorrect. The version of SUS that is installed has no bearing in this situation, therefore Answer **D** is incorrect.

9. Your global network is operating in Windows Server 2003 functional mode at both the domain and forest level and is geographically dispersed over 25 locations in North America and Western Europe. You have installed and configured SUS servers that have subsequently been placed in all remote locations on your network. All Group Policy configuration is performed at the corporate headquarters in Massachusetts. You have OUs corresponding to each remote location on your network. How should you configure the Specify intranet Microsoft update service location option for each of your OUs?

   A.   You should point the clients in all OUs towards the SUS server that is located in your corporate headquarters.

   B.   You should point the clients in North American OUs to Western European SUS servers for redundancy. Likewise, you should point the clients in the Western European OUs to North American SUS servers.

   C.   You should point the clients in each OU towards the local SUS server located at that location.

   D.   You should point the clients in all OUs towards all available SUS servers for maximum reliability.

   ☑ **C**. Since you have taken the time and effort to create a distributed network of SUS servers, you would best be served by configuring a GPO for each site's OU that points the clients located at that site towards the SUS server that is also located at that site.

   ☒ **A, B, D**. You should not point all clients towards the corporate SUS servers since you have created a distributed network of SUS servers, therefore Answer **A** is incorrect. You should not point clients in one OU towards the SUS server in another location because each location has its own SUS server for increased performance, therefore Answer **B** is incorrect. You cannot point clients at more than one SUS server, therefore Answer **D** is incorrect. You can, however, create SUS server NLB clusters to improve reliability and availability if desired.

10. Your global network is operating in Windows Server 2003 functional mode at both the domain and forest level. Your network is geographically dispersed over 25 locations in North America and Western Europe. You have installed and configured SUS servers that have subsequently been placed in all remote locations on your network. All Group Policy configuration is performed at the corporate headquarters in Massachusetts. You have 1,500 Windows XP Professional SP1 desktop clients and 700 Windows 2000 Professional SP4 portable computer clients on your network. The portable computers are often not attached to the network during the scheduled update installation time of 3AM. What can

you do to ensure that these portable computer clients will automatically download and install available approved updates the next time they are started while connected to the network?

A. Enable the **Configure Automatic Updates** option and select an installation time of 1P.M. daily.

B. Enable the **Specify intranet Microsoft update service location** option and enter the URL of your SUS server.

C. Enable the **Reschedule Automatic Updates scheduled installations** option and configure a time delay of 10 minutes.

D. Enable the **No auto-restart for scheduled Automatic Updates installations** option.

☑ **C.** You will need to configure Automatic Updates to be rescheduled for clients that are not powered on or are not connected to the network during the configured update installation time in order for them to download and install available updates the next time they are powered on while connected to the network.

☒ **A, B, D.** You already have Automatic Updates configured and scheduled for 3A.M. daily, therefore Answer **A** is incorrect. Configuring the SUS server URL, while required, is not the correct solution to this problem, therefore Answer **B** is incorrect. Configuring Automatic Updates clients to not automatically restart after installations have been performed is not advisable and is also not a solution to this problem, therefore Answer **D** is incorrect.

11. You have recently installed and configured an SUS server for your 5,000 Windows XP Professional SP1 clients to use to download and install approved updates from. All clients are located in one of the ten OUs that correspond to the various departments within the company, with approximately 500 computers per department. You have also configured Automatic Updates in Group Policy at the domain level to point all of your clients towards the SUS server. After a week has gone by, you have determined through performance monitoring that your single SUS server is being slightly overloaded. You decide to configure a second SUS server that your clients can connect to. How should you configure your clients so that half of them connect to the first SUS server and half of them connect to the second SUS server without disrupting any of the other existing Group Policies you have in place and does not require any extra administrative effort on your part?

A. Create two new OUs and move half of the client computers into each of the OUs. Configure a new GPO for each OU that points the Automatic Updates clients towards one of the two SUS servers. Remove the Automatic Updates GPO that is linked to the domain.

B. Create two new GPOs, with one of them pointing Automatic Updates clients towards the first SUS server and the other pointing clients towards the second SUS server.

Link each of the GPOs to five of the ten departmental OUs you have. Remove the Automatic Updates GPO that is linked to the domain.

C. Create a new GPO for each of the ten OUs. Configure five of the new GPOs to point at the first SUS server and the other five new GPOs to point at the second SUS server. Remove the Automatic Updates GPO that is linked to the domain.

D. Create two new OUs within each of the 10 existing OUs. Create two new GPOs, with one of them pointing Automatic Updates clients towards the first SUS server and the other pointing clients towards the second SUS server. Link one of the new GPOs to one of the new OUs and link the other new GPO to the other new OU in each of the departmental OUs. Move half of the client computers in each departmental OU to each of the new OUs created within the departmental OU. Remove the Automatic Updates GPO that is linked to the domain.

☑ **B.** The best (most administratively efficient) option that meets the requirements is to create two new GPOs and link each of them to five of your ten departmental OUs. This solution does not require you to move any OUs or clients around, possibly disrupting the processing of your existing Group Policies.

☒ **A, C, D.** Moving client computers from their existing GPOs will likely result in disruptions to the processing of existing policies, therefore Answer **A** is incorrect. Creating ten new GPOs is not required, as two will suffice, therefore Answer **C** is incorrect. Creating 20 new OUs is not required, as you can accomplish the required result by simply creating two new GPOs, therefore Answer **D** is incorrect.

12. You have recently installed and configured an SUS server for your 5,000 Windows XP Professional SP1 clients to use to download and install approved updates from. Automatic Updates works fine the first day after you configure it, but after that time, no updates have been downloaded and installed by your clients even though you have approved several new updates. You have accessed the SUS server and can find nothing wrong with the server's operation. What is the most likely cause for this problem?

A. Your clients are pointing at the wrong SUS server.

B. You have not configured rescheduling of missed scheduled updates.

C. You have not configured clients to automatically restart after installation of updates.

D. You have not enabled Automatic Updates to occur with a scheduled installation day and time.

☑ **C.** Clients will not be able to detect any new updates until they have been restarted following the installation of updates.

☒ **A, B, D.** Your clients are obviously pointing at the correct SUS server URL as they were able to download and install updates correctly the first time, therefore Answer **A** is incorrect. Configuring missed updates to be rescheduled is a good idea, but is not the solution to this problem, therefore Answer **C** is incorrect. You have configured update installation to occur as evidenced by the fact that your clients have previously installed available updates on the first day, therefore Answer **D** is incorrect.

13. Your network is operating in Windows Server 2003 functional mode at both the domain and forest level. You have recently installed and configured an SUS server for your 3,500 Windows XP Professional SP1 clients to use to download and install approved updates from. All of your Windows XP Professional clients can successfully download and install updates from the SUS server. You have just hired three temporary contractors who require network access so that they can reach the Internet to check their e-mail and browse Web pages. You want the Windows XP Professional SP1 portable computers these contractors are using to also contact your SUS server to ensure that they are not the cause of a security breach on your network. You do not want to join these computers to your domain; however they must still be allowed to contact your SUS server. How will you configure these three portable computers to enable Automatic Updates from your SUS server?

A. Install the updated version of the Automatic Updates client.

B. Manually create and configure the
HKEY_LOCAL_MACHINE\SOFTWARE\Policies\Microsoft\Windows\WindowsUpdate
Registry key.

C. Manually create and configure the
HKEY_CURRENT_CONFIG\SOFTWARE\Policies\Microsoft\Windows\WindowsUpdate
Registry key.

D. You cannot accomplish this without joining the three portable computers to your Active Directory network.

☑ **B.** As long as the required version of the Automatic Updates client is installed (which it is), you can manually create and configure the Registry values required to point the computer towards an SUS server.

☒ **A, C, D.** The required version of the Automatic Updates client is installed by Windows XP SP1, therefore Answer **A** is incorrect. The Automatic Updates entries in the Registry are located under the *HKEY_LOCAL_MACHINE* root key, therefore Answer **C** is incorrect. You can accomplish this task by manually creating and configuring the Registry values required to point the computer towards an SUS server, therefore Answer **D** is incorrect.

14. You are the assistant network administrator; the regular administrator is on vacation for the next two months. Your network is operating in Windows Server 2003 functional mode at both the domain and forest level. Before going on vacation, the regular administrator installed and configured an SUS server for your 3,500 Windows XP Professional SP1 clients to use to download and install approved updates from. Where can you quickly determine what updates the regular administrator had approved before she left on her vacation?

A. You should view the approval log on the SUS server.

B. You should view the SUS IIS logs.

C. You should view the synchronization log on the SUS server.

D. You should view the SUS server options.

☑ **A.** You should view the approval log to quickly determine what updates the regular administrator had approved before she went on vacation.

☒ **B, C, D.** The IIS logs, while very useful, will not easily lend themselves to quickly determining what new updates have been downloaded to the SUS server, therefore Answer **B** is incorrect. The synchronization log will detail what new updates have been downloaded from the Windows Update Web servers, therefore Answer **C** is incorrect. Monitoring the server will only tell you how many updates are available, not which ones are new since the last time you looked, therefore Answer **D** is incorrect.

15. You have installed and configured an SUS server and configured the Automatic Updates to automatically download and install updates on a daily basis. After three days, you determine that your clients have installed no updates. When you attempt to access your SUS administration page, you cannot access the page and receive the following error from IIS: "The page you are looking for is currently unavailable. The Web site might be experiencing technical difficulties, or you may need to adjust your browser settings." What is the most likely cause for this problem?

A. The Software Update Synchronization Service has stopped functioning normally.

B. The World Wide Web Publishing Service has stopped functioning normally.

C. The WebClient Service has stopped functioning properly.

D. The SUS server is not properly identified in the Automatic Updates options.

☑ **B.** In this case, where you cannot even access your SUS administration page, the most likely cause of your difficulties is that the World Wide Web Publishing Service is not functioning correctly. In most cases, restarting the service will remedy the problem.

☒ **A, C, D.** If the Software Update Synchronization Service was not functioning properly, you would still be able to access your SUS administration page, therefore Answer **A** is incorrect. The WebClient Service has nothing to do with SUS or Automatic Updates, therefore Answer **C** is incorrect. The SUS server not being properly identified in the Automatic Updates options would not cause the SUS administration page to become unavailable, therefore Answer **D** is incorrect.

Managing Updates for Legacy Clients

16. You have a Windows Server 2003 network that is operating in Windows Server 2003 functional mode at both the domain and forest level. All of your Windows 2000 Professional and Windows XP Professional clients are using an SUS server to download and install required updates. You also have an assortment of Windows 98 and Windows Millennium Edition computers that you are responsible for supporting. Using Windows Update locally on each of the legacy computers is not an option as they are distributed over six locations up and down the East Coast. You have network connectivity will all remote locations through VPN connections that have been created over the Internet and link each remote location with the home office. Each remote location has an ISDN connection to the Internet using a local ISP. You need to be able to keep all of your legacy clients up to date with required security patches and updates. You also are the only person authorized in your companies Information Technology (IT) policy to distribute security updates. How can you accomplish the required goal? (Choose two correct answers)

A. Create computer accounts for the Windows 98 and Windows Millennium Edition computers in Active Directory Users and Computers.

B. Use the Windows Update Catalog to locate and download required updates. Create a script that will install the updates remotely over your VPNs on the required computers.

C. Use the Windows Update Catalog to locate and download required updates. Use SMS to install the updates remotely over your VPNs on the required computers.

D. Instruct users at each location on how to use Windows Update to download and install required updates locally.

☑ **B, C.** By using the Windows Update Catalog, you can install the updates using your choice of methods, including but not limited to, scripting or SMS.

☒ **A, D.** While you can create computer accounts for your legacy computers in Active Directory, it won't have any effect, therefore Answer **A** is incorrect. Company policy prohibits any other user from installing security updates, therefore Answer **D** is incorrect.

Index

128-bit encryption, 258
401 errors, 262
404 errors, 258–259
503 errors, 262–263

A

access
  Account Lockout Policy node options
    (table), 430
  directory service, auditing, 462
  object, auditing, 463–464
account policies
  Account tab, account Properties (fig.), 45
  activating Terminal Server Licensing server,
    108–110
  audit management, 460–462
  password policy node options (table), 428–429
Active Directory
  adding computer account object to, 537
  adding contact objects to, 538
  adding group objects to, 539
  adding OUs to, 540
  adding user objects to, 540
  and BIND servers, 395
  command-line tools, 536–592
  delegating administrative authority, 41
  displaying computer properties in, 558
  displaying contact properties in, 559
  displaying domain controller properties in, 562
  displaying group properties in, 560–561
  displaying OU properties in, 561
  displaying partition properties in, 566
  displaying quota specification properties in,
    565–566
  displaying site properties in, 565
  displaying subnet properties in, 564
  displaying user group properties in, 562
  domain controller control of, 65
  and domain environments, 4
  hierarchical structure of, 340
  importing and exporting data, 58–60, 568–570
  integrated zone features (table), 347
  modifying computer properties, 543
  modifying contact properties, 543–544
  modifying properties of groups in, 544–545
  modifying properties of OUs in, 545–546

  modifying quota specifications in, 548
  modifying user properties in, 546–548
  moving and renaming objects in, 549–550
  querying for computer information, 550
  querying for contact information, 550–557
  querying for domain controller
    information, 554
  querying for group information, 552
  querying for OU information, 553
  querying for partition object information,
    556–557
  querying for quota specification
    information, 556
  querying for site information, 553
  querying for user information, 555
  removing objects from, 549
Active Directory Users and Computers console
  changing group scope from, 26–27
  converting group type from, 24–25
  deleting groups from, 28–29
  illustrated (fig.), 15
Active Server Pages. *See* ASPs
adding
  computer account objects to Active
    Directory, 537
  connections with Remote Desktop
    Connection utility, 172–173
  contact objects to Active Directory, 538
  DNS server records to zones, 581
  group members, 19–21
  group objects to Active Directory, 539
  new groups, 18–22
  OUs to Active Directory, 540
  quota specifications to directory partition, 542
  user objects to Active Directory, 540
  users to Remote Desktop Users group,
    141–142
Address tab, account Properties (fig.), 45
administering IIS remotely, 266
Administrative Tools folder, 129–130
administrators
  backup operations, configuring, 308–309
  control over backups, 328
  daily tasks, 128
  delegating administrative authority, 41
  delegation of user rights by, 4
  IIS 6.0 installation, 209

required group memberships, 17
update control, 488
using principle of least privilege, 404–405
adminpak.msi, 136
Advanced Digest authentication, 201–202
Advanced Research Projects Agency Network
    (ARPNET), 338, 339
Advanced tab, DNS server, 363–364
ampersand (&), DNS forward lookup zone, 373
anonymous authentication, 244
answer files, parameters for IIS unattended setup,
    218
AOL Instant Messenger, 147
application pooling, 207, 260
application servers, 210
applying user rights to groups, 32–34
approval logs for updates, 508
architecture
    ASP.NET, 207–208
    IIS 6.0 request processing, 206
archive attribute, 278
ARPNET (Advanced Research Projects Agency
    Network), 338, 339
ASP.NET
    authorization, 204
    IIS 6.0 content errors, 258
    and IIS integration, 207–208
    pages returning as static files, 260
    working with, 238–239
ASPs, execution and implementation, 204
ASR (Automated System Recovery)
    Self Test, 329–336
    using, 312–314
ASR Wizard, 295
assigning
    IP addresses restrictions to Web site (fig.), 252
    NTFS permissions to groups, 34–35
    user rights to groups, 31–34
audit policies, 430–432
Audit Policy node options (table), 432
auditing
    security events, 458–468
    solutions, configuring and implementing,
        469–472
authentication
    Advanced Digest, 201
    anonymous, 244

and authorization, 204
backing up across domains, 309
basic, 245
client certificate mapping, 248
configuring user, 249–252
configuring Web site, 250–251
Digest Authentication, 246–247
hashing and, 201
IWA (Integrated Windows
    Authentication), 246
methods supported by IIS, 244
.NET Passport, 205
supplying user credentials, 57
troubleshooting user, 52–53
authorization described, 204
Automated Recovery System. See ASR
Automated Recovery System Wizard, 313–314
Automatic Updates
    configuring in Registry, 503–507
    grayed out options, 524
    installing client, 490, 497–507
    key values (table), 505
    troubleshooting, 512–513
AXFR zone transfers, 348

B

backing up
    IIS configuration, 598
    IIS metabase, 239–242
    system state data, 288–289, 307
backup data, restoring, 309–312
Backup or Restore Wizard, 287
Backup tab, Windows Backup Utility (fig.), 296
Backup Utility. See Windows Backup Utility
Backup Wizard, 302–308, 310–312
backups
    basics of, 277–286
    command-line tools, 607–608
    configuring jobs using Backup Wizard,
        303–308
    configuring security for, 308–309
    managing, 607–608
    media for, 279–286
    naming, 297
    offsite storage, 282
    planning, 276–286

Self Test, 329–336
using Windows Backup Utility, 287–308
bandwidth
Remote Desktop Connection utility, settings
(table), 170
and terminal session latency, 82
basic authentication, 245
batch files or scripts, command-line
utilities in, 134
Berkeley Internet Name Domain (BIND), 342
best practices
auditing, Microsoft recommendations,
468–469
shadow copies, 324
BIND servers and Active Directory, 395
boot files, backing up, 308–309
brute force hacking, 430
buffering, response, 262
Builtin container, default groups in (tables),
10–14

C

caching
ASP.NET levels, 208
flexible (IIS), 207
Caching API, 208
CAs (certificate authorities)
40-bit SGC, 202
Server-Gated Cryptography and, 202
and SSL-secured communications, 253–256
CD-R/RWs, 281
centralized computing environment (fig.), 77
certificate authorities. See CAs
certificates
client, mapping, 248–249
server, requesting, 253–256
SSL, IP addresses and Web sites, 237
changing
See also modifying
domain functional levels, 15
group scope, 26–27
Citrix MetaFrame, 74
client certificate mapping, 248–249
Client Settings tab, RDP-Tcp Properties dialog
box (fig.), 97–98
clients
deploying software for shadow copies, 322

managing updates for clients, 513–518
requests timing out, 262
using Remote Desktop Web Connection
utility, 177–180
clipboard problems, troubleshooting, 111
clustering Terminal Services, 119
CNAME records, 387
color resolution, Terminal Services, connection
problems, 119
COM + class registration database, 307–308
command line
See also specific commands
assigning user rights from, 31
changing group scope from, 27
converting group type from, 25
creating, modifying computer accounts from,
54–56
deleting user accounts from, 51
extended functionality of, 2
groups, creating new, 18–22
MCSA command-line reference, 535–608
quotation marks, use of, 19
removing groups from, 28
removing members from groups, 23
resetting user account passwords, 40
utilities described, 134
commands. See specific command
common resource record types (table), 388–389
computer accounts, creating, 53–58
computers
in Active Directory, modifying properties of,
543
displaying properties in Active Directory, 558
joining to domains, 56–57
querying Active Directory for information
about, 550
computing, centralized versus distributed, 75–76
configurations, duel boot, and shadow copies,
324
Configure Your Server Wizard, 88, 134, 210–215,
352–360
configuring
application performance properties (IIS), 261
auditing solutions, 469–472
backups using Backup Utility Backup tab, 297
DNS server options, 360–368
DNS Service, 352–360
DNS zone options, 368–381

domain level security policy (fig.), 422

File System Security Inheritance Behavior (fig.), 454

IE 6.0 for use with Remote Desktop Web Connection utility, 180

IIS metabase backup, 241

IP address/domain restrictions, 252

Registry security, 450–452

Remote Assistance for use, 145–146

Remote Desktop Connection utility, 164–170

Remote Desktop for Administration, 140

Restricted Groups node, 445–447

saved Remote Connections, 173

security event log policies, 442–443

security templates, 428–458

shadow copy schedule (fig.), 320

SMTP virtual server default domain, 229

software update infrastructure, 488

SSL properties for Web site (fig.), 257

SSL-secured communications, 253–258

SUS (Software Update Services), 490–495

Terminal Services, 92–105

user account properties, 44–46

user authentication, 249–252

user logon restrictions, 46–48

virtual directory permissions, 235

volume shadow copies, 316, 318

Web security, authentication using SSL, 256–258

Windows Backup Utility options, 289–292

connecting

  to Emergency Management Services, 185–186

  to remote DNS servers, 382

connections

  allowing users to make Remote Desktop for Administration, 140

  establishing with Remote Desktop Connection utility, 175–176

  troubleshooting errors (IIS), 260

connectivity, troubleshooting, 111

consoles

  Computer Management, 136–137

  default Domain Controller Security Settings, 32

  DNS management, 381

  Group Policy Editor, 310

  IIS Manager, 219

  Local Security Settings (fig.), 421

  Security, 409–411

Terminal Server Licensing, 106–108

contacts

  displaying properties in Active Directory, 559

  querying Active Directory for information about, 551

Content Management Server (CMS), content replicator, 266

converting

  group type, 23–25

  IIS log files, 208

cookies, vulnerability to attacks, 248

copy backups, 279

copying

  IIS metabase, 603

  user accounts, 41–42

  volume shadow. *See* volume shadow copy

Corporate Windows Update Web site, 524

creating

  ASR backup, 277

  ASR set, 313–314

  backup job, 297–302

  backup plan, 276

  CNAME record (fig.), 387

  computer accounts, 53–58

  custom MMCs, 132–134

  DNS forwarder, 361–362

  FTP sites, 596–597

  FTP sites using FTP Site Creation Wizard, 224–227

  groups, 2–5, 13, 17–19

  IIS 6.0 Web sites, 593–594

  NNTP virtual servers, 229–233

  rollback templates, 607

  Security Console, 409–411

  security templates, 419–420

  shadow copies, 315

  SMTP virtual servers, 227–229

  user accounts, 36–53

  virtual directory for FTP site, 598

  virtual servers, 233–235

  Web sites using Web Site Creation Wizard, 220–224

Cryptographic Service Provider (CSP), 203

cryptography

  selectable service provider, 203

  server-gated, 202

csvde command, 568–570

csvde (CSV Directory Exchange) utility, 58–60

customizing
  MMCs, 131–133
  security templates, 419–420

D

DACLs (Discretionary Access Control Lists)
  described, 25
  and distribution groups, 4
daily backups, 279
DAT (Digital Audio Tape), 280, 281
data, backing up, 276–325
databases
  DNS, 339
  security, 413–417
DDLs, execution permission, 223
DDS format tapes, 280–281
Debug Logging tab, DNS server, 365–367
defense in depth, 404
delegated namespaces, 342–343
delegated zones, 386
delegating administrative authority for backups,
    309–310
Delegation of Control Wizard, 41
deleting
  DNS server records from zones, 581
  groups, 27–28
  IIS metabase backup copy, 601
  user accounts, 50–52
  virtual directory for FTP sites, 598
Denial-of-Service (DoS) attacks, 143, 444
differential backups, 278–279
Digest Authentication, 246–247
Digital Audio Tape (DAT), 280
Digital Data Storage (DDS) format, 280
Digital Linear Tape (DLT), 280
directories
  adding quota specification to partition, 542
  configuring IIS security properties (fig.), 244
  virtual. See virtual directories
directory partitions
  changing resident zone of, 584
  modifying, displaying DNS application
      information, 577–578
  modifying properties in Active Directory, 548
directory service access, auditing, 462
disabling user accounts, 42–43
disaster recovery

creating backup plans, 276–286
Exam Objectives Summary, 325
disconnecting with Remote Desktop
    Connection utility, 175–176
Discretionary Access Control Lists. See DACLs
disk space, adequate for shadow copies, 319
Display tab, Remote Desktop Connection
    utility, 165
distributed computing environment
  versus centralized, 75–76
  described (fig.), 78
distribution groups described, 3–4
DLT (Digital Linear Tape), 280
DNS (Domain Name System)
  changing registry values, 572–577
  clearing cache, 572
  committing changes, 584
  configuring reverse lookup zone options,
      378–381
  configuring server options, 360–368
  configuring zone options, 368–381
  debug logging, 366–367
  deleting specific server records, 581
  determining namespace requirements, 342
  determining forwarding requirements,
      348–352
  displaying information, troubleshooting,
      589–592
  displaying, modifying directory partition
      information, 577–580
  displaying server zone information, 580
  displaying statistics on specified server, 583
  Exam Objectives Fast Track, 391–394
  Exam Objectives Summary, 390–391
  Fully Qualified Domain Name (FQDN), 338
  hierarchical database system (fig.), 339
  hierarchical namespace, 340–341
  installing service, 352–360
  introduction, 338
  log, and EventComMT tool, 477
  management tools, 570–592
  managing service and servers, 381–389
  managing zone settings, 386–389
  name resolution process (fig.), 350
  planning service, 338
  reason for using, 395
  removing servers from directory partition
      replica set, 583
  resource record types (table), 388–389

Self Test, 396–402
server setup and Active Directory setup, 352
time-stamping resource records, 571–572
verifying and troubleshooting records, 589
zone type requirements, 345
DNS forwarder, creating new, 361–362
DNS servers
connecting to remote, 382
starting, stopping, pausing, 385
dnscmd command, 570–588
dnslint command, 589
domain controllers
displaying properties in Active Directory, 562
modifying properties of, 546
querying Active Directory for information
about, 554
domain environments
and forest functionality, 5
versus workgroup environments, 4
domain functional levels
changing, 15
described, 5
and group nesting, 9
groups scope behaviors versus (table), 7
raising, 16
domain licensing, 106
domain local groups, scope, using, 6
Domain Name System. *See* DNS
domains
backups for users in multiple, 309
configuring to restrict users, 252
creating computer accounts by joining, 55–56
Group Policy application order (fig.), 455
root, top level, 339, 341
DoS attacks, 143, 444
dsadd command, 537–542
batch file or script, 65
creating computer accounts, 55
creating new user account, 38–39
switches (table), 18
user account properties, 44
dsget command, 31, 558–566
dsmod command
disabling user accounts, 43
group conversion, 25–27
verifying results of (fig.), 22
dsquery command, 550–557
dsrm command, 51

duel boot configurations, shadow copies on, 324
Dumpel.exe, 477
DVDs, 281
Dynamic Host Configuration Protocol. *See*
    DHCP
Dynamic Link Libraries. *See* DDLs
dynamic updates, 379, 395

E

eCommerce and application pooling, 207
e-mail
distribution and security groups, 23
requesting help for Remote Assistance, 149
Emergency Management Services (EMS),
    183–186
enabling
ASP.NET support, 239
Digest Authentication for user account (fig.),
    247
Health detection (IIS), 241–242
IIS 6.0 Web Service Extensions, 232
Remote Assistance (fig.), 145
Remote Desktop for Administration, 140
shadow copies, 315–316, 321–322
user accounts, 42–43
encryption
128-bit, 258
and FIPS compliance, 113
TLS, and SMTP servers, 227
enterprise licensing, 106
Environment tab, RDP-Tcp Properties dialog
    box (fig.), 96
error messages
404 errors, 258–259
'The certificate has failed to verify,' 202
'This Initial Program Cannot Be Started,' 111
errors
401 errors, 262
404 errors, 258–259
503 errors, 262–263
file not found, 263
in Registry, 502
Event Logging tab, DNS server, 367
event logs
configuring event log policies, 442–443
configuring for network security, 414
examining SUS, 510
parsing, 477

EventComMT tool, 477
events
    configuring logon, 462
    system, auditing, 467
Exam Objectives Fast Track
    disaster recovery, 326–328
    DNS, 391–394
    managing user, computers, groups, 61–64
    network security, 474–476
    remote server management, administration,
        188–189
    software updates, 523–524
    Terminal Services, 115–117
    Web server management, maintenance,
        264–266
Exam Objectives Summaries
    disaster recovery, 325
    DNS, 390–391
    network security, 473
    remote server management, administration,
        187–188
    software updates, 522
    Terminal Services, 114
    Web server management, maintenance, 264
Exclude Files tab, Windows Backup Utility,
    292–295
.EXE files, 131
Experience tab, Remote Desktop Connection
    utility, 169–170
Expert, Remote Assistance, 138–139
exporting
    Active Directory data, 568–570
    IIS metabase, 602
    security templates, 419, 605
Extensible Markup Language. See XML

F

fat clients, 75–76
File Allocation Table (FAT), 287
file authorization, 204
file not found errors, UNIX, Linux, 263
File System Security node, configuring options,
    452–454
File Transfer Protocol. See FTP
FIPS compliant encryption, 113
firewalls, 362
flexible caching (IIS), 207
floppy disk, ASR restoration, 314, 329

forests
    and domain functionality, 5
    hierarchical structure of, 340
forward lookup zones, 348, 368–372
forwarder (DNS server), 350
Forwarders tab, DNS server, 360–361
forwarding requirements (DNS), 348–352
FQDN (Fully Qualified Domain Name), 172,
    338
FrontPage, enabling Server Extensions (IIS), 212
FTP application described, 210
FTP Site Creation Wizard, 224–227
FTP sites
    access points to different, 266
    creating, 224–227
    management tools, 596–598
Full Security option, Terminal Services, 91
Fully Qualified Domain Name. See FQDN

G

General tab
    forward lookup zone, 369–372
    RDP-Tcp Properties dialog box (fig.), 94
    Remote Desktop Connection utility, 164–165
    reverse lookup zones, 378
    Windows Backup Utility options (table), 291
GFS media rotation system, 284–285
global groups, 6, 8
gpresult command, 567
Grandfather, Father, Son (GFS) media rotation
    system, 284–285
group members described, 2
group nesting, 9
Group Policy
    advanced Terminal Services configuration,
        102–105
    application order (fig.), 455
    configuring Automatic Updates via, 498–502
    deploying Group Policy with, 454–457
    displaying settings and RSoP of users, 567
    Editor console, 310
    managing Terminal Services with, 118
    security extensions, 420–421
Group Policy Objects (GPOs), 32, 420–421
group properties, modifying, 28–29
group scope, 6–7, 26–27
group type, converting, 23–25
groups

adding group object to Active Directory, 539
advantages of managing users through, 64
assigning user rights, 31–34
common tasks performed in relation to, 15
creating, 2–5, 17–19
default, 10–14
deleting, 27–28
determining user membership of, 30–31
displaying properties in Active Directory, 560, 563–564
local, 3
managing and modifying, 14–17
nesting, 9
querying Active Directory for information about, 552
Remote Desktop Users, 141–142
restricted, 414
types, 3–5

H

hacking, brute force, 430
hard disk space, adequate for shadow copies, 319
hardening Windows Server 2003, 441–442
hashing, MD5, 201
headers, viewing Web site information (fig.), 237
health detection, IIS 6.0, 206
Health detection (IIS), 241–242
help requests
  management feature for, 190
  Remote Assistance, using Windows Messenger, 148
home directory, entering for a Web site (fig.), 223
hosting multiple Web sites, 235
hours, logon, 46–48
HTML, Remote Administration component, 181–182
HTTP
  MD5 hash and, 201
  requests, and IIS handling of, 207
HTTP.SYS kernel driver, 206
Hyper Text Transfer Protocol. *See* HTTP

I

icons, security analysis, 412–413
identifying logged on users, 567
IIS
  See also IIS 6.0

access methods, default, 210
Locked Down mode, 210
metabase, backup and restoration, 239
security management, 243–258
IIS 6.0
  ASP.NET authorization options, 204
  backing up and restoring configuration, 598
  command-line tools, 592–607
  creating new Web sites, 593–594
  HTTP.sys kernel mode device driver, 206–207
  installing, 209–219
  kernel and user modes, 206–207
  lockdown, default status, 203
  managing, 219–243
  managing configuration settings, 601–603
  metabase backup, restoration, 598–601
  .NET Passport authentication, 248
  new features, 200–209
  new IIS management commands, 592–603
  options, examining (fig.), 216
  reliability features, 205
  Server Role dialog box (fig.), 212
  troubleshooting, 258–264
  Web Service Extensions, enabling, 232
  work process described, 205
  XML metabase, 208
IIS Certificate Wizard, 256–258
IIS servers
  remote administration of, 266
  requesting server certificates for, 253–256
iiscnfg.vbs utility, 601–603
iisftpdr.vbs utility, 598–599
iisftp.vbs utility, 596–598
iissuba.dll, 262
iisvdir.vbs command, 594–596
iisweb.vbs utility, 593–594
implementing auditing solutions, 469–472
Import Template dialog box (fig.), 416
importing
  Active Directory data, 58–60, 568–570
  IIS metabase, 602
  security templates, 606
  security templates at domain level, 457–458
  security templates at OU level, 455–457
incremental backups, 278
inetinfo.exe process (IIS), 206
.inf files, 415
Information Technology. *See* IT
installing

Automatic Updates client, 497–507
DNS Service, 352–360
IIS 6.0, 200, 209–219
IIS 6.0 using unattended setup, 217–218
IIS 6.0 with Configure Your Server Wizard, 210–215
IIS 6.0 with Windows Component Wizard, 215–217
Previous Versions Client, 324
Remote Administration (HTML), 182–183
Remote Desktop ActiveX Control, 178
Remote Desktop Connection utility, 161
Remote Desktop Web Connection utility, 176
SUS (Software Update Services), 489–497
Terminal Server Licensing, 107–108
Terminal Services, 87–92
Integrated Windows Authentication (IWA), 246
Interfaces tab, DNS server, 360
Internet, history of, 338
Internet Information Services. See IIS
Internet Protocol (IP) address. See IP addresses
Internetwork Packet Exchange/Sequenced Packet Exchange. See IPX/SPX
IP addresses
    configuring to restrict users, 252
    DNS resolution, 338
    for FTP site, 225
    multiple Web sites, 235
    setting to specified DNS server, 582
    SMTP virtual servers, 228–229
IPX/SPX, protocol use, 338
ISAPI filters, not visible as properties on Web site, 263
IT backup capability, 278
IWA (Integrated Windows Authentication), 246
IXFR zone transfers, 348

J

joining computers to domains, 56–57

K

Kerberos authentication, 246
Kerberos Policy node options (table), 431
KiXart, 128

L

Last Known Good Configuration (LKGC) and ASR, 312

LDAP directory services, importing and exporting data, 568–570
ldifde command, 568–570
ldifde (LDAP Data Interchange Format Directory Exchange) utility, 58–60
leaf, term described, 341
licensing
    Microsoft, Web site information, 106
    Terminal Services, 105–111
    time limits, 118
Lightweight Directory Access Protocol. See LDAP
Linux, 'file not found' errors, 263
LKGC (Last Known Good Configuration), 312
local groups created during installation of Windows Server 2003, 3
Local Resources tab, Remote Desktop Connection utility, 166
local security policies, 431–442
Local Security Settings console (fig.), 421
locating forward lookup zone options, 368–369
lockdown, IIS 6.0, default status, 203
logging
    debug, 366–367
    event. See event logs
logon
    account, audit events, 459–460
    configuring user properties, 46–48
    events, auditing, 462
    password assignment, 38
    Terminal Services, troubleshooting, 110
Logon Settings tab, RDP-Tcp Properties dialog box (fig.), 95
logs
    approval, 508
    backup, configuring, 293
    event. See event logs
    security. See security logs
    synchronization, viewing, 507
    system, viewing, 510–511
    Terminal Services configuration, 89

M

Manage Your Server utility, 93, 134
management tools
    DNS, 570–592
    types of, 128–137
managing
    client connections, 118

disaster recovery, 276–325
DNS service and DNS servers, 381–389
DNS zone and record settings, 386–389
IIS 6.0, 219–243, 592–603
IIS security, 243–258
security templates, 603–607
SUS (Software Update Services), 507–512
updates for legacy clients, 513–518
users generally, 2
mbschema.xml, 209
MCSA command-line reference, 535–608
MD5 (Message Digest 5), 201
media
backup, 279–286
backup rotation, 282–286
floppy disk, ASR restoration, 314
volume shadow copy storage, 319
Member Of tab, account Properties (fig.), 50
members, group, 2
adding, 19–21
removing, 23
Message Digest 5 (MD5), 201
messages, error. *See* error messages
metabase
backing up, restoring, 598–600
copying, saving, 603
IIS, backing up, 240–242
XML, 208
metabase.xml, 209
Microsoft Trustworthy Computing campaign, 405
Microsoft Cryptographic API, 203
Microsoft Management Consoles. *See* MMCs
MIME, IIS 6.0, valid file format, 259
mixed environments
described, 80–81
designing to specific situation, 119
thin and fat clients, 76
MMC shell, creating security management console, 409–411
MMCs (Microsoft Management Consoles)
console modes (table), 131
customizing, 131–133
models, isolation mode and worker process, 205–206
modifying
See also changing

Active Directory objects, contract properties, 543–544
computer properties in Active Directory, 543
domain controller properties, 546
group properties, 28–29, 543
shadow copies, 328–329
user accounts, 37
monitoring SUS servers, 508
Monitoring tab, DNS server, 367–368
moving objects in Active Directory, 550
.MSC files, 130
MSN Messenger, 147
Multipurpose Internet Mail Extensions. *See* MIME

N

name resolution
See also DNS
troubleshooting with nslookup, 385
Name Servers tab
forward lookup zone, 374–375
reverse lookup zones, 379
namespaces
delegated, configuration (fig.), 344
DNS hierarchical, 340
internal and external, 342
naming backups, 297
naming conventions, Terminal Services, 84
nesting groups, 9
.NET framework and ASP.NET, 208
.NET Passport authentication, 248
NetBIOS and TCP/IP, 376
Netscape, HTTP 1.1 support, 201
Network Adapter tab, RDP-Tcp Properties dialog box (fig.), 98
Network News Transfer Protocol. *See* NNTP
network security
configurable areas, 413
Exam Objectives Fast Track, 474–476
Exam Objectives Summary, 473
introduction, 404
principle of least privilege, 404
secedit.exe command, 423–427
Self Test, 478–485
networks, peer-to-peer, 4
New NNTP Virtual Server Wizard, 229–233

New SMTP Virtual Server Wizard, 227–229
New Technology File System. *See* NTFS
NNTP in IIS Manager, 219
NNTP virtual servers, creating, 229–233
nodes described, 341
Novell ZENWorks, 338
Novice, Remote Assistance, 138–139
nslookup command, 385, 589–592
NT File System. *See* NTFS
ntbackup.exe, 312, 607–608
NTFS (New Technology File System)
   authentication, 246
   formatted drive, IIS installation, 209
   permissions, 34–35, 405

O

object access, auditing, 463
Opera , HTTP 1.1 support, 201
Organization tab, account Properties (fig.), 49
organizational unit. *See* OUs
Other tab, Remote Desktop Connection utility,
   175
OUs (organizational units), 405
   adding to Active Directory, 540
   displaying properties in Active Directory, 561
   modifying properties in Active Directory,
     545–546
   querying Active Directory for information
     about, 553
out-of-band management, 192
Outlook Express and Remote Assistance, 149

P

Partial Response Maximum Likelihood
   (PRML), 280–281
partition objects, querying Active Directory for
   information about, 556–557
partitions, displaying properties in Active
   Directory, 566
Password Policy node options (table), 428–429
passwords
   See also permissions, user rights
   account policies, 428–429
   age policies, 429
   assigning temporary user account, 38
   authentication and, 244–249
   backups and, 308–309

principle of least privilege, 404–405
Remote Assistance, 150, 158–160
resetting user account, 39–41
strong, 143
Web sites access, 224–226
PC Anywhere, 138
PDAs and DNS zones, 371
peer-to-peer networks, 4
performance
   configuring application properties (fig.), 261
   configuring Web site, 238
periods, DNS forward lookup zone, 373
permissions
   See also passwords, user rights
   access, assignment, 414
   assigning to groups, 31–34
   assigning to user accounts, 52
   backups and, 308–309
   configuring virtual directory, 235
   NTFS. *See* NTFS permissions
   principle of least privilege, 404–405
   universal and global groups, 8
   Web sites access, 224–226
Permissions tab, RDP-Tcp Properties dialog box
   (fig.), 99
Personal Digital Assistants. *See* PDAs
planning
   for auditing, 468–469
   backups, 276–286
   disaster recovery, 329–330
   DNS namespaces, 342
   network security, 404–405
.pol files, 477
policies
   audit, 430–432, 459
   changes, auditing, 465–466
   password, 39
   Remote Assistance, 158–160
port 443, SSL default, 256
port 3389 vulnerability, 143
port numbers for FTP site, 225
Previous Versions Client, 324
principle of least privilege, 404
PRML (Partial Response Maximum
   Likelihood), 280–281
process tracking, auditing, 466–467
Profile tab, account Properties (fig.), 48

Programs tab, Remote Desktop Connection
  utility, 167–169
properties
  computer, 543
  contact, 543–544
  groups, 544–545
  Health detection, examining (fig.), 243
  OUs, 545–546
  partition, 566
  quota specifications, 565–566
  site, 565
  subnet, 564
  user, 546–548
  user account, 44–46
  user group, 562
  Web site, examining (fig.), 236

Q

queries
  DNS, 348–350
  recursive, 352
querying
  Active Directory for computer information,
    550
  for FTP site information, 597
  for information about IIS 6.0 Web sites, 594
  for information about virtual directories,
    594–596
  for Web site virtual directory information, 598
quota specifications
  adding to directory partition, 542
  displaying properties in Active Directory,
    565–566
  modifying in Active Directory, 548
  querying Active Directory for information
    about, 556
quotation marks (" "), use of in command-line,
  536

R

reassigning user accounts, 51
record scavenging, manually initiating, 384
recovery, performing ASR, 314, 329
recursive queries, 352, 363
Redundant Array of Independent Devices. *See*
  RAID
references, virtual and existing directories, 233

Registry
  backing up, 307–308
  changing values on DNS server, 572–577
  configuring Automatic Updates in, 503–507
  displaying DNS server settings, 580–5581
  editing manually, 502
  security, configuring, 450–452
Relaxed Security option, Terminal Services, 91
Release to Manufacturing (RTF), 109
remote administration, using Terminal Services
  components for, 137–160
Remote Administration (HTML)
  installing, 182–183
  using Web interface for, 181–182
Remote Assistance
  administration tool described, 138–139
  on Expert's computer (fig.), 154
  on Novice's computer (fig.), 156
  operation described, 144–145
  requesting help, 146–147
  security issues, 158–160
  sending e-mail request, 149
  sending file-based request, 152–158
  using, 144
remote configuration, 418
Remote Control tab, RDP-Tcp Properties
  dialog box (fig.), 97
Remote Desktop Connection utility, 118,
  160–170
Remote Desktop for Administration, 138,
  140–144
Remote Desktop Protocol (RDP), 138
Remote Desktop Web Connection utility,
  176–180
Remote Desktops console, 170–171
remote server management, administration, 266
removing
  DNS servers from DNS management console,
    383
  members from groups, 23
  objects from Active Directory, 549
renaming user accounts, 64
replicating Web content on multiple servers, 266
requests
  client's, timing out, 262
  DNS, 348–350
resetting user account passwords, 39–41
resource records, 371, 388–389, 571–572
resources

authorization to use, 204
enabling shadow copies on shared, 315
response buffering, 262
Restore tab, Windows Backup Utility, 292
Restore Wizard, 295
restoring
  backup data, 309–312
  Backup or Restore Wizard, 287
  configuring restore options on Backup Utility,
    292
  IIS configuration, 598–600
  IIS metabase, 239
  previous versions of files, 322
Restricted Groups, configuring, 445–447
restrictions, account logon, 46–48
Resultant Set of Policy (RSoP), displaying user
    settings, 567
reverse lookup zones, 348, 378–381
RFC-compliant naming rules, 364
rights
  See also passwords, permissions
  user. See user rights
rolling out Terminal Services, 82
root domain, 339
Root Hints tab, DNS server, 365
rotation, backup media, 282–286
Run as command, 135

S

SAC (Special Administrative Console), 184
scalability of Terminal Services, 84
scavenging resource records, 371–372, 582
schedule, backup (fig.), 302
scheduling shadow copies, 320
Screen Options tab, Remote Desktop
    Connection utility, 174
scripts
  ASP.NET, 238
  security analyses, 424
Scripts and Msadc virtual directories, 263
secedit.exe command, 418, 423–427, 476,
    604–607
securews.inf, 413
security
  analyzing using Security Configuration and
    Analysis, 415–417
  auditing events, 458–472
  configuring event log policies, 442–443

configuring for backup operations, 308–309
configuring Restricted Groups, 444–447
file system, 452–454
Group Policy extensions, 420–421
Group Policy versus security templates, 423
IIS 6.0, new features, 200–204
initiating analysis, 604
local policies, 431–442
Registry security, 450–452
Remote Assistance issues, 158–160
Remote Desktop for Administration issues,
    143
reversing policies, 477
SSL access information, 267
Terminal Services, 112
Web, configuring with SSL, 256–258
Security Configuration and Analysis snap-in,
    411–415, 476
Security Configuration Manager, 409
security groups described, 3–4
security logs, viewing, 472
Security Options node, local policies options
    (table), 436–441
security templates
  configuring, 428–458
  deploying, 605
  deploying via Group Policy, 454–457
  versus Group Policy security, 423
  importing, exporting, 419, 455–458, 605–606
  .inf files, 415
  management tools, 603–607
  preconfigured, 405
  validating, 607
  Windows Server 2003 (table), 406–409,
    412–413
Security Templates and user rights assignments,
    32
Security Templates snap-in, 419–420
Self Tests
  disaster recovery, 329–336
  DNS, 396–402
  group creation and management, 66–68
  network security, 478–485
  remote server management, administration,
    192–197
  software updates, 525–534
  Terminal Services, 120–125
  user account creation and management, 69–71

Web server management, maintenance, 268–273
server certificates
    and SSL-secured communications, 253–256
    using on multiple Web sites, 267
Server-Gated Cryptography (SGC), 202
Server Web Administration welcome page (fig.), 182
servers
    accessing over the Web, 181
    BIND, and Active Directory, 395
    DNS, 340
    identifying logged on users, 567
    IIS. *See* IIS servers
    shutting down decisions, 444
    slave, 350
    SMTP virtual. *See* SMTP virtual servers
    SUS (Software Update Services). *See* SUS servers
Service Packs, updating, 489
service providers, cryptographic, 202–203
Session Directory Service, 119
sessions, Remote Assistance, 147
Sessions tab, RDP-Tcp Properties dialog box (fig.), 96
setup, IIS 6.0, unattended, 217–218
shadow copies
    best practices, 324
    creating, 315
    and backups, 329
    enabling, configuring, 321–322
    Self Test, 329–336
shared folders
    locating for shadow copying, 323
    making shadow copies of, 315
    shared resources, accessing via groups, 34
    shutting down servers, 444
sites
    displaying properties in Active Directory, 565
    querying Active Directory for information about, 553
slave servers, 350
SMS, 488, 521
SMTP virtual servers, creating, 227–229
snap-ins
    MMC, 131
    Remote Desktop MMC, 191

Security Configuration and Analysis, 411–415
Security Template, 419–420
security template management, 603–607
sniffing authentication information, 201
SOA tab, reverse lookup zones, 379
Software Update Services (SUS), 488–495
software updates
    Exam Objectives Fast Track, 523–524
    Exam Objectives Summary, 522
    infrastructure, installing and configuring, 488–495
    introduction, 488
    Self Test, 525–534
    SMS and third-party applications, 521
    Windows Update Catalog, 518–521
Special Administrative Console (SAC), 184, 191
SQL servers, backups on, 289
SSL
    configuring Web security and authentication using, 256–258
    security access information, 267
SSL-secured communications, configuring, 253–258
SSL/TLS, 202–203
standard zones (DNS), 346–348
Start of Authority (SOA) tab, forward lookup zone, 372–374
storage options, volume shadow copies, 318
strong passwords and Remote Desktop for Administration, 143
Structured Query Language. *See* SQL
stub zones, 346
subnets, displaying properties in Active Directory, 564
SUS (Software Update Services), 488–495
    and Automatic Updates, 524
    managing, 507–512
    troubleshooting, 512–513
synchronization logs, viewing, 507
sysocmgr.exe, difference from winn32.exe, 218
system events, auditing, 467
system logs, viewing, 510–511
System Policy information Web site, 53
System Security node, configuring options, 448–449
system state data, 277, 288–289, 307
Systems Management Server. *See* SMS

T

tape backups, 279–286
TCP, port 3389 vulnerability, 143
TCP/IP
    support history, 338
    UNIX and, 376
Telephones tab, account Properties (fig.), 49
templates
    account, 41
    rollback, generating, 607
    security. *See* security templates
Terminal Server External Connector
        (TS-EC), 106
Terminal Services
    advanced configuration via Group Policy,
        102–105
    client tools, using, 160–183
    and computer environments, 75–82
    Configuration console, using, 93–101
    configuring, 92–105
    design issues, 81–82
    Exam Objectives Summary, 114
    installing, configuring, 87–105
    introduction, 74, 83–86
    licensing, 105–110
    Management console, using, 101
    NLB cluster (fig.), 85
    Remote Desktop for Administration, 137
    security issues, 112
    troubleshooting, 82, 110–113
    using for remote administration, 137–160
testing
    disaster recovery plans, 328
    new CNAME record, 387
    software updates, 497
tests. *See* Self Tests
thin clients
    Web site information about, 79
    common (table), 341
    Terminal Services, management, 80
Threats and Countermeasures Guide, 441
time-stamping resource records, 571–572
Time To Live (TTL), 374
timing out, client requests, 262
TLDs
    common (table), 341
    FQDN (Fully Qualified Domain Name)
        suffix, 341

tools
    Admin Pack, 136
    Administrative Tools folder, 129–130
    management, types, 128–137
top-level domains (TLD), 339
Total Cost of Ownership (TCO), 76
Tower of Hanoi media rotation system, 285–286
Transmission Control Protocol/Internet
        Protocol. *See* TCP/IP
trees, term described, 341
Trojans, 143
troubleshooting
    DNS servers, 589–592
    DNS with nslookup, 385
    IIS 6.0, 258–264
    SUS and Automatic Updates, 512–513, 524
    Terminal Services, 82, 110–113
    user authentication issues, 52–53
two-way trust relationships, backups and, 309
types, group, 3–5

U

Unicode Transformation Format 8 (UTF-8), 208
universal groups
    scope, 6
    using, 8
UNIX
    file not found errors, 263
    and TCP/IP, 376
updates
    dynamic, 379, 395
    software. *See* software updates
updating
    computer using Windows Update, 514–518
    DNS server zone file, 384
    URL authorization, 204
user accounts
    assigning rights and permissions, 52
    configuring properties, 44–46
    copying, 41–42
    creating, 36–53
    default (table), 36
    deleting, 50–52
    disabling, enabling, 42–43
    enabling Digest Authentication for (fig.), 247
    managing, Exam Objectives Fast Track, 61–64
    modifying, 37

options (table), 46
reassigning, 51
renaming, 64
User Principal Name (UPN), 38, 57
user rights
administrator delegation of, 4
assigning to groups, 31–34
assigning to user accounts, 52
assignments node options (table), 433–435
auditing, 466
backups and, 308–309
and NTFS permissions, 34
in security groups, 4
users
determining group membership of, 30–31
displaying information about logged on users, 567
displaying user group properties in Active Directory, 563–564
FTP site user isolation, 226
modifying properties of, in Active Directory, 546–548
querying Active Directory for information about, 555
Users container, default groups in (tables), 12–13
utilities
command line, 134
Manage Your Server, 134
Remote Desktop Connection, 118

V

VeriSign, obtaining certificates from, 202
viewing
approval logs, 508
backup schedule, 302
certificate request summary (fig.), 256
group manager details (fig.), 30
group members (fig.), 21
previous backup versions (fig.), 323
Remote Assistance requests, 158, 162
secedit.ext analysis, 425
security logs (fig.), 472
SUS IIS logs, 512
synchronization logs, 507
Web Service Extensions (fig.), 233
virtual directories
management tools for, 594–596
managing for FTP sites, 598–599

Scripts and Msadc, 263
Virtual Private Networks. *See* VPNs
virtual servers
creating, 233–235
NNTP. *See* NNTP virtual servers
SMTP. *See* SMTP virtual servers
volume shadow copy
and Windows Backup Utility, 287
working with, 314–324
VPNs , remote users, and Terminal Services, 84

W

Web-Based Enterprise Management (WBEM), 136
Web Distributed Authoring and Versioning (WebDAV) and Advanced Digest authentication, 202
Web servers. *See* IIS
Web Service Extensions (IIS), 232
Web Site Creation Wizard, 220–224
Web sites
ASP and ASP.NET information, 205
Citrix MetaFrame, 74
configuring authentication, 250–251
configuring performance, 238
configuring SSL properties for, 257
Corporate Windows Update Web site, 524
creating new, 593–594
creating with Web Site Creation Wizard, 220–224
hosting, 235–236
ISAPI filters not automatically visible as properties, 263
KiXart, 128
Microsoft licensing, 106
Microsoft Resource Kit, 135
Remote Assistance, 151
restricting users, 252
session directory, Terminal Services, 86
System Policy information, 53
Terminal Services features, test objectives, 74
thin client information, 79
Threats and Countermeasures Guide download, 441
TLD listings, 341
using server certificates on multiple, 267
Windows Update (fig.), 515
whoami command, 567

Windows 2000
  40-bit encryption support, 202
  and TCP/IP, 338
Windows Backup Utility
  Advanced mode, 292–295
  Advanced options (table), 302
  command-line tools, 607–608
  configuration options, 289–292
  managing backup operations, 607–608
  using, 287–308
Windows Component Wizard, 87, 90, 107–108,
    215–217
Windows Internet Naming Service (WINS),
    339
Windows Management Instrumentation (WMI),
    86
Windows Messenger, using to request Remote
    Assistance help, 147
Windows Resource Kits, 135
Windows Server 2003
  Administration Tools Pack, 136
  centralized computing environment with
    (fig.), 79
  command-line utilities, extended functionality,
    2
  DNS integration in, 342
  hardening, 441–442
  managing user, computers, groups, 2–61
  network security. See network security
  Resource Kits, 135
  security templates (table), 406–409, 412–413
  Terminal Services. See Terminal Services
Windows Update, 488, 514–518
Windows Update Catalog, 518–521
Windows XP, Remote Assistance in, 139
winnt32.exe, difference from sysocmgr.exe, 218
WINS-R tab, reverse lookup zones, 380
WINS tab, forward lookup zone, 376
WINS (Windows Internet Naming Service),
    339, 347
wizards
  ASR, 295
  Automated Recovery System, 313–314
  Backup or Restore, 287
  Configure Your Server, 88, 210–215
  Configure Your Server Wizard, 352–360
  Delegation of Control, 41
  FTP Site Creation, 224–227
  IIS Certificate, 256–258

New NNTP Virtual Server, 229–233
New SMTP Virtual Server Wizard, 227–229
Restore, 295
understanding, 134
Web Site Creation, 220–224
Windows Component, 87, 215–217
Windows Component Wizard, 107–108
worker process
  isolation mode model and, 205–206
  sessions lost due to recycling, 259
workgroups versus domain environments, 4
World Wide Web. See Web
World Wide Web Service dialog box (fig.), 217
WWW Publishing Service, 203

X

XML metabase, IIS configuration settings, 208

Z

ZENWorks, 338
zone transfers, 345, 395
Zone Transfers tab
  forward lookup zones, 377
  reverse lookup zones, 380
zones
  changing directory partitions on, 584
  configuring again, scavenging for all, 383
  configuring DNS options, 368–381
  deleting specified, 585
  described (DNS), 341
  determining type requirements, 345
  displaying resource records, settings, 585–588
  displaying specific server information, 580
  secondary, reason for, 396
  standard (DNS), 346–348